Wisdom by the Week

The Weekly Torah Portion as an Inspiration
for Thought and Creativity

Wisdom by the Week

The Weekly Torah Portion as an Inspiration for Thought and Creativity

Editor: Naftali Rothenberg

THE MICHAEL SCHARF PUBLICATION TRUST
OF THE YESHIVA UNIVERSITY PRESS
NEW YORK

and

THE VAN LEER JERUSALEM INSTITUTE

מכון ון ליר בירושלים
THE VAN LEER JERUSALEM INSTITUTE
معهد فان لير في القدس

ISBN 978-1-60280-199-8

Translated by Shmuel Sermoneta Gertel

Co-Published by
The Michael Scharf Publication Trust of
Yeshiva University Press
500 West 185th Street
New York, NY 10033

THE VAN LEER JERUSALEM INSTITUTE
43 Jabotinsky Street
Jerusalem, Israel 91040

Distributed by
KTAV Publishing House, Inc.
888 Newark Avenue
Jersey City, NJ 07306
Tel. (201) 963-9524
Fax. (201) 963-0102
www.ktav.com
bernie@ktav.com

On the cover: Riki Rothenberg, at *The Foot of Mount Sinai*

Dedicated to the Memory of
Professor Nehemia Levtzion

Acknowledgments

The Van Leer Jerusalem Institute (VLJI) is grateful to the Michael Scharf Publication Trust of Yeshiva University Press and to Professor Jeffrey S. Gurock for taking the publication of this book upon themselves.

Sincere thanks to Professor Moshe Sokolow, the academic editor on behalf of the Press for his valuable professional and scholarly work.

Wisdom by the Week—The Weekly Torah Portion as an Inspiration for Thought and Creativity was published in Hebrew (*Hogim BaParasha*) by the Van Leer Jerusalem Institute and Yediot-Sfarim publishing house in Tel Aviv. We wish to thank the people at Yediot-Sfarim for their dedicated work in bringing this book to press and for unceasing efforts in the successful distribution of the book in Hebrew.

The book was admirably translated from Hebrew into English by Shmuel Sermonita-Gertel, and we wish to express our thanks to him for his skilled translation.

Thank you to Keren Keshet—the Rainbow Foundation.

Our sincere appreciation goes to Professor Gabriel Motzkin, Director of the VLJI for his support and to Dr. Tal Kohavi, Yona Ratzon, Dafna Schreiber, Shira Karagila, and Danae Marx for making this project possible.

Thank you, also, to Adam Bengal of KTAV Publishing House, Inc.

Last but not least we are honored to express our gratitude to every one of the forty-seven scholars who wrote and contributed their works to this book—together they have created a colorful mosaic.

Naftali Rothenberg

Contents

Introduction

Culture Creates Culture:
The Weekly Torah Portion as a Source of Inspiration for Thinkers, Writers and Artists throughout the Ages

This book offers readers an unusual cultural experience. Here they will discover not only the thoughts and views of contemporary authors, but the ideas, observations and dreams of forty-eight thinkers, writers and artists through whose work they have chosen to explore the weekly Torah portions. Their choices represent 1,800 years of constant cultural activity, from the third century CE to the present.

All creative endeavors draw upon three sources: personal experience, natural phenomena, and previous cultural achievements. Thought and creativity are born of and intensified by cultural influences, as *culture creates culture*. Only a handful of classical works throughout history have served as constant sources of creative inspiration, and the Bible—the unrivaled bestseller of all times—is certainly the foremost example of such works. No other book has inspired thinkers and artists to such an extent, leaving a clear and lasting impression on philosophy, literature, music, theatre, and the plastic arts. It is an incredible cultural phenomenon, in no way weakened by the secularization process of the past three centuries. On the contrary, secularization has also given rise to vibrant new approaches to Scripture. The innovation, audacity, and renewed challenge in contending with the Bible, has heightened its impact on creative works of all kinds.

Various factors have contributed to this remarkable phenomenon—most notably, the spread of Christianity. It is noteworthy that the processes of separation of church and state and the weakening of the religious establishments did not diminish the Bible's influence on thinkers, artists and writers. On the contrary, the more the Church's authority waned, the freer access to the biblical texts became, and as education and literacy became more widespread, the clergy began to lose its monopoly over Scripture.

These processes, which have unfolded in European and related cultures over the past three hundred years, were a fundamental part of Jewish culture over two thousand years ago. This is the rationale behind the practice of reading from the Torah on the Sabbath; that Scripture might be freely accessible, without intermediaries, to each and every Jew. The Midrash offers the following explanation: "'And they went three days in the wilderness, and found no water'—The commentators say: 'They did not find water'—that is words of Torah, which are compared to water. They had not studied Torah for three days, and that is why they rebelled. The prophets and the elders therefore decreed that the Torah should be read on the Sabbath, Mondays and Thursdays" (*Yalkut Shimoni, Beshalah*; *BT Bava Kama* 82a). The public reading of the Torah on the Sabbath, Mondays and Thursdays (and at Sabbath afternoon prayers—a practice adopted somewhat later) was intended to afford the Israelites a constant source for thought and discourse, lest three days pass without engaging in intellectual activity. Torah study is a search for answers to difficult questions, an attempt to discover the truth, and an endless opportunity for creative thought.

The weekly Torah portion has thus served as a wellspring for cultural development in general. For some thirteen centuries, the great majority of creative works were based on and inspired by the Torah portions and their public reading. Most of the aggadic and midrashic literature—originally spoken and later written down—is directly linked to these weekly readings. Halakhic literature on the other hand, broke away from the biblical text at an earlier stage, with the redaction of the Mishnah and the Tosefta. Its eventual independence, as a cultural work in its own right, was established with the closure of the Talmuds.

There is evidence that halakhic discourse originally adhered closely to the biblical texts, as witnessed by the opening phrase of the Babylonian Talmud: "Where does the *tana* [in the mishnah] stand, that he taught 'From what time [is the Shema recited]'?" (i.e., to what biblical passage is the *tana* referring; *Berakhot* 2a). This is, however, the last time such a question is asked in the Talmud. Maimonides too was unsuccessful in his efforts to reestablish the direct connection between Halakhah and Scripture. In the introduction to his *Yad Ha-Hazakah*, he declares: "That is why I have called this work *Mishneh Torah* (*Repetition of the Law*), as one may first read the Written Law and then read this work and know the entire Oral Law from it, requiring no further, intermediary works." Maimonides' magnum opus not only failed to restore the link between Halakhah and Scripture, but in fact achieved the opposite result. The fact that Maimonides did not cite his sources compelled students to search for them in the Talmuds and the geonic responsa rather than relying exclusively on Scripture. Halakhah became a world in itself, independent of the verses of the Torah.

At the same time, Jewish thought was undergoing a similar process. The tenth century saw the appearance of systematic philosophical works that no longer followed the order of the biblical portions, although they were still clearly bound to Scripture. This continued dependence on Scripture was the result of two main factors: (1) Jewish thought was greatly influenced by contemporary Christian and Muslim philosophy, which drew inspiration from the Bible or the biblical ethoi in the Koran. (2) As noted above, the reading of the Torah on Sabbaths, Mondays, and Thursdays was central to Jewish life, and the homilies delivered in the synagogue and elsewhere almost always related to some aspect of the weekly Torah portion. Many midrashic works thus continued to follow the order of the weekly readings. Let it suffice to mention the Zohar and the tremendous influence it has exerted. Although the Zohar is considered the final Midrash to attain canonical status, the creation of Midrash did not end in the 13th century, and in fact continues to this day.

The content of the portions themselves naturally inspired philosophers, writers, poets, composers, and artists in an epitome of creative culture. The creation of culture is the creation of the world. When we speak of the Torah as a source of inspiration for thinkers, writers, and artists, we are in fact recapitulating the words of the Sages, who said that the Torah preceded the world and was the inspiration for all creation, as in the following passage from the beginning of Genesis *Rabbah*:

> Rabbi Hoshaya began: (*Prov.* 8:30) "Then I was by Him, as a nursling (*Amon*)" ... [that is] a craftsman (*uman*). The Torah says: I was the instrument of the Holy One's craft. It is the way of the world that a mortal king who builds a palace does not do so of his own accord, but employs a craftsman. And the craftsman does not build it of his own accord, but employs parch-

ments and tablets, to help him design its rooms and doors. So the Holy One, blessed be He, looked into the Torah and created the world. (Genesis *Rabbah*, 1).

Men and women who have wished to resemble God have looked into the Torah and built their own creative worlds. That is what the Rabbis of the Talmud and the Midrash, Saadiah Gaon, Judah Halevi, Maimonides, Hume, Spinoza, Kierkegaard, Rembrandt and many others have done. Philosophers, writers, painters, composers and poets, thinkers and artists have all looked into the Torah and created worlds.

The idea of reversing the sequence of events, of the Torah having preceded the world, has deep dialogical roots. The Torah was given at Sinai, but Sinai, according to this approach, is not a one time historical event—sublime and momentous, but nonetheless a part of the past. It is rather, a source of hope for the future, as the Jerusalem Talmud teaches us in the tractate of *Shabbat*:

"It was Rabbi Yehoshua ben Levi's custom to hear a Torah lesson from his grandson every Sabbath eve. One day he forgot, and went to bathe at the baths in Tiberias. He was leaning on the shoulder of Rabi Hiya bar (Ab)ba, when he remembered that he had not gone to hear his grandson's lesson, and got up and left. What [exactly] happened? Rabbi Drosai said: It happened as described. Rabbi Lazar (Eleazar) son of Rabbi Jose said: He was unclothed [at the time]. Rabbi Hiya bar Abba said to him: Did you not teach us that "if one has begun (to bathe, etc.), he may continue"? He [Rabbi Yehoshua ben Levi] said to him: Hiya, my son, is it a trifling matter to you that one who hears a lesson of Torah from his grandson, it is as if he has heard it from Sinai? Why is that so? [As it is written] (Deut. 4): "Make them known unto thy children and thy children's children; the day that thou stoodest before the Lord thy God in Horeb" (JT, *Shabbat* 1,2).

We learn from here that the Sinai of the past is not enough; that we must claim and aspire to the Sinai of the future: the Sinai we will hear from our grandchildren. The singularity of the Sinai experience lies in the fact that it encompasses and enables all future Sinaitic experiences.

This idea also appears in *Derekh Etz Ha-Hayim*, by Rabbi Moshe Hayim Luzzatto (Ramhal). The Torah, says Ramhal, subsumes a multiplicity of views and meanings—not only in the eye of the beholder, but in its very essence. The Torah's many and varied interpretations are thus not imposed from without, by students, scholars, and artists, but are inherent to its nature. The Torah's exegetical pluralism is immanent and a priori, independent of its commentators. Ramhal compares the Torah to embers that burst into flame when fanned by those who dedicate themselves to its study:

And he who strives to engage in [Torah study] will cause a great and varicolored flame to burst forth from every letter, the hues of which are the knowledge that lies concealed within that letter...

For the lights [that shine] upon the letters embody their every aspect ... And when a man strives to understand, and reads and contemplates, rereads and further contemplates, these very lights ignite and blaze like a flame from a glowing ember.

The knowledge concealed within the Torah and revealed to all who study and contemplate it is not monolithic. It also entails a personal aspect, revealed differently to each and every student. The intensity of the flame depends upon the personal dedication and efforts of those who engage in its study. Its manifold interpretations and meanings are like the colors in a bursting flame:

And when the flame bursts forth, as I have said, it is varicolored and comprises a great many matters. There is something more, however, for ... the ancients taught that the roots of all of the souls of Israel can be found in the Torah, so that the Torah has sixty myriad interpretations, corresponding to the sixty myriad souls of Israel. The Torah can thus be said to explode into many sparks, for it bursts into flame, displaying all of the lights pertaining to a given matter, which shine in sixty myriad ways in the sixty myriad [souls] of Israel.

The specific way in which each individual grasps the Torah is not extraneous to it, but an integral part of the Torah itself. Individual understanding is thus not imposed upon the text, but discovered—as one discovers oneself, one's own particular hue—within it. This book represents only a small fraction of the possible interpretations and meanings found in the Torah. Its contribution lies in the fact that it highlights this essential aspect of the Torah: that it can be interpreted in sixty myriad ways, corresponding to and flowing from the sixty myriad souls of Israel.

Fellows of the Van Leer Jerusalem Institute felt that the power of the biblical text, as a source of creative inspiration, goes far beyond its weekly reading in the synagogue. They therefore decided a number of years ago to conduct a lecture series at the Institute in Jerusalem and at various other venues throughout the country. The lecturers in the series represent a broad range of interpretations and approaches to the Torah. The large and varied audiences that have filled the lecture halls at the Van Leer Jerusalem Institute and elsewhere have greatly contributed to the series' success. It is the "weekly Torah portion" as a cultural concept that lies at the heart of the entire *Pothim Shavua* ("The Week Opening") initiative. It is our intention to reinforce this concept and its standing within Israeli culture, while stressing the legitimacy of all cultural exponents as biblical commentators. It is to this end that we decided to publish the product of the lecture series in books in order to increase the circles of the dialogue between commentators and learners.

Wisdom by the Week is a unique attempt to go beyond the interpretations of the lecturers and authors presented here, to consider the portions of the Torah through the prism of those upon whose work they have drawn. Readers are thus invited to embark upon a journey straddling two worlds: the world of the book's authors and that of the philosophers, artists, and writers who have inspired them.

This book is dedicated to the blessed memory of Prof. Nehemia Levtzion (1935–2003). In the Van Leer Jerusalem Institute, Nehemiah initiated the establishment of the Framework on Contemporary Jewish Culture and Identity and saw The Week Opening lecture series as the capstone of its activities. The breadth of commentary on the weekly portion, the diversity of the lecturers, and, no less important, the participation of the large and highly diverse audiences that filled auditoriums at the Institute in Jerusalem and throughout the country each week—all of these represented for Nehemiah the fulfillment of a personal dream. He dreamt of Judaism without divisions, of an experiential and intellectual common denominator for Jews coming from varying backgrounds and living diverse lives.

Naftali Rothenberg
The Van Leer Jerusalem Institute

Bereshit – Genesis

Hamutal Bar-Yosef

Bereshit – In the Beginning

Abraham B. Yehoshua on the Story of Cain and Abel

If thou doest well, thou shalt prevail; and if thou doest not well, sin coucheth at the door; and unto thee is its desire, but thou mayest rule over it (Genesis 4:7).

A.B. Yehoshua is best known in Israel as one of the most important authors of his generation—the generation of the birth of the Jewish state (*dor ha-medinah*). His approach to Israeli reality is rooted in Freudian psychoanalysis. During the 1960s and 70s, Yehoshua saw an Israeli experience characterized by complexes, a subconscious, pathological repression, and a need for psychotherapy in order to recover its sanity. This approach is clearly reflected in his collection of essays *Between Right and Right* (*Bizkhut ha-normaliyut*) (1980), in which he attempts to define Zionist goals in psychoanalytical terms, that is sane Israeli existence, free from Diaspora complexes and all types of spiritual and behavioral extremism. The views that Yehoshua expresses in this series of essays and in another collection entitled *The Wall and the Mountain* (*Ha-kir ve-ha-har*) represent the standpoint of secular Israeli Zionism, which aspires above all to afford Israelis the possibility of living quiet and productive lives in their own land, free of the anxiety and pressures engendered by "the situation."

In his book *The Terrible Power of a Minor Guilt* (*Kohah ha-nora shel ashmah ketanah*) (1988)—the product of a series of university lectures—Yehoshua begins his introduction with a complaint about the state of literary criticism, which he believes has failed to relate to the ethical aspect of literature:

It is only on rare occasions that we hear a reader voice words of protest or admiration for the ethical stance of a story or author of a literary work of any kind.... The catchwords of literary criticism, both professional and personal, are: "plausibility," "complexity," "depth," and especially "originality." It is only on rare

3

occasions indeed that words such as "ethics," "values," "truth," and "goodness," come up (p. 11).

Furthermore, he claims, "of late, literature itself has begun to obfuscate the natural ethical conflicts that appear within the fabric of the text; relegating them to the backstage" (p. 16). Yehoshua asks why this happens and offers a number of possible explanations. First and foremost, he asserts, the cause "lies in the growth and heightening of psychological knowledge, allowing us to better understand the sources of human failure and deviant behavior, significantly reducing our willingness to pass ethical judgment" (*ibid.*).

Psychological understanding pulls the rug out from under ethical judgment, claims Yehoshua. The more sophisticated our psychological insight, the harder it is for us to identify with ethical judgment: psychology has accustomed us to think that there is no such thing as a bad person, only a disturbed, affection-starved, paranoid, frustrated person suffering from some complex or other, inflicted by parents or society. It has also accustomed us to the notion that there is no such thing as a good person: good in its accepted meaning being merely a reaction formation to repressed and deviant desires that, despite their righteous exterior, could be harmful to the person's environment. Dostoevsky, claims Yehoshua, could never have written *Crime and Punishment* today without addressing Raskolnikov's childhood and his relationship with his mother and his sister (although Freud himself was deeply influenced by Dostoevsky). Moreover, the habit of psychological thinking also affects our reading of texts centered on ethical dilemmas. Sophocles' plays—*Antigone* for example—have been the subject of a number of psychoanalytical interpretations that have focused on the heroine's complexes and inhibitions, asserting that Antigone was driven to suicide by her frustrated sexual desires. A similar approach is taken by Dan Miron in his books *Taking Leave of the Impoverished Self* (*Ha-pridah min ha-ani he'ani*) (1986) and *A Butterfly from the Worm* (*Parpar min ha-tola'at*) (2001)—on the young Bialik and the young Alterman, respectively. Miron also adopts a psychological approach to the texts he treats, although they can easily be read from an ethical standpoint as well.

Surprisingly, Yehoshua's own early works, such as the stories *The Yatir Evening Express* and *Three Days and a Child*, could be cited to illustrate his point. These works also seem to relegate the ethical dilemma to the sidelines, emphasizing the Freudian psychological mechanism that governs the protagonists' behavior and justifies it. The characters in *The Yatir Evening Express* derail a train with the sole purpose of alleviating the bleakness of the village of Yatir. In *Three Days and a Child*, the protagonist nearly kills a small child in order to free himself from his obsession with the child's mother—his former lover. Yehoshua's words in his introduction to *The Terrible Power of a Minor Guilt* would thus seem to represent a significant change of worldview, an attempt to free himself from the psychoanalytical approach in which he had been trapped for many years.

Let us now look at Yehoshua's interpretation of the story of Cain and Abel. This story, like all of the stories addressed in *The Terrible Power of a Minor Guilt*, is treated as a literary work within which the author has placed an ethical message. God's behavior in the story of Cain and Abel, claims Yehoshua at the beginning of the chapter, is perplexing. The reader's basic sense of justice would expect murder to be punished with death, and God—the epitome of justice—to impose just such a sentence upon Cain. After all, a reader in ancient times might have claimed, God himself said to Noah and his sons, after the flood: "Whoso sheddeth man's blood, by man shall his blood be shed" (9:6). How can Cain's punishment be reconciled with the ethos of "an eye for an eye" (Ex. 21:24), he would have wondered? The question is equally relevant, however, to the modern Israeli reader who, at least according to Yehoshua, shares the same basic sense of justice that gave rise to the principle of "an eye for an eye."

Yehoshua thus suggests the following interpretation: God, as an omniscient being, was fully aware of Cain's inner weaknesses—including his homicidal tendencies—before they were ever manifested. The punishment that he imposed was thus essentially internal as well. "A fugitive and a wanderer," according to Yehoshua, refers to a lack of mental stability, living in a permanent state of neurosis. This punishment continues to plague Cain long after his external life has been rehabilitated.

The first thing we are struck by is the fact that Yehoshua, despite all of his criticism of psychoanalysis and its influence on contemporary culture, seems to have been unable to escape it himself. His interpretation of the Cain and Abel story also betrays the influence of European literature, deeply influenced in turn, by Christian thought. Contrary to the commonly held belief regarding the importance of action in Jewish ethics, Yehoshua credits the author of the story with an ethical code that judges a man's morality on the basis of his individual psychological makeup. Cain's punishment, according to Yehoshua, thus resembles Raskolnikov's inner torment, making the story more accessible to the modern reader, in a culture that places great value upon man's individuality, judging him by his mental and emotional characteristics—factors taken into consideration even by the courts.

Personally, I find the story of Cain and Abel perplexing from the very beginning, even before the punishment stage. Verse 5 reads: "But unto Cain and to his offering He [God] had not respect." What is the meaning of this unexplained preference? Does God not understand the feelings of one who brings his beloved possessions, the fruits of his labor, in order to express love and devotion, only to be rebuffed by the recipient? Could God not have understood and known the anguish Cain would feel at the sight of his brother's gift being preferred over his, without any apparent reason, as well as the consequences of such feelings? Are knowledge and wisdom not the traits we most expect of God (as manifest in the Garden of Eden story, for example)? Is such behavior just? Can it serve as a model for human behavior? In my opinion, such behavior—on a human level—is insensitive, unwise, and—on a divine level—can be understood as even intentionally cruel.

I believe that God wished to test Cain, like his parents before him, by offering him an ethical choice. The alternatives are made absolutely clear to Cain: "For if thou doest well, thou shalt prevail/bear [the Hebrew word *se'et* is ambivalent and grammatically strange]; and if thou doest not well, sin coucheth at the door." The verse is puzzling. A choice is clearly being offered between two courses of action, one good and the other bad, but what exactly are the choices? And why does God speak to Cain in such an enigmatic fashion when he is already confused and in a state of emotional turmoil? The linguistic difficulties presented by the verse would seem an accurate reflection of Cain's state of mind: agitated, confused, unsure of the right path, of the precise meaning of the divine voice. The most difficult word in the verse is *se'et* (literally: "bear," translated above as "thou shalt prevail" –tr.). The traditional biblical commentators suggest various interpretations, most of which assume *se'et* to be the predicate of a sentence in which the subject is God. According to Onkelos, Rashi, Radak (David Kimhi), and the *Da'at zekenim miba'alei hatosafot*, it is God who will bear Cain's sin, that is will grant him forgiveness if he mends his ways. Ibn Ezra explains that God will restore Cain's dignity and will let him prevail; while Nahmanides suggests that God will prefer Cain over his brother; and Seforno—that he will make Cain great. In the opinion of Rabbi Bahye ben Asher of Saragossa, *se'et* signifies "bringing a gift"—God is thus asking Cain to bring him a better offering, worthy of being accepted. Only the much later interpretation of Rabbi Joseph Dov Soloveichik stresses Cain's role—"Do not despair, for you still have the power to improve your situation." It is unclear, however, how the word *se'et* lends itself to such an explanation. The basis for all of these explanations would appear to be the appearance of a word deriving from the same Hebrew root (*nasa'*) in verse 13, understood in the sense of "forgiveness"—"my sin is too great [for God] to forgive (*mineso*)".

Avraham Even-Shoshan, in his dictionary of the Hebrew language, cites this verse as an example of the verb's use in the sense of forbearance, as in "Surely our diseases he did bear" (Is. 53:4) and "I am weary to bear them" (*op. cit.*1:14). In other words, verse 7 may be referring to the possibility that it was Cain's duty to forbear his anger, aroused by the unequal treatment afforded to the two brothers—treatment which he perceived as intolerable favoritism.

Initially, some may find the interpretation I am about to propose difficult to accept. Was God suggesting that Cain do nothing about Abel? Many have remarked on the enigmatic phrasing in verse 8: "And Cain spoke unto Abel his brother and it came to pass when they were in the field that Cain rose up against Abel his brother and slew him." What did Cain say to Abel? To my mind, this is the crux of the matter, because in fact, he said nothing. Anger stifled his ability to speak to Abel. This silence is a crucial part of Cain's "possession" by the beast of sin; the process whereby he loses his divine image. Cain, like his parents before him, fails the ethical test that God sets before him, and his failure is greater than theirs, because its price is the life of his brother. Now, he must be punished—perhaps even more severely than his parents. Why then does God shield him and allow him to rebuild his life?

The answer can be found later in the chapter, in the story of Lemech. This story appeals to the basic human urge to exact revenge from someone who has caused you harm, giving him his comeuppance—or more—in order to assuage the rage and the pain. And indeed, that is what Lemech, a descendant of Cain's, does in verses 23–24. "I have slain a man for wounding me, and a young man for bruising me. If Cain shall be avenged sevenfold, truly Lemech seventy and sevenfold," he informs his two wives, apparently with pride. What is the biblical author's opinion of Lemech, and why did he append his story to that of Cain and Abel? With typical biblical economy, Lemech's terrible song weaves the thread that leads from violence to murder and yet more murder. Long before Shakespeare's *Macbeth* and Dostoevsky's *Crime and Punishment*, the author of this text draws a direct line from Cain, who murdered because he could not overcome his jealousy, to Lemech, who murdered merely for having been wounded or bruised. Revenge is a human impulse, esteemed in many cultures (not limited to the Orient or the ancient) as supremely ethical and manly; e.g., the dueling tradition in European culture, or Nietzsche's attitude—adopted by Micha Josef Berdyczewski—to the masculine lust for revenge.

Revenge could have been considered a positive value by the biblical author and his contemporaries as well—a fact evidenced by the Bible itself: "Whoso sheddeth man's blood, by man shall his blood be shed" (9:6). Yet in the story before us, the author denounces impulsive revenge and spurns revenge as a value. He offers Cain a choice between natural impulsivity on the one hand and self-control and the ability to engage in dialogue—as should an intelligent human being created in God's image—on the other. Like Adam and Eve, Cain too fails, and his failure reveals the tenuousness of God's image in man.

The light punishment that Cain receives is emblematic of the type of divine response that was beyond Cain. It demonstrates the difference between human impulsivity and divine wisdom. Cain is punished, not with death or vengeful murder, but in a manner that allows him to re-build his life. God does not engage in impulsive revenge, nor does a human being capable of distinguishing between good and evil. This is how Joseph behaves when he reveals himself to his brothers. Nothing would have been more natural than to take revenge at such a time. He treats his brothers coldly, speaks harshly to them, accuses them of being spies, and locks them up for three days. The meeting is very painful to him—"And he turned himself about from them, and wept" (42:24)—but he exercises great restraint. When he saw Benjamin, "he sought where to weep... and came out; and he refrained himself" (43:30–31). Absalom behaves in the opposite manner when he murders Amnon for the wrong he had done to their sister, and sets fire to a field in order to secure a meeting with his father (2 Sam. 13–14). Absalom's selfishness and vengeful impulsivity will exact a heavy price later in the story. When we read such stories, we get the impression that the author (assuming a single author) places great ethical value upon wisdom, moderation and self-control, and decries vengefulness and impulsivity. Leviticus 19:18 commands: "Thou shalt not take vengeance, nor bear any grudge." And although it is also written "The Lord is a jealous and avenging God" (Nahum 1:2), the latter belongs to the apocalyptic world of the Later Prophets—quite different from that of the author of Genesis in whose eyes, knowledge is the mark of the divine image in man, not jealousy and revenge.

Yehoshua's interpretation is a midrash. He strives to make the story more accessible to contemporary readers who live in a culture that ascribes great value to man's individuality—judging people by their psychological and emotional traits—even taking these things into consideration in matters of law and social standing. However, Yehoshua's interpretation changes the ethical code at the heart of the story in the hope of finding affirmation for prevailing concepts in our culture. The story was written in an entirely different cultural context, although—and therein lies its greatness—it addresses human instincts and impulses that remain as powerful as they ever were, and thus still require ethical guidance.

In conclusion, Cain—like other protagonists in Genesis—is given an ethical choice, and he—like Adam and Eve before him—acts in a fashion that exposes his basic frail humanness. When jealousy gives rise to an uncontrollable desire for violent revenge, he is unable to resist, yet he is able to say "my sin is too great to bear", and so accept responsibility for his evil deed—something Lemech does not even consider. Were Cain God, he might have been capable of total self-control, but the author of the biblical narrative does not expect man to be God.

David Ohana

Noah

Nimrod—From Nehama Leibowitz to Yitzhak Danziger

And Cush begot Nimrod; he began to be a mighty one in the earth. He was a mighty hunter before the Lord; wherefore it is said: "Like Nimrod a mighty hunter before the Lord" (Genesis 10:8–9).

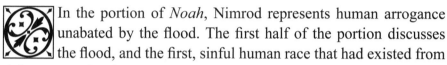In the portion of *Noah*, Nimrod represents human arrogance unabated by the flood. The first half of the portion discusses the flood, and the first, sinful human race that had existed from Adam to Noah. The remainder of the portion relates to the second human race, which was supposed to have been homogeneous and equal, but which—like its predecessor—was quick to stray from the path of equality and brotherhood.

In this chapter, I will present two approaches to the figure of Nimrod: the "Jewish" interpretation of biblical scholar Nehama Leibowitz, and the "Canaanite" interpretation of sculptor Yitzhak Danziger. I will attempt to show that the labels "Jewish" and "Canaanite" with regard to Nimrod, are too simplistic; and through Daniziger's *Nimrod*, I will attempt to create a dialectic between the Jewish-universal and the Canaanite-particular.

Nimrod is the first king mentioned in Bible; the first man to have his name associated with the concept of kingship. The man who "began to be a mighty one in the earth" is also the man whose kingdom had its beginnings in the land of Shinar. He is not a concrete ruler, but a Mesopotamian paradigm of kingship, a paradigm of the rulers of Assyria in the first millennium BCE. To use the term coined by sociologist Max Weber, Nimrod—the father of all kings—is the "ideal type" of kingship, and that is his role within the Bible. The precise genealogy of Nimrod is thus irrelevant, as is his identification with a specific Assyrian or Babylonian king. The first king is real, but also metaphorical; he is not an imaginary king or legendary hero, nor is he a literary figure, but an existential representation of a father-ruler and paradigm for all future kings.

The biblical Nimrod is an embodiment of man-king, not God but man—unlike, the hero-king Gilgamesh, for example, to whom divine origin is ascribed. The story of Nimrod, which lacks mythological elements, shows clear traces of a prebiblical Mesopotamian source; a distant echo of a historical memory. The story is a myth, but in the sense afforded by Martin Buber: a narrative containing a kernel of real historical memory, passed down from generation to generation.

In Nehama Leibowitz' *Studies in* Bereshit, Nimrod represents the polytheistic tendency toward power-seeking, hubris, boldness, and differentiation that stems from the refusal to accept Jewish monotheism's universalistic message. Leibowitz highlights the commentaries of M.D. Cassuto, Isaac Abravanel, and David Kimhi (Radak), who criticize the tendencies represented by Nimrod. Cassuto explains that the new human race created after the flood—like the human race that preceded it—was supposed to have been homogeneous and equal. This view also serves as the basis for later, universalistic eschatological prophecies. The second human race also fails to live up to expectations: humankind becomes fragmented rather than united, strengthening divisions between strong and weak; repression supplants equality; and power-seeking supersedes brotherhood. The representatives of these tendencies are Nimrod and the generation of the builders of the Tower.

Nimrod, as noted above, represents human kingship, as opposed to divinely imposed rule (essentially a concept of reign without subjects— prophetic monarchy). Commentators known for their adherence to the plain meaning of the biblical text, such as Gersonides (Ralbag), Abravanel, and Naphtali Zevi Yehudah Berlin (Netziv), explain that Nimrod invented the concept of "kingship", i.e., rule by dominion. The Sages of the Talmud asserted that the invention of the concept of kingship in a generation that recognized the creator in itself constituted rebellion: "Nimrod the wicked, who with his kingship, incited the entire world against me in rebellion" (*Pesahim* 94b). Abravanel writes as follows: "The Torah wished to tell us our sin, that until that time men were all of equal standing, all descendant from a single man; and Nimrod came and began to dominate and rule over the members of his generation"— something he accomplished as a mighty and cunning hunter. Abravanel also finds fault with Nimrod for having "made towers and strong fortified cities from which to rule over the entire land". Nimrod's tyranny, like that of all tyrants, is accompanied by delusions of grandeur, given expression in the construction of towers and monuments. Abravanel associates Nimrod with the builders of the Tower of Babel and details his sins: possessiveness, power-seeking, and the greatest sin of all—the abrogation of human equality. In his rebellion, Nimrod strove to abrogate the universality of mankind—fruit of the Jewish revolution.

In highlighting the word "began" (*hehel*)—"he began to be a mighty one in the earth"—the biblical commentators expose a human tendency that waxed stronger from generation to generation: from Enosh to the generation of the flood, and from the generation of the flood to the generation of the Tower of Babel. Rabbi Ze'ev Wolf Einhorn, in his commentary (*Perush Maharzu*) on *Rabbah* 23,7 writes: "'*hehel*' derives not from the root *HH"L* (to begin), but from the root *ḤL"L* (to desecrate), that is to say, idolatry. '*Hehel lihiyot gibor*'—Nimrod, with his might, overcame the weak, killed them and stole from them". Rashi on the other hand, explains the word '*gibor*—mighty one' as follows: "to incite the entire world to rebellion against God, with the stratagem of the generation of the Dispersion." "A mighty hunter," according to Rashi, means: "he ensnared men with his words, and misled them to rebel against God" (10:8–9). Rabbi Yehudah Loew of Prague (Maharal), in his commentary *Gur Aryeh* (p. 70), adds: "Nimrod began to be a mighty one before God, when he should have been submissive. The gravity of the rebellion was a matter of idolatry. Nimrod was not merely a mighty hunter, like other hunters, but cunning in divine matters and thus led others to rebel."

A number of characteristic elements are thus associated with Nimrod: kingship, mightiness (mightiness in the hunt rather than in war), rebellion, conquest, construction, and wickedness. Nimrod is a mighty hunter in a utopian kingdom, whose ruler is not an architect of victory but of the hunt of animals, proud of his cruel occupation. Of all the biblical heroes, only Nimrod an Esau are characterized as hunters—"like seeks like", according to A.Y. Kook. Nimrod is proud of his contemptible hobby—God's displeasure—and the fact (of which he is fully aware) that only in his time, two generations after the flood, did the Torah grudgingly permit the eating of flesh, notwithstanding.

The boundaries of "Nimrod's land", which we call Mesopotamia, stretch from Babylonia to Assyria. The Mesopotamian hero is not satisfied merely with the kingdom of Babylon and the cities of Shinar, and thus sets out to conquer Assyria. In addition to the city and tower, later called Babel—construction of which the Talmud ascribes to Nimrod—he builds seven other cities: Erech, Accad, Calneh, Nineveh, Rehoboth-ir, Calah, and Resen. The Sages reinforce his negative image as a rebel against God and builder of the Tower of Babel, identifying him with Amraphel, who cast Abraham into the fiery furnace. Abraham defied Nimrod-Amraphel when the latter sought to replace Abraham's divine religion with his own human one. Abraham represents a turning point in ancient history, while Nimrod represents an earlier era—an era of idolatry, differentiation between men, and the sanctification of polytheistic mythology.

"Nimrod" may be an epithet attached to him by members of his or subsequent generations, due to his rebellious behavior, or perhaps a name of his own choosing, reflecting his intentions. The latter possibility seems the more likely, since a name employed by others would probably have taken the form *yimrod* ("he will rebel") or *mored* ("rebel") rather than *nimrod* ("let us rebel")—in the future tense of the first person plural. The voluntary—as opposed to hereditary—selection of names indicates awareness of the possibility of constructing one's own identity. Such awareness is manifest in the hebraization of foreign names among the "new Hebrews"—product of the first waves of Zionist immigration to Palestine, and the "Canaanite" influence on native-born Palestinian and Israeli Jews. In selecting his own name rather than merely inheriting one, Nimrod may have set a precedent for leaders such as Pharaoh, Abimelech, or Stalin, who sought to shape their image in the eyes of future generations by assuming a name of their own choosing. Nimrod may, however, have been his name from birth, making his actions the result rather than the source of his name as a kind of self-fulfilling prophecy. Nimrod was raised, of course, in the house of Cush son of Ham—the impudent branch of Noah's family—in an atmosphere of rebelliousness.

It was his incitement to rebellion against God that created the image of Nimrod the wicked, from the late biblical period to mishnaic and talmudic times. Josephus describes him as having incited the generation of the Tower to rebellion against God and the Talmud imputes acts of deception and incitement to him. Nimrod's kingship is in itself perceived as rebellion against God by virtue of the dominion it sought to impose. The Tower of Babel, identified with the actions of Nimrod, came to be known as the House of Nimrod. There is general consensus among the commentators that Nimrod personifies malevolent dominion authority exercised not before God, but against God. Nimrod's reign—history's first monarchy—typifies the evil kingdom of Assyria and Babylon, in rabbinic literature. Biblical theology views the desire for power, dominion, and conquest among kings and kingdom, as a direct challenge to the exclusive reign of the Hebrew God. Human monarchy in itself is a product of rebellion against the King of Kings.

According to Bible scholar Yehezkel Kaufmann, biblical religion was revolutionary inasmuch as its approach to the world was not mythological; conceptually, the Israelite God of faith stood beyond myth. The role of biblical religion was thus the eradication of pagan phenomena—vestiges of mythological belief. There is absolutely no evidence, claims Kaufmann, that the Israelites intermingled with the Canaanites, assimilating elements of their religion. There is no mention anywhere, he maintains, of idolatrous influence exerted upon Israel by Canaanites within Israelite territory. Idol worship—as significant as it may be in its own right—is not synonymous with paganism and in no way contradicts the concepts of divine unity or incorporeality. Although popular paganism did exist among the Israelites, it was never true polytheistic worship with temples and priests.

Kaufmann is the radical spokesman of a school of thought that asserts that paganism was never a fertile, culture-producing force in Jewish history. Although idol worship did exist among Jews, it assumed the form of a national cult. According to Kaufmann, the claim that idolatry could not have developed among the Israelites because it was forbidden in the Decalogue is without basis—for it did in fact exist, despite the prohibition. If idolatry did not develop in the presence of belief in divine unity, it was not due to any formal prohibition, but rather to the lack of a mythological tradition capable of serving as a living source for pagan religious art. Israelite paganism was ritualistic, magical, and fetishist, and as such, unable to attain the level of a creative cultural force. The

Bible does not even recognize the possibility of symbolic idolatry; idol worship itself, according to the Bible, is the worship of other gods.

A. G. Horon (also known as Adia Gurevitch and A. Gur) took a completely different approach to the relationship between the Israelite tribes and the Canaanite peoples. Horon dedicated his life's work to revealing the Jewish people's Hebrew past, attempting to prove that a single land, language, and people stretched from the Egyptian frontier to the Euphrates River. Archaeological discoveries at Ebla near Aleppo in Syria, at Mari on the banks of the Euphrates, and at Ugarit on the Syrian coast, strengthened Horon's conviction regarding the existence of a common regional Canaanite-Israelite identity. He made a clear distinction between "Hebrew" and "Jewish"—the former designating national-territorial identity, and the latter communal identity applicable throughout the Diaspora. The "pagans" were thus our "Hebrew" ancestors in the Land of Canaan prior to the Babylonian exile. Jewish monotheism was born during this exile, with Ezra serving as the new religion's lawgiver. Horon drew attention to the biblical redactors' manipulative invention of a mythological story about Nimrod, son of Cush. According to Horon, the redactors included this story in the genealogy of the various peoples of the earth, despite the geographical discrepancy it entailed.

The figure of Nimrod came to symbolize the Canaanite movement and its ideas—from the first issue of *Alef* (organ of the "Young Hebrews") which appeared in 1948, bearing *Nimrod* on its cover, to a special supplement of *Haaretz* in honor of Israel's 50th anniversary, which featured an article by Aharon Amir accompanied by a photograph of Danziger's *Nimrod*.

Following a dramatic encounter with Horon in Paris in the late 1930s, the poet Yonatan Ratosh returned to Palestine and formed an ideological circle adopting Horon's historical and cultural views as the basis for a political movement. One of the first to join Ratosh was the young sculptor Benjamin Tammuz, who also introduced his teacher, Yitzhak Danziger—recently returned from England and France, where he had studied sculpture—to the circle. Danziger, while a student at London University's Slade School of Fine Arts, signed his works "Yitzhak ben Baruch" and adorned his sketches with biblical verses. In Europe he had chosen to highlight his Jewish identity. Upon his return to Palestine, however, he preferred a Hebrew identity.

The sub-heading of Tammuz' article *"Nimrod, The Beginning of Is-raeli Rebirth"*, read: "1939: Yitzhak Danziger Gives Birth to *Nimrod*, Symbol of the New Israeli. 1939: The Old Jew is Led to Auschwitz" (*Globes* 9/4/96). Despite its dramatic dichotomy and the fact that Jews were in fact led to Auschwitz only three years later, the title manages to convey the revolutionary message that many ascribed to the work and the tragic significance of its timing—as if it were a crossroads at which the old world was razed to the ground and a brave new world sought to emerge from the ruins, borne by the new Hebrew. Did "the ancient hunter Nimrod become a Palmah fighter (like Danziger himself), and the symbol of the new Jew, a monument to the spirit of rebellion of the generation of '48"? For that is what appears as Danziger's source of inspiration in *Nimrod*'s catalogue listing.

In the spring of 2000, Danziger's *Nimrod* was removed from its per-manent location in the Israel Museum's Israeli Art Wing, for a brief stay in the museum's restoration department. In white coats, as if in an operating theater, members of the department worked for a number of weeks to create a negative of the original, and cast two plaster copies. The statue had been copied before, by Danziger himself, in the private foundry of Yossef Zaritsky. This time however, the work was carried out with careful precision. The statue was wrapped in plastic and smeared with a modelling-clay and epoxy mixture. When the clay was removed, the resulting cavity was filled with silicone. Following the copying pro-cedure, *Nimrod* came to rest in the museum's storehouse as well. The entire procedure was but the latest chapter in the history of Israel's most significant work of art; a work that has become, since its creation in 1939, an artistic icon, a symbol of Israeli identity and a founding myth in Israeli culture.

No other Israeli work, it would seem, has been the object of such wide-ranging and conflicting interpretations. For over 60 years, Dan-ziger's sculpture has served as a prism of Israeli identity; a kind of Rashomon of Israeli self-awareness and identity. *Nimrod* is an axis—with the "new Hebrew" warrior in the tradition of Zionism's Canaanite cult at one extreme (an approach also reflected in Avraham Melinkoff's

Tel Hai Memorial—1926), and the post-Zionist challenge at the other extreme, seeking to expose the shame of the Israeli-Zionist-Hebrew hunting god, and presenting a counterweight to the Zionist ethos of heroism, in the form of the Jewish Nimrod: a wandering, studious, *tefilin*-wearing, antihero.

This kind of polarity came to the fore once again in 1988, in two key interpretations by leading figures in the world of Israeli art who set out to bless and to curse *Nimrod*. Tammuz, who had witnessed the work's creation, and was a member of the hard core of the Canaanite group, was surprised to discover *Nimrod* in the Israel Museum after having wondered about the sculpture's whereabouts for decades. "I ran toward the statue, embraced it, and kissed it. Only then, moving away, looking at it through a shadow of tears, did it strike me that I had been guilty of idol-worship, for I had kissed a statue! Was I really one of those madmen who kiss the ground at political rallies of messianic lunatics?" (Tammuz, *ibid.*).

In that same year, art critic and museum curator Sarah Breitberg-Semel wrote, in what is perhaps the most important critique of the work to date: "Today, he annoys me, like the shameful, pointless, youthful indiscretion of one of our greatest artists—divorced from and drained of history, charged with graceless myths, unaware of the image he projects? What do he and I have in common?" (*Agripas Neged Nimrod, Yediot Ahronot*, 1/9/88).

Nimrod conveys an internal contradiction between the Canaanite ideal and the bearer of that ideal or its symbol, which is of biblical origin. *Nimrod's* Canaanite representation, its form and occupation, is a rebellion against Judaism inasmuch as it leaps thousands of years back in time to mythological and pagan culture, and in so doing, rejects the idea of Jewish cultural continuity. The conscious mythologization of Canaanite aesthetic sought to create a rift in the textual thread of Jewish history. Furthermore, not only is *Nimrod* not a text—the Jewish creative form par excellence—but a statue associated with Canaanite place striving to repudiate the unity of abstract belief by offering an alternative, regional identity in which physical place supplants metaphysical place.

The awakening of Jewish national consciousness in the late 19th century, given expression in the birth of Zionism, changed the attitude of many Jews to the ethos of heroism. The heroes of the Jewish renaissance were no longer associated with the intellectual tradition of rabbis and scholars, saints and mystics, but with "real" heroes—sword-wielding adherents of "muscular Judaism".

The heroic myths of Jewish history began to inspire a Jewish revolutionary ethos, or in the words of Berdyczewski: "The people's ancient heroes and their exploits shall be a symbol and staff of strength in the hands of the next generation" (M. J. Berdyczewski, *Toladah, Baderekh* 3 p. 20). The new-old heroes are Simeon and Gideon, Saul, Joab and Abimelech, Herod and Eleazar ben Yair, and, of course, Nimrod. Berdyczewski's heroes are "those who conquered Canaan by the sword, and not those who returned from Babylon by their tears" (Aliza Klausner-Eshkol, *Hashpa'at Nietzsche Veschopenauer al M.Y. Bin-Gurion*, 5711/1951). The result is a selective view of Jewish history that nevertheless aspires to what anthropologist Claude Lévi-Strauss defined as the desire to find unity in history through myths. In terms of Nathan Rotenstreich's philosophy of history, it is not a unity of continuity, but of revolution.

Nimrod—the warrior and the rebel—was shaped and nurtured by the Canaanites as a metaphor for their rebellion against Zionism, which continued to sustain the Gordian knot binding Judaism and "Hebrewism". Boaz Evron asserts that "the rebel is, after all, raised within the conceptual framework against which he rebels, and his thought is conditioned first and foremost by the prevailing concepts within that framework" (*Haheshbon Haleumi* p. 354). "Canaanitism" was a rebellion against Zionism precisely because the latter had attained its goals: the return to Zion and the definition of nationality exclusively in terms of ties to the homeland. The process of marginalization of Judaism—begun by figures such as Berdyczewski, Saul Tchernichowski, and David Ben-Gurion, who had sought to replace the "Jew" with the "Hebrew"—culminated in Canaanite ideology that severed the ethnic connection between "Jew" and "Hebrew"—the native speaker of the Hebrew language who resides in his Hebrew homeland.

"Nimrod died in late 1947," declared Amos Kenan in the final chapter—entitled "From *Nimrod* to the Holocaust Pyramid"—of *Shoshanat Yeriho* (*Rose of Jericho*). *Nimrod*, according to Kenan, stands as a memorial to the ideals of 1948, the generation of the Palmah, the "golden age" of Jewish settlement in Palestine—a period spanning 30 years, coming to a close with the War of Independence—the "Hebrew Age". Kenan claimed that the sculpture *Nimrod* had fomented a revolution:

> [It fomented] the pulsating revolutionary spirit of the early forties.... *Nimrod* was a revolution, but a revolution embraced with enthusiasm by a younger generation that found expression in it. It was the expression of a spirit, a feeling of exhilarating creativity, a longing for Hebrew expression in general: in music and dance, in the connection to the land. There was a longing for Hebrew farmers, fishermen, sailors and warriors, thinkers and artists. *Nimrod* expressed this longing (*Shoshanat Yeriho*, 1998, p. 278).

This longing died a premature death in 1947. Uri Avneri refers to the end of the era of Hebrew culture as "The Death of Nimrod" in an article by that name. He places its birth in the 1930s and its demise in the 1940s. Using the concepts developed by Oswald Spengler and Arnold Toynbee, he portrays culture as a living organism that grows, withers, and decays. The new Hebrew culture in Mandatory Palestine, according to Avneri, thus "struck root, flowered and died" (*Omanut Hapisul Beyisrael: Hipus Zehut*, 1988, p. 25).

Hebrew culture was born in the 1930s, because it was only at that time that it began to see itself as a historical subject; a new society fully aware of its own power and hunger for cultural expression. The new Hebrew language and the new Hebrew nation sustained one another. In response to the question, "What is the new Hebrew culture, and how is it expressed?", Avneri said: "Formal beginnings can be observed in literature, poetry and art. Some see Yitzhak Danzger's sculpture *Nimrod* as a symbol of this culture, although it was also influenced by foreign styles" (*ibid.*).

Shlomo Shva does not see *Nimrod* as a tragic symbol of a culture that is no more, but as one of "the first expressions of vague stirrings in the hearts of a few young people, who wished to return to the primeval dawn hinted at in the ancient words of the Bible, and written on stones and clay tablets throughout the Middle East" (*Makom Tahat*

Hashemesh, op. cit., p. 21). The sense of homeland and belonging was not self-evident to the children of immigrants to Palestine. Their parents "considered themselves foreigners—transients. They had no connection to the landscapes that lived inside them." Upon their arrival, they felt as if they had been reborn: discovering "love for the place, the region, the country, the homeland." Wondering how they might live in this new-old place, they concluded that they must incorporate ancient "Eretz-Israelitism" into Hebrew culture and art, make a temporal leap, and reclaim the ancient life of this land. That is how Canaanitism was born; the paradoxical fruit of Jewish extremism.

Shva is one of the few cultural critics to address the dialectic process of creating the new from the ancient. Attitudes to Canaanitism and the Land of Israel were in fact the product of Jewish yearning—having "known no home, land or nature—for land and nature. This Jewish longing also produced the intensely anti-Jewish Canaanite movement" (*ibid.*). One might say that Danziger—the "Eretz-Israelite and foreigner" who sought after the ancient land—"served as a guide for his own work—executed in the image of ancient art". Painter Michael Segen-Cohen writes: "It is interesting that this Canaanite hero bears a biblical name. Yet the Canaanite-pagan approach is a correct one. Rashi says of the hero from the book of Genesis, that he would incite the people against God. In other words, the Nimrod of the Rabbis was a rebel against God." Art critic Gideon Efrat also addressed the Jewish-Canaanite dialectic, writing in his book *Nimrod Bitfilin* (Nimrod in *Tefilin*) that "Nimrod in *tefilin* is a paradox, a conflicted soul, torn between its Israeli and Jewish identity, between setting down roots and wandering" (*Nimrod Bitfilin, Beheksher Mekomi*, p. 315–323).

Danziger's sculpture has undergone a fascinating transformation: if at first *Nimrod* embodied the "new Hebrew" striving for rootedness and absorption into the region, in recent years, the work has begun to represent the longing for wandering and exile: *Nimrod* went from "new Hebrew" to "wandering Jew". Sarit Shapira, curator of the exhibit *Maslulei Nedudim* (Wandering Routes), sees *Nimrod* as a mighty hunter, living in a nomadic society, "a figure that represents an approach to local culture through the desert. Nomadism is... an energy that eliminates boundaries" (*Studio* 29, p. 9). The Jew puts aside his land in order to write text.

Moses, who writes the Torah in the desert, is the ultimate exponent of the principle of rootlessness. The concept of rootlessness in Jewish and Israeli culture thus assumes a new form, inasmuch as nomadism is portrayed as the true identity of the Jew and the Israeli.

Other critics share this post-Zionist approach. Smadar Tirosh notes that it is no wonder that Danziger, who at the age of 23 had spent more time in Europe than in Palestine, possessed a "local identity that was more aspiration—based on the declared ideal of man's integration into his environment—than undeniable fact; and hence, paradoxically, entailed an element of foreignness" (*Mishkafayim* 22, pp. 17–19).

Nimrod has not escaped the prevailing iconoclastic atmosphere in Israel—characterized by its destruction of Zionist symbols. The following titles are typical of critical articles on the subject, published in the late 1990s: "We Don't Want another Hero" by Ruth Direktor; "How the Mighty have Fallen" by Gideon Efrat; "Nimrod is just a Doll" by Rami Rosen; "I am not Nimrod" by Shlomit Steinberg. Even a simple account of a court ruling regarding a copy of Danziger's statue, appearing in the *Maariv* daily, was given the headline "Destroy Nimrod!"

Gitit Holzman

Lekh-Lekha – Get Thee Out

Melchizedek King of Salem: Priest of God the Most High
In the Thought of **Elia Benamozegh**

And Melchizedek king of Salem brought forth bread and wine; and he was priest of God the Most High. And he blessed him, and said: "Blessed be Abram of God Most High, Maker of heaven and earth" (Genesis 14:18–19).

Lekh-lekha, the third portion in the book of Genesis, comprises six chapters and recounts familiar and important events. The portion opens with God's words to Abraham: "Get thee out of thy country, and from thy kindred, and from thy father's house, unto the land that I will show thee" (12:1). It goes on to describe his arrival in the land of Canaan, his descent to Egypt due to famine, and his return to Canaan, accompanied by his parting of ways with his brother's son Lot. Chapter 13 ends with the divine promise to give the land to Abraham and to his seed forever. Chapter 14 describes Lot's kidnapping by the king of Sodom, and his rescue by Abraham. Chapter 15 includes God's promise to give Abraham seed, and of course, the "Covenant of the Pieces" (*berit bein habetarim*). Chapter 16 tells the story of Hagar's flight from Sarah's wrath and the birth of her son Ishmael. In chapter 17, Abraham and his seed are commanded to keep their covenant with God and recall it through the rite of circumcision.

In light of all of these weighty matters, the choice of Melchizedek—mentioned only briefly in a few verses in chapter 14—as the focus of this discussion seems a little odd. Clearly, this king and his meeting with Abraham do not figure among the portion's more important matters. The decision to focus on the figure of Melchizedek did not naturally come to mind reading the chapters of *Lekh Lekha*, but was the result of having studied the unique commentary of Elia (Elijah) Benamozegh on this

portion in particular and on the Pentateuch in general, further influenced
by the desire to contribute to familiarity with this original thinker and
his exegetical works. (An outline of the thought of Elia Benamozegh can
be found in my article *"Universaliyut Ule'umiyut, Yisrael Vehe'amim,
Bemishnat Harav Eliyahu Ben Amozegh," Pe'amim*, pp. 104–130.)

Benamozegh's commentary on the Pentateuch, entitled *Em Lamikra*, comprises five volumes, published in Leghorn in 1862–1863, and
disseminated throughout the Jewish communities of the Mediterranean
basin. The commentary's originality and innovativeness—combining
Kabbalah, mythology, and scientific knowledge—was received with enthusiasm, as well as intense debate. Among the rabbis of Aleppo, Benamozegh's ideas aroused such strong opposition, that his books were
burned—along with the words of the Torah itself! The rabbis of Aleppo
were so incensed by Benamozegh's writings that they urged the Jews of
Damascus to burn all of the copies of *Em Lamikra* in their possession,
and berated all who failed to do so. Benamozegh responded publicly to
the various accusations levelled at him, and found supporters in the communities of Salonika and Izmir. (This affair is treated extensively in Yar-
on Harel's article *"Ha'ala'at Em Lamikra Al Hamoked: Haleb* 1865".)
Nevertheless, the extreme reaction to his biblical commentary undoubtedly discouraged Benamozegh from publishing his *Em Lamasoret*—a
broad commentary on the writings of the Rabbis. The burning of *Em
Hamikra* may also offer a partial explanation for the fact that few copies
of the work have survived. What was it about this commentary, written
some 140 years ago, that aroused such extreme reactions?

Benamozegh's treatment of the figure of Melchizedek king of Salem, explained in light of other ideas appearing in his work, provides
an example of his unusual approach to the Bible and Jewish tradition
in general, as well as insight into the intense opposition this approach
engendered.

Genesis 14 begins with a description of the war of the four kings
against the five kings waged in the vicinity of the Dead Sea. During the
course of the war, Lot is taken prisoner following the defeat of the king of
Sodom, and Abraham comes to his rescue. The chapter tells of the meeting between Abraham and the defeated king of Sodom, but interrupts the
story in order to describe Abraham's meeting with Melchizedek: "And

Melchizedek king of Salem brought forth bread and wine; and he was priest of God the Most High. And he blessed him, and said: 'Blessed be Abram of God Most High, Maker of heaven and earth'" (14:18–19). In his commentary on these verses, Benamozegh stresses that Salem (*Shalem*) is the ancient name for Jerusalem, citing Psalm 76:3: "In Salem also is set His tabernacle, and His dwelling-place in Zion", which creates a parallel between the names "Salem" and "Zion"; as well as the Midrash in *Rabbah* (56,10) that explains the name Jerusalem (*Yerushalayim*) as a composite of the names *Yireh* and *Shalem*. Benamozegh also discusses the name of the king of Jerusalem, Melchizedek (King of Zedek), maintaining that Zedek (righteousness) too was one of the city's ancient names, as for example, in Isaiah (1:26): "Afterward thou shalt be called the city of righteousness (*zedek*), the faithful city." For this reason, he explains, the kings of the city were known by the name Zedek, and it is in this vein that he understands Isaiah 1:21 "righteousness (*zedek*) lodged in her"; and Jeremiah 23:5–6: "Behold, the days come, saith the Lord, that I will raise unto David a righteous shoot, and he shall reign as king and prosper, and shall execute justice and righteousness (*zedek*) in the land. In his days Judah shall be saved, and Israel shall dwell safely; and this is his name whereby he shall be called, The Lord Is Our Righteousness (*Zedek*)".

Benamozegh bases his assertion that Jerusalem was sacred even to the people who resided there before Israel on the premises that Salem is Jerusalem and that its ancient king was priest of God the Most High— i.e., the God of Abraham. He thus concludes the existence of a certain affinity between the religions known as pagan and the Jewish religion: "For the Israelites were not averse to building their Temple citadel in a place where the peoples before them had worshipped God the Most High, to show that the two services are one, with the latter merely perfecting the former" (*Em Lamikra*, Gen. 14:19).

"The two services" are the cult known as pagan and branded "idol worship" and worship of God. Benamozegh believed that in essence, there is no difference between the two cults and that the two should be viewed as different stages of a single path. He intimates that the source of this affinity is the fact that a single divine force stands behind the various cults that seem so different from one another. It is this force that

guided Israel to choose as their holy place specifically the place that was
sacred to their enemies:

> This too is a sign that it was the divine spirit among Israel [that
> determined their] remaining near or going further afield and not
> their king, for without the will of Heaven the People of Israel
> could not—after having dispossessed the land's inhabitants,
> their bitter foes—have chosen to worship God in a place that had
> been sacred to the first inhabitants, had it not been for a divine
> command. And He who forbade the high mountains and the hills
> permitted Jerusalem and Mount Moriah (*ibid.*).

"He who forbade the high mountains and the hills" refers to the
prohibition against worshiping in places formerly used for idolatry, as
it is written: "Ye shall surely destroy all the places, wherein the nations
that ye are to dispossess served their gods, upon the high mountains,
and upon the hills, and under every leafy tree" (Deut. 12:2). Ostensibly,
this injunction should have applied to Jerusalem as well, having served
as the cult site of Melchizedek. Not only is Jerusalem not prohibited
however, it is chosen by the Israelites as the primary focus of their divine worship. Benamozegh believed that this strange phenomenon of a
people deliberately choosing the holy place of its "bitter foes" as its own
holy site can only be explained if we understand that they were imbued
with and guided by the sprit of God.

In his book *Israel and Humanity* (1994), Benamozegh again discusses the name "Jerusalem", claiming that the name itself is a symbol
of the affinity between Judaism and other religions. In support of this
claim, he cites a passage from the Midrash:

> Abraham called it *Yireh*, as it is written (Gen. 22) 'And Abra-
> ham called the name of that place *Adonai-yireh*; as it is said to
> this day: In the mount where the Lord is seen'. Shem called it
> *Shalem* (Salem), as it is written (Gen. 14) 'And Melchizedek
> king of Salem'. God said, if I call it *Yireh* as Abraham called
> it, Shem, a righteous man, will object. And if I call it *Shalem*,
> as Shem called it, Abraham, a righteous man, will object. I will
> therefore call it Jerusalem, as both called it: *Yireh-Shalem*" (*Rab-*
> *bah* 56:10).

Benamozegh notes that one element of the name Jerusalem belongs to Israel and one to paganism, and so is a mark of the affinity that exists between Israel and the nations. He points out that the name Jerusalem appears in the dual form, intimating a historical duality, a perpetual affinity between Judaism and paganism and other monotheistic religions (*Israel and Humanity* pp. 317—323).

Elsewhere in his commentary and other writings, Benamozegh attributes this perpetual affinity to the fact that it is the God of Israel who stands behind all of the world's many and varied cults and religions. This audacious approach is closely related to Benamozegh's understanding of the Kabbalah. On the one hand, he saw the Kabbalah as an ancient and original Jewish doctrine that spread throughout the ancient world. On the other hand, he identified the Kabbalah with the Oral Law, believing it to be the esoteric teachings given to Moses, passed down to future generations.

Benamozegh believed that the essence of Jerusalem as the chosen city was part of these esoteric teachings. He notes that there is no reference to Jerusalem in the Pentateuch, as the future site of the Temple. Nevertheless, the choice of Jerusalem for this purpose was not a matter of chance, nor was it a human act, but the work of God. In support, he cites Deuteronomy 12:5: "But unto the place which the Lord your God shall choose out of all your tribes to put His name there, even unto His habitation shall ye seek, and thither thou shalt come." In the expression "the place which the Lord your God shall choose," the Written Law offers a clue regarding the place in question, while the explicit name—Jerusalem—was revealed, according to Benamozegh, in the orally-transmitted esoteric tradition.

Benamozegh found evidence for this assertion in two verses in Genesis: "The Lord said unto Abram: 'Get thee out of thy country, and from thy kindred, and from thy father's house, unto the land that I will show thee'" (12:1); "And He said: 'Take now thy son, thine only son, whom thou lovest, even Isaac, and get thee into the land of Moriah; and offer him there for a burnt offering upon one of the mountains which I will tell thee of'" (22:2). In neither verse does God explicitly state the name of the place to which Abraham is required to go. Nevertheless, Abraham finds his way both to Canaan and to the mountain, which he recognized from afar. In these verses, Benamozegh found evidence that certain things, including the sanctity of Jerusalem and the Land of Israel, were conveyed directly by God to his elect and subsequently passed down in the Oral Law.

Thus far, we have seen that the selection of Jerusalem as Israel's sacred place manifests an affinity between Judaism and other religions, and that the very name "Jerusalem" attests to the existence of a spiritual affinity between the various religions and peoples. Elsewhere in Benamozegh's commentary, he asserts that the name and city of Jerusalem attest not only to an affinity between Israel and the nations, but also to a connection between the temporal and the divine worlds.

In his comments on the expression *ashterot tzonekha* (Deut. 28:4), Benamozegh cites the ancient practice of naming cities after deities, and discusses the source of the name Jerusalem and its meaning. He explains the word *ashterot* to mean "ewes", based on the well-known fact (according to Benamozegh) that "*Ashtoreth* was a 'detestation of the Zidonians' in the form of a ewe":

> And in honor of the goddess, the city was called Ashtoreth, just as Jerusalem was named after the Holy One, blessed be He, as explained by our Sages who were more familiar with the ancients than some of late would think.... And Jerusalem is the name of the *Sefirah* of *Malkhut* (Kingdom), which is the matrix of all the female deities and is also called *Rahel* (ewe) by the kabbalists, just as her consort *Tiferet* (Beauty) is called *Seh* (lamb). And all of this shows that the root of wisdom burst forth in ancient times—times in which these names were common and well-known to adherents of religion—unlike today, when it is [widely] believed that the kabbalists' words are pure invention. And so the earthly and the heavenly Jerusalem are both called Zedek and Zion and the City of David, just as Ashtoreth was both the name of a city and of a female deity, and as Athena is the name both of a Greek goddess and of the famous city of wisdom: Athens (*Em Lamikra* 107a).

These remarks include a number of basic principles in the thought of Elia Benamozegh, which we will explain below.

The word *Ashtaroth* appears in the Bible as a place name, and the word *Ashtoreth* as the name of a goddess. Ashtaroth was one of the cities of Og, king of Bashan, mentioned in Deuteronomy (1:4), and a number of times in the book of Joshua (9:10; 12:4; 13:12). Following the conquest of the kingdom of Og, Ashtaroth fell to the lot of the sons of Machir son of Manasseh (Jos 13:31), and was designated a Levite city (1 Chron. 6:56). Ashtoreth was a Canaanite goddess, whom the Bible calls "the detestation of the Zidonians" (2 Kings 23:13), and to whom Solomon is said to have built high places in Jerusalem, where she was worshiped until Josiah came and destroyed them. The source of Benamozegh's assertion that Ashtoreth was represented in the form of a ewe is unclear. It may derive from the expression *ashterot tzonekha* that associates ewes with the goddess, or perhaps evoke an ancient custom of presenting newborn lambs to Ashtoreth. The Bible, in any event, uses the expression in contexts stressing the fact that the offspring of live-stock are a gift from God—apparently to repudiate the ancient practice (Deut. 7:13; 28:4).

Benamozegh would appear to have hit the mark in associating the name of the city with the name of the goddess, for it is almost certain that Og's city and other places of the same name were so designated be-cause they practiced the cult of Ashtoreth. He finds further confirmation of this ancient practice in the example of Athens, named for the goddess Athena.

Benamozegh asserts that the Sages—i.e. the kabbalists, whom he saw as sages of antiquity—"were familiar with the ancients", i.e. the pagans. Similarly, he claims, Jerusalem was named after God; although in the case of Jerusalem, the name does not represent an individual god or goddess, but a more complex system of divinity. He explains that Jeru-salem is the name of the *Sefirah* of *Malkhut*, the lowest of the ten Sefirot enumerated by the kabbalists—the *Sefirah* that links the world of the Sefirot to the physical world. Through this *Sefirah*, identified with the *Shekhinah*, the godhead is revealed and *shefa* (divine abundance) from the upper Sefirot is channelled to our world. Benamozegh also mentions the names Zedek, Zion, and the City of David that, in his opinion, de-note both the earthly and the heavenly Jerusalem.

Jerusalem indeed appears in the Zohar as one of the names of the *Se-firah* of *Malkhut*, as does the designation *Zedek*. The name *Rahel* is also mentioned in the Zohar as one of the names of *Malkhut*, but in the sense of *Rahel* (Rachel), wife of Jacob, rather than in the sense of "ewe". As Benamozegh notes, the *Sefirah* of *Malkhut* is linked to the *Sefirah* of *Tif-eret*—identified with the patriarch Jacob. In fact, the unification of the *Shekhinah* with *Tiferet* is one of the purposes of prayer and observance of the precepts. The fact that Benamozegh mentions that the *Sefirah* of *Malkhut* is also known as *Rahel* can be seen as an attempt to associate this *Sefirah*—and the *Sefirot* in general—with the cult of Ashtoreth. This would seem to be in the spirit of his previous assertion that the two serv-ices—idolatry and worship of God—are in fact one and the same, the differences between them being a matter of degree rather than essence. This would also seem to be his intention in the statement "And Jerusa-lem is the name of the *Sefirah* of *Malkhut*, which is the matrix of all the female deities" (*Em Lamikra* 106b)—i.e. the *Sefirah* of *Malkhut* is the source, the image in which all of the "female deities" were made. He may even have been intimating that the source of the ancient custom of naming cities after goddesses lies in the connection between the earthly Jerusalem and the Temple, the heavenly Jerusalem, the *Shekhinah*, and the *Sefirah* of *Malkhut.*

We may now ask, in what way is the *Sefirah* of *Malkhut* the "ma-trix" of all the "female deities"? Was he referring to a cultural influence exerted by the People of Israel on the nations of the world, or an actual process of outflowing or emanation (*atzilut*) of additional divine forces from the *Sefirah* of *Malkhut*? An answer to this question can be found in Benamozegh's commentary on the verse "Thou shalt not plant thee an Asherah of any kind of tree beside the altar of the Lord thy God, which thou shalt make thee" (Deut. 16:21):

> And who knows if Astarte-Ashtoreth is not also the Asherah, with a difference in inflection, and it seems to me now that the meaning of the word Ashtar or Isthar (Ishtar) in Persian is the planet Venus, which was, in the eyes of the ancients, a female deity who commands desire, eventually called Asherah by the Hebrews, in order to bring it closer to the Holy Tongue ... And Astarte and Ashtoreth and Asherah ... are the same Isthar [men-

tioned] in the Talmud, in the tractate of *Megilah* (13), by which name the Persians call Esther, after Isthar, that is the planet Venus, the goddess of sexual intercourse, like Asherah and Ashtoreth. And from the connection and dependence of all of these on the quality (*midah*) of *Malkhut*, as we have written, the Talmud states (*Hulin* 139b): Where is Esther mentioned in the Torah? 'And I will surely hide (haster astir) my face in that day for all the evil which they shall have wrought, in that they are turned unto other gods' (Deut. 31:18). They modified the Persian word, as they concede, to a Hebrew form, as was their wont, in order to reveal the matter and its sublime root, and that is the *Shekhinah* or *Malkhut* that hides or reveals her face in accordance with the actions of those on earth" (*Em Lamikra* 68a–b).

Benamozegh explains the prohibition against planting an Asherah in that it is a symbol of one of the gods of the nations. He postulates that the god with whom the Asherah is associated is Ashtoreth and denounces her cult due to the licentiousness it involved. He goes on to identify Ashtoreth with the Persian Isthar, noting that the Sages of the Talmud find the Hebrew origin of the name in the verse "And I will surely hide (*haster astir*) my face in that day" (Deut. 31:18). According to Benamozegh, the Sages' intention in this was to convey that Esther is "the *Shekhinah* or *Malkhut* that hides or reveals its face in accordance with the actions of those on earth" (*ibid.*). The name Esther is one of the names the Zohar ascribes to the *Sefirah* of *Malkhut*, apparently associated with the queenly role played by the biblical Esther. According to Benamozegh, the pagan cults of Asherah, Ashtoreth, and Ishtar are all connected to and dependent upon the quality of *Malkhut*. This can be understood to mean that that the "female deities" are indeed emanations from the *Sefirah* of *Malkhut*, i.e. whence their metaphysical force derives. If so, it is not merely a matter of cultural influence, but a far more significant spiritual phenomenon.

Benamozegh's remarks regarding the *Shekhinah* hiding or revealing her face, would thus appear to refer to the various manifestations of the goddess among different peoples. Proof of the fact that Benamozegh did not necessarily view these goddess cults in a negative light is the fact that he mentions Athena, with whom he associates "the famous city of wisdom: Athens" (*Em Lamikra* 107a). The aspect of the goddess that appears to each people; the nature of each cult; the direction in which it leads—whether physical or spiritual—is determined by the actions of those on earth: the ways and habits of the people who feel the presence of the *Sefirah Malkhut*, and choose to worship her.

At the beginning of this chapter, we explained Benamozegh's belief that Jerusalem was holy both to the peoples that resided in the land before the Israelites and of course to the Israelites themselves. This paradox—the fact that the Israelites had chosen to build their temple specifically in a place that had been sacred to their enemies—proves, in his opinion, that it was not a chance or arbitrary choice. It is God who instructed his believers to choose Jerusalem as their holy city, an instruction passed down in esoteric tradition through the generations. The reason for this, and for the fact that Abraham, David, and their descendents were not deterred from choosing the city of Melchizedek as a site central to their own religious cult, was their understanding that the earlier cult was not in essence different from their own. Abraham did not hesitate to accept Melchizedek's blessing and in addressing the king of Sodom, adopted the very same formula employed by the king of Salem "God Most High, Maker of heaven and earth": "And Abram said to the king of Sodom: 'I have lifted up my hand unto the Lord, God Most High, Maker of heaven and earth'" (14:22).

The appearance of the Jewish People and religion on the stage of history was thus marked by respect for earlier religions, and reliance upon them. Consequently, the advance of Judaism did not negate the validity of other religious traditions. Benamozegh believed that God is not only a distant and unknown entity; and inasmuch as he viewed the Kabbalah as the core and essence of Judaism, he adopted its doctrine of a vast and complex system of divine forces at work in the universe. It is this dynamic and pluralistic approach that would appear to have led Benamozegh to show openness and tolerance toward the variety of religions and cultures of the ancient world, and toward those still extant in his day.

In the Kabbalah, Benamozegh saw the esoteric tradition transmitted as Oral Law. In his commentary on Numbers 3, he writes: "The wisdom of Kabbalah is the soul of the Torah." He found elements of Kabbalah in the works of the Sages, and even in the writings of Maimonides: "The words of Maimonides and the words of the Kabbalah are one" (commentary on Ex. 6:3). Benamozegh further expanded upon this harmonious view. Not only did he consider Kabbalah the wellspring of the Torah and Jewish thought in general, but believed it to be an ancient source of many and varied spiritual systems. He was of the opinion that the seeds of Kabbalah were sown in the hearts of men before they were scattered upon the face of the earth—finding proof of this in the similarity between the various spiritual systems known in his time. In his commentary on Exodus 6:3, he asserts that the "unity of origin of the human race" and its "unity of belief before men were separated from one another" can be proven. The evidence that he offers is based on the words *El Shaddai*. Benamozegh explains that *Shaddai* derives from the word *dai* (sufficient), and signifies that God is "sufficient for all who trust in him". He claims that both the Latin *deus*, and the Indian *dao* derive from this word. He was aware of the fact that *dao* does not refer to a personal god of any kind, but means "way". This posed no difficulty however, to Benamozegh: "Among the names of God, *Shaddai* is the name that denotes the quality of *Yesod* (Foundation) called *Shaddai*, known among the kabbalists simply as 'way' (*derekh*); and in this, the name *Shaddai* and its significance among the kabbalists can be compared to the name *dao* and its meaning among the Indians, whence the other similar names of the Creator issued, each after their tongues, in their lands, after their nations" (*Em Lamikra* 20a).

The affinity between Judaism and other religions is thus explained by the fact that each religion was influenced by different aspects of the esoteric wisdom of the Kabbalah. Hence, all worship the same God or one of His various aspects—each people in its own unique way.

Hagai Dagan

Vayera – And the Lord Appeared

The Human God and the Divine God
Based on the Thought of Søren Kierkegaard

And Abraham drew near, and said: "Wilt Thou indeed sweep away the righteous with the wicked? Peradventure there are fifty righteous within the city; wilt Thou indeed sweep away and not forgive the place for the fifty righteous that are therein? That be far from Thee to do after this manner, to slay the righteous with the wicked, that so the righteous should be as the wicked; that be far from Thee; shall not the Judge of all the earth do justly?" (Genesis 18:23–25)

In *Vayera* we find two separate incidents, presenting different and even opposing approaches to the connection between religion and ethics. In the first incident (*ibid.* 23–33), Abraham engages in debate with God, who has decided to destroy Sodom and all its inhabitants. The decision is not stated explicitly, but arises from the dialogue between Abraham and God—initiated by Abraham. The story begins with Abraham "standing before God"—not kneeling or prostrating himself. Thus throughout the difficult and poignant exchange, Abraham stands his ground and demands that God address the ethical ramifications of the course of action he intends to pursue. Abraham does not humble himself, plead, bow, or scrape. His tone is assertive, firm, coherent, and to the point—albeit not without cunning—typical of negotiation in general, although it is human life that hangs in the balance here.

Asserting a point of ethical principle, Abraham begins the discussion with the question/demand: "Wilt Thou indeed sweep away the righteous with the wicked?" (verse 23). He then goes on to quantify his argument. The discussion itself is a little perplexing, since it concludes with God's agreement not to destroy the city for the sake of ten righteous men. Whether he would have agreed not to destroy the city for less is unclear. In the end, we know that God destroyed the city, allowing the sole righteous man and his family to escape. The discussion ends however, and Abraham departs, perhaps reluctant to demand more of God—that he not destroy the city for the sake of a single righteous man. It would appear from the discussion that, in principle, God was prepared to accept Abraham's argument, contingent upon certain "practical" quantitative considerations. In other words, the city should not be destroyed if it numbers righteous men among its inhabitants. One righteous man however, does not generate sufficient "righteous mass" to prevent its destruction. Similarly, for example, the State of Israel opposes the killing of innocent civilians, even those who belong to a collective defined as the enemy. If the opportunity arises for the "targeted execution" of an enemy operative however, and it involves the killing of a number of innocent passers-by, their innocence is not sufficient to prevent the murder of the "wicked" man. The answer to "Wilt Thou indeed sweep away the righteous with the wicked?" is thus: in principle, no, but in certain quantitative circumstances, yes.

With this one reservation, God appears receptive to ethical arguments and even demands. He is portrayed as a normative god, who places his ethical aspect above all others. In the Bible, on the other hand—and even more so in post-biblical literature—God is depicted as possessing two conflicting sets of characteristics. He is transcendent, that is external, above and beyond human reality, and thus able to rule the world without being bound by its rules and constraints. He created it from without, governs empirical and historical reality, and is omnipotent (contrary to the created and the present). He is therefore not bound by reason or human norms. In other words, God is neither rational nor ethical. Despite attempts to claim that God possesses his own reason and his own ethics above human reason and ethics and therefore beyond human understanding, this insight is irrefutable, for the simple reason that reason and ethics are human categories. Anything that stands "above" them cannot, by definition be ethical or rational. The claim that "God is good, but his good is not the same as ours" is thus completely without basis. If I lack the ability to understand and judge his reason and ethics, I can have no way of determining that he is good. Abraham demonstrates this to great effect: he demands that God conform to the demands of human ethics. You are good? Then you must not sweep away the righteous with the wicked. That is the only good there is, and there is no other. The resounding demand, "shall not the Judge of all the earth do justly," is meaningless if the rulings of the Judge of all the earth are incomprehensible to those who come before him in judgment. And God in fact accepts this logic. In a certain sense, Abraham—in his direct and courageous manner—compels God to appear as an ethical god. He frees God from the initial ambiguity of a decision that seemed to require no further explanation, and takes him to court—a Torah court, if you will—in the earliest and most basic sense of the word. In so doing, he denies God his omnipotence, placing him instead at the opposite pole: that of an ethical being whose decisions must be clear and accessible, keeping with the norms of human ethics. The ethical God of the discussion concerning Sodom, is a more human God than the one that destroys all of humanity in the flood; more human and less divine.

This is not the case in another incident recounted in this portion, that of the *Akedah*—the Binding of Isaac (chapter 22). The story of the *Akedah* is one of totality, murderousness, and great silence. Here Abraham no longer stands before God, no longer argues, voices opinions, or demands explanations. He utters but one word: *hineni*—"here am I". He is passive, submissive and acquiescent. And the fate to which he acquiesces is not only terrible, but completely absurd, utterly incomprehensible. The Danish philosopher and writer Søren Kierkegaard (1813–1855) addresses this issue in his essay *Fear and Trembling*. God appears absurd to the extreme, making demands that run counter to human reason (inasmuch as he contradicts his own promises that had shaped the course of Abraham's life), and human ethics (demanding that a father murder his only son). He does not reveal himself, but remains external, incomprehensible, lurking in his impenetrable heavens, whence he issues orders that are heartless, senseless, murderous, illegitimate, and odious by any human ethical standard. Nevertheless, Abraham obeys. All he has to say is *hineni*. And Sarah has nothing to say at all, or perhaps the biblical author did not consider the things she might have said appropriate. She too, in her silence—as roaring as it may be—accepts the will of an incomprehensible and estranged God. Out of her silence and his obedience flows the evil and mad course of events, and the one and only God appears in his transcendent and omnipotent form. It is an external God, whose externality is total and final. In the face of such externality, one can only obey and keep silent. Dialogue and comprehension are pointless. Reason, according to Kierkegaard, can only lead to the conclusion that God is absurd, and ethical judgment can only lead to the conclusion that he is bloodthirsty. Faith however, is on a higher plane, requiring a "movement of infinity" and the renunciation of any attempt to understand or justify. This "movement" is the special quality of the "knight of faith", and Abraham, prepared to murder his son, is Kierkegaard's knight of faith. This Abraham, in his opinion, stands on a higher plane of faith than the Abraham who stood before Sodom, trying to draw his God into a discussion of the ethical. In order to be a "knight of faith", one must do the opposite—renounce the ethical for the religious, i.e., violate its laws. The external God must not be brought down to the human plane, but man must strive to attain the divine, which Kierkegaard considers the authentic plane of human existence.

The biblical text expresses no opinion in the matter, unless we ascribe significance to the fact that the *Akedah* story comes after that of Sodom. The two stories offer two paradigms of divine and human behavior; two types of god within the same deity and two types of believer within the same man. The two paradigms, I believe, represent two religious tendencies. The one—that of the *Akedah*—springs from a sense of fear and trembling, of encounter with the absolute other. This is the extreme that gave rise to the monotheistic desert God; an abstract, incorporeal god that demands far more than it is prepared to give, and which in its midrashic and Christian manifestation is willing to give primarily in the world to come and not in this life. Religious philosophers such as Kierkegaard, whose religiosity is infinitely demanding, are the culmination of this process. Theirs is a demanding, Sisyphean, rigid, and ascetic religiosity that finds its highest expression, according to Kierkegaard, in Abraham's willingness to sacrifice the most precious of all—Isaac. It is a religiosity that willingly renounces the human need to understand and to justify, while wholly internalizing the figure of God the terrible and the awe-inspiring in his absolute otherness; revealed as something that cannot truly be revealed, the utter foreignness of which—antithetic to all that is human—must be maintained.

The second paradigm presents a God who seeks to approach man, and is prepared to relinquish some—if not all—of the unbridgeable gap inherent to his being. Contrary to those who seek to keep God at a distance, to prevent his reification, his coming down to earth; contrary to those who seek to preserve the distance by virtue of which everything human is declared illegitimate or paltry in comparison to God's total, dazzlingly pure nothingness—the God of the story of Sodom is a God who strives to approach, the God of those who would bring him close. This tradition, at some point termed "dialogical religion", sought to bring God closer to the world, to draw him out of his absolute, celestial isolation, to deliver him from his unyielding and inexplicable solitude, to bring him closer to the human, the rational, but first and foremost—to the ethical.

Consistent pursuit of this approach would of course, eventually, make God redundant, for what use is there in a god who is entirely human and present? Religious feeling however, is not a consistent philosophical progression, and generally seeks to preserve the externality of God, while bringing him a little closer, making him a little less alien, different and beyond comprehension. Religious feeling would appear to present both paradigms, but like the biblical text in *Vayera*, expresses no preference.

Things are not that simple however. Upon closer examination, we find that Kierkegaard viewed the subordination of man's will to the will of God, as a higher manifestation of human will. Kierkegaard believed that in order to reach the foundations of the soul, the pure self, where "I" is only "I" and nothing else—one must first renounce all forms of universal doctrine, which are applied equally to everyone and impose the general upon the personal. Reason—like Kantian ethics that aspired to this kind of universal validity—is just such a doctrine. Abraham's inexplicable behavior—behavior that cannot be contextualized or justified—thus stems from a totally liberated state of consciousness; and the voice of God in fact springs from the pristine depths of the soul, uncorrupted by generalization and rationalization. Hence, nothing remains of the external God but the voice that springs from the depths of the soul; retaining God's exteriority only inasmuch as it remains incomprehensible, inaccessible and unjustifiable. The depths from which the voice springs are no longer the abysses of divine otherness, but the depths of human existence, solitude and absolute silence that generate unjustifiable and inexplicable behavior like that of Abraham. The sacrificing Abraham thus stands on a higher plane than Abraham the ethical negotiator, since authenticity takes precedence over ethics, and is therefore not ethical.

Total obedience of the divine voice is thus obedience of one's primordial self, as opposed to the standards of normative behavior. This self does not lend itself to positive description, because any positive description would place it on a general, contextualized and rational plane. It is therefore fated to remain a sort of primordial nothingness, the *hyle* that precedes all existence, the true hero, the knight of faith, who creates *ex nihilo*, but is sometimes swept up again into the nothingness.

Thus Abraham, prepared to murder his only son, becomes one who in his action and presumed state of consciousness does not obey God, but recreates himself in the primordial void, as the spirit of God hovering over the face of the waters, prepared to create and recreate darkness from darkness.

Eliezer Schweid

Hayei Sarah – The Life of Sarah

The Promise of the Land of Canaan to the Patriarchs and Their Descendants and the Manner of Its Fulfillment in the Thought of Nahmanides, Maimonides, and A. D. Gordon

> I am a stranger and a sojourner with you: give me a possession of a buryingplace with you, that I may bury my dead out of my sight (Genesis 23:4)

According to Rashi's introduction to the book of Genesis (citing the *tana* Rabbi Yitzhak), the purpose of the creation story is to provide moral justification for the conquest of the Land of Canaan by the Israelite tribes. At first glance, the broad range of messages conveyed by the creation story and their significance as the foundations of a biblical worldview would seem to imply that Rashi's approach is a rather narrow one, stemming from the premise that the Torah's essence lies in its statutes, laws, precepts, and the reasons behind them, rather than in imparting truths for their own sake. This impression changes however, upon closer examination of the history of humanity as conceived by the book of Genesis. Mankind's population of the world created for it and the role of the People of Israel—born of another people that had already settled its land—in this enterprise are issues of vital moral and religious importance, addressed in Genesis and the other books of the Torah and the Prophets. Judging by the manner in which these issues are treated in the Bible, Rabbi Yitzhak—and Rashi in his footsteps—would appear not to have overestimated the central importance of the moral-religious dilemma posed by the Israelite conquest of the Land of Canaan. According to the creation story, mankind—the descendants of Adam and Eve—was destined to populate the entire world, conquer and rule it, and thereby proclaim the kingdom of the heavenly God on earth. In keeping with this plan, God apportioned the earth to all of the various peoples, providing each with a patrimony to be distributed in turn to its respective tribes, clans, and families.

I won't go into all of the difficulties that impeded the implementation of creation's original plan, from Adam's sin in the Garden of Eden to the sins of the Israelites as they journeyed toward their land, and after they had taken possession of it. The story of the People of Israel is clearly a crucial part of the effort to bring this plan to fruition, ostensibly in the "end of days", requiring repeated corrective measures. The land to which Abram the Hebrew was sent, that he might bequeath it to his seed, destined there to become a blessing to all the nations, was originally intended for Canaan son of Ham, who committed a great sin against his father and his God. Abraham, a descendant of Shem, was sent to the Land of Canaan to inherit it and to purge it of the idolatrous sins of the Canaanite peoples. In so doing, he was to rectify the situation, allowing creation's plan to be realized in the distant future. This is the conceptual context within which all of Abraham's efforts in Canaan should be viewed. They were attempts to claim the land to which he had come as a "stranger", and in which he strove—with only sporadic success—to be a "sojourner".

In this sense, *Hayei Sarah* is fundamental. It tells of Abraham's final effort at a time when he was required to pass on the legacy of the divine promise to Isaac, the son in whom his seed would be called. It represents an important juncture and provides a fundamental approach to the appropriate manner in which one might lay claim to a land still in the possession of another people. Two noteworthy points emerge: First, the land promised to Abraham's descendants is consistently referred to, throughout the Bible as the "Land of Canaan" and not the "Land of Israel". The name "Land of Israel" (*Eretz Yisrael*) appears only three or four times, all of which clearly refer only to the region in which the kingdom of Israel was located, just as the "Land of Judea" is used to designate the realm of the kings of Judah. We thus learn that from a biblical perspective, the name of the land and its frontiers are determined by national-collective sovereignty, through the establishment of a national kingdom. The land promised to Israel in the future is therefore referred to by the name of the people in whose national-sovereign possession it was at the time: Canaan. The second point that emerges is that the divine promise per se does not determine national sovereignty. The people to whom the land has been promised are required to perform a worthy act through which the promise might be fulfilled. The important thing, for the purposes of this discussion, is that such an act cannot derive its legal-moral justification solely from the divine promise. It must comply, in and of itself, with the standards of justice that are determined by God's Torah but enjoy universal validity. This requirement applies equally to all peoples, because God promised every people a domain of its own in which to live in justice. In other words, a people wishing to exercise its promised right must do so justly with regard to rival claims, if any such claims exist.

The story of Abraham the Hebrew's efforts to lay claim to his land illustrates these two basic points. First, Abraham knows from the very outset—further repeated and confirmed in the "Covenant of the Pieces" (Gen. 15:17–18)—that the Promised Land will not belong to him, but to his descendants in the distant future. Secondly, in his travels throughout the Land of Canaan, he seeks to take symbolic possession of the land promised to his seed in the future, without violating the divine law by which all mankind is bound. He remains faithful to his great mission— to proclaim the kingdom of the most high God, creator, lawmaker, and master of the universe—while at the same time striving to afford legal status to the clan he heads in a land that is, from a national standpoint, not yet its own.

His commitment to these two converging goals is reflected in the two methods he employs in establishing his presence in the land. First and apparently foremost is the ritual consecration of the land promised to Abraham's seed by God, to God. To this end, Abraham crosses the Land of Canaan from north to south. In a few places, probably precincts of ancient temples, he builds altars to God upon which he renews the covenant promising the land to his descendants. The story of the binding of Isaac, recounted in the portion immediately preceding *Hayei Sarah*, would appear to serve the same sacred purpose. The binding of Isaac is quintessential symbolic ritual drama. It can be seen as the final and most important act of consecration performed by Abraham in order to bind his descendants to the land destined to be theirs, and thereby ensure fulfillment of the promise. The object of the ritual story is to establish the Temple site atop Mount Moriah as the place in which God is destined to establish his divine presence in the Promised Land and among the people to whom it was promised. In any event, the main purpose of the story is to symbolize—and thus establish—the unbreakable bond between Abraham's seed and the land at the heart of which stands Mount Moriah. The purpose of the symbolic ritual act (it is obvious even to Abraham from the very outset that Isaac will not actually be sacrificed: he is clearly told in the previous chapter that "in Isaac shall thy seed be called") is to consecrate Isaac to God in the place where God is to establish his divine presence among the People of Abraham. Isaac is thereby bound to God in the place consecrated to him, in much the same fashion that Samuel is later consecrated to God before the priest at Shilo. Through symbolic ritual, the divine promise to reside in the land among the seed of Abraham, becomes more than just a pledge. It becomes timeless, eternally binding, ritual reality. In other words, through the act of binding, Isaac inherits the divine promise as an absolute and irrevocable right; a right he will one day be able to bequeath to his own son in whom his seed shall be called as his patrimony. This is demonstrated to great effect in *Hayei Sarah* and the rest of Isaac's life story: one consecrated to God in the consecrated place can never leave the sanctum. Isaac, as we know, was commanded never to leave his promised land, not even to seek a bride in his father's birthplace. Abraham sends his slave to seek a wife for his son on the absolute condition that she agree to leave her native land in order to marry Isaac in his land—notwithstanding the fact that it is not yet his land.

The second method Abraham employs in his efforts to bring about the fulfillment of the divine promise is to strive to secure permanent legal status within the land in which he is a guest. Abraham constantly seeks formal alliances with local kings, hoping thereby to attain the legal right to dwell independently in the land alongside its kings and their peoples. Occasionally he is successful, but such treaties are short-lived. *Hayei Sarah* tells of Abraham's final attempt to secure independent status in the land in which he dwells—valid and irrevocable according to the law of the land. The legal thought invested in this story would be a worthy subject for further study.

Abraham seeks to buy a plot of land with a cave on it, in which to bury Sarah. He is clearly concerned with his own burial as well as that of Sarah, since the portion concludes with the death of Abraham and his burial in the very same cave. He presents himself as a "stranger-so-journer", the significance of which becomes clear in comparison to the expression "people of the land" used to denote the status of the town's citizens, who are the lords of the land. Inasmuch as they are the lords of the land, it is called by their name—Canaan. Abraham insists on his status as a "stranger-sojourner": one who is not a citizen of the land but enjoys permanent status in his place of residence. It is precisely this status that Abraham desires, because it affords a permanent claim without the need to renounce his national and personal identity. Note how Abraham politely but firmly rejects the Hebronites' enticing offer that he take the land for free, as he is "a prince of God among us". The words "among us" expose the trap: they are suggesting that he become a citizen of the Hittite-Canaanite city, one of its notables and priests.

The reason for Abraham's refusal is very clear: he insists upon his independence in two senses. First, he is not one of the "people of the land". He is a member of another people. Abraham jealously guards his status as such. He is an Aramaean from Haran, and he preserves his affinity to another "homeland". Secondly, although a "prince of God", his God is not the same as that of the "people of the land", but the Most High God whose worship brought him from Aram-naharaim, and is the legacy of his forebear Shem, son of Noah. In these two senses, Abraham insists on remaining independent. Nevertheless, he wishes to gain ownership of the field and its cave in perpetuity, that is ownership that could be passed down to his descendents. To this end, he insists that his acquisition be absolute, irrevocable, not only in the sight of God, but mainly in the sight of the lords of that land. He presents strict legal conditions: that the previous owners renounce any claims they might have to the property in question in return for payment of what they consider to be its full value. He is meticulous about every aspect of the negotiations, lest there be any doubt of the transaction's validity: full agreement to sell, full payment of the price demanded by the seller, all conducted in full view of the entire community. It is this public validation that takes the acquisition out of the realm of private transactions, affording it lasting collective-political significance.

The promise is thus fulfilled by means of a ritual act of sanctification requiring profound religious commitment alongside a legally and morally binding acquisition. A study of other books of the Bible that deal with the fulfillment of the promise of the land to the people reveals that they too are rooted in the fundamental principles established in Genesis. There are of course differences between the views of the prophets, for example, who emphasize the legal-moral aspect, as the primary path to gaining and retaining possession of the land; and that of the priests, who stress ritual as the key to consecrating the land to the people and the people to the land. An examination of postbiblical rabbinical literature paints a similar picture: despite variations in emphasis and different legal or philosophical approaches, all revolve around a central axis combining these two elements—the legal-moral and the ritual—as two sides of the same religious *Weltanschauung*.

I would like to begin the discussion on the basis of the views of two central halakhic and philosophical figures of the Middle Ages, whose influence can be felt to this day: Rabbi Moses ben Nahman (Nahmanides or Ramban) and Rabbi Moses ben Maimon (Maimonides or *Rambam*). To these two, I will add a third, modern voice, that of Aaron David Gordon, whose interest in this topic stemmed from his Zionist beliefs. His approach is a modern, humanistic synthesis of principles taken from Nahmanides and Maimonides, while drawing directly upon the biblical source.

I will begin with Nahmanides, although he came later than Maimonides, because the latter's views, which tend toward those of the prophets, are easier to understand in light of the sacerdotal-cultic views of the former. Maimonides was familiar with the sacerdotal-cultic approach from the writings of Judah Halevi, to which he had access, and to which he apparently replied. Judah Halevi's vision of *Eretz Yisrael* has a lot in common with that of Nahmanides. The affinity between the two is also reflected in the fact that both drew practical conclusions from their approaches and settled in the Holy Land. Nahmanides, however, was not only a philosopher, but also a halakhic scholar, and thus parallels Maimonides.

The sacerdotal-cultic approach is based on the perception of sanctity as a divine trait that may permeate certain objects to become part of their internal essence. The Land of Israel, according to this approach, is imbued with divine sanctity and thus differs from all other lands, just as the People of Israel differ from all other peoples. This distinction can be defined in terms of the steps or *Sefirot* of reality: *Eretz Yisrael* is an intermediary between all lands and the spiritual step of reality that is the source of sanctity. The same characterization also applies to the relationship between the Jewish people and all other peoples.

The status of *Eretz Yisrael* was determined when it was made the first object of creation. As a mystic, Nahmanides understood this in terms of the doctrine of *Atzilut* (Emanation), the influx of divine essence into earthly vessels. As the object with which the creation process began, *Eretz Yisrael* lies at the center of the earthly cosmos and is the nexus between the spiritual *Sefirot* that emanate from the source of the *Ein-Sof* and the earthly vessels. When its link with the *Sefirot* of Emanation is undiminished, *Eretz Yisrael* draws and fills with transcendent spiritual abundance. When the link is marred, however, it is held captive by the deficient earthly traits, open to the elements of evil in reality, and thus controlled by the idolatrous essence of Canaan. *Eretz Yisrael* is open both to the sanctity above and to the impurity below, and as such, is subject to Providence both for reward (direct divine presence) and for punishment (divine concealment and abandonment to the laws of nature), more than any other land. Its status depends, in this sense, upon that of the Jewish People, determined of course by its conduct as a people. If it attains the spiritual-Torah heights to which it is destined and to which it is commanded to aspire, it connects to its land and ascends to its proper *Sefirah* of reality, thereby allowing blessedness to flow out to all the nations. If, on the other hand, it descends into sin, the land will vomit it out and will be taken over by forces of evil, plummeting, and ruled over by idolatrous peoples that hate the People of Israel.

We can thus draw a number of conclusions regarding the worship of God by his people in its land. God resides among his people only when they are in their land; only in that place, at the heart of which lies Mount Moriah, can they build the Temple and engage in his sacerdotal-cultic worship. It thus follows that only in *Eretz Yisrael* can a Jewish kingdom be established in accordance with Jewish law. Many other precepts are also associated with the people's inhabitancy of their land in justice and charity, some of which depend upon the land itself and can be observed nowhere else. Furthermore, the power of prophecy, which is a direct connection between God and his people, can be granted only in *Eretz Yisrael*; and only in the Land of Israel does God rule over his people directly and supernaturally. Similarly, prayers offered in *Eretz Yisrael* and in the Temple are superior to those uttered anywhere else.

The question of the promise of the land to the people is thus explained, according to this cultic approach, by means of the essential affinity that exists between the land and the people and between these and the flow of divine Emanation; the promise is inherent to the order of creation from its very inception. It must therefore be defined not as a right, but as an absolute commandment to the people to gather in their land, live in it according to the Torah, and be a chosen people. The promise is thus fulfilled in the following manner: when the Jewish people rise to the level of its destiny, they become worthy to enter their land, establish their kingdom, build their temple, and fulfill all of their obligations to worship God. As long as they continue to observe these precepts and do not deviate from the path of the Torah, they will live as a free people in its land. Exile is the result of sin, and the way to return from exile is to abandon evil and return to God, possible only through constant striving to return to the land even when it lies desolate and in ruins under the rule of strangers. When the slightest opportunity for return arises, if only for individuals, each and every one who has the opportunity to do so is commanded to do everything in his power to help reestablish national life and thereby raise the land to its rightful level from the time of creation.

This is thus the one and only way in which the promise can be fulfilled, leading to certain practical halakhic conclusions. Since the commandments directly associated with the Land of Israel are incumbent upon the entire People of Israel for all eternity, the obligation to settle in the land in order to restore it to a state in which all of the commandments of the Torah can be observed is also incumbent upon the entire people for eternity. Hence, when conditions for the fulfillment of this obligation arise, each and every Jew who is capable of observing the commandment must do so. That is how Nahmanides ruled, and that is the ruling he applied to himself. When circumstances permitted, in his opinion, he travelled to the Holy Land and settled there. Hence the decisive influence of Nahmanides as a philosopher and halakhic authority, on religious Zionism.

Nahmanides' halakhic views derive from his philosophy. Most of the ideas cited above were taken from his commentary on the Torah, written in *Eretz Yisrael*. This is not the case with Maimonides, whose philosophy derived from his halakhic opinions. The issue of the people and the land does not appear in *Guide for the Perplexed*, but is discussed at length in his halakhic works, *Sefer Hamitzvot* and *Mishneh Torah*—particularly in *Hilkhot Beit Hebehirah* (the section that deals with laws pertaining to the Temple), *Hilkhot Terumot* (tithes), and *Hilkhot Melakhim* (kings). His decision to address this issue in a halakhic rather than philosophical context was based on philosophical-methdological considerations. It is rooted in Maimonides' understanding of the concept of sanctity. Contrary to the sacerdotal-cultic approach of Rabbi Judah Halevi and Nahmanides, Maimonides' prophetic approach views sanctity as separation from physicality, which is rife with deficiencies, unlike perfect mind-spirit that lacks nothing. Physical matter is the cause of every flaw and deficiency, all evil and impurity. The word "holy" can only be used to describe spiritual things when they are distinct from the physical elements that mar them. Physical objects cannot be considered holy in and of themselves. They can be sanctified only as a means toward spirituality and thus symbols representing the truly spiritual things that lie beyond them.

A land therefore, cannot be holy in its essence; a house cannot be holy in its essence; a book cannot be holy in the essence of the pages and ink it comprises; and a man cannot be holy in the essence of his physical being. A land, a house, a book, or man can, however, be sanctified—by force of moral-spiritual behavior that relates them to God by pure thought and pure action. In fact, determining the purity of thoughts, feelings, and actions is the province of Halakhah.

The question of the sanctity of the Land of Israel and its connection to the People of Israel is therefore a matter of the ways in which the land can be sanctified by the people. Maimonides thus returns to the point of departure of the biblical passages discussed above. The land takes on the name of the people that take possession of it as such, i.e. establish their kingdom in it. The land is thus defiled when it hosts a pagan kingdom and its accompanying ritual, moral, social, and political order; it is sanctified when inhabited by a kingdom devoted to the true God, committed to his laws and statues, moral injunctions, and commandments.

In order to better explain the halakhic significance of these things, I will stress the fact that, according to Maimonides, the obligation to reside in *Eretz Yisrael* and the prohibition against leaving it, except temporarily and for specific purposes, applies only when there is a legitimate kingdom in the land founded on the principles of the Torah. The boundaries of *Eretz Yisrael* are, for these purposes, the boundaries of the kingdom that may shrink or expand according to circumstances. When no such kingdom exists, the obligation to reside in *Eretz Yisrael* does not apply. This is how Maimonides ruled and consequently how he conducted himself—when he fled North Africa with his family due to persecution, they settled in *Eretz Yisrael* for a time, but eventually departed for Egypt, which offered greater possibilities as an important economic center and seat of Jewish learning.

Does this mean that the sanctity of *Eretz Yisrael* dissipated and the binding halakhic bond between the Jewish People and its land was severed upon the destruction of the Temple and the Jewish kingdom? Can the commitment to the Land of Israel not be expressed in exile as well? And most importantly—when the Jewish People is in exile, is its claim to the land revoked, and are the non-Jews who rule over it as a result of conquest and expulsion of its former inhabitants its legal owners? The answer to these questions in the halakhic literature is an unequivocal no. Maimonides attempts to explain the basis for this halakhah by distinguishing between "first sanctity" and "second sanctity". The first sanctity was conferred following the conquest of Joshua and the establishment of the House of David; the second sanctity was conferred at the time of the return from Babylonian exile, sanctioned by Cyrus and led by Ezra and Nehemia. Maimonides terms the first sanctity "temporary" and the second "eternal".

What then is the source of the halakhic distinction between first and second sanctity? Maimonides' explanation is that the first sanctity was based upon the violent conquest of the land from its former inhabitants. That is not to say that Maimonides negated the conquest per se. What is more, a Jewish king may engage in war for the sake of conquest if sanctioned by the Great Rabbinical Court, and conducted according to the Torah's laws of war. The territories thus acquired become part of *Eretz Yisrael* as long as there is territorial contiguity with the original Land of Israel. The conquest of the land destined to be the patrimony of the Jewish People among the nations would thus appear to be sanctioned by the Torah when there is no other way of claiming it. Sanctity based on the dispossession of the land's previous inhabitants however, is valid only as long as the kingdom stands. When another people comes along and conquers the land destroying its Temple and its kingdom, the sanctity comes to an end.

This is not the case, however, with the second sanctity, which was determined not by conquest but by the declaration of Cyrus, who ruled over the land and wished to establish a temple there to the God of Israel, "God of the Heavens", God of mankind. The legal basis for the Jewish People's return to its land was the fact that the land was considered—both by the Jews who returned to it and by Cyrus—a "patrimony" to which the descendents of its owners were entitled. The halakhah is therefore that sanctity based upon conquest is abrogated by further conquest, but sanctity based on inheritance is a perpetual legacy passed from father to son that no conquest can revoke. Thus, even if the Jewish People is in exile and the land is ruled over by others, such foreign conquest is no longer legitimate, but an injustice. The bond between people and land—within the frontiers determined by the second sanctity—remains, and must be given expression, even in exile. When the right messianic-utopian conditions arise, enabling the Jewish kingdom to be restored and the Temple reconstructed, all Jews will be obligated to return to their land.

There is more, however, to the issue of the sanctity of the Land of Israel. Halakhah affords Jerusalem, and particularly the Temple Mount and the Holy of Holies, a unique and absolute status. It is a kind of sanctity that never dissipates and is the source of its being the only place in the world in which the Temple can be built and the cult of God established. Does this mean that the place designated for the Temple at the time of creation is independently sacred? This is what even Maimonides' cautious phrasing would seem to imply. Upon careful examination, however, we discover that Maimonides was not referring to the inherent sanctity of the mount or the rock, but to a state of absolute sanctification by a unilateral act of divine will, independent of the people's response—like creation itself, like the giving of the Torah at Mount Sinai, like the choosing of the People of Israel.

The element of absolute unity in the actions of the one and only God is reflected in the sanctification of the one and only place for his worship; and it is God himself who chooses this place for his cult. This sanctification is reflected in a series of singular events initiated by God who, according to Rabbinical tradition, chose Mount Moriah not only for the binding of Isaac, but for a number of sacred encounters both prior and subsequent. The validity of these encounters is eternal, rendering the sanctity conferred through them upon the place in which they occurred eternal as well.

These principles are also important in terms of the relationship between the Jewish People and its land while in exile. A number of well-known precepts reflect this commitment, such as the requirement that one face toward Jerusalem and the Temple during prayer. The most important precept, however, the observance of which serves to regulate the order of Jewish national life—one based on the sanctity of time—pertains to the halakhic validity of the Jewish calendar. The precept in question is that of sanctifying the months and establishing leap years. Without it, the Jewish People would have no calendar to regulate its cycle of time. Observance of this precept requires eyewitness testimony and a decision by the Great Rabbinical Court, which can only be convened in Jerusalem, and only when the Temple is in existence. Although the algorithm for determining the dates of the festivals has been known since the time of the return from Babylonian exile, the obligation to do so by means of the Rabbinical Court based upon the testimony of eyewitnesses still remains. This ritual bears special significance as a symbol of the relationship between God and his people and was therefore carefully observed throughout the Second Temple period.

How can the sanctification of the months and determination of leap years retain their validity when the Temple lies in ruins and there is no rabbinical court with sufficient authority? Maimonides replies that we rely on the decision of the Great Rabbinical Court to permit the mathematical calculation of the calendar. That this decision might have current validity—renewed annually, although the Great Court no longer exists—Maimonides writes that there should be a Jewish community in Jerusalem, with a halakhically-competent rabbinical court. Of course this is merely a symbol intended to preserve a memory, but even as such, should not be taken lightly—by virtue of the obligation it entails, it has the power to safeguard the eternal bond between the Jewish People and its land. As noted above, Maimonides does not consider settlement in the Land of Israel to be a halakhic obligation in the absence of a Jewish kingdom. Nevertheless, he believes that the institutions that represent the Jewish People as a whole must ensure the constant presence of a Jewish community—at least in Jerusalem—in order to preserve the living connection between the people, and the land that is its sacred patrimony.

The philosophy of A. D. Gordon, as noted above, comprises a synthesis of ideas deriving from the works of Judah Halevi, Nahmanides, and Maimonides—in the spirit of a modern humanism firmly rooted the Bible. I will first stress the humanistic element in Gordon's work. He rejected the religious-Zionist approach to the Bible as the Jewish People's "deed" to its land, with Scripture providing documentation of the divine promise. First, a divine promise is not ownership, and secondly, the promise documented in the Bible obligates only those who believe in it, and not members of other peoples—neither those who reside in the land nor those who rule over it. In other words, the moral basis for the Jewish People's return to its land should be universal values rather than subjective Jewish belief. That is not to say that the Bible—as a national creation of the People of Israel produced in the Land of Israel and in the Hebrew language—is not vitally important as a point of departure for the right of the people to return to its land. As a national creation, the Bible embodies the unique bond that exists between the Jewish People and its land. It is the intense embodiment of this bond that attests to the fact that the people that created it in the land are the people of that land, whose unique national culture flows from the unique characteristics of the land. Indeed, even in exile, the Jewish People continued to draw its creative inspiration from the Bible and the literature that developed from it in *Eretz Yisrael* and later in exile.

The Bible offers further support of the people's right to its land. The fact that the Jewish People once created the Bible in the Land of Israel attests to a past claim, upheld from generation to generation, in the continuity of Jewish creation based on the Bible. The proof that the Jewish People is still the people of its land lies in the national creativity that it will once again exercise in that land, with the very same creative essence revealed in the Bible, or in the words of Gordon, "with biblical force". The Jewish People returned to its land in order to create its life's work by virtue of that essential creative force. That is all the proof it owes to itself and to others, for one cannot deny a people the right to live a full and independent life in the only land to which it is bound as its homeland. Gordon naturally applied this principle equally to all peoples. Formal possession created by force or even purchase was, in Gordon's view, existentially meaningless and without moral legitimacy. The right of a people in its land is the right to create life and developing culture, for its own benefit, and for the benefit of all who come into contact with it. In other words, if the Jewish People were to return to its land, settle there, make its deserts bloom, bring forth from it a wealth of physical and spiritual creation—enough to sustain full national life—it would prove its right through the realization of that right. There is no other kind of right and therefore no need of any other kind of proof.

What is the basis for this claim? How does it relate to Jewish sources? In terms of the bond between the Jewish People and its land, this is a humanistic interpretation of the ideas expressed by Judah Halevi and Nahmanides. Gordon presumes the human animal to be the organic product of the sum total of his natural environment, and human society—a step above the social interaction of other animals. The culture of every dynamic human society thus stems from the aggregate of its natural environment: landscape, resources, natural abilities and shared experiences. Together, these things constitute the sources that nourish and shape the unique characteristics of every family, community, and nation, as integral organic social units.

Nahmanides saw the creation of the collective life of the people as the downward flow of *Atzilut* from the upper *Sefirot* into the physical vessels. Gordon, on the other hand, saw it as an upward flow emanating from nature: from the inanimate to plant life, from plant to animal, and from animal to man. Nevertheless, as a religious philosopher, he too saw the secret of creation as rooted in the "Hidden Mind", whose actions we cannot see or even grasp—the sublime source from which the energy of life and creation flows out upon the universe, guiding its development, and inspiring it to attain the spiritual *Sefirot*. We thus conclude that there is an organic bond between every people and its homeland, and that they belong to one another. Like all peoples, the Jewish People also has a natural-original bond with its homeland and can exist as a unique people only through this bond with its origins. Its existence in exile is therefore weakened, impoverished, one-sided, only when it returns to its land to fully live its national life there will its unique essence emerge in the whole of its cultural activity.

In this existential sense, the bond is the right, and it is in this that Gordon drew upon Nahmanides' views. What then creates the bond between the land and the people upon which the right is based? Certainly the fact that it is a patrimony in the broadest and most tangible sense, for *Eretz Yisrael*, according to Gordon, is the exclusive source of the spiritual legacy that sustains the Jewish People passed down from generation to generation.

Regarding realization of the right, Gordon adopted Maimonides' approach: it is not created through conquest but through life and creation. This is true for the Jewish People as it is for any other people. In certain aspects, Gordon's philosophy indeed resembles that of Maimonides. In others, however, it differs significantly. Maimonides was a political philosopher who saw constitutional monarchy—physically, morally, and spiritually—as the necessary framework for cultural development. The collective possession of a land by its people was therefore conditional, according to Maimonides, upon the establishment of a kingdom. Gordon, on the other hand, saw monarchy as a "mechanical" system based on coercive power. As such, he considered it entirely unacceptable and the source of all that is evil and awry in modern culture. The utopia that Gordon saw in his vision of the "end of days"—in the spirit of Isaiah's vision of peace—entailed brotherhood between peoples, each residing in its own land, on the basis of organic familial-communal-national collectivity. Cohesion is internal, arising from a moral spirit, rather than imposed from without, by a coercive framework. In other words, Gordon believed in the establishment of a national society without armed forces and other trappings of power that serve no purpose except to satisfy the wickedness of the selfish rulers who desire them.

In fact, the renunciation of sovereignty formed the basis of Gordon's proposal for the resolution of the budding conflict between Zionism and Palestinian nationalism. Gordon did not renounce the primacy of the Jewish People's right to the homeland from which it had been forcibly exiled. Nevertheless, he did recognize both the individual and the national rights of the Arab inhabitants who lived and worked on the land. He therefore believed that if both peoples wish to live in their homeland developing its resources as well as their own skills and abilities, then *Eretz Yisrael* can sustain them both—each in their respective villages and settlements, treating one another as good neighbors in a spirit of cooperation and mutual responsibility. Furthermore, such an arrangement could be to the advantage of both sides, as long as each people approaches its own development for its own sake and not out of a sense of hatred and jealousy toward the other, and as long as both are prepared to renounce sovereignty, which lies at the heart of the violent conflict between them.

Gordon knew that his was a utopian vision demanding a higher level of morality than the prevailing one. Nevertheless, he knew with absolute certainty that humanity must aspire to such morality if it is to avoid utter destruction. He saw clear signs of this in the First World War, the Bolshevik revolution, and the environmental havoc wreaked by the insatiable appetite of modern industry. On the basis of these critical observations, Gordon concluded that the utopian is essential, and if mankind wishes to survive, it must rise above itself and attain a different level of human life. For the Jewish People, this was particularly urgent. The situation, however, was no less desperate for most Palestinians, who suffered extreme deprivation and exploitation at the time. Cooperation was thus essential and to the advantage of both sides. That is why Gordon insisted upon utopia as the only hope for salvation: if successful, it would serve as a model for all peoples and would usher in a new era in the history of mankind.

Irit Aminoff

Toledot – And these are the generations of Isaac

*"Each Hastening to Slay the Other"—The Midrashic Approach of **Rabbi Yohanan** and **Rabbi Shimeon Ben Lakish***

And the Lord said unto her: Two nations are in thy womb, and two peoples shall be separated from thy bowels; and the one people shall be stronger than the other people; and the elder shall serve the younger (Genesis 25:23).

Toledot, one of the richest portions in the book of Genesis, focuses on the story of birth, childhood, and coming of age of the twin brothers Esau and Jacob and Esau's breaking away from the central branch of the Patriarch's family. Esau's is the third such departure, following that of Lot from Abraham, and Ishmael from Isaac. Esau parts from his twin brother Jacob and the entire family of the Patriarchs; a parting between brothers, peoples, and cultures. That is how we parted ways with Amon and Moab (descendents of Lot), the nomadic peoples (descendents of Ishamael), and now the branch of Edom.

Three dramatic episodes are recounted in Toledot, in an unusually striking manner. **First**: The barren Rebecca is remembered by God, and feels pain and disquiet at the strange struggling inside her womb. She turns to ask—"to inquire of the Lord." The reply she is given bears an important revelation:

"Two nations are in thy womb, and two peoples shall be separated from thy bowels;
and one people shall be stronger than the other people; and the elder shall serve the younger"

Toledot and the subsequent portions try to fill this revelation with content.

Second: The twins come of age, and each chooses his own path in life. A passing need causes Esau, the hunter and man of the field, to sell his birthright with its many advantages, to his younger brother.

56

The birthright is sold for a pottage of lentils. (This dramatic scene is mirrored in the next portion, *Vayetze*, when Leah, the eldest, is selling; Rachel, the youngest is buying; 30:14–17.) In the description of the sale, the story presents the seller as an innocent lacking wisdom and wit, even foolish, driven by fleeting desire. The buyer, on the other hand, is wise, even cunning—a careful planner who attains his goal.

Third: The portion's climax and the heart of the entire book of Genesis—the scene in which Jacob steals the blessing is masterfully constructed, with each of its seven complex tableaux and general theatrical structure warranting separate attention. The story is constructed layer upon layer: conspiracy, deception, discovery and awakening, hatred and escape. *Vayetze* opens with Jacob's flight from his father's house, his country, and his kindred to another land, another family, and an unfamiliar home—the first chapter in his adult life, as he begins to step into his role as father of the nation. On the other hand, Jacob's flight brings to a close the personal story of Esau, father of Edom, offering only a brief description of his family life, far removed from Jacob's role as hero of Genesis.

Toledot has spawned many ideas in the history of Jewish thought. Of particular importance, is Jewish history's attitude toward Esau and all that he represents. Talmudic-midrashic literature (tannaitic and amoraic) identified Esau—the father of Edom—with the mighty Roman Empire. The figure of Esau as a typological concept and symbol was shaped in Palestine in the first centuries CE—the height of aggadic literary development. It was greatly enhanced by significant historical and spiritual events in the life of the Jewish people: the Great Revolt that led to the destruction of the Temple; the Diaspora Revolt and its impact on the lives of Jews in Palestine; the Bar-Kokhba Revolt and the anti-Jewish measures that followed in its wake; and the rise of Christianity among Palestinian Jews with its many and far-reaching ramifications.

Incessant pressure from within and without thus weighed heavily on attitudes toward Rome, overshadowed by its longstanding rule over Judaea, during the course of which hatred of Esau served to reinforce hatred of Rome. Pagan and Christian Rome were explained typologically through the figure of Esau. The range of human traits condemned by the Sages were similarly associated with Esau, who became a catchall for everything evil—mendacity, larceny, adultery, incest, bloodshed, disbelief, and atheism—the archetype of all reprehensible behavior. Everything the Sages wished to say about the Roman Empire—and they had a great deal to say—was said through the literary channel of Esau=Edom=Rome.

This also helps to explain the basic difficulty presented by the portion of *Toledot*: What caused the Jewish People to blacken the name of the biblical Esau, making him blacker than black (or redder than red—as he is called Edom) throughout its history? What is the source of the paradox between the biblical figure of Esau—innocent, decent, practically the "perfect gentleman" (see *Vayishlah*)—and the midrashic-talmudic figure of the murderous, incestuous, idolatrous, lying, hypocritical, licentious sodomite and general evildoer?

In this chapter, I will briefly present a number of midrashim on the portion of *Toledot* taken from the earliest and most important anthology of Palestinian aggadic Midrash—*Genesis Rabbah*—and will try to shed some light on the problematic identification of Esau with Rome. Since this book deals with the portions of Torah according to the philosophy and thought of Jewish scholars, I will focus on those passages that reflect the thought of Rabbi Yohanan bar Nafha and Rabbi Shimeon ben Lakish, disregarding dozens of parallel midrashim.

Like the other Matriarchs, Rebecca too was barren. Her husband, Isaac, prayed to God concerning his wife's inability to conceive, and God answered his prayer:

"And Isaac entreated (*vaye 'tar*) the Lord" (25:21) –
Rabbi Yohanan and Resh Lakish –
Rabbi Yohanan said: [It means that] he poured out his prayers in abundance.
Resh Lakish said: [It means that] he overturned the [divine] decree, and that is why a pitchfork is called *atra*—for it overturns the threshing floor (*Genesis Rabbah* 63,5).

"'Because she was barren (*akarah*)'—Rabbi Yudan in the name of Resh Lakish: She lacked the main uterus and God engraved/carved a womb for her" (*ibid.*).

The Midrash presents a discussion between Rabbi Yohanan and Resh Lakish (Shimeon ben Lakish), regarding the meaning of the word *vaye'tar*. Rabbi Yohanan interprets *vaye'tar* as deriving from the word *atir* (*ashir*—abundant), indicating that Isaac prayed abundantly. Resh Lakish on the other hand, explains *vaye'tar* as deriving from *atra* (*atar*—pitchfork), so named because it turns over the grain on the threshing floor. According to Resh Lakish, Isaac attempted with his prayers to reverse the heavenly decree that Rebecca remain barren; like the pitchfork (*atra*) that turns over the grain, he sought to overturn the decree of barrenness. While Rabbi Yohanan does not relate to the context of the word *vaye'tar*, merely offering a linguistic interpretation, Resh Lakish uses his midrashic interpretation of the word, with the help of agricultural imagery, to address its broader context.

Resh Lakish also understands the word *akarah* (barren) as reference to Rebecca's lack of womb, lack of the main thing (*haikar*). As a result of Isaac's devotions, God engraved/carved a womb for her—renewing his creation—that she might conceive. Isaac thus succeeded in reversing a divine decree with his prayers. This is a very significant assertion. Rebecca is disconcerted by the struggling in her womb and goes to "inquire of the Lord". The plain meaning of the text is that Rebecca, pregnant for the first time, failed to understand the strange movements in her belly. However the word *vayitrotzetzu* ("and they [the children] struggled together"), serves Rabbi Yohanan and Resh Lakish as a wonderful pretext to explain the deep-seated differences between the twins already manifest in the womb:

"And the children struggled together
(*vayitrozezu*) within her" (25:22) –
Rabbi Yohanan and Resh Lakish –
Rabbi Yohanan said: Each hastening (*ratz*) to slay the other.
Resh Lakish said: Each abrogating the laws (*matir tzivuyo*) of the other.
...
"And the children struggled together within her" –
When she stood near synagogues and houses of Torah-study,
Jacob would struggle to come out, as it is written
"Before I formed thee in the belly I knew thee" (*Jer* 1:5);

and when she passed near houses of idol-worship,
Esau would struggle to come out, as it is written
"The wicked are estranged from the womb" (*Ps* 58:4) (*Genesis Rabbah*. 63,6).

"And they struggled together", along with its various midrashim, is the essence of the struggle that persists to this day. At first glance, Rabbi Yohanan's interpretation appears the harsher of the two: "Each hastening to slay the other", i.e. striving for the total physical annihilation of his brother. Resh Lakish, on the other hand, relating to *vayitrotzatzu* as a contraction of *vayatiru tzivuyim* (and they abrogated laws), refers to a state of never-ending war, which is not a war for physical destruction but a clash of cultures, values, and religions—a war of worldviews. The profound conflict represented by Rabbi Shimeon ben Lakish is a war of spiritual rather than physical conquest, a *kulturkampf*, the war of Judaism against the new sect-religion that emerged from it and turned against it.

It is important to note that at this stage, in the 3rd century, pagan Rome no longer posed a threat to Judaism's religious status. An increasingly Christian Rome, however, posed an enormous threat. The divergence of worldviews, as presented by Resh Lakish rooted in his midrashic interpretation of the word *vayitrotzetzu*, draws an opposite line between: "Houses of idol worship," represented by the new church on one pole, and the Jewish "synagogues and houses of Torah-study," on the other pole. It is only in the early fourth century that Christianity became the official religion of the Roman Empire, yet in Rabbi Shimeon ben Lakish's midrash of *vayitrotzetzu,* we hear echoes of the debate between Judaism and the young religion to which it gave birth and which subsequently spread throughout the Roman world, abrogating and repudiating all of Judaism's fundamental laws. Such a state of affairs was far more bitter than a war of physical annihilation.

The words of Resh Lakish are thus far more serious than those of Rabbi Yohanan, which may possess literary beauty and are certainly accurate historically but are less profound than those of Rabbi Shimeon. While Rabbi Yohanan plays on the word *vayitrotzatzu*, based on the Hebrew roots RU"Z and RZ"Z—"each hastening to slay the other",

Resh Lakish explains the word *vayitrotzetzu* as a contraction of *vayatiru tzivuyim*—"and they abrogated laws." The Christians abrogate the laws of Judaism, and the Jews will abrogate the laws of Christianity—and there can be no compromise or bridging of the gap that exists between the two.

Note the contrast of "synagogues and houses of Torah-study" with "houses of idol-worship" that characterizes the twins from the very beginning. The physical struggling in the womb is explained by the ardor of the fetuses as they sense the "odors" of the houses of Torah-study and conversely the houses of idol-worship when the pregnant mother passes by their doors. The twins would appear to have manifested their respective religious and cultural preferences from the very earliest stages of their development. The profound differences between them are thus imprinted upon their very being, even before birth. The dichotomy between synagogue and house of idol-worship is a central element in all of the midrashim pertaining to the lives of Jacob and Esau—Israel and Rome.

We learn about the babies' respective characters from the description of their birth:

"And the first came forth ruddy (*admoni*), all over like a hairy mantle; and they called his name Esau" (25:25) –
Rabbi Abba bar Kahana said: Wholly a shedder of blood.
And when Samuel saw David was 'ruddy', as it is written:
"And he sent, and brought him in. Now he was ruddy" (*1* Sam. 16:12), he was afraid and said: is this one too a shedder of blood like Esau!?
God said to him: "and withal of beautiful eyes" – Esau kills on his own authority, but this one will do so [only] on the authority of the Sanhedrin (*op. cit.* 63,8).

The midrash of Rabbi Abba bar Kahana, a disciple of Rabbi Yohanan, on the word *admoni*—("ruddy") is highly significant. The midrash seems to play upon the contrast between the two important *admonim* in Jewish history. Outwardly, there is a close resemblance between the two, and Samuel therefore fears that the second *admoni* will be just like the first. God reassures him and points out the difference between them. The difference can be found in the verse describing the young shepherd, David son of Jesse, brought before Samuel the seer who sought the boy whom he would anoint king among the children of Jesse: "And he sent, and brought him in. Now he was ruddy, and withal of beautiful eyes, and goodly to look upon" (1 Sam. 16:12).

Rabbi Abba bar Kahana explains "and withal of beautiful eyes,"— meaning the eyes are always with him. EYE in Hebrew (in gematria) is 70, so the eyes of Israel, i.e., the Sanhedrin (71), are always with David at his side in every decision that he takes. While the first *admoni* (Esau-Rome) killed on his own authority, the second (David, king of Israel) killed only on the authority of the Sanhedrin.

The importance of this passage is immense, inasmuch as it juxtaposes David, king of Israel, and Herod, king of Judaea (by the grace of Rome). Both kings were great builders and great conquerors, and both shed a great deal of blood. While the latter killed of his own accord, however (perhaps referring to the execution of those who took part in the Gallilee Revolt led by Hezekiah under the reign of John Hyrcanus when Herod was governor of the Galilee), David only put people to death on the authority of the Sanhedrin. (For the purposes of this midrash, the talmudic passages accusing David of having murdered Uriah the Hittite without Sanhedrin sanction are ignored: "'Uriah the Hittite thou hast smitten with the sword'—You should have brought him before the Sanhedrin, yet you did not"—*Shabbat* 56a.)

On the one hand, we find a comparison between two judicial systems: the Roman system, in which people are executed without trial; and the Jewish system, based on the rule of law and the decisions of an authoritative judicial body—in this case, the Sanhedrin. (The suggestion that David would have enjoyed the support of the "Sanhedrin" is, of course, a Rabbinical anachronism.)

On the other hand, the midrash offers a comparison between two great kings—David and Herod—with the intention of exonerating the former of murder, a fact explicitly stated in the Bible. Esau-Herod, ruler by the grace of Rome, shed blood without trial, like the empire that afforded him its patronage, while David's executions were all judicially sanctioned and in keeping with the principles of law and justice. For the purposes of this midrash, Esau=Edom=Herod=Rome, and as such demonstrates the talmudic-midrashic identification of the biblical Esau with historical Rome.

The second formative stage in the lives of the brothers is their coming of age. From this moment forth, they manifest all of their future characteristics and the paths they will choose:

> "And the boys grew; and Esau was a cunning hunter, a man of the field; and Jacob was a quiet man, dwelling in tents" (25:27) – Rabbi Levi said: Like a myrtle and a briar growing side by side, when they reach maturity and blossom, the one offers its fragrance, and the other its thorns. So, in their first thirteen years, they both went to school and returned from school.
> At thirteen however, the one went to the houses of Torah-study, and the other to the houses of idol-worship (*Genesis Rabbah* 63,10).

According to the parable, the two boys were provided with the same conditions and opportunities. They are compared to a myrtle and a briar growing side by side, intertwined, and indistinguishable until they have "come of age" and flowered, i.e. manifested their individual characteristics—the one its fragrance and the other its thorns. Thus, the two boys, who were given the same education ("they both went to school and returned from school" an anachronistic use of the term "school"—*betsefer*—characteristic of the Midrash), were indistinguishable. At their coming of age, however, they began to manifest their individual characteristics—the one is drawn to the synagogue and study-hall and the other to pagan temples, just as they struggled while still in the womb whenever their mother passed by such places. This image will become a permanent fixture of their representations and annals.

The parable stresses the fact that, despite having been raised in the same environment, by the same parents, each of the brothers (peoples) developed his own proclivities, beliefs, religion, and culture.

> And Esau was a cunning hunter, a man of the field (25:27) –
> Rabbi Hiya said: He made himself free to all, like the field.
> Said Israel unto to Lord: Master of the universe,
> is it not enough that we are enslaved by the seventy nations [of the world],

but must we also be enslaved by this one who is lain with as a woman!? (*ibid.*).

The plain meaning of "man of the field" disappears, and the field becomes synonymous with licentiousness. Like a woman who makes herself sexually available to all and sundry, so Esau "made himself free like the field, as if saying: come and get me." In addition to the bloodshed and idolatry that the Midrash ascribes to Esau-Rome, we now enter the realm of incest, licentiousness and homosexuality, with which the Sages frequently characterize Rome and its culture.

In describing Rome as a nation that is "lain with as a woman," Rabbi Hiya asserts that all Romans are plagued with homosexuality—an abomination according to the laws of the Torah. Such sexual license is seen as characteristic of all Romans.

Having established Esau's immoral character and wanton ways, the word *hale'iteni* ("let me swallow down") is also interpreted as expressing crude and brutish behavior typical of gentiles (see e.g. "Rabbi Yithak bar Ze'ira said: The wicked one opened his mouth wide, like a camel"—Gen. *Rabbah* 63:12).

> And Esau said to Jacob: "Let me swallow down, I pray thee,
> of this red, red pottage; for I am faint" (25:30) – Rabbi Yohanan
> and Resh Lakish – Rabbi Yohanan said: Of it and its *patron*.
> Resh Lakish said: Of it and its like. He is red and his dish is red,
> his land is red, his heroes are red, his clothing is red,
> and his retribution will come from One who is red, clothed in
> red (*ibid.*).

Esau's innocent request ("let me swallow down") provides the midrashic basis for a demonstration of the bloodthirstiness of Esau-Rome. The debate between Rabbi Yohanan and Resh Lakish concerns the significance of the repetition: *Min HaAdom HaAdome Hazeh*—i.e., from the Reddish Red Pottage. The midrash offers two levels of meaning—the manifest and the hidden.

On the manifest level, Rabbi Yohanan says: It (the red lentils) and its *patron* (red blood). Resh Lakish says: It (the red dish) and its like (other things that are red in color).

On the hidden level, Rabbi Yohanan says: He (Esau) and his patron (the red Roman Empire and its murderous dominion). Resh Lakish says: He and his like (Esau and those who are like him, i.e. all members of the murderous and bloodthirsty Roman people).

While Rabbi Yohanan refers to the institutions and dominion of the Roman Empire—corrupt judges who condemn people to death without trial and thereby shed innocent blood—Resh Lakish relates to the entire Roman people as bloodthirsty murderers, whose hands and clothing are soaked in blood, and for whom bloodshed is a part of their very essence. The greater intensity of Resh Lakish's hatred for the Romans is evident in most of the midrashim.

(According to talmudic accounts of his life, Rabbi Shimeon ben Lakish was forced by poverty to sell himself to the *ludari*—agents who provided gladiators for the arenas of Rome. The occupation itself was disgraceful, and Rabbi Yohanan implored him to change his ways, promising him the hand of his beautiful sister in marriage [*Bava Metzia* 84a]. The Talmud tells of Resh Lakish's return from iniquity to the world of Torah, and his rapid development as a scholar, eventually becoming second only to Rabbi Yohanan at the *yeshivah* of Tiberias. Resh Lakish's firsthand knowledge of Hellenistic and Roman society of his time, afforded him greater familiarity with the Romans. His views of Rome may therefore have been not without basis.)

The famished Esau fails to appreciate the value of a birthright that does not seem as concrete and real to him at the time compared to the tangible lentil pottage, filling his nostrils with its tantalizing aroma.

And Esau said: "Behold, I am at the point to die;
and what profit shall the birthright do to me (*velamah zeh li bekhorah*)?" (25:32) – Resh Lakish said: He began to curse and blaspheme, for it does not say *lamah li,* but *lamah zeh li,*
showing that he repudiated *zeh eli*—"this is my God" (*Ex.* 15:2)"
(*Gen. Rabbah, op. cit.*).

"And he said: Because the Lord thy God sent me good speed" (27:20) –
Rabbi Yohanan said: Like a raven bringing fire to its nest.
When he said "Because the Lord thy God sent me good speed",

Isaac said: I know that Esau does not mention the name of God,
and this one is doing so: it must not be Esau, but Jacob.
Since Jacob had affirmed [that he was Esau], he [Isaac] said:
"Come near, I pray thee, that I may feel thee, my son" (*ibid.*
65,19).

Rabbi Yohanan and Resh Lakish took different views of the religious beliefs of Esau-Rome. In the phonic midrash on the words "*lamah
zeh li*" (*lamah zeh eli*), Resh Lakish speaks of repudiation of the God
of Israel—clearly referring to Christian Rome, for the failure of Roman
pagans to recognize the Jewish God would hardly have been noteworthy. It is at Esau the Christian that Resh Lakish aims his barbs when he
accuses him of having repudiated the God of Israel.

In the midrash on the verse "Because the Lord thy God sent me
good speed" (from the story of the theft of the blessing), Rabbi Yohanan
explains, with great delicacy that Esau was not in the habit of mention-
ing God's name. It was therefore clear to Isaac that the man standing
before him was not Esau, but Jacob. In this—the fact that Esau does not
mention God's name—Rabbi Yohanan was implying that he does not
worship him either.

In comparison, Resh Lakish's interpretation of the verse, "And what
profit shall the birthright do to me (*velamah zeh li bekhorah*)?" is remarkably blunt. He asserts that Esau began to curse and blaspheme,
repudiating *zeh eli* ("this is my God")—i.e. he recognized God, yet rejected him. This repudiation of the God of Israel was, in the eyes of the
Jews of Palestine, a hallmark of the Christian religion rapidly spreading
throughout the Roman Empire.

At the climax of the blessing story, Isaac remarks to his impostor
son: "The voice (*kol*) is the voice of Jacob, but the hands are the hands
of Esau" (27:22). This verse is, without a doubt, the key to understanding the abyss that lay between the two brothers. As such, it has given
rise to hundreds of midrashic passages that have played a central role in
shaping the perennial conflict between Jacob and Esau throughout the
course of Jewish history.

Rabbi Yohanan said: The voice of the Emperor Hadrian
who killed eighty thousand myriads at Bethar (*ibid.* 65, 21).

Another version of the same midrash reads:

Kol—The Emperor Hadrian killed eighty thousand myriads at Bethar (*Lamentations Rabbah* 2:4); and another:

The voice of Jacob cries out for that which the hands of Esau inflicted upon him at Bethar (*Yerushalmi, Ta'anit* 4:8).

Rabbi Yohanan, master of the Midrash: "Each hastening to slay the other", offers a historical interpretation of the central verse in *Toledot*: The hands of Esau are none other than the hands of the wicked Emperor Hadrian who put down the Bar-Kokhba Revolt, killing eighty (thousand) myriads at Bethar". The trauma of Hadrian's repression of the revolt has haunted the Jewish People for millennia, persisting even to this day (witness frequent discussions in the media, scholarly articles, books, plays, debates, symposia, etc.).

Rabbi Yohanan presents the Bar-Kokhba Revolt (132–135 CE) and the persecution that followed in its wake (135–138) as the essence of the struggle between the voice of Jacob and the hands of Esau. Over a century after the Revolt, Rabbi Yohanan—in keeping with his midrash "*vayitrotzetzu,* each hastening to slay the other"—identifies with deep grief the terrible massacre at Betar as that which the hands of Esau had wreaked upon Jacob.

This is not the only midrash in which Esau is associated with Hadrian. The following interpretation, for example, not ascribed to any specific source, appears earlier in the portion: "'Two nations are in thy womb, and two peoples shall be separated from thy bowels' (25:23): the prides of two nations are in thy womb, the one taking pride in its world and the other in its empire. The prides of two nations are in thy womb: Hadrian among the idolaters and Solomon of Israel" (Gen. *Rabbah* 63,7).

The anonymous midrashist simply and naturally compared Hadrian (Emperor of Rome: 117–138) to Solomon, King of Israel. Hadrian (who appears to have harbored no ill will toward the Jews at the beginning of his reign; on the contrary, he strove to win their favor, and possibly even contemplated rebuilding the Temple) was so despised by the Jews that the imprecation "*shehik tamya*" ("may his bones be ground to dust") was added to his name. Hadrian was credited with the greatest persecution ever suffered by the Jewish population of Palestine in the period following the repression of the Bar-Kokhba Revolt (as noted above). From the manner in which the midrash compares Hadrian and Solomon, it is clear that the Sages felt a certain amount of respect and admiration for the emperors of mighty Rome and for Hadrian himself, who, in the scope of his construction and restoration projects, reminded many of Solomon.

The comparison of Hadrian to Solomon is an indication of the former's status and worth in the eyes of the author. Most of the midrashim that evoke the name of Hadrian, do so in order to illustrate the wickedness of Esau and the cruelty of Rome. In this particular midrash, for one brief moment, Esau is clad in imperial purple, placed opposite Solomon, King of Israel, builder of the Temple as Rome the glorious, the creative, and the constructive. For the most part, however, the Esau portrayed in the Midrash is hardly glorious, but rather ugly, revolting and foul. So, for example, in the midrash on the verse "And he came near, and kissed him. And he smelled the smell of his raiment, and blessed him" (27:27):

> Rabbi Yohanan said: There is no odor more foul than that of goat skins, yet [the verse] says "and he smelled the smell of his raiment and blessed him"!?
>
> Rather when our father Jacob came before his father, the Garden of Eden entered with him, as it is written:
>
> "See, the smell of my son is as the smell of a field which the Lord hath blessed" (*ibid.*).
>
> And when Esau came before his father, Gehenna entered with him, as it is written: "When wickedness cometh, then cometh shame" (*Prov.* 11:2)
>
> (*Gen. Rabbah* 65,22).

And similarly:

> "And Isaac trembled very exceedingly" (27:33) –
>
> Rabbi Yohanan said: When one has two sons, and one goes out and the other comes in, does he tremble!?
>
> Rather, when Esau came before his father, Gehenna entered with him (*op.cit.* 67,2).

The hundreds of midrashim that describe the gulf between the two brothers developed a set of contrasting images to represent the brothers' antithetical worldviews: black and white, good and evil, light and darkness, truth and falsehood, wisdom and foolishness, righteousness and wickedness, this world and the next, the Garden of Eden and Gehenna, fragrance and foulness, flower and thorn, house of Torah-study and house of idol-worship, prayer and killing, etc. The brothers thus become a pair of diametrical opposites, to the best of the midrashists' ability and imagination, in a genre that tends toward the extreme. With a certain amount of naiveté, Rabbi Yohanan describes the two brothers— two peoples, two cultures—as the contrast between Eden and Gehenna, adding a further, more tangible dimension to their smells: the fragrance of the Garden of Eden as opposed to the stench of Gehenna.

In the biblical narrative, Esau introduces a second, midrashic interpretation of Jacob's name, from which we understand that it was not Jacob's holding his brother's ankle that gave him the name Jacob, but rather his twisted nature.

And he said: "Thy brother came with guile,
and hath taken away thy blessing" (27:35) –
Rabbi Yohanan said: He came with the wisdom of his Torah.
And he said: "Is not (*hakhi*) he rightly named Jacob (*Ya'akov*)?
for he hath supplanted me (*vaya'keveni*)" (27:36) –
Resh Lakish said: He cleared his throat as one about to spit,
and spat out the word *hakhi* (*op. cit.* 67,4).

The word *mirmah* (guile), uttered by Isaac, is a condemnation of Jacob. Rabbi Yohanan cleverly turns it around, replacing guile with the cunning and wisdom of the Torah, i.e. experience and worldliness. This midrash is emblematic of Rabbi Yohanan's approach to Jacob and all that he represents.

The Jacob of the book of Genesis is not deceitful but wise, worldly, and cunning; traits born of the difficult circumstances of his life that honed his mind and enabled him to survive in the face of persecution. Rabbi Yohanan cleverly leads us from "guile" to "cunning", from "cunning" to "wisdom", and from there to "Torah wisdom"—and we hardly notice the difference between the first characterization and the last.

Resh Lakish describes Esau's reaction when he discovers the deceit that has changed his life, as typically Roman in its vulgarity. Esau clears his throat and spits, in keeping with his vulgar, ill-mannered and common—in the pejorative sense of the word—nature. Once again we find Resh Lakish's penchant for exaggeration, in his denigration of Rome by means of a crude depiction of the biblical Esau.

Despite all of the condemnation and denigration of Esau in the Midrash, we cannot ignore Esau's role as one of the protagonists of the portion of *Toledot*, a figure with whom the biblical text—in its plain meaning—finds no fault or malice. Let us conclude therefore with a little of the little praise that Jewish tradition has for Esau:

"And Rebecca took the choicest garments of her eldest son Esau, which were with her in the house" (27:15)—

In which [garments] he was wont to serve his father.

Rabban Shimon ben Gamliel said: I have served my father all my life, yet I have not done one hundredth of the service that Esau did his father.

For when I served my father, I would do so in soiled clothing, and when I went out of the house, I would put on clean clothing.

Esau however, when he served his father, would do so only in royal raiments, saying "it would be disrespectful to my father to serve him in anything less than royal raiments",

as it is written: "which were with her in the house" (*op. cit.* 65, 16).

Rabban Shimon ben Gamliel, President of the Sanhedrin, son of Rabban Gamliel of Yavne and father of Rabbi Yehudah Hanasi—prince among princes—invents a fictional "self" whom he contrasts with Esau—Rome.

This fictional Rabban Shimon ben Gamliel—president of the Sanhedrin and representative of the Jewish people—is compared to Esau the hunter—man of the field, the simple Roman. Here it is the personal Esau who is the subject of comparison, symbolizing the people of Rome, rather then Rome's empire and ruling class.

Rabban Shimon ben Gamliel makes the following confession: I (i.e. the Jewish People), who am commanded to honor my mother and father, have failed to do so properly, preferring my own honor in the eyes of others to that of my father. I was therefore meticulous about my clothing before going out in public, but served my father in soiled clothes. Esau (the people of Rome), on the other hand, has always shown great devotion in observing this commandment, and we should therefore learn from his example. He served his father, dressed in his finest garments, out of a sense of respect.

Other midrashim tell of Esau's scrupulous observance of the precept "honor thy father:"

"It can be inferred *a fortiori*, if kings and rulers run to cleave to Esau, who observed only a single precept—
honoring his father—how much more so Jacob ..."
(*Sifre, Deut.* 336 ; Gen. *Rabbah* 82,14).

That Esau loved and honored his father, we learn from the Bible itself—the rest is the wonderful art of midrash. Rabban Shimon ben Gamliel—who was certainly not required to serve his father personally, due to his standing and wealth—compares himself to Esau, with the obvious literary goal of highlighting the difference between them. In other words, the Patriarch asserts, we Jews should learn from Roman custom to honor our parents and observe the commandment "honor thy father and mother". In order to obtain maximum effect, Rabban Shimon ben Gamliel, prince among princes, juxtaposed himself with Esau, hunter among hunters, that readers might draw a conclusion *a fortiori*: If the Patriarch of the Jews knows that one must learn to honor one's parents from the simplest of Rome's citizens, all the more so ordinary descendants of Jacob. Similarly, the Talmud contains a wealth of stories regarding a certain Dama ben Netina—a gentile of Ashkelon, who is praised and held up as a paragon of filial devotion (*Yerushalmi Pe'ah* 1,1; *Kidushin* 30b).

Summary

Toledot offers readers a number of wonderful episodes, among the most dramatic in all of Hebrew literature. We are drawn from the biblical narrative to the talmudic-midrashic interpretations of early Common Era Palestine, which afford the biblical stories such vivid historical expression that we can almost hear the din of ancient Rome and the clatter of Roman cohorts in the streets of occupied Judaea. Between the lines, we feel the Sages' repressed hatred toward Rome and everything it represented.

The biblical Esau was not given the benefit of fair treatment over the course of Jewish history, since it was his misfortune to have been identified with the wicked Roman Empire—the greatest enemy of the Jewish People until the Modern Era. The simple, candid figure that arises from the chapters of *Toledot*, is replaced by the crude and violent features of Rome—assumed by Esau, its historical representative.

We must not, however, overlook the fair-mindedness of the talmudic-midrashic Sages who—when and where they felt they owed Rome and its leaders a debt of honor—were even prepared to hold up Esau as a role model. Thus, beyond its hermeneutical value, the Midrash on the portion of *Toledot* provides an important lesson regarding the commandment "honor thy father and mother"—a precept of paramount importance, of which it is written, "That thy days may be long upon the land which the Lord thy God giveth thee" (*Ex.* 20:11).

Yeshaya Steinberger

Vayetze – And Jacob went out

Jacob and the Boundaries of Truth In the Teachings of
Rabbi Eliyahu Eliezer Dessler

And Jacob outwitted Laban the Aramaean (Genesis 31:20).

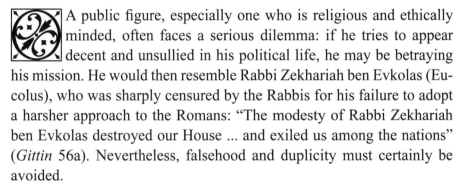A public figure, especially one who is religious and ethically minded, often faces a serious dilemma: if he tries to appear decent and unsullied in his political life, he may be betraying his mission. He would then resemble Rabbi Zekhariah ben Evkolas (Eucolus), who was sharply censured by the Rabbis for his failure to adopt a harsher approach to the Romans: "The modesty of Rabbi Zekhariah ben Evkolas destroyed our House ... and exiled us among the nations" (*Gittin* 56a). Nevertheless, falsehood and duplicity must certainly be avoided.

I believe that Jacob has shown us the way in this matter, and "the actions of the fathers are an example for the sons." The Patriarchs represent symbolic values in the thought of the Sages of the Talmud, Midrash and Kaballah. Jacob represents the quality of truth, as we find in the verse "Give truth to Jacob" (*Micah* 7:2; and commentaries there). In the kabbalistic world of the *Sefirot*, Jacob is identified with the *Sefirah* of *Tiferet* (Beauty), which conveys the abundance that flows from the higher *Sefirot* to the *Sefirot* below. In the Bible however, many of Jacob's actions appear deceitful. Jacob's appropriation of Esau's blessing is characterized as follows: "Thy brother came with guile, and hath taken away thy blessing." In other words, Jacob's disguising himself as Esau, by which means he obtained the blessings, is nothing short of scandalous.

Jacob appears fully aware of his manipulative abilities, and even takes pride in them. According to the Rabbis, Jacob sends his uncle Laban a clear message, prior to their first encounter: "'And Jacob told Rachel that he was her father's brother'—If he seeks to deceive me, I too am his brother in deceit!" (*Megilah* 13b; Rashi on Gen. 29:12). That is to say, one must treat Laban the deceitful Aramaean (the Hebrew words *arami*—Aramaean—and *ramai*—deceitful, comprise the same letters) in kind; and not only is the quality of truth not diminished thereby, but it is that very quality that dictates such a response. A study of Jacob's experiences and the many instances in which he was forced to resort to oblique ways, may offer some insight into the boundaries of truth.

Laban mirrors Jacob's behavior precisely—as a frame of reference and window on a world full of deceit. In this sense, *Vayetze* is a direct continuation of *Toledot*. Jacob's response to the falsehood that besets him—first from Esau, then from Laban—is one and the same.

The first episode we will examine is that of the sale of the birthright: "And the boys grew; and Esau was a cunning hunter, a man of the field; and Jacob was a quiet man, dwelling in tents. Now Isaac loved Esau, because he did eat of his venison; and Rebecca loved Jacob" (25:27–28). The picture seems quite clear: Esau is virile and impetuous, a fighter and hard-working hunter—a respectable profession in his day. Isaac, who is rather fond of his food, prefers the elder, who plies him with delicacies. Jacob, on the other hand, is the fragile, innocent child, removed from the bustle of life—the "field"—and detached from society. The mother, sympathetic toward her delicate child, takes him under her wing (we can assume that Jacob's pottage-cooking skills were the result of long hours spent at home, in the kitchen, at his mother's apron ...). Unlike his brother, Jacob is physically weak and uninitiated in the manly pursuits, but compensates for these shortcomings with his cunning and mental prowess—a typical reaction to physical disadvantage. In order to defeat Esau, Jacob the schemer lays a trap for his tired and gluttonous brother, and thereby manages to wrest the birthright from him.

The biblical narrative could be a precursor to Shakespeare's *Merchant of Venice*: Shylock, the Jewish usurer (a lowly and exploitative occupation) demands a pound of flesh from Antonio, the honest, hardworking gentile, who is late in paying his debt. Could Christian-European anti-Semitism—which demonized the Jew as a schemer who takes advantage decent Christians—find early justification in Jacob's treatment of Esau?

Nothing could be further from the truth. The Bible itself presents Esau as a wicked man. It is wrong to presume that the Bible saw hunting as a respectable profession. The biblical description of Esau resembles that of Nimrod: "And Cush begot Nimrod; he began to be a mighty one in the earth. He was a mighty hunter before the Lord; wherefore it is said: 'Like Nimrod a mighty hunter before the Lord'" (10:8–9). Nimrod was certainly considered wicked, regardless of any conclusion we may reach with regard to Esau. The expression "before the Lord" and his very name (*Nimrod*—"let us rebel"), imply that he was a man who "knew his Maker and intended to rebel against him" (Rashi, *ibid.*). If the Bible stresses Nimrod's skill as a hunter, this should be taken in a pejorative sense, as Rashi indeed remarks: "He ensnared men with his words, and misled them to rebel against God". If we compare the two figures, Rashi is correct in presenting Esau in a similar light: "'For he would [place] game in his mouth'—in Esau's mouth, who would ensnare his father with deceitful words." Indeed, the hunter outwits the animal with his cunning in setting traps and snares. It is therefore entirely within reason to characterize Esau as one who fooled his old father, manipulating him with lies. The idea that Isaac—certainly portrayed in the Bible as a righteous man—would have loved Esau purely out of gluttony, is preposterous. Esau's ruddiness, too, recalls blood and bloodthirstiness. How else do we explain his predilection for this particular color: "And Esau said ... 'Fill me, I pray thee, some of this red, red pottage...' Therefore was his name called Edom" (25:30)? Such a trivial matter as color would not have been stressed, were it not indicative of character. The color red is a symbol of murder or sexual license in other cultures as well.

Jacob's character, too, is masterfully described—in positive terms this time. The word "*tam*" (25:27) can be understood to mean righteous, as in the characterization of Noah as "a man perfectly righteous (*tzadik tamim*)" (6:9); or naive and simple, like the "simple son" in the Passover Haggadah. Neither of these interpretations is congruous with deceitfulness. Jacob's "dwelling in tents" is also—rightly—interpreted in a positive sense. The tent is a symbol of holiness and modesty, as we find for example in the expressions "the tents of Shem" (9:27), or "'Where is

Sarah thy wife?' And he said: 'Behold, in the tent'," on which Rashi comments: "for she was modest" (18:9).

In light of the above, the tendency of the Sages to ascribe positive intentions to Jacob, and negative ones to Esau, is comprehensible. The text describing the sale of the birthright also offers a number of indications in the same vein. Esau's faintness is mentioned twice in the text— perhaps understandable, considering the nature of his occupation. He goes too far, however, when he asserts "Behold, I am at the point to die" (28:32)—unless the faintness in question is no ordinary case of fatigue, but the existential faintness of one who espouses the philosophy, "Let us eat and drink, for tomorrow we shall die!" The contrast is thus not between an honest hard-working man and a conniving parasite, but between a nihilistic, brutish hunter, and a sensitive, intelligent man of the spirit.

Note the subtle humor in the biblical description of Esau, as explained by Rashi: "'And Esau said to Jacob: Fill me (*hale'iteni*), I pray thee'—I will open my mouth, and you pour a lot into it; as we have learned 'one may not force-feed a camel, but may fill it'" (Rashi, 25:30). Esau is then ... a camel—a brute animal with no table manners. (Rabbi Joseph Dov Soloveitchik, in one of his essays, discusses the differences between man—specifically Jewish man—and beast, in terms of their respective approaches to food. Animals pounce upon their prey, often unable to restrain themselves. Man, on the other hand, is capable of self-control. That is why virtually every human society has developed rituals pertaining to food, drink, and table etiquette. In Judaism, the entire subject has been imbued with sanctity, hence the many laws and customs associated with it.)

Ostensibly, it is Esau who is taken advantage of. His brother used his weakness in order to get him to "sign" away the birthright. The end result may have been legal, but such behavior has little of "beauty" (*Tiferet*) or "truth" in it.

And in fact, Esau protests to his father, equating the two wrongs he has suffered. Jacob's appropriation of the birthright is no less grave in Esau's eyes than his appropriation of the blessings: "he hath supplanted me these two times: he took away my birthright; and, behold, now he hath taken away my blessing" (27:36). Careful reading of the biblical text, however, clearly shows that Esau was hardly a victim. Until Jacob had taken the blessings, he did not feel exploited or cheated. It is human nature, when one is lured into a deal by temptation, to protest vociferously as soon as desire has been satisfied, and it becomes apparent that one has been cheated. Esau does nothing of the kind: "and he did eat and drink, and rose up, and went his way. So Esau despised his birthright" (25:34). In other words, even after having satisfied his desire, he remained convinced that he had made a terrific deal. He enjoyed an excellent meal practically for free—offering only a birthright of dubious value in exchange. The birthright had no bearing on financial matters, i.e. the right of the firstborn to a double share of any eventual inheritance. Were it not so, Esau would never have treated it with such contempt. He was not stupid. Only a complete fool would not have regretted such a terrible "deal"—inheritance rights in return for a meal—especially after having wiped the final morsels from his lips.

The birthright must therefore have a deeper meaning; pertaining, as Rashi explains, to the future right to worship in the Temple. We thus begin to understand—from the biblical narrative itself—the Rabbis' benevolence toward Jacob and aversion to Esau. It is not a matter of bias, but of a correct reading of the text.

In short: Had the birthright—symbolising future divine worship and in effect the destiny of the Jewish People—been important to Esau, he would never have renounced it for a tasty meal, as hungry as he may have been. The expression "sold his birthright for a pottage of lentils" is used to mock one who would forfeit his future in exchange for some fleeting pleasure. Esau, the firstborn, failed to appreciate what he had been given, due to his ignorance and vulgarity. Jacob, on the other hand, man of the spirit that he was, fully grasped the significance of this eternal legacy, and strove with all his might to deliver it from the hands of his wicked brother. Jacob, however, faced a grave theological dilemma: it was God after all, who had chosen to give the birthright to Esau. Did he, Jacob, have the right to deny his brother his God-given right? On the other hand, could he just sit idly by—knowing, as he did, that Esau and his descendents were likely to squander this divine gift: the birthright symbolising the future of the Chosen People? (This dilemma in fact reflects the famous contradiction between God's foreknowledge and man's freedom of choice, which requires him to act and aspire to change. See Maimonides, *Hilkhot Teshuvah*, chapters 5 and 6).

I will try to illustrate with a contemporary example. There was a case a number of years ago in which a U.S. Air Force pilot suffered a stroke while flying a sophisticated aircraft. Among the passengers were two pilots: one, a cadet not yet licensed to fly, but with a reputation as a prodigy, capable of flying just about anything; and the other a licensed, high-ranking pilot lacking the knowledge and skill necessary to fly the sophisticated craft. The brilliant young aviator was aware of the fact that his senior colleague could crash the plane if allowed to fly it. A violent argument erupted between the two, during the course of which the ace struck the licensed pilot, took command of the aircraft, and landed it safely. He was court-martialed for flying without a license, insubordination and striking a senior officer. His attorney argued that not only was he not worthy of punishment, but that he deserved a citation, for having exercised responsible judgment, to the best of his knowledge and conscience, to save the aircraft and its passengers. He understood that in such cases, licenses and regulations have little meaning. To the prosecution's claim that the cadet's actions could lead to others taking the law into their own hands, the defense replied that from the perspective of an onlooker, safe on the ground, the licensed pilot should certainly have been preferred over the unlicensed one. In an emergency, however, saving the plane and its passengers must take precedence over all such considerations. The cadet was acquitted.

The plane is the birthright, the vehicle for the spiritual future of the Jewish People, the passengers, the descendents of Abraham and Isaac; the cadet, Jacob, and the older, licensed pilot, Esau. Clearly, the law was broken in both cases. It is equally clear in both cases, however, that the specific circumstances warranted the application of principled judgment, in the spirit of "a well-intentioned transgression is preferable to a meritorious act with ill intent."

Consequently, Jacob did not veer from the path of truth, but on the contrary, it was precisely this path that required him to act as he did. The alternative—blind adherence to the formal letter of the law—would have resulted in falsehood and injustice. It is thus not merely a case of a positive precept taking precedence over a negative one—i.e., the imperative of preserving life coming before the prohibition against mendacity—but rather a bolder, more profound definition of truth and falsehood.

Since Jacob had already won the birthright, his claiming the blessings would appear justifiable (as Rashi on 27:36 indeed implies). His behavior in the matter is rather distasteful nonetheless. How unbecoming of the qualification "*Tiferet*" is the third patriarch's impersonation—clothed in hairy goatskins—of Esau, in order to deceive his aged, blind father, as well as his brother.

I will try to demonstrate, using the method of one of the foremost halakhic authorities of the Middle Ages, that Jacob was compelled to act as he did, and it was in fact this very action that earned him the title defender of truth of all ages. Rabbi Eliezer of Metz (13th century), author of the *Sefer Yere'im* on the 613 precepts of the Torah, writes the following regarding the precept "keep thee far from a false matter:"

> One must be most careful in this matter, lest one cause harm by his lie ... and all who fear God will take heed to keep far [from falsehood], for one may thereby cause harm ... The Torah however, did not forbid a lie that causes no harm ... Beit Shamai said: According to you (Beit Hillel), how can one say a bride is beautiful and gracious if she is lame or blind, for the Torah said ...keep thee far from a false matter"? [The Torah was only referring to falsehood] that causes people harm (*op. cit.*, 235).

According to the *Yere'im*, falsehood is determined by the harm it inflicts; in the above example, whether or not one causes a man distress by falsely praising his lame bride. When there is no harm, there is no lie, or at least not of the kind forbidden by the Torah. Let us thus complete the equation, inferring the positive from the negative: If a lie produces objective benefit, it is not a lie but a truth. In other words, although the end generally does not justify the means, the end in this case "defines" the means! A lie is measured not by the words uttered, but by the results it produces: whether it creates a false or true reality.

The story of Jacob, although not mentioned specifically by the *Yere'im*, may help to prove the validity of the above assertion. Any justification of Jacob's devious ways is, after all, little more than apologetics. Why, then, do the Rabbis see Jacob, of all people, as a symbol of truth? Only if we find that Jacob—more than anyone before or since—developed profound and original principles for understanding the innermost essence of truth, will we be able to consider him the father of this quality. According to the *Yere'im*, it is these very principles that we find in these chapters—not only in the sale of the birthright, but in all of Jacob's ostensibly dishonest dealings. His attitude toward Laban, "if he seeks to deceive me, I too am his brother in deceit," conveys the message that the path of deceit is in fact the true response to an Esau or a Laban—a response in kind; not merely a necessary evil, but truth itself.

Rabbi Eliyahu Eliezer Dessler, revered spiritual director of the Ponevezh Yeshivah in Bene-Berak, does not explicitly cite the *Yere'im*, but presents similar ideas, which he employs in his portrait of Jacob's spiritual greatness (see *Mikhtav Me'eliyahu*, vol.1, pp. 94–6). A similar approach is often ascribed to another giant of the *Musar* Movement, Rabbi Yeruham Leibovich of Mir. Moreover, as a *haredi* leader and thinker, Rabbi Dessler indirectly helped shape the ethos of *haredi* politics. The *haredim* have always taken a pragmatic, goal-oriented approach to politics—not coincidentally termed "blackmail" by critics and opponents. The *haredi* approach to politics undoubtedly draws inspiration and justification from ethical concepts shaped in the study hall, and particularly from the thought of Rabbi Eliezer Menahem Shach—a later successor of Rabbi Dessler's, and another of Ponevezh's well-known leaders.

Although a lie that does no harm does not violate the biblical precept "keep thee far from a false matter," the Rabbis forbade it. Various sources trace this prohibition to a verse in *Jeremiah*: "they have taught their tongue to speak lies, they weary themselves to commit iniquity" (*Jer.* 9:4). One must preserve the purity of one's tongue, and not conceal the truth. Further examples can be found in talmud and midrashic literature. One must return a lost item to a rabbinical scholar (*tzorva mirabanan*) for example, solely on the basis of his recognition of the item (without the required "signs"), on condition that he is known as one who never conceals the truth. On occasion, however, even such a scholar is required to conceal the truth for social reasons. Thus, for example, he may give a lukewarm appraisal of his host's table—although truthfully speaking the food may have been of the highest quality—lest the latter be overburdened by guests (*Bava Metzia* 23b). God's words to Abraham regarding Sarah's laughter are also interpreted in this vein: Sarah laughs and says of Abraham, "my lord is old," but God, for the sake of peace, changes her words: "Wherefore did Sarah laugh, saying: ... I ... who am old" (18:13). The example cited by the *Yere'im* regards the manner in which one should dance before a bride. According to Beit Hillel, one must sing "beautiful and gracious bride" even if the bride is ugly and covered in boils—in order to praise the groom's "purchase". If he has decided to marry her, why spoil things?

There would thus appear to be two distinct categories: "falsehood" and "concealing the truth". The biblical prohibition, "keep thee far from a false matter," is contingent upon intent and context, and often does not apply at all. If a statement promotes peace, it was never a falsehood to begin with. "Concealing the truth," on the other hand, is independent of context and intent, and therefore always applicable. In certain cases however, one may conceal the truth for the sake of peace (see *To'afot Re'em* on *Sefer Yere'im*, section 1, who cites the dissenting view of the *Ritva*.

Note how meticulous Jacob was in matters of truth and falsehood. As we have seen, according to all of the Sages' ethical-halakhic criteria, Jacob was permitted and even obligated to rescue the birthright and the blessings from his wicked brother. Nevertheless, the Torah recounts how Jacob was loath to obey his beloved mother who had devised the plan for stealing the blessings, and only when she took responsibility upon herself, saying "upon me be thy curse, my son" (27:13) and implored him, did he acquiesce. She probably alluded to the prophecy she had received before his birth: "and the elder shall serve the younger" (25:23). Jacob felt uncomfortable with such subterfuge, which ran counter to his nature, and cooperated in spite of himself.

With the help of the above, perhaps we can understand Rashi's commentary on *Vayetze*, in which he twice gives Jacob the benefit of the doubt, employing seemingly sophistic semantic arguments. When Jacob says to his father "I am Esau thy first-born," Rashi inserts a comma into the phrase: "I am [before you], Esau [is] thy firstborn." When Isaac insists: "Art thou my very son Esau?' And he said: 'I am.'" (27:24), Rashi again mitigates the lie: "'And he said: I am'—He did not say 'I am Esau', merely 'I am'." Is Rashi, God forbid, underestimating our intelligence?

We have already established that Jacob's words did not constitute a violation of the injunction against falsehood (were this not the case, Rashi's rationalizations would hardly have afforded sufficient justification). Jacob, however, was wary of "concealing the truth"—a concept which certainly applied here—and that is the difficulty that Rashi attempted to resolve by changing the punctuation of the verse. For Jacob, the righteous man of Halakhah and truth, was scrupulous even with regard to such minutiae.

Those who are not convinced, and insist on seeing Jacob in a negative light (see for example Alan Dershowitz, *The Genesis of Justice*, p. 132 *et seq.*), will find it hard to explain the fact that Isaac, who loved Esau and was ostensibly tricked by Jacob, does not censure him in any way. Furthermore, he reconfirms the blessings he has given to Jacob: "yea, and he shall be blessed" (27:33, see Rashi there; Nahmanides offers a different interpretation, but admits that Isaac did not reprove Jacob). Isaac then blesses Jacob yet again (28:1), and in one mind with Rebecca and Jacob, sends the latter to find a suitable wife, in obvious contrast to the sins of Esau, who married the daughters of the land. This would have been strange indeed, had Isaac himself not concluded that Jacob had done the right thing; a conclusion he must have reached on the basis of the principles we have presented here.

The symbolism associated with Jacob has a negative side as well, inasmuch as Jacob represents Jewish exile throughout the ages, in keeping with the rabbinic principle of "the actions of the fathers are an example for the sons." As long as he bears the name Jacob—before the angel (Esau's guardian according to the Sages) concedes the blessings (see 32:25; Rashi *ibid.* 27)—he represents crookedness, hardships that can only be overcome by resorting to behavior devoid of *"Tiferet"*. (Rashi 32:22 beautifully encapsulates the tragedy that plagues Jacob throughout his life: "'So the present passed over before him'—He too was angered that he must suffer all of this." In other words, Jacob felt wretched and reproached, forced by his fear of Esau to resort to tricks of survival unworthy of him.) This is the essence of exile, marked by a lack of *"Tiferet"*: "The glory is departed (exiled) from Israel" (*1* Sam. 4:21). And this is how Jacob's descendents have been perceived throughout the generations, particularly in medieval Christian-European culture and the anti-Semitic myths to which it gave rise.

From the moment the angel concedes the blessings, however, Jacob's character is wholly changed. The name "Israel" attests to his inherent dignity and the restoration of his lost honor. Deriving from the word *serarah*—authority, the name Israel symbolizes redemption. Upon careful examination, however, we will find that, in truth, this *Tiferet* existed secretly, all along.

Summary

Like our father Jacob, Jews throughout the ages have been perceived as thieving, conniving exploiters, who live at the expense of ostensibly honest gentiles. Like Jacob, whom Laban left no choice but to herd "the rest of Laban's flocks", i.e. "Jacob was given the weakest among them" (Rashi 30:36), Jews were for the most part forced by a hostile society into unworthy occupations. Jews were not allowed to engage in respectable and productive professions, and were compelled to earn heir living as moneylenders, tax collectors, etc. Shakespeare, too, in the *Merchant of Venice*, ignores the historical background and vagaries of survival that forced Shylock to enter his despicable profession (the *Oxford English Dictionary* still lists the word "jew" as a verb, meaning "to cheat"). Sadly, such phenomena persist to this day—the stereotypical characterization of certain groups, portrayed as living at the expense of honest, productive society. Although such generalizations may be justified at times, we must guard against the prejudices that often lie behind them.

We have much to learn from the path of Jacob. It was he who gave us the religious political ethic. Leaders and public servants must not delude themselves that they will always manage to preserve their images and good names in the battle for Judaism's sacred values. Humiliation and even character assassination are sometimes the price that one must pay for the hidden inner good in a world of falsehood. Thus, only the courageous—undeterred and imbued with the justness of their cause—will succeed in changing the world for the better.

Clarification

Despite all of the above, the approach of the *Yere'im*—whereby the definition of falsehood is contextual, so that a lie that serves a positive end is permissible—is not universally accepted. (See Rabbi N. Yabrov, *Niv Sefatayim*; and Rabbi Dr. J. J. Schachter, "Facing the Truths of History", *Torah U'Madda*, vol. 8, p. 200 *et seq.*) The words of the *Yere'im* pertain to the realm of personal conscience; between man and God. In modern society, such principles may be difficult to apply, and there is the danger that they may be exploited in an unscrupulous fashion. Such practical considerations however, do not change the basic definitions of truth and falsehood we have presented here.

Erella Yedgar

Vayishlah – And Jacob Sent Messengers

Ethical Judgment in the Commentary of **Nehama Leibowitz***:
The Shekhem Affair as a Test Case*

And Jacob said to Simeon and Levi: "Ye have troubled me, to make me odious unto the inhabitants of the land, even unto the Canaanites and the Perizzites; and, I being few in number, they will gather themselves together against me and smite me; and I shall be destroyed, I and my house." And they said: "Should one deal with our sister as with a harlot?" (Genesis 34:30–31).

One who approaches Scripture with a sense of religious commitment or national-cultural identification, expects the fathers of the nation—God's chosen—to be paragons of virtue, a source of pride and inspiration. Surprisingly, the Bible is full of cases in which the Patriarchs' conduct appears to contradict natural ethics or the ethics of the Torah itself. These present exegetes and educators with a religious, hermeneutical and ethical challenge. In this chapter, I will discuss some of the ways in which Nehama Leibowitz met this challenge in her two best-known works: *Gilyonot Le'iyun Beparashat Hashavua* ("Study Sheets"), and *Iyunim Beparashat Hashavua* ("Studies").

Nehama Leibowitz pursued a twofold educational goal: exegetic–to teach a responsible approach to Scripture and its commentaries; and moral—to impart their religious, moral and philosophical messages. The relative weight ascribed to each of these goals varies in accordance with the type of work in which they appear. In her *Study Sheets,* for example—intended for an educated audience—primacy is given to exegesis, and moral lessons are veiled. In her *Studies*, on the other hand—intended for a general audience—she clearly leads the reader to the moral lessons deriving from the text and its homiletic interpretations. In other words, pedagogical knowledge of her target audience led her to employ different approaches to educated and general readerships, without changing her basic ethical position.

A comparison of the positions reflected in the two types of work will thus demonstrate the full extent of her ingenuity.

Nehama also wrote "Teachers' Guides" (*Alonei Hadrakhah*)—for teachers who used the *Study Sheets* in their hermeneutics and education classes—which she later included in her corresponding *Studies*. The *Teachers' Guides* offer greater insight into the moral positions reflected—directly or implicitly—in both types of her work; shedding light on her general philosophical outlook. A comparison of the *Study Sheets*, *Studies* and *Guides* will thus contribute to our understanding of Nehama's approach to moral judgment in the Patriarch narratives.

A wonderful example of this can be found in Nehama's writings on the conduct of Jacob's sons in the Shekhem affair. She addresses the various aspects of the affair in the *Studies* and in a number of the *Study Sheets*, both in her commentaries on the episode itself—recounted in the portion of *Vayishlah*—and in the context of Jacob's blessings in *Vayehi*. This chapter will focus on Nehama's approach to the brothers' conduct, in the study entitled "The Story of Dinah" (*Studies on* Bereshit pp. 380–387), as compared to her approach in the *Teachers' Guides* and, in passing, to the corresponding *Study Sheets* as well.

Genesis 34 recounts the story of the rape of Dinah and her brothers' reaction. At first reading, the story raises a number of grave moral questions regarding the brothers' conduct: the demand that all of Shekhem's men circumcise themselves, which appears from the outset to have been merely a ruse; their betrayal, after they had complied with the conditions set by Jacob's sons; the killing of residents of the city who had not been involved in the rape; the taking of spoils and of the city's women—ostensibly no better than Shekhem's own actions.

Yet the Bible itself offers no unequivocal moral guidance. Although Jacob's blessing in *Vayehi* may suggest sweeping condemnation of the brothers' actions, in *Vayishlah*, he cites purely practical considerations for his displeasure. Jacob thus appears to see nothing inherently wrong with his sons' conduct. God too, seems to intervene on the brothers' behalf—leading us to believe that even he condoned their actions. Moreover, the Bible gives the brothers the last word. The overall impression created by the biblical text is thus one of agreement with the brothers' motives, if not with their actions.

Indeed, many commentators clear the brothers of all charges of deceit and violence for its own sake. Some claim that Jacob's sons acted in the capacity of judges. Accordingly, they explain that the people of the city knew about the rape and collaborated with Shekhem—a capital offense in its own right. Some believe that the brothers were on a rescue mission to secure the release of their captive sister. They were therefore justified in deceiving the kidnappers and even killing all of Shekhem's men, who had collaborated with their leader and were defending him. Others view the entire incident as a struggle between two peoples, and even a defensive war: the brothers saw Shekhem's action as the provocation of a powerful local ruler, well-connected with the people of the land, against the small, foreign, and defenseless family of Jacob. Such a provocation could have led to far worse attacks on the part of the surrounding peoples, and therefore warranted a disproportionate, deterrent response.

Nehama, however, rejects all of these approaches. She believed the actions of the brothers to be morally and religiously inexcusable. Most of her objections relate to the brothers' violence and killing of innocent people, although she also addresses their duplicity against the Hivites. This unequivocal condemnation is apparent in every aspect of the study: in its structure; in the focus of her questions; in her choice of analytical method and commentators; and in the way she presents her personal views.

In her introduction to the Study, she states in no uncertain terms: "In chapter 34, we find a tale of murder: the murder of an entire town—men, women and children. Can this act be justified? Does the fact that it was a retaliatory raid (*pe'ulat tagmul*), in reprisal for a heinous crime, really offer any justification?"

At first glance, Nehama appears merely to present the questions that will be addressed in the discussion to follow, without expressing an opinion. The Hebrew phrasing of the latter question however (employing the interrogative *ha'umnam*, as opposed to the simple *ha'im*), implies a negative response: No, there can be no justification for their actions. Moreover, Nehama questions the brothers' murder of "an entire town—men, women and children", although according to the biblical text, they killed only the males (and perhaps only adult males; those termed "all that went out of the gate of his city" in the preceding verse), taking the women and children captive (34:29). Twice she uses the word *retzah* (murder), and once the expression *pe'ulat tagmul* (the very same expression used to denote the Israeli military reprisals of her day). She would thus appear to be expressing sharp condemnation of the actions of Dinah's brothers—stemming also from her objections to such retaliatory raids per se.

This sense of disapproval is reflected throughout the Study: in the wording of the questions and in the background discussion of Jacob's view of Simeon and Levi's conduct. In this discussion, Nehama reinforces her initial position, claiming that her evaluation of the brothers' actions is guided by Jacob's own point of view. His rebuke at the end of the chapter seems to be rooted entirely in practical considerations: "Ye have troubled me ... they will gather themselves together against me and smite me" (*ibid.* 30). Nehama asserts, however, that Jacob rejected their actions per se, for moral reasons. She bases this claim on Jacob's words upon his deathbed:

> Then, many years had elapsed since the incident; Jacob dwelt safe and sound in Egypt, in the shelter of Joseph, the viceregent of the realm. He had left the Canaanites and Perizzites far behind him, There was nothing to fear from them and no such motives of expediency could be said to motivate his condemnation of the deed which he had evidently not been able to forget: "Cursed be their anger, for it was fierce, and their wrath, for it was cruel" (49:7) (*ibid.* p. 381).

Yet, Jacob's words before his death are open to interpretation. Some commentators ascribe Jacob's condemnation of Simeon and Levi (*ibid.* 5–6) to their role in the sale of Joseph (*mekherotehem/mekhirotehem* ... *ish* ... *shor*—sale ... man ... bull; ['bull' being a reference to Joseph; see *Deut.* 33:17]), rather than to the Shekhem affair. Others claim that Jacob made a distinction between the act itself and the character traits that it reflected. He cursed the trait of anger ("anger" "wrath"), which he saw as boding ill for the future, but did not disapprove of their conduct in this specific incident. Nehama however, does not raise either of these possibilities, asserting rather, that Jacob's view of the incident was entirely negative.

She reiterates this position in the phrasing of her next question: "And if Jacob could not find justification for the act itself—*inasmuch as it was an unjustifiable and heinous crime* (emphasis mine)—why did he acquiesce?" (*Iyunim* p. 264).

In the *Teachers' Guides* 5717/5731 (1956/1971), Nehama seems to take the opposite view, cautioning against an offhanded, shallow reading of the biblical text: "With regard to the act of Simeon and Levi, one must take special care to avoid a one-sided and emotional approach. The story strikes too close to home and many have already drawn rash and superficial conclusions, comparing this episode to our current state of affairs". In light of this admonition, one would expect the author to provide readers with a number of possible approaches to the brothers' actions that are neither emotional nor one-sided.

Indeed, in the *Study Sheets*, intended for a more educated readership, Nehama cites interpretations that justify the brothers' actions, while raising questions regarding the weaknesses of these interpretations, as well as their textual basis. She thus provides the reader with the opportunity to contemplate the brothers' motives and the course of action they chose to pursue, despite her own, unequivocal rejection of their approach. In the *Studies* however, accessible to a wide variety of readers, she was not prepared to engage in such dialectic, perhaps for fear that some readers might not share her conclusion that justification of the brothers' actions is "rash, one-sided and emotional". Her approach is based on the premise that the brothers' actions included untoward behavior. Her role is not to defend or explain them, but to reveal the lesson she believes the Torah wishes to teach us here. She therefore brings readers to adopt the premise that the brothers were wrong to inflict collective punishment, before discussing the subject in detail. The ensuing discussion might then limit, explain or mitigate, but not deny the basic premise.

Once she has established this point, Nehama turns to the rest of her analysis. She begins with a literary analysis of the story, citing Nahmanides, who discusses the brothers' actions in light of the circumstances, and concludes with a discussion of the episode based on its consequences. She thus proceeds from an introduction, in which she asserts that the circumstances do not justify the act, to the study's conclusion, in which she argues the consequences are equally unable to provide justification.

The author poses three questions in the introduction, to which she replies in the study. Two are explained fully: The question regarding Jacob's reaction: If the action was justified, why was he angry with his sons? And if it was not justified, why did he not try to prevent it? And the question regarding the brothers' motives: Can the massacre of an entire town by the brothers (who were essentially righteous) be justified by the fact that it was an act of reprisal? The third question, regarding God, she posed without further explanation. The author then reiterates the questions, as formulated by Nahmanides, of whom she writes: "Of all our commentators, Nahmanides is the most astute in his observations on this chapter." She thus finds support not only for her final conclusions, but for her initial questions as well.

She then turns to literary analysis, specifically the negotiations between the brothers and the Hivites. She examines the wording of Shekhem's request to marry Dinah, juxtaposing Shekhem and Hamor's words to the brothers with those addressed to their own townspeople. This analysis is a turning point in the discussion, in two senses. First, it examines the circumstances of the case. Nehama thus intimates that one cannot judge an action by abstract, ideal criteria, without trying to understand the real context in which it occurred. Secondly, while Nehama relates only to the brothers' actions in the introduction, she now introduces a further element that one must consider before passing moral judgment: Was the other side really attempting to make amends, only to be cruelly deceived?

The marriage proposal appears to have been sincere: following the rape, Shekhem fell in love with the girl, recognizing her qualities and lineage (34:3). Some therefore contend that Shekhem's father, Hamor, proposed an honorable solution to the entire unfortunate affair, along the lines of the one prescribed by the Torah: one who rapes a virgin must pay her father fifty shekels and marry her, never to divorce her (*Deut.* 22:28–29). Nehama's strives, in her literary analysis, to rule out this possibility.

She claims that the detailed account of the negotiation process was intended to show that the Hivites were far from innocent. They address Jacob and his sons in a respectful manner: "The soul of my son Shekhem longeth for your daughter. I pray you give her unto him to wife" (34:8).

Dinah is referred to as "your daughter" and the decision to "give" her in marriage is left entirely up to her family. The tone of the conversation between Shekhem and his father, however, is quite different: "Take me this child to wife" (34:4). She is a mere "child", and the father is asked to "take" her, that is to say the matter is entirely in his hands. Their respectful request for Dinah's hand is deceitful, inasmuch as it ignores both the rape and the fact that she is still captive in their house. They speak in a smooth and courteous manner, when in fact they are practicing blackmail. Jacob's sons are not fooled by their smooth words. From their perspective, they have no choice but to resort to trickery or force in order to free their sister from captivity.

A discrepancy between Hamor's words to Jacob and his sons, and the words he addressed to the people of his city, also attests to the Hivites' lack of good faith, as shown in the following table:

Hamor to Jacob and his sons	Hamor to his fellow-citizens
(verses 9–10)	(verses 21–22–23)
I. "And make ye marriages with us; give your daughters unto us, and take our daughters unto you."	II. "Let us take their daughters to us for wives, and let us give them our daughters."
II. "And ye shall dwell with us; and the land shall be before you; dwell and trade ye therein, and get you possession therein."	I. "These men are peaceable with us; therefore let them dwell in the land, and trade therein; for, behold, the land is large enough for them."
--	III. "Shall not their cattle and their substance and all their beasts be ours?"

The two versions are similar, yet differ in such a way as to clearly reveal the Hivites' hypocrisy. Both versions may be divided into two parts: domestic—intermarriage; and political—settlement and possession. When addressing Jacob, Hamor begins with the subject of marriage, wherein lies his main interest, followed by the subject of settlement—in the framework of which he offers both settlement and possession in return for intermarriage. When father and son come before the people of the city, however, they place the political before the do-

mestic, and omit the offer of possession. The domestic part that follows
is presented in terms of the public interest, rendering intermarriage a
by-product of the commercial gains to be garnered from the association
with Jacob's family.

In support of this interpretation, Nehama cites Rashi, who highlights the difference between the marriage arrangements Hamor proposes in his negotiations with sons of Jacob, and those he presents to
the townspeople—"give your daughters unto us, and take our daughters
unto you" (34:9), to which Jacob's sons reply: "then will we give our
daughters unto you, and we will take your daughters to us" (*ibid.* 16).
The wording is reversed, however, in Hamor's report to the people of
his city: "let us take their daughters to us for wives, and let us give them
our daughters" (*ibid.* 21). According to the latter phrasing, argues Nehama, the initiative is left entirely to the Hivites. It is they who will give,
take and reap the benefits.

The Hivites' intention of taking advantage of Jacob's family is particularly evident, according to Nehama, in the detail that Hamor and
Shekhem add to their report to the town, but fail to mention to the brothers: "Shall not their cattle and their substance and all their beasts be
ours?" (*ibid.* 23).

> For that is the way of the world: The stranger comes, settles, toils
> and may even prosper, but in the end, all that he has produced—
> he has produced for us; all he has amassed—he has amassed for
> us; *and when the time comes, we will know how to get rid of him*
> (emphasis mine). Is it not worth our while to welcome them and
> even accede to the strange condition they have stipulated? It is
> indeed worth our while.

Here, Nehama takes her specific observations to a general plane:
"for that is the way of the world." Her prose becomes florid and emotional. Moreover, she ascribes to Hamor and Shekhem something that
they do not explicitly say: "and when the time comes, we will know
how to get rid of him." The Shekhemites thus become a paradigm for
any group that exploits strangers, ultimately to eliminate them and appropriate their property (and perhaps non-Jews who allowed Jews into
their lands, exploited them, expelled them and seized their property, in

particular). Comparing Hamor's words to Jacob's sons and to the people of Shekhem, we find justification for the brothers' assessment of the situation. They conclude that it is justified to resort to force against Hamor and Shekhem and perhaps even against the entire city, because it is the Hivites who are the exploiters and the deceivers, while Jacob's sons are constrained to act as they do, in order to rescue their raped and captive sister. Nehama thus finds some justification for the brothers' duplicity, although she does not say so explicitly: the only way to deal with liars may be to resort to their method.

The Study, at first reading, leaves the impression that Nehama intended, in her literary analysis, to mitigate the one-sided, negative approach to the brothers, particularly with regard to their act of deception. They may not have acted correctly, but the conduct of the Shekhemites should be regarded as an extenuating circumstance. This impression arises both from the emotional generalization to which she resorts in describing the wickedness of the Shekhemites, and from her remarks in the *Teachers' Guides*: "Students should be shown that the visit by Shekhem and Hamor to Jacob's house and the proposal they put forward hardly attest to their sincere desire to make amends and to forge a true alliance with Jacob." Later in the *Guides,* however, she reaches the opposite conclusion: "At the same time it should be stressed that Nahmanides—*although fully aware of all of this* (emphasis mine)—stands by his harsh characterization of the actions of Simeon and Levi."

This last sentence explains why Nehama placed her literary analysis within her discussion of Nahmanides' commentary, rather than following it, as she did in the *Study Sheets.* Had she placed her analysis after Nahmanides' commentary, it would have appeared as if she were presenting an interpretation of her own, at odds with that of Nahmanides. She wished to make it clear however, that he was fully aware of the things of which we are aware. She bases this assumption on the fact that Rashi, with whom Nahmanides was familiar, offers a similar analysis. The context of the brothers' conduct is thus their perception of the people of Shekhem as rapists, deceivers and exploiters; casting the brothers in a fairer and more balanced light, although not absolving them of guilt.

Her approach to Nahmanides—as to the story as a whole—differs from the *Study Sheets* to the *Studies.* In the *Study Sheets* (5708; 5726;

5731), Nehama first cites Maimonides (quoted by Nahmanides), who justifies the brothers on the grounds that they acted as judges seeking not only to punish the people of Shekhem for their past deeds, but to prevent them from causing further harm to society (that is how she explains Maimonides' interpretation in the *Study Guides*, stressing the importance of this view and how difficult it is to understand). Only then does she turn to—and accept—Nahmanides' opposing view. The experienced Bible student is thus encouraged to take a more complex view of the moral dilemmas faced by the protagonists. In the *Studies*, intended for a wider audience, she cites only Nahmanides' view, as if unwilling to put the readers' judgment to the test. In both works, readers are expected to draw negative conclusions regarding the brothers' behavior. This is also reflected in the opening passage of the *Study Guide*:

> This lesson, primarily concerned with evaluating the brothers' actions, should begin with an attempt to understand Jacob's words and approach to his sons' behavior ... at this point teachers should present Nahmanides' commentary ... *which condemns Simeon and Levi's actions in no uncertain terms*" (emphasis mine).

Nahmanides' condemnation is neither simplistic nor unbounded. It provides a different perspective of the circumstances in general, and of the roles played by Jacob and the other brothers.

Nahmanides addresses the issue of "Jacob and his sons" based on the assumption that Jacob could not have consented to Dinah's marriage to Shekhem. That is how he explains Jacob's passivity during the incident, and his subsequent anger. According to Nahmanides, Jacob foresaw two possible scenarios. The first, most logical and likely scenario was that the people of Shekhem would refuse to be circumcised. Consequently, the bothers would be able to justify a raid on the city, for the sake of rescuing their sister. According to the second, less likely scenario, the Shekhemites would agree to circumcise themselves—in which case, the brothers would enter the city when its people were in pain, and take Dinah, without hurting anyone. Nahmanides thus claims that Jacob and all of his sons had agreed upon a course of action. Simeon and Levi however, violated that agreement, and murdered the city's inhabitants with a "vengeful sword." Hence, Jacob was not involved in the killing, and was justified both in his silence during the meeting, and in his subsequent anger.

In his discussion of Simeon and Levi's behavior, Nahmanides distinguishes between the men and their actions. He presumes that the two were fundamentally righteous (stating this at the very beginning of his commentary), but cannot condone their negative behavior. On the one hand, he attempts to mitigate their deception by explaining their point of view. They did not believe the circumcisions—performed only to curry favor with the prince—to be sincere, and therefore felt no obligation to keep their promise. At the same time, he absolves the other brothers of all responsibility. On the other hand, he utterly rejects the massacre of the people of Shekhem, asserting—based on Jacob's words on his deathbed—that Simeon and Levi committed an act of violence ("weapons of violence their kinship") against the people of the city, who had trusted them and done them no wrong, and who might have turned to God. Moreover, (according to Nahmanides on *Vayehi*, cited in the study here) "they caused profanation of the Divine Name, [causing people to think that a prophet had committed violence and pillage]. This is the implication of the phrase: 'Let my soul not come into their council,' (49, 6). It disclaims Jacob's responsibility for their conspiracy when they answered with guile and declares he was not a party to their assembly when they came down on the city and slew them." Nahmanides thus charges Simeon and Levi with duplicity, murder, thwarting the Shekhemites' conversion, and profaning the name of God.

Nahmanides is a spiritual-religious authority. His words, with which Nehama brings to a close her discussion of the circumstances of the brothers' behavior, serve to reinforce her initial claim that even if the circumstances can be said to extenuate their culpability, they cannot justify the deed itself. Their intentions were not pure, their chosen course of action unwarranted, and its after-effects negative.

The final part of the Study (also mentioned in the *Study Guides*, but not in the *Study Sheets*) entails an equally negative evaluation of the events at Shekhem. At this point, Nehama addresses the third, unexplained question, raised at the beginning of the study: The fact is that the direct result of the brothers' actions was to their advantage: "and a terror of God was upon the cities that were round about them, and they did not pursue after the sons of Jacob" (35:5). The question is: can divinely-aided success be considered proof of divine acquiescence, as many commentators have asserted?

Nehama might have refuted this view by dismissing the expression "terror of God" (*hitat elohim*) as hyperbole, as in "*ir gedolah l'elohim— an exceeding great city*" (*Jonah* 3:3); or by means of contextual analysis: divine assistance came only after Jacob had purified his household of strange gods, and commanded his family to go up to Beth-El. God's intervention may in fact have been contingent upon this purification; atonement for the sons' misdeeds at Shekhem. These explanations, however, both pertain to the specific, while Nehama preferred a more conceptual approach. Her reply is not rooted in the traditional commentaries, but reflects a personal approach—one that is reiterated throughout the *Studies*, and lies at the heart of this particular study:

> Is the fact that a miracle occurred not proof of God's approbation? In answer to this we would say—as we have pointed out a number of times in our Studies—that the Torah stresses time and again that a miracle or a supernatural "sign" does not constitute proof of the truth. The Egyptian magicians also succeeded in their sorcery, and even false prophets (*Deut.* 13:2–6) are sometimes capable of producing signs and wonders in the heavens and the earth. As we observe in our daily lives and as we have seen throughout history, falsehood often gains the upper hand. This in no way proves—nor can we deduce from the fear of the sword that has fallen upon nations who live by the sword and frequently understand no language other than that of force—that an action is justified and good in God's eyes. As a contemporary thinker once said, nowhere among the many and varied names of God that attest to His attributes, do we find the name "success" (*Iyunim*, p. 263).

Nehama's reply comprises two separate arguments, while gently hinting at their relevance to contemporary Israeli reality, and particularly the retaliatory raids: (1) Miraculous, supernatural acts in no way attest to the truth of the claims of those who perform them; witness the false prophet and the Egyptian magicians. (2) The natural success of a despotic people, that lives by the sword and terrorizes its neighbors, is no indication of the justice of their actions (even when they themselves understand only the language of force). Both arguments are essential to understanding the event. The success of Jacob's sons in casting fear into the hearts of the surrounding peoples brings to mind the natural reality addressed by the second argument. The biblical text, however, makes explicit reference to divine intervention in the natural order: "and a terror of God was upon the cities." Such intervention is more reminiscent of the type of event addressed in the first argument. Nehama thus concludes that divine intervention in human affairs—whether by natural or supernatural means—cannot be seen as condoning human behavior.

When discussing the primary moral lesson of a study, Nehama generally works her way inward, from shell to core—from the specific example to the general, abstract value it embodies. This value is, in effect, the goal of the entire study, inasmuch as she believes it to be central to Torah thought and relevant to the lives and education of her readers. She thus begins the study with a question regarding the morality of the brothers' behavior within its specific context, while alluding to a much broader question: are there any circumstances in which collective punishment can be justified? She then asks whether divine intervention can be interpreted as divine acquiescence to human actions or values and concludes with a discussion of the relationship between inner truth, in the philosophical and theological sense, and its visible manifestations (citing the wonders performed by the Egyptian magicians and the signs of the false prophet—which belong to the realm of religious truth rather than morality).

In the study's closing discussion, she also employs strong rhetorical devices: florid language; the first person plural—identifying with her readers, as the Torah's target audience; expressions that evoke the subject's relevance to current events. The purpose of these devices is to bring the reader to identify with her words on an emotional level, and to incorporate them into her or his value system, as well as understanding them on a rational level. We thus discover Nehama's hidden purpose in her study on the Shekhem affair. The brothers' actions serve merely as a means by which to convey a fundamental message: (1) Our actions are judged by their merits, not their results; (2) The Torah requires all of us, the fathers of the nation included, to act truthfully and morally, even in the most difficult of circumstances; (3) Immoral behavior cannot be justified retroactively, using pseudo-religious arguments to assert divine sanction, based on material success. We thus gain insight into Nehama Leibowitz' moral-religious, dialectic approach, one that she combines with her exegetical approach. This method is particularly evident in the *Study Sheets* and *Study Guides*, in which she presents readers with moral dilemmas and alternative interpretations, but can also be found in the *Studies*, despite their apparent disregard of such dilemmas—due to the general audience for which they were intended. On the one hand, she defends the brothers in the *Studies*, clearly sharing Nahmanides' conviction regarding the brothers' fundamental righteousness. She justifies their actions—as they originally planned to rescue Dinah from her captivity—thereby mitigating their duplicity; she limits responsibility for the unwarranted and unjustifiable massacre to Simeon and Levi—asserting that Jacob and the other brothers had remained faithful to the original plan; she hints at the complexity of the situation faced by the brothers and establishes the guilt of the Shekhemites. Consequently, neither side was wholly guilty or wholly innocent.

On the other hand, she clearly condemns the brothers' conduct, unequivocally characterizing their actions as negative. The phrasing of her questions does not allow for the possibility that Jacob's sons may have been justified in acting as they did. She cites Nahmanides as an authority, without discussing his methodology or the textual basis for his view; she does not cite alternative commentaries; she provides broad support for her position, comparing the account here to Jacob's reference to the episode in his blessing; and finally, she extends the discussion to the general lesson it has to offer: one must judge every action based on its own merit, regardless of its consequences.

Her conclusion is unequivocal: there is no justification for the brothers' actions. Her treatment of the affair in the *Study Sheets* and *Study Guides,* however, shows that this conclusion was not automatic, offhanded or one-sided, but the result of serious moral contemplation, rooted in responsible didactic thought and a principled religious outlook, while honestly addressing the moral values behind the brothers' behavior.

This approach is emblematic of Nehama's approach to the sins of the patriarchs in general. She acknowledged the fact that her own religious orientation was primarily ethical: "In teaching the book of Genesis, one should teach the ethical dimension of the stories of the patriarchs" (*Pirkei Nehama* p. 427). Although she believed that "all of the actions of our forefathers, even the mundane, were a tabernacle to God," she also believed that the Bible makes no attempt to conceal the patriarchs' weaknesses (*Study Guides: Vayishlah* 5717/573; *Toledot* 5727; etc.). From a pedagogical point of view, she maintained that one need not focus on the greatness of biblical figures in order to create a sense of identification with them. The lives of the fathers of the nation should be viewed in their entirety—the shadows as well as the light. We will thus come discuss the moral values they reflect, learning both from the actions of the fathers and their consequences. According to Nehama, the essence of the Torah lies in the lessons that it conveys:

> [The assumption of our commentator is that] the stories of the Torah are not biographies of important figures of the past, or a history of mankind or the Jewish People, but wholly *torah*—i.e. instruction and testimony; providing lessons and guidance, and bringing us closer to divine worship (*Limud Parshanei Hatorah Udrakhim Lehora'atam* p. 83).

Nehama thus raises the possibility of moral-religious interpretation, tempered by humility, balance and respect for the text and its protagonists. Many of her studies imply a clear distinction between overall character judgment and the moral evaluation of a single act. On the one hand, she strives to portray the patriarchs in as positive a light as possible, explaining the complexity of the circumstances surrounding their actions. Her religious convictions led her to approach Scripture and the patriarchs, who are "the divine chariot", with a sense of reverence. Her exegetic convictions gave rise to her responsible, multifaceted and balanced (as opposed to "rash and one-sided") approach to the text. Her pedagogical convictions led her to avoid phrasing that might degrade the patriarchs—and the Bible in general—in the eyes of students. On the other hand, her moral judgment is completely uncompromising. Unacceptable behavior is always unacceptable. She believes that the purpose of the Torah is not to discuss the actions of its protagonists for their own sake, but to provide the reader with the tools to judge the biblical figures' values and choices for her/himself, in view of the constraints of reality, and in light of moral-religious ideals. In her opinion, even when one is driven by circumstances to pursue an undesirable course of action, one's intentions, alternatives and moral justification come under scrutiny. Moreover, the fact that the need for a particular action can be explained in a given context, does not necessarily make it moral or good. According to Nehama, the Torah teaches us—both as individuals and as a society—that we must judge all of our actions, in times of national prosperity and in times of crisis, by the combined standard of truth, conscience and religious ideals.

Shimon Gershon Rosenberg (Shagar)

Vayeshev – And Jacob Dwelt

Joseph the Dreamer:
*The Imagination According to **Rabbi Nahman of Breslov***

And Joseph dreamed a dream, and he told it his brethren; and they hated him yet the more. And he said unto them, Hear, I pray you, this dream which I have dreamed: For, behold, we were binding sheaves in the field, and, lo, my sheaf arose, and also stood upright; and, behold, your sheaves stood round about, and bowed down to my sheaf. And his brethren said to him, Shalt thou indeed reign over us? Or shalt thou indeed have dominion over us? And they hated him yet the more for his dreams, and for his words (Genesis 37:5–8)

The chapters of the Torah that deal with Joseph "the dreamer" have been fertile ground for commentators and homilists from talmudic times to the present. The attention devoted to Joseph and his dreams is no less than that devoted by modern psychology to the subject of dreams and the imagination. Naturally, the story of Potiphar's wife and her unsuccessful attempt to seduce Joseph is an important element of the discussion. The connection between dreams and imagination and sexual temptation features in the hermeneutical literature as well.

In his blessing to Joseph, Jacob says: "The archers have sorely grieved him, and shot at him, and hated him: But his bow abode in strength, and the arms of his hands were made strong" (*Gen* 49:23–24). The first verse is understood as a reference to his brothers and to the wife of Potiphar, who made Joseph's life miserable, as recounted in the biblical narrative. Regarding the second verse, Rashi cites the Aramaic translation of Onkelos—*vetavat behon nevi'utei* ("his prophecy was fulfilled in them"). This translation affords the opportunity to associate Joseph's imaginings and trials with prophecy. The connection between imagination, dreams and prophecy is explicitly mentioned in the Torah, and a number of prophecies were said to have appeared in a dream. The verse in the book of *Hosea* (12:11): "and by the ministry of the prophets have I used imagery," has often been cited in support of the existence of a connection between imagination and prophecy.

A talmudic interpretation attributed to Rabbi Yohanan (*Sotah* 36b) adds further substance to the verse's homiletic associations: "'But his bow abode in strength'—Rabbi Yohanan said in the name of Rabbi Meir: his bow returned to its strength; 'and the arms of his hands were made strong'—he clutched the ground with his hands, and his seed exuded from [beneath] his fingernails." Joseph, who according to kabbalistic-Hasidic tradition is the righteous one who upheld the Covenant (of circumcision), is portrayed by Rabbi Yohanan as having wasted his seed in order to resist temptation—a very grave sin, according to these same traditions. This sin is caused by the fantasies of the imagination, and its consequences—as described in the Talmud and the Kabbalah—the generation of demons and evil spirits. Fantasies emerge as demonic spirits.

Vayeshev is generally read in the synagogues on the Sabbath before Hanukah, at a time of year when we recall Hellenistic culture, which saw the Jews as lacking creative imagination. This negative characterization was based on Judaism's injunctions against the creation of graven images and other likenesses, the intellectualism of the Jewish study hall, and the paucity of Jewish works in the plastic arts, as compared to Greek accomplishments. Torah study was the focus of divine worship. Josephus Flavius quotes Apion's criticism of the Jews: "We Jews have not had any wonderful men amongst us, not any inventors of arts, nor any eminent for wisdom" (*Against Apion* II,13 –tr. W. Whiston). Generally speaking, Hasidism accepted this description of Judaism, although it did not consider it ideal, but rather the result of Jewish decadence. According to the Hasidic view, this state of affairs, whereby the intellect had become the central and virtually exclusive path to the divine—was not the way that things should be. It was directly related to the disappearance of prophecy that was tantamount to the disappearance of imagination all together. Prophetic imagination was supplanted by intellectual mind.

These are some of the many thematic and homiletic associations that provided the backdrop for Rabbi Nahman of Breslov's philosophy of imagination. By way of an introduction to the thought of Rabbi Nahman, I will present two well-known approaches to the subject of imagination by the medieval Jewish scholars Judah Halevi and Maimonides, typological positions that will help us to place Rabbi Nahman in the spectrum of Jewish philosophy.

What is the power of imagination? Maimonides (*Guide for the Perplexed* II, 36 –tr. M. Friedlander, Routledge, London, 1904) writes that, "Imagination is certainly one of the faculties of the body." It is a faculty related to the senses, but distinct and antithetical to the action of the intellect.

You will observe that most animals possess imagination ... Man's distinction does not consist in the possession of imagination, and the action of imagination is not the same as the action of the intellect, but the reverse of it. For the intellect analyses and divides the component parts of things, it forms abstract ideas of them, represents them in their true form as well as in their causal relations, derives from one object a great many facts, which—for the intellect—totally differ from each other, just as two human individuals appear different to the imagination; it distinguishes that which is the property of the *genus* from that which is peculiar to the individual, and no proof is correct, unless founded on the former; the intellect further determines whether certain qualities of a thing are essential or nonessential. Imagination has none of these functions. It only perceives the individual, the compound in that aggregate condition in which it presents itself to the senses; or it combines things which exist separately, joins some of them together, and represents them all as one body or as a force of the body. Hence it is that some imagine a man with a horse's head, with wings, etc. This is called a fiction, a phantasm; it is a thing to which nothing in the actual world corresponds. Nor can imagination in any way obtain a purely immaterial image of an object, however abstract the form of the image may be. Imagination yields therefore no test for the reality of a thing (*ibid.* I, 73).

The action of the intellect, according to Maimonides, is abstraction and generalization. The imagination, on the other hand, merely perceives the aggregate of images provided by the senses. Sights, sounds, colors and even smells—are the stuff of the imagination. It absorbs the fleeting and the ephemeral, and from these it fashions boundless fantasy worlds, melodies and characters, in a realm of freedom trapped within the confines of sensory images. The intellect treats the imagination with profound mistrust. The chimeras of the imagination, the intellect cautions with disdain, are but empty illusions, or at best, sources of aesthetic pleasure. The intellect takes an interest in the sensory only to the extent that it is a means to abstraction, material for future experimentation, for reduction to a general formula, a mathematical equation; for dour, compelling and constant truth. Man is not unique in his imaginative abilities with which the animals are also endowed.

Maimonides views factual analysis as the only path to truth, since it allows one to grasp the principle behind a tangible, often transitory and random event; a principle that is far from imagination.

Maimonides focuses his discussion of imagination on two main topics: prophecy and the sin of the Tree of Knowledge:

> Prophecy is, in truth and reality, an emanation sent forth by the Divine Being through the medium of the Active Intellect, in the first instance to man's rational faculty, and then to his imaginative faculty; it is the highest degree and greatest perfection man can attain: it consists in the most Perfect development of the imaginative faculty … You know that the full development of any faculty of the body, such as the imagination (*ibid.* II, 36).

Prophecy, according to Maimonides, is a form of inspiration in which true intellectual enlightenment is cloaked in the sensory images that express it. Maimonides views understanding as a far better instrument than imagination for attaining truth. A prophet is a philosopher with imaginative abilities, whose advantage lies only in the social function with which she or he is charged. The influence of descriptive imagery on the masses is much greater than that of intellectual arguments.

Imagination is also discussed in connection with the Tree of Knowledge. According to Maimonides, the sin of the Tree of Knowledge led to man's degeneration—his ability to grasp the fundamental difference between truth and falsehood supplanted by a subjective perception of good and evil. Imagination recast post-transgression man as a subject, an "ego" guided by considerations of "good for me" and "bad for me," imagining a fictitious reality tailored to his own pleasure and needs, whereas his previous existence had been one of objective conscious-ness, guided simply by recognition of the truth. According to some in-terpreters of Maimonides, the snake that causes man to sin is none other than the imagination. "All this is the work of the imagination, which is, in fact, identical with 'evil inclination'. For all our defects in speech or in character are either the direct or the indirect work of imagination" (*ibid.* II, 12).

The dual representation of imagination—as an instrument of proph-ecy, on the one hand, and the snake (the source of sin), on the other—re-flects Maimonides' ambivalence toward it. Imagination in fact assumes two entirely different meanings in the thought of Maimonides. Imagina-tion is fantasy—in the sense of man's ability to create tangible images in his mind's eye—which becomes prophecy when it acts in the service of intellectual enlightenment. The prophet, as noted above, is a philoso-pher with imagination. In its negative sense, imagination is simply fic-tion.

In principle, Rabbi Judah Halevi accepts the Maimonidean ap-proach to prophetic imagination in the service of the intellect, where-by the prophet attains intellectual-divine enlightenment by virtue of imagination. He differs from Maimonides, however, on two essential points. According to Halevi, imagination enables the prophet to see on-tic reality. Imagination is thus not merely an expression of intellectual consciousness—a projection from the internal to the external—but a vision of reality. This approach is related to Halevi's "Glory of God" doctrine, whereby the prophet sees real beings, created to represent the divine. The two approaches differ with regard to the ontic reality of such visions, but not the instrument by which they are conveyed, i.e. the imagination—which Halevi numbers among the senses. Halevi also contends—in keeping with his view of the "the divine" as transcending "the intellectual"—that the prophet's understanding is greater than that of the philosopher. The "mystical" world is tangible, and imagination is the sense with which the mystic sees this world above the world of wisdom. The prophet's ability should therefore not be seen only terms of the social function he fulfills. The imagery and visions he perceives afford a cognitive as well as a sociopedagogical advantage:

The Creator was as wise in arranging this relation between the exterior senses and the things perceived, as He was in fixing the relation between the abstract sense and the uncorporeal substratum. To the chosen among His creature He has given an inner eye which sees things as they really are, without any alteration. Reason is thus in a position to come to a conclusion regarding the true spirit of these things, He to whom this eye has been given is clear sighted indeed ... It is possible that this eye is the power of the imagination as long as it is under the control of the intellect. It beholds, then, a grand and an awful sight which reveals unmistakable truths. The best proof of its truth is the harmony prevailing among the whole of this species and those sights. By this I mean all the prophets. For they witnessed things which one described to the other in the same manner as we do with things we have seen.... Those prophets without doubt saw the divine world with the inner eye; they beheld a sight which harmonized with their natural imagination. Whatever they wrote down, they endowed with attributes as if they had seen them in corporeal form ... If a prophet sees with his mind's eye the most perfect figure ever beheld in the shape of a king or judge, seated on his throne, issuing commands and prohibitions, appointing and deposing officials, then he knows that this figure resembles a powerful prince (*Kuzari*, tr. H. Hirschfeld, Schocken, 1964, pp. 207–208).

Another important element of Halevi's approach, emphasized by Rabbi Nahman, is the distinction that he makes between prophetic imagination—the result of inspiration, and the imagination of the *hasid* at worship—an act of volition, intended to summon images that will help him to attain *devekut* (communion with the divine). The efficacy of the prophetic imagination stems from its spontaneity and so too its high degree of certainty and reality, as compared to that of the *hasid*, who strives to bring his imagination to a point at which he might find the strength of conviction.

> He ... charges his imagination to produce, with the assistance of memory, the most splendid pictures possible, in order to resemble the divine things sought after. Such pictures are the scenes of Sinai, Abraham and Isaac on Moriah, the Tabernacle of Moses, the Temple service, the presence of God in the Temple, and the like (*Kuzari*, p. 138).

> For there can be no faith in that which the intellect comprehends. Faith begins where the intellect ends. It is where comprehension fails, that faith is needed. And when one's intellect fails to comprehend, all that remains is the power of imagination, and that is where faith is needed (*Likutei Moharan, Tenina* (2), 8,7).

The intellectual rationalist, lacking in imagination, is therefore incapable of faith. The freedom of the imagination, which Maimonides believes to be random and therefore inferior—is, according to Rabbi Nahman, the very quality that renders imagination the means to faith. This view stems from the broader conception that "faith begins where the intellect ends." Contrary to Maimonides, who considered the intellect to be the source of faith (which is demonstrable), and unlike Halevi, who did not see the intellect as the source of faith but claimed there could be no contradiction between the two, Rabbi Nahman believed philosophical inquiry to be antithetical to faith. The philosopher is bound by the natural order of things, which runs counter to faith, inasmuch as faith is based upon the principle of God's omnipotence, which cannot be subject to order of any kind. Articles of faith such as belief in divine reward and punishment, Providence and miracles, are inconceivable in a world governed by a strict natural order. Faith requires a medium through which it can be revealed, because it cannot appear as an abstraction. And that medium is imagination.

> Let Him be described—that is with attributes and qualities that lie within the power of imagination. For all the attributes and qualities we ascribe to God, lie in the realm of imagination. In purely intellectual terms, God is entirely abstract, beyond all

qualities and attributes. All attributes and qualities thus lie in the realm of the imagination (*ibid.* 8,12).

The connection between Rabbi Nahman and Rabbi Judah Halevi, who viewed the imagination as a sense by means of which one may see the divine, is clear. Unlike Halevi, however, who considered the imagination superior only in its sensory ability, but otherwise subservient to the intellect, Rabbi Nahman saw this sensory capacity as an independent instrument, unhindered by the intellect, and thus fit to serve as a means to faith.

Imagination is the prophetic inspiration—the charisma—of the Hasidic rebbe. The rebbe can channel this spirit of inspiration to his followers.

> One must therefore earnestly seek out a true leader, in order to draw near to him. For each and every leader possesses the power of prophecy ... "another spirit" (*Num.* 14). And this other spirit that the leader possesses, is the holy spirit, the spirit of prophecy ... For one who has the good fortune to draw near to a true leader, by drawing near to him his power of imagination is perfected and clarified by the leader's spirit of prophecy ... And by the perfection of imagination, holy faith is perfected and clarified (*ibid.* 8,8).

Rabbi Nahman cautions against the false charisma of "a false leader", "a lying spirit", calling it "the pollution of the serpent": "For the commingling and confusion of the imagination, commingled and confused with false beliefs, is the pollution of the serpent." False prophecy, which originates in the imagination of diviners and augurs, spreads false beliefs, nonsense and lies.

If the leader is a true leader however, imagination is not only an expression of faith. Its power of persuasion, inasmuch as it is spontaneous inspiration granted from without, as noted above in the words of Judah Halevi, is itself belief! Rabbi Nahman goes a step further; imagination becomes the guiding force in changing the face of reality.

> And through faith, the world will be renewed.... This is the meaning of faith that hinges upon the power of imagination....

Then the world will be conducted in a wondrous fashion.... For there is a melody that is the natural way, in the sense of "the heavens declare the glory of God, and the firmament showeth his handiwork"—praising God for the current manner in which the world is conducted, that is in the natural way; but in the future a new song will awaken, one of wonders, and of Providence (*ibid.* 8,9).

The renewal of the world, the creation of a utopia in which the world is released from the grasp of the natural order, attaining the freedom of "wonders", also hinges upon the prophetic inspiration of the imagination. These ideas are reminiscent of modern utopian philosophers, whose beliefs differ greatly from those of Rabbi Nahman, but who equally balk at the stranglehold of "instrumental rationalism".

Rabbi Nahman was of course referring to the renewal of the world through the imagination of faith, but his description of the wondrous melody, the new song that will be sung at the end of days, is tinged with aesthetic freedom. In any event, Rabbi Nahman would have agreed that freedom of imagination is the remedy for the ills of reality, and that it has the ability to penetrate the world and transform it into a utopia.

Rabbi Nahman devoted a good deal of attention to the subject of preservation of the Covenant, i.e. the struggle against sexual desire. The figure of Joseph the dreamer—who according to Kabbalah and Hasidism represents the *Sefirah* of *Yesod* (the *Sefirah* of the Covenant of circumcision) and the righteous one who resisted temptation and upheld the Covenant—was seen as embodying the connection between prophetic inspiration of the imagination and sexual passion. Rabbi Nahman describes such passion as a spirit—in its perfected form the very spirit of prophecy and faith that will renew the world, and charge it with the tension of devotion and wonder. One might say that Rabbi Nahman considered the mystical spirit to be a form of desire, perfected through the preservation of the Covenant.

In a number of places, he cites or refers to the following wonderful talmudic exegesis:

And even Rahab the harlot said to the messengers of Joshua ... "neither did there rise any more spirit in any man"—that [their

members] did not even harden. And how did she know this? As
it has been said: There was no prince or nobleman who did not
lie with Rahab the harlot (*Zevahim* 116a).

According to the Gemara, Rahab the harlot knew of the impending
defeat of the Canaanite inhabitants of the land, from the fact that they
had lost their virility—"neither did there rise any more spirit in any
man". It is on this talmudic interpretation that Rabbi Nahman bases his
view of the transformation of sexual energy—to the point of becoming
holy spirit and the charisma of the *Zaddik* : "And this is the perfection
of the Covenant, that is the holy spirit, that is 'neither did there rise any
more spirit in any man' (*Likutei Moharan, Kama* (1), 19,3).
     And so too with regard to imagination:
     And 'the dream of Pharaoh is one' (Gen. 41), that the dream of
Pharaoh, the power of imagination, an idle power—as it is written (*Ex.* 5): "do ye hinder the people"—comes from 'one', that
is love [because 'one' is love, as explained elsewhere]. That is to
say, from fallen love, in the sense of "my people are destroyed
for lack of knowledge: because thou hast rejected knowledge,
etc." … And thus one falls from love of God to brutish love, and
is then overcome by the power of imagination, that is the power
of brutishness (*ibid.* 54,6).

The imagination is fallen love; love that has become brutish desire.
Like Maimonides, Rabbi Nahman, too, expresses ambivalence toward
imagination, even employing similar terms, referring to imagination as
an animal force.
     In this context, Rabbi Nahman cites the *Zohar* on demons created
at twilight. God failed to provide them with bodies, leaving them to
search for bodies to inhabit. The demonic imagination seeks out Torah
sages whose scholarship is only brilliant on the surface. Torah scholarship, by which heaven and earth are created—in this case creates "false
heavens", provoking famine. Criticism here is aimed not at the imagination of false *Zaddikim*, false prophets who spread false beliefs, but at
scholars whose learning is dazzling but superficial—aesthetically pleas-

ing but essentially meaningless and without substance. The utopia of imagination turns to false renewal and illusion in the mouths of these false scholars.

Here, and in one of his famous tales, "The Seven Beggars", Rabbi Nahman portrays Joseph as one who controls and perfects the spirit. Rabbi Nahman also teaches that the perfection of the Torah scholar (called "Jewish demon" in the *Zohar*) can be found in Joseph.

> And his perfection is Joseph, as in (Gen. 30:23) "God hath gathered in my reproach". For he sweetens the evil that is like famine, as in (*Ezek.* 36:30) "that ye may receive no more the reproach of famine among the nations". And it is he who "gathered in the spirit, etc.", as in (Gen. 41:38) "a man in whom the spirit of God is". And of whom it is said (*ibid.* 46:4) "and Joseph shall put his hand upon thine eyes". For by the hand, the eye is guarded against the power of imagination.

Joseph is thus the antigen of the "Jewish demon"—the brilliant but false Torah scholar. The role that Rabbi Nahman assigns to the *Zaddik* is quite different from that of the prophet. The *Zaddik* controls the spirit, has the ability to shape it into a melody that brings inspiration to the prophet who hears it. The image that Rabbi Nahman evokes is of a musician's hands, rising and falling, imparting rhythm and structure to the spirit. The *Zaddik* is an artist who shapes the spirit, as a sculptor shapes stone. The hands, that are the instruments of action and control, control the spirit itself. Such is the *Zaddik*'s ability to shape the spirit of the world. In Hasidic thought, this action is termed the "service of clarification"—separating good from evil, and gleaning the "sparks"—the positive forces within evil. Hasidism places the emphasis on releasing the holy sparks from the *kelipot* (the "shells" of impurity), like a sculptor who releases the form trapped within the stone, by removing all of the superfluous material. The *Zaddik* composes the melody and plays it to the prophet, to whom it brings inspiration—a division of labor that forms the basis of a number of Rabbi Nahman's tales. According to Kabbalah, the upper *Sefirot* require human service before they can pour out their *shefa* (divine abundance) upon them. The prophet is an instrument of inspiration, but the creator of that inspiration is the *Zaddik*, who shapes and sculpts and clarifies thΛ3e spirit, affording the prophet the inspiration he needs. The *Zaddik* is thus greater than the prophet.

The two figures work closely together; the one in need of a muse, and the other able to control, shape and guide it at will. Rabbi Nahman himself belonged to the second category, and took great pains in the preparation of his teachings and tales. (The story is told of one of the founders of Hasidism—Dov Baer (the Maggid) of Mezhirech—that he would fall silent from time to time while teaching. When asked why this was so, he replied that every time he heard his own voice, the *Shekhinah* would cease speaking through him, forcing him to stop, until he had once again forgotten himself. This is an example of teaching by inspiration. He had to make himself a passive instrument that the inspiration might pass through him.)

In the chapters of *Vayeshev*, Joseph and his brothers—particularly Judah—are at odds with one another, undoubtedly foreshadowing the historical rift between the kingdoms of Judah and Israel. In Hasidic thought, however, Judah and Joseph are perceived as two archetypes of righteousness, differing in their respective spiritual approaches to divine service. This dispute is seen as a constant element throughout Jewish history—stretching all the way to the days of the Messiah, as reflected by the two messianic figures: the Messiah ben Joseph and the Messiah ben David. Rabbi Nahman himself certainly identified with the figure of Joseph—interpreting the biblical passages accordingly.

The dispute between Joseph and his brothers was not an accidental lapse, but a vital part of Joseph's development of his method, as dispute was to Rabbi Nahman as well. Joseph is the charismatic *Zaddik*, whose charisma derives from his acute imagination and the dreams that he shares. Imagination, as explained above, is the means to faith and divine revelation. It is the holy spirit that brings Joseph to the audacious behavior that irritates his brothers and causes them to turn against him. The dispute between them is not over power, but over the future of the Jewish People. The brothers fear Joseph's method, and fear that Jacob's special love for him will lead to his triumph and their exclusion from the leadership of the People. The most striking expression of this is Joseph's sale and descent to Egypt. In hasidic terms, this descent is interpreted as Joseph's descent into the *kelipot* to release the sparks that had fallen there—one of Hasidism's central tasks. According to this doctrine, it is specifically in the depths of evil and impurity that the highest values and "lights" can be found; higher even than those that lie within the traditional precincts of faith. The role of the *Zaddik* is to descend to those places, in order to gather the lights, and incorporate them in divine service. Such incorporation, however, requires an extension of the boundaries of faith, and the adoption of a "new Torah"—a term Rabbi Nahman was not loath to use in various contexts. The brothers, on the other hand, are portrayed as conservative in their approach, lacking the will and audacity for true renewal. Joseph, the *Zaddik*, draws his conviction and audacity from his dreams, i.e. from the imagination that brings the spirit upon him, which he is then able to convey to his flock.

Judah's opposition to Joseph leads to his sale; an event that in fact serves Joseph's purposes—descent into the *kelipot* in order to gather up the sparks that are there. Joseph's temptation, his attempted seduction by Potiphar's wife (associated with imagination, as explained above), adds a further dimension to the conflict between Joseph and Judah. The Torah—even at the basic narrative level—obviously wished to juxtapose Joseph's resistance to temptation with Judah's behavior toward his daughter-in-law Tamar, foremother of the Davidic dynasty and the Messiah ben David.

The description of Joseph as being of "beautiful form and fair to look upon" also lends itself to this interpretation. In a number of his teachings, Rabbi Nahman portrays the *Zaddik* as possessing grace. Here, too, Rabbi Nahman places unusual emphasis upon the aesthetic-artistic aspect of spirit. Beauty is not only a source of enjoyment, but a source of truth as well, inasmuch as it reflects the divine rhythm; the cadence and melody of *Ein-Sof*. Grace is the meter, the original rhythm of the *Zaddik*'s charisma. Hence, Rabbi Nahman's application of his own artistic skills to his tales and teachings. Rabbi Nahman frequently laments the departure of "grace" from the Jewish People, to reside among the gentiles; and finds redress in the grace of the *Zaddik*.

Hasidism strives to discover the internal logic of the biblical narrative. Not satisfied with the plain meaning of the text, it seeks the message or insight at its core. The story of Joseph and his brothers, and the figure of Joseph, are interpreted by Rabbi Nahman in light of his own self-perception as *Zaddik* of his generation—the controversy that he and his followers aroused merely serving to vindicate their approach, for such is the fate of all who come bearing a new and anticonventional truth.

Michael Rosenak

Miketz – And it Came to Pass

Righteous Indeed? **Maimonides, Yeshayahu Leibowitz** *and* **Nehama Leibowitz** *Discuss Joseph*

And Joseph was the governor over the land, and he it was that sold to all the people of the land. And Joseph's brethren came, and bowed down to him with their faces to the earth. And Joseph saw his brethren, and he knew them, but made himself strange unto them, and spake roughly with them; and he said unto them: "Whence come ye?" And they said: "From the land of Canaan to buy food." And Joseph knew his brethren, but they knew him not (Genesis 42:6–8).

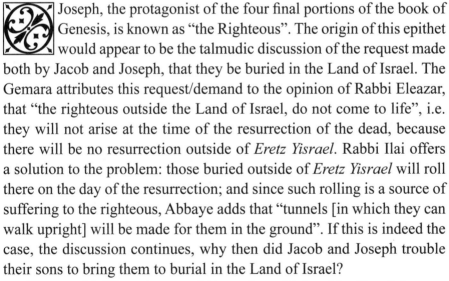 Joseph, the protagonist of the four final portions of the book of Genesis, is known as "the Righteous". The origin of this epithet would appear to be the talmudic discussion of the request made both by Jacob and Joseph, that they be buried in the Land of Israel. The Gemara attributes this request/demand to the opinion of Rabbi Eleazar, that "the righteous outside the Land of Israel, do not come to life", i.e. they will not arise at the time of the resurrection of the dead, because there will be no resurrection outside of *Eretz Yisrael*. Rabbi Ilai offers a solution to the problem: those buried outside of *Eretz Yisrael* will roll there on the day of the resurrection; and since such rolling is a source of suffering to the righteous, Abbaye adds that "tunnels [in which they can walk upright] will be made for them in the ground". If this is indeed the case, the discussion continues, why then did Jacob and Joseph trouble their sons to bring them to burial in the Land of Israel?

Karna said: There is something to be said for this. Our father Jacob knew that he was completely righteous, and if the dead outside the Land of Israel come to life [at the time of resurrection], why did he trouble his sons? Rather, [he feared] that he might not merit tunnels. Similarly "And Joseph took an oath of

115

the children of Israel ...";; Rabbi Hanina said : Joseph knew that
he was completely righteous, and if the dead outside of the Land
of Israel come to life, why did he trouble his brothers [to carry
his coffin] four hundred parasangs [to the Land of Israel]? [He
too feared] that he might not merit tunnels (*Ketubot* 111a).

The son follows in the footsteps of the father. They are both completely righteous, yet both fear that they will not be granted the privilege
of walking upright through the tunnels on the day of redemption. Was
it from this point forth that Joseph was referred to as "the Righteous"
whereas Jacob—like all the Patriarchs—retained the title "our father"?
The question that has troubled readers and students of the Torah is:
How does this man—who first appears at the beginning of the portion
of *Vayeshev* as an ill-mannered boy who goes on to become a rather
unpleasant adolescent—of all people, come to be called "Joseph the
Righteous"? How did this righteousness manifest itself, and what was
so unusually great about Joseph, that he alone of all the figures in the
Torah, would be forever remembered as "the Righteous"? How did a
spoiled, insensitive child, who told tales about his brothers and used his
dreams to appear interesting and important in the eyes of his father and
brothers suddenly become "righteous"?
The reader wonders whether the two portraits—that of the unpleasant
youngster and that of the man "officially" titled "Righteous"—can
be reconciled. How do we approach the task of reconciling these two
sets of data: references to the character of the boy, and evidence of the
qualities that warranted the epithet "the Righteous"? One way in which
both types of information can be addressed seriously, is to treat the entire
story as one of personal development, portraying the process that leads
to emotional and spiritual maturity. If this is the path we intend to follow,
we will expect to see gradual improvement in Joseph's character, and
observe his attempts at self-correction. Joseph would thus appear as a
man who abandons his weaknesses and faults, marshalling his inherent
good qualities, or those developed through his experiences. And we do
in fact witness the appearance of such qualities in Joseph. He resists
the temptation to sleep with Potiphar's wife, and takes responsibility
and initiative in his dealings with those—such as Potiphar or the keeper

of the prison—who place their trust in him. Later, he takes determined action on behalf of society as a whole, saving a great many from hunger. Moreover, Joseph declares, on more than one occasion, that his ability to interpret dreams is not his own, but comes from God, who guides him. At the end of the process, Joseph is reconciled with his family as well.

The question remains, however, at what stage of the story, at which moment can we say with certainty that Joseph has not only grown up and overcome his impulses, but changed so drastically that he can henceforth be seen as a paragon of righteousness. At what point does Joseph come to mind when we think of a righteous person—his way of life enriching our definition and understanding of righteousness? This question leads to another: What brought Joseph to this moment of spiritual accomplishment? Was it his inherent qualities merely waiting to be "activated" by the right circumstances? Or perhaps his father had raised him to be righteous, knowing full well that the fruits of "character education" are slow to mature, so that he was not surprised—neither by the faults of the boy, nor by the excellence of the adult?

But does this really explain Jacob's tolerance of the young Joseph's outrageous behavior? The father does rebuke his son the dreamer, and it appears—at least according to the Midrash—that the father indeed managed to teach the son a certain amount of self-control: the Midrash recounts that when faced with Potiphar's wife's attempts to seduce him, "he saw his father's image" (*Tanhuma, Vayeshev* 8). We must ask, however: Is self-restraint all there is to righteousness? Furthermore, perhaps Joseph's behavior was due to certain reasonable but far from righteous considerations—fear evoked by his father's presence, for example? After all, he did not exhibit similar self-restraint in other situations. He tormented his brothers when they came before him, and even failed to contact his father, grieving over his loss, in the Land of Israel. Rashi cites a well-known midrash:

"And Joseph was of beautiful form and fair to look upon." Since he saw himself in charge [of the household of Potiphar], he began to eat and drink and curl his hair. God said: Your father is grieving and you are curling your hair, I will set the bear [Potiphar's wife] upon you (Gen. 39:7).

We must assume that the Rabbis who established Joseph's status as "Joseph the Righteous" had a certain conception of righteousness, the embodiment of which they saw in Joseph. They too must have asked themselves how one achieves righteousness, and when did Joseph attain the lofty spiritual and religious status that warranted such a characterization.

To help answer these questions, let us invite three scholars to join the discussion. First, Maimonides—whose views on the subject of righteousness as perfection are unequivocal. Secondly, Yeshayahu Leibowitz—who will teach us the essential process he believes one must undergo on the path to righteousness. In other words, Leibowitz will provide a kind of educational theory for the intelligent tutelage of those who aspire to righteousness. The third member of the group is the eminent educator, Nehama Leibowitz. Her role in our discussion will be to describe—combining biblical texts with passages from the Midrash and classical commentary—different views on what it means to be righteous, and various approaches to the process of becoming righteous. We can also expect her to address further questions, such as: How does a righteous person change, and how does she or he relate to her or his past? What happens to a righteous person and her or his surroundings following her or his attainment of righteous perfection?

First however, there is a fundamental question we must address; one that will undoubtedly be of interest to our three guests as well: Is the story of Joseph an appropriate framework for a discussion of righteousness? The story is marked by inherent tension between determinism (theological and historical) and free will. It is this tension that fascinated the great German writer Thomas Mann. In the final line of his novel, *Joseph and his Brothers*, he writes: "Thus ends the divine story of Joseph". The reader wonders whether Mann means to say that this is Joseph's story about God, describing the struggle of a servant of the Lord to live according to his commandments, striving to draw closer to him in a difficult and complicated world, overcoming hatred, and giving life to a great multitude, that he might merit "tunnels in the ground", the ability to walk upright in a world of death and horror. On the other hand, it might be God's story—seeking to fulfill his promise made at the "Covenant of the Pieces", and doing so through the story of Joseph, who is, along with his entire family, but clay in the hands of the (divine) potter? Is it a story that teaches us that senseless hatred leads to exile and enslavement, or does it perhaps demonstrate how even hatred between brothers can serve the divine plan, for all is in the hands of heaven?

Let us now turn to our scholars. Maimonides should clearly be the first to speak, due to his venerable status, and the originality of the questions he posed and answered. In *Guide for the Perplexed* (III, 27), he discusses the "object of the Law", i.e. the ideal performance of society and of man as an individual—which he believes to be twofold. The first object he calls "the perfection of the body", and the second, "the perfection of the soul". The perfection of the body is achieved, writes Maimonides, when human beings learn to avoid that which is morally wrong and harmful, fostering that which is good and beneficial in their relations with one another, and maintaining a just society. The perfection of the soul regards the consummation of the human spirit—the possession of true knowledge, to the best of one's ability. Maimonides asserts that the ultimate purpose of human existence is the well-being and perfection of the soul, but that such perfection cannot be achieved without first ensuring the well-being of the body, that is the perfection of the social structure—which is the object of most of the Torah's precepts.

The chapter in the *Guide for the Perplexed* that deals with this twofold "perfection", in accordance with the "object of the Law", would appear to be addressed to educators and leaders of society. They must understand their roles, as well as their limits: they are not responsible for the perfection of the soul, but must communicate basic truths in a fashion comprehensible to the masses—i.e. "allegorically"—through stories and metaphors, that translate lofty matters into simple and comprehensible language.

In the final chapter of the *Guide for the Perplexed* (III, 54), on the other hand, Maimonides discusses four types of perfection, apparently addressing those striving for their own perfection. He cites two types of perfection greatly esteemed by the masses: the perfection of possession and property, that is external to man, imaginary and transient; and the perfection of the body, its health and its strength. This perfection is also imaginary: not only common to both man and animal—and therefore not a perfection of man as man—but also ephemeral. The third perfection—moral perfection—also concerns the "perfection of the body", and is indeed essential to society, and the subject of most of the biblical precepts. It, too, however, cannot suffice for the characterization of the ideal man, primarily because it is entirely dependent upon the presence of another, the object of moral behavior. True perfection is of the fourth kind: "The possession of the highest intellectual faculties: the possession of such notions which lead to true metaphysical opinions as regards God. With this perfection man has obtained his final object; it gives him true human perfection; it remains to him alone; it gives him immortality, and on its account he is called man" (*Guide for the Perplexed*, translated by M. Friedlander, Routledge, London, 1904, III, 54).

Maimonides, the philosopher, turns to the path of Midrash, in the effort to link this Aristotelian insight to Jewish sources—and the practical ideal they represent:

> The prophets have likewise explained unto us these things, and have expressed the same opinion on them as the philosophers. They say distinctly that perfection in property, in health, or in character, is not a perfection worthy to be sought as a cause of pride and glory for us: that the knowledge of God, i.e., true wisdom, is the only perfection which we should seek, and in which we should glorify ourselves. Jeremiah, referring to these four kinds of perfection, says: "Thus saith the Lord, Let not the wise man glory in his wisdom, neither let the mighty man glory in his might, let not the rich man glory in his riches; but let him that glorieth glory in this, that he understandeth and knoweth me" (*Jer.* 9:22,23).

Maimonides adds that understanding, seemingly the essence of the fourth perfection, does not encompass its full scope. This too can be learned from the words of Jeremiah at the end of the very same verse: "that I am the Lord who exercises lovingkindness, judgment, and righteousness, in the earth". From this, we learn that man's ultimate purpose is indeed "the possession of the highest, intellectual faculties ... which lead to true metaphysical opinions as regards God", but also that "the Divine acts which ought to be known, and ought to serve as a guide for our actions, are, *hesed*, 'loving-kindness,' *mishpat*, 'judgment,' and *zedakah*, 'righteousness'" (*ibid.*). In other words, one who attains the fourth perfection engages in loving-kindness and judgment, not as a loyal member of society, party to a social contract, but as a consequence of the knowledge that the intellectual faculties lead to the action of striving to resemble God. He thus engages in such action because his knowledge would be empty and incomplete without the action that brings it down to earth, the action dictated by knowledge itself (knowledge of God).

Yeshayahu Leibowitz joins our discussion as a philosopher who addressed—often directly—questions pertaining to Jewish education. As a Maimonides scholar and disciple of "The Great Eagle", he showed great interest in Judaism as a key to understanding the nature of living correctly. He thus dealt with Judaism's ability to provide a guide to living a full personal life; one that aspires to truth and righteousness that is—according to Maimonides—the fourth perfection.

This great follower of Maimonides, however, would appear to have advocated an educational approach that runs counter to that of Maimonides. Leibowitz' educational vision seems to focus entirely upon perfection of the body. In his well-known essay *Hinukh Lemitzvot* (in *Yahadut, Am Yehudi Umedinat Yisrael*), Leibowitz criticizes educators who purport to "impart" perfection of the soul. Those who do so, according to Leibowitz, mistakenly believe that Judaism is a religion of "innermost thoughts and sensibilities". Not so! The Jewish faith is "institutional", i.e. a religion of laws, a religion that is not a means to any value or emotional need, but a system that is entirely *lishmah*, for its own sake; serving no interest, not even the most lofty. Observance must therefore be the object of religious education. A closer look at Leibowitz' approach, however, reveals that the matter is not at all straightforward: If we consider the subjective aspect of consciousness and individual tendencies and feelings, as well as the objective aspect of lifestyle and [adherence to] a certain regimen—how can one educate to ideal life? Do you instill lifestyle, institutions and practice by shaping a person's spiritual character, or perhaps this character is merely a function of lifestyle? This is the fundamental question of education ... [and Maimonides writes] "and how should a man cultivate opinions that they might take hold? He should perform, repeat and repeat again, actions consistent with [those] opinions ... and repeat them always ... and the opinions will be fixed in his heart" (*Hilkhot De'ot* 1,7).

That is to say, that the "institutional" precepts must not only be observed "for their own sake", but constitute a system of habits that groom one for wisdom; for, as we have seen, perfection of the soul (intellectual understanding that is also applied in practice) can only be achieved through perfection of the body, which the Torah strives to facilitate through the precepts and Halakhah. The "for its own sake" of Halakhah is thus knowledge and love of God—the fourth perfection. It is in this vein that we can understand the following passage:

> Religious education merely imposes the yoke of Torah and the precepts, although it is quite clear that Torah study and observance of the active precepts are not the be all and end all of the Torah. The Torah—despite being an end in itself—comprises elements that are means and elements that are ends (Maimonides' first and second "objects"). The very essence of religion is "And thou shalt love [the Lord thy God]". Nevertheless, religious education can only provide the tools of religion—the active precepts. No education in the world can do more than prepare the ground for attaining the ultimate goal ... Religious education is not the inculcation of values but preparation for their acquisition. Religious values cannot be inculcated; they can only be acquired (Leibowitz, *Yahadut, Am Yehudi Umedinat Yisrael* p. 59).

If Joseph was a righteous man, it would therefore have been the result of Jacob having taught him "Torah and the precepts", thereby preparing him to withstand the great trials of his life. The subjective, emotional aspect that brought tears to his eyes at meeting with his brothers, stemmed from the habits acquired from his father Jacob, that over the course of time created the perfect *tzadik*, who loved and knew God and exercised loving-kindness, judgment and righteousness. Leibowitz, therefore, provides an educational-developmental approach to ideal man, i.e. Maimonides' righteous man.

Nehama Leibowitz joins our discussion of "Joseph the Righteous", not as a philosopher or the sister of Yeshayahu, but as an educator who taught two generations a different approach to the Torah: confronting the dilemmas posed by the biblical texts with a special combination of literary analysis and moral evaluation, through the works of midrashists, commentators and writers as demonstrated by Dr. Marla Frankel, in her dissertation (*"Iyun Vehora'ah—Havharat Shitatah Shel Nehama Leibowitz"*, Hebrew University of Jerusalem, *Tevet* 5758, pp. 221–228). She perceived the text as reflecting a combination of unique, transcendental, demanding, normative religion, on the one hand, and internal religiosity, on the other: driven by religious and moral experience, emotion and insight, together with universal consciousness—all presuming the existence of a connection between the various forms of religious life and the experiences that derive from them.

The importance of her contribution to the discussion lies in her vision of the protagonist's journey to righteousness. As Frankel demonstrates in her study, Nehama was particularly fond of the Joseph stories, which—unlike the story of the binding of Isaac, for example—take no clear theological position. The story does raise challenging and even provocative theological questions, but it offers no unequivocal answers. This allows the reader to take an active part in the search for the meanings hidden within the text. We have already noted one of the story's central issues: Are the choices made by the characters—Joseph in particular—their own? Or is it perhaps God who makes the decisions and conducts the events according to his will? This is a fundamental question, because if everything is in the hands of heaven—what is the meaning of heroism?

Nehama finds, in her readings and studies, support for the view that certain aspects of divine Providence are manifest in historical events. In her *Iyunim Besefer* Bereshit (*Studies in* Bereshit), a book intended for laymen seeking contact with the Torah and its messages, she emphasizes Nahmanides' interpretation of verses 14–17, in chapter 37, in which Jacob sends Joseph to his brothers in Shekhem, and he does not find them there. This was supposed to have "spared" the young man an encounter with his brothers, who hated him in any case. Then however—"And a certain man found him, and, behold, he was wandering in the field: and the man asked him, saying, What seekest thou? And he said, I seek my brethren: tell me, I pray thee, where they feed their flocks. And the man said, They are departed hence; for I heard them say, Let us go to Dothan. And Joseph went after his brethren, and found them in Dothan". Since Joseph was destined to be sold, that he might save the lives of a great many people, and draw his family down to Egypt, that the "Covenant of the Pieces" might be fulfilled—the midrashists explain that the "man" he encountered was no ordinary passerby, but an angel. Nahmanides remarks as follows (as cited by Nehama):

> And the Bible goes on at length ... to teach us that the [divine] verdict is truth and [man's] efforts falsehood, for God summoned a guide to lead him *unwittingly* to them. And that is what our Rabbis meant when they said that such figures are angels, that the entire affair was not in vain, but to inform us that (*Prov.* 19:21): "the counsel of the Lord shall stand" (*Iyunim Besefer Bereshit* p. 276).

From this passage, Nehama would appear to view Joseph's righteousness as no more than a divine decision or "counsel", for "the [divine] verdict is truth and [man's] efforts falsehood". Nahmanides continues in this vein later in the story, when Joseph snubs his brothers, explaining that it was God's counsel that they bring Benjamin as well, to fulfill the dream of the 11 sheaves bowing down to him, and eventually Jacob—in order to fulfill his second dream—"that all might come there and all his dreams be fulfilled". In the spirit of Thomas Mann, we can encapsulate as follows: Joseph knew that he was a character in "God's story", having but to read the script ushering the characters toward a predetermined ending. It is clear, however, that Nehama is uncomfortable with an approach that releases man from all moral responsibility for his actions. She therefore cites Rabbi Isaac Arama, author of *Akedat Yitzhak*, who asserts that Joseph's behavior was in fact improper. His considerations should have been humane and moral: "he should not have sinned against his father".

Nehama does not agree with Arama's conclusion—"let He who grants dreams provide their solution"—and cites examples of human actions designed to fulfill divine promises and prophecies:

> And so we find that Jeremiah told the Babylonian exiles that in seventy years time, God would restore them "to this place"—

and they, the exiles, did not say "let He who grants prophecies fulfill them", but rather at the end of the seventy years, Zerubbabel and Jeshua the son of Jozadak and the "chief of the fathers of Judah and Benjamin" arose and went up to the Land of Israel … to fulfill the prophecy (*ibid.* p. 327).

Nehama combines the two approaches: one must recognize the will of heaven, and act to bring it to fruition. This does not, however, release man from the obligation to act morally and compassionately: "Could Joseph not have brought about the fulfillment of his dreams without inflicting so much pain upon them and his father?", she asks.

In fact, it is Joseph's cruelty that brings about the brothers' repentance. Not only do they recognize their wrongdoing, feel remorse at having sold Joseph, confess their sin, and resolve never to repeat it, but they achieve complete repentance. Maimonides explains "complete repentance" as follows: "What is complete repentance? When one encounters the object of a previous transgression, has the opportunity to sin, but withdraws and does not sin—not for fear or lack of ability, but because he has repented," (*Hikhot Teshuvah* 2, 1). Joseph, in his cruelty, creates an existential situation for his brothers' benefit, remarkably like the circumstances of his sale: he favors the younger brother, son of Rachel, in the presence of all the others, and then offers to buy him as a slave. In other words, he sets the stage for another sale, that of Benjamin, in which he is the instigator, and the brothers need only comply! How do they react? Not only do they not offer to sell their younger brother, but they categorically refuse to do so; and one of them, Judah, the same brother who suggested that they sell Joseph, nearly a generation earlier, intervenes on Benjamin's behalf, offering himself in his place.

It is not this event, however, that precipitates the decisive moment in which Joseph reaches maturity and righteousness. As we have seen, Nehama is not averse to acts that further the divine script, but demands that they be performed without cruelty, without causing others pain. In the chapter entitled "*Yosef Hatzadik*" (Joseph the Righteous), in her book on Genesis—the chapter in which she documents Joseph's progression toward righteousness—she does not mention the ruse that results in the brothers complete repentance. Instead, she cites the words that Joseph utters immediately thereafter, upon revealing his identity to his brothers: "And God sent me before you to give you a remnant on the earth, and to save you alive for a great deliverance (Gen. 45:7), and explains:

> All his arrogance and pride have dissipated, and the dreams are no longer a sign of dominance, but of responsibility, of vocation. His lot is one of servitude, not domination. Joseph, the viceroy, now begins to show himself to be the true servant of his brothers and his father, an instrument in God's hands, for their salvation (*ibid.* p. 309).

Joseph has thus learned to act generously, within the framework of the divine story, rather than continuing to excuse his own cruel behavior by evoking predestination, against which he himself is powerless.

Nehama is not satisfied however with this kind of righteousness, and this is not her final word on the subject. In her last comment on the book of Genesis and the Joseph narrative ("Is it permitted to change [facts] for the sake of peace?) she cites the *Pesikta Rabbati*, which asks—and explains—why Joseph needed to hear from others that his father was ill (*ibid.* 48:1):

> For Joseph's greatest virtue was his zeal in honoring his father … and had others not come and told him that his father was ill, would he not have known? Rather, to highlight his righteousness, that he did not want to be alone with his father, lest [his father] ask him "what did your brothers do to you?"—and he would curse them … Therefore, he refrained from visiting his father too frequently (*ibid.* p. 404).

Here, she quotes Nahmanides, who was of the opinion that Jacob had never been told that the brothers had sold Joseph. After the death of their father, the brothers ask Joseph for mercy, and report to him, as if Jacob had commanded them to do so: "So shall ye say unto Joseph, Forgive, I pray thee now, the trespass of thy brethren, and their sin; for they did unto thee evil: and now, we pray thee, forgive the trespass of the servants of the God of thy father" (*ibid.* 50:17). The brothers' assumption that Joseph (who had in fact, "brought unto his father their evil report", in the past) had told Jacob of the affair, pains him, and he weeps and comforts them. He is not only moral in their regard as he was when he brought about their complete repentance, but he understands the meaning of the entire story and the responsibility of one who understands all that there is to understand to exercise judgment and loving-kindness. A moral person might not have hesitated to tell his father how he had been mistreated. After all, the father "deserves" to know the facts, and the son deserves to see his brothers punished. So why didn't he tell?

At this point, Yeshayahu Leibowitz might remark that it was Joseph's halakhic education that proved itself at the critical juncture. Joseph was no longer dependent upon his father's indulgence, his own sense of righteous indignation, or any of the social justifications for the morality of perfection of the body. Here, he had attained, on the basis of "education to observance of the Law", the very perfection of the soul that is the supreme object of the Torah.

Maimonides might also add, that when Joseph understood that he must not tell his father the truth, for the sake of domestic peace, and when he felt his brothers' pain at the death of their father and "comforted them and spake kindly unto them", he attained the fourth perfection, that alone can raise a person to the lofty degree of one who is "Righteous".

Eliezer Schweid

Vayigash – Then Judah Came Near

Judah and Joseph: Two Different Paths to Kingship
Criticism of the Monarchy in the Thought of Don Isaac Abravanel

Then Judah came near unto him, and said: "Oh my lord, let thy servant, I pray thee, speak a word in my lord's ears, and let not thine anger burn against thy servant; for thou art even as Pharaoh" (Genesis 44:18)

In *Vayigash*, the clash between Judah and Joseph reaches its climax and resolution. It is a struggle for leadership of the clan of Jacob, and subsequently of the people that sprung from its "fruitfulness and abundant increase". It seems to conclude with Judah's acceptance of Joseph's victory. Joseph is "as Pharaoh", and Judah bows before him, calling him "lord" and referring to himself as Joseph's "servant". He also describes his brothers and even his father as Joseph's "servants". Later in the story, when the whole family goes down to Egypt and settles in the land of Goshen, and Joseph completes his program for the subjugation of all Egypt to Pharaoh, which had earned him the position of viceroy, his brothers and their offspring relate to him as a fearsome tyrant. Joseph's dream of kingship, for which his brothers had despised him and Judah had sold him into slavery, was thus fully realized. The fact, however, that Joseph's rule was marked by tyranny and subjugation—eventually leading to the enslavement of all of his brothers' descendants—is, to the ironic author, proof that Joseph's victory is in reality a moral defeat, and as such will be short-lived. Thus, in terms of significance for the future—as reflected in Jacob's blessings to his sons—Judah, who humbles himself before Joseph in order to save his family and keep his promise to Jacob, is the one who assumes the mantle of leadership, emerging the victor. The issue here is certainly not the rivalry between the two brothers, but rather the ethical and philosophical nature of legitimate rule and how it is attained.

128

As noted above, the conflict reaches both its climax and its resolution in the portion of *Vayigash*—which must therefore be seen as the central and unifying axis of the story of Joseph and his brothers. As the name implies, Joseph would appear to be the story's sole protagonist. A closer reading, however, suggests that a more apt title might be: "The Story of Joseph and Judah in Jacob's Family". This would also maintain the literary integrity of the narrative, otherwise inexplicably interrupted—following the sale of Joseph into slavery—with the episode of Judah and Tamar. Although the two stories may appear wholly unrelated to one another, the connection is plain if we see Judah as coprotagonist of the cycle: The story of Judah, his sinful sons, and daughter-in-law found to be righteous in her sin and thus destined to become mother of kings, closely parallels the story of Joseph and his master's sinful wife, who has him cast into prison, whence he is raised to the throne. Both protagonists are thus portrayed here as engaged in a struggle to fulfill their respective destinies as leaders of their family and people. In the background stands their first fateful encounter (as recounted in *Vayeshev*), in which Judah appears the winner, but it is in fact Joseph who has won (having been set on the path to realising his dreams). Before us, we find their second confrontation, in which the victor will appear to be Joseph, but will in reality be Judah (who, in standing up to Joseph for the sake of justice, steps forward as a leader and savior of his family and his people).

Let us take a brief look at the story from the very beginning, from its preface, in which the two protagonists are not even mentioned by name—i.e. the incipient struggle between Jacob and his sons, and between the brothers themselves, for leadership of the family, including the task of settling in Canaan. I refer to Jacob's attempt at permanent settlement in the vicinity of Shekhem, by peaceful means: the building of an altar, and the forging of economic, social and political alliances with the people of the land. He is nearly successful, but fails in the end, as a result of the leadership dispute between father and sons. Simon and Levi rebel against their father, wrest leadership from him, and in a bid to defend the family's honor—in their own murderous way—seal its fate. In their terrible revenge, they turned the alliances their father had sought to make into a state of eternal hostility, thereby forcing the small clan to flee. Their apparent victory was in fact a moral failure and miserable defeat.

In the distant future, the characteristic zealotry manifested by Simon and Levi would be drawn upon to lead the people to receive the Torah and take lawful possession of the Land of Canaan. It would have risen up from the lowly zealotry of defending family honor to the exalted zealotry of defending the honor of God and his commandments. Moses and Aaron were Levites, and the Levites, who stood by Moses during the crisis of the Golden Calf, would come to play a unique leadership role. Following their horrific actions at Shekhem, however, the two brothers were simply deposed and cursed. The leadership returned to the hands of a frustrated and bewildered Jacob, who had little choice but to return his family to the state of "sojourner," the most his father and grandfather had ever managed to obtain in Canaan.

As a result of their failure to secure a foothold in the land, the Patriarchs were never able to realize the promise that their small family would become a great nation. Abraham did in fact have numerous progeny, making him a "father of many nations", but the nation that was to bear his name had to arise in Canaan, where his legacy was sufficient for but one son: Isaac. Isaac too, despite his economic success, could be inherited in Canaan by only one of his two sons, forcing the other to seek out another land. Moreover, Abraham and Jacob themselves were compelled to abandon Canaan during times of hardship. Isaac, too, was forced to leave his home, although not Canaan itself, due to famine. We thus begin to understand Jacob's intentions at Shekhem. By forging a political alliance uniting his family with the "people of the land", he hoped to enable all of his sons and their descendants to inherit in Canaan and make the transition from family to nation. It was thus the undermining of his plan, by his sons, that eventually forced the family to go down to Egypt for a period of exile lasting centuries. Only in Goshen could the family be fruitful and multiply, remain together and become a great nation, without being assimilated by their hosts. That was Joseph's mission, although he failed to understand this until his final confrontation with Judah. From the outset, he had sought power exclusively for its own sake, since it had in fact made him both tyrant and slave to Pharaoh, and in this sense, a slave to his own lust for power.

After Simon and Levi, came the turn of Reuben, Jacob's firstborn from his first wife, Leah. The leadership was, after all, his birthright. In Abraham's family, however, elder sons had been passed over, generation after generation, in favor of younger sons, chosen by God, by virtue of their own spiritual qualities. Jacob, who had bought his birthright and stolen his blessings from his elder brother, ignored the firstborn son of his firstborn wife. In order to claim that which he believed to be rightfully his, Reuben was driven to an act that clearly reflected his rash and impetuous nature, showing him unfit to lead. He tried to force matters, by lying with Bilhah, the concubine given to his father by Rachel and mother to Rachel's children following the latter's death. In trying to seize control of the family, he proved beyond all shadow of a doubt that he was not destined to be its leader, not only because of the grave sin he had committed, but because of the petty-mindedness, impetuousness, and short-sightedness that had brought it about. The family of Jacob needed a leader capable of bearing responsibility and striking a path, not one focused on satisfying his own desires.

The fact that Reuben was not the right man was later confirmed in two failed attempts to repair the damage he had done and prove his trustworthiness. On the first occasion, he attempted a ploy to rescue Joseph from the brothers' ire. He was thwarted, perhaps unwittingly, by Judah. Had his machinations borne fruit, restoring Joseph to his father after the brothers' act of revenge, the inevitable result would have been even greater conflict to the point of an irrevocable rift!

In light of the above, the solution proposed by Judah, who had stepped forward at that point not only in a bid for the leadership, but as acting leader, was clearly the right one. Despite its high price, it was the only way to preserve family unity. Judah, acting as judge—speaking firmly, openly and directly—rejected the brothers' plan for vengeance, that would have brought an eternal curse upon their heads, before their father and before God. He also rejected the suggestion put forward by Reuben, who had thought of himself, but not of the price that the brothers and even their father would have to pay—upon discovering how the mission he had imposed on Joseph as a punishment, might have ended. Judah, on the other hand, proposed a solution that was both just and right for the family: for the ambivalent Jacob, unhappy with the domineering airs put on by the son he had dressed in a coat of many colors; for the brothers, who could not stand their arrogant, talebearing brother; for Judah himself, who claimed the leadership as his destiny; and finally for Joseph. Although Judah could not have known all of this at the time, what he did know was quite sufficient. He knew that he had to send Joseph away by punishing him in a manner that would befit his crime. Since Joseph had sought to enslave his brothers and even his parents, he himself was sold into slavery. The divine irony was that this expiatory punishment would lead to the realization of his dream, and thereby to the fulfillment of the mission with which he had been charged by Jacob, for his own sake and for the sake of all of his brothers.

Judah's decision marks the beginning of the conflict that culminates in the brothers' encounter in *Vayigash*. At the same time, Judah presents an approach to kingship that differs sharply from that of Joseph, one that will not lead to exile and slavery, but rather to laying down roots in Canaan on the basis of alliances with its inhabitants; the same approach that Jacob tried to pursue, following the example of Abraham and Isaac. This assertion is further supported by the story of Judah and his wife—the daughter of Shua, and his daughter-in-law Tamar; which is in fact a record of Judah's consistent efforts to forge alliances with the people of the land, and to uphold them with justice. It is precisely the Canaanite women that he took for himself and for his sons, that enabled Judah to found the Davidic dynasty, Israel's rightful kings—up to and including the Messiah, destined to settle his people securely in their land, and make a covenant of peace between them and all the nations of the world!

The second confrontation between Reuben and Judah occurs at the juncture when it is again decided that they must go down to Egypt, setting the stage for the reconciliation between Judah and Joseph. Reuben tries to convince his father to allow him to take Benjamin to Egypt with all of his brothers in order to placate the Pharaonic ruler and bring home provisions and fails: "And Reuben spoke unto his father, saying: 'Thou shalt slay my two sons, if I bring him not to thee; deliver him into my hand, and I will bring him back to thee'. And he said: 'My son shall not go down with you; for his brother is dead, and he only is left; if harm befall him by the way in which ye go, then will ye bring down my gray hairs with sorrow to the grave'" (42:37–38). Judah however, succeeds where Reuben has failed: "And Judah said unto Israel his father: 'Send the lad with me, and we will arise and go, that we may live, and not die, both we, and thou, and also our little ones. I will be surety for him; of my hand shalt thou require him; if I bring him not unto thee, and set him before thee, then let me bear the blame for ever. For except we had lingered, surely we had now returned a second time? And their father Israel said unto them: 'If it be so now, do this'" (43:8–11).

In what way is Judah more persuasive than Reuben? First of all, he addresses his father as the head of the family, reminding him of his responsibility toward the entire family. He must not allow his concern for Benjamin and for himself, were he to lose him, to take precedence over the welfare of the family as a whole; all the more so in the present circumstances, for if they do not go to Egypt to procure provisions, both he and Benjamin will perish, along with the rest of the family! Secondly, Judah explains to Jacob that Benjamin's presence is essential. Were the brothers to return to Egypt without abiding by the tyrant's wishes, they would be endangering their own lives, and Jacob would risk losing all of his sons. And finally, Judah takes the responsibility upon himself and proves that he can be trusted, that he will act appropriately, that he will do everything in his power to avert disaster, and if disaster should strike, that he will not rest until Benjamin is safely restored to his father. His words demonstrate to Jacob that he will follow in his footsteps and act as he himself would, in keeping with his covenantal obligations. Indeed, Judah attains all of his goals: Jacob reassumes leadership of the entire family and takes responsibility for the decision to send Benjamin. Note that after Judah's appeal, not only does Jacob agree to allow Benjamin join his brothers, but commands them to go and to take Benjamin with them, instructing them on how to avoid further mishap. The difference between Judah and Reuben is manifest. Clearly, Jacob cannot trust the rash son who suggests that he murder his two young grandsons to avenge the loss of his youngest son. Reuben is a petty, selfish and vindictive man, incapable of worthy conduct. Only one such as Judah can be trusted as Jacob trusted himself with the leadership of the family when he went to meet Esau. Note further that Jacob commands his sons to placate the Pharaonic tyrant just as he placated Esau when he went out to meet him.

This complex web of relations and intentions serves as the backdrop for the final confrontation between Judah and Joseph, in *Vayigash*. In order to understand Joseph's position in the conflict we must first ask: what was the point of the game of cat and mouse that he played with his brothers, from the moment he recognized them among those who had come to buy grain in Egypt? Was he seeking revenge for their having sold him into slavery? Why then did he not do so immediately and openly? If, despite his resentment, he felt responsibility toward his aged father and younger brother, and recalled that he had not been entirely blameless, and that in any case it had all worked out for the better—why then, did he not act like Judah? As noted above, Judah had acted as a judge, punishing the guilty in a commensurate fashion, and benefiting the innocent. The explanation of Joseph's behavior can be found in the way in which he toys with the brothers' fate. Due to his imperious nature, he was unable to enjoy the spectacle of his own victory to its full extent, until they had recognized him as he had recognized them. They had to see the fulfillment of his dreams with their own eyes, fully recognizing how blind, petty, and mean-spirited they had been in their treatment of him. He wanted them to despair in the realization that they had foolishly treated him with disdain, and brutishly punished him—at their own peril—because in so doing they had, with their own hands, granted him the power of which he had dreamed. The one thing for which Joseph cannot forgive his brothers, from the moment he discovers their presence in Egypt, is the fact that they did not recognize him. Why? Obviously because in their stupid, petty, little minds, they could not imagine that the proud, self-assured Pharaonic ruler before them could be their boastful brother. They were still convinced that in selling him into slavery they had once and for all, refuted his dreams.

Joseph's caprices are thus explained. He torments his brothers, inexplicably vacillating between generous hospitality and terrible humiliation. His behavior is evasive and tortuous. On the one hand, he cannot hide his heartfelt interest in the welfare of his father and younger brother. He longs to know whether the brothers still remember him, whether they regret their treatment of him and long to see him alive; whether his father and younger brother still remember him, love him, and long to see him alive; or whether they have perhaps forgotten him and live well enough without him. Nevertheless, he does not reveal himself to the brothers, waiting for them to recognize him of their accord. Interestingly, all of his torments are coded messages, clues, and gestures by means of which they might have discovered his identity, had they not been so entrenched in their belief that the Pharaonic ruler could not possibly be their brother whom they had sold into slavery. Joseph's anger grows due to his inability to understand his brothers' indifference. Are they not puzzled by the gentile ruler's particular interest in them? Do they not ask themselves why he has singled them out—alternately to their advantage and disadvantage? Do they not wonder why he is so suspicious of them, although they have done nothing to arouse such suspicion? Are they not perplexed by his interest in matters that have nothing to do with their activities in Egypt? And do they not find it curious that in his intimate questions he betrays knowledge of things that only a family member could know?

The failure of Joseph's efforts to bring his brothers to discover his identity explains his growing anger and ever-greater demands from them, culminating in the framing of Benjamin—a pretext to separate him from the brothers, detain him, and send them back to their father without him, that they might once again face their father as they did when they sold his darling Joseph into slavery! This is the most terrible revenge that Joseph could have exacted from his brothers and his father. He knows that it is beyond their endurance, but the brothers should have realized at long last that such revenge could only have been devised by their betrayed brother.

This is the decisive moment in which Judah "comes near" to the Pharaonic ruler, as if to put a stop to his despotic games and unmask him, that he might finally tell them what it is that he wants from them, why he is tormenting them so, and what they can do to satisfy him. We, the readers, already know what Joseph is waiting to hear from Judah, the man who lifted him out of the pit and sold him into slavery, who has now come forward and stands before him, face to face. Has he guessed by now? Will he ask forgiveness? Will he admit that the dreams that had been the cause of their hatred had come true?

No, Judah had not recognized his brother beneath the Pharaonic exterior. He was plainly not plagued by guilt. On the contrary, he remained convinced that what he had done at the time had been just. He saved his brother from death, and the family from the strife that Joseph had caused. As he approached the tyrant, he could find no conceivable justification for his treatment of them. He therefore sought not forgiveness, but justice, speaking as if presenting a case before a judge, in accordance with the laws and principles of justice associated with the covenant. If we look beyond his deferential manner, at the arguments themselves, we find that Judah speaks as an accuser remonstrating against an injustice rather than refuting allegations of wrongdoing. Nonetheless, or rather, precisely because of this, he achieved his goal. At the end of his speech, it was not he who broke down before Joseph, but Joseph who broke down before him. Joseph burst into tears—not very appropriate behavior for a Pharaonic ruler, but most apt for a son of Jacob, who wept with his brother Esau when they met in peace. He reveals his identity to them, not only by saying his name, but also in the tears, embraces, and kisses of one who has not seen his brothers in a very long time.

What was it in Judah's speech that brought about this sudden change in Joseph? Let us first take note of the fact that Judah, in his wise leadership, even without recognizing Joseph or admitting that his dreams had been fulfilled, met some of Joseph's expectations. Although he did not know who the man was, Judah judged his character, and found him to be arrogant and power-hungry; one who treats all around him as slaves, and expects everyone to grovel before him. Proud Judah, confident in his own justice and worth, without expecting others to humble themselves before him, had no difficulty providing one who thirsted for external signs of submission, with his desire; on the assumption that he would thereby be moved to do his royal duty, i.e. to judge the case on its merits. In almost every verse, Judah refers to the ruler before him as "my lord", and to himself as "thy servant", thereby seeking to placate him and assuage his anger toward his humble "servants". Joseph appreciates it and responds, because he views such comportment as conveying a dual message: not only his proud brother's acceptance of his sovereignty, but also, retroactive acknowledgment of his dreams, i.e. of the mistake that the brothers made in his regard. Joseph, eager for his brothers' recognition, found the irony in this state of affairs irresistible. His royal brother was bowing down before him, as a servant before his lord, without knowing who he was. The brothers and their father were all presented as his servants, without knowing who he was. How could he resist the temptation of saying to them: Miserable servants, do you know who I, your lord, am?

It was, however, merely a shallow, external gesture. In the process of revealing himself to the brothers, something unexpected happens to Joseph: he experiences an outburst of love for his hated brothers! Why? Let us take a look at Judah's speech from Joseph's perspective. He learns that despite the many years that have passed, his memory is still alive in the family; that his father has never ceased mourning for him and that his love for him persists; that his concern for Benjamin stems from this love; and that the brothers have a heightened sense of responsibility toward their father as a result of his disappearance. He also learns that his father and brother Benjamin believe him to be dead. That is why they had never searched for him or sought to ransom him. That is why the brothers had not been looking for him. That is why they did not dare consider the possibility that Joseph might be alive and that the man who held their lives in his hands was none other than their lost and presumed-dead brother. Such a discovery would have been too much for them—from the frying pan into the fire! Joseph learns all of this from Judah's speech, because—without knowing who he was—Judah spoke to him about family matters, as if he were a member of the family. He sensed that, for some reason, this "lord" took a greater interest in the family than a mere stranger would have; making him, Judah, all the more indignant at the undeserved ordeals to which they had been subjected. In other words, beneath the veneer of "servant" and "lord", the Egyptian courtiers and administrators were witness to an intimate discussion between brothers, in which Joseph clearly required no translator to understand Judah's words and be moved by them. In this intimate discussion however, their positions seem to have been reversed: Judah is the elder, recognized representative of the family—of the father's authority; while Joseph is the younger brother obligated to treat his elder brother and father with respect. Indeed, to Joseph—who knew full well with whom he was speaking—Judah's words appeared to be a rebuke for having neglected his duty toward his elderly father and younger brother, and toward the family; a family that had wronged him (albeit not without his having wronged them first), but still deserved his loyalty, perhaps even more than Pharaoh.

In these two senses, Judah—conversely—lived up to Joseph's expectations; thereby preparing the ground for the emotional turning point that returned Joseph to the bosom of his family. It is Judah's legal argument, however, that breaks Joseph's resolve and it is this legal argument that lies at the heart of the confrontation. Ostensibly, Judah recognizes the gentile ruler as his "lord". In reality, however, it is Judah who dictates the terms of the discussion. A Pharaonic ruler owes no explanations. Judah, however, holds him to the standards expected of a judge—according to the covenantal ethic of his family, which presumes that a judge, like all human beings, is judged in turn by God, who is the source of the law. In a lengthy discourse, Judah unfolds before the Pharaonic ruler, all of the tribulations to which he had subjected him and his brothers—the brothers' words, intentions and deeds, as well as the ruler's words and deeds. He then demands that the ruler—by virtue of his office—act as judge, witness and accused, and recognize the fact that the brothers had given him no cause for the suspicions, accusations and shameful punishments inflicted upon them, but acted in good faith and broke no laws. Yet he treated them unjustly and arbitrarily; unless he knows something that Judah does not, in which case it is time he revealed his true motives!

Judah's use of the words "lord" and "servant" is thus tinged with irony. It is only in his outward gestures and language that Judah yields to the ruler, as a servant. In the content of his speech, he stands upright before God, and speaks as if to an equal. The opening phrase of *Vayigash*: "Then Judah came near unto him, and said: 'I pray thee, my lord'", encapsulates the irony of the entire situation. The expression "came near" implies rising up to stand face to face with the ruler, in order to speak to him "man to man". The expression "I pray thee, my lord" on the other hand, is a respectful request for permission to freely express his opinion on the subject at hand. Judah's meaning is clear: circumstantially, you may be lord and I your servant, but in moral terms, you are in an inferior position. Justice is on my side, and it is justice that determines the outcome of a trial, not position. Henceforth, every time he uses the words "lord" and "servant", we hear the same ironic tone, as if he is declaring: my lord, you have used your lordship unjustly, and I am in the right. In this fashion, Judah forces Joseph, for the first time, to use his position as a judge, to judge himself and to answer for what he has done to his elderly father and younger brother, to all of his brothers, and even to himself—as a member of the family. Hence the intensity of Joseph's emotional reaction: "And Joseph said unto his brethren: 'Come near to me, I pray you'. And they came near. And he said: 'I am Joseph your brother, whom ye sold into Egypt'" (45:4). Note that Joseph uses the same word previously used to describe Judah's approach to him: "*geshu*—come near"; reaffirmed in the verse: "and they came near". The implication is that there was movement on both sides: Joseph crossed the distance from his lordship over his brothers, and they travelled the distance from their servitude to him. They are now able to relate to one another on the same plane of human relations, i.e. that of kinship between brothers.

So far, we have discussed the direct personal significance of the confrontation described in *Vayigash*. Beneath the surface, however, lies the much broader issue of legitimate kingship, and the difficulties it entails. Seen from this perspective, the conflict between the figures here is in fact the conflict between Pharaonic despotism—represented by Joseph—and constitutional monarchy, based on the covenant established before God, who is the true "Lord". Therein lies the essential difference. The Pharaonic ruler is a man of power, for whom dominion is his life's goal. He assumes it by force and maintains it by the constant application of such force—without any regard for the principles of justice. Conversely, according to the covenant, a king is—first and foremost—a judge, committed to God's constitution and the administration of justice. The goal of such a ruler is the welfare of his subjects. He attains his high office by virtue of the fact that he is universally recognized as one who has proven himself a man of truth and justice. In other words, his adherence to the will of God attests to his divine election.

The continuation of the story as it unfolds in *Vayigash* clearly shows that the sudden change in Joseph was the result of an emotional upheaval, which found expression only in his attitude toward his brothers. It affected neither his despotic nature nor his Pharaonic worldview. He made peace with his brothers and allowed them to benefit from his high standing at Pharaoh's court, yet as Pharaoh's regent over all Egypt—his brothers included—he continued to fulfill his duty with the ruthlessness characteristic of Pharaonic rule and its logic of force. Prior to his brothers' arrival, his actions were justified, inasmuch as they were intended to save Egypt, as well as the surrounding peoples, from starvation. Following the brothers' arrival however, Joseph turned his wise counsel that food be stored in times of plenty, into a tool by means of which Pharaoh came to control all of Egypt's land and water; enslaving all of his subjects. As long as Joseph was alive, and as long as Egyptian rulers remembered him and were grateful to him, the Children of Israel enjoyed a certain degree of freedom. When a new king "who knew not Joseph" arose, however, they became the most oppressed slaves in all Egypt.

In *Exodus,* we discover that during their sojourn in the land of Goshen, the Children of Israel became a nation—based upon the covenantal constitution of their family, within the framework of the "community" (*edah*), and in keeping with its laws. It is to this community that Moses and Aaron appealed when they came to lead their people to freedom. This was the legacy of Judah, reinforced and institutionalized by Moses at Sinai, in anticipation of the settlement of Canaan. Thus, in their encounters with Pharaoh and his magicians, Moses and Aaron—who had come to lead their people to freedom—followed in the footsteps of Judah and his "legal" confrontation with the Pharaonic regent, Joseph. This time however, the confrontation was on a national level.

In closing, I will briefly mention—by way of confirmation and further elaboration upon the above interpretation of *Vayigash*—the political philosophy of one of the greatest biblical commentators: Don Isaac Abravanel (1435–1508). Don Isaac's insights into the portion of *Vayigash* are of particular interest, due to the unique connection between the ideas he presents and his personal life experience. Don Isaac was a leader of the Jews of Portugal—a position he attained by virtue of his standing at the Portuguese royal court. He served as minister and advisor to a gentile king, just like Joseph in Egypt. He was dismissed from his various positions and exiled a number of times, but was always reinstated, thanks to his abilities, trustworthiness and loyalty to the monarchy. In this sense, he was irreplaceable. Don Isaac was of course thoroughly acquainted with the science of government and the inner workings of power. He would thus have had first-hand experience of the lust for power and the pleasure obtained from its satisfaction. He would also have been familiar with the ruthlessness without which power cannot be wielded efficiently. He was never deterred from the execution of his duties of state—to the best of his ability—yet he harbored no illusions. He related to them as an unfortunate necessity of the real world. Had he not done so, he could never have offered his people the kind of protection that he did, considering the difficult times in which he lived. He saw this as his mission, on behalf of his people—adding a crucial element to the discussion of the confrontation between Judah and Joseph. Don Isaac grappled with the problems of human existence in the world, in light of which he approached the problem of relations between Israel and the nations.

His struggle stemmed from the fact that he did not perceive his position as a vocation, by means of which he might aspire to the highest spiritual goals. The ideal of every Jew—to worship God and live a righteous and compassionate life of Torah study and observance of the precepts—was not served by his political office. During periods in which he was removed from office, Abravanel applied himself to an ambitious project in the field of Torah scholarship, imbued with a longing for the redemption of Israel and the establishment of the Heavenly Kingdom on earth. As a statesman he embodied the essence of Joseph's Pharaonic rule, while as a Torah scholar, he represented the critical stance of the Prophets, rooted in the ethical outlook of the covenant: the legacy of Judah.

In his commentary on Genesis, Don Isaac traces the source of the development of human civilization to the sin of Adam. What was his sin? He was not content with the divine gift bestowed upon him and his fellow creatures, for the benefit of all, but sought mastery over the land, in order to draw from it more than it would give of its own accord. He desired wealth, honor and power for their own sake, and was therefore made a slave to toil and to his craving for power and honor. He made man's dominion over the civilization he had created for himself, repressive, exploitive and humiliating. This is also the punishment to which he condemned Adam's descendants: unrest within and bloody wars without.

In this, Don Isaac saw the root of the conflict between despotic paganism and the Torah of Moses and the Prophets. Moses and the Prophets rose up against Pharaonic idolatry. They wished to restore humanity to its Edenic existence, to living modestly, taking only what is truly necessary, based on the just distribution of nature's gifts among all human beings and creatures of the earth. But what is human happiness? According to the Torah, it lies in devotion to divine service—the one area in which no limit is placed on our aspirations, in which the more we achieve the better—through Torah study and observance.

It is not only the nations who are guilty of the sin of discontent. It happened in the days of Samuel, when Israel sought a king "like all the nations", rejecting God, "that [He] should not be king over them". For this sin, they eventually lost their kingdom and were sent into exile. It is in this vein that the Prophets' vision of redemption should be understood. They sought to restore man to his original, Edenic state—under divine, rather than human kingship. Abravanel espoused a coherent theory of history and the interaction between Israel and the nations, on the basis of which he determined that the end of days would come in his time. The essence of his theory is that through observance of the precepts of the Torah in exile, and acts of martyrdom, God's Kingdom will be revealed on earth and Israel will be restored to its land, which will flow with milk and honey—bringing forth the plenty of Eden, without toil or servitude. The Jewish People will thus live in peace with the nations, since the land will provide for the needs of all. Don Isaac learned all of these things from the story of the Exodus. The Israelites went forth into the desert, leaving behind the corrupt pagan civilization that had been their "house of bondage". In the wilderness, they were content with the manna—the justly-distributed gift of God that sustained them—and lived in obedience to the word of God. So it will be in the end of days: the Kingdom of God will be restored, the kingdom of man abolished, and the Jewish People redeemed. In the way of messianic dreamers throughout history, Abravanel believed that time to be close at hand.

As we well know, however, the messianic kingdom of Judah has not yet been established, and the kingdom of Pharaoh, shaped by Joseph's counsel, is alive and well in the world. In other words, humanity—the Jewish People included—has not yet renounced wicked civilization as the path to earthly happiness and success. Everyone longs for a messianic age of boundless, effortless plenty. Most individuals and all nations, however, hope to attain this Eden through competition and force; taking most of the plenty for themselves and turning the rest of humanity, including their own people, into slaves. It goes without saying that those condemned to slavery are not satisfied with their lot, although they generally wish merely to replace their "masters". Evidently, the familial-national-universal debate between Joseph and Judah is still far from resolved, among Jews and gentiles alike.

Yeshaya Steinberger

Vayehi – And Jacob Lived

Joseph: Father of the Battle against Assimilation
in the Teachings of Rabbi Yitzchok Hutner

Joseph is a fruitful vine, a fruitful vine by a fountain; its branches run over the wall (Genesis 47:22).

Joseph is the most complex and mysterious of Jacob's sons. His destiny sets him apart from his brothers. He is the firstborn of the beloved wife who died. The father finds comfort in his orphaned son who resembles his mother. Joseph is comely, wise, sensitive, and spoiled—just like Rachel. The special treatment he receives from his father and his inherent otherness get him into trouble with his brothers and arouse their jealousy. Joseph has difficulty communicating with them. His social isolation adds to his sense of isolation as a motherless child. His only close friend is his aging father. Hence his tendency to contemplate the mysteries of life, typical of one detached from the active society of his peers, and so too, his dreams and dreaminess, understood by his father as the prophetic visions of his gifted child (see Rashi and Nahmanides on Gen. 37:10). The gap between Joseph and his brothers turns to hatred, culminating in attempted murder. Only at the last minute do the brothers decide merely to sell him into slavery. In so doing, they believe they have condemned him to permanent exile from his home, society, and people.

It is in exile that Joseph's genius is revealed. The very traits that had made him the object of his brothers' hatred were the source of his success in the house of his Egyptian master. His grace and talent combined with the mystical ability to interpret dreams paved the Hebrew slave's way to the pinnacle of Egyptian society and power. It is interesting to note that every time Joseph glories in his remarkable success, he is struck down (see Rashi on the words "And Joseph was" in 39:6; see also Rashi on 40:23).

144

Joseph recovers after every fall. He is tempered in every sense by the vicissitudes of life. From the moment that he comes to power: as he waxes in strength outwardly as Pharaoh's regent, so he grows inwardly in righteousness, an "everlasting foundation". He becomes a symbol of resistance to temptation; proudly preserving his Jewish identity in foreign surroundings. So for example: "If one says, I was handsome and troubled by the evil inclination, he is asked: Were you more handsome than Joseph? It is said of Joseph the Righteous that Potiphar's wife would entice him every day ... Joseph [in his conduct] condemns the wicked" (*Yoma* 35b).

Moreover, as one who believed that Providence had sent him into exile in order to preserve his people, he bore no grudge against his brothers. In his old age, Joseph devoted his energies to raising his children in the ways of his forebears. His final appeal to his brothers, in which he expresses his desire to be buried in the Land of Israel, and assures them of their eventual redemption, reflects his deep sense of loyalty to his people and his land (see the final verses of the book of Genesis). The magnanimity that Joseph displays is the product, first and foremost, of the excellent education he received at the hands of his father and teacher.

The story of Joseph is a model and precedent for the Diaspora experience. First, on a general plane: if we substitute "Jewish People" for "Joseph" and "the nations" for "his brethren", the resulting scenario offers a compelling explanation of Israel's standing among the nations and the root causes of anti-Semitism. Like Joseph, the Jewish People is inherently other in terms of its destiny, in the sense of "Before I formed thee in the belly I knew thee". God refers to Israel as "my firstborn son", and its qualities and origins elicit God's favor from the dawn of creation: "In the beginning God created—for Israel, who are called 'beginning'", explains Rashi on the first verse in Genesis. Israel is compared to the heart amidst the organs of the body (*Kuzari*, Part 2, 36). Its otherness, however, also condemns it to isolation: "a people that shall dwell alone, and shall not be reckoned among the nations". This, and particularly God's special treatment of his chosen people, have engendered hatred toward Israel. "Why was it called *Sinai*? Because that is where hatred (*sin'ah*) for the Jewish People began" (*Shabbat* 89b). The giving of the Torah at Sinai—the source of Israel's otherness, as "a kingdom of priests, and a holy nation" (*Ex* 19:6)—is also the root cause of anti-Semitism. Rabbi Saadiah Gaon asserts that "our nationhood derives exclusively from the Torah". This definition of nationhood would, in itself, appear to arouse the envy of other nations and hostility toward Israel—leading to murder, or (at best) exile. Against all odds, the Jewish People has survived and, at times, even managed to rise to the top of gentile society. The very characteristics that engendered hatred against Jews, have also become an asset. Acuity, foreignness and exotic charm—as well as a sense of internal cohesion, forged by adversity—have made Jews excellent merchants and bankers, mediators and financiers; cosmopolites who stimulate and invigorate the economies and cultures of the lands in which they are dispersed.

The negative aspect of the Joseph analogy is equally valid. When the Jews begin to feel at home in the Diaspora, forgetting the *Shekhinah*—who weeps, as it were, for her sons—God "stirs up the bear" against them (see Rashi 39:6). The object of their desires thus becomes the source of their downfall; revealing the fatuous anomaly of Diaspora life.

The story of Joseph's resurgence and triumph is also a token for future generations. Despite its trials and tribulations, the Jewish People is never completely destroyed. Like the mythological phoenix, it arises again even from the flames. When redemption comes, Israel will be revealed as the savior of mankind, perfecting the world under the Kingdom of God. Then, there will be no revenge, just justice and perfection. The end of Joseph's life is also an analogy for redemption—return to the Land of Israel, and the advent of the End of Days as envisaged by the Prophets (see *Maharal, Gevurot Hashem*, 11: "There is an affinity between Joseph and the Jewish People. Therefore that which befalls the Jewish People has befallen Joseph").

The story of Joseph is far more than an analogy. It offers each and every Jew a practical approach to exile and its pitfalls. The dangers and opportunities inherent to life in exile are given particular prominence in *Vayehi*.

There is a glimmer of hope in Joseph's plight, from the very outset. The *Shekhinah*—the divine presence that goes into exile with Israel—accompanies Joseph as he joins the Ishmaelite caravan, indicated by the fact that it bore spices rather than the resin and pitch generally carried by such caravans (see Rashi on 37:25; *cf.* Rashi *ibid.* 6:14, on the word "pitch").

We are left with the feeling that the protagonist's adventures are far from over. The story in fact goes on to become a dominant theme in Jewish history—stretching well beyond the Ten Martyrs (the well-known *piyut* "*Eileh Ezkerah*", recited in the *Musaf* service on the Day of Atonement, asserts that the martyrdom of the ten, at the hands of the Romans, was belated retribution for the sin of the sale of Joseph), to include all of Israel's exiles. Furthermore, the manner in which Joseph approached his own exile, would serve to safeguard Jews against the dangers of future encounters with foreign cultures, in the sense of "the actions of the fathers are an example for the sons".

As Israel's mentor with regard to life in exile, Joseph—a son, one of the tribes—becomes one of the fathers of the nation. Joseph's sons are thus afforded the status of tribes in their own right: "And now thy two sons, who were born unto thee ... Ephraim and Manasseh, shall be even as Reuben and Simeon are to me". The word "father" (*av*) in fact appears time and again in reference to Joseph, as for example: "And they cried before him: *Avrech*—a father in wisdom" (Rashi on 41:43, citing Rabbi Yehudah); "and He hath made me a father to Pharaoh" (45:8; see also Rashi on *Num.* 22:26).

My rabbi and teacher, Yitzchok Hutner, one of the greatest *yeshivah* deans of the previous generation, considered the meaning of this fatherhood. Nahmanides, in his introduction to the book of *Exodus*, defines Genesis as the "Book of the Fathers", and *Exodus* as the "Book of the Sons". Genesis closes, as it happens, with the death of Joseph. His death, the first among the brothers, thus provides the closing notes of the magnificent symphony of the lives of the fathers that is Genesis. In other words, Joseph belonged to the era of the Patriarchs. The story of his life therefore comes to end in Genesis, whereas those of his brothers spill over into *Exodus*.

Rabbi Hutner explained the respective contributions of the fathers, as the foundations of the nation, to its creation. Abraham, Isaac and Jacob were all founders, each adding a layer to the structure of the House of Israel. Isaac adds to Abraham's contribution, for it is he alone who continues the legacy of his father, according to the verse: "for in Isaac shall seed be called to thee" (21:12), as opposed to Ishmael or the sons of Keturah, who are not sons of the covenant. "In Isaac—and not all of Isaac"—to exclude Esau, who does not carry on the lineage of the chosen people. The Jewish People per se begins only with Jacob, whose "couch was complete," i.e. all of his sons were worthy of carrying on his lineage (*Pahad Yitzhak, Sukot*, 12).

Once Jacob has established the Jewish People and nothing remains to be perfected or further refined, what is there for Joseph to add, in his capacity of "father"? Rabbi Hutner answers (*ibid.*):

Jewish continuity is still in peril, for the child of a Jewish man who marries a gentile woman will be a gentile like its mother. The bastion of Judaism is far from impenetrable—practical and halakhic assimilation are still possible. That is where Joseph's contribution as a patriarch lies. He established the principles of contending with assimilation. The moment that Joseph found the courage and spiritual resources to break away from the wife of Potiphar—rushing out to embrace the memory of his heritage (the image of his father that appeared to him in a window—see *Sotah* 36b)—he set a precedent for victory against the scourge of assimilation. Joseph was a patriarch because he sealed this possible breach. One who seals the cracks in a wall is counted among its builders.

In Joseph's example, "He that called the generations from the beginning" would appear to have touched upon the danger of assimilation that has plagued recent generations. When is the danger of assimilation most acute? Is it when Jews live as humiliated second-class citizens in gentile society, or is it when they have successfully scaled the social ladder in the lands of their dispersal? Experience has shown that it is precisely in those places in which Jews are granted equal rights and are embraced by the cream of society that the danger of assimilation is greatest.

From the time that Napoleon granted the Jews under his dominion equal rights, and emancipation penetrated most of the lands of Western and Central Europe, it took only one generation before there was hardly a single thriving center of Torah study in any of these lands. In the less enlightened lands of Eastern Europe on the other hand, where anti-Semitism was generally a part of official policy, and in the Sephardic communities, authentic, vibrant Judaism continued to flourish. The greater the number of Jews in high places—in government, culture, science and the arts, as well as in commerce—the greater the level of assimilation, and the more imminent the threat of Jewish spiritual annihilation.

The victims of today's spiritual holocaust that is reducing the number of Jews in the world at an alarming rate far outnumber the victims of anti-Semitism and of Europe's physical Holocaust. Anti-Semitism and danger are the surest ways to drive Jews back to their roots. This has been made manifestly clear by the renewed interest in Judaism and Israel in the countries of the CIS (FSU) and South Africa a decade ago, and more recently in Western Europe, in places where anti-Semitism has reared its head. Prosperity and especially acceptance at the highest and levels of society are driving the Jewish People to extinction. This is the essence of the spiritual holocaust suffered by Jews throughout the Western World.

The Sages of the Talmud and the Midrash, always refer to Joseph as "the Righteous", or "the righteous everlasting foundation"—an unusual designation, to say the least. The image of the successful, handsome, ruler sought after by women is difficult to reconcile with the image of the "righteous one" (Rashi 49:22: "Its branches [lit. daughters] run over the wall. The daughters of Egypt would walk on the walls to gaze at his beauty. 'Daughters' [*banot*—in plural form]—for there were many. 'Run' [*tza'adah*—in singular form]—for each sought out a place of her own, from which to gaze upon him"). When we think of someone who is righteous, the image that comes to mind is one of detachment from the material world and total absorption in study, prayer and charity. Righteousness in fact, however, lies in the ability to face the most elaborate of temptations, and resist them. We must remember that Joseph could have found ideological justification for his sin, since the Sages explain that the intentions of Potiphar's wife were good, having foreseen that she would bear Joseph's children—a prophecy that was fulfilled when he married her daughter.

Nevertheless, the handsome young man, far from home, courted by a socialite filled with true spiritual love for him, and whom he himself loved as well—conquers his passion and preserves his inner purity. Few people would not have been swept up by such temptations, and Joseph is held up by the Rabbis as the ultimate answer to those who yield to their passions.

There is a striking contrast between the humiliation that Joseph suffers at the hands of his brothers, and the success he enjoys in Egyptian society. His family shuns him and abuses him: "The archers have dealt bitterly with him, and shot at him, and hated him" (49:23; on which Rashi comments: "His brothers became adversaries"), but in Egypt, where he should have met with hostility, he was welcomed with open arms, against all odds, until Pharaoh himself was greater than he in title alone. In presenting Joseph to Pharaoh, the chief butler stresses his lowly status, highlighting the absurdity of the possibility of his promotion to a senior position: "And there was with us there a boy, a Hebrew, servant" (41:12). Rashi, ever aware of the subtle meanings of every verse, explains: "He refers to him with contempt: 'boy'—a simpleton, unworthy of greatness; 'Hebrew'—who doesn't even know our language; 'servant'—it is written in the statutes of Egypt that a servant may not rule or don ministerial garb". In the end, as we know, Joseph fulfills his childhood dreams and prophecies. He becomes regent to the king of Egypt, and his brothers and parents come to bow down before him.

Remarkably, one who was actively abandoned by his people/brethren and welcomed enthusiastically by strangers, remained faithful to his national heritage, preserving his inner purity: "And Joseph was in Egypt—highlighting Joseph's righteousness. The Joseph who was in Egypt and had become king there, was the very same Joseph who had herded his father's sheep" (Rashi on *Ex.* 1:5; see also Rashi on Gen. 47:31).

When a young religious man leaves Israel, or a student leaves the *yeshivah*, to learn a trade or to pursue professional academic studies at an institution near home—there is no cause for alarm. The Jewish future of such a young man is more or less assured. When the purpose, however, is to attend a prestigious university on an isolated campus with a vibrant social life interacting with male and female students of the gentile social elite, then the danger of assimilation becomes very real. The average traditionally-minded young Jew is invulnerable to inter-marriage, as long as gentile society does not offer him the chimera of wealth and prestige. When a social bond is created with the sons and daughters of the gentile elite, and "fitting in" appears a worthwhile and feasible goal, then assimilation becomes a distinct possibility. The United States is emblematic, inasmuch as the process described above is the story of economically and socially integrated third generation American Jews. Reform Jewry generally lacks even a second generation, due to such assimilation processes.

Joseph proved that even one who has been accepted into the highest echelons of gentile society, may remain a faithful Jew. He was not bedazzled and did not go astray. His fortitude is awe-inspiring. The warm but restrictive social and familial framework that often defines religious affiliation clearly meant nothing to Joseph. The threads that bound him to his heritage passed directly between Joseph and his God, requiring no further external support.

The secret of Joseph's strength that enabled him to cope with his family's rejection, with the temptations at court, and with the unfamiliar surroundings in which he found himself lay in his profound faith. This unshakable faith can be traced to three sources: his education, his unique personality and extraordinary approach to life. Joseph received an excellent Jewish education. The special bond that existed between Joseph and his father Jacob would appear to have played a crucial role in his spiritual success. The excellence of his education was the result of three factors: deep personal identification with his teacher, stemming from the closest of relationships between father and son; the subject matter offered a profound and comprehensive philosophy of life; instruction was on an individual basis, conforming to the student's specific needs.

Identification between father/teacher and son: The Talmud asserts (later reiterated in the writings of Maimonides) that ideally fathers should teach their own sons, rather than sending them to school. Rabbi Hutner (in a discourse in Yiddish, published in the *Shavuot* section of *Pahad Yitzhak*), cautioned against misunderstanding this principle. Yehoshua ben Gamla was praised for having founded a school. This is not to say, however, that his accomplishment was a manifestation of progress. On the contrary, it was in fact an expression of regression. Previously, fathers had been versed in the Torah and were thus able to teach their sons without having to send them to school. It is after all, incumbent on a father to teach his son Torah and a trade (*Kiddushin* 29a). That is why Maimonides (in *Hilkhot Talmud Torah*) stresses this obligation. Only one who is unable to teach his son may hire a teacher. Maimonides makes no reference to schools as an "obligation". In other words, the ideal situation was and remains one in which fathers capable of teaching their sons do so, rather than sending them to school. With the passage of time, however, as the number of fathers knowledgeable in Torah and capable of teaching it decreased, and the number of children whose education was neglected increased, the need arose for a public education system. It is for meeting this need that Rabbi Yehoshua ben Gamla was praised, and rightly so. It is a well-known fact that many sons of scholarly families, even in recent times, have studied with their fathers rather than in *yeshivot*, including the *Or Sameah* (Meir Simhah of Dvinsk), the *Hazon Ish* (Avraham Karelitz), and members of the Soloveitchik family.

The bond between father and son is central to Torah study—so central in fact, that it is used in the talmudic and midrashic literature as a metaphor for the relationship between teacher and student in general. "One who teaches the son of another the Torah, it is as if he had begotten him" (*Sanhedrin* 19b). This deep bond first appears in the case of Joseph. "Now Israel loved Joseph more than all his children, because he was the son of his old age (*ben zekunim*)" (37:3), and Rashi explains: "And Onkelos translated *bar hakim* (wise son) ... he taught him everything he had learned from Shem and Eber. Another interpretation—he was the image (*ziv ikonin*) of his father". What we find here is a doubly intense bond. The first interpretation reflects the fact that the father was the son's teacher, who taught him everything he knew. The second interpretation, which complements the first, notes the total identification between son/student and father/teacher. The first interpretation relates to the giver's relationship to the receiver, while the second pertains to the receiver's relationship to the giver.

Joseph is not only Jacob's beloved son and chief disciple, but also his spiritual double and biographical "clone". The expression *ziv ikonin* (lit. "radiance of features") denotes a spiritual resemblance; a resemblance of radiance, of inner light. It is to this resemblance that Rashi refers in 37:2:

> Joseph was the image of his father, and everything that had befallen Jacob befell Joseph—the former was despised and the latter was despised, the brother of the former sought to kill him and the brothers of the latter sought to kill him, and so forth at length in Genesis *Rabbah*.

This is the secret of Joseph's fortitude. Thus, when he is overcome by passion, his father's image appears to him in the window, saving him from sin. It is by virtue of the deep educational bond that Joseph shared with his father, that he manages to survive his golden exile in Egypt. The appearance of one's teacher—in this case the student's father—at a difficult juncture, is proof of a successful education. The teacher, who is like a divine messenger, makes such a deep impression, that the student carries his image with him, beyond the time and even the field of instruction. An ideal teacher is one who "goes into exile with his student" (see *Makot* 10b). Thus, whenever a problem arises, the student will ask himself: what would Rabbi have said about this? Woeful is an educational system that lacks such educators—whose "image" accompanies students long after they have left the halls of learning.

Education as a profound and comprehensive philosophy of life: The education that Jacob provides consists entirely of piety and fear of God, described as follows by Maimonides: "And Jacob taught all of his sons ... the way of God and observance of the precepts of Abraham" (*Hilkhot Avodat Kokhavim* 1:3). This, coupled with Jacob's fears regarding his sons' ability to resist temptation, explains some of the more puzzling aspects of the patriarch's meeting with his lost son. Rather than rejoicing, he is plagued by doubt. The brothers tell him not only that Joseph is alive, but that he is "ruler over all the land of Egypt. And his heart fainted, for he believed them not" (45:26). The elderly father is full of apprehension: What are the chances that his lost son has remained faithful to the precepts? And what of his grandchildren—members of the Egyptian nobility?

And when was Jacob's spirit revived? "When he saw the wagons (*agalot*) which Joseph had sent to carry him". Rashi explains: "He sent with them a sign, indicating the [Torah] portion he had been studying when he departed from him, that of the 'beheaded heifer' (*eglah aru-fah*)" (*ibid.* 27). Only when Jacob is certain that Joseph remembers his Torah studies does he rejoice, and the spirit of prophecy returns to him.

Joseph's behavior is also curious. He sends his father "aged wine—appreciated by old men" (Rashi, *ibid.* 23). Is Jacob an alcoholic, a connoisseur of fine wines, whose son indulges his fancies? Here, too, Joseph would appear to have been sending a message to his father, re-assuring him that despite the external appearance of an Egyptian ruler, he had remained a faithful Jew. The aged wine symbolizes the spirit of Judaism, which retains its redolence, even in a new and different vessel.

The dramatic meeting between father and beloved, long-lost son, should have been marked by joyous celebration. Again the reader is in for a surprise: Jacob does not even kiss Joseph. According to the Rab-bis, it is precisely at that moment that he finds it opportune to recite the *Shema*, (Rashi, 46:29). In so doing, he in fact declares that only profound faith can give meaning to such an emotion-laden and intimate personal encounter.

Jacob is not satisfied until he is convinced of the continuity of his legacy: he must ascertain not only that Joseph has remained righteous, but that the next generation, his grandchildren raised in Egypt in a non-Jewish environment, are committed to the Torah and its precepts. Jacob studies Torah with his grandson Ephraim.

Jewish education—measured by its ability to achieve continuity of Torah study within the family—comes to fruition in this chapter. The chain of tradition is preserved for more than three generations. That is the meaning of Joseph's keen interest, in his final years, in raising as many generations as possible (see the final verses in the book of Gen-esis).

Instruction was on an individual basis: Joseph's education was tailored to his specific needs. As noted above, Jacob transmitted to Joseph—and apparently to him only—all that he himself had learned. On the assumption that the other sons were not party to this legacy,

Jacob and Joseph studied alone. Even the gift of the coat of many colors that set Joseph apart from his brothers, was meant by Jacob as an educational exercise. Through this gift, Jacob sought to exalt his beloved son, and to set him on the path to greatness. Perhaps he wished to help realize his son's dreams, which he considered prophecies.

"Bring up a child according to his nature" (*Prov.* 22:6) is an ancient piece of advice, advocating an individual approach to education. In mass education, individuals become ciphers, without personality or voice. The Rabbis, who said: "Their opinions are unique [just as] their faces are unique", could never promote such an approach. Jacob, the paradigm of human perfection, was fully aware of this. In the remarkable attention he lavished upon his beloved son, he unwittingly prepared him for his unique destiny—his "many colors". Rashi explains that the word "*pasim*" ("of many colors")—an acronym of the parties to whom he would later be sold: **P**otiphar, **S**oharim (traders), **I**shmaelites, and **M**idianites—presages Joseph's tribulations (37:3).

My Rabbi and teacher, Yitzchok Hutner, would meet with students individually, relating to each on a personal basis. "An idea or moral teaching suited to 'Reuven' may not be suited to 'Shimon'", he used to say. He believed that an indiscriminate, wholesale approach to education completely misses the point.

Joseph is fearless, and by virtue of his fanaticism—a quality much maligned today—manages to resist temptation. The object of Joseph's fanaticism was his own desire, although fanaticism itself has its place, even when directed against others, in extreme circumstances—when the very foundations of Judaism are in peril. Those who lack the capacity for fanaticism are thus liable to fail miserably in such circumstances.

When Joseph is nearly seduced by Potiphar's wife, his response is unequivocal: "And he left his garment in her hand, and fled, and got him out" (39:12). Rabbi Hutner explains Joseph's flight as rooted in the kind of fanaticism that is mandated only on rare occasions—the best known of which is the duty to slay a "*bo'el aramit*"—one who fornicates with a pagan woman (*Sanhedrin* 81b). Were Joseph to have begun reasoning and weighing matters, he would have been overcome by the evil inclination. Initially he was able to offer a cogent reply to her repeated pleas: "But he refused, and said ... there is nothing too great in this

house for me; neither hath he kept back any thing from me but thee ...
How then can I do this great wickedness, and sin against God?" (*ibid.*
8–9). Rational arguments are powerless, however, once he is overcome
with desire; at which point only fanaticism and near-hysterical flight can
save him.

As a result of his fanaticism, Joseph was able to defy nature and
overcome his desires. So great was his accomplishment, that God overturned the laws of nature on his behalf, splitting the Red Sea for his
descendants. "'The sea saw it, and fled'—It beheld Joseph's coffin approaching. God said let it flee before he who fled, as it is written: 'And
he left his garment ...'" (*Yalkut Shimoni* 873). For relations with a pagan
woman are not merely a transgression. It constitutes assimilation, inasmuch as it combines the sins of fornication and idolatry. One who has
relations with the "daughter of a strange god" (*Mal.* 2:11; see also *Sanhedrin* 82a), embodies the great peril of assimilation, in which man's
two strongest impulses converge.

Joseph, who was saved from the virtually irremediable sin of assimilation, by virtue of his fanaticism, stood in the breach and set an example for future generations. Although it is said that the ways of the Torah
"are ways of pleasantness, and all her paths are peace" (*Prov.* 3:17),
there are times when audacity is required. In a state of emergency, there
is no place for civility and propriety. When the danger of assimilation
threatens to destroy everything—particularly when it assumes the form
of socializing between men and women—a modicum of fanaticism is
certainly called for. Joseph the Righteous was successful, because his
fanaticism was imbued with love of God devoid of violence—directed
inward rather than at others. Moreover, Joseph skillfully cloaked his
fanaticism in sophistication and propriety, as we shall see below.

Joseph is always described as handsome and graceful. Particularly
striking are the words of Nobel Laureate Thomas Mann, in his epic
Joseph and his Brothers (*The Stories of Jacob*, tr. John E. Woods):

> What all has not been proclaimed and asserted, in song and saga,
> in apocrypha and pseudepigrapha, in praise of his appearance ...
> That his countenance could have shamed the splendor of sun and
> moon is the least of what became fixed in memory. It has been
> said that he literally had to cover his brow and cheeks with a veil

so that people's hearts might not be ignited by earthly passion for this man sent from God ... Oriental tradition ... A Persian bard of great authority outdoes even that ... if all the world's beauty were melted into a single coin weighing twenty-four drachms, then twenty drachms, so our poet enthuses, would have fallen to him, the incomparable paragon.

Such emphasis is understandable coming from a secular writer, but rather embarrassing, to say the least, when expressed by the Torah and the Rabbis. Would anyone today dream of extolling the physical virtues of a saintly rabbi? "Grace is deceitful, and beauty is vain" (Prov. 31:30)! The beauty and grace of Rachel's children—and particularly Joseph— is renowned. The Rabbis, however, interpreted the verse that praises Joseph's beauty—"Joseph is a fruitful vine, a fruitful vine by a fountain; its branches run over the wall" (49:22)—as referring to the encounter with Esau, praising the son for having stood before his mother, in order to hide her from his rapacious uncle.

Joseph's beauty is a symbol of his *modus operandi*– a unique approach to interaction with this world; a way of dealing with a hostile material world, using the enemy's own weapon. External appearance is something that this world can appreciate, and Joseph is thus constantly associated with dress: the many-colored coat his father made for him, changing his garments before meeting with Pharaoh, the changes of clothing he gives his brothers. Joseph's beauty also embraced remarkable communication skills; the ability to find favor through the external interpretation of internal secrets. The capacity to interpret dreams coincides with the ability to apply the internal to the external, i.e. the physical world. That is why Joseph was called *Zaphenath-Paneah*—"he who reveals what is hidden" (41:45). His knowledge of all the world's languages, including Hebrew,—the source of his superiority over Pharaoh, according to the Talmud—further complemented his ability to dominate his surroundings as a consummate communicator. His ability to reign lay precisely in these traits. This is the true meaning of the dream in which the brothers bowed down before him; a dream that eventually came true.

Joseph's behavior in exile was marked by an outward appearance of assimilation, coupled with fanatical internal observance. In other words, Joseph may have been able to allow himself to use popular idioms such as beauty and grace, language and clothing, because inside, he burned with "divine fire". Joseph's inner ardor, his fanaticism, safeguarded his hold on divine truth, despite the dangers entailed in resorting—albeit outwardly—to the earthly tools of the gentile world. Put another way, when one is compelled to engage in worldly affairs, internal fanaticism is invaluable as a counterbalance.

Joseph's beauty is merely a tactic. His external appearance is a tool in his struggle with an environment that threatens to engulf him. By virtue of his charm, he succeeds against all odds. This method has a price however—accelerated "burnout". That is why Joseph dies before his brothers; why Joshua the son of Nun (of the tribe of Ephraim) dies at a relatively young age, why the kingdom of Ephraim was short-lived, and why the "Messiah ben Joseph" will be killed in combat.

In his book *Hamesh Derashot*, Rabbi Joseph Dov Soloveitchik asserts that the path of Joseph—engaging in worldly life—is the way of Modern Orthodoxy everywhere, and of Religious Zionism in Israel. Those who adhere to this way of life believe that one should deal with cultures that are foreign and even hostile to Judaism and the Torah, by infiltrating the ranks of the "enemy" and harnessing the forces of externality to the cart of holiness.

To a large extent, this is the path of Rabbi Samson Raphael Hirsch and his disciples—advocates of *Torah im Derekh Eretz* ("Torah with worldly involvement"); of Rabbi Abraham Isaac Kook and the followers of Torah Zionism; of Rabbi JD Soloveitchik and devotees of *Torah Umadda* ("Torah and secular knowledge"); and, to some degree, of many, many others—including my rabbi and teacher, Rabbi Yitchok Hutner, of blessed memory. The opponents of this approach have been legion and often fierce, and the controversy—a dispute for the sake of heaven—which rages to this day, may persist until the coming of the Messiah. In the Diaspora, however, where circumstances have compelled Jews both to interact with gentile society and to fight those who would destroy Judaism from within, the method learned from Joseph the Righteous has been widely accepted. In conclusion, the story of Joseph is the story of contending with foreign culture. There is nothing new under the sun. The problems with which Joseph grappled in his time, are the classic problems of our time, and his solutions, for the most part, remain effective even to this day.

Shemot – Exodus

Pnina Galpaz-Feller

Shemot – Now these are the Names

Moses and Monotheism in the Thought of Sigmund Freud

And Moses said unto God, Behold, when I come unto the children of Israel, and shall say unto them, The God of your fathers has sent me unto you; and they shall say to me, What is his name? What shall say unto them? And God said unto Moses I WILL BE THAT WHICH I WILL BE: and he said, Thus shalt thou say unto the children of Israel, I WILL BE hath sent me unto you (*Exodus* 3:13–14).

The portion of *Shemot* describes God's appearance to Moses at Mount Horeb, in the burning bush. The God who appears before Moses and reveals his name to him is the God who created the universe; the God who is all that becomes—"I will be that which I will be" (*ibid*, 13). Moses thus proclaims monotheism—a unique event in a polytheistic world. But is ancient Israel really the source of this belief, and Moses its herald, as implied by the biblical author; or was it perhaps borrowed from another culture, its foreign origins veiled? This question was addressed by psychoanalyst Sigmund Freud.

Freud studied the figure of Moses and the monotheistic belief associated with him—not in the same fashion as archaeologists, historians, Bible scholars, or 19th and 20th century writers, but in a wholly new way: through psychoanalysis. To Freud, Moses, monotheism and the destiny of the Jewish People, were merely research tools in a study that was, in effect, an addition to his psychoanalytical work *Totem and Taboo*, on the development of religion. While presenting a fundamentally psychoanalytical theory, Freud also managed to integrate Jewish history into general history. In this chapter, we will not discuss the psychoanalytical aspects of Freud's approach to monotheism and the life of Moses, but will focus rather on his views regarding its origins.

In 1934, inspired by Thomas Mann's *Joseph and his Brothers*, Freud began to write a historical novel on the subject of Moses and monotheism. He never finished it, but in 1937, published two articles on Moses' origins, in the psychoanalytical journal *Imago*. He did not write *Moses and Monotheism*, however, until after his flight from Nazi Europe to England, in 1938. Freud's focus on the Jewish topic of Moses and the source of monotheism in his final years is particularly interesting in light of the fact that he was then suffering from a terminal illness and knew that this would be his final work.

Freud's approach rests on three principles: (1) Moses was an Egyptian; (2) The origins of monotheism lie in Egypt; and (3) Moses the Egyptian, who liberated the Israelites from slavery, gave them laws and proclaimed the monotheistic faith, was murdered by them, and another Moses, a Midianite, replaced him.

Freud bases his theory of Moses' Egyptian origins, primarily on an analysis of the story of his birth and childhood in Pharaoh's house, and especially on the identification of the name Moses with the Egyptian name *mose*" or "child"—an abbreviated form employed in theophoric names. Freud posits that Moses was Egyptian, and that the religion named for him, the "Mosaic religion", was thus an Egyptian religion.

With the exception of a very short period, the religion of the ancient Egyptians was always polytheistic, although changes did occur over the course of history in the hierarchical status of many gods in the Egyptian pantheon. The Egyptians worshiped the wonders of nature and the wondrous qualities of animals, through divinities conceived in human or animal form, or in the forces of nature. The Mosaic faith is strikingly different. It is a monotheistic faith that believes in the existence of a unique and exclusive God, who cannot be looked upon or worshiped through a statue or image, whose name cannot even be taken in vain. The Egyptian religion thus differed from monotheism throughout its history. Monotheism strictly forbade the use of magic, to which the Egyptians resorted on a daily basis. The monotheistic religion completely renounced the concept of immortality—contrary to the Egyptian belief in man's eternal life in the hereafter. Due to these fundamental differences, Freud saw the Egyptian cult as a religion in its primitive stages of development, and monotheism as the religion of exalted abstraction. How then can we resolve the contradiction between the Egyptian religion and the principles of monotheism described in the Bible while ascribing both to Moses?

Freud explains that it was not the widely-accepted polytheistic Egyptian religion that Moses bequeathed to his people, and had prevailed in Egypt for millennia but the unique religious philosophy of Amenhotep IV, that is Akhenaton. This king conceived a new religious idea, based on the belief in a single God—the sun-god Aton. His attempt to impose this faith on Egypt was in fact the most radical religious revolution in Egyptian history.

Worship of the solar disk, Aton, is rooted in Egyptian tradition dating from the Old Kingdom Period. In the days of the father of Amenhotep IV, Amenhotep III, worship of the physical aspect of the sun was revived: the sun was featured on the royal barge, some of the king's guards and military officers were named after the god Aton, and Amenhotep III built a special palace in the god's honor. Nevertheless, the official national god remained Amon-Ra, whose status continued to rise, and whose cult enjoyed ever greater political and economic power, centered around the elaborate temple at Karnak.

Initially, Amenhotep IV built special structures at Karnak for the cult of Aton, while continuing to worship the sun-god Ra in his aspect of Ra-Harakhte ("Horus of the two horizons"). In the third year of his reign however, he established Aton as the preferred sun-god. Henceforth, Aton was represented in the form of a solar disk adorned with the Uraeus (the upright cobra), from which emanated rays terminating in human hands holding the Egyptian hieroglyphs for "power" (*was*) and "life" (*ankh*). In the fifth year of his reign, Amenhotep's religious beliefs radicalized, and he began to see Aton as a unique and exclusive god. He even changed his own name, Amenhotep, which included the name Amon, to the name Akhen-aton, based on the name Aton. Between the sixth and ninth years of his reign, Akhenaton established a carefully planned new capital, Akhetaton, now called El Amarna. The new capital was built north of Thebes on virgin land with no connection to Egypt's previous religious tradition and was consecrated exclusively to Aton. Within a short time, Akhenaton's religious revolution had transformed Egypt's entire religious culture. Temples were closed; depictions of the various gods and their statues were destroyed. The names of the other gods were erased and their cults discontinued. These changes left an impression on Egyptian language and art as well (Pnina Galpaz-Feller, *Yetziat Mitzrayim Metzi'ut o Dimyon*, The Exodus from Egypt Fact or Fiction, pp. 47–60).

The principles of Akhenaton's religion can be learned from the iconographic and epigraphic finds in the temples he built at Karnak, and in the rock tombs of his courtiers, discovered on the outskirts of the city. The best preserved inscription—found in the tomb of Ay, the king's chariot-master—consists of a hymn to the sun-god, which clearly expresses the new religion's vision of the king as teacher of Aton's creed, and reflection of the sun on Earth. Freud acknowledges the fact that the author of the hymns would appear to have been Amenhotep himself (Sigmund Freud, *Moses and Monotheism*, Vintage Books, 1955, p. 23). In the religion established by Akhenaton, Aton was afforded the status of unique god; no longer associated directly with a graven image, but a celestial being merely represented in the form of a solar disk. He was perceived as the center of the universe, its prime mover; nourishing, supporting and renewing it daily. The king's philosophy affirmed the rays of the sun as physical manifestations of the god's power—thereby providing an accessible image. The god Aton was seen not only as a national deity, but as a universal god. Evidence of widespread, systematic and intentional effacement indicates that the king ordered the name and symbols of Amon-Ra expunged from existing structures, along with the names of other gods appearing on monuments and temple walls.

Akhenaton's new approach ignored earlier theological ideas, like that of the primordial hill and the primordial waters, ideas that had existed in Egypt for thousands of years. Tomb decorations ceased to give prominence to the deceased in their journey to the afterlife: descriptions of struggles against the demons that lie in wait for the souls of the dead. The religion of Amarna focused exclusively on the present, on the "here and now".

The religious revolution that marked all areas of life, failed nevertheless, to capture the imagination of the masses. Ordinary people found themselves unable to renounce a world full of gods, that would have been extremely real to them, in order to suddenly embrace a belief in an abstract world and a single god. The fact that the king was designated sole intermediary between man and god made things even more difficult for the average Egyptian, who would have found the new religion hard to swallow in any case. The religion of Aton was never a popular religion and, as Freud stresses, was probably limited to a small circle of high officials, close to the king's person.

King Akhenaton died in 1358 BCE (according to Breasted's chronology, adopted by Freud), having ruled for only seventeen years, and was succeeded by his son-in-law Smenkhkara, husband of his eldest daughter. The latter lacked the qualities essential to a head of state, especially in light of the political, social and religious upheaval that followed the death of Akhenaton. He remained at El Amarna, but ruled with a weak hand, and when Akhenaton's other son-in-law, Tut-ankh-aton, rose to power, the previous king's religious reforms were all abolished, El Amarna abandoned, and its temples destroyed. The cult of Amon-Ra was restored to its former state, and the new king returned to Egypt's old capital, to the joy of the traditional priesthood. He even changed his name to Tut-ankh-amon, and scorned the memory of Akhenaton "as that of a felon" (*ibid.* p. 26).

According to Freud, Moses the Egyptian remained faithful to the religion of Aton, and refused to come to terms with the restoration of the old religion. He was, apparently, a high-ranking official (perhaps a member of the royal house), and showed himself to be a man of initiative. When Akhenaton died, Moses decided to choose a new people to whom he would offer the religion that the Egyptians had rejected. He was, it would seem, governor of the region of Goshen at the time, and chose the enslaved Hebrew- Israelite tribes; teaching them belief in the one God, Aton. The Hebrews accepted his religious message, in return for their liberation from Egypt—rendered possible in the period following the death of Akhenaton. Over time, Moses radicalized his religious approach and rejected any connection with the cult of the Egyptian sun-god. The religion he developed was based on belief in a universal moral god, the rejection of magic and cult worship, and adherence to the principles of justice and truth. Moses established the Egyptian custom of circumcision as a sign of membership in the new religion.

Freud appreciated the difficulty in comparing the religion of Aton to that of Moses due to the paucity of Egyptian finds. The traditional priests of Egypt, the priests of Amon, meticulously destroyed all record of that religion, and the religion of Moses we know only in its final form, when its principles were committed to writing, hundreds of years after the fact. Nevertheless, Freud concludes: "If Moses was an Egyptian and if he transmitted his own religion to the Jews, then it was that of Akhenaton, the Aton religion" (*ibid.* p. 27).

Freud's theories shocked and angered many. He himself had doubts regarding the accuracy of his premises:

> "To my critical faculties, this treatise, proceeding from a study of the man Moses, seems like a dancer balancing on one toe" (*ibid.* p. 71) ... "When I use Biblical tradition here in such an autocratic and arbitrary way, draw on it for confirmation whenever it is convenient, and dismiss its evidence without scruple when it contradicts my conclusions, I know full well that I am exposing myself to severe criticism concerning my method and that I weaken the force of my proofs. But this is the only way in which to treat material whose trustworthiness—as we know for certain—was seriously damaged by the influence of distorting tendencies" (*ibid.* p. 30 n.1).

Theologians attacked him as a heretic, and historians dismissed him as lacking credibility. To this day, his work is hardly mentioned under the entry "Moses" in encyclopedias.

Freud understood the monotheistic period in Egypt as an iconoclastic one; a period in which the "sacred cows" of Egyptian polytheistic religion were slaughtered. In his psychoanalytical interpretation, Freud gives prominence to the historicity of the figure of Moses, the man who abandoned Egypt with his followers, gave them laws and precepts, and created the Hebrew nation. These actions were merely the means however, to the real end: saving "Atonism", the belief in one god. The process was not spontaneous but occurred gradually over the course of time, part of the ebb and flow of human civilization. Moses, who liberated the Israelites from slavery, made them into a people and led them through the desert, failed to change their stiff-necked nature, and eventually met his death in one of their many rebellions. The people abandoned his teachings, although the seeds of monotheism he had sown would reemerge centuries after his death, through the Prophets. According to Freud, it was in fact Moses' death and the abandoning of his teachings that enabled later generations to approach repressed memories from the distant past with renewed force, resulting in the triumph of the Mosaic religion: monotheism.

Even today, some 70 years after Freud's death, most of his claims regarding Moses the man cannot be corroborated. Only the influence of the Amarna religion on Moses' belief can be examined more closely, thanks to recent philological developments and the discovery of further Egyptian documents, as well as methodological developments in the field of biblical criticism. The questions that interest scholars today are whether Mosaic religion was monotheistic from the very beginning, i.e. rooted in the firm belief in a single god, or was it henotheistic—recognizing one supreme deity, an *"el elyon"*, above a more extensive pantheon; and if it was monotheistic, were its tenets drawn from the Egyptian court?

Both historians and anthropologists rejected Freud's theories, and tried to demonstrate that the roots of monotheism can be found in descriptions of the figure of Abraham, styled "the first monotheist". Nevertheless, when we examine the beliefs of the Patriarchs, we find them fundamentally different from those of Moses. In the days of the Patriarchs there were no festivals, no constitution, and no clear and established path to divine worship; moreover, the divinity was not known by name. The Rabbis, who noticed these differences, cited the giving of the Torah at Sinai as their source. In other words, they agreed that the Israelite faith before Sinai differed from the one that came after.

It is clear from the Bible that a religious revolution took place in Moses' time, resulting in the framing of a religious constitution, ascribed to him. Clans became tribes, and the monotheistic approach emerged—although tenuous and not yet universally accepted. Also, the God of Israel was given a name, the Tetragrammaton, thereby affording the tribes a national character. God, although still identified as God of the Fathers, is no longer the intimate "God of Abraham, Isaac and Jacob", but a jealous god, the Lord of Hosts. He dwells in the Tent of Meeting, as befits the god of a nomadic society.

Monotheism continued to develop under the Jewish kings, who established it as their state religion, by means of the prophets and the Temple cult. It would thus appear to be less of an original phenomenon that took history by storm, than one that developed slowly and came into its own in the fifth and sixth centuries BCE, at the earliest, as claimed by Freud.

Identifying the religion of Moses with the tenets of Amarna is not that simple. Biblical monotheism requires belief not only in the unique existence of the God of Israel, but in the singularity of his worship as well. Although God sometimes appears in anthropomorphic form, his uniqueness lies in his otherness; in his utter exaltedness. He transcends all natural laws and phenomena. The essence of this belief is reflected in the unique and exclusive character of his worship.

It is hard to compare the two religions. The religion of Amarna has been the subject of a great deal of research, but scholars have failed to agree as to whether it was purely monotheistic, or the religion of a particular god, Aton, whose divine existence was believed to be independent of that of other gods. Another matter is the fact that the religion of Amarna endured only 17 years, during which time it failed to be applied or adopted. Moses' monotheism on the other hand, was only in its infancy at the time—becoming the fully developed religion we know, primarily in its later stages. In the religion of Moses, the priests were charged with the task of teaching and spreading the faith, whereas at Amarna, Akhenaton was the religion's sole teacher. In the Mosaic religion, the king is subject to the law (2 Sam. 2, 11–12; 1 *Kings* 21; etc.), although invested with sanctity, as reflected by his ritual anointment with oil (1 Sam. 15:1; 16:1; 1 Kings 1:39). Akhenaton, the earthly manifestation of God, enjoyed a much higher level of sanctity, to the point that it sometimes seems that Akhenaton (venerated in his own right), rather than Aton, was the real god of the Amarna period. The father-son relationship appears in the Bible as an allegory for the relationship between the Jewish king and his God (2 Sam. 7:14; *Ps.* 2:7). Akhenaton on the other hand, is seen as the actual son of God, called "the beautiful child of the Sun", or "the son born of thy body". To this day, no code of law from the Amarna Period has been discovered, while the religion of Moses is rooted in positive and negative precepts. Freud, too, recognized the difficulty in comparing the two religions: "The Mosaic religion we know only in its final form as it was fixed by Jewish priests in the time after the Exile, about eight hundred years later" (*ibid.* p. 27).

Today, it is widely presumed that the Exodus occurred during the reign of Ramses II, not Akhenaton, as Freud believed (K.A. Kitchen, "Egyptians and Hebrews, from Ra'amses to Jericho", *Beer-Sheva* 12, 65–131). Moses would thus have lived 100–150 years after Akhenaton; born a Hebrew and raised in Pharaoh's palace, as described in the Bible. It is possible that while in the royal palace, he may have come across hymns to Aton that had survived from the Amarna Period, despite concerted efforts to destroy them. They were preserved in reliefs, for example, and in fragments on bricks reused after the destruction of the buildings erected by Akhenaton. Moses may thus have become acquainted with the abstract approach to God and his representation in the solar disk, with the demand that he be worshiped exclusively, and with the idea of a jealous and unique God—as witnessed by the effacement of various monuments in the days of Akhenaton.

As we have seen, the religious revolution in Egypt was short-lived. Its influence on biblical culture however, persisted for centuries. A comparison between the hymn to the sun inscribed on the walls of the tomb of Akhenaton's chariot-master Ay, and *Psalms* 104, gives the impression that the author of the psalm intentionally addressed the approach adopted by the Egyptian hymn (Y. Hoffman, *"Tehilim Kof-dalet, Iyun Sifruti,"* Psalms 104, A Literary Analysis, *She'arei Talmon: Mehkarim Bamikra, Kumran Vehamizrah Hakadmnon Mugashim Leshmaryahu Talmon*, 1992, pp. 13–24).

Freud understood that the Divine Name *Y-H-W-H*, which denotes the religious revolution and monotheistic belief in the Bible and appears in the portion of *Shemot*, derives from an ancient nomadic source. The Children of Israel accepted the cult of the god YHWH in the Sinai Peninsula, apparently under Midianite influence. This god was apparently worshiped by other tribes in the area as well. Freud stresses however, that there is no connection between Moses the Egyptian—who gave the people their new religion—and the name YHWH. Over time, the supporters of the "Egyptian" Moses, who cherished the Exodus experience, ascribed the act of liberation to the new god YHWH. The name YHWH appears in Egyptian records, in relation to areas in the vicinity of *Se'ir*. The fact that the divine revelation in the Bible is described as having taken place in the Sinai, supports the nomadic origins of the name YHWH, as Freud believed, based on the work of the historian Eduard Meyer. Contrary to the name of God however, which is not the name of an Egyptian divinity, some of the manifestations of God in the Bible bear clear traces of Egyptian influence.

The God YHWH is described in his theophanic form as "shining" and possessing "rays": "The Lord came from Sinai and shined forth from Seir" (*Deut.* 33:2), and "God cometh from Teman and the Holy One from Mount Paran ... And a brightness appeareth as the light; and he hath rays [coming forth] from his hand" (*Hab.* 3:3–4). An inscription discovered at Kuntillet 'Ajrud (about 50 km south of the biblical Kadesh Barnea), and dated to the 9th century BCE, reads: "*wvzrḥ... 'l br wymsn-hrm ...*", that is "when God shines forth the mountains melt" (N. Shupak, "*Ha'el Haba Miteman Ve'el Hashemesh Hamitzri: Iyun Mehudash Behabakuk 3:3–7,*" The God who Comes from Teman and the Egyptian Sun-God: *Habakuk* 3:3–7 Reconsidered, *Teshurah Leshmuel*, pp. 409–432).

In these sources, we find traces of Egyptian religion from the El Amarna period, and the solar disk described as having rays and hands bearing the symbol of life. It is possible that in these physical descriptions, the biblical authors associate the appearance of YHWH, the God of Moses' message, with the El Amarna conception of God. Moses, like Akhenaton, enjoys a special relationship with the god. This is manifest in the fact that Moses is the only man to see God face to face: "And the Lord spoke unto Moses face to face" (*Ex.* 33:11), or "whom the Lord knew face to face" (*Deut.* 34:10). Furthermore, the description of Moses—the skin of Moses' face sent forth beams (*Ex.* 35)—evokes descriptions of Akhenaton as reflecting the rays of Aton.

There are to this day no definitive findings proving the influence of Akhenaton's philosophy on Moses. That is not enough, however, to rule out such influence. According to Freud, Moses was the conduit through which the ideas of El Amarna reached the Hebrews. It is difficult to assess the extent of Moses' contribution. It is clear however, that during the Amarna Period, there were close ties between Egypt and Canaan, which was under Egyptian rule. It is also possible that impressions of Egyptian religion may have reached scribes at the Jerusalem court, through the medium of Canaanite scribes.

The uniqueness of Moses' belief lies in the fact that it appeared when the time was ripe for it, allowing it to achieve full development. This was not the case however, with the religion of Akhenaton, which died with the king—although a handful of zealots may have continued to adhere to it in secret. All that remains of it are a few literary inscriptions and works of art. Egyptian historiographers tried to blot out the memory of Akhenaton, and they nearly succeeded; while the religion of Israel—in which the name YHWH has served as a manifest symbol of monotheistic belief linked to the name of Moses, developed, evolved, and lives on to this day.

Freud's theory of monotheism and its Egyptian origins explains how an ethical-abstract conception—foreign to a polytheistic world—took root in the Jewish People. By means of psychoanalytical processes, Freud tried to understand how a people of slaves, apparently no different from other peoples, developed in an entirely different way, leaving its mark—through Moses, herald of monotheism—on world history. Freud thus transformed the figure of Moses from a concrete historical figure to a timeless, universal one.

Bryna Jocheved Levy

Va'era – I Appeared

Samuel David Luzzatto's Interpretation of the Ten Plagues

The Lord said to Moses, "Early in the morning present
yourself to Pharaoh and say to him, 'Thus says the Lord,
the God of the Hebrews: Let my people go to worship Me.
For this time I will send all My plagues upon your person,
and your courtiers, and your people, in order that
you may know that there is none like Me in all the world'."

(*Exodus* 9:13–14)

Throughout the generations, thinkers have sought to discover meaning within the *extraordinary chastisements* which we call the *ten plagues* (*makkot*). Little wonder, after all; since the Creation they represent the greatest act of intervention by God in the natural order. There were those commentators who analyzed the structure of the plagues, others who dealt with content, but all in an effort to understand just exactly what was the nature of the ten plagues inflicted upon the Egyptians. The controlling purpose behind the extensive and multi-faceted analysis was to establish that the plagues were not random vicissitudes of nature (although they were natural disorders), but rather, deliberate and purposeful acts of Divine will.

In the realms of philosophy and theology, the *ten plagues* provide the key to unlocking the mysteries of God's governance of the world; on the level of *peshat* (the literal reading of Scripture) their intent is portrayed as three dimensional—coercive, retributive, and educative.

According to the Torah, the intended purpose of the plagues was to force the Egyptians to let the Israelites out of Egypt. At the burning bush, God informs Moses: "Yet I know that the king of Egypt will let you go only because of a greater might. So I will stretch out My hand and smite Egypt with various wonders which I will work upon them; after that he shall let you go." (*ibid.* 3:19-20).

This refrain appears again and again throughout the plagues, as for example in the case of the plague of frogs "If you refuse to let them go, then I will plague your whole country with frogs." (*ibid.* 7:27); and the plague of the locusts: "For if you refuse to let My people go, tomorrow I will bring locusts on your territory" (*ibid.* 10:4).

What is missing from these verses is some mention of the fact that the plagues were just that—*makkot*—severe punishments inflicted incessantly upon the Egyptian people. It is interesting that the Bible does not state the obvious, the correlation between the Egyptians' crimes and their punishment, in terms of cause and effect; something along the lines of "since they have enslaved you mercilessly, I will therefore bring My *makkot* upon them." This, it would seem, is self-explanatory.

· The biblical account does, however, stress the fact that the plagues were intended to demonstrate the presence, power, and supremacy of the God of Israel. Regarding the plague of blood, the Bible states: Thus says the Lord, "By this you shall know that I am the Lord." See, I shall strike the water in the Nile with the rod that is in my hand, and it will be turned into blood" (*ibid.* 7:17); and of the plague of wild beasts "But on that day I will set apart the region of Goshen, where My people dwell, so that no swarms of insects shall be there, that you may know that I the Lord am in the midst of the land" (*ibid.* 8:18). The same idea is repeated twice in the verses pertaining to the plague of pestilence: "For this time I will send all My plagues upon your person, and your courtiers, and your people, in order that you may know that there is none like Me in all the world" (*ibid.* 9:14); and "Nevertheless I have spared you for this purpose: in order to show you My power, and in order that My fame may resound throughout the world" (*ibid.* 16); reaching a climax at the time of the plague of hail: "Plead with the Lord that there may be an end of God's thunder and of hail. I will let you go; you need stay no longer, so that you may know that the earth is the Lord's" (*ibid.* 29).

Philosophers and biblical commentators alike, in their analyses of the biblical narrative, focused on the efficacy of the plagues as instruments of punishment and instruction. Maimonides presents the plagues as a fitting and commensurate punishment for Pharaoh's crimes:

And a man may commit a sin so great or many sins, that when he is called to justice before the True Judge, his punishment for the sins he has committed willingly and knowingly will be that he will be denied [the opportunity] to repent, and will be prevented from returning from his iniquity, so that he will die and perish in the sin that he committed ... And that is why it is written in the Torah "and I will harden Pharaoh's heart". Because he first sinned of his own volition and inflicted harm upon the Israelites living in his land, as it is written "come let us deal wisely with them", it was decreed that he be denied [the opportunity] to repent, until he had been punished. And that is why God hardened his heart, and why he sent Moses to him, telling him to let [them] go, and to repent, although God had already said to him you will not let them go, as it is written "but as for thee and thy servants, I know." For this reason however, I have made thee to stand, that the world might know that when God prevents a sinner from repenting, he cannot repent, but will die in the iniquity that he first did of his own volition (*Hilkhot Teshuvah* 6,3; *cf.* Maimonides' Introduction to *Avot—Shemonah Perakim*, 8).

Maimonides cites the biblical story of the plagues in his discussion on the subject of free will and Divine providence; attempting to explain why Pharaoh was punished for refusing to let the Israelites out of Egypt, when it was, in fact, God who had prevented him from doing so, by hardening his heart. This question is only legitimate if one begins the story from the end. It is without basis, however, if we regard the hardening of Pharaoh's heart as a deserved punishment in itself, for his unforgivably cruel treatment of the Hebrew slaves, over a period of many years. Maimonides' contention is that the intransigence of Pharaoh was necessary in order to dole out to him the full measure of punishment he deserved for his sordid past.

Toward the end of the passage however, Maimonides also addresses the issue of the punishment's ultimate purpose. God did not annihilate the Egyptian people in an instant, or mete out a single punishment that would have compelled them to let the Israelites go. He carried out their sentence in a relentless fashion, blow by blow, locking the gates of repentance, effectively teaching Pharaoh and the world a lesson in the workings of divine justice.

Maimonides' explanation concerns the overarching purpose of the punishment, rather than the specific calamities with which God chose to smite the Egyptians. This aspect of the plagues was addressed by the Rabbis, who viewed them as embodying the principle of *lex talionis*; whereby not only the measure of punishment was commensurate with the transgression, but the specific plagues themselves were designed to fit the crime. A well known example of this notion is found in *Midrash Tanhuma* (*Va'era* 14):

> The Ten Plagues were all measure for measure. Blood: why did He bring blood upon them? Because they [the Egyptians] did not allow the daughters of Israel to purify themselves from their [menstrual] impurity, that they might not procreate ... Why did he bring frogs upon them? Because they enslaved the Israelites, telling them to bring them unclean foods. Therefore, "and the frogs came up" ... Why lice? Because they made the Israelites sweep the streets and the markets. Therefore, their dust was turned to lice and they would dig one cubit by one cubit and there was no dust there, as it is written "all the dust of the land became lice".

Midrash Tanhuma describes the correlation between crime and punishment. Other midrashic renditions provide an even more expansive account of the Egyptians' crimes, in order to explain and justify each and every plague. The following passage goes so far as to proviztians.

> God brought the plagues upon them according to the stratagems of kings. When a city rises up against a king of flesh and blood, he sends legions against it to surround it. First, he dams their aqueduct. If they mend their ways, well and good. If not, he brings noise-makers to harass them. If they mend their ways, well and good. If not, he plies them with arrows. If they mend their ways, well and good. If not, he assails them with barbarian forces. If they mend their ways, well and good. If not, he afflicts them with disease. If they mend their ways, well and good. If not, he fires pitch at them. If they mend their ways, well and good. If not, he hurls missiles at them. If they mend their ways, well and good. If not, he sets a multitude upon them. If they mend their

ways, well and good. If not, he imprisons them. If they mend their ways, well and good. If not, he kills their leaders. So God, came upon Egypt according to the stratagems of kings. First, he dammed their aqueduct, as it is written (*Ps.* 79) "and turned their rivers into blood". They did not mend their ways. He brought noise-makers upon them—these are the frogs. Rabbi Jose bar Hanina said that their croaking was worse than the destruction they wrought. They did not mend their ways. He fired arrows at them—these are the lice, as it is written "and the lice were in man and in beast', they pierced the flesh of the Egyptians like arrows" (*Tanhuma Bo* 4).

According to these midrashim, the choice of plagues was not arbitrary, but specifically designed to bring about Egypt's defeat. God neither forgave nor forgot the sins of the Egyptians. He fought fire with fire and meted out justice punishment by punishment for every heinous felony.

Both *Midrash Tanhuma* and Maimonides thus assert that the plagues were in fact punishments for the cruel treatment suffered by the Hebrew slaves under the Egyptian lash. By accentuating their literary architecture, the *makkot* become not only retributive but provide an educational dimension, an ultimate lesson in the workings of the Supreme Judge.

Further important pedagogic lessons can be derived from the plagues, as demonstrated by Samuel David Luzzatto (Shadal) in his commentary on the book of Exodus. Luzzatto's interpretation of the plagues provides a response to the method adopted by 18th century protestant Bible scholars—most notably, German historian and Bible scholar Johann Gottfried Eichhorn (1752–1827), considered one of the pioneers of modern biblical scholarship, in his book *Einleitung in das Alte Testament* (Göttingen, 1823–1824).

In his discussion of the purpose of the plagues, he contends that they were widespread and well-known natural phenomena in ancient Egypt. They were devoid of any miraculous content. His motivation to identify the plagues with natural occurrences was so strong that he even asserted the slaying of the firstborn was caused by the smallpox virus (*variola pestifere*), a virus he claimed struck only males!

Although Shadal rejected this approach from beginning to end—
from "blood" to "firstborn"—he was perfectly willing to accept the underlying principle behind it. He writes as follows:

"And all the waters that were in the Nile were turned to blood."
Eichhorn and others who follow in his footsteps assert that the
blood and all the other plagues were natural phenomena, occur-
ring annually in Egypt, and that Moses' intention was, in fact, to
make Pharaoh understand that it is the God of the Hebrews who
is behind all of these events, and that He rules the entire earth. Indeed it is well known that the waters of the Nile, when they have
risen over the Land of Egypt in the month of Tamuz, appear red
and thick (whether from the redness of the Ethiopian soil near
the source of the Nile, or from the proliferation of organisms that
redden the water in other lands as well, causing common folk to
believe that blood has rained down from heaven), and become
putrid, and are insalubrious to drink ... Moreover, it is inconceivable that Moses would have thought to persuade Pharaoh using
natural annual occurrences, without having first performed some
preternatural wonder" (commentary on *Exodus* 7:20).

According to Eichhorn, the plague of blood was one of two common
natural phenomena that give the Nile a reddish tint: the presence of red
silt from the river's sources, or large quantities of single-celled organisms in the water. Both phenomena give the impression that the water
has indeed turned to blood.

Shadal does not reject the premise that this plague was in fact a well-
known natural phenomenon. On the contrary, he incorporates it into the
theory of "miracle through a natural course of events," to which he sub-
scribes. He does, however, present a strong argument against Eichhorn
and his successors: if these were in fact common natural occurrences,
what value would the plagues in general—and the plague of blood in
particular—have had, in persuading and compelling Pharaoh to let the
Israelites go? Shadal resolves the dilemma in his own fashion:

It is well-known that even in His wonders, the Creator likes to
preserve the natural order somewhat. And so it was with the
plagues of Egypt. In my opinion, it is likely that these plagues

were familiar in Egypt to some extent, some in one year and some in another. However, they would not all have occurred in a single year. Moreover, there was some new dimension in each one—some aspect of the supernatural. In the case of the plague of blood, for example, we see that the intensity of the redness of the water was accompanied by something new and exceedingly detrimental that caused the fish to die—an occurrence of which not recorded in the reports of eye witnesses, thus proving that the putrefaction of the water was much greater than in other years and was preternatural, as if the water had actually turned to blood (*ibid.*).

Shadal offers two possible solutions to the problem of "why is this plague different from all other plagues" to which Egypt was accustomed? The first regards the time and frequency of the plagues: "And so with the plagues of Egypt, it may be the case that they occur naturally in Egypt, to some extent: some in one year and some in another. However, they would not all have occurred in a single year." (*ibid.*)

The Torah does not tell us how long the plagues lasted, individually (apart from blood and darkness), or in total. The Rabbis of the Mishnah (*Eduyot* 2,10) set the duration of "the judgment of the Egyptians" at twelve months. It is in reference to this time frame that Shadal suggests that the plagues were natural disasters, and that their frequency—within the span of a single year –would have aroused wonder in the hearts of Pharaoh and his subjects. He develops this idea further, in two directions. In the case of frogs, lice, wild beasts and darkness, he suggests that it may have been the intensity of the occurrences that was out of the ordinary. Regarding the plagues of locusts, the slaying of the firstborn, and again of frogs he cites the timing of the plagues themselves, how and when they commenced and ended, as proof of their miraculousness. Shadal's second solution pertains to the supernatural in all of the plagues as he notes: "and what is more, in each plague there was embedded a supernatural element".

The plagues of Egypt were in this regard natural disasters with a supernatural dimension. In the case of blood, for example, it was "... the putrefaction of the water. Although the reddishness of the water was a well-known phenomenon, on this occasion it resulted in the destruction of all living creatures in it, something of which there is no mention in the annals of Egyptian history". This principle plays an important role in Shadal's explanations of the nature of the various plagues. Regarding the plague of murrain he remarks: "And I will not deny that there was a natural element to it, but rather that it was accompanied by an element of the miraculous and the preternatural" (*ibid.* 9:3). He also addresses Eichhorn's claim that the plagues of lice and wild beasts precipitated an infestation of vermin that laid eggs on the vegetation, thereby infecting the flocks with murrain. He is prepared to accept this claim, but draws the line at Eichhorn's explanation of the fact that the flocks of the Hebrews were unaffected "because they were skilled in the art of healing livestock". Shadal argues rather that "*this* was the miraculous element!"

In his dispute with Eichhorn, Luzzatto employs further arguments. If the plagues were indeed common natural phenomena, the biblical account is sorely lacking. Eichhorn believed that the plague of boils was in fact an advanced stage of the plague of murrain. Luzzatto remarks (citing Ernst Freidrich Karl Rosenmüller, 1768–1835) that one would then have expected human beings to die, as well as livestock—a detail "Moses would not have failed to mention". With regard to the plague of darkness, which Eichhorn identifies as a *khamsin* (sandstorm), Luzzatto reaches the following conclusion:

> Eichhorn gains nothing by this, for that wind does not generally result in complete darkness, to the point that one may not see his fellow within his house. We know that great darkness has sometimes occurred in Egypt, but it has always been caused by a great sand storm, of which there is no mention here (*ibid.* 10:21).

Scripture's silence regarding these important details speaks for itself. Eichhorn presents the lack of Egyptian historiographical documentation of unusual plagues of remarkable force, as further proof of the fact that they were indeed ordinary occurrences. Shadal returns the ball to Eichhorn's court, asserting that the lack of documentation of these or similar plagues would seem to indicate that they were out of the ordinary. Concerning the plague of frogs, for example, he writes: "See the lengths to which this unbeliever will go in his insolence—claiming that the proliferation of frogs and their stealing into homes was a natural phenomenon in Egypt that occurs every year, despite the fact that no one has ever witnessed or mentioned any such thing!" (*ibid.* 7:27).

The be all and end all is Eichhorn's presentation of the final plague—the slaying of the firstborn—either as a virus that struck only firstborn males, or as the direct result of the actions of Moses and his followers, who passed through Egypt with swords drawn to slay all the firstborn. Shadal responds as follows: "See how many absurdities the unbelievers will heap upon themselves merely to avoid accepting the fact that God performs miracles on earth—'so as to bring about the present result—the survival of many people'—that knowledge of His unity and His virtues may be perpetuated, for the benefit of all mankind" (*ibid.* 12:29).

This view, proposed by 18th century biblical criticism, was taken up again the in the 1950s, by scholar Greta Hort, who published two articles on the subject ("The Plagues of Egypt", *ZAW* 69, 84–103; *ZAW* 70, 48–59). Not only does Hort claim that each plague was consistent with prevailing conditions in Egypt at the time, but she links the plagues to one another through a logical, natural chain of events. The plague of blood was caused by flagellated protozoa of the *euglena sanguinea* and *haematococcus pluvialis* species that resulted from an over-oxygenation of the waters of the Nile. This over-oxygenation killed the fish, thereby changing the frogs' ecological biotope, and forcing them onto land. The frogs' deaths brought about the proliferation of the anthrax bacteria (*bacillus anthrax*), and precipitated the proliferation of the stable flies (*stomoxys calcitrans*) that transmitted the bacteria to livestock, causing the plague of murrain, and so forth. Like Eichhorn, Hort faced the problem of the plague of the slaying of the firstborn—a manifestly miraculous plague. She found a creative solution however, replacing "firstborn children" with "first fruits", in order to avoid the complications created by the interpretive limitations she herself had imposed!

Shadal's method of "miracles through a natural course of events" offers a further advantage, inasmuch as it shifts the center of gravity in terms of the purpose of the plagues. Emphasis is thus placed not on punishment, but on the important lesson the plagues provided, regarding the forces of nature and the real power behind them. According to Shadal, the plagues made a deep theological impression on the Egyptians.

The Egyptian pantheon comprised over five hundred deities. There was no force of nature that was not represented in this pantheon. The plagues as supernatural "natural disasters" were thus an attack against the gods of Egypt, as the Bible indeed states: "For that night I will go through the land of Egypt and strike down every first-born in the land of Egypt, both man and beast; and I will mete out punishments to all the gods of Egypt, I am the Lord." (*Ex.* 12:12).

Accordingly, the first plague of blood was directed against the Nile, in its capacity a chief deity in the Egyptian pantheon. It may have been intended as an attack on either the god Khnum, creator of water, or the Nile-god Hapi. The plague of frogs was directed against the god Heket—goddess of fertility, whose symbol was the frog. The uncontrolled proliferation of the frogs was intended to prove which god was truly in charge! This approach is further corroborated by the plague of darkness, which usurped the authority of the sun-god *Ra*. According to Shadal, it is, in fact, the supernatural element in each plague that attests to God's supremacy: through the plagues, the transcendent God of the Hebrews outstretched His mighty hand and vanquished the gods of Egypt.

We may ask: if the purpose of the plagues of Egypt was instruction, who were the students, the objects of that instruction? Shadal does not address the question directly, but the Bible itself would appear to provide a clear answer: that the Egyptians might finally know "that there is none like Me in all the world". However, the lesson of theological fine tuning regarding the plagues may have been directed not only towards the Egyptians, but towards the Hebrews who resided in their midst.

This is indeed the opinion of Don Isaac Abravanel:

The purpose of the plagues was to demonstrate the greatness of God ... The truth is, in my opinion, that Egypt was a metropolis full of idols defying and undermining the very foundations of God's divinity. There were those among the Hebrews who did not believe in His existence, those... who believed in His existence, but not in His providence over the lower world ... and some who believed His power to be limited, like that of other heavenly hosts ... These [*makkot*] therefore proved that His existence is irrefutable, that His providence regards Israel in particular, and that His ability is boundless ... You will thus find that Moses first said "In this thou shalt know that I am the Lord", that is the existence of a First Cause, and brought three plagues to verify this: blood, frogs and lice ... And before the fourth plague, that is wild beasts, he said "that thou mayest know that I am the Lord in the midst of the earth", that He is omniscient and exercises providence over all men. And to verify this came three plagues: wild beasts, murrain and boils ... And before the seventh plague, that is hail, he said "that thou mayest know that there is none like me in all the earth", that God is all-powerful, and to this end came the four final plagues: hail, locusts, darkness and the slaying of the firstborn (Abravanel, Commentary on *Exodus*, 7, pg. 63).

Abravanel depicts the Hebrews as estranged from the knowledge of the Lord, God of Israel. There were those among them that no longer believed in Him at all, and those that did not believe in His Providence, and others that thought His power limited like that of other gods. The plagues were divided in three categories; corresponding to these three misconceptions. Through them the Hebrew spirit might be mended, awakened from its religious slumber, that it might know that God exists, that He is provident, mighty and awesome for all eternity.

We have thus seen that the plagues of Egypt were not merely a method by which to punish the Egyptians, but they had an educational purpose as well. Luzzatto saw the plagues as pedagogical tools. Through them, it was possible to learn and teach God's way in governing the world, according to the principle of "miracles through a natural course". Luzzatto's hermeneutical method provided a response to the biblical critics who sought to eradicate the miraculous component of the plagues, describing them rather as manifestly natural phenomena. In his interpretation of the plagues, Luzzatto tried to strike an appropriate balance between the critical approach based on prevailing conditions in ancient Egypt, and the profound belief in God's ability to perform miracles. His goal, as he explained, was to lead to deeper understanding: "that God performs miracles on earth—'so as to bring about the present result—the survival of many people'—that knowledge of His unity and His virtues may be perpetuated, for the benefit of all mankind" (commentary on *Exodus* 12:29).

Shlomo Tikochinski

Bo – Go to Pharaoh

Miracle and Nature in the Thought of Nahmanides

And thou shalt tell thy son in that day, saying: It is because of
that which the Lord did for me when I came forth out of Egypt.
And it shall be for a sign unto thee upon thy hand, and for a memorial between thine eyes, that the law of the Lord may be in thy
mouth; for with a strong hand hath the Lord brought thee out of
Egypt (*Exodus* 13:8–9)

Bo is a key section of the Torah, containing the Exodus and
the commandment to observe the Passover, as well as precepts
intended to preserve the memory of the Exodus for posterity.
Rabbi Moses ben Nahman (Nahmanides, or Ramban) concludes his
commentary on *Bo* with a special homily on these commemorative precepts. He relates specifically to the precept of *tefilin*, which appears toward the end of the portion, and which belongs to this category:

And now I will tell you a basic principle, underlying many of
the precepts. For since the advent of idolatry in the world, in the
time of Enosh, opinions in matters of faith have become confused ... "And they said the Lord hath forsaken the land." When
God elects a certain group or individual, and performs a miracle for them contrary to the natural order, the falseness of these
opinions becomes manifest to all, for the wondrous sign proves
that the world has a renewing, omniscient, providential and omnipotent God ... evidencing Providence; that they have not been
left to chance, as they believe ... For the Egyptians denied or
doubted all of this, and the great signs and wonders bore faithful
witness to belief in the Creator and in the entire Torah.

And because the Holy One, blessed be He, does not perform
signs and wonders in every generation, before every wicked person or unbeliever, He commanded us always to make a memorial

and token of that which our eyes had seen, and to convey this to our children and our children to their children and their children, until the end of days ... And we are required to write all that has been shown to us, truly, with signs and wonders—on our arms, and between our eyes, and on the doorposts of our homes, and utter it morning and evening ... and make a tabernacle every year, and so all of the many similar precepts commemorating the exodus from Egypt; to serve in every generation, as a testimony to the wonders, lest they be forgotten, and to silence unbelievers who would deny divine belief. For one who buys a *mezuzah* for one coin and affixes it to his doorpost, with the correct intention, thereby affirms the [constant] renewal of creation, and acknowledges the Creator and His Providence, as well as prophecy, and belief in all aspects of the Torah" (Nahmanides, *Commentary on the Torah*, Exodus 13:16).

In other words, the purpose of miracles is to proclaim God and His Providence to all creation. Unlike the generation of the Exodus however, not every generation or individual is worthy of witnessing God's supernatural intervention in history. Symbolic acts were instituted, therefore, to convey the experience of the divine presence to future generations. The precepts given as "a remembrance for the Exodus from Egypt" were not intended merely to afford meta-historical significance to the great miracles, but primarily as a means to "refute false beliefs," to heighten awareness of the miraculous, and to foster faith in perpetuity. The daily and annual rituals established in the generation of the Exodus serve to transmit the experience of the miraculous to the next generation which did not witness it, and must therefore be satisfied with rituals that embody the faith-idea behind the miracle.

The role of such precepts does not end there however. Nahmanides ascribes an educational purpose to them—to teach those who observe the commandments to believe in the perpetuity of miraculous Providence. Although the miracles of the exodus were unique events, they were intended to demonstrate God's involvement in everything around us, at all times. Nahmanides offers a brief summary of his views on miracles:

And from the great and renowned miracles one acknowledges the hidden miracles, that are the very foundation of the Torah, for a man can have no share in the Torah of Moses until he believes that everything that befalls us, whether collectively or individually, is a miracle, beyond nature and natural order. If one observes the commandments his reward will make him successful, and if he violates them his punishment will destroy him— entirely by heavenly decree, as noted above; while on a collective level, the hidden miracles are revealed in the fulfillment of the Torah's promises (*ibid.*).

Similarly, in his famous sermon, "*Torat Hashem Temimah*" (*Kitvei Ramban*, C. B. Chavel ed., vol.1, p. 153), Nahmanides writes:

Upon careful examination, we discover that one can have no share in the Torah of Moses until he believes that everything that befalls us is a miracle, beyond nature and natural order, for the promises of the Torah are wholly miraculous and wondrous. For there is no apparent difference between a righteous man who lives out his span of eighty years, in peace and safety, without illness, and one who eats of the priestly tithes and dies.

Some have identified Nahmanides' views with those of the medieval Islamic school of the *Kalam*, which categorically denied the existence of natural laws, attributing the natural order of the universe to the constant renewal of divine will. Maimonides, in *The Guide for the Perplexed* (III, 17), attacks both the Mutazilites and the Asharites, refuting their respective positions by philosophical argument. Nahmanides' commentary on *Job* (36:7) attenuates this conclusion somewhat, inasmuch as it limits miraculous Providence to the select few who faithfully cleave to God:

He withdraweth not His eyes from the righteous—This verse explains a matter of great importance with regard to Providence; one addressed in many verses. For men of Torah and perfect faith believe in Providence: that God watches over and preserves members of the human race ... And for this reason, He preserves the righteous, for just as their hearts and eyes are always with Him, so the eyes of the Lord are upon them from the beginning

of the year even unto the end of the year; to the point that one
who is utterly pious—who cleaves to his God always, and is
not separated from him in his thoughts by mundane concerns—
will always be safe from chance occurrences, even in the natural
course of events, and will be miraculously preserved from them,
as if part of an exalted group, not subject to nature and the vagaries of time. As he cleaves to God, so will be his preservation.
And he who is distant from God in thought and deed, even if
he does not deserve death for his sin, will be cast out and left
to chance ... And this is the subject of many verses: David [*sic*]
said: "He will keep the feet of His holy ones, but the wicked
shall be put to silence in darkness". That is to say that those who
are close to Him are preserved absolutely, while those who are
far from Him are left to chance, with no one to save them from
harm, like one who walks in the darkness and is apt to stumble if
he is not cautious and does not walk slowly ... And because most
of the world belongs to this middle group, the Torah commanded
that some be exempted from battle by the priest anointed for
war—that those who are frightened might return home, lest they
melt their brethren's heart as their own; and so the order of battle set forth in the Pentateuch and the Prophets ... For if they are
worthy, they may go out to war in few and be victorious without
weapons, and if they are destined to be defeated, a great host
will not avail them, for they are rightly subject to the natural
order and the vagaries of fortune.

Providence is thus a direct function of man's adherence to God, in
thought and deed. One whose mind does not stray from God for a single
moment sets Providence in motion, and even intensifies its effect. One
who is distant from God, however, is abandoned by Providence, "cast
out and left to chance," subject to the vicissitudes of the natural order
of the universe. Between these two extremes, lies the "middle group"—
those who do not adhere sufficiently to God—which comprises most of
mankind. Accordingly, this group is governed not by Providence, but by
the fixed laws of nature. The Torah therefore includes many commandments that pertain to the "way of the world", such as war, statecraft, ag-

riculture, etc. Nahmanides, in his commentary on the Pentateuch (*Deut.* 11:13), further clarifies this position: "And know that miracles, for good or for ill, are performed only for the wholly righteous or the wholly wicked. Those in between are treated, for good or for ill, in keeping with the natural order of the world, 'by their way and by their doings'."

Nahmanides' approach to Providence and miracles demands further study, particularly in relation to other thinkers of his day. What is the relationship between the miraculous and the natural order? Is the difference inherent or merely semantic, in keeping with one's proximity to the divine? Are Providence and the miraculous one and the same in the thought of Nahmanides?

In his article "*Torat Ha-ness Ve-hateva Etzel Ramban, Ve-zikata Le-rabi Yehudah Halevi*" [Nahmanides' Theory of Miracle and Nature, and its Relation to Rabbi Judah Halevi (*Daat* 17, 5746)], Michael Zvi Nehorai argues that Nahmanides' approach is based entirely on the philosophy of Rabbi Judah Halevi, as presented in the *Kuzari*. Halevi posits two types of creation: one, an immediate expression of divine will, such as the heavens or the first tablets given to Moses; the other is an act of constant renewal and generation through natural causes, like fire that burns what is in its path. He explains that although the manifestly miraculous can be distinguished from the natural order, the natural cannot be distinguished from the miraculous. He denies the independent existence of natural forces, ascribing their perpetual function to the divine will that acts through them. Divine will thus plays a role even in the ever-renewing phenomena of nature, inasmuch as material causes lack the power of renewal—but for the divine cause. It is the latter cause that affords form to everything endowed with form, determining the appearance, extent and context of every act of nature.

In the same vein, Nahmanides distinguishes between manifest miracles and "natural" miracles—i.e. those that appear to stem from the normal order of things. It is only those acts performed before all of Israel and explicitly described in the Bible as such, that Nahmanides ascribes to manifest miraculous Providence. Nahmanides defines all other events that occur to individuals or even the Jewish People, as natural miracles, concealed within the ordinary workings of the universe. These "natural miracles" are indeed paradoxical and beyond our understanding, since we do not, intuitively, identify occurrences governed by natural laws, as miracles. Nahmanides addresses this difficulty in his commentary on *Exodus* 6:2:

> For good will not be visited upon a man in reward for his observance of the precepts, or ill as punishment for their violation, except by miracle. If a man is abandoned to nature or fortune, his actions can neither benefit nor harm him. The Torah's rewards and punishments in this world however, are all hidden miracles, perceived as part of the natural order, when they are in truth man's punishment and reward.

Rabbi A. I. Kook (*Orot Hakodesh, Mussar Hakodesh*, 17) made a similar distinction. He asserted that the world is governed according to principles of general morality, applied to personal morality in the form of reward and punishment—reflected in the divine name *Elohim*. There is however, a higher level of Providence, associated not with morality and free choice, but with a supernal vision that transcends temporal considerations and time itself. That is the meaning of the Tetragrammaton (*YHWH*)—a name that comprises past, present and future (metatemporal); and that is the Providence associated with the chosenness of Israel.

In any event, according to Nahmanides, miracles—whether manifest or hidden—pertain exclusively to the application of divine will to the People of Israel, the principal nation among men.

Miraculous Providence also provides a framework for Nahmanides' three tenets of faith, established in *Torat Hashem Temimah:* constant renewal of creation (*hidush*), omniscience (*yedi'ah*), and Providence (*hashgahah*). The particular importance of miracles is reflected in the prominence given to precepts that exemplify and perpetuate the signs and wonders performed by God in the Jewish People's formative period—including, *inter alia*, the precepts of *mezuzah, tefilin*, Passover, *sukah*, and the Sabbath.

We will not go into all of the differences between Nahmanides and Maimonides with regard to miracles and the natural order. Let it suffice to note that there is a clear difference between the two in terms of the emphasis accorded the connection between the precepts and the principles of faith. Due to Maimonides' tendency to attach philosophical significance to the tenets of Judaism, most of his principles do not correspond to specific precepts. Nahmanides on the other hand, views specific precepts as ends unto themselves—as illustrated in the classic passage cited at the beginning of this essay concerning the precept of *mezuzah*. In fulfilling the precept of *mezuzah*, with the appropriate intention, one affirms all of the principles of Judaism: the constant renewal of creation, omniscience and Providence.

The concept "hidden miracle" or "natural miracle" comes to resolve the apparent contradiction between belief in divine Providence, and the fact that such Providence is not felt in the world, nor is there any clear historical evidence that it has ever been so. The theological justification for such miracles is that God does not wish His presence to be overly felt, because this might undermine the principle of free choice. The Rabbis of the Talmud and the Midrash thus show a general aversion to miracles and manifest signs (as seen in the story of Akhnai's Oven, *Bava Metzia* 59b), since ideally one should not need miracles to sustain one's faith.

What then is a "miracle"? Before we embark upon a discussion of miracles, we must first establish a definition of the term. The Hebrew word *nes* has two meanings: (1) something wondrous, out of the ordinary, inexplicable; and (2) a flag or banner. Etymologists have suggested a common source for both meanings. The Bible tells the story of the copper snake, fashioned by Moses and placed atop a pole: "And Moses made a serpent of copper, and set it upon the pole (*nes*); and it came to pass, that if a serpent had bitten any man, when he looked unto the serpent of copper, he lived" (Numbers 21:9). The pole was high, visible from a distance, possibly indicating its uncommonness, or in other words, a miracle. The word *nes*, in the sense of a wondrous occurrence, does not appear in the Bible, which refers to such events as "wonders" (*moftim*) or "signs" (*otot*). The current usage of *nes*, in the sense of "miracle", can be traced to the talmudic and midrashic literature. The word *teva* (nature), used to denote the unmiraculous, has its origins in medieval, rather than biblical or even talmudic-midrashic literature.

A miracle is thus a deviation from the natural order of things. Nahmanides however, views the perpetual order of creation as a "natural miracle". In many ways, this approach coincides with that of the Bible itself, which often describes the permanent order of the universe as expressing God's praise. Jeremiah, for example, declares: "Thus saith the Lord, Who giveth the sun for a light by day, and the ordinances of the moon and of the stars for a light by night, who stirreth up the sea, that the waves thereof roar, the Lord of hosts is His name: If these ordinances depart from before me, saith the Lord, then the seed of Israel also shall cease from being a nation before me for ever" (31:34–35). That is to say that God's hosts—the light of the sun, moon and stars, the stirring sea and the roaring waves; all part of the natural order—are the Creator's true praise. The destiny of the Jewish People is also contingent upon the fixed order of these hosts—the perpetual order of creation.

Many talmudic legends reflect this idea of the miraculous concealed within the natural, asserting that God's might should be seen in the fixed order that He established. We find for example, in the tractate *Ta'anit* (7a):

> Rabbi Abahu said: A day of rainfall is greater than the resurrection of the dead, for the resurrection of the dead benefits only the righteous, while the rain benefits the righteous and the wicked alike ... Rabbi Yehudah said: A day of rainfall is greater than the day on which the Torah was given, as it is written, "My doctrine shall drop as the rain" (*Deut.* 32:2)—and doctrine is Torah, as it is written, "For I give you good doctrine; forsake ye not my teaching" (*Prov.* 4:2). Rava said: Greater than the day on which the Torah was given, since it is written "My doctrine shall drop as the rain"—a lesser thing is compared to a greater one.

What then is the role of the supernatural miracle? According to Nahmanides, it is the exception that proves the rule. Its main purpose is to strengthen the belief that all is governed by God, highlighting the order and natural laws He created in His universe, rather than drawing attention to its own extraordinariness. In the succession of supernatural events associated with the Exodus, the restoration of natural order is an essential part of each and every miracle. Thus when Moses turns the serpent back into a rod, when his leprous hand regains its normal aspect, and when nature returns to its course after each of the plagues—as a fundamental part of the miracles themselves—God's power over creation is manifested. The need for the aberration is explained by the fact that the laws of nature are constant—concealing God's intervention in a confusion of details. Only a miracle can demonstrate God's ability and will to uphold them and ensure their continuity. The difference between the natural order and the aberration is purely a matter of perception, or more precisely, habit. To the master of both order and aberration, they are one and the same. We however, must experience the aberration in order to discover the true nature of the universal order and God's might. It is this idea that Nahmanides sought to convey, in asserting that "from the great and renowned miracles one acknowledges the hidden miracles"—i.e. the principle of the "natural miracle".

What is the difference between a "natural miracle" and "Providence" in Nahmanidean thought?

On the subject of Providence in rabbinical literature, Ephraim E. Urbach wrote (*Hazal: Pirkei Emunot Vede'ot*, p. 228):

> The concept of *hashgahah* (Providence) was, as we know, invented by the Ibn Tibbons. The Sages had no similar term, but found references to the idea of Providence throughout the Pentateuch, Prophets and Writings, and frequently observed its ways, contemplated its nature and pondered its meaning. This Providence has two facets, the first of which concerns the superintendence of the universe—governing nature and providing for the needs of all creatures. This type of Providence is extended to all, even the wicked and the idolatrous nations. The other facet of Providence is the scrutiny of human beings and their actions, described as follows by the prophet Jeremiah: "great in counsel, and mighty in work; whose eyes are open upon all the ways of the sons of men, to give every one according to his ways, and according to the fruit of his doings" (34:19). God is a judging God and a God of justice, and therefore necessarily oversees the actions of his creatures and knows their doings. Only one who denies his existence will say "there is neither justice nor judge" (*Leviticus Rabbah* 28,1).

The question arises, what is the relationship between these two facets of Providence? What is the connection between providing for the needs of all creatures and the system of divine retribution, i.e. the scrutiny of their actions? Can the actions of man, possessed of free choice, and eliciting reward or punishment, influence the ways of Providence? Or are man's actions too, merely details within processes wholly governed by divine will? Are the actions of both the righteous and the wicked—like their punishments and rewards—in fact determined by God? Is twofold Providence really no more than a "twofold decree"—ordained not by fate or natural law, but by God? This question engaged medieval philosophers, such as Saadiah Gaon, Maimonides, Judah Halevi and others.

Nahmanides theory of Providence would appear to support the first possibility, whereby the system of personal retributive Providence exerts an influence on the general Providence that establishes the fixed order of the universe. In other words, the "natural miracle" stresses the aberration within the natural order, because it concerns the majority of mankind, who have not yet attained the highest levels of adherence to God. Nahmanides would certainly agree with Maimonides on a basic level, that "Divine Providence is related and closely connected with the intellect, because Providence can only proceed from an intelligent being ... Those creatures, therefore, which receive part of the intellectual influence, will become subject to the actions of Providence in the sane proportion as they are acted upon by the Intellect" (*Guide for the Perplexed* III, 17 –tr. M. Friedlander, Routledge, London, 1904). In keeping with his views regarding miracles as cornerstones of faith however, Nahmanides would not concur with Maimonides' metaphysical observations. According to Nahmanides' kabbalistic conception of the centrality of the Jewish People to creation, and Israel's unique status as God's chosen people, it is in upholding the Covenant that one will come to cleave to God and believe in his general Providence. It is only this belief, embodied in the precepts given as "a remembrance for the exodus from Egypt"—emphasizing the miraculous in nature—that the natural order is maintained, eventually leading to individual Providence, i.e. the supernaturally miraculous.

Yehoyada Amir

Beshalah – When Pharaoh had Let the People Go

"The Kingdom of Heaven" in the Thought of *Spinoza*, *Mendelssohn and Buber*

And it came to pass, when Pharaoh had let the people go, that God led them not by the way of the land of the Philistines, although that was near; for God said: "Lest peradventure the people repent when they see war, and they return to Egypt" (*Exodus* 13:17)

Beshalah describes the historic moment between the Israelites' departure from Egypt and their receipt of the Torah. It opens with the Hebrew slaves' dramatic removal to the desert. God does not lead them "by the way of the land of the Philistines, although that was near" (*ibid.*). He knows that this band of newly freed slaves is as yet unable to contend with liberty and struggle for a place in the world. They must first wander in the desert, shaping their personal and collective identity, before they can enter the Land and wage war against its inhabitants. Although the Israelites themselves feel as if they have gone out "with a high hand" to fulfill their destiny, a casual observer might be tempted to remark: "They are entangled in the land, the wilderness hath shut them in" (14:3). This is the backdrop for the Israelites' final encounter with their former enslavers. At first, they are seized with terror, stranded on the seashore, with the Egyptian host fast approaching. The encounter concludes however, with the miraculous splitting of the sea, the drowning of the Egyptians and the knowledge that the divine promise "for whereas ye have seen the Egyptians to-day, ye shall see them again no more for ever" (*ibid.* 13) has been fulfilled. The sons and daughters of Israel are now free to sing songs of praise and thanksgiving.

The Israelites are finally free to pursue their destiny. They have left slavery behind, and no longer fear pursuit. They find themselves in the

195

desert, and must seek out their physical and spiritual path. The God of their fathers appeared to them and took them out of Egypt, but the land of the fathers is still a long way off. Although given "a statute and an ordinance" at Marah—the very first encampment after the crossing of the sea—and their first commandment regarding the Sabbath, shortly thereafter; these are mere hints of the great drama to come: the giving of the Torah and the establishment of their distinctive spiritual path. Only at Mount Sinai—described at length in the portion of *Yitro*—will they receive the Ten Commandments and the entire code of Torah law. *Beshalah* describes the very beginning of their journey.

This state of having left the sovereign authority of one nation, but not yet having developed another form of sovereignty, captured the imagination of Baruch (Benedictus) Spinoza (1632–1677), the first modern Jewish thinker. Spinoza subscribed to the theory of the "social contract", which developed over the course of the 17th and 18th centuries—particularly among French and English philosophers such as Thomas Hobbes, John Locke and Jean-Jacques Rousseau—and presaged a turning point in the history of political philosophy.

Advocates of social contract theory strove to examine the significance of man's political existence from a new perspective. The mere Aristotelian observation that man is a naturally political animal did not suffice any more; they were seeking to discover the full implications of the fact that the state is a human construct. The existence of states—or more precisely, the fact that human society, at any given time and place, exists within a political framework—means that the state fulfills a function in human life. In order to understand the essence of this function, they argued, one must discover what would be lacking were there no state, and how the state satisfies this deficiency. To this end they sought, each in his own way, to describe human society in a pre-state condition they termed the "state of nature"—i.e. a state of existence entirely lacking political or legal structures. In the state of nature, individuals live life to the best of their ability to fulfill their needs and desires; associating with others on a purely temporary and voluntary basis.

Some of the social contract philosophers stressed the fact that the state of nature precludes the realization of man's full spiritual and cultural potential; and in this they saw its deficiency—the very deficiency that justifies its abandonment in favor of the political state. To others, Spinoza included, the essence of the state of nature lies in the fact that it places no legal strictures upon man's actions. Each and every individual does as she or he pleases, on the sole condition that they are able to do so. This absolute freedom is also the freedom to murder, steal and rape. Its real meaning is thus perpetual insecurity and anxiety. For even if I succeed in taking what I desire today, eventually someone stronger than me will take the bread from my mouth, threaten my life or make it a living hell. Accordingly, the reason behind the decision to abandon the absolute freedom of the natural state is the desire to create a framework that will guarantee individual needs and security, by establishing and enforcing a set of basic rules. The "state of nature" is abandoned when a group of people living in that state choose a sovereign and entrust their rights to that sovereign. Henceforth, members of the group may do only that which the sovereign permits, but may also rest assured that those around them will not harm them.

This description is generally cited for purposes of theoretical analysis. The social contract philosophers, for the most part, did not claim that human beings had actually lived in a state of nature up to a certain point in time, at the dawn of human history or shortly thereafter, when contracts were drafted, establishing the various states. The biblical narrative provides Spinoza with the opportunity to lend historical substance to this theoretical construct. The newly liberated people of slaves described in *Beshalah*, is portrayed in his *Theologico-Political Treatise* as existing in a state of nature. The Israelites are no longer subject to Egyptian authority, with all of its horrors; they are in the desert, in no-man's land, and must choose a sovereign, who will assume the task of legislation.

The Israelites indeed choose a sovereign who gives them a code of law, thereby establishing the political framework that would govern national life for many generations. Unlike all other peoples however, the Israelites did not elect a flesh and blood sovereign, but God, as king and legislator of the state established in the desert, who—if obeyed—would guarantee the citizens of the new theocracy internal order and the purported security of political existence.

What does this mean? Spinoza did not believe in a supernatural God who reveals Himself to man and addresses his needs and hardships. God, in Spinoza's eyes, was identical to the natural order of the universe. His will is the laws of nature, and His decisions are events deriving from that order. The assertion that Israel chose its God as sovereign and that the events at Mount Sinai exemplify this choice can be understood in one of two ways. Spinoza may have seen the entire matter as an illusion. The people believed that they had chosen God as their sovereign and that He had revealed Himself to them, when in fact they had merely witnessed a natural phenomenon—volcanic or otherwise—for God does not reveal Himself or speak. In any event, the Torah itself recounts how, during the course of the event, the people– frightened by God's speech—renounced their right to experience the revelation directly, asking of Moses: "Speak thou with us, and we will hear; but let not God speak with us, lest we die" (20:15). In this, Spinoza identifies the first crack in the Israelites' theocracy. Henceforth, the people are no longer guided directly by the word of God; Moses is given the exclusive right to interpret God's commandments, and it is his word alone that is afforded the force of law.

Spinoza's analysis can also be understood in another vein—one intimated in Thomas Hobbes' *Leviathan* (originally titled: *Leviathan, or The Matter, Forme and Power of a Common Wealth Ecclesiasticall and Civil*), with regard to the natural laws and "The Kingdom of God by Nature". According to this approach, Spinoza believed that God was in fact sovereign of the state founded at Sinai. The divine imperative arising from the first two commandments—those that, according to the Midrash, the people heard directly from God (e.g. *Song of Songs Rabbah* 1)—is essentially the imperative of rational ethics. A state of which God was supposed to have been sovereign, would have been established on the basis of these ethics, and citizens of such a state would have been expected to conduct themselves accordingly, without recourse to human law or enforcement. True theocracy is thus a state governed solely by the laws of ethics, requiring nothing else. The people's unwillingness to hear the divine injunction directly, preferring to vest authority in Moses, meant the *de facto* renunciation of theocracy; rendering their state like all others—governed by a human ruler and lawmaker. The laws of the resulting state no longer coincided with those of rational ethics; at best, bearing a partial resemblance to them.

Whatever the explanation, the laws of the state founded in the desert remained in force for as long as it continued to exist. As in any state, citizens were required to obey its laws—whether of the kind found in any civil constitution, or whether of a particular nature, such as the Sabbath or dietary laws. They became void upon the destruction of the state, as would be the case with any other state and any other constitution. For the very same reason that Jews were required to obey only the laws of their state, they must also obey the laws of other states in which they reside. The fact that the Jews stubbornly continued to obey laws no longer in force, is inconsequential. It is merely a testament to their incomprehensible obstinacy.

Spinoza, thus used a historical analysis of the passage from *Beshalah* to *Yitro* as a springboard for the subversion of Jewish existence. In the prevailing conditions in the 17th century, even in a liberal country such as Holland, there was no Jewish existence beyond the communities founded upon observance of Jewish law. The paradoxical assertion that consistency with the path set out by the Torah requires that we forsake the very same Torah as no longer valid, challenged the very existence of the Jewish People—in effect calling for its demise. What is more, this analysis provided the philosophical basis for the path taken by Spinoza himself—who openly and blatantly abandoned any semblance of religious observance, compelling the Jewish community to excommunicate him and strike him from its ranks. Excommunication allowed Spinoza to define himself as one who lived beyond all religious communal affiliation. He was no longer a member of the Jewish community, nor did he belong to any of the Christian communities. He was a citizen of the state, and no more; a unique and unprecedented state in the social and political environment of 17th century Europe. This state would be the province of all Jews who adopted Spinoza's approach, drawing its practical conclusions. They would be giving up their distinctiveness as members of the Jewish community, but in so doing would acquire a far more unique status—as founders of a supra-national society, impervious to the boundaries of religious communities and the authority of the religious establishment.

In questioning the very meaning of Jewish existence and the legitimacy of continued adherence to it—rooted in the Israelites' passage from the state described in *Beshalah* to the one described in the subsequent Torah portion—Spinoza presented modern Jewish thinkers with an inescapable challenge. If Jewish thought is the reflective and scholarly exploration of questions pertaining to Jewish existence, then all thought after Spinoza is, to a large extent, a direct or indirect attempt to address this challenge.

The first to take up the challenge was Moses Mendelssohn (1729–1786). Mendelssohn lived in Berlin, a generation before the French Revolution, and was one of the city's leading intellectuals. In his book *Jerusalem*, he addresses the claims of Christian intellectuals that an enlightened approach must necessarily lead an upstanding and broadminded man such as himself to Christianity and the renunciation of irrational Jewish beliefs. In the book, Mendelssohn evokes the history of the Jewish state founded in the desert. He does not mention Spinoza specifically, but clearly seeks to address the views of the great Jewish thinker of the previous century. He too sees the type of existence described in *Beshalah* as a state of nature, and also explains the events at Mount Sinai as the moment at which the law was given and the state established, with God as its sovereign. Mendelssohn however, does not see this merely as an expression of human choice, but first and foremost, as divine revelation. The law given at Sinai is the law of the state, but it is also God's law. Its validity is both political and religious. A Jew, as such, was therefore bound to uphold it, both as state law and divine imperative. The destruction of the state—many generations later—deprived the law only of its political authority, but could not abrogate its significance as a religious command.

What does this mean? To Mendelssohn, the essential difference between state and religion lies in the different social functions that each of these man-made institutions fulfills. Both aspire to a decent society, pervaded by truth and justice. The role of the state however, is to enforce certain types of behavior, without which there can be no security or justice. It has sufficient force to compel such behavior, but its strength is also its weakness. Coercion, by its very nature, can only affect actions; while human thoughts and feelings remain the private affair of the individual. The state can influence behavior, but only as a coercive force. It cannot educate. That must be the task of another social institution; one that would refrain from compulsion, concentrating rather on persuading and educating people to act honestly, because that is what both reason and God command. Such an institution is public religion.

There are two aspects to Mendelssohn's assertion that halakhic law is still religiously binding for contemporary Jews, although its political force expired with the fall of the Second Commonwealth. On the one hand, Mendelssohn believed with all his heart that a Jew must observe the halakhic precepts. No one has the right to abrogate divine commandments, and a good person must uphold them. This belief however, has no political ramifications. No one has the right to enforce the precepts by means that are the exclusive province of the state. It is paramount that the Jewish community refrain from exerting force or pressure upon its members to ensure their halakhic observance. It must resort to the courses of action particular to religion: persuasion, education and edifying discussion. In other words, Jewish halakhic existence—which Mendelssohn wished to preserve amidst the changing reality of his generation—is relegated entirely to the individual, and is contingent upon personal choice. One who chooses, as did Spinoza a century earlier, not to observe the precepts—commits an error; while one who seeks to compel other Jews to observe their religious obligations, as did the community to which Spinoza belonged—commits a sin. Mendelssohn—drawing upon the exodus and Sinai narratives—thus establishes modern Jewish existence, as voluntary. Unlike Spinoza however, he calls upon Jews to take part in that existence, and believes that it has religious value and meaning. Contrary to the statutory status afforded to Jewish communities throughout the Middle Ages, he wished to see the Jewish community as a free association of Jews who choose to affiliate with it and shape their lives in accordance with its laws.

Spinoza and Mendelssohn also differ in their respective approaches to the biblical Jewish state. As we have seen, Spinoza saw the moment of the state's founding as the moment at which it also began to stray from its intended path. The seeds of its own demise were sown in the very same generation, when Moses violated the natural social order, whereby the duty to bring offerings was performed by the firstborn of every family; granting his own tribe—Levi—exclusive control over sacrificial cult. Mendelssohn identified another moment entirely as the historical point at which the fabric of the divine state began to come undone—the investiture of Israel's first king. He adopts the position taken by the book of *Judges*, and views Israel's lack of a monarch as a mark of God's direct rule over his people. The installation of a king—even with God's consent—is the first rent in this fabric. Mendelssohn's approach recalls God's words to Samuel, who was appalled by the people's request for a king: "for they have not rejected thee, but they have rejected me, that I should not be king over them" (1 Sam. 8:7). Henceforth the rift between political rule and religious authority would only grow wider. Many generations would pass before the downfall of the Jewish state, but the root cause can be found here, in the people's decision not to be directly and exclusively ruled by God.

A century and a half later, the exegetical thread started by Spinoza was taken up by another Jewish thinker: Martin Buber (1878–1965). Like his two predecessors, Buber wove his exegesis within the spiritual context of his philosophical outlook. Like them, he made his understanding of this narrative, a pillar of his approach to contemporary Jewish existence.

Scripture, according to Buber, is suffused with dialogue between God and man. God provides man with absolute measures of good and evil; and man is free to decide whether to obey God's command or to rebel against it. This dialogue is conducted not only between God and individuals, but primarily between God and the People. The plane on which man's adherence to God's is measured, according to Buber, is a collective one: the quality of society, its treatment of the stranger, the orphan and the widow. The biblical imperative—rooted in "I will be that which I will be" (3:14)—is that individual, society, nation and mankind all adhere to the same moral standards of truth, kindness and charity. That is the profound sense of standing before God, sole creator of heaven and earth, before whom there are no divisions and no separate domains.

This imperative culminates in the choice of the desert-going people to accept the word of God uttered at Sinai. The people-of-slaves becomes truly free, not at the moment when their Egyptian shackles are cast off, but when they loudly proclaim: "All that the Lord hath spoken will we do, and obey" (24:7). At that exalted moment, the "Kingdom of Heaven" was founded, and God alone was chosen to lead his people. The period of the Judges, despite its many failures and shortcomings, was—in Buber's eyes—a supreme expression of this heavenly kingdom. When external circumstances demanded organization and leadership—a judge was appointed; when the problem was resolved –exclusive divine rule was restored. Gideon, who declined the people's offer to make him king, is the true hero of this period. His words—"I will not rule over you, neither shall my son rule over you; the Lord shall rule over you" (*Jud.* 8:23)—are the sublime essence of this approach. Buber was well aware of the fact that the people of that time did not always take the path of truth and justice, and sometimes committed grave errors, as recounted at length in the Bible. Their actions however—both good and ill—were performed before God, and were not dictated by any human authority. They had only their own sense of obligation to uphold God's command.

Like human beings in general, the Israelites of that period found it difficult to face the challenge of living as a people before God. Time and again, they sought a king to rule over them—eventually succeeding in their efforts. Thus began the Kingdom of Israel, a period with many glorious moments, but one that supplanted the full and direct rule of Heaven.

To Buber, this was not merely ancient history. Zionism had placed the Jewish People, once again, in a *Beshalah*-like situation. Again, they had won their freedom from foreign political and cultural domination. Again, they were able to choose their destiny, to fill their freedom with positive content. Again, they were called upon to elect God as their sovereign. Again, there was the danger that those who desired a king like all the nations might prevail, reducing a sublime idea to the grey reality of empty sovereignty. Buber thus called upon those who stood on the threshold of freedom, to choose the Kingdom of Heaven.

These three appeals—voiced by Spinoza, Mendelssohn and Buber—belong to the past—just like the story of the Israelites' passage from liberation (described in *Beshalah*) to acceptance of God's command (described in *Yitro*). Like the biblical story, they too pertain to the consciousness that pervades Jewish history. None of these appeals was ever fully heard or acted upon. Nevertheless, each has something to offer us, at the dawn of the 21st century. One who listens to Spinoza from a contemporary Jewish perspective, will not hear a call to abolish distinctive Jewish existence outright, but to recognize the fact that this existence can have other meanings, beyond the religio-halakhic. One who listens to Mendelssohn today, will hear the voice of tolerance and the categorical demand that religion forswear the mechanisms of state power; and the assertion that the life one lives before God must be a matter of conscience and personal conviction, without pressure or coercion. Those who listen to Buber, will find themselves compelled to ask what each and every one of us can do that we may be gathered under the wings of the Kingdom of Heaven—affording formative and legislative significance to the desert purity reflected in *Beshalah*. They will have to ask themselves whether we are still capable of immediate and unreserved acceptance of the divine imperative that demands "therefore choose life, that thou mayest live" (*Deut.* 30:19).

Yehoyada Amir

Yitro

*Scripture and Life: On **Franz Rosenzweig's** Concept of Torah*

Now mount Sinai was altogether on smoke, because the Lord descended upon it in fire; and the smoke thereof ascended as the smoke of a furnace, and the whole mount quaked greatly. And when the voice of the horn waxed louder and louder, Moses spoke, and God answered him by a voice (*Exodus* 19:18–19).

Yitro depicts God's public revelation to His People at Mount Sinai, with broad brushstrokes and bold colors. The portion itself presents the Ten Commandments as the direct content of this revelation, firmly establishing the connection between biblical monotheism—as reflected in the first two commandments—and the fundamental principles of religious ethics: "thou shalt not murder", "thou shalt not commit adultery", "thou shalt not steal". These commandments acquired the force of categorical imperatives, becoming milestones in the course of human development. Sabbath- observance and honoring one's parents, taking God's name in vain and bearing false witness against one's fellow—embody the two facets of the revelation that have given the text its eternal force and singularity.

Rabbinic tradition goes much further, viewing the revelation at Sinai as the heart of the giving of the Torah, including both the written Pentateuch and the Oral Law. Accordingly, every new interpretation a "faithful student" may put forward in this generation or another (see e.g. *Leviticus Rabbah* 22,1), was already given at Sinai. Future halakhic content, provided by sages throughout the generations, thus assumes divine and binding status. This special status influences midrashic interpretation, and makes it a point of departure for ongoing and developing halakhic and theological discussions—a focus for the entire sense of Jewish religious authority.

Regarding the significance of the giving of the Torah *per se*, traditional explanations are far from monolithic. Talmudic-midrashic literature and medieval commentaries paint diverse pictures of the essence of the giving at Sinai, and the relationship between this event and the written text. In some sources, Moses is depicted as a "clerk", who wrote the words of the Torah with his own hand, as dictated by God. As such, he was able to add certain remarks during the course of his work, and to rail against Heaven (see e.g. Genesis *Rabbah* 8,3). Elsewhere, Moses appears as ascending the heavens, walking among the angels, even to the Throne of Glory—where he receives the Torah, concealed beneath the Heavenly Throne since before creation (see e.g. *Shabbat* 88b). Some are careful to portray the giving of the tablets in such a way as to preserve the fundamental distance between God and man. According to this version of the story, neither the *Shekhinah* descended upon the mountain, nor did Moses ascend to heaven, (*Sukah* 5a). Rabbi Berekhiah, for example, asserts that at the time of the giving of the Law, God held the two upper hand's-breadths of the tablets, and Moses the two lower. The two hand's-breadths between them represent the distance that can never be bridged between God and man (*Exodus Rabbah* 28,1).

These varied accounts demonstrate both the importance the Rabbis attached to the giving of the Torah, and the caution they exercised in addressing this decisive moment in Jewish history. Should the Torah be seen as a something metaphysical and divine, given to man? Is the essence of the giving of the Torah the fact that man transcended the physical, or that God descended among men? Or perhaps we should view the concept of "Torah from Heaven" as a figurative description of what we are otherwise unable to grasp or depict. This is the path that Maimonides follows in his "Thirteen Principles of Faith" (Commentary on the Mishnah, Introduction to *Perek Helek*, 8th principle). He makes belief in the divine provenance of the Torah entirely contingent upon the uniqueness of Moses' prophecy. Moreover, he asserts that belief in "Torah from Heaven" ensures the reliability and originality of the extant text, and that we are charged to believe that the Torah "came to us entirely from God, in a manner that we call metaphorically: 'speech', but no one knows the nature of its delivery, except for [Moses] of blessed memory, to whom it was delivered. And he was as a clerk, who writes down all that is said to him, its dates and stories and precepts, and he is thus called lawmaker" (*Ibid*).

Maimonides prudently contradicts himself, calling Moses both "clerk" and "lawmaker"—two very different roles—in the same sentence, in order to emphasize the fact that his was not an actual description of the giving of the Torah—something of which only Moses would have been capable.

In kabbalistic hermeneutics, beyond the stories and laws of the Torah, beyond the text's plain and homiletic meanings—lie the secret names of God Himself. The Torah is thus in itself a revelation, and "Torah from Heaven" is Torah that reveals Heaven. The giving of the Torah at Mount Sinai continues, every time a mystic studies Torah in the "true fashion", and even every time a simple Jew studies its plain and homiletic meanings.

It is in this context that modern discourse regarding the relationship between the Torah and Hebrew Bible developed—beginning with the new status afforded to the Bible by Jews and Christians alike in the Modern Era. In Christianity, this tradition began with Protestant reformer Martin Luther, who advocated the restoration of Scripture—including both Old and New Testaments—to the status of the word of God, and the binding authority such standing accords. It is therefore not Church dogma or authority that stands at the heart of Christian religious life, he argued, but Scripture and its Word—experienced directly, without intermediaries. He gave expression to this view in his translation of the Bible into German, in order to enable even those who lacked a theological education to read it. The Bible thus became accessible to every literate man and woman; greatly reducing believers' dependence upon the Church and its institutions.

Among Jews, such a radical revolution could not occur, because The Hebrew Bible had always been accessible to anyone who could read—i.e. every Jewish male with a basic education. Nevertheless, the call to return to the Bible, and to establish it as the central text of Jewish religious life, was to have a decisive impact. Rather than reading Scripture through the eyes of exegetical tradition and halakhic authority, Halakhah and tradition were now seen through the eyes of Scripture. If previously, it had generally been believed that "a sage is preferable to a prophet", prophecy now lay at the heart of Jewish understanding, serving as hermeneutical tool and moral standard for the evaluation of everything that was to follow. This development, spanning at least three centuries, opened the way for many of Judaism's modern movements, from Haskalah and Reform to Zionism.

This return to Scripture was not without pitfalls however, from a religious perspective. Reading Scripture as it is written, and making it the focus of our ethical understanding, can also be seen as giving license to critical reading of the Bible, undermining many of the convictions that tradition takes for granted. This development began with the thought of Baruch (Benedictus) Spinoza, and his use of Scripture to question Jewish and Christian religious principles, the idea of Jewish chosenness and the obligation of contemporary Jews to observe the halakhic precepts. Spinoza's powerful ideas pose an extremely complex challenge to every modern Jewish thinker who strives to maintain a critical position, viewing the Bible as an evolving, human-made text; while at the same time, considering it the Torah of life and the word of God. Such thinkers must address the meaning of the Sinaitic revelation, the authority of the written text, and the relationship between viewing Scripture as written and developed by human beings—no different from any other man-made text—and considering it the expression of God's word and command.

One of the most interesting and prolific 20th century Jewish thinkers to deal with these questions was Franz Rosenzweig (1886–1929). In his magnum opus, *The Star of Redemption*, he draws upon a wealth of biblical sources, alongside other Jewish and Christian texts, weaving various stories into a dazzling homiletic tapestry, and developing innovative hermeneutical approaches. These focus primarily on the various layers of language, and their expression in the story of creation, in the dialogue of revelation—above all in *Song of Songs*—and in communal prayer as shaped by *Psalm* 115.

The greater part of Rosenzweig's judgments concerning Scripture would come later however, while translating the Bible into German; a task he shared with his friend Martin Buber. At that point, he felt the need to find a theoretical explanation for the way in which he related to this book, for the relationship between its revelational status and its use of "human language", and for the place of traditional Jewish commentary. The central and unique standing of Scripture in Rosenzweig's world, both as a book that has exerted a unique influence on human history in general, and as the foundation upon which he, the Jew Franz Rosenzweig, built his own religiosity, is manifest in the answers he provided to these questions.

The question thus arises, regarding Rosenzweig's attitude to modern biblical scholarship. Rosenzweig often approaches such scholarship with caution, by no means accepting each and every one of its theories. Ultimately however, it is clear to him that matters of textual development and philological value cannot be determined on the basis of theology and belief "in the holiness, namely uniqueness, and revelational character" of the Torah (Franz Rosenzweig, *Zweistromland: Kleinere Schriften zu Glauben und Denken, R. and A. Mayer* ed., p. 831). He further clarifies this position, asserting that Scripture "is human throughout" (*ibid.*, p. 761). Rosenzweig even wondered at the insistence of Jewish Orthodoxy—contrary to its Christian counterpart—on repudiating this scholarship in toto. Far from feeling alienated by the Orthodox position however, he was greatly drawn to it. Alongside his assertion that one cannot draw conclusions regarding the literary genesis and textual accuracy of Scripture on the basis of theological views, Rosenzweig firmly believed in the revelational character of the text and its divine provenance.

This complex position is based on Rosenzweig's commitment to the spiritual and textual unity of Scripture, capable of redressing any discrepancies between the various sources. Rosenzweig, who was prepared in principle, to accept the positions of Documentary Hypothesis regarding the sources and processes of scriptural development, argued that the process should be approached from the perspective of the final redactor, i.e. that of the religio-cultural decision to unite the various sources and weave them into a literary whole. He adopted the symbol "R", generally used to represent the hypothetical redactor, as if referring to *rabeinu* ("our teacher"), i.e. he who shaped from all these sub-sources the text of the Torah in which we believe. "We do not know who he was; we cannot believe that it was Moses ... he is our teacher, his theology is our teaching" (*ibid.* 831.).

This commitment to unity had a profound effect on Rosenzweig's textual interpretations. It allowed him to distinguish between different sources, while exploring the unified message revealed through their juxtaposition. It also lent itself to the concept of "leading words", to which Rosenzweig and Buber both resorted in their commentaries, linking various parts of the Bible. It is important to note that this commitment to a unified reading of the text springs from the conviction that it is the Torah of life, and should be treated as such. Through deep reflection, claims Rosenzweig, we may discover its underlying unity—both in terms of the text itself, and in terms of the relationship between the text and rabbinical exegesis throughout the ages. The Jewish reading he advocates knows the history of the text, is familiar with its sources and various levels of interpretation, but aspires to the unity inherent in a Torah of life that speaks from the past and commands in the present.

What does the biblical text offer those who read it? What is the significance of its "revelational character"? It is specifically as a human creation that Scripture has the ability to present a human account of God's word to man. The encounter with God that pervades Scripture is always described by human beings, and from a human perspective. This in no way detracts from its being the story of the revelation however, or mitigates the claims it makes upon the reader. The prophet attests to the truth of God's word to him, although the prophecy and its specific wording are his. The story of the revelation is an "objective" one, inasmuch as it reports an actual encounter. It is a testimony of the impression that the experience of the encounter left upon man. In that alone it may be the word of God speaking to the reader.

And so Rosenzweig writes, in one of his letters: "What stands in the Bible one can learn in two ways: 1. in that one hears what it says, 2. in that one hearkens to the beat of the human heart... The Bible and the heart say the same thing. That is why (and only why) the Bible is 'Revelation'" (*Franz Rosenzweig and Jehuda Halevi: Translating, Translations, and Translators*, Barbara Ellen Galli, McGill-Queen's University Press, 1995, p. 352) Listening to the beating of the human heart is not simply a metaphor. Our hearts, minds and experience form the basis of our ability to hear—through the human inscription of the Bible and the testimony of the revelation that was—the word of God truly speaking to us. Rosenzweig approaches the Bible, open to the possibility of believing and denying, at once embracing and turning away. This openness is the willingness to find in Scripture that which arouses belief—in him and in the reader—without preconceived ideas that merely seek confirmation. He offers the following description of one who reads Scripture correctly:

> As a searchlight detaches from darkness, first one section of the landscape and now another, and then leaves these again dimmed, so for such a man the days of his own life illumine the Scriptures, and in their quality of humanness permit him to recognize what is more than human, today at one point and tomorrow at another, nor can one day ever vouch for the next to yield a like experience. ... This humanness may anywhere become so translucent under the beam of a day of one's life, that it stands suddenly written in his innermost heart; and the divine in human inscription becomes as clear and actual to him for that one pulse beat as if—at that instant—he heard a voice calling to his heart. Not everything in the Scriptures belongs to him—neither today nor ever. But he knows that he belongs to everything in them, and it is only this readiness of his which, when it is directed toward the Scriptures, constitutes belief (Nahum N. Glatzer (ed.), *Franz Rosenzweig: His Life and Thought*, Hacket Publishing Company, 1998, p. 252).

Scripture is human myth. It tells of human life, and is written in human language. It bears witness, from a human perspective, to man's encounter with God. The account of such an encounter is always human and subjective, while the revelation itself remains an objective fact—*the* objective fact. Rosenzweig however, challenges us to admit the possibility that the "days of our own lives" can transform this myth into revelation. It is not the text itself that is credited with the ability to effect this metamorphosis, but the character of the individual believer, her or his personal history and willingness to listen. It is this boundless and wholly unpredictable ability that makes reading and studying the text a religious act, and affords Scripture the force of a true source.

Rosenzweig devotes little attention to the story of the giving of the Torah at Mount Sinai, the central focus of *Yitro*. He prefers to listen to the word of God speaking to him through the divine command and call, through the testimony of those to whom the command was addressed.

In so doing however, he restores the relevance of the giving of the Torah and the centrality of revelation. One who follows in Rosenzweig's footsteps must determine how best to respond to this call, and how to make it the center of her or his life. The Bible-reader envisioned by Rosenzweig is always autonomous, free to reject and criticize, rail against Heaven and repudiate. Those who choose to pursue this path however, must also be prepared to believe, to hear, to listen and to respond to the divine command that speaks to them through the Torah—given by Moses, according to tradition, to all future generations of Israel.

Yotam Benziman

Mishpatim – Now These Are the Ordinances

"And they saw the God of Israel": The Apologetics of **Martin Buber**

And they saw the God of Israel; and there was under His feet the like of a paved work of sapphire stone, and the like of the very heaven for clearness (*Exodus* 24:10).

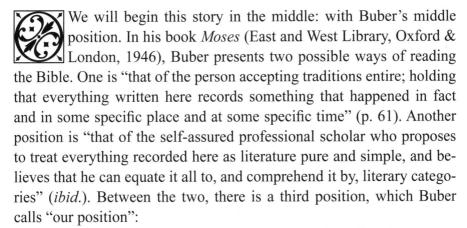 We will begin this story in the middle: with Buber's middle position. In his book *Moses* (East and West Library, Oxford & London, 1946), Buber presents two possible ways of reading the Bible. One is "that of the person accepting traditions entire; holding that everything written here records something that happened in fact and in some specific place and at some specific time" (p. 61). Another position is "that of the self-assured professional scholar who proposes to treat everything recorded here as literature pure and simple, and believes that he can equate it all to, and comprehend it by, literary categories" (*ibid.*). Between the two, there is a third position, which Buber calls "our position":

We must adopt the critical approach and seek reality, here as well, by asking ourselves what human relation to real events this could have been which led gradually, along many by-paths and by way of many metamorphoses, from mouth to ear, from one memory to another, and from dream to dream, until it grew into the written account we have read. It is certainly not a chronicle which we have to work on, but it is equally not imaginative poesy; it is a historical saga. But that is a concept the employment of which should not calm the scientific conscience; it must stir it up (*ibid.*).

The term "historical saga" combines the approach that sees the Bible as factual account, with the approach that sees it purely as literature.

It is a hybrid that at first glance appears impossible. It would seem to violate all of the laws of logic. Every hypothetical event is supposed to be defined as one that happened or did not happen, and there is no middle road. Closer examination of Buber's hermeneutical approach however, sheds more light on his understanding of historical saga. Certain events happen, and they are engraved in the hearts of the people who experience them, shaping their consciousness. People interpret such events, give them meaning, and recount them. They do so through saga. Hence, "the saga is the predominant method of preserving the memory of what happens" (*ibid.* p. 15)—even if the narrative that people create is myth, for "here, unlike the concept familiar in the science of religion, myth means nothing other than the report by ardent enthusiasts of that which has befallen them. And it may very well be doubted whether, in the last resort, the report of an unenthusiastic chronicler could have come closer to the truth" (*ibid.* p. 17).

The truth is the story of the person who experiences the event and is enthused by it. Not all of the stories in the Bible meet this criterion. That is to say, that not all of the stories in the Bible faithfully reflect the authentic experiences of those who lived, took part, were amazed and moved by the events described. The Bible includes many later, polished reworkings of these primordial experiences. The historian thus requires sharp literary instincts in order to isolate the core from its wrappings; to distinguish between the experience's kernel of truth and that which was added later. Thus for example:

> The choice of words in a given section, and in this connection the original meaning of the words and the changes in meaning, as well as the sentence structure to be found on each occasion, have to be carefully studied. In particular, however, a special function is exercised, in my view, by the principle of repetition. By the fact that the identical sounds, words, and sentences recur, whether in the same passages or in other corresponding ones, our attention is drawn in part to the specific meaning of single motifs, and in part to common analogies and completions of meaning as between them (*ibid.* p. 7).

Buber indeed devotes "careful study". The story of the burning bush, for example, he classifies as true. But when Moses receives the command to prove to the people the revelation he experienced:

The style differs here from that in the undoubtedly genuine parts of the narrative of the burning bush; it is more loose, more expansive, more wordy. Here necessity does not hold sway as it does there; the purposeful repetitions are replaced by casual ones; and finally a rhetorical note is to be heard. The hard rhythm has become a thin absence of rhythm, the firm composition has become negligent; even the structure of the sentences is careless. The contents do not resemble those of the genuine parts... (*ibid.* p. 46).

Had Buber been satisfied merely to provide a literary analysis of the biblical narrative, his work on Moses would have afforded readers a fascinating lesson on how to approach a text, its rhythm and its drama. The emphasis he places on the "real parts" however, constitutes a fundamental flaw in his method. "The real parts", according to Buber, were written by people who had in fact experienced the events described. In other words, the hermeneutical approach proposed by Buber can only be applied to events that one can reasonably assume to contain some element of historical truth. This method creates an apologetic approach to the text. Rather than seeing the Ten Plagues as a rich literary text, without committing oneself to its historicity, Buber characterizes the plagues as "extraordinary, though not necessarily in any way supernatural, in order to have an effect as a sign" (*ibid.* p. 63). The plague of frogs is thus explained by the fact that in the summer ("the season for the flood"— *ibid.* p. 67), the frogs come up from the Nile; and the plague of hail is something that occurs in very harsh winters. The plague of blood merely reflects the fact that "the river ... was red, as was frequently the case" (*ibid.*). Buber is aware that the slaying of the firstborn, as it appears in the Bible, is completely implausible. According to the Book of *Exodus* (12:29): "And it came to pass at midnight, that the Lord smote all the firstborn in the land of Egypt, from the firstborn of Pharaoh that sat on his throne, unto the firstborn of the captive that was in the dungeon; and all the first-born of cattle." Inasmuch as such a course of events would not be realistic, Buber cites only the slaying of Pharaoh's firstborn as the motive for the Israelites' release. He does not even mention the plagues of lice, wild beasts, murrain or boils.

Similarly, Buber trivializes the beautiful description of the encounter between Moses, Aaron and his sons, the Seventy Elders and God. The Bible recounts: "And they saw the God of Israel; and there was under His feet the like of a paved work of sapphire stone, and the like of the very heaven for clearness" (24:10). Buber explains:

They have presumably wandered through clinging, hanging mist before dawn; and at the very moment they reach their goal; the swaying darkness tears asunder (as I myself happened to witness once) and dissolves except for one cloud already transparent with the hue of the still unrisen sun (p. 117).

The description of the "paved work of sapphire stone" appears toward the end of the portion of *Mishpatim*. It is the division of the Pentateuch into "portions" that sets Mishpatim apart as a distinct unit. The story begins however, with the giving of the Ten Commandments, in the previous portion of *Yitro*. Immediately following the Commandments, it is written: "And all the people perceived the thundering, and the lightning, and the voice of the horn, and the mountain smoking: and when the people saw it, they trembled, and stood afar off" (20:15). The people thus stood back, while "Moses drew near unto the thick darkness where God was" (*ibid.* 18), and God gave him the entire Torah "on one foot". It begins with "Ye shall not make with me gods of silver, neither shall ye make unto you gods of gold" (*ibid.* 20); and proceeds with "Now these are the ordinances which thou shalt set before them" (21:1—the opening verse of *Mishpatim*). Then, in three dense chapters, God summarizes for Moses—who was within "the thick darkness where God was"—the essence of the precepts; the very same precepts that remain ingrained to this day.

Among the injunctions cited are: "But if the servant shall plainly say, I love my master, my wife, and my children; I will not go out free; then his master shall bring him unto God, and shall bring him to the door, or unto the door-post; and his master shall bore his ear through with an awl; and he shall serve him for ever" (*ibid.* 5–6); "eye for eye, tooth for tooth, hand for hand, foot for foot" (*ibid.* 24); "And a stranger shalt thou not wrong, neither shalt thou oppress him: for ye were strangers in the land of Egypt" (22:20); "Thou shalt not follow a multitude to do evil; neither shalt thou speak in a cause to turn aside after a multitude to pervert justice" (23:2); "Keep thee far from a false matter; and the innocent and righteous slay thou not: for I will not justify the wicked" (*ibid.*7); "And six years thou shalt sow thy land, and shalt gather in the produce thereof: but the seventh year thou shalt let it rest and lie fallow; that the poor of thy people may eat: and what they leave the beast of the field shall eat. In like manner thou shalt deal with thy vineyard, and with thy oliveyard" (*ibid.* 10–11); "Six days thou shalt do thy work, and on the seventh day thou shalt rest; that thine ox and thine ass may rest, and the son of thy handmaid, and the stranger, may be refreshed" (*ibid.* 12); "Three times thou shalt keep a feast unto me in the year" (*ibid.* 14); "The first of the first-fruits of thy land thou shalt bring into the house of the Lord thy God. Thou shalt not seethe a kid in it mother's milk" (*ibid.* 19).

Here God reveals His leadership, and the fitting way of life He wishes to convey to the people. Soon, the encounter will come to an end, and God will disappear. For the moment however, He is here, conversing, accessible—reach out and touch Him. At first He speaks only to Moses, and then He is beheld by Aaron, Nadab and Abihu and the Seventy Elders. What they see is not, as Buber himself saw, clouds and "clinging, hanging mist", but "the God of Israel", as the verse clearly states. And as if to prove Buber wrong, the next verse adds: "And upon the nobles of the children of Israel He laid not His hand; and they beheld God, and did eat and drink".

What is Buber afraid of? Why does he insist on forcing the events described in the Bible stories into the straitjacket of the likelihood of their occurrence? In so doing, he strips the text of its symbolic meaning, its power, and a significant amount of its content. The rich figure of Moses is also denied its due. Moses, who ascends to God to receive the Torah, comes down with the tablets, breaks them, goes up a second time, fasts for forty days and forty nights, returns to earth, his skin glowing from his encounter with God. This is Moses in all his glory, literary magnificence and force of character—as portrayed in the Bible, and as perceived by subsequent generations. Buber however, insists: "If we wish to keep before us a sequence of events possible in our human world, we must renounce all such tremendous scenes" (p.139).

Buber is wrong to reject the approach that sees the biblical text as literature. It is not "literature pure and simple", as he calls it, but literature at its best. Such literature elicits, as has often been said, the "suspension of disbelief". God is one of the main characters in the Bible, if not *the* main character, from the very first verse of Genesis. There is no need to put him in parentheses, or to seek clumsy scientific analogies for his portrayal as creator of heaven and earth. Let us see him in all his majesty. Here He is the Creator. Here He descends upon Mount Sinai and addresses the people. Here the people perceive the thundering. It is not the approach "of the self-assured professional scholar who proposes to treat everything recorded here as literature pure and simple". It is the approach of an enraptured reader, enchanted by the story, unabashedly believing it with all his heart, for as long as he is reading it. And then, when he looks up from his reading, he may very well decide that God never existed. Just as he relates to Hamlet, Jean Valjean or any other literary figure.

Buber, whose book on Moses is filled with wonderful examples of attentive and sensitive reading of biblical texts, is unwilling to apply his analytical ability to some of the Bible's most beautiful passages. This shortcoming is unfortunate with regard to the plagues for example, but particularly regrettable when it comes to the God of Israel, under whose feet "there was the like of a paved work of sapphire stone, and the like of the very heaven for clearness"; a beautifully lyrical description. This passage is open to numerous and varied interpretations, yet Buber leaves God in the darkness. We do not know what is "under the feet of God" that is compared to "a paved work off sapphire stone", and we certainly do not know what God Himself looks like. The repeated emphasis of the fact that Moses and Aaron, Nadab and Abihu, and the Seventy Elders saw Him, leaves the remainder of the people—and future readers—in a state of perpetual seeking.

God descends to the people—reach out and touch him—but he is elusive, conceals Himself, disappears. Where is He: In a thick cloud (19:9)? Upon Mount Sinai (*ibid.* 19)? In the darkness (*ibid.* 18)? In heaven (*ibid.* 19)? And what does the verse "and the appearance of the glory of the Lord was like devouring fire on the top of the mount in the eyes of the children of Israel" (24:17) mean? Perhaps that the people could not see God Himself: His glory appeared "like devouring fire on the top of the mount in the eyes of the children of Israel", but in fact "the cloud covered it six days" (*ibid.* 16), and the people saw nothing but the cloud.

Only Moses, Aaron, his sons and the Elders actually saw God. Buber would say that such sight is not possible in our "human world". Moses and the others however, do not transcend "the human" here. They eat and drink as human beings, unlike Moses' later experience, of which it will be said: "And he was there with the Lord forty days and forty nights; he did neither eat bread, nor drink water" (34:28). The Midrash interprets Moses' not eating as rendering him like God or the angels: "When he went up to heaven—[he was as] God. Just as the angels do not eat or drink, so he neither ate nor drank" (*Devarim Rabbah* 11, 4).

How can one approach God in a human fashion, as flesh and blood, reach out and touch Him? Here, I would like to discuss another interpretation of the word "God" (*Elohim*), arising it would seem, from a verse in *Mishpatim*. Emanuel Levinas writes in his first Talmudic reading: "God (*Elohim*) generally symbolizes authority, power, and therefore often 'judge' as well" (*Nine Talmudic Readings*, Heb. ed., p. 15). Yehonatan Etz-Chaim reproaches Levinas for resorting to "high words, rather than simply citing the verse that states: 'the cause of both parties shall come before the *elohim*; he whom [the] *elohim* shall condemn, shall pay double unto his neighbor' (*Ex.* 22:8), from which it is clear that in the language of the Bible, the word '*elohim*' also means judge" ("*Keriah Hereshet Batalmud*", *Haaretz* 19/4/2002).

Etz-Chaim claims that the word *elohim*, as it is used here, simply means flesh and blood judges, and not God, creator of the universe. He is not the first to make this observation. The talmudic passage discussed by Levinas (in reference to a different verse) also asks: "What is *elohim*? A judge" (*Yoma* 87a). Nevertheless, this is not the word's plain meaning. The plain meaning of the word *Elohim* is God, not man.

The verse that Etz-Chaim cites refers to a situation in which someone was charged with the safekeeping of another's property, but the property was stolen. The preceding verse however, reinforces the natural reading of the word *elohim* as referring to God: "If the thief be not found, then the master of the house shall come near unto the *elohim*" (22:7). Is the verse referring to a flesh and blood judge? The verb *nikrav* ("shall come near") is reminiscent of mythical ceremonies of "coming near" in which *elohim* is *Elohim*, appearing in all His glory, and intervening (perhaps reluctantly) in matters pertaining to the here and now.

Thus for example in the circumstances described in *Numbers* (5:12)—"If any man's wife go aside, and act unfaithfully"—in which the priest blots the Holy Name into an earthen vessel containing the water of bitterness, immediately after he has "brought her near (*hikriv*), and set her before the Lord" (*ibid.* 16). So too in the case of Saul, who wished to do battle against Philistines: "Then said the priest, Let us draw near (*nikrevah*) hither unto God. And Saul asked counsel of God, Shall I go down after the Philistines? wilt thou deliver them into the hand of Israel? But He answered him not that day" (1 Sam. 14:36–37).

The *elohim* to which one draws near is "the" *Elohim*. Inasmuch as God is the ultimate other, as He is termed by Levinas, one cannot really draw near to Him in the fullest sense. The sanctity ascribed to Him and to all that surrounds Him, creates a barrier between Him and any who stretch out their hands to touch Him. The existential state we all share is embodied by the phrase "draw not nigh hither", which Moses hears from within the bush (*Ex.* 3:5). It appears that not only does "come near to the *elohim*" refer to approaching God Himself (as opposed to a judge or other human being); it denotes a singular, unique almost-contact, with what is in theory unattainable, untouchable; with something never-present, something called "I will be" (*ibid.* 14).

Why the does Etz-Chaim interpret the verse in *Exodus* as a reference to human judges? Probably due to the end of the verse. The beginning, "the cause of both parties shall come before the *elohim*", can perhaps be understood as referring to God. The ending however, is disappointing, petty, mundane, prosaic: "he whom [the] *elohim* shall condemn, shall pay double unto his neighbor". The *elohim* of this verse, whoever he/they may be, functions as an arbitrator, who sets the level of compensation that one found guilty must pay to one he has wronged. If an encounter with God is a unique experience—glorious, sublime and awe-inspiring—it is wholly inconceivable that such a One would engage in the pettiness of awarding damages. Consequently, *elohim* here must be a human judge, an official of some kind—not the creator of the universe.

On the other hand, let us recall that the verse discussed earlier, appearing in the same biblical portion, uses the very same word *elohim*, in all its abstract incorporeality: "And they saw the God of Israel; and there was under His feet the like of a paved work of sapphire stone, and the like of the very heaven for clearness. And upon the nobles of the children of Israel He laid not His hand; and they beheld God, and did eat and drink" (24:10–11). Despite His abstractness, His sublime otherworldliness, He is described as something that can be beheld. One can thus approach God with fear and trepidation, fasting for forty days and forty nights; or one can look directly at Him, behold Him, and eat and drink. And God Himself, sometimes appears with great terribleness, signs and wonders, and sometimes deals with the petty and the human—with two people squabbling with one another, in need of an arbitrator, as in the story of the master of the house and his neighbor. God shows both of these faces in the very same portion.

The God of *Mishpatim*, like the God of the Pentateuch in general, is both sublime and distant, and near and approachable. Sometimes He has "under His feet the like of a paved work of sapphire stone, and the like of the very heaven for clearness"; and sometimes, as Tirza Attar writes in her poem "Birthday Prayer", He is "behind the cypress tree", "the one who bent his head to mine". Buber also makes God accessible. He is prepared to see him, but is unwilling to see him as God, only as sunlit clouds.

The God of Tirza Atar bent his head to hers, but at the time of the giving of the Torah, He was beheld only by very few: Moses and Aaron, Nadab and Abihu, and the Seventy Elders. Was such a sight denied to the people? Perhaps not. One might say that they beheld Him when they "perceived the thunderings, and the lightnings, and the voice of the horn, and the mountain smoking" (20:15). This description however, notes only the clamor and confusion, without God Himself. Perhaps "the Lord is not in the commotion" (1 *Kings* 19:11).

The people may in fact have seen God however, as described in the second half of the previous verse: "and when the people saw it, they removed, and stood afar off". Their removal and standing afar may cause the reader to miss the moment. It is as if these actions "demand" that the preceding word—spelled *vav-yod-resh-aleph*—be vocalized *vayera* ("and [the people] were afraid"), rather than *vayar* ("and [the people] saw"). The word remains as it was however, denoting sight, not fear. But what did the people see? Perhaps a tremendous revelation, inexpressible in words; perhaps a fleeting, intimate touch, "behind the cypress tree", equally inexpressible.

Perhaps the people saw God, and perhaps they didn't. Moses, Aaron and his sons, and the Seventy Elders did see Him. Moses was to receive a further, personal revelation, face to face (33:11). He was, according to the Bible, the only one. One of the Torah's final verses reads: "And there hath not arisen a prophet since in Israel like unto Moses, whom the Lord knew face to face" (*Deut.* 34:10). By virtue of this relationship, Moses was granted a singular burial. "And he buried him in a valley in the land of Moab over against Beth-peor" (*ibid.* 6). Buber concludes his book with the following explanation: "there can be no doubt that YHVH himself is regarded as the digger of the grave of His servant" (*Moses* p. 201).

This is God as he appears in the Torah: God who buries and gives life, whose voice walked in the garden in the cool of the day, who creates, plants, regrets, is saddened, enraged, performs miracles, is childish and willful, argues and becomes convinced, reveals Himself and disappears, resides in the darkness and speaks with the fathers of the nation, a mighty and terrible figure, a literary figure.

Hava Pinhas-Cohen

Terumah – Take for Me an Offering

The Figure of the Artist in the Works of Shmuel Yosef Agnon

Neither shalt thou go up by steps unto mine altar, that thy nakedness be not uncovered thereon (*Exodus* 20:22).

And let them make me a sanctuary, that I may dwell among them
(*Exodus* 25:8).

The making of a sanctuary, according to the above verse is, first
and foremost, an internal, national obligation, centered on the
"making"—physical, sensual construction. In order to explain
the essence of this sanctuary and promulgate the idea, it must first be
constructed through language. It must be created with words with precise language and heightened awareness of the materials and substances
suited to building. "And let them make me a sanctuary" implies a common national creation.

In the words of Mircea Eliade, it is a celestial model (*The Myth
of Eternal Return*, Bollingen, Princeton, 1971, p. 7) that David gives
to Solomon, assuring him that "All this the Lord made me understand
in writing by His hand upon me, even all the works of this pattern" (1
Chron. 28, 19). Eliade adds:

For the moment, what we wish to emphasize is the fact that the
world which surrounds us, civilized by the hand of man, is accorded no validity beyond that which is due to the extraterres-
trial prototype that served as its model. Man constructs according to an archetype. Not only does his city or his temple have
celestial models; the same is true of the entire region he inhabits
(*ibid.* p. 10).

The Bible continues in its description of the archetype: "According
to all that I show thee, the pattern of the tabernacle, and the pattern of
all the furniture thereof, even so shall ye make it" (25:9)—reflecting

the longing to realize an idea, to capture an abstract concept and make it reality; to turn nothingness into something visible, tangible, present. This is the passage between the abstract, its expression in words, and its physical realization. Realization also entails the anxiety of knowing limits, of understanding plans and instructions, and of bringing them to fruition. In its precise specification of materials colors and forms, the text displays a thorough understanding of limits; in its imperative language, it leaves no room for doubt regarding the sacred source of its content. Sacred collective creation will be the bond between the sanctuary and the people.

Raphael was a scribe. Agnon's "The Tale of the Scribe" ostensibly begins with an account of his life.

"This is the story of Raphael the scribe. Raphael was a righteous and blameless man who copied Torah scrolls, phylacteries, and *mezuzot* in holiness and purity. And any man in the household of Israel who was childless, Mercy deliver us, or whose wife had died, Mercy deliver us, would come to Raphael the scribe and say: "You know, Reb Raphael my brother, what are we and what are our lives? I had indeed hoped that my sons and my sons' sons would come to you ... And Raphael then would sit and write a Torah scroll to give the man and his wife a name and remembrance in the household of Israel" (S. Y. Agnon, *Twenty-One Stories*, Nahum N. Glatzer ed., Schocken Books, New York, 1970).

In other words, the writing of a Torah scroll is not just for the sake of its liturgical use, but rather, in the act of copying and objectifying the text, one preserves a memory—or, in more general terms, art is memory. In the portion of *Yitro*, Moses is given instructions for the construction of an altar to God:

And the people stood afar off; but Moses drew near unto the thick darkness where God was... Thus thou shalt say unto the children of Israel: Ye yourselves have seen that I have talked with you from heaven. Ye shall not make with me—gods of silver, or gods of gold, ye shall not make unto you. An altar of earth thou shalt make unto me, and shalt sacrifice thereon thy burnt offerings, and thy peace-offerings, thy sheep, and thine oxen; in every place where I cause my name to be mentioned I will come unto thee and bless thee. And if thou make me an altar of stone, thou shalt not build it of hewn stones; for if thou lift up thy tool upon it, thou hast profaned it. Neither shalt thou go up by steps unto mine altar, that thy nakedness be not uncovered thereon (20:17–22).

In both cases, the Israelites are commanded to build something associated with divine worship. In *Yitro*, when Moses ascends the mountain to speak to God, it is into "thick darkness"—something intangible, vague and airy. God's instructions thus include an explicit prohibition against the consecration of material images to him, in silver or in gold.

The text does, however, stipulate specific materials and forms of worship. The altar must be of earth or stone, and the offerings sheep and oxen—animals associated with agriculture (i.e. not fowl). In the case of a stone altar, the type of masonry is also specified; proving the speaker's consciousness of construction materials and their symbolic significance. In his commentary on this verse, Nahmanides writes:

Thou shalt not build it of hewn stones—For in taking up any iron [tool] to make them so, you take up your murderous and many-victimed sword, and profane them. There was therefore, no iron in the Tabernacle, for even its pins—that are better made of iron—were of brass; and so in the Temple, no iron tools were used, with the exception of knives ....

Such consciousness of material and form, expression and significance, continues in *Terumah*, and further increases in the portions that follow—regarding the fashioning of the Tabernacle, the *menorah* and the cherubim.

This consciousness in fact comprises four distinct elements, which together provide the basis for understanding Jewish art and the role of the Jewish artist: consciousness of process, material, form and significance. In *Terumah,* the relationship between the believer and God, the object of her or his belief, is not relegated entirely to the realm of the spiritual, but is afforded the possibility of expression in the realm of the physical, and elaboration in the realm of memory.

I believe that the question of the artist's fundamental nature and role in the world vis-à-vis God, of her or his existence in the place between thick darkness and earth and stone, between faith and art—is a recurring theme throughout the work of Agnon. It is a question that hangs, suspended between the faces of the cherubim and the ark of the testimony. One cannot approach heaven, it would seem, without touching the earth, create without submitting to passion, or truly touch matter without understanding its essence, significance and symbolic meaning.

"The Tale of the Scribe" appears to revolve around the figure of Raphael, who undoubtedly reflects the figure of the artist in general, a metaphorical representation of the artistic-poetic. Appropriately, the story is dedicated to "my wife Esther, who tarries at home". The story describes the life of a couple: Raphael the scribe, and his modest and pure wife, Miriam. He devotes his life to the holy calling of writing, and she devotes her life to him: "Raphael the scribe sat and wrote, and his wife, most blessed among women, the pious Miriam, stayed home and made life pleasant for him in a fine house with fine utensils ... so that her husband would do his work in a clean and pure atmosphere". There is a clear division of labor. She creates the holy atmosphere in which he may engage in his holy work.

To her mind, a woman's role in the world is to bear children, and her place is determined by the fruit of her womb. In the story however, Miriam sits with Raphael in their modest apartment adjacent to the great synagogue and the old house of study and the ritual bath, a single room divided by a partition. He sits and writes:

> On the other side of the partition there was an oven and a range for pots, and between oven and range the pious and modest mistress of his house sat, and she cooked and baked and preserved and wove and knitted and looked to the needs of her home. Children they had none. Because the Holy One, blessed be He, desires the prayers of the righteous, He closed her womb.

By definition, Miriam's creativity is the product of her adversity.

She longs to have children and therefore knits and sews for orphans, for those who need her.

Raphael writes *mezuzot, tefilin*, and Torah scrolls. These are works that create identity for others. A Torah scroll written in memory of one who has departed this life is a monument, a name and remembrance ("And Raphael then would sit and write a Torah scroll to give the man and his wife a name and remembrance in the household of Israel"). It is their only memorial in the community in which they lived. *Mezuzot* and *tefilin* afford those who use them a sense of identity and place. Raphael's creation appears to be flawless, since it has nothing of its creator's ego, desires or passions; serving merely as a tool in the hand of its maker.

In her article *"Lesugiyat Hayetzer Vehayetzirah Besipurei Agnon"* (On Desire and Creativity in Agnon's Stories; *Kovetz Agnon*, 5754–1994), Malka Shaked posits the following:

Agnon's attitude to the act of artistic creation and to that of writing in particular, oscillates between two fundamentally different approaches—the second cloaked within the first. The first is the classic approach of Jewish (and not only Jewish) tradition, declared explicitly in a number of Agnon's works. At its core lies the rejection of artistic writing in general, and the conviction that true writing is something entirely different, the purpose of which lies not in the realm of the aesthetic, but in the realm of the religious and the ethical (p. 295).

Art as presented in the opening verses of *Terumah* is not art for art's sake, but a means to an end, toward which each and every one of its components is applied. Every detail is laden with symbolism and meaning—hence a consciousness of the place of beauty and aesthetics in the artistic act.

This is the traditional approach. It is also the approach presented in "The Tale of the Scribe", which poses the question of the artist and his loyalty to his art. The tale maintains that there is no higher form of art than the copying ancient works on ancient parchment (see Shaked, p. 296). The present is sustained by the past, and the copying faithful—sanctified by virtue of its source, its antiquity and its endless repetition.

"The Tale of the Scribe" was written in 1917, while the novel *Only Yesterday* was published in 1945. These two works, decades apart, show how intrigued Agnon was by the subject of art and artists. The later artist in Agnon's work, Samson Bloykof in *Only Yesterday*, adds a further dimension: painting that is not art, which demands perfection. Bloykof was a good teacher to Isaac Kumer, instructing him not only in his trade, but also in the theory of art:

Bloykof was an experienced teacher and knew how to make his pupils love their trade. When he sat with Isaac to teach him, he told him, Here's a sheet and here are paints. Ostensibly, they have nothing in common, but you want to mate them. So, try to make the mating succeed ... Pick up your brush and don't spare your efforts, for you are not the main thing, but what you do, and what you do isn't the main thing, but the act itself (*Only Yesterday*, Princeton University Press, 2002, pp. 249–250).

In his portrayal of the traditional artist, Agnon places the artistic act before the artist. The artist possesses the ability to couple tangible paper and paint with the intangible act. The artistic act is thus procreative, fundamentally erotic, judged solely on the basis of its outcome.

Elsewhere, Agnon discusses the meaning of the word *sofer*. He is fully aware of the apparent contradiction between its original and modern usages: "Unintentionally, I have mentioned that I am a writer. Originally, the word denoted the scribe, who wrote the words of the Torah. But since everyone who engages in the craft of writing is called a writer, I am not afraid of arrogance in calling myself a writer" (S. Y. Agnon, *A Guest for the Night*, Naftali C. Brandwein and Allen Mandelbaum eds., Schocken Books, New York, 1968, p. 448).

The traditional definition of literature and art is community-oriented, extending from the national to the personal. Emphasis is placed upon the individual's ability to contribute to the group, as opposed to simply declaring her or his own individuality. Copying and drawing the past into the present heighten the meaning of the historical in the life of the individual. Rather than asking "who is the copyist?", we ask "in whose memory was the scroll copied and created?". In other words, the emphasis shifts to the object—the scroll—and to the one in whose name it was written and by which it will always be remembered. Agnon goes on to speak of poets, or more specifically, liturgical poets:

I have told elsewhere the story of the poet ... And where did he get the Laments? The bees who had given him their honey stung him, and out of that pain he wrote the Laments for the Ninth of Av. There are other poets who were not privileged in the same way as Rabbi Eleazar Hakalir, but because they were humble and modest, they regarded their misfortunes as part of the community's misfortunes and made them songs and lamentations for the House of Israel; so a man reads them as he reads a lamentation over himself (*ibid.* p. 448).

Here Agnon draws a portrait of the traditional Jewish poet, whose individual pain is inexorably linked to that of the community; who can only understand communal pain in terms of his own. The poet's words at once refer both to the community and to himself, allowing the reader to see his personal pain, i.e. his world, reflected there. Agnon thus describes the artistic triangle, comprising personal narrative, national narrative, and the reader. The work's reflection in the eyes of the reader however, is a thoroughly modernistic dimension of art. In *Only Yesterday*, Agnon places a more practical view in the mouth of Bloykof: "Once Bloykof looked at him, and said, what is it, Kumer, you've abandoned your world. Another time Bloykof looked at him and said, there's a special quality you've got and I don't know what it is. Too bad you weren't born an artist. Because a person doesn't become an artist unless he is born an artist, but he can learn [a craft] that is an art, so he started teaching him sign-painting".

Bloykof makes a clear distinction between craft and art, showing respect for the former, as a means by which one may earn a living—certainly a measure of the standing and dignity of art. Raphael represents the traditional approach, which serves the ritual needs of the community and preserves the memory of its individual members, and as such is always near to death. The more conscious one is of the proximity of death, the more intense one's fear of being forgotten. Agnon thus establishes Raphael as a "good advocate" for those who have died childless—in a partnership between the silent seed of the name's owner, and his own abilities as a scribe. This approach, represented by the character of Raphael, a relatively simple artist, persists in the characters of other artists in Agnon's work: Adiel Amzeh and Bloykof:

> Samson Bloykof was about thirty years old, suffered from a weak heart and weak lungs, and knew that his death was near, and so he worked diligently to accomplish in his life what he wouldn't accomplish after his death, for when a person is dead, he can't paint, and furthermore, at the moment when he is passing to the nether world, all his images return and pass before his eyes and are thousands and thousands of times sweeter and finer. And he wants to stretch out his hands and paint. ... He no longer paints the pictures that made him popular in his generation, and he doesn't make frames for pictures, but paints what Heaven shows him. And even though he knows himself that he is the slightest of the slight and keeps neither Torah nor Commandments, he knows that Heaven is gracious to him and gives him strength to see and to paint, and the Omnipotent Creator of the World must have a special intention for future generations to know the splendor of Jerusalem, even in her destruction. And they will know that there was one Samson Bloykof who looked favorably upon her (pp. 217–218).

In other words, Bloykof would be remembered by future generations for his ability to see the beauty of Jerusalem. He too, like Raphael, is shown a heavenly ideal, which he seeks to realize through his talent (the name "Bloykof" or *blau-kopf*, meaning "blue head", denotes both one whose head touches heaven and one who employs the color blue in his work).

Fully aware of his impending death, Samson Bloykof makes "a name and a remembrance" for himself—not by the traditional means of a Torah scroll, but through his individualistic expression in painting.

Returning to "The Tale of a Scribe", we find that even the traditional artist faces the dilemma of the modern, individualistic artist. Raphael writes and fashions the Torah scroll entirely on his own. His is a kind of existential solitariness, a part of his independent personality, wholly devoted to the most important thing in his life: the Torah.

Raphael came forward, went to the Ark, accepted the scroll from the cantor, and walked at the head of the procession. The elders stood and clapped their hands, adding to the rejoicing ... But when Raphael began to sing his melody all hands became still and everyone stood motionless without saying a word ... Raphael held the scroll in his arm, walking in the lead with all the other youths following him in the procession around the pulpit. At that moment a young girl pushed her way through the legs of the dancers (*ibid.* p. 23).

The description of Raphael's dance with the Torah scroll expresses erotic intimacy, shortly before his first meeting with Miriam. The *Simhat Torah* dance foreshadows his *danse macabre* with the scroll written as a name and remembrance for his beloved wife.

Raphael's foremost trait however, is his sexual abstinence—to the point of avoiding all physical intimacy with his wife. His erotic energy is channeled into his creative efforts, into the writing of the Torah scroll. His wife is supplanted by the Torah. "The artist's devotion to his work bears the mark of sexual arousal, and the act of artistic creation itself would appear to be a substitute for the erotic and sexual fulfillment never achieved in the marriage bed. Its consummation thus compels him to complete social and sexual abstinence" (Shaked, *ibid.*).

The more that Raphael devotes himself to his work—and dialectically, the more individualistic the manner in which he does so, and the more he sees it as a goal to be achieved—the closer it comes to perfection. At the cost however, of his wife's childlessness, and eventual death.

Here Agnon engages in inter-textual debate with the position of the Rabbis in the matter of Rabbi Rehumi, who also devoted himself entirely to the Torah, to the point of forgetting or ignoring the emotional and physical needs of his devoted wife.

It was the custom of Rabbi Rehumi, who studied before Rava in Mahoza, to return home every Yom Kippur eve. One day, he was deep in study [and forgot to go home]. His wife was expecting him, [thinking] "now he will come, now he will come". [When] he did not come, she became discouraged and shed a tear. He

was sitting on a roof [at the time]. The roof gave way beneath
him and his soul departed (*Ketubot* 62b).

In the talmudic tale, Rabbi Rehumi is the one who dies—the lover
of the Torah who devotes himself to it, even to the death. Both his wife's
power and her weakness lie in her longing, in the pain and sorrow encapsulated in her tear. The power of that single tear is so great, because
it is the expression of all of the sorrow in her world. His love of the
Torah and devotion to it are juxtaposed with her love for him and her
pain. The power of her tear is greater than the power of his love, and it is
her pain that (like the prayers of barren mothers for which God yearns)
pierces the heavens, killing her husband. In "The Tale of the Scribe", it
is the wife who pays the price, perhaps because the scribe must—according to Agnon—remain to write the Torah scroll that will remember
and tell the story.

For the Rabbis of the Talmud, the story of Rabbi Rehumi was a literary tool for the transmission of a cultural and educational message, and
that is why the legend ends with Rabbi Rehumi's death, for although
he rightly studied Torah, he went too far. He upset the balance, making creativity the object of his desires and ignoring a wife who longed
for him, and lacked an alternative Torah world of her own. Miriam and
Raphael lived side by side, but the gap between them, embodied in the
partition, was like the gap between Rabbi Rehumi and his wife.

> Raphael the scribe sat and wrote, and his wife, most blessed
> among women, the pious Miriam, stayed home and made life
> pleasant for him in a fine house with fine utensils which she
> scrubbed and cleaned and purified, so that her husband would do
> his work in a clean and pure atmosphere. She delighted him with
> delicate foods and savory beverages ... Thus the pious Miriam
> sits, drawing thread after thread, and a thread of mercy is drawn
> ... And if her hands were not busy with her work, one might mis-
> takenly think that every day is Sabbath (*ibid.* pp. 8–14).

The home of Raphael and Miriam stands near the house of study
and the ritual bath, and is divided by a partition. "It had only one room
which was divided in the middle by a partition made of boards. On the

other side of the partition there was an oven and a range for pots, and between oven and range the pious and modest mistress of his house sat, and she cooked and baked and preserved and wove and knitted and looked to the needs of her home. Children they had none". Not only is the apartment located next to the synagogue and the house of study, but even within the house itself there is a partition separating the holy from the profane. Such a partition is completely justified from a halakhic perspective: "One may not have sexual relations in a house in which there is a Torah scroll, until [the scroll] is removed. And if one is unable to remove it, he must erect a partition before it" (*Shulhan Arukh, YD*, 282). And so: "And one may not treat it with disrespect. One may not place a Torah scroll in a bedroom". In other words, the utilitarian partition became an absolute one. The presence of the Torah scroll eclipsed the fact that this was the home of a man and a woman, meant to procreate: "And when Raphael returns home after the prayers and sees his wife in her true beauty reflected in the mirror, he is immediately attracted to her. He goes toward her to make some pleasing remark. But when he is near her, His Name, may He be blessed, flashes before him out of the mirror. Immediately he stops and recites devoutly and in holiness".

Raphael is not blind to his wife's beauty, and still desires her, but God stands between them. God emerges, metaphorically, from the mirror—a well-known metaphor for art. Consequently, each avoids the other, and physical intimacy becomes impossible. The mirror, which occupies a central place in the house, assumes the central place of the wife in the home.

It hangs on the western wall, opposite and reflecting the east-wall embroidery that Miriam made in her youth.

It depicts a garden full of fruit trees, with a palace in the garden, and two lions watching over the garden. The lions' faces are turned toward each other, lion facing lion, one tongue reaching out toward the other; and stretching from tongue to tongue there is an inscription in large letters of gold, which says, "The earth is the Lord's and the fullness thereof," as if it were one mighty roar ... Facing the east-wall embroidery, on the opposite wall, there is a mirror, and on top of its frame lies a bundle of willow twigs.

The garden is the erotic, the garden of the *Song of Solomon*, and the lions represent the cherubim—the cherubim described in *Terumah*, placed atop the ark cover, facing one another. This face-to-face posture is the erotic encounter between male and female, but also the encounter between man and artist and the duality within her/himself.

The mirror duplicates everything. It has the power of propagation, but it is the propagation of art, the propagation of culture, the propagation of man's ability to express her/himself. In this story however, it is precisely the mirror—multiplier of images in the world—that represses reproduction. This is the power of the artist who devotes himself utterly to the act of cultural creation, repressing the power of human procreation. The beaten willow branch, symbol of fertility, sits dry and wilted above the mirror. Raphael and Miriam's home is quiet, peaceful, holy, as if enveloped in an eternal Sabbath. The reigning holiness upsets the natural balance, and precipitates death.

The idea that man was created in God's image—a fundamental principle in the Bible (see Yair Lorberbaum, *Tzelem Elohim*, p. 100, n.62)— is expressed metaphorically in the idea of the mirror, which reproduces and multiplies the image, in its reflections. Sometimes the reflection is direct, as in the case of Jacob's struggle with the angel, of which he says: "for I have seen God face to face, and my life is preserved" (Gen. 32:31).

Although man's face is the image of God, its reproduction results in distortion and duality, for example: "male and female created He them"—a duality that exists within the godhead as well; and "... man strikes a number of coins with the same die, and they all resemble one another. The King of Kings, the Holy One, blessed be He, cast all men in the stamp of Adam, yet none resembles his fellow" (*Sanhedrin* 4:5). Ibn Ezra stresses the duality of man created in the image of God, and compares human procreation to the creation brought forth by the waters—a substance that is at once, vital, elusive and reflective: "And Adam was first created with two faces and he was one but also two. And 'in the image of God' [means in the image of] the angels. And he [Adam] was created male and female, and the expression '[be] fruitful and multiply' in man, is a blessing, just as it is with regard to the creation [brought forth by] the waters" (Ibn Ezra, commentary on Gen. 1:26). All of the motifs are there: divine image, male and female, and the blessing of procreation. Artistic creativity is thus—like a reflection in the water—a refinement of the desire to procreate rather than a substitute for it. It is precisely this balance that Raphael is unable to strike.

Agnon was familiar with the biblical source and its rabbinical exegesis, but focused instead on the psyche of the artist. In this, Agnon was a modernist, concerned primarily with self-reflection. The artist's psyche is a mirror reflecting the Creator, and as such is an abstract altar of earth, the altar described in *Terumah*, the altar of the written word. Sometimes, in the struggle between the desire to serve God and the desire to recognize one's self and essence, the desire to procreate is lost. To renounce procreation is to choose death.

Similarly in "Agunot", Ben Uri needs Dinah's inspiration, but abandons her—despite his love for her—once she has served her purpose: "But as Ben Uri pursued his work, he cleaved more and more to it, until both eyes and heart passed into the Ark; no part of him was free of it. Memory of Dinah fled him; it was as though she did not exist" (*Twenty-One Stories*, pp. 33–34). He makes his own, individualistic existence, his entire world; filling himself up until there is no room for anyone else—a situation that cannot possibly end well. In Lurianic Kabbalah and other traditions, God Himself is said to have "withdrawn" for the sake of creation, compelled as it were, to reduce his Infinite Light, that there might be a "void" in which the worlds might be created—for the sake of His Kingship, the ultimate purpose of creation.

These literary characters, both the scribe and the ark-maker, serve as metaphors for Agnon himself. Cast in his image, they are artists who abstain from life for the sake of their art. In this, Agnon affirms that there can be no artistic creation without abstinence and abandonment—the price both artist and wife must pay for his art. Artistic creation thus entails a kind of immorality, and sets the self-identified artist above the normal balances of Jewish life.

The outcome of "The Tale of the Scribe" shows that Agnon had no intention of leaving Raphael without the woman in his life—his artist's life. He needed her, because she was his daughter. Carefully selecting his figurative materials, Agnon describes Raphael's symbolic erotic union with his wife, Miriam, after her death, upon completing the Torah

scroll he has written in her memory. When he removes the covering from the mirror, he comes face to face with the motifs that fill his life:
At that moment his soul stirred and he returned to the table ... and he leaped and danced and sang in honor of the Torah. Suddenly Raphael stopped, puzzled about the melody he was singing in honor of the completion of the scroll. He felt sure that he had heard this melody before, but could not remember where he had heard it ... Where had he heard this melody?

The melody is the memory of his first meeting with Miriam. It was in the synagogue, on the night of *Simhat Torah*, when he held the Torah and danced with it, in a state of joyous rapture:
At that moment a young girl pushed her way through the legs of the dancers, leaped toward Raphael, sank her red lips into the white mantle of the Torah scroll in Raphael's arm, and kept on kissing the scroll and caressing it with her hands. Just then the flag fell out of her hand, and the burning candle dropped on Raphael's clothing.

The melody, like the Torah scroll, is a repository for personal as well as collective memory. At this particular moment, it is the personal that predominates.

Death—like the altar of his art—separates the artist from his love, but also binds him to her for all eternity.

Elhanan Yakira

Tetzaveh – Command the Children of Israel

On Obedience and Freedom:
Spinoza's Critique of Biblical Theocracy

And bring thou near unto thee Aaron thy brother, and his sons with him, from among the children of Israel, that they may minister unto me as priests, even Aaron, Nadab and Abihu, Eleazar and Ithamar, Aaron's sons. And thou shalt make holy garments for Aaron thy brother, for splendor and for beauty. (*Exodus* 28:1–2).

The portion's primary focus would appear to be a series of ritual acts: the lighting of the "continual lamp" (and the provision of olive oil for that purpose); the preparation of the priestly garments to be worn by Aaron and his sons when ministering in the Tent of Meeting (28:2–43); the actions prescribed "to hallow them, to minister unto me as priests" (29:1–37); the order of the "continual offering" (29:38–42); the construction of the "altar to burn incense upon" and the burning of the "incense of sweet spices" (30:1–10). Two additional matters are addressed briefly. At the very beginning of the portion (28:1), Moses charges the Israelites as follows: "And bring thou near unto thee Aaron thy brother, and his sons with him, from among the children of Israel, that they may minister unto me as priests, even Aaron, Nadab and Abihu, Eleazar and Ithamar, Aaron's sons". The portion's final verse establishes an annual expiation ritual to be performed by Aaron: "And Aaron shall make atonement upon the projections of it once in the year; with the blood of the sin-offering of atonement once in the year shall he make atonement for it throughout your generations; it is most holy unto the Lord.

The opening verse of *Tetzaveh* drew the attention of many biblical commentators. God says to Moses: "And thou shalt command (*tetzaveh*) the children of Israel". Elsewhere—in *Terumah* for example, when detailing the contributions required for the construction of the Tabernacle—God tells Moses to "speak" (*daber*) to the Children of Israel. The commentators explain that the word *tetzaveh* implies immediate compliance and eternal validity. The *Midrash Hagadol* for example, remarks: "And thou shalt command—Why was the 'commanding' rather than the 'speaking' form used? As an impetus to act—immediately and in future generations ... Although the Sanctuary has been destroyed and the lamps abolished, synagogues and houses of study that kindle them are called 'little sanctuaries', as it is written (*Ezek.* 11:16): 'yet have I been to them as a little sanctuary'" (for further examples, see Nehama Leibowitz, *New Studies in Shemot*, pp. 370–371).

The commentators thus explain the use of the imperative form as establishing a temporal context: a pressing demand that the required action be performed immediately, swiftly and continually. While the first two elements clearly pertain to the verb's ordinary meaning, the reference to the future is not so readily apparent. In any event, it is not a natural part of our general perception of the grammatical imperative. In *Tetzaveh* however, it is repeatedly stipulated—explicitly, consistently and at more or less regular intervals—that its precepts must be observed "continually" (*tamid*), in the sense of a nonimmediate time frame. For example: "And thou shalt put in the breastplate of judgment the Urim and the Thummim; and they shall be upon Aaron's heart, when he goeth in before the Lord; and Aaron shall bear the judgment of the children of Israel upon his heart before the Lord continually (*tamid*)" (28:30); "And it shall be upon Aaron's forehead, and Aaron shall bear the iniquity committed in the holy things, which the children of Israel shall hallow, even in all their holy gifts; and it shall be always (*tamid*) upon his forehead, that they may be accepted before the Lord" (*ibid.* 38). This final *tamid* is unclear—is it limited to Aaron's lifespan, or does it refer to a broader time frame? Elsewhere, little room is left for doubt: "And thou shalt make them linen breeches to cover the flesh of their nakedness; from the loins even unto the thighs they shall reach. And they shall be upon Aaron, and upon his sons, when they go in unto the tent of meeting, or when they come near unto the altar to minister in the holy place; that they bear not iniquity, and die; it shall be a statute for ever unto him and unto his seed after him" (*ibid.* 42–43); "And when Aaron lighteth the lamps at dusk, he shall burn it, a perpetual (*tamid*) incense before the Lord throughout your generations" (30:8).

Whether the commentators' understanding is a product of profound linguistic insight or merely based on the general context, some of the precepts in *Tetzaveh* are undoubtedly intended for "the generations". This being the case, how do we explain the discrepancy between the brevity with which the perpetual validity of the precepts is expressed, and the extensive and detailed attention given to the "technical" aspects of the rituals prescribed? The demands upon the Israelites are far from trifling: binding not only those present, but all future generations as well. Moreover, the idea of a covenant or a treaty entails voluntary acceptance, and hence the possibility of non-acceptance as well. The demand that the Israelites' acceptance be "perpetual" and "throughout the generations" however, denies future generations this freedom. It is a grave responsibility, yet the Bible takes this perpetuity for granted, focusing instead (as noted above) on the precise requirements of ritual and ceremony.

The two matters addressed with extreme brevity at the beginning and end of the portion are paramount. One is the designation of Aaron and his sons as priests to God—thereby establishing the institution of the priesthood; with far-reaching implications for the social order, cult, law and image of historical Israel. The other is the creation of what would later become the most important day in the Jewish calendar: Yom Kippur. This contrast between the extreme economy with which "truly" important issues such as the eternal validity of the precepts are treated, and the careful and detailed attention given to descriptions of the priestly garments, the sacrificial cult and the form of the altar, is puzzling, to say the least.

Upon closer examination, we find that matters of cult and ritual are closely interwoven with juridical, and what we might call "divine" matters—practically forming a single, organic unit: "And thou shalt put in the breastplate of judgment the Urim and the Thummim; and they shall be upon Aaron's heart, when he goeth in before the Lord; and Aaron shall bear the judgment of the children of Israel upon his heart before the Lord continually" (28:30). The classic commentators pay little attention to the relationship between ritual and more "substantive" issues. Some explain that the beauty of the priestly garments was intended to inspire respect in all who beheld them. Rashi however—on the verse "And thou shalt make holy garments for Aaron thy brother, for splendor and for beauty" (*ibid.* 2)—explains that it was the garments themselves that consecrated Aaron as a priest to God. In other words, the "splendor and beauty" of the garments was inherent, independent of the feelings they evoked. Ritual and ceremony are central to all religious tradition and, from a biblical perspective, there is no real difference between ritual and law, no distinction between commandments governing the ceremonial and the juridical. The traditional commentators' failure to address this issue shows that they too found no particular difficulty in the matter.

Some however, have considered the integration of ritual and law worthy of closer scrutiny. It is primarily critics of religion who have questioned the relationship between ritual practices or ceremonial objects such as those described at such length in *Tetzaveh*, and general mores. Religious philosophers who have addressed this issue have generally done so in an apologetic fashion, in response to the critics' assertions. Western philosophy has, from its inception, harbored a tradition of religious criticism; and among those philosophers and intellectuals in western culture who have taken a critical approach to religion, Spinoza stands out, as one of the sharpest and most important. He was also one of "Rabbinic" Judaism's most scathing critics—in matters that would undoubtedly resonate with modern Israeli readers.

In his youth, Spinoza studied at Amsterdam's Ets Haim seminary. According to biographers, his teachers—the rabbis of the community—expected great things of him. We can reasonably assume that he was one of the best students at the school, and one of the most promising disciples of its dean, Rabbi Saul Levi Morteira. He was certainly familiar with the exegetic and homiletic methods of traditional Jewish literature. Spinoza himself often engaged in exegesis, and his *Theologico-Political Treatise* (henceforth the *Treatise*) includes not only exegesis, but a comprehensive hermeneutical system for the interpretation of Scripture. Spinoza is often considered one of the founders of modern biblical criticism. The hermeneutical principles he formulates however, and espe-

cially the interpretations he offers, not only differ from traditional exegesis, but seek to undermine its very validity. His exegesis can thus be
termed subversive: employing methods and modes of expression taken
from tradition—and thus acceptable to readers who are familiar with
them and acknowledge their authority—but in fact intended to undermine their foundations.

It is in this fashion that Spinoza interprets *Isaiah* 58. After criticizing the superficial and empty observance of the religious precepts, the
prophet exclaims:

Is not this the fast that I have chosen? to loose the fetters of
wickedness, to undo the bands of the yoke, and to let the oppressed go free, and that ye break every yoke? Is it not to deal
thy bread to the hungry, and that thou bring the poor that are cast
out to thy house? When thou seest the naked, that thou cover
him, and that thou hide not thyself from thine own flesh? Then
shall thy light break forth as the morning, and thy healing shall
spring forth speedily; and thy righteousness shall go before thee,
the glory of the Lord shall be thy rearward (58:6–8).

Later in the same chapter, Isaiah says:
If thou turn away thy foot because of the Sabbath, from pursuing
thy business on my holy day; and call the Sabbath a delight, and
the holy of the Lord honorable; and shalt honor it, not doing thy
wonted ways, nor pursuing thy business, nor speaking thereof;
Then shalt thou delight thyself in the Lord, and I will make thee
to ride upon the high places of the earth, and I will feed thee with
the heritage of Jacob thy father; for the mouth of the Lord hath
spoken it (*ibid.* 13–14).

It is interesting, almost amusing, to see how Spinoza interprets these
verses, or rather manipulates them to serve his purposes. It is worth
noting here, that the *Treatise*, was intended for a non-Jewish audience,
whose familiarity with Scripture (the "Old Testament", as Spinoza himself refers to it), and particularly the Hebrew language, would have been
rather limited. Spinoza, who was also a grammarian (one of his lesser
known works is a compendium of Hebrew grammar), often demon-

strates his knowledge of the language; although here too he bends and shapes meaning to his own ends. This method of reading into Scripture—as opposed to interpretation that seeks the plain meaning of the text—offers those who employ it a great deal of freedom and room for creativity.

Regarding verses 6–8, Spinoza observes that the prophet "commends liberty and charity towards one's self and one's neighbors" (*Theologico-Political Treatise*, V, 17 –tr. R. H. M. Elwes). These are the primary elements of what can loosely be termed Spinoza's ethical philosophy. These "ethics"—also the title of his most important work—are the ethics of personal happiness or even "salvation". Fundamentally, it is a utilitarian approach to ethics. Spinoza also engaged in political philosophy, but viewed knowledge of "the right way of life"—wherein lies man's happiness—as the ultimate goal of philosophy. This happiness depends, to a large extent, upon the liberty and autonomy of the individual, as well as her or his self-concern. Hence Spinoza's incorrect attribution of the word "liberty" to the prophet; and his interpretation of words such as *besarkha* "thine own flesh" (referring—as also explained by the commentators—to others) and *arukhatkha* "thy healing", in terms of concern for oneself. In a footnote, Spinoza adds that the word *ya'asfekha* (translated "shall be thy rearward" in the JPS 1917 edition –tr.), refers to death, and derives from the Hebrew expression "to be gathered unto one's people". Here too Spinoza exercises interpretive liberty—contrary to the traditional commentators' understanding of the word—possibly with his Christian (and particularly Calvinist) readers in mind, for whom the reward of the righteous and the elect is eternal life.

Spinoza's purpose in citing these verses however, goes even further. He finds an original difference—i.e. one that none of the traditional commentators had, or could have noticed—between the first group of verses and the second. "Thus the prophet," Spinoza writes, "for liberty bestowed, and charitable works, promises a healthy mind in a healthy body, and the glory of the Lord even after death; whereas, for ceremonial exactitude, he only promises security of rule, prosperity, and temporal happiness" (*ibid.*). Spinoza's reading of these verses is clearly biased. What renders his interpretation really explosive however, is the distinction he makes between "liberty and charitable works" and "ceremonial exactitude". As noted, such a distinction between the verses would not have occurred to traditional commentators, because to do so would have been to question their own vocation—based, *inter alia*, on the assumption that the personal and inner religious meaning of Scripture cannot be separated from its authority in temporal matters. And this was precisely Spinoza's intention—to undermine the authority of scriptural interpretation as a religio-political institution. Undermining the authority of institutional interpretation was in effect only part of a much broader campaign. Spinoza fought an uncompromising battle against religion in general, or more precisely, against its purporting to serve as a basis for social, i.e. political, life. He argued against its pretension to absolute authority—the authority of truth—for its assertions and precepts; its claim to be the final arbiter of good and evil; and the generally formative status it accords itself within the human experience.

The ramifications of Spinoza's broad campaign against religion are many and varied. It bears special significance however, with regard to Judaism and the Jewish People. Spinoza has occupied an important place in Jewish group consciousness throughout the ages, in different ways and for different reasons, some symbolic and some philosophical. In many ways he is often seen as the principal harbinger of Jewish modernism, with all the problems and contradictions, hopes and dangers, it entails. Spinoza was perceived by many proponents of the *Haskalah* as embodying the inherent promise of the emancipated Jew; freed of the shackles of religious prejudice and superstition, released from the ghetto into the world of enlightenment and science. To secular Zionists such as Ben-Gurion (perhaps the most prominent, but by no means the only one), he represented the possibility of Jewish political existence. Others viewed his life and thought as a betrayal of his people and a danger to its continued existence. Regardless of one's perspective, Spinoza undoubtedly embodies or symbolizes—in his unusual life story as well as the many-faceted content of his philosophy—the great shift in Jewish history, toward modernity. Leo Strauss, for example, justifiably concludes his introduction to *Spinoza's Critique of Religion* with the assertion that, in the end, the two great alternatives that lie before modern Judaism are Spinoza or Orthodoxy. Similarly, Eliezer Schweid contends that Spinoza is the most important challenge faced by modern Jewish thought.

Spinoza was, as we know, excommunicated by the Amsterdam community in which he was born and raised. Contrary to other members of the Portuguese community of Amsterdam who, unable to withstand the rigors of life outside the community, shamefacedly returned to its ranks (the dramatic case of Uriel da Costa is perhaps the best known), Spinoza never sought readmission. He severed all ties with the community, and in effect would appear to have shunned the community no less than it had shunned him. This is a highly symbolic element of the Spinozist challenge. Inasmuch as this renunciation of Jewish solidarity is rooted in a historical and philosophical analysis that seeks to undermine its legitimacy, or at least its importance and benefit—the "Spinoza case" indeed becomes a significant intellectual, and possibly existential, challenge. The reason that Spinoza was able to serve as a symbol and point of reference for *maskilim*, Zionists and many others not necessarily seeking to cast off their ties to the Jewish People or their sense of Jewish solidarity, lay in part in the fact that Spinoza was one of secularism's greatest thinkers, if not *the* greatest. From the moment in which the viability of secular Judaism—as a nation, a state and a culture—became apparent, Spinoza could again be seen as a symbol of a valid Jewish alternative. One could also speculate that, had the possibility of leading a secular Jewish life been open to Spinoza (an option that only became historical reality about a century after his death), he might have embraced it. In any event, his sharp and sweeping criticism of religion was seen by proponents of Jewish secularism to meet their theoretical and ideological needs.

This sweeping opposition to religion can be found in all of Spinoza's writings. His magnum opus, the *Ethics*, strives to present a comprehensive alternative to religion as a basis for the right way of life, and salvation. It is perhaps the most far-reaching attempt in the history of western thought, to propose a secular version of this religious concept. Religious criticism in the strict sense of the term however, i.e. the direct and explicit questioning of its fundamental principles, can be found in the *Treatise*. This work—of no less importance to the development of western thought than the *Ethics*—poses a number of problems. Beyond difficulties of interpretation to be found in every philosophical work worthy of the name, the *Treatise* presents readers with questions of a methodological or "textological" order. The *Treatise* differs from Spinoza's other writings in that it is the only one of his works in which the views he presents are not aimed at a select audience of "philosophers". It is intended rather, for readers who accept the authority of religion and the leadership of its ministers, and his apparent premises are those that would normally be acceptable to such a readership. Its critical message—or at least the radical aspects of that message—is conveyed indirectly and in such a fashion as to outwit not only the censors, but readers as well. Deciphering the precise nature of this message is thus a delicate matter and has been the source of a good deal of controversy.

Let us now return to Spinoza's interpretation of the verses in *Isaiah*. Spinoza asserts, as noted above, that the first group of verses (*Is.* 58:6–8) promises healing and personal salvation; while the second group (*ibid.* 13–14) promises mainly material success and "security of rule". Of course, the distinction between personal, and public or national religion, runs counter to the spirit of Jewish tradition. More important however, is the fundamental distinction that Spinoza makes between Scripture's eternally-valid inner message (liberty and charity/love) and its limited, obsolete aspect ("ceremonial exactitude"). The chapter in which these matters are addressed is the fifth, entitled "Of Religious Ceremonial Observance, and Faith in Historical Narrative. Of the Reasons why Rites and Ceremonies are Useful, and of those who Find them Necessary" (tr. Robert Willis, Trübner, London, 1862). Divine law, Spinoza writes—summarizing the previous chapters' conclusions for his readers—is universal law, common to all men. Fundamentally, this is an objective truth concerning the way in which men should live their lives, if they truly seek happiness. This law is the valid part of Scripture, and was given to the great lawgiver Moses and to the prophets, who grasped it purely by intuition (but not by philosophical inquiry). "But with regard to the ceremonial observances which were ordained in the Old Testament for the Hebrews only, and were so adapted to their state that they could for the most part only be observed by the society as a whole and not by each individual, it is evident that they formed no part of the Divine law, and had nothing to do with blessedness and virtue" (Elwes, V, 2). The ceremonial observances were thus valid only as long as there was a Hebrew kingdom, i.e. as long as the Jews enjoyed political independence within a state of their own. Moreover, the entire purpose of these ceremonies was "that men should do nothing of their own free will, but should always act under external authority, and should continually confess by their actions and thoughts that they were not their own masters, but were entirely under the control of others" (*ibid.* 58), i.e. their leaders—Moses and his successors. Since the Israelites were, at the time, a people of slaves, and thus unaccustomed to the orderly and mature exercise of sovereignty, Moses wisely established statues and ordinances that would ensure the people's willing—rather than fearful—compliance. "Moses, therefore, by his virtue and the Divine command, introduced a religion, so that the people might do their duty from devotion rather than fear" (*ibid.* 55).

The main purpose of the religious ceremonies and biblical narratives was thus to overcome the Hebrews' obstinacy and elicit their compliance. The subversive implications of Spinoza's analysis steal into a single brief phrase: "obedience," he explains, "consists in acting at the bidding of external authority". In other words, "obedience" is the opposite of liberty. And liberty, according to Spinoza, is the autonomy of the necessity of reason, i.e. a rational man or philosopher has no need of external authority (Scripture and its narratives, ceremony, the coercive power of the state, pastors and priests, rabbis and doctrinaires of all kinds) in order to conduct himself in accordance with divine, eternal and universal law. In this sense, he is like one who deduces the qualities of a triangle from its definition: the deduction is necessary, but involves no obedience of "authority". Liberty is also the quality of those who live life in accordance with reason, and as such is the ultimate goal of philosophy and the key to true happiness. Furthermore, liberty—more than security or peace—is also the purpose of the state, and therefore the criterion by which its rationality is measured. That is why Spinoza considers democracy the preferred form of government. Accordingly, we may conclude that a state resembling the biblical state—based on the law ordained by Moses, i.e. on obedience—is a state that is less free, and thus less rational and less desirable.

The implications are far-reaching, in terms of religious criticism. The line of argument in the *Treatise* proceeds simultaneously on a number of planes, some more and some less evident. The most direct and obvious of these lies in the realm of political theory. Spinoza criticizes the principle of authority in the context of his criticism of the theocratic state, that is a state founded on the principle of religious authority. He feared the struggle of Calvinist theologians against the relatively tolerant and proto-democratic bourgeois elite that ruled Holland at the time. Calvinistic orthodoxy had struck an alliance with royalists who sought to invest the House of Orange with full power over country. The theological grounds on which the Calvinists based their struggle were seen by Spinoza as advocating the establishment of a monarchy by divine right, i.e. a theocracy. His criticism of the biblical state, as presented in the *Treatise*, is in fact criticism of the prototypical theocracy. His interpretation of the Mosaic constitution, as essentially designed to elicit obedience—rather than bearing a message of "truth"—expresses his concern that theocracy will undermine the ultimate purpose of the state: liberty.

The conclusion Spinoza would seem to wish readers to draw from his analysis of the reasons for the failure of the biblical state—and hence of theocracy in general—is the need for "separation of church and state". Things are not that simple however, and beyond this ostensibly moderate and essentially liberal conclusion, lies a far more radical position. When Spinoza questions the validity of the principle of authority, he is in fact questioning a fundamental tenet of religion that extends to areas apparently unrelated to politics. Spinoza's criticism of the role that religion seeks to fulfill in the political domain is, in effect, sweeping criticism of the validity of the religious position in general, in all areas. Although Spinoza appears to allow for the continued existence of religion within its own sphere, it is of a kind that is wholly subordinate to the (essentially secular) state. Religion is supposed to help the authorities to obtain the obedience of the masses—incapable of autonomous, rational action. Spinoza rejects the idea that an institution or tradition may, by virtue of supernatural privilege, possess a special truth that affords it absolute authority. Spinoza dismisses as mere illusions, such concepts as "revelation", "miracle" and "prophecy", which religion generally cites as the source of its privilege. Such authority can only stem from autonomous reason; the truths that can be proven as one proves the truths of geometry.

Ceremony is thus merely a peaceable means by which to obtain the obedience of a state's subjects. It has no source beyond the wisdom or shrewdness of the sovereign, and no value or essence beyond its "didactic" function. This claim is of course, not new, and has always been asserted, in one way or another, by critics of religion. The priestly garments described in such detail in *Tetzaveh* are also, ostensibly, ceremonial objects. Indeed, the commentators who discuss the purpose of these garments, their richness and particular design, explain that they were intended to inspire the Israelites' awe and respect. Once again however, beyond the seemingly simple and rather hackneyed contention, the popular psychology cum cliché, lies a much deeper matter.

Let us return once again to Spinoza's interpretation of *Isaiah* 58. It was, as we have seen, an example of the type of "proof" he found in Scripture of his distinction between eternal law, which leads to true salvation, and ceremony, which can only result in external, material and public (or political) success. As an example of such a ceremony, Spinoza cites the Sabbath and its observance. This choice of example, it is safe to assume, was not a random one; as evidenced perhaps by the artificiality of his interpretation of *Isaiah*. Spinoza specifically chose the Sabbath, because he was aware of its significance in Jewish life and history, and the shaping of the distinctive character of the Jewish People. The cultural, sociological and even economic impact of the Sabbath was such that Jewish history would have been quite different without it.

Above all however, the Sabbath is one of the highest expressions of Jewish religious consciousness—and it is precisely this aspect of the Sabbath that Spinoza had in mind when he referred to it as "ceremonial". The Sabbath is undoubtedly one of the core elements of the experience of holiness in Jewish religion and tradition. The concept of "holiness" or "the holy" is central to attempts in the field of religious studies to distill the "essence" of religion or "religiosity" in general, from the history and sociology of religion. Rudolf Otto or example, in his well-known book *The Idea of the Holy: An Inquiry into the Non-rational Factor in the Idea of the Divine and its Relation to the Rational*, offers a "phenomenological" analysis of religious consciousness. He seeks to demonstrate that the unique nature of this consciousness, or the experience termed "religious", can be explained by means of "the holy". There is a unique type of experience that cannot be understood in terms of other experiences, such as the experience of beauty called "aesthetic". Otto denoted the object of the religious experience, the "moment" encapsulated in the holy: "the numinous". In this sense, one might refer to the Sabbath as a "numinous object".

This by no means implies acceptance of Otto's analysis of the holy. His is but one of many attempts—albeit a particularly interesting one—to provide justification for religion's claim to unique, irreducible status. Spinoza's inclusion of the Sabbath in the category of "ceremonial exactitude", asserting that it is essentially a means by which to maintain political order, effectively rejects of the idea of the unique nature of the religious object. Graver still, it questions the legitimacy of the religious experience. Otto's phenomenological analysis of the experience of the holy and the conclusions he draws regarding its uniqueness and irreducibility also provide the justification for the religious experience itself. Although Spinoza would not of course have been familiar with Otto or modern jargon such as "phenomenology of religion", his criticism of religion is not merely the result of his democratic and liberal convictions, but would also appear to question the validity of interpretations such as Otto's that accord religion *sui generis* status. In other words, the sphere of religion should be limited and confronted—along with all of its rituals and mores—with its true source; a source Spinoza identifies with the political. As we have seen, these ceremonies serve no purpose other than to secure the obedience of the masses, by appealing to their imaginations. Imagination is easily swayed by the beauty and splendor of ceremonies carefully devised with a keen understanding of human nature. As everyone knows, even the most secular of states abounds in ceremonies and symbols designed, *inter alia*, to inspire loyalty in its citizens.

When God instructs Moses, in *Tetzaveh*, to command the Children of Israel to consecrate priests, he also directs him to "speak unto all that are wise-hearted, whom I have filled with the spirit of wisdom, that they make Aaron's garments to sanctify him, that he may minister unto me in the priest's office" (28:3). What kind of wisdom was it that filled the craftsmen charged with the task of preparing the priestly garments? Were they merely wise in their craft, skilled at cutting and sewing? Or were they endowed with the same political and legislative wisdom that Spinoza ascribed to Moses; the ability to control the ignorant masses with beautiful sights and wondrous visions? The Bible offers no further explanation, and remains open to both interpretations. As a number of commentators point out however, the expressions "wisdom", "wise-heartedness" and "spirit of wisdom" generally refer to other matters, beyond sartorial skills. As the verse states, these garments will be for Aaron "for splendor and for beauty"—a manifestly religious expression, repeated a number of times in *Tetzaveh*, and generally associated with the phenomenon described above as the experience of "the holy", for it is often used in reference to God Himself.

Thus, contrary to Spinoza's approach, the priestly garments may be seen as "numinous objects", in the full sense of Otto's term. For example, the Rabbis explain the verse "And thou shalt make a plate of pure gold, and engrave upon it like the engravings of a signet, holy to the Lord (YHWH)" (28:36) to mean that the words "Holy to YHWH" themselves—the Tetragrammaton, the utmost expression of the numinous in Jewish tradition—should be engraved upon Aaron's front plate. The priestly garments are also often referred to as the "holy garments", and the response they are meant to elicit in those who behold them (and it is of course impossible to isolate their visual effect from the ceremonies in which they are worn) is a religious one. This response—at least in terms of the verse itself and the views that can be ascribed to it as a religious document—cannot be attributed to feelings of wonder, astonishment and dread, which derive from another psychological source. The breastplate of judgment and the Urim and Thummim worn by the high priest further strengthen this impression. They can certainly be considered numinous objects inasmuch as they evoke religious experience through their symbolic function.

The priestly garments, breastplate and Urim and Thummim are not the only numinous objects that strike "fear and trembling" into the hearts of believers however. The priesthood itself is such an object as well. *Exodus* 19:6 equates the word "priest" with the word "holy": if they uphold the covenant, Moses tells the people, they will be "a kingdom of priests, and a holy nation". And so elsewhere. The fact that the priesthood is restricted to a specific group (Aaron and his descendants in *Tetzaveh*; in other sources, e.g. *Deut.* 10:8–9, the entire tribe of Levi) is a further expression of the holiness of the priesthood. The custom of the Priestly Blessing offers sufficient evidence of the fact that a number of elements of the symbolic function of the priesthood persist to this day.

The priests fulfilled a number of roles in biblical society; some ritual, others of a somewhat different nature. Among other things, they served as judges (although apparently not exclusively) and teachers. Spinoza devotes considerable attention to the subject of the priests and the priesthood, but credits them with a purely political role. Spinoza's approach to the priesthood is entirely in keeping with his approach to ceremony. He views the ostensibly religious component of the priesthood as stemming from, and serving, its political and social functions.

Like most of the *Treatise*, Spinoza's discussion of the priests and the priesthood is a mixture of explicit and implicit messages. For example, he asserts (VII, 187) that one cannot infer the absolute authority of the papacy to interpret Scripture from the authority afforded to the priests in the interpretation of biblical law. He thus uses Scripture to express views concerning the political and theologico-political disputes of his day. He ascribes the interpretative authority of the biblical priests to a political source: "the laws of Moses being also the ordinary laws of the country, necessarily required some public authority to insure their observance"; immediately adding: "With religion the case is widely different. Inasmuch as it consists not so much in outward actions as in simplicity and truth of character, it stands outside the sphere of law and public authority" (*ibid.* 188–189). What appears to be an attack on papal authority in matters of scriptural interpretation was in fact addressed to a Reformist (Calvinist) audience that would have rejected such authority in any case. We must therefore assume, here as in similar passages, that Spinoza indulges his readers somewhat, in order to lead them to ideas they would not otherwise have entertained.

Of greater interest to us however, is Spinoza's understanding of the institution of the priesthood and its sources. Historically speaking, it is of little value—completely disregarding the priesthood's roots in ancient Near Eastern culture, for example; a subject of which Spinoza may in fact have been ignorant. The importance of Spinoza's views in this matter derives from their significance in terms of political theory. The unique character of the ancient Hebrew state—conferred by Moses and his Law—is termed "theocracy" by Spinoza. Indeed, Spinoza portrays Moses as a wise lawgiver, who transformed the multitude of slaves he had taken out of Egypt into a people. Moses successfully turned an ignorant horde, wholly lacking what might be called "political maturity", into a nation guided by a constitution, capable of sustaining an organized state. The seeds of the Hebrew state's demise however, lay in its very constitution.

Contrary to other states—defined as monarchies, aristocracies or democracies, depending on the individual or group in possession of political power—all powers in the Hebrew state were conferred upon God. According to the Hobbesian model, the source of sovereign power is the act whereby citizens effectively transfer their "natural rights" to the sovereign. While Hobbes believed that such a "commonwealth by institution" should be governed by a "sovereign absolute", Spinoza applied this model to all the chief forms of government. Those who decide to establish a commonwealth may thus transfer their rights to an individual, a group or themselves (the people). In the unique case of the Hebrew state, these rights were transfered to God. What could be simpler or more reasonable than explaining the covenant between God and his people in this fashion? Things are not quite so simple however, and Spinoza's analysis reveals an irreconcilable contradiction between the idea of a covenant between ruler and subjects based on the voluntary transferal of the rights, and the idea that such a covenant can be made with God. The contradiction stems from the absoluteness of transfering one's rights to God on the one hand, and the fundamental impossibility of total abdication. This impossibility is inherent to the "human condition". Spinoza does not say this explicitly, but his conclusions regarding the Hebrew state and its ruin can be understood in this fashion. Since the "natural right" of each individual is, in effect, her or his ability to exist and act, the complete renunciation of these rights would be tantamount to self-annihilation—something Spinoza considers a logical impossibility. This intrinsic contradiction soon comes to light within Hebrew political reality, i.e. the state established by Moses.

The Hebrews thus surrendered their rights, not to another human being, but—all together and with one voice—to God, before whom they were therefore all equal, as if in a democracy. Spinoza's description is ironic. In fact, the equality between the Hebrews was closer to that of the natural state than to the equality of democracy, since (of course Spinoza never says so explicitly) their rights were not transfered to anyone and no sovereign was appointed. The true ruler was Moses, who became—by popular will, according to Spinoza's reconstruction of the biblical narrative—intermediary between the divine ruler and his human subjects, sole interpreter of God's laws and in effect, sole ruler. What set the Hebrew state apart from ordinary monarchies was the fact that Moses chose no heir; clearly distinguishing between political power and the authority to interpret the law. Aaron and his sons, the priests, were made interpreters of God's law. This first separation of powers helped to avert the ills of absolute rule—too much power in the hands of the sovereign, resulting in popular unrest—allowing the existence of the Hebrew state for a time.

The reason for the state's downfall was, in the end, the very same constitution that had fostered its establishment and existence—more specifically, the entrusting of matters of cult to the Levites and the priests. So disastrous was this decision that Spinoza wrote: "When I reflect on this change, I feel disposed to break forth with the words of Tacitus. God's object at that time was not the safety of the Jews, but vengeance" (XVII, 167–168). In other words, setting one tribe apart from the rest of the people, granting them exclusive control over cult rites and interpretation of the law, ultimately and inevitably led to such social discord that the commonwealth—more than succumbing to external enemies –simply collapsed from within. Jealousy of the Levites' privileges, resentment of the obligation to support them and other such human feelings, resulted, according to Spinoza, in endless strife and unrest. Eventually, the Hebrews installed a king, but kings are "above all things jealous of a precarious rule, and can in nowise brook a dominion within their own", he writes. As the commonwealth's affairs continue to deteriorate, it becomes clear that Moses failed to provide it with the necessary political tools. Since the laws were the exclusive province of religious leaders—Levites and prophets who sought only to undermine the power of the kings—it was impossible to abrogate them or adapt them to changing needs. "And they shall have the priesthood by a perpetual statute" (29:9), we are told in *Tetzaveh*. It is this perpetual statute that destroyed the Hebrew commonwealth.

Spinoza's first conclusion from "the successes and the histories of the Hebrews" is that "the concession to ministers of religion of any power of issuing decrees or transacting the business of government" is extremely harmful both to religion and to the state (XVIII, 40). Nevertheless, he asserts that the commonwealth of the Hebrews "might have lasted for ever", although "it would be impossible to imitate it at the present day, nor would it be advisable so to do" (*ibid.* 1). This is because a covenant based on citizens transfering their rights to God, as they would to a human sovereign, would also require the explicit consent of God. "God, however, has revealed through his Apostles that the covenant of God is no longer written in ink, or on tables of stone, but with the Spirit of God in the fleshy tables of the heart" (*ibid.* 3). This remark is of course aimed at Christian readers, and would mean little to a fellow Jew. Its general message however, is that if a covenant or charter between man and God for the establishment of a state is to be upheld, God must play an active and explicit role not only in forging the covenant itself, but also—in fact primarily—in administering state and government affairs, for by virtue of the covenant He is its sovereign. No great effort is needed to understand that knowing God's will is only possible through interpretation. In other words, political divine will, expressed directly and without intermediaries, is pure invention. Either it is a personal matter, relegated to the heart, and thus of no political value; or it is a matter of interpretation, and thus a clear recipe for political destruction. In any case, religion and priests must remain outside the political arena.

It is plain to see why no one would wish to imitate the Hebrew commonwealth. God's will can no longer be ascertained without intermediaries, assuming for the sake of argument that such revelation was indeed granted to the Hebrews. But why would it not be "advisable"? The reason is that the word "law" (*hok*) as it is used in Jewish tradition—or in

Halakhah, to extend matters beyond the Bible, to the historical context in which Spinoza lived and to which he related—is misleading. Law, according to Spinoza, is an expression of divine intellect, rather than will. It results not from a sovereign will, but from the nature of the thing in question. Despite occasional appearances to the contrary, Spinoza views the concept of "natural law" as preceding and giving rise to juridical "law". Indeed, some see the term "natural law" as an analogy borrowed from the juridical world. Bodies are thus said to fall in accordance with Newton's law of gravity, ostensibly because "someone" made this law. Spinoza however, views the concept of "natural law"—and for the modern reader there is nothing new in this—as describing the way in which things behave or occur according to their "nature", and so refers to them as "eternal truths" rather than "divine decrees" (IV, 56). The "law" in this sense is an assertion regarding a thing and its nature—determining not how it must act, but how it usually does. It does not impose an obligation but establishes what is true, and geometry offers the greatest examples of such "truths".

If the law is not an expression of sovereign will but of knowing and thinking intellect, if it is "true" in its essence, and a command only in its external form, then its violation—even the violation of the clearest possible law, i.e. divine law—is not a "sin" and involves no culpability, but rather harmful error and ignorance. It is only as a result of his ignorance that Adam believed the injunction against eating from the tree of knowledge to be a divine command. In effect, it was eternal truth, and "would have involved a contradiction that Adam should have been able to eat of it" (IV, 58). God only told Adam not to eat from the tree, but did not reveal to him the inevitability of the evil that would result from it. The prohibition was therefore perceived as a law, that is a commandment, and not as truth. As Gilles Deleuze (one of Spinoza's more interesting interpreters) remarked, Spinoza's divine law is more like a doctor's prescription, than a moral or religious command. Ostensibly, a prescription is also a command—it says "do this!". In fact however, it is a theoretical assertion or "truth", regarding the necessary effect—as a natural law—that certain things (drugs, for example) will have upon others (illness, for example).

This is the archetype of "legality", according to Spinoza, and human law should also be understood in this light. The will of the legislator is neither the foundation upon which human law—that is state law—rests, nor the source of its authority. To some extent, modern legal terminology and certain schools of thought still preserve the notion of a fundamental link between "law" and "will". The concept of "sovereignty" for example—central to political theory in Spinoza's time and a little before—derives, not surprisingly, from the theological realm (in the thought of Jean Bodin, for example), although a harbinger of the secular perception of the state (Hobbesian, for the most part). Spinoza's great originality lay in the intensity with which he questioned all of the religious or theological sources of modern perceptions of the state and the law. The concept of "sovereignty" is a case in point. Spinoza questions its status as the source of authority and validity of the law. (Human) law is an expression of truth regarding the damage or benefit entailed by certain modes of behavior. Spinoza defines the law as "a plan of life laid down by man for himself or others with a certain object" (IV, 15). And this object is justice, for which Spinoza accepts the Aristotelian definition, i.e. the equitable distribution of benefits and burdens. He thus rejects the biblical perception of justice as compliance with God's will and commandments.

If Spinoza's approach can be said to challenge the concept of sovereignty as the source of juridical authority, his position vis-à-vis the perception of the law as commandment is all the more manifest. The commandments are perhaps the most quintessentially numinous objects in the Jewish religion. Just as Spinoza rejects the religious significance of priestly ritual and status, he rejects the idea that the law derives its authority solely from the fact that it is commanded, imposed—the expression of a sovereign, legislative, and even arbitrary will. A fundamental characteristic of the biblical approach is, as noted above, a lack of distinction between the legal-political and the religious. Justice and law are no less of a religious obligation than ritual. In fact, they constitute a single unity—just like the priestly garments, the Urim and the Thummim ("the inscription of the Tetragrammaton," according to Rashi) and the breastplate of judgment. In making a sharp distinction between the two apparently autonomous spheres—religion and state, law and faith, philosophy and theology—Spinoza in effect contests the validity of the religious concept of "commandment", arguing that law must lie beyond the scope of religion, inasmuch as it is not, by its very nature, commanded. It is thus with good reason that Spinoza is considered the greatest challenge to modern Jewish thought.

Yair Tzaban

Ki Tissa

"Monism and the Jewish Mind"—According to **Ber Borochov**

And he received the gold at their hand, and fashioned it with a graving tool, and made it a molten calf; and they said: "This are thy gods, O Israel, which brought thee up out of the land of Egypt" (*Exodus* 32:4).

The Torah cautions us, lest we make an idol of any thing that God has commanded us (Rabbi Menahem Mendel of Kotsk).

There is something artificial in associating the weekly Torah portion with a particular philosopher. But longstanding exegetic and homiletic tradition however, has made the "artificial" almost essential to any exposition on the weekly portion.

Efforts by the Van Leer Jerusalem Institute to revive this ancient tradition are warranted, in my opinion, to the extent that they are able to transcend the constraints of conservatism, and offer new perspectives on the ancient texts. Yosef Dan, in his book *Sifrut Hamusar Vehadrush* (1975, p. 268), stresses that the exegetic and homiletic literature, by its very nature, demands a considerable degree of conservatism, inasmuch as it adheres closely to the ancient texts and requires every new or revisited idea to be firmly rooted in the inveterate chain of tradition. This tendency was, in the past, reinforced by the fact that preachers and exegetes generally owed their living to influential community members and leaders. While occasionally, some would defy communal authority; this was the exception rather than the rule.

The idea of associating each weekly portion with a particular intellectual figure indeed offers the possibility of breaching the confines of conservatism. In choosing Ber Borochov (1881–1917), one of the fathers of Socialist Zionism, I have attempted to afford meaning to this break with the past, in terms of current relevance and content as well as form.

It is of particular significance at this time, as we observe the inaptitude and even indifference displayed in the face of grave social problems: rising unemployment that denies so many families not only their means of support, but also their dignity; growing inequality that earns our society such a shameful position in international rankings of social disparity; spreading poverty; the plight of the disabled, who have been forced to go on strike to make their voice heard.

The sense of solidarity once so prominent in the social consciousness of many has been jettisoned, no longer paid even lip service. The intellectual pursuit of ideas intended to provide a social vision and long-term social goals has withered, become desolate—a few oases notwithstanding.

The connection between *Ki Tissa* and Borochov may be spun out of three separate strands: monism, the moral ethos and *Eretz Yisrael*.

Ki Tissa is replete with events: the affair of the "atonement money"; the service of the Tent of Meeting, the anointing oil and incense and the craftsmanship of Bezalel; the laws of the Sabbath; Moses' receipt of the tablets is marred by the affair of the golden calf; Moses descends from the mountain and breaks the tablets; the Levites kill the revelers; God reaffirms his commitment to bring the people to the promised land; the Tent of Meeting is pitched outside the camp; Moses enters the Tent of Meeting and the people see the pillar of cloud; Moses is commanded to fashion new tablets; Moses goes up the mount for the second time; God repeats some of his principal commandments; after forty days have passed, Moses descends and "knew not that his face shone."

Clearly, this combination—of the Revelation at Sinai, on the one hand, and the total, absolute and uncompromising rejection of the golden calf, on the other—is the pinnacle of this ancient demonstration of monotheism, the central pivot on which the *Ki Tissa* portion turns.

The year 1903 saw the publication of Borochov's first philosophical essay—"On the Nature of the Jewish Mind" (in *Ketavim Filosofi'im*, 1994, pp. 27–54)—which focuses on the central claim that the Jewish mind naturally aspires to extreme monism, a fact clearly evidenced already in the Bible. Borochov was 22 at the time and the essay was based on a lecture he had given two or three years earlier.

Upon completing his secondary school studies in his hometown of Poltava, Borochov traveled to Yekaterinoslav (now Dnipropetrovsk). The two years he spent there were crucial to his ideological development. Alongside his activities in the Russian Social Democratic Party—a revolutionary party founded in 1898 to unite a number of radical groups, and later headed by Lenin—he was also active in Zionist circles, led at the time by Menahem Ussishkin (1864–1941). Ussishkin invited him to lecture in his home before a select group of Zionist activists and members of the local intelligentsia. Borochov lectured on "The Nature of the Jewish Mind," and made a tremendous impression. The two would later become allies in their ardent struggle against Herzl's "Uganda Plan," but remain divided in matters of ideology—due to Ussishkin's firm opposition to any attempts to link socialism and Zionism.

The essay that followed the lecture was published, as noted above, two or three years later, in a Russian-language Zionist almanac. Although this first philosophical essay clearly displays the young Borochov's talent, acuity, broadness of horizons and writing skills, it does bear some of the marks of a first and immature work.

In the essay, Borochov ascribes unique and specific characteristics to the Jewish People: "The Jews share common and distinct intellectual characteristics that not only bind them to one another, but also distinguish them from other peoples. These characteristics of the Jewish mind are utterly unique and original, and are not the result of influences exerted upon them by the nations among whom they have lived. On the contrary, the latter often received them from the Jews." He later abandoned this idea.

He argued that the Jewish manner of thinking has been marked, throughout history, by an "intellectual stringency," which seeks a single, "monistic" principle, from which all things derive, and on the basis of which reality can be explained. The Jewish mind aspires to what he terms "strict monism."

The roots of this approach can be found in the quintessentially monotheistic Jewish religion of the Bible. Borochov rejects the claim that the Jewish religion is fundamentally dualistic, inasmuch as it distinguishes between "God" and "the world." This dualistic separation appeared only after the Babylonian exile, under Persian influence, and was integrated into Jewish theology.

Considering the limitations of this theology, Maimonides attained a high level of monistic unity in his approach. Borochov sees in Spinoza—whose pantheism and divine immanence in the world contain not a "shred of dualism"—the height of Jewish monistic thought, an approach in which "God" is immanent to "the world".

Borochov does not make do with a discussion of philosophical doctrines, and he highlights the contributions to social science and political economy of two prominent Jewish thinkers: Ricardo and Marx. On the basis of principles introduced by Adam Smith, Marx managed to overcome the dualism and internal contradictions of his predecessors, by means of the monistic principle that labor is the basis of value; replacing Smith's concept of "value of labor" with the new concept of "value of labor-power" as a commodity. Marx's philosophical materialism (which Borochov described as "the first example of a scientific approach to history"), explains all of human history in terms of a single (monistic) principle: the development of relations of production and the class struggle.

The essay includes a number of interesting observations regarding "the Jewish character," but in attempting to generalize and establish fixed patterns for the development of Jewish thought, he also draws conclusions that reality has proven false. For example, he argues that Jewish monism is "subjective monism," resulting in a Jewish tendency toward music, lyric poetry, ethics and social activism, as opposed to the natural sciences. "Not one important discovery in the field of mathematics or natural science is associated with the name of a Jew," Borochov (wrongly) declares. Four years after the publication of Borochov's essay, the Jewish physicist Albert Michelson, won the Nobel Prize. He was the first of many: of the 88 Nobel laureates in physics over the course of the prize's first 70 years (1901–1971), seventeen—nearly one fifth—were Jewish, including of course, Albert Einstein.

According to Borochov, dualism and pluralism are essentially monistic in that they purport to organize the sum total of human experience under a single philosophical system. Jewish thought, however, aspires to absolute monism. In this, Judaism differed from other civilizations in the ancient world—Egypt, Babylonia, Persia and Greece—all of which were guilty of the sins of dualism and pluralism. India was the only other exception to the rule.

In particular, Borochov highlights the difference between Jewish and Greek culture, noting that the latter espoused dualistic and pluralistic approaches. Of course, Borochov was not the first to contrast the "Jew" and the "Hellene." His understanding of the contrast however, was quite different. Heinrich Heine, famously wrote that "all men are either Jews or Hellenes." Heine was referring to cultural, rather than ethnic characteristics. One might be born a Jew, yet become a "Hellene," or vice versa. Judaism is characterized by severity, asceticism and martyrdom; Hellenism by its pursuit of beauty. Heine believed that Judaism, together with its offspring, Christianity, had "given the world religious fanaticism" and "all that holy torture which has cost the human race so much blood and so many tears." The God of the Jews and the Christians is a jealous and despotic deity, who represses free emotions and binds them in chains of severe spirituality. Greek paganism spoke to Heine at that time.

Borochov's approach to the contrast between "Jew" and "Hellene" was very different. According to Borochov, it is in fact absolute monism, in all its apparent austerity, that fosters perfect love and compassion for all creatures. A unified view of the world allows one to treat the other as another aspect of the same reality of which one is oneself an organic part. Only strict monism could give rise to rules such as "Love thy neighbor as thyself" or "Love ye therefore the stranger." Borochov thus presents perfect morality as the main characteristic of Jewish monism: "The other—is a monistic concept; altruism—is monistic morality. Neither ancient religion nor ancient philosophy ever attained this level of morality."

It is in this spirit, we can assume, that Borochov would have addressed the events at Mount Sinai as they are described in *Ki Tissa*—for the event of the giving of the Torah symbolizes, more than anything else, the idea of monotheistic belief, belief in one God, monistic belief. And such was the Jewish religion, according to Borochov, in its early stages.

Rachel Elior, in an excellent article on the changes in Israelite belief and God concepts, distinguishes between biblical literature, "which reflects a perception of God as absolute unity," and the Qumran literature for example, "which represents a dualistic approach to God and the world." She then discusses the philosophical approach of the Middle Ages, "which sought to resolve the contradiction between the idea of an impersonal deity, based on the principles of total abstraction and unity; and the personal God of revealed religion," as well as the kabbalistic approach that asserts a "divine unity comprising many different forces of varying importance, due to processes within the godhead as well as human actions." Elior thus concludes that "there was no single God concept, but a divinity recreated in the image of each and every era" (*"Temurot Bemusag Ha'el Bamahshavah Hayehudit,"* *Free Judaism*, 11–12, pp. 30–36).

Borochov, seizes on those periods in which the monistic character of Jewish thought—both traditional-religious (biblical and philosophical) and nontraditional (such as Spinoza and Marx)—was pronounced. In focusing on this monism, Borochov underscores the ethical aspect of Jewish thought.

The story of the Revelation at Sinai and the Ten Commandments must certainly have served as a major source of inspiration for Borochov in his perception of the moral image of Jewish monotheism. Jewish monotheism was born thanks to Moses' genius. Philo of Alexandria, who brought Jewish monotheism to an even higher level, was the next link in the chain, followed later by Maimonides and Ibn Gabirol in the Middle Ages, Salomon Maimon in the early modern age, and still later—Marx and Lassalle. Some believe that Borochov harbored a hope at that time that he might serve as a modern link in that chain of monistic Jewish geniuses.

A leading expert on Borochov, Matityahu Mintz, points out that the young Borochov had hoped to found a new philosophical school. He had planned to publish a comprehensive philosophical work entitled *Critique of Pure Ethical Experience*—a title clearly reminiscent both of Kant's *Critique of Pure Reason* and of the *Critique of Pure Experience* by Richard Avenarius, a philosopher whom Borochov greatly admired at an early stage.

The outline he prepared for this work, five or six years after the publication of his first philosophical essay, indeed demonstrates considerable philosophical pretension. What is of interest to us, however, for the purposes of this chapter is Borochov's focus on the ethical.

During the same period (1907–1908), Borochov wrote another philosophical essay on the subject of ethics: "Virtualism and the Religious-Ethical Problem in Marxism" (*Ketavim Filosofi'im*, 1994, pp. 55–160). The essay sharply attacks those who sought, according to Borochov, to turn socialism into a "new religion." The essay closes with a dramatic appeal: "We have straightened our backs, bent for thousands of years. Please do not suggest that we bend our heads before something we have ourselves created. We have eradicated idolatry and risen up from our knees. Please do not entice us to fall prostrate before ourselves."

With the same determination with which he rejected all forms of clericalism and attempts to promote a new faith—"the godless religion of socialism"—he also rejected extreme anticlericalism. The Jewish experience, he believed, demanded a closing of ranks in pursuit of common goals. "We must declare all-out war against [...] irresponsible one-sidedness. The future demands synthesis [...] Synthesis is fertile only when it mercilessly rejects the extremes and boldly stands in their place" ("To Destroy or To Build? [1913]," *Ketavim* 3, 1966, pp. 375–380).

Borochov distinguishes between two types of ethical consciousness: behavior ethics and life ethics. Behavior ethics are based primarily on prohibitions, since they must ensure a minimal level of harmony, in a society rife with essentially disharmonious class differences. The norms of behavior ethics answer the question "How should one act?" Life ethics on the other hand, answer the question "How should one live?" inasmuch as they challenge the social status quo and aspire to a society free of class disharmony.

In the specific context of our Torah portion, he writes: "The Mosaic Decalogue is the archetypal behavioral-ethical constitution" ("Virtualism and the Religious-Ethical Problem in Marxism" p. 136). In striving to avert interpersonal conflict, ethics cannot but limit man's freedom of action. In a society fraught with conflict, order cannot be maintained other than through the imperative injunction: Thou shalt not! And that is why most of the Ten Commandments begin with these words.

Borochov mentions Kant's categorical imperative ("Act only according to that maxim whereby you can at the same time will that it should become a universal law"), and notes that Schopenhauer had already remarked that Kant's imperative was merely a wonderful paraphrase of Hillel's maxim "That which is hateful to you, do not unto your fellow." Borochov does not reject behavior ethics per se, but stresses that only when these are "illuminated by life ethics" can they rise above the decadence of the mundane.

To what extent however, did the "moral impulse" influence Borochov's approach to the national issues of the day and his practical and theoretical efforts to synthesize Zionism and socialism? Did he view the establishment of a Jewish socialist society in Palestine as the realization of the "life ethics" that addressed the question of how one should live?

In March 1906, the founding convention of the Jewish Workers' Social Democratic Party in Russia—*Po'alei Zion*—was held in Poltava. Borochov, only 25 at the time, was without a doubt the leading ideological figure there. In the counterrevolutionary atmosphere that followed the 1905 Revolution, many of the conference's participants—including Borochov himself—were arrested. Over the course of the following months, in conjunction with the other members of the organization's leadership, he wrote "Our Platform"—a proposed program for *Po'alei Zion*.

Borochov then began a period of exile that lasted over seven years, marked by difficult material circumstances. He wandered between Austria, Galicia, Belgium, Holland and Switzerland. Throughout this time, Borochov continued to study, research and write. Borochov was an autodidact par excellence. He taught himself all of the major European languages, as well as the classical languages. He also mastered philosophy, history and economics and deepened his knowledge of Hebrew and particularly Yiddish—of which he would become a leading scholar.

After the outbreak of the First World War, in early 1915, he departed for the United States, where he also continued his research and public activities. Following the revolution of February 1917 (the Kerensky Revolution), he returned to Russia, filled with hope for the future. In August 1917—between the February and October revolutions (the Bolshevik Revolution)—a *Po'alei Zion* convention was held in Kiev, at which Borochov was received with great enthusiasm.

The "Congress of Nations," to which Borochov was a delegate, was convened in September, in the same city. There, he argued that the Russian Federative Republic—sole heir to the Russian Revolution—would be a socialist republic, for only in this way could anarchy and destruction be averted.

Traveling through Russia, he came down with a cold, contracted pneumonia and died in December 1917, at the age of 38. He was survived by his wife Luba (Meltzer) and their two children.

Borochov's ideas were recognized as a conceptual system, "Borochovism" but, as often happens in such cases, debate ensued among the Borochovists as to the correct interpretation of his ideas. We must recall however, that Borochov's own ideas, both his Socialist Zionism and his general philosophy, underwent significant changes over the years.

Borochov believed in territorialization, the creation of a sovereign territorial base—necessarily in Palestine—as the solution to the Jewish problem. In the absence of such a base, as an exterritorial people living in a capitalist society—matters would only get much worse. Only in *Eretz Israel* could they achieve economic and subsequently political independence. This would also serve as the strategic base for the struggle of the Jewish proletariat to realize its dream of a socialist society.

At first, Borochov believed that Jewish migration to Palestine would be a "stychic," that is an unorganized or elemental process, completely unplanned, a natural consequence of Jewish life, Jewish adversity and the nature of Jewish emigration. There was therefore no need of concerted action on the part of the Jewish proletariat for the realization of the Zionist idea. Initially, the stychic processes must be allowed to run their course, while enabling the Jewish bourgeoisie to build the country's economic infrastructure. In time, class struggle would inevitably develop over the direction that of the new society would take. Toward the end of his life, Borochov changed a number of elements in his approach. He saw the first fruits of Zionist activities in Palestine and was no longer satisfied with stychic processes. He therefore recommended that his movement take a more active role in guiding the processes and in participating in the realization of the Zionist idea. Contrary to *Po'alei*

Zion's previous position, Borochov now supported the idea of establishing cooperative workers' settlements in Palestine.

Borochov devoted a great deal of energy, along with remarkable rhetorical skills, to the struggle against the "territorialists," those who advocated a national solution to the Jewish problem in any available territory, not necessarily Palestine. Borochov however, also distanced himself from those Zionist thinkers who based their Zionist views regarding the present and the future entirely on the legacy of the past. He did not underestimate the value of historical consciousness in the construction of a national homeland: "The national ideal is very closely linked to historical destiny, because there can be no nationalism without a past." Nevertheless, he claimed, we look to the past as a result of our current adversity, our inability to feel a sense of homeland in the places where Jews live. "We cannot but love *our homeland*, when we are not permitted to feel a sense of homeland in the Diaspora." Elsewhere, he writes: "We all *love Eretz Yisrael*, the people and its culture, because Zion is *dear* to us all; and it is *dear* not because it is a tradition, but because it is *ours*" ("On the Question of Zion and Territory [1905]," *Ketavim* 1, 1955, p. 90).

Borochov's refusal to rely on tradition as a justification for Zionism did not mean that he was indifferent to it; on the contrary, in 1913, he published an essay entitled "Passover Musings of a Heretic," which was infused with tremendous pride in his Jewish identity and heritage, alongside sharp criticism of the Rabbinical world on the one hand, and Jews in the workers' movement who sought to renounce that heritage, on the other.

He praises the ability of the Jewish People to take a cosmic, spring festival, and turn it into the holiday of freedom. He rejects the idea that our people is ailing and debilitated, and points to the contrasts it has harbored in its midst throughout its history: courage and cowardice, cringing servility and bold defiance—or in the words of Ahad Ha'am: "Slavery in Freedom." With regard to the Haggadah, he takes a different approach to the "wicked" son, and criticizes the Sages for having made him the object of their scorn. It is precisely this son—branded "wicked" by the rabbis—that Borochov sees as the cornerstone of Jewish regeneration. In his view, it is those who are condemned by the ultra-Orthodox as "wicked," those freethinkers that embrace freedom and life, who will resolve the contrast of "Slavery in Freedom."

As noted, there are three concepts that reverberate between Borochov and *Ki Tissa*. The monotheistic message of Sinai and its uncompromising rejection of alternative cults (the golden calf) corresponds to Borochov's conception of absolute monism as a primary characteristic of Jewish thought; God's commitment to bringing the people to the promised land corresponds to Borochov's fierce opposition to the Uganda Plan and his devotion to the realization of Zionism in *Eretz Yisrael*; and the moral ethos, as derived from the Ten Commandments and adopted by Western culture as a whole corresponds to the centrality of ethics in Borochov's philosophy.

The story of the golden calf—a story that has attracted the interest of commentators and preachers, scholars and philosophers, writers and poets—is relevant to all three of these connections. The source of this unique tale, in which Aaron plays such a negative role, is a fascinating subject in itself, treated at length by Bible scholars. It is impossible not to associate this affair with the story of the two golden calves erected at Beth-El and Dan by Jeroboam son of Nebat, king of Israel, who declared: "Behold thy gods, O Israel, which brought thee up out of the land of Egypt" (1 *Kings* 12:28)—the very same words used in reference to the golden calf in *Ki Tissa*. Scholars have spilled seas of ink in attempts to discover the hidden meaning of these stories: the golden calf; the implication of Aaron; the story of Jeroboam's golden calves; and the connection between the two narratives.

In her book, *Hidden Polemics in Biblical Narrative* (2003, pp .120–122), Yaira Amit explains the story of the golden calves that Jeroboam placed at Beth-El and Dan as a partially hidden polemic, conducted on behalf of the Kingdom of Judah, apparently at the time in which Josiah sought to establish the status of Jerusalem as an exclusive cult center, and to undermine the legitimacy of other centers—Beth-El, in particular. According to Amit, the author resorted to the images and phrasing of the golden calf—regarded as an unparalleled sin—that his readers and listeners might associate Jeroboam's actions at Beth-El with the nefarious events at Sinai.

Israel Finkelstein and Neil Asher Silberman, in their book *The Bible Unearthed* (2001, p. 168), link the Bible's sharp criticism of Jeroboam's actions to Josiah's war for the status of Jerusalem as exclusive cult center: "Under Josiah, however, the time comes for Judah to rise to greatness. But in order to revive the golden age, this new David needs first to undo the sins of Solomon and Jeroboam. The path to greatness must pass through the cleansing of Israel, mainly the destruction of the shrine of Bethel."

Yair Zakovitch and Avigdor Shinan, in their book *Lo Kakh Katuv Batanakh* (2004, pp. 96–102) also attribute the condemnation of the desert golden calf and Jeroboam's golden calves as blasphemy, to a source representing the interests of the Kingdom of Judah. They posit that the golden calves were in fact a widespread ancient tradition, since "it is inconceivable at a time of crisis—the breakaway from the House of David—that Jeroboam would have effected far-reaching change, advocating a form of worship wholly unknown to his or the Israelites' forebears." The authors thus presume the existence of a tradition that viewed calf worship as something pleasing to God. They suggest that the calf story in *Ki Tissa* was also written in the interest of condemning Jeroboam.

The story of the golden calf has long since transcended its original context, serving preachers as a constant source of inspiration, for a variety of homiletic purposes. Worth noting in this context is a sermon delivered in the 1940s by Moshe Avigdor Amiel, chief rabbi of Tel-Aviv, and one of the spiritual leaders of the religious-Zionist Mizrachi movement (those were the days!). At the height of the Second World War, as the Holocaust raged, Amiel looked to the furthest, broadest possible horizon, in an attempt to understand and explain the terrible tragedy that had befallen our people, and in fact all of humanity. He said as follows:

Indeed, militarism itself is the result of the golden calf. For so Moses, chief among the prophets, tells us: "And it came to pass, as soon as he came near to the camp, that he saw the calf and the dancing", and it was declared "Put every man his sword by his side [...] and slay every man his brother, and every man his companion, and every man his neighbor". (Ex. 32:19, 27). And if today, we see millions observing this commandment of "slay every man his brother" with such great devotion, and all of the world's clerics have promised them exceeding reward in the world to come, then we must know that the reason for this is the golden calf that exists in the world even in times of peace.

And further:
The rich are the golden calf itself, and it is the poor who dance around the golden calf. It is the poor who kneel and prostrate themselves, and acknowledge, "Holy, holy, holy!" before every golden calf. And all the world is measured only against the standard of the golden calf [...] and as long as this order reigns in the world, so too the order of 'slay every man his brother' will reign. For the calf is too small for all the nations and kingdoms of the world to ride upon and they must therefore kill one another. Only when this terrible world order is changed will the intoxicating effect of the water of the golden calf that we have drunk wear off.

The golden calf has from the start served as a metaphor for greed, veneration of the wealthy and the betrayal of virtue. Shaul Tchernichovsky uses the metaphor in his wonderful poem "I Believe":
For my soul still aspires to freedom,
I have not sold it to a golden calf,
For I still believe in man,
And in his spirit, his bold spirit.

His spirit will cast off the chains of vanity,
Will raise him up on high;
Workers shall not die of hunger,
Freedom for the soul, bread for the poor.*
* Translator unknown

The poem was written in Odessa in 1894, when Borochov was only thirteen years old. If a poem can attest to a philosophy and way of life, then these verses affirm the beliefs of those who, like Borochov, reject all forms of subjection to the golden calf and look toward a society that will ensure "freedom for the soul, bread for the poor." Borochov's writings still have a great deal to offer those who harbor such hopes.

To Borochov, the legendary figure of Moses symbolized the people's struggle for freedom. In honor of the third anniversary of the death of his former fierce adversary, Theodor Herzl, he wrote:

> Like the legendary Moses, whose soul departed on the threshold of the Promised Land, and who did not live to taste the boundless pleasure of a life's work completed—Theodor Herzl fell into everlasting sleep, his gaze still fixed upon his ideal. [...] As the Bible so movingly recounts, God did not want to give Moses the satisfaction of witnessing the triumph of his labors and his struggle; but God has never allowed any man this incredible joy. God is history, and we know that Moses and Theodor Herzl are no exceptions; we know that their fate is a universal law ("Theodor Herzl," *Ketavim* 2, 1958, p. 118).

I believe that Borochov also felt that he stood atop Mount Nebo, alongside Moses and Herzl: seeing the Promised Land afar off, but destined never to enter.

Avi Katzman

Vayakhel – And Moses Assembled All the Congregation of the Children of Israel

Sabbath, Tabernacle, and Candelabrum:
*Jewish Culture in the Teaching of **Mordecai Kaplan***

The candlestick also for the light, and all its vessels, and its lamps, and the oil for the light (*Exodus* 35:14).

The freedom which means the release of selfhood consists in the right to be different and the right to be creative (Mordecai Kaplan, *The Meaning of God in Modern Jewish Religion*, 1962, p. 278).

Vayakhel begins with a reiteration of the commandment regarding the Sabbath, and goes on to discuss the labors of the Tabernacle—in inverse order to their first appearance. Commentators have pondered the meaning of this repetition and inversion of the Sabbath and the Tabernacle, offering a variety of explanations, emphasizing the important religious principle that places the Sabbath above the labors of the Tabernacle—thus establishing the 39 categories of actions prohibited on the Sabbath. The religious principle, however, tends to overshadow a greater human principle: the institution of the 39 categories, and the acceptance of the responsibility that comes with action.

Where the Sabbath, realm of the sacred, ends, labor, the profane, the realm of man, begins. The conflict between the two realms is unresolvable, and man's efforts to worship God in fact constitute recognition of the profound contradiction between sacred and profane. In *Vayakhel* we find expression of the sacred, of the contradiction between sacred and profane, as well as a wonderful expression of the recognition of this contradiction—of man and his rebellion.

Preceding action, labor and toil, with the Sabbath—as a reversal of the order of creation—introduces a new, human order. God created the world in six days, as man's dwelling place, and following the creation of man, rested from his labors. Here, following the giving of the Torah and the Sabbath precepts, begin the days of human labor delimited by the Sabbath. Action is possible, only because its boundaries have been set first. Human labor begins with the construction of the Tabernacle—God's dwelling place—delimiting man's place in the world. Human creativity—the founding of human civilization—begins with the construction of sacred symbols and the establishment of the boundaries that also represent acceptance of responsibility. God created the world out of *tohu* and *bohu*. Man creates within his own confines. It is the recognition of these confines and their acceptance that enable man to gain mastery over them—to plan, to create, and to soar.

The Tabernacle is a symbol and paradigm of human creation, the dawn of man's creativity. God concludes his labors—the creation of the universe—with the creation of man; man begins his labors, the creation of his world, with the construction of a dwelling place for God.

The human creativity embodied in the construction of the Tabernacle converges upon a unique symbol, the *menorah*—a candlestick of pure gold, resembling the tree of life. Unlike the other appointments of the Tabernacle, the *menorah* has no specific function, no role in the sacrificial cult, no instrumental purpose of any kind. The Bible offers no explanation of the drama it represents. Such explanations can be found however, in the traditional sources, and in many popular myths. What then does the *menorah* symbolize?

Perhaps it is the light of the Torah, or the first act of creation; the "let there be light". The giving of the Torah, the culmination of God's labors, concludes with the injunction "Ye shall kindle no fire throughout your habitations upon the Sabbath day"—a commandment that takes note of the fact that all human civilization began with the kindling of fire (an idea raised by Yeshayahu Leibowitz in *Sheva Shanim shel Sihot al Parashat Hashavua*, Jerusalem, 2000). The Talmud points out the interesting parallel between the beginning of God's labors and the beginning of man's labors and the first blessing it entails, "who createst the lights of fire": "One does not bless the light but at the conclusion of the Sabbath, for that is when it was first created ... And at the conclusion of the Sabbath, God gave Adam understanding, following the example of heaven, he brought two stones, rubbed them against one another, and produced light" (*Pesahim* 54a).

One of the best-known myths is that of Prometheus, which corresponds to the narrative in Exodus on a number of points. The Titan Prometheus, the foreseer, was the savior of mankind in Greek mythology. He taught them the crafts and stole fire for them from the gods, taking a spark from the chariot of Apollo, hiding it in a hollow stalk, descending from the mountain and bringing fire to downtrodden man. For this he was punished by Zeus, banished to a mountain in an unknown location, where, for many years, an eagle fed daily on his liver, which was regenerated by night.

The struggle between man and God over fire—light, understanding, independence—epitomized by the myth of Prometheus, is embodied in the golden *menorah*, as a continuation of the narrative begun in the previous portion, *Ki Tissa*: the compromise between the human and the divine following the affair of the golden calf.

This portion—the only one to begin with the word "*vayakhel*" ("and he [Moses] assembled")—underscores the social aspect of human creativity, not mentioned in the previous chapters: "whosoever is of a willing heart", "every wise-hearted man among you", "every one whose heart stirred him up, and every one whom his spirit made willing", "and they came, both men and women, as many as were willing-hearted", "and all the women that were wise-hearted with their hands", "and all the women whose heart stirred them up in wisdom", "the children of Israel brought a willing offering", "every man and woman, whose heart made them willing", and the climax:

> And Moses said unto the children of Israel, See, the Lord hath called by name Bezalel the son of Uri, the son of Hur, of the tribe of Judah. And He hath filled him with the Spirit of God, in wisdom, in understanding, and in knowledge, and in all manner of workmanship. And to devise skilful works, to work in gold, and in silver, and in brass, and in cutting of stones for setting, and in carving of wood, to work in all manner of skilful workmanship. And He hath put in his heart that he may teach, both he, and Oholiab, the son of Ahisamach, of the tribe of Dan. Them hath He filled with wisdom of heart, to work all manner of workman-

ship, of the craftsman, and of the skilful workman, and of the embroiderer, in blue, and in purple, in scarlet, and in fine linen, and of the weaver, even of them that do any workmanship, and of those that devise cunning work (35:30–35).

This detailed list implies creation *ex nihilo*, for as Rabbi Bahye ben Asher of Saragossa and other commentators have noted, the Israelites in Egypt did no "fine work", only hard labor in mortar and brick.

The very "technical" orientation of the chapters of *Vayakhel* conceals their subversive basis: the designs behind the "design". Beneath the surface of the holy work we find the element of human ingenuity— "to work all manner of workmanship, of the craftsman, and of the skilful workman, and of the embroiderer ... and of those that devise cunning work". Although the holy work of the Tabernacle, as noted by the commentators, was meant to correspond to, and atone for, the sin the golden calf, its illicit ardor persisted, as it is written: "And all the wise men, that wrought all the work of the sanctuary, came every man from his work which they made. And they spake unto Moses, saying, The people bring much more than enough for the service of the work, which the Lord commanded to make" (36:4–5). The redundant phrase "the service of the work" is none other than a euphemism for idolatry, in this case in the guise of holy work. The twist in the plot comes, however, when the holy work itself is superseded by holy service—its antithesis, the Sabbath, of which it is written: "whosoever doeth any work therein shall be put to death".

The Sabbath takes precedence over the Tabernacle, which, along with the *menorah* that illuminates it, is thereafter rendered possible, as the beginning of new activity; following the human order of creation. This arrangement constitutes a compromise between God and the creature he made in his image, in divine recognition of his creative passion, willingness of heart, wisdom and understanding. It offers a resolution to the conflict between the human and the divine, in the form of peaceful coexistence: "And let them make for me a sanctuary, that I may dwell among them"—a great concession on God's part. The human side of the arrangement lies in the harnessing of "all manner of workmanship, of the craftsman, and of the skilful workman, and of the embroiderer"—with hidden emphasis on the word "all", repeated continuously throughout the passage—to the construction of the Tabernacle and the wondrous *menorah*, that "shall be made", as if of its own accord.

Thus, as God completes the course of his actions, man begins the course of his—with the sacred. The construction of the Tabernacle tells the story of creation in reverse, its symbols corresponding to all of the acts of creation. This time, however, the world created is a human world, the dawn of civilization.

Civilization is everything that man is not granted by nature; everything that a group of people must achieve and create together, by virtue of their energy and wisdom, inspiration and memory, desires and sensibilities, courage and generosity. Ever-changing, dynamic and controversial, civilization is the product of bitter struggles, and the fruit of actions taken by powerful individuals and groups. It is on this principle that the philosopher of religion Rabbi Prof. Mordecai Menahem Kaplan (1881–1983) based his thought.

Kaplan claims that the rabbinical focus on the minutiae of Halakhah—applying the religious precepts to ever-greater areas of life, by means of "fences" and decrees of the past, rather than developing the precepts themselves—has created a breach between them and the people, in the reality of their lives. The resulting disintegration of the depth and inner essence of the *mitzvot* is accompanied by an over-emphasis on external appearance—creating an incurable rift between human civilization and the divine word. Depressing conformism, fear of change, reticence and avoidance of the duty to adapt, result in an embalming of the *mitzvot*, impoverishing them and depriving them of any connection to reality, thereby creating many small golden calves, by making them symbols of symbols.

Over time, such an approach destroys the profound principles we find in *Vayakhel*: Moses assembles "all the congregation of the children of Israel"—all of Israel, in all its diversity. God offers humankind—men and women alike—the opportunity to dedicate the wisdom and generosity of their hearts to the holy work of the Tabernacle. He reduces his own presence, in order to dwell among them in the Tabernacle they have created for him; affording the sacred, precise measurements. *Vayakhel* advocates change and renewal, concession for the sake of existence, adaptation to changing conditions, and the permanence of intent, rather than the permanence of content. It recognizes human psychology and sociology, and highlights the tension between the temporal (the Sabbath) and the territorial (length, breadth and height); the tension between extreme abstraction and the tangible—represented by the work of the Tabernacle. It celebrates the eternal flame of human creativity that shines forth from the *menorah*.

Vayakhel teaches us that civilization means discourse, involving the entire congregation of the children of Israel. Mordecai Kaplan sought to create just such Jewish discourse. Born in Lithuania, he lived in New York City from the age of eight, and toward the end of his life, made his home in Jerusalem. Eight years after his *aliyah*, at the age of 98, he fell ill, and returned to New York, where he died. Kaplan, who departed from his traditional upbringing, studied at the Jewish Theological Seminary, and was later to become one of its leaders, although he disagreed with the approach of the Conservative Movement—without cutting off ties with it—and founded the Reconstructionist Movement. His seminal work, *Judaism as a Civilization*, represented a return to the ardent spirit of *Vayakhel*. His socio-ethical sensibility is virtually unique in 20th century Jewish thought. His knowledge was vast, including the fields of classical and modern literature, philosophy, theology, history, political science, psychology and sociology, in addition to Jewish thought throughout the ages. His long life was filled with initiative and achievements. In *The Meaning of God in Modern Jewish Religion* he writes:

... Loyalty to Jewish tradition does not mean the closing of our minds to present experiences and of our hearts to present needs. It does not mean that our ancestors can tell us what we ought to think, or how we ought to act. They can tell us how they though about similar problems, and how they acted in similar situations, but the responsibility for the decision is our own, and there can be no responsibility without freedom. Our responsibility to our forefathers is only to consult them, not to obey them. Our responsibility to our descendants is only to impart our most cherished experiences to them, but not to command them. These responsibilities, though limited, are real and important. Their wholehearted acceptance is implicit in the ideal of covenantship, and suggests the method by which Judaism in our day may serve as a way of salvation to the modern Jew and make him feel his Judaism to be a privilege rather than a burden (pp. 97–98).

His approach never found fertile ground in Israel. The anti-messianic and antiviolent spirit of his religio-ethico-political philosophy could not resonate with the messianic subcultures that developed on both the right and the left in Israel. His too-rational humanism was deemed superficial, and his great enterprise—the founding of a new Jewish civilization, firmly rooted in the present, but without casting off the treasures of the past—fell by the wayside.

In effect, Kaplan sought to build a new Tabernacle, or more precisely, to reestablish a Tabernacle—not to God, but to Jewish civilization, its literature and its art—the center of which he saw in Israel. He viewed God as a formative and guiding concept in the history of human culture; the ultimate validation of all that is human; or in other words, the sum total of creative forces that pulse within man and give his life meaning—but only within the context of a national collective, a culture that defies narrow nationalism, imperialism and capitalism.

Kaplan, in essence, understood the spirit of Judaism as the fulfillment of man's ability to cope with arbitrariness in his world, through belief in the existence of meaning and in the ability of every individual to overcome the arbitrary by accepting responsibility and striving to make things as they ought to be. He writes: "If civilization is to survive, we must find a way of reinstating men's faith in the moral law. Cold logical reason will not do it" (*ibid.* pp. 306–307).

Such words may strike contemporary ears as naive and simplistic, imbued with a positivist-pragmatic-universalist spirit that has lost its charm—without mystery, twilight or shadow; critical in the less sophisticated sense of the word, clinging too firmly to the poor and narrow horizons of the social sciences. The importance of Kaplan, the Jewish liberation theologian, lies not in the solutions he offered, or in his failing Kantianism, but in the direction he indicated. His reduction of the religious to a response to human needs, of the transcendent to a kind of general problem solver or "heavenly Google", in no way detracts from the originality of his message. He was, above all, a religio-social existentialist who sought meaning beyond every imperative, and readers should not be deterred by his awkward phrasing. "Salvation must be conceived mainly as an objective of human action," he wrote, "not as a psychic compensation for human suffering" (*ibid.* p. 54). It is precisely this idea that we find between the lines in *Vayakhel*; an idea, the religious force of which has resounded in Jewish culture in all its forms, throughout history.

After all, how does the construction of the Tabernacle really differ from the fashioning of the golden calf? Both drew upon the same materials, and upon the same kind of participation—in action, purpose and zeal. In the case of the Tabernacle however, idolatrous passion is refined, and "Up, make us gods" is superseded by the *menorah*, as an integral part of man's relationship with the transcendent.

Judaism chose its symbol at the time of the exodus from Egypt. Its great sages asserted that in every generation, every Jew must see himself as having gone out of Egypt, and the meaning of the exodus lies in turning one's back on the past and looking toward the light, toward the new dawn. Kaplan sought to renew Judaism in this spirit of looking forward, setting its goals in the future. In *Vayakhel*, the entire community takes part in the work of building the Tabernacle, i.e. the task of turning their backs on Egypt and its culture of the dead, rooted in sanctification of the past. At the crucial juncture, the people are filled with "wisdom of heart", ushering in a new creativity, looking forward from Egypt. It is no coincidence that the story of the building of the Tabernacle ends, in the portion of *Pekudei* (40:33), with the words "So Moses finished the work"—echoing the enigmatic verse at the end of the creation story: "And on the seventh day God finished His work which He had made" (Gen. 2:2). The fact that these words also conclude the book of *Exodus* (the subsequent five verses notwithstanding), serves to indicate that in the work of the Tabernacle, Moses—and the people—completed the great enterprise that was the exodus from Egypt. Not only did the Israelites leave Egypt with their bodies, but henceforth, they also left it with their hearts. At least some of them did.

Kaplan sought to free Judaism from its stagnation, from its looking back to the exodus from Egypt—representing the exodus itself as an ongoing process, an expression of the divine:

The moral implication of the traditional teaching that God created the world is that creativity, or the continuous emergence of aspects of life not prepared for or determined by the past, constitutes the most divine phase of reality (*The Meaning of God in Modern Jewish Religion*, p. 62).

Egypt constantly assumes new forms, as does the Tabernacle borne from place to place throughout the world—the spirit of creation and creativity, the joy in cultural activity, seeking to free itself from the yoke of slavery and stagnation, from the chains of arbitrariness, toward the glimmering light.

Ben Z. Schreiber

Pekudei – These are the Accounts

*Vision and Visualization in the thought of **Rabbi Avraham Krol***

These are the accounts of the tabernacle, even the tabernacle of the testimony, as they were rendered according to the command-ment of Moses, through the service of the Levites, by the hand of Ithamar, the son of Aaron the priest (*Exodus* 38:21).

In *Pekudei*, we find a meticulous account of all of the materi-als used in constructing the Tabernacle. Many commentators ask why Moses saw fit to provide such a detailed record. Two explanations are offered: the first, that Moses was merely complying with stringent halakhic requirements concerning the collection and al-location of funds; and the second, that Moses had learned from bitter personal experience, having been suspected by the Children of Israel (according to the Midrash) of embezzlement.

Regarding the first explanation, the Talmud (*Bava Batra* 8b) states: The Rabbis taught: A collector of funds for charity who has no one to whom to distribute them—may exchange [copper coins for more durable silver ones] with others, but not with himself. A collector of foodstuffs for charity who has no one to whom to distribute them—may sell [the foodstuffs] to others, but not to himself. Charity money may not be counted by twos, but rather one by one.

In other words, those in charge of public funds must exercise ex-treme caution, and count them "one by one"—in keeping with the verse: "then ye shall be clear before the Lord, and before Israel" (*Num.* 32:22).

The second explanation raises the possibility that Moses' extreme caution with public funds may have been the result of previous allega-tions against him. On the verse "Hew thee two tables of stone" (34:1), Rashi comments: "Hew thee—He showed him a quarry of sapphire from within his tent, and told him 'the remnants shall be thine', and

Moses thus became very wealthy". If we accept this interpretation, it is no wonder the Israelites were jealous of Moses' riches. And indeed, *Midrash Tanhuma* (Buber, *Pekudei* 4) reads as follows:

These are the accounts of the Tabernacle—Why did Moses render accounts to them? God trusted him, as it is written "My servant Moses is not so; he is trusted in all my house", and yet he said to them come let us render accounts. Rather, Moses heard talk behind his back, as it is written: "And it came to pass, when Moses went out unto the Tent, that all the people rose up .. and looked after Moses". And what did they say? Rabbi Yitzhak said that they would speak well of him—blessed be she who gave birth to one such as him; the Lord speaks with him all his days; all his days he is faithful to God. Rabbi Hama said that they would speak ill of him—look at that neck, look at those thighs, all that Moses eats comes from the Jews, and all that he drinks comes from the Jews, and all that he has comes from the Jews; and his friend would reply: would you not expect one who has overseen the work of the Tabernacle to be rich? When Moses heard this, he said to them: As you live! When the Tabernacle is finished, I will render accounts to you, as it is written "These are the accounts of the Tabernacle".

This midrash—surprising in its questioning of Moses' authority and purity of intentions, yet true to human nature—is a fitting introduction to the interpretive approach of Rabbi Avraham Krol. In his book, *Befikudekha Asihah*, Rabbi Krol offers an interesting commentary on the subject of Moses' accounts:

All of the commentators ask why Moses provided a full account of all he had made of silver and brass, but not of gold? Nahmanides explains that they were unable to calculate the amount of gold in the vessels that were merely overlaid with gold. My great-grandfather, in his book *Torat Aharon*, explains that it was because the Ark was made of gold, and it is said (*Sotah* 38a) that the Ark would carry its bearers. Would it not then have carried itself as well? As it is written (Jos. 4:11) "And it came to pass, when all the people were clean passed over, that the ark of the

Lord passed over". It would thus have been entirely weightless, because it would never have weighed upon or tilted the scales. And because they did not know the weight of the Ark, they could not know the weight of the remainder, for if any gold was missing, they would say that more had been used in the Ark (*ibid.* p. 198).

According to Rabbi Krol, since the Ark—which was overlaid with gold—carried itself and was therefore weightless, it would have been impossible to calculate the quantity of gold used in its manufacture. This interpretation is typical of Rabbi Krol's commentary on the Pentateuch—employing a visual-associative approach that breathes life and relevance into the abstract.

This approach was facilitated by his phenomenal memory, which afforded him complete mastery over the rabbinic literature and the ability to paint halakhic and aggadic reality in vivid colors, as if they were events unfolding before the very eyes of his readers and those who attended his lectures. This method of bringing the text to life in a kind of *son et lumière* may have been the result of his remarkable homiletic skills, combined with the desire to be understood by everyone. The visual-associative approach to Scripture is far more likely to leave a lasting impression on the minds and memories of readers than standard homiletic and exegetical methods. Indeed, it was King Solomon's memorization techniques that earned him the title "wise", as the Talmud (*Eruvin* 21b) states:

> What is the meaning of "And besides that Koheleth was wise, he also taught the people knowledge; yea, he pondered, and sought out, and set in order many proverbs"? ... He taught the people knowledge—He taught them [mnemonic] diacritical marks, and explanations by means of analogy.

Solomon thus taught the people by analogy and diacritical marks. This method—well-known in the field of memory research—is cited in Rabbi Krol's commentary on the talmudic tractate of *Berakhot—Mimayenei Haberakhot: Hidushim Vehe'arot al Masekhet Berakhot Ufer-*

ek Helek (Defus Monzon, 5744–1984), regarding the appropriate way in which one should take leave of a friend:

> "One should take leave of one's fellow with a halakhic lesson, for in this way, he will remember him". It is written in the Mishnah (*Pe'ah* 6): "That which is before him is not forgotten [see *Deut.* 24:19 –tr.], and that which is behind him is forgotten". It is also written in the *Yerushalmi* (*Shabbat* 1,2): "One who repeats something he has heard from another in the name of he who said it, will see the one who said it, as if he were standing before him". What does this mean? "Surely man walketh as a mere semblance" (*Ps.* 3:7). Thus, if one pronounces a halakhic lesson, and his friend wishes to repeat it, he will necessarily see him as if he were standing before him—and that which is before him is not forgotten. In this way, he will remember him (p. 51).

Rabbi Krol suggests that one may recall a halakhic lesson by calling to mind the "semblance" of the source of that lesson—based upon the *mishnah* in *Pe'ah*, concerning the laws of the "forgotten sheaf" that must be left for the poor. The *mishnah* distinguishes between the area in front of the harvester, in which the sheaves are not considered forgotten, and the area behind him, which he no longer sees.

Underlying Rabbi Krol's associative-visual approach to the Pentateuch and the Talmud are man's primary senses: hearing and sight. We will cite a number of examples that illustrate the experience of reading a dry text, while subjecting it to careful analysis.

First, let us cite an example of his use of the sense of hearing. In *Deuteronomy* (17:14–20), we find the laws governing the appointment of a king over Israel. According to most commentators, the appointment of a king is neither compulsory nor desirable. Indeed, when the people came to ask Samuel for a king, it is difficult to ascertain from the text itself, the extent of the prophet's approval or disapproval.

Rabbi Krol attributes this to the difference between the intentions of the elders and those of the ignorant younger generation (*Befikudekha Asihah*, 5738–1978, pp. 377–378). The elders wanted a king that he might enforce the laws of the Torah upon the people, while the ignorant wanted a king that they might be like all the nations, as it is written:

"And they said unto him: 'Behold, thou art old, and thy sons walk not in thy ways; now make us a king to judge us like all the nations'" (1 Sam. 8:5); "And Samuel said unto all Israel: 'Behold, I have hearkened unto your voice in all that ye said unto me, and have made a king over you" (*ibid.* 12:1). Rabbi Krol explains:

> We must understand the significance of the expression "unto your voice" (*bekolkhem*), for it would have sufficed [Samuel] to say "I have hearkened unto you in all that ye said unto me". Rather, they said: "make us a king to judge us like all the nations", but the word "judge" is unclear. Does it refer to what precedes or to what follows. In other words, does it mean to judge us that we might obey the laws of the Torah, or does it mean to judge us like all the nations?

Here Rabbi Krol links the verses in *Samuel* to the Talmud in *Sanhedrin* (18a), which makes a distinction between the elders and the ignorant younger generation:

> It is taught, Rabbi Eliezer said: The elders of the generation asked rightly, as it is written (1 Sam. 8:6) "give us a king to judge us"; but the ignorant among them spoiled matters, as it is written (*ibid.* 20) "that we also may be like all the nations; and that our king may judge us, and go out before us, and fight our battles'."

The situation that Rabbi Krol paints for us is one in which Samuel actually hears the inner desires of the two groups addressing him—the elders and members of the ignorant younger generation—in their respective tones of voice.

> And Samuel understood, from the inflection of their voices, that their intentions were not equal. For the elders paused after the words "to judge us", and their intentions were for the sake of Heaven—that a king might judge them in accordance with the Torah. The young men on the other hand, made the words "to judge us" flow into the words "like all the nations", and in this they spoiled matters. And that is why he reproved them, saying "Behold, I have hearkened unto your voice"—that is from the

inflection of your voice I know the intention behind your request, that your requests are not equal.

Later, when Samuel rebukes Saul for having disobeyed God's command to destroy Amalek, Saul twice justifies his actions before admitting his sin. He is punished nonetheless—or in the words of the Talmud, his sin was "counted against him". Once again, Rabbi Krol offers an explanation based on the sense of hearing:

It is said in the tractate of *Yoma* (22b): "Saul [sinned] once and it was counted against him; David twice and it was not counted against him". Rather, when Samuel came to Saul regarding the matter of Amalek, he tried to justify himself, saying "I have performed the commandment of the Lord" (1 Sam. 15:13). When Nathan came to David on the other hand, he confessed immediately, saying "I have sinned against the Lord" (2 Sam. 12:13), to which Nathan replied "The Lord also hath put away thy sin" (*ibid.*). The Gaon, Rabbi Elijah of Vilna remarked: Was he really forgiven for the sake of a single word—'*hatati*' (I have sinned)? Rather, the words "I have sinned against the Lord" were followed by a pause, for he truly wished to say more, but was choked by tears, and had reached the point of total self-abasement. The prophet sensed this and said "The Lord also hath put away thy sin", and that is why it was not counted against him. Saul however, who did not confess immediately and attempted to justify his actions, had his sin counted against him (*Befikudekha Asihah* pp. 265–266).

This interpretation is typical of Rabbi Krol's way of depicting reality: drawing forth from the "dry text" the true remorse that brought David to tears, remorse worth a thousand of Saul's words.

In the biblical account of the exodus, Rabbi Krol notes the use of two different forms to denote the Israelites' supplications to God: *ze'akah* and *tze'akah*. *Exodus* 2:23 reads "And the children of Israel sighed by reason of the bondage, and they cried (*vayiz'aku*)"; while chapter 14, verse 10, reads "And the children of Israel cried out (*vayitz'aku*) unto the Lord". Rabbi Krol explains the distinction as follows:

For there is a difference between *ze'akah* and *tze'akah*. *Ze'akah* is the cry of an aching heart, as it is written (*Is*. 15:5) "My heart crieth out (*yiz'ak*) for Moab", and the "*Metzudot*" explain: "bitterness of heart". *Tze'akah* on the other hand, is a raising of the voice, as in *Exodus* 22:26: "and it shall come to pass, when he crieth (*yitz'ak*) unto me, that I will hear".

And this explains the different forms employed in *Psalms* 107, with regard to four types of people who must give thanks to God. The cry of the wanderers in the wilderness is called *tze'akah*, as is that of the seafarers. The cry of the prisoners however—those who sit in darkness and the shadow of death—is termed *ze'akah*; and so when the sick cried (*vayiz'aku*) unto the Lord, "He sent His word, and healed them". The reason is that the cry of desert and sea-goers is uttered in a place of total desolation, and is thus directed toward God alone, with no hope of human salvation. The sick and the imprisoned on the other hand, reside among people and place their trust in physicians and in their family and friends, and that is why their cry is called *ze'akah*. As for the Israelites at the time of the exodus from Egypt, they passed from *ze'akah* to *tze'akah* (*ibid*. p. 149).

According to the author, the Children of Israel initially placed their trust in Moses, and that is why their first cry is called a *ze'akah*. When the Egyptians drew near however, and they saw that they could not be saved by natural means, and that God was their only hope for salvation, they cried out to him—*vayitz'aku*.

The other sense to which Rabbi Krol resorts in his commentary on *Pekudei*—in order to illustrate the reality that lies within the "dry text"—is that of sight.

Rabbi Krol explains the words of the prophet Isaiah (*Is*. 11:9) "for the earth shall be full of the knowledge of the Lord, as the waters cover the sea", evoking our ability to penetrate the depths of the sea:

The meaning is as follows: Observed from the surface, the sea floor would appear to be uniform. When we descend to the depths however, we discover that there are in fact considerable differences. In some places, the bottom is deeper, and thus cov-

ered by a greater quantity of water, while elsewhere, there is less
water because the sea floor is higher, and the sea itself shallower.
It is in this fashion that the earth shall be full of the knowledge
of the Lord—wisdom and knowledge will be equal throughout,
as the waters cover the sea (*ibid.* p. 372).

This explanation distinguishes between current and future reality, by
means of a visual image. Today, understanding of the Torah and knowledge of God vary greatly from person to person—like the differences
between the mountains and valleys of the sea floor. At the end of days
however, "knowledge of the Lord" will be equal and uniform, "as the
waters cover the sea", i.e. everyone will understand the Torah equally,
just as the level of the sea appears the same everywhere.

Sometimes Rabbi Krol uses small variations in the biblical text to
explain questions with which the commentators have struggled. For
example, Rashi on *Numbers* 16:7 asks, based on the Midrash, what
brought Korah "who was clever", to rebel against Moses? Rabbi Krol
explains Korah's behavior with the help of a distinction between one
who observes the world with one eye and one who observes it with two:

> "And what did Korah, who was clever, see in such folly? His eye
> misled him" [(Rashi, *ibid.*)]. Note: "eye" not "eyes". We find in
> *Sotah* (30b) that "when the Israelites came up from the [Red]
> Sea, their eyes were set on singing God's praises". Man has two
> eyes: one with which to see God's greatness, and the other with
> which to see his own insignificance. When they came up from
> the sea, they saw the greatness of the Creator, but did not lose
> sight of their own insignificance, and they were thus prepared to
> sing God's praises. As the Talmud states, they "set their eyes",
> that is they saw with both eyes. And that is also the meaning of
> the verse "The eyes of the Lord are toward the righteous" (*Ps.*
> 34:16)—who see with two eyes. Korah however, was misled by
> his eye, in that he saw only the greatness of God, but not his own
> insignificance (*ibid.* p. 299).

Similarly, the author completes the missing text in the matter of one
who rolls up the Torah scroll (*ibid.* p. 421): "We find in the tractate of

Megilah (32a): 'One who rolls up the Torah scroll takes the reward of all [who have participated in the reading]. The reward of all? Rather a reward equal to that of all [the others combined]'." In other words, according to the Talmud, one who raises and rolls up the Torah scroll merits a reward equal to that of all of the participants in the preceding reading. Why?

Rabbi Krol explains this passage with the help of an image taken from current Torah- reading practice. One who is called up to the Torah stands next to the reader and faces the reader's side of the scroll rather than his own, just as the reader looks toward the opposite side of the scroll. The one who raises (and rolls) the scroll on the other hand, lifts it up and turns to all sides, so that the congregation may see both sides of the scroll. For this reason his reward equals that of all the others combined.

The meaning is as follows: When the Torah scroll is open [on the lectern], part of the Torah lies to the right, and part to the left. Some might then say that they will observe only part of the Torah, but not the Torah in its entirety. That is why one who [raises and] rolls up the scroll, and takes it upon himself to observe the entire Torah, merits a reward equal to that of all the others.

Among the many examples of Rabbi Krol's homiletic method, his explanation of Solomon's statement in *Proverbs* (3:17)—"Her ways are ways of pleasantness, and all her paths are peace"—is particularly interesting. Rabbi Krol explains why "ways" (*derakhim*) are associated with pleasantness, and "paths" (*netivot*) with peace.

The meaning is as follows: There are two types of road, one public and one private. Each has both an advantage and a disadvantage. The public way can be confusing, but offers a sense of security. The private path is exactly the opposite. It is not confusing, but one who travels it does so in fear (*ibid.* p. 166).

The public thoroughfare has many forks and crossroads, so that one who travels it may lose his way, but since it is frequented by many, offers relative safety. The private path on the other hand, is clear and easy to follow, but fraught with fear, due to its isolation. Solomon's promise to those who study Torah is thus that they will enjoy pleasantness, or peace of mind, on the public way—i.e. they will suffer no anxiety at its forks and crossroads. Conversely, its private paths will offer them peace. "And King Solomon came and praised the ways and paths of the Torah, which are unlike any other, in that its ways—i.e. its public thoroughfares—are pleasant; and its paths—i.e. its private trails—peaceful" (*ibid.*).

As we have seen in the above examples, Rabbi Krol's approach to the Pentateuch and Rabbinic literature sets him apart from most commentators, from his day to the present. The unique method he employed was the result of a rare combination of traits and abilities: a phenomenal memory and vast knowledge of the Torah, an associative mind, a visual imagination and wonderful didactic ability.

Rabbi Krol possessed the ability to connect diverse subjects by means of original associations, and to infuse the dry text with vivid colors and variegated voices. He did so carefully and deliberately, bearing in mind the needs of the general public. Indeed, his book *Mimayenei Haberakhot*, written for a more scholarly audience, includes fewer interpretations of this type, so frequent in his commentary on the Pentateuch.

His explanations of elliptic texts by means of *son et lumière* representations of the reality to which they pertain—drawing further support from the vast "sea" of Talmud and Midrash—not only resolve difficulties the reader may have, but also provide the means with which to remember their solutions. This approach is consistent with Rabbinic texts that recommend using the primary senses—sight and hearing—as well as various formulae and devices, to improve one's ability to remember the Torah's teachings. The Talmud in *Menahot* (43b) thus offers the following explanation of the verse "that ye may look upon it, and remember all the commandments of the Lord, and do them" (*Num.* 15:38): "Looking leads to remembering; remembering leads to doing". And so, with regard to hearing: "Rabbi Shefatyah said in the name of Rabbi Yohanan: He who reads without melody and studies without song—of him it is said, 'Wherefore I gave them also statutes that were not good, and ordinances whereby they should not live' (*Ezek.* 20:25)" (*Megilah, ibid.*). The *tosafot* explain: "They would study the Mishnah with a melody, for it was studied orally and would thus be remembered with greater facility".

Many years after his passing, those fortunate enough to have heard Rabbi Krol's Sabbath afternoon or midweek lessons, still remember his pearls of Torah wisdom, as if they had just been spoken. One of the reasons for this is the *son et lumière* visualizations he imparted to his listeners.

Vayikra – Leviticus

Shmuel Wygoda

Vayikra – And the Lord Called

Holiness as Ethics in Light of the Philosophy of
Emmanuel Levinas

Ye shall therefore sanctify yourselves and ye shall be holy; for
I am holy ... For I am the Lord that bringeth you up out of the
land of Egypt, to be your God: ye shall therefore be holy, for I
am holy (Leviticus 11:44–45).

The concept of holiness, central to all religions, plays a key
role in the book of Leviticus. An entire portion is named for
the imperative expressed in its opening verses: "Ye shall be
holy." It is not only in that portion however, that holiness appears as
a fundamental precept, but throughout the entire book. The first seven
chapters of Leviticus detail the various laws pertaining to the sacrificial
cult. Throughout these chapters, the concept of holiness is a recurrent
theme, associated with all of the various types of offerings. Chapters
8–10 describe the consecration of Aaron and the altar, while chapter
11 discusses which animals may be consumed—emphasizing that "Ye
shall therefore sanctify yourselves, and ye shall be holy; for I am holy".
Chapters 12–15 address the laws of ritual purity and impurity pertaining
to childbirth, leprosy and bodily discharges, and chapters 16–27 deal
with various matters of holiness of place ("thus shall Aaron come into
the holy place"), time (*Yom Kippur* and the other holy days), man—in
his religious, inter-personal and social conduct—and the Land of Israel,
as expressed in the Sabbatical and Jubilee years, and in the laws of inheritance. The laws governing the assessment of vows of dedication that
appear in the book's final chapter also relate to the concept of holiness,
and indeed the penultimate verse reads: "both it and the change thereof
shall be holy". Leviticus is thus a book in which the concept of holiness
serves as a kind of ideological framework for a broad range of topics
and precepts.

As noted above, the idea of holiness is fundamental to all religious approaches, and there is hardly a religion that does not place it at the heart of its worldview. But what is holiness? Is it a purely theological concept or can it be understood philosophically, i.e. by means of the rational dialogue of universal reason? This question was the subject of heated debate in the late-19th and 20th centuries. In the following chapter, I will focus on the views of Emmanuel Levinas (1905–1995), one of the 20th century's greatest philosophers. First however, let us take a brief look at the views of two other scholars, on the subject of holiness.

Historian of religion Rudolf Otto (1860–1937) strove, in his book *Das Heilige (The Idea of the Holy*, Oxford University Press, London, 1958)—first published in 1917—to define holiness as a uniquely religious phenomenon, distinct from ethical behavior. The beginning of the second chapter reads as follows:

"Holiness"—"the holy"—is a category of interpretation and valuation peculiar to the sphere of religion. It is, indeed, applied by transference to another sphere—that of ethics—but it is not itself derived from this. While it is complex, it contains a quite specific element or "moment", which sets it apart from "the rational" in the meaning we gave to that word above, and which remains inexpressible—an ἄρρητον or *ineffabile*—in the sense that it completely eludes apprehension in terms of concepts (Rudolf Otto, *The Idea of the Holy*, Oxford University Press, London, 1958, p. 5).

Otto thus seeks a category unique to the field of religion, transcending reason, and primarily differing from ethics; thereby underscoring his rejection of the identification—found predominantly in 19th century Protestant theology—of holiness with ethics. To denote the particular realm of the holy in the history of religion, Otto coined a new term, "the numinous", which he associated with the "moments" and emotional states marked by wonder and astonishment, elicited by encounters with what he termed the *mysterium tremendum*. This mystery is a combination of awe and fear of something incredibly immense, with "blank wonder" and a desire to adhere to the source of that ineffable wonder. The numinous, or the holy, according to Otto, is thus that which people perceive as divine; that which is mysteriously and tremendously bound to a force or forces beyond human comprehension. This Something, that can be a place, a time or an object, serves as a kind of sensory testimony to an extrasensory reality—hence the sense of dread aroused by the numinous. Otto's entire book is an attempt at the phenomenological description of the numinous as a uniquely religious category.

Another figure who addressed the idea of holiness and sought to define it, was the historian and scholar of religion Mircea Eliade (1907–1986). In his research, Eliade focused on myth and its role in the development of religion and society. In 1956, he was asked to write a small book, a kind of introduction to religious phenomenology that he titled *Das Heilige und das Profane* (*The Sacred & the Profane*). Eliade's approach is based on that of Otto, but he goes a step further, describing religion as something "wholly other". According to Eliade, holiness is simply divine revelation, or "hierophany", which man identifies within the framework of time and place: holy places, time, objects or actions. Eliade believed such revelations however, to be the province of primitive man, living in a culturally undeveloped society. For modern man, free from the superstitions characteristic of primitive man, all of these things—time, place, objects and actions—have completely lost their otherness, and remain ordinary everyday time, place, objects and actions, comprehensible by means of the scientific and cultural tools at man's disposal.

Having presented this basic dichotomy in the introduction to his book, Eliade devotes a chapter to the definition of sacred space in the eyes of religious man, another to sacred time, one to the sacredness of nature and religious man's approach to it, and finally, a chapter on the sanctity of human life. Eliade relates to a wide variety of religions in his study, and although he makes a number of distinctions between groups of religions, his characterizations are based on the broadest possible common denominators.

Eliade's analyses may be of interest to scholars of religion or sociologists, but would appear to have little to offer in terms of understanding the positive meaning of holiness. To this end, let us return to the philosopher with whom the discussion began: Emmanuel Levinas.

Levinas, born in Kovno (Kaunas, Lithuania), was educated first in the land of his birth and then in Ukraine—to which his family fled during the First World War—and eventually at the universities of Strasbourg (France) and Freiburg (Germany) where he studied with E. Husserl and M. Heidegger. His original thought is marked by its attempt to offer metaphysics based not on ontology, but rather on ethics.

In his lifetime, Levinas published phenomenologically-inspired philosophical works, and from the early 1960s on, works of Jewish thought as well. He was extremely careful however, to keep the two fields apart, even going as far as employing two separate publishers. The following citations belong to the purely philosophical part of his thought. According to Levinas, fundamental wonder pertains not to existence, but to the encounter with the other and the responsibility that derives therefrom. In an interview he gave in 1986, published a year later in a biographical work about him (edited by François Poirié), Levinas speaks of the place of holiness in his philosophy:

Are ethics then, above all?

The word "ethic" is Greek. I think a lot more, especially now, of holiness; the holiness of the face of the other or the holiness of my obligation as such. There is holiness in the face [of the other], but above all there is holiness or ethics with regard to the self in approaching the face as a face, where the obligation toward the other, is to consider the other, to give precedence to the other (F. Poirié, *Emmanuel Levinas. Qui êtes-vous?*, Editions La Manufacture, Lyon, 1987 p. 95).

Elsewhere in the book, Levinas further elaborates on the meaning of holiness for modern man:

The idea is that, after all, the real, indisputable value, which it is not ridiculous at all, is the value of holiness. It has nothing to do with self-privation, but lies in the certainty that the other must be given priority—from an "after you" at an open door, to the willingness—hardly possible, but demanded by holiness—to die for the other.

In this approach to holiness, there is a return to the normal, natural order of things, the persevering in being of the ontology of all things, to the extent that it is for me, the moment in which the human evokes in my mind that which lies beyond existence: God. If you will, the circumstances that bring God to mind are neither miracles, nor the contemplation of the mystery of creation ... The shock of the divine, the breach of immanent order, the order I can embrace, the order I can grasp in my mind, the order that can become mine, is the face of the other (*ibid*. p. 93).

Contrary to Otto and Eliade, who speak of holiness in terms of the numinous and the "wholly other", Levinas relates to holiness in a far more prosaic fashion. A simple "after you" is a mark of holiness. Why? Because in this simple act I give expression to the fact that I am aware of a reality beyond myself and give it precedence as a result of my obligation toward it. Levinas calls this reality: The other. Moreover, according to Levinas, in the very ability to give precedence, I recognize not only the other, but God as well, because he too is evoked by means of the face of the other. It is important to emphasize that these are not the words of a preacher in a house of worship, but of a 20th century philosopher, in his purely philosophical writings. How then can we understand, from a philosophical point of view, the connection between giving precedence to another and standing before God? In order to do so, let us look at the first time holiness appears in the Bible: "And God blessed the seventh day and sanctified it; because on it He rested from all his work which He had created" (*Gen* 2:3). Rashi, in his commentary on the Bible, explains as follows: "And He blessed and He sanctified: He blessed it with the manna that fell [in the amount of] one measure per person on every day of the week, and in a double measure on the Sabbath eve; and sanctified it with the manna that did not fall at all on [the Sabbath]".

There is something surprising in Rashi's interpretation: sanctity is manifested in the absence of something. The sanctity of the Sabbath is manifested in the fact that on that day, the manna that nourished the Israelites on their journey through the desert, did not appear. Contrary to the view of holiness as something that actually appears in places, times and objects, this approach perceives holiness as nonappearance, and is thus the antithesis of Eliade's conception of holiness as hierophany and "wholly other". It is important to note that although this understanding of holiness—based on Rashi's commentary on Genesis 2—appears in a specific context, its validity is universal. From the sanctity of the Sabbath, we learn the meaning of sanctity in general: abstention. The sanctity of place, as found in traditional Jewish sources, clearly leads to the same conclusion. The holiest place in the Tabernacle and the Temple—the Holy of Holies—is that place which may not be entered, with the exception of the high priest on the Day of Atonement, and only as the representative of the entire Jewish People. Virtually all of the references to "holiness" (*kedushah*) in the Bible display a similar approach. Holiness is thus not something mystical or "numinous", in the words of Otto, reflecting some *mysterium tremendum*, but something that pertains directly to man: abstention and restraint.

I believe this is what lies at the heart of Levinas' assertion regarding the centrality of holiness. As a philosopher however, Levinas effects what he calls a "translation into Greek", i.e. the translation of Rashi's religious language into philosophical language; a language that can be understood even by one whose cultural background is not that of Judaism. And so he remarks in one of his last books:

"..the fundamental feature of being is the preoccupation of each individual being with its own being. Plants, animals, all living things hang onto their lives. For each one, it's the struggle for survival. And matter, too; isn't it, in its essential hardness, closure and collision? And then comes the human, with the possible advent of an ontological absurdity: the concern for others is greater than the concern for oneself. This is what I call ["holiness"][1]. Our humanity consists in being able to recognize the priority of the other (Emmanuel Levinas, *Unforeseen History*, University of Illinois, 2004, p. 128).

Levinas derives the basic intuition behind this approach from his understanding of the concept of holiness in Jewish tradition. In the process

---

[1]Although *sainteté* is often translated "saintliness" in Levinas' published works in English, I have taken the liberty, throughout this chapter, of replacing "saintliness" with "holiness", as more in keeping with the Hebrew concept of *kedushah*.

of its translation into philosophical language however, it collides with another, perhaps far more dominant approach in the history of philosophy. The foremost proponent of this approach in the 20th century was the German philosopher Martin Heidegger (1889–1976), with whom Levinas studied at Freiburg in the 1920s. In his early thought, Heidegger sought to re-examine the meaning of the relationship between existence and existents. In his most important work, *Being and Time*, Heidegger stresses the aspiration of everything that exists to continue to do so, or in other words, of every entity (*Seiendes*) to persist in its Being (*Sein*). This aspiration is in essence what we call the fight for survival, and—*à la guerre comme à la guerre*—the object is to win, and there is no place for gestures toward the other side. But who is the other side? Clearly, it is anyone who is not the "entity" itself, or in the terminology of Levinas: the other. It is no wonder then that in the philosophy of Heidegger there is very little room for ethics, and in its classical sense, none at all. Such an approach is manifestly antithetical to that of Levinas. He seeks to understand the self on the basis of its encounter with the other, and sees such an encounter as a response to the imperative "thou shalt not kill"; not only in its obvious sense, but in a broader fashion—as an asymmetrical responsibility for the welfare and needs of the other. He sees holiness as abstention and the willingness to give priority to the other. In light of this understanding, let us now look at Nahmanides' remarkable interpretation of the words "ye shall be holy" (*Lev.* 19:2):

The *Sifra* (1,2) simply [explains], ye shall be abstinent (*perushim*). And so it is written there (*Shemini* 12,3) "Ye shall therefore sanctify yourselves and ye shall be holy; for I am holy—just as I am holy so you shall be holy, just as I am abstinent so you shall be abstinent". In my opinion, this does not refer to abstinence from forbidden relations, as asserted by Maimonides, but to abstinence as it appears throughout the Talmud, the authors of which are called abstinent (*Perushim* or Pharisees). And the matter is that the Torah cautioned against illicit relations and forbidden foods, but permitted a man to have sexual relations with his wife and to consume meat and wine. A voluptuary may be lecherous with his wife or with his many wives, and a glutton and a drunkard, and speak of all manner of filth, which is not explicitly forbidden by the Torah, and will thus be a scoundrel within the boundaries of the Torah.

Nahmanides addresses the difficulty that lies in a general injunction to "be holy", without any specific designation. Rashi, in his commentary, emphasizes the element of illicit sexual relations, while Nahmanides—based on the *Sifra*—extends the obligation to be holy to many other areas as well. He makes it a general rule of behavior, rooted in abstention and the recognition of that which lies beyond the self. Although Nahmanides' words can also be taken in a much narrower sense, such an approach would undermine the very generality he sought to underscore. The issue here is not one or more particular areas of behavior, as important as they might be, but a general obligation based on a worldview in which self is not the focus of existence—with all that entails in terms of the myriad situations that life presents.

I have cited Rashi on Genesis 2 as a possible source for Levinas' approach to holiness. Nahmanides on Leviticus 19 could be another—a proposition requiring further investigation. Was Nahmanides referring to some form of asceticism that man undertakes in order to purify himself before his creator? Or does holiness, according to Nahmanides, reside in the imperative against overindulging one's appetites, lest one "wax fat and rebel". Nahmanides' remarks on the *Sifra* and Rashi's interpretation of "and He blessed and He sanctified" in Genesis 2, both appear to lead to a single conclusion, further heightened by Levinas' statement here, and elsewhere in his philosophical works. Reality is a given and man strives to understand it. The more man understands, the greater his sense of control. And indeed, when we want to say that we understand something, we say that we "grasp" it. Grasping—or understanding—creates a sense of security, of having overcome the unexpected. Holiness challenges this desire in man. Holiness, as we have defined it, is abstention; a kind of "no entry" sign that denies man the grasping that affords him his sense of control. It is worth noting that Levinas constantly reiterates, throughout his philosophical writings, the surprising nature of the other. The other is not a reflection of the self, an alter ego, but other, that is different, and in that sense, a constant surprise. Holiness as interpreted by Nahmanides thus meets holiness as reflected in Levinas' philosophical definition. In this context it is worth noting that when the Pentateuch speaks of holiness, it is as a commandment, i.e. a normative demand from man. Even before the giving of the Torah at Mount Sinai, God says to Moses: "Now therefore, if ye will obey my voice indeed, and keep my covenant, then ye shall be mine own treasure from among all peoples; for all the earth is mine. And ye shall be unto me a kingdom of priests, and a holy nation" (*Ex.* 19:5–6). Read together, these two verses underscore the connection between "if ye will obey" and the imperative to be a holy nation. In Leviticus 19, the Torah also commands "ye shall be holy". Holiness is not a given; it is a demand from man, and an asymptotic one at that, inasmuch as man can never attain holiness, but can only strive toward it. The only one who is ever called "holy" is the Holy One blessed be He. In human terms, we might say that only in the case of God is the adjective "holy" also the name we employ to give expression to his essence.

Let us now address another aspect of holiness in the philosophy of Levinas: the distinction between two concepts that are very similar in terms of their plain meaning: *sacré* (sacred) and *saint* (holy). Levinas makes a clear distinction between the two. *Sacré* refers to something sanctified, i.e. something to which people tend to ascribe the value of holiness, out of a sense of numinous dread. *Saint*, on the other hand, means holy in the sense of abstention, as described above. Levinas explains the difference between the concepts in the following passage in *Difficult Freedom*, his first book on Jewish thought, published in 1963:

For Judaism, the goal of education consists in instituting a link between man and the [holiness] of God and in maintaining man in this relationship. But all its effort—from the Bible to the closure of the Talmud in the sixth century and throughout most of its commentators from the great era of rabbinical science— consists in understanding this [holiness] of God in a sense that stands in sharp contrast to the numinous meaning of this term, as it appears in the primitive religions wherein the moderns have often wished to see the source of all religion. For these thinkers, man's possession by God, enthusiasm, would be consequent on the [holiness] or the sacred character of God, the alpha and omega of spiritual life. Judaism has decharmed the world, contesting the notion that religions apparently evolved out of enthusiasm and the Sacred. Judaism remains foreign to any offensive return of these forms of human elevation. It denounces them as the essence of idolatry.

The numinous or the Sacred envelops and transports man beyond his powers and wishes, but a true liberty takes offense at this uncontrollable surplus. The numinous annuls the links between persons by making beings participate, albeit ecstatically, in a drama not brought about willingly by them, an order in which they founder. This somehow sacramental power of the Divine seems to Judaism to offend human freedom and to be contrary to the education of man, which remains *action on a free being*. Not that liberty is an end in itself, but it does remain the condition for any value man may attain. The Sacred that envelops and transports me is a form of violence.

Jewish monotheism does not exalt a sacred power, a *numen* triumphing over other numinous powers but still participating in their clandestine and mysterious life. The God of the Jews is not the survivor of mythical gods ... Monotheism marks a break with a certain conception of the Sacred. It neither unifies nor hierarchizes the numerous and numinous gods; instead it denies them. As regards the divine which they incarnate, it is merely atheism (*Difficult Freedom: Essays on Judaism*, Johns Hopkins University Press, Baltimore, 1997, pp. 14–15).

Levinas thus makes a sharp distinction between the two concepts. He does not accept the sacred as holy at all, because this category, which he identifies with the numinous, artificially transports man beyond himself. Various forms of ecstasy and enthusiasm deny man his cognizance and ability to exercise his judgment at any given moment. And if there is no clear judgment, there can be no responsibility. A person who is in a trance is detached from reality and therefore loses all responsibility toward it. Levinas intimated as much in the quote from Rashi on Leviticus 11:2, which he chose as an epigraph for the first part of *Difficult*

Freedom: "Let them not enter the Sanctuary drunk". He cites Rashi's words as a kind of subheading for the book's opening section, which he entitled "Beyond Pathos". Levinas rejects both the approach of Rudolf Otto and that of Mircea Eliade, which he identifies with the concept of sacredness. His sharp words at the end of the above passage speak for themselves: "As regards the divine which they incarnate, it is merely atheism". That is to say that if the sacred, the numinous or the hierophanic represent the divine, then Judaism is a-theistic, godless. Contrary to his attitude to the *sacré*, Levinas identifies the *saint* with holiness. The following was first presented by Levinas at an interfaith conference held in Morocco in 1957. Some three years later, it was published in an article included in *Unforeseen History*. In this article, he offers a succinct definition of holiness as he understood it:

> The sacred does not consume, does not uplift believers, does not indulge in the liturgical thaumaturgy of human beings. It is manifest only when man recognizes and welcomes others. Ancient authors qualified Judaism as impious or atheistic because of its opposition to this idolatry of the sacred. Jewish ritualism serves as method and discipline of its morals. It does not acquire sacramental significance. No proselytism attempts to impose it. Ethical relations, impossible without justice, not only prepare religious life, flow from this life; they are this life itself. According to Jeremiah 22:16, knowledge of God lies in "being good to the poor and unfortunate." The Messiah is defined first and foremost by the establishment of peace and justice—that is by the consecration of society. No hope of individual salvation— however it is imagined—can operate or be conceived outside the social accomplishment whose progress echoes in Jewish ears like the very footsteps of the Messiah. To say that God is the God of the poor, the God of justice, is to make a statement not about his attributes, but about his very essence. Which leads to the idea that *human relations, independent of all communion that is, narrowly speaking, religious, constitute in a sense, the supreme liturgical act, autonomous with regard to all manifestations of ritual piety*. In this sense the prophets certainly prefer justice to sacrifices at the temple. The prophet never speaks of

human tragedy as determined by death; he is not concerned with the immortality of the soul. Man's misfortune lies in the misery that tears apart and destroys society. Murder is more tragic than death. It is told in the tractate Baba-Bathra that a Roman asked Rabbi Akiba, "If your God is the God of the poor, why does he not feed the poor?" And the Jewish scholar replied, "So that we will not be doomed to Gehenna." It is up to man to save man: the divine way of relieving misery is not through God's intervention. The true correlation between man and God depends on a relation of man to man in which man takes full responsibility, as if there were no God to count on (*Unforeseen History*, pp. 116–117).

Here, Levinas identifies holiness with social justice, with one's obligation toward every human being, even those who are economically or socially inferior. This brings to mind the words of Isaiah: "And God the Holy One is sanctified through righteousness" (*Is.* 5:16). In other words, God's holiness is not manifested in religious ecstasy, or in the unbridled enthusiasm with which man deludes himself and his surroundings that he "communes" with God, but in the pursuit of justice, i.e. the ability to exercise restraint and consideration for that which lies beyond the self. As Rabbi Akiva replied to Turnus Rufus, there are indeed problems of social inequity in the world, and holiness is nothing more than the normative aspiration to do one's utmost to rectify that.

And in light of the words of Isaiah, perhaps Levinas' thoughts will serve as a warning against a number of disconcerting phenomena we have witnessed of late in our own society.

Warren Zev Harvey

Tzav – Command Aaron and his Sons

Gersonides on the Sacrificial Cult, Prophecy, and Philosophy

> This is the law of the burnt offering: it is that which goeth up on its firewood upon the altar all night unto the morning; and the fire of the altar shall be kept burning thereby (Leviticus 11:44–45).

Tzav, like *Vayikra* before it, deals with the laws of the temple sacrifices. I would like to discuss the approach of the Provençal Jewish philosopher Rabbi Levi ben Gershom (Ralbag or Gersonides, 1288–1344) to the sacrificial cult, and especially the surprising connection he finds between the sacrifices, prophecy and philosophy.

Gersonides is undoubtedly the most important Jewish Aristotelian philosopher after Maimonides. He was an outstanding scientist, who made original contributions to the fields of mathematics, physics and astronomy. His proofs regarding harmonic numbers were the subject of recent discussion in the context of Catalan's conjecture and Fermat's last theorem. The navigational instrument he invented, known as "Jacob's staff" (*baculus Jacobi*), was in use on the open seas until the 17th century. And there is a crater on the moon named after him: the Rabbi Levi crater. He wrote at least 10 commentaries on Averroes' commentaries on the works of Aristotle; commentaries that would become required reading for generations of Jewish students who wished to study Aristotle. His great systematic philosophical work, *The Wars of the Lord*, significantly influenced the course of Jewish philosophy. Some critics judged the book too extreme in its rationalism, jokingly referring to it as *The Wars against the Lord*. In addition to his scientific and philosophical works, Gersonides also wrote numerous commentaries on the books of the Bible, including a commentary on the Pentateuch, and his commentary on the book of Leviticus naturally includes the portion of *Tzav*.

Gersonides' commentary on the Pentateuch was one of the first Hebrew books to be printed. It was printed in Mantua before 1480, in Venice in 1547, and many times since. A recent edition, published by

307

Mossad Harav Kook (Jerusalem, 1992–2000), is quite good. The best edition however, is that of Hotza'at Ma'aliyot, the publishing house of Yeshivat Birkat Moshe (Ma'ale Adumim, 1993; 2000), although thus far it includes only Genesis, *Exodus* and Leviticus. All page numbers cited below refer to the Venice edition.

Although Gersonides followed in Maimonides' footsteps on many philosophical issues, he did not do so on the subject of sacrifices. His approach to the sacrificial cult is in many ways the antithesis of that of Maimonides. Maimonides asserts in *Guide of the Perplexed* (III, 32) that God established a sacrificial cult not for its own sake, but because it was the only form of worship with which people of that time were familiar, and as Aristotle teaches the *Nicomachean Ethics* (II, 1, 1103b 24–26), human beings cannot change their habits overnight. The Torah, explains Maimonides, used a "ruse": it borrowed the sacrificial cult from idolatry, transfering it to the worship of God. Therefore, Maimonides asserted, there is no point in seeking reasons for the various elements of the sacrificial cult, and those who do so suffer from a "prolonged madness" (*Guide of the Perplexed,* III, 26, tr. S. Pines, University of Chicago, Chicago, 1963, p. 509). The Arabic word Maimonides employs here is *hadhayān*—"delirium." One who seeks reasons for the details of the sacrificial cult is not engaging in rational scholarship, but is delirious.

Gersonides was not afraid to be accused of being "delirious". In his commentary on the chapters of the Pentateuch dealing with the sacrificial cult, he seeks reasons for each and every element. In his commentary on Leviticus (*Tzav* 134d), he offers an original interpretation of the biblical injunction to add salt to every sacrifice:

> That we might take to heart the intentions of the Law in the sacrifices, that are multifarious and very useful, ... the Law commanded that salt be brought with every offering (*Lev* 2:13: "with all thy offerings thou shalt offer salt") in order to make us aware, lest we deem the sacrifices insipid or without *ta'am* [The Hebrew word "*ta'am*" means both taste and reason]. Something is called "insipid" [Heb. *tafel*] if it lacks salt, that is, lacks a reason, as it is written: "nor ascribed ought without reason [Heb. *tiflah*] to God" (*Job* 1:22). Now, that which is salted is the opposite of insipid, that is, it is something that has a reason and *ta'am*. And

this should lead us to delve into the matter of the sacrifices, that
we might comprehend their intention, for "it is no vain thing for
you" (*Deut* 32:47).

The addition of salt to the offerings comes to teach us that the sacrificial cult is not "insipid", and that each and every detail has a reason.
For what is salted is not insipid, but has taste, reason. This metaphor
invites us to "delve into the matter of the sacrifices", and seek reasons
for each and every detail of its service. This interpretation of "with all
thy offerings thou shalt offer salt" is in itself an example of the type of
unexpected "intentions" that Gersonides discovers in the details of the
sacrifices.

Although Gersonides completely rejects Maimonides' approach
whereby seeking reasons for the details of the sacrificial cult is a "prolonged madness", he does not reject the notion that the Jewish sacrificial
cult is linked to that of idolaters. He finds in the war against idolatry a
reason to engage in sacrificial worship, stressing however that there are
other reasons as well (*Tzav* 131c):

And you should know that the Torah is wont to use one matter
for many purposes, as we have explained above regarding the
Sabbath (on *Ex.* 20, *to'elet* 10 [6]). And one of the intentions of
the sacrifices was to distance them from the sacrificial cults of
idol worship upon which they had been raised, as it is written
in *Aharei Mot*: "To the end that the children of Israel may bring
their sacrifices, which they sacrifice in the open field, even that
they may bring them unto the Lord ... And they shall no more
sacrifice their sacrifices unto the satyrs, after whom they go
astray" (*Lev.* 17:5–7). Similarly, this would appear to be one of
the intentions in building the Temple and designating the Priests
for this service.

Nevertheless, it is not appropriate that the sacrifices should not
have a utility in their own right. Otherwise, the ordinance of
these services would not have been set out in so wondrous a
fashion, but there would merely be a commandment to bring offerings to God, no more.

Indeed, the Law wisely afforded them a utility in their own right
... and to this end God ordered the rituals of the sacrifices in such
a wondrous fashion ... and similarly the rituals of the Temple
were ordered in so wondrous fashion.

Gersonides claims that just as the Sabbath has many reasons ("remembrance of creation", "remembrance of the exodus from Egypt", refraining from work, etc.), so the sacrificial cult has many reasons, some
of which pertain to the sacrifices "in their own right", and not as a means
to something else, or a "ruse". The Torah, Gersonides asserts, would not
have set forth the minutiae of the sacrifices, were there not great significance in such details.

Gersonides first voices his criticism of Maimonides' views on the
sacrificial cult in his commentary on the portion of *Noah*, in the book of
Genesis. It is written there: "and Noah builded an altar unto the Lord;
and took of every clean beast, and of every clean fowl, and offered burnt
offerings on the altar" (Gen. 8:20), and Gersonides asks: if the sacrifices have no value beyond the struggle against idolatry, how is Noah's
sacrifice to be understood? And so he writes (Commentary on Genesis,
Noah 21a–b):

Let us now examine the matter of the sacrifices brought by
Noah. We shall try to resolve here a objection concerning them
that is of no little difficulty. For Maimonides explained (*Guide
for the Perplexed* III, 32 and 46) that the matter of the sacrifices
about which we were commanded in the Law is without intrinsic
meaning but only a means to another end, to wean Israel from
the practices to which they were accustomed in those times, as in
the cults of idolatry ... But if this were indeed the case, why were
the prophets inspired to build an altar and bring burnt offerings
upon it, as we find in the case of Noah (Gen. 8:20), and of Abraham on numerous occasions (*ibid.* 12:7–8; 13:18; 22:13), and
Isaac (*ibid.* 26:25), and Jacob (*ibid.* 33:20; 46:1), and Moses (*Ex.*
24:4–5). And in the case of Balaam as well (*Num.* 23:1; 14:29).
Now, if we were to say that it was a means to another end, it
would have been more fitting had these prophets commanded

those who came after them to perform these offices, or to bring people to do these offices for the sake of God. We may say that the sacrifices indeed seem to be a means to another end; nevertheless they are also an end in themselves. The aspect of them in which they are a means to another end involves many of the sacrifices about which Israel was commanded, and the aspect of them in which they are an end in themselves involves their being an instrument to the attainment of prophecy.

And that is why Balaam said to Balak, after he had built the altars and offered up a bullock and ram: "Stand by thy burnt offering, and I will go, peradventure the LORD will come to meet me" (*Num.* 23:3).

This is why you will find the advent of prophecy in many places in which the building of an altar is mentioned, as in the case of Noah, above. And so in the case of Abraham: "And the Lord appeared unto Abram" (Gen. 12:7), "And the Lord said unto Abram", followed by "and he built there an altar" (*ibid.* 13:14–18); "and Abraham built the altar there", followed by "And the angel of the LORD called unto him out of heaven" (*ibid.* 22:9–11). And so in the case of Isaac ... (*ibid.* 26:24–25), and Jacob ... (*ibid.* 35:7–9).

The testimony of the Bible, Gersonides argues, refutes Maimonides' position, because it demonstrates that Noah and other prophets built altars and brought sacrifices not for political reasons or to wean the masses from idol-worship, but for the spiritual purpose of attaining prophecy. The scriptural evidence that Gersonides offers indeed shows a connection between sacrifice and prophecy. How can this connection be explained? Gersonides tries to explain it follows (*ibid.* 21a–b):

It will become clear from my words that the act of the sacrifices has an effect on the attainment of prophecy. Now it has already been explained in the second book of *The Wars of the Lord* (6, vi) that in the act of prophecy the intellect must be isolated from the other faculties of the soul. This cannot occur without the nullification of those faculties from their actions. To this end, the prophet, when he wishes to prophesy, would need to arouse the intellectual faculty and numb the other faculties. Therefore, you will find among the prophets, those who performed certain actions to attain prophecy, as Elisha said: "But now bring me a minstrel. And it came to pass, when the minstrel played, that the hand of the LORD came upon him" (*II Kings* 3:15).

You will find regarding the sacrifices that they arouse the intellect and numb the sentient faculties. This is because in the sacrificing the animal, cutting it into pieces, and burning it in fire, the sentient soul is necessarily subdued. For the sentient faculties, just as they are aroused by the perception of sensible objects that appear before them, so they are subdued and numbed by the destruction of the objects that were before them. In addition, a human being, on this account, will take it to heart that corruption is the end of all terrestrial things. The animal soul will be subdued by this and harried and its faculties numbed. Then intellect will be awakened as the individual contemplates the animal parts and the wisdom in their creation.

According to this intriguing psychological theory, the sacrifices play a role analogous to that of music in preparing the soul for prophecy. In order to prepare the soul for prophecy by relaxing its nonrational faculties, one can listen to music or—bring a sacrifice. The slaughter of a sacrificial animal removes sensory and emotional impressions from the soul, thereby liberating the soul from them, and preparing it for the concerted intellectual effort required for prophecy. The killing of the animal brings about the nullification of the animal in the human being, and in turn awakens the nonanimal, i.e. the intellectual. Thus, the bringing of sacrifices prepares the soul for prophecy. In addition, Gersonides mentions two further ways in which the sacrifices prepare the soul for prophecy. First: the bringing of sacrifices reminds man of the ephemerality of everything in our material world, and this existential consciousness prepares the soul for prophecy. Secondly: from the biological observation involved in bringing sacrifices, man recognizes the wisdom of the Creator.

A clear example of Gersonides' philosophical interpretation of the sacrifices can be found at the beginning of *Tzav*, which begins with the laws of the `olah*—the burnt offering. "And the Lord spoke unto Moses, saying: Command Aaron and his sons, saying: This is the law of the burnt offering: it is that which goeth up on its firewood upon the altar all night unto the morning; and the fire of the altar shall be kept burning thereby ... And the fire upon the altar shall be kept burning thereby, it shall not go out; and the priest shall kindle wood on it every morning; and he shall lay the burnt offering in order upon it" (*Lev.* 6:1–2;5; *cf. ibid.* 1:7). Gersonides interprets these verses as follows (*Commentary on Leviticus, Tzav* 131c):

> Wood is placed on the altar when the pieces of the daily burnt offering (*tamid*) are brought to the fire (*Lev.* 1:7; 6:5), that the fire might burn the wood, and by means of it consume the parts of the burnt offering. It was done in this way in order to bear witness to the fact that the living creature is consumed by that which is similar to it in its *hyle*, that is, similar to its vegetative body, and not by something that is similar to its form. Thus, the destruction of the parts of the animal was done by means of the wood. For form will strive as far as possible to maintain the being of which it is the form. In general, the good comes to a thing by virtue of its form, and bad by virtue of its matter.

> Now this will lead to the contemplation of form in all its levels, and this contemplation will conclude with God, blessed be He. In this way the act of the daily burnt offering will also lead to the attainment of prophecy for one who is prepared for it. We have offered in the portion of *Noah* another explanation regarding the connection between sacrifice and prophecy.

The `olah*, or burnt offering, according to Gersonides, teaches us an important ontological lesson. Why does the Torah insist on the use of wood to burn the sacrificed animal ("And the fire upon the altar shall be kept burning ... and the priest shall kindle wood on it every morning")?

WISDOM BY THE WEEK

Gersonides explains that the animal burnt upon wood symbolizes man's animal soul, that is, his form as an animal being; whereas the wood on the altar symbolizes man's vegetative soul, which is the matter—or *hyle* in Greek—of the animal soul. It is the wood on the altar that brings about the consumption of the animal; that is to say—destruction lies in matter and continued existence lies in form. It is man's animal soul that keeps him alive; for form is the principle of perseverance in being, Spinoza's *conatus*. "For form will strive as far as possible to maintain the being of which it is the form" (*ibid.* ll. 19–20). It is not the animal soul that brings about man's death, but the vegetative soul—i.e. matter—that does so. Man lives by virtue of the animal soul, and dies by virtue of physical, material, vegetative forces. The good of being always comes from form, and the ill of demise always comes from matter. The first source of good is the First Form—God. Indeed, contemplation of the role of the wood on the altar leads a human being to contemplate the process of generation and corruption, the relationship between form and matter, and finally, to know God as the First Form that benefits all. This knowledge of God is the prophet's knowledge. We thus discover that according to Gersonides, the sacrifices serve as an instrument not only for the education of the masses, but also for the education of the intellectuals, and even that of the prophets.

Gersonides emphasizes that there are special sacrificial laws for the intellectuals. He remarks, for example, that the sin-offering of the anointed priest and the High Court differs from an ordinary sin-offering. The blood is sprinkled on the golden altar, i.e. the altar of incense that is in the Tent of Meeting, rather than on the bronze altar, the altar of burnt offering in the Tabernacle court. He explains (*ibid.* 130d):

> As for the sin-offering for the sin of perfect individuals, like an anointed priest or a High Court that erred in its ruling (*Lev.* 4:3–21)... [the blood] was sprinkled at the horns of the golden altar (*ibid.* 6–7)… Furthermore, it was uniquely for these perfect individuals that the sprinkling was performed upon this altar, because this altar symbolizes a being more perfect than the one symbolized by the outer altar. ... Since these individuals had perfected their souls and cognized the *intelligibilia* in actuality, the sprinkling of the blood was performed for them on this altar that

symbolizes the existence of the human form ... It is as if it were saying: since the cause of the transgression was a lack of perfection of the soul in rational thinking, due to matter and material things, one must try in every possible way to subdue the material forces, that their actions be directed exclusively to the service of God.

Gersonides describes the anointed priest and the members of the High Court as "perfect individuals" who have "cognized the *intelligibilia* in actuality"—that is, he describes them as intellectuals or philosophers. According to his interpretation, the bronze altar symbolizes the world of the four elements that comes into being and perishes; and the golden altar symbolizes the human being, who comprises the four elements and comes into being and perishes, but also possesses an immortal intellect (see Gersonides, Commentary on *Exodus*, *Tetzaveh* 30:1–10, 110a; *Terumah* 27:1–8. 105d). The blood of sacrifices brought by perfect individuals, with perfect intellects, is sprinkled on the golden altar, symbolising the human being who has an eternal intellect. Gersonides' discussion of the perfect individuals—i.e. philosophers—and the golden altar, and ordinary people and the bronze altar is reminiscent of Plato's Myth of the Metals (*Republic* III, 415a *et seq.*).

Rabbi Jacob Anatoli, a philosopher who agreed with Maimonides on the subject of the sacrifices, wrote: "God does not desire sacrifice except in the sense that a good physician desires the ingestion of his drug" (*Malmad Hatalmidim, Vayikra*). In his commentary on *Tzav*, Gersonides also employs the analogy of physician and medicine with regard to the sacrifices, but refers to a "perfect physician" rather than a "good physician" (Commentary on Leviticus 132d):

It is similar to perfect physician who sees a patient not following his advice and pursuing a bad regime. He will attempt to cure him precisely by means of the bad things themselves, if possible. For example, if the patient wishes to eat a food that is inappropriate for his illness, the physician will add such things to it that will counteract its ill effect and turn it into something that cures him of his illness.

The remedy of Anatoli's good physician is effective only when a person is ill, but has no value for someone who is well. The remedy of Gersonides' perfect physician is always effective, and of great value even to a healthy person.

Contrary to Maimonides and Anatoli, Gersonides believes that the sacrificial cult is of great value even to those of healthy intellect, including prophets and philosophers.

At the end of his commentary on *Tzav*, Gersonides, the rigorous scientist and rationalist philosopher adds a prayer to God, with innocent and obvious fervor (Commentary on Leviticus 133a; *cf.* a similar prayer at the end of *Shemini* 139b):

> May the Creator of All be praised for all the great good He has bestowed upon the House of Israel. We give Him thanks for what He has revealed to us in his mercy and great loving kindness regarding the reasons for these deep matters, about which we have found no mention by others.... May the Creator of All be praised for having placed such things in our heart.

Gersonides did not have the privilege to bring a sacrifice at the Temple in Jerusalem, but did have the privilege to study and interpret the sacrificial cult, and he received from God—in prophecy?—its reasons, reasons he had not found in the work of other commentators. Contemplation of the details of the sacrifices was certainly a profound intellectual experience for him, an experience that was possibly prophetic but certainly philosophic.

Michael Zvi Nehorai

Shemini – And it Came to Pass on the Eighth Day

*The Vegetarian Ideal in the Thought of **Rabbi Avraham I. Kook***

These are the living things which ye may eat among all the beasts that are on the earth (Leviticus 11:2).

In *Shemini* (*Lev.* 11), the Children of Israel are told which creatures they may and may not eat. The latter, it turns out, are far more numerous than the former. Many explanations have been offered for the Torah's restriction of the consumption of meat to a limited number of species. In this chapter, we will explore the views of Rabbi Abraham Isaac Kook on the subject, as expressed in his polemical essay *"Talelei Orot"* ("Fragments of Light"), first published in *Tahkemoni* (Berne, 1910), and reprinted in *Ma'amarei Ha-Reiyah* (Jerusalem, 5740–1980).

Many adherents of the 19th-century Haskalah Movement cast off religious observance and sought to attenuate their Jewish and national identity. By way of justification, they cited the lack of cultural-aesthetic standards in precept-observant society, at a time when all enlightened nations were embracing liberal and universal culture.

Like many others before him, Rabbi Kook strove to defend the bastion of religion, choosing to this end, a path reminiscent of the words of the angel to the king of the Khazars: "Thy way of thinking is indeed pleasing to the Creator, but not thy way of acting" (tr. Hartwig Hirschfeld). Rabbi Kook thus addressed the aforementioned group, welcoming their moral vision, but cautioning them that it must grow within the Israelite camp, if it is to bear fruit.

He asserted that the Torah and its precepts encompass the finest moral ideals, yet these remain largely unknown. He therefore called upon the *maskilim* to draw attention to them—characterizing the need to evaluate the moral significance of the religious act as one of the methods by which the Torah is interpreted: "Individual feeling and conscience must not be sacrificed on the altar of collectivity, [for] the dead praise not the Lord" (*"Afikim Banegev"*, *Hapeles*, 5663–1903, pp. 600–601). In this, Rabbi Kook followed in the footsteps of Maimonides, who cited Aristotelian philosophy for the purpose of establishing the principle of creation: "The relationship of the doctrine of evolution—in all its ramifications—to Judaism, and its fundamental concepts in our time, is similar to the ancient confrontation of the teaching about the eternity of the universe with Judaism in the time of the spiritual polemic with the Greeks. Here we need to follow resolutely, the scientific method of Maimonides, although the methods of reasoning have changed with the changing times. With all the scientific defects in the theory of evolution, which is presently at the inception of its development and in its early stages, let us take courage to base the triumphant affirmation of Judaism on the basis of its assumptions, which, on the face [of] it, seem so antagonistic to us" ("Fragments of Light", in *Abraham Isaac Kook: The Lights of Penitence, The Moral Principles, Lights of Holiness, Essays, Letters, and Poems*, Ben Zion Bokser ed., Paulist Press, Mahwah, New Jersey, 1978, p. 306). Rabbi Kook thus expresses his views on the clash between the traditional approach to creation and modern Darwinist theory. He saw the debate as corresponding to the historical confrontation between the scriptural account of creation, and the Aristotelian theory of the eternity of the universe. Maimonides, as we know, did not reject Aristotelian theory, but in fact used it to establish the biblical principle of *ex nihilo* creation. Rabbi Kook thus exhorted educated Jews of his day to take up the scientific challenge, as did Maimonides. He also affirmed that "Judaism can no longer be explained by means of ancient philosophies" (*Igrot Ha-Reiyah*, 1, 183), and that every new idea must therefore be carefully weighed in terms of its potential to reveal the Torah's hidden moral content:

> And all the nations, when they hear these statutes and their workings, will undoubtedly exclaim: "Surely, a wise and understanding people, this great nation that hath statutes and ordinances so righteous as all this law, which I set before you this day" (*Deut.* 4:6–20)—I set before you such statutes and ordinances today, that they might be esteemed in a distant time (*Hapeles*, p. 717).

The last phrase—"esteemed in a distant time"—would appear to apply to the theory of evolution; i.e. the Torah contains universal, humanistic messages that could not be revealed until the present. So for example: "Evolution, despite its advancement, cannot decry the injustice that occurs when we murder living creatures in order to satisfy our appetites. That is but a pleasant dream of extreme idealists" (*ibid.*).

Here, Rabbi Kook draws our attention to the Torah's didactic method. The concept of vegetarianism is presented as a moral ideal rather than an element of normative behavior, because the time is not yet ripe for its fulfillment.

This ideal is implied in two places in the Bible: (1) In the verse that instructs Adam, who naturally represents the ideal man, to eat only of the herbs of the earth and the fruit of the trees, but not of the flesh of animals (Gen. 1:29). According to Rabbi Kook, it stands to reason that humanity will one day return to this level of existence, because "it is inconceivable that the Creator would have established an eternal law of this kind in the world he had created, allowing man to slaughter living creatures" (*ibid.* p. 656). (2) In the verse that permits the consumption of flesh—"and thou shalt say: 'I will eat flesh', because *thy soul desireth* to eat flesh; thou mayest eat flesh, *after all the desire of thy soul*" (*Deut.* 12:20). The Bible stresses the fact that meat is permitted only as a concession to man's desire. According to Rabbi Kook, one can hear, in the spirit of the verse, the admonition: "You may eat meat as long as you are not as morally sickened by the consumption of the flesh of animals as you would be by that of humans" (*ibid.* p. 657).

Intimations of this kind can also be found in the Talmud, as in the story of the calf that hung on the skirts of Rabbi Yehudah Hanasi and cried as it was led to slaughter (*Bava Metzia* 85a). Rabbi Yehudah sent it away, saying: "Go. That is what you were created for". He was subsequently visited with terrible afflictions, which ceased only when he showed compassion toward the cats in his house.

Rabbi Kook then goes on to list a great many precepts—including those in *Shemini*—intended, he believed, to inculcate this ideal in human consciousness.

The fact that the Torah (in Leviticus 11) prohibits such a large number of species—as well as certain parts of permitted animals—suggests that it sought to limit the consumption of animal flesh in general. The fact that kosher animals are mostly domestic, further strengthens this message, as members of the household tend to become attached to them (*Hapeles*, p. 663).

The obligation to cover the blood of game—"And whatsoever man ... that taketh in hunting any beast or fowl that may be eaten, he shall pour out the blood thereof, and cover it with dust" (Leviticus 17:13)— draws attention to the fact that the slaughter of animals is "bloodshed" and as such, should be a source of shame and embarrassment. Rabbi Kook believed such practices will "bear fruit" and "in the course of time people will be educated" ("Fragments of Light", *ibid.* p. 319).

The prohibition against mixing wool and linen is intended to convey the idea that one must distinguish between the property of a living creature and that which is acquired from the plants of the field: "The legal inequity in the ownership of property is registered in the prohibition of wearing a mixed garment of wool and linen. We are inhibited in the free mixing of wool, which was taken by robbery from the innocent sheep, with flax, which was acquired by equitable, pleasant and cultured labor" (*ibid.* 320).

The verse "Thou shalt not seethe a kid in its mother's milk" (*Ex.* 23:19) evokes the cruel image of a man who kills a kid and cooks it in its mother's milk, in order to satisfy his desires. The Torah's intention in evoking this image is to prevent all who consume meat with milk from sinking to such an abomination. The same is true of the precepts concerning ritual slaughter—i.e. that one must slaughter in a prescribed fashion, in order to minimize the animal's suffering. Precepts such as "wanting time" (an animal unfit for sacrifice because it is less than eight days old) or "sending away the mother bird" (*Deut.* 22:6–7), are meant to impress upon man "that he is dealing with a feeling, living creature, worthy of compassion" (*Hapeles*, p. 663). Rabbi Kook encapsulates the Torah's intention in this matter, as follows: "And thine ears shall hear a word behind thee, the mighty voice of the Lord, thou shalt not seethe a kid in its mother's milk... The animal does not exist merely to feed your sharp teeth, honed and polished by your base and gluttonous appetite for flesh; and the milk was not intended as a seasoning for the satisfaction of your base desires" (*ibid.* 714).

Rabbi Kook saw the prohibition against eating an animal killed by another animal as extending the obligation to visit a sick person to the animal kingdom as well, for one naturally feels more compassion toward the sick than the healthy: "Just as the rule to cover the blood extends the sway of "You shall not murder" to the domain of the animal, and the prohibition of mixing meat and milk and the banning of linen and wool in a garment extends the injunctions, "You shall not rob" and "You shall not oppress" ("Fragments of Light", *ibid.* p. 321).

The prohibition against eating an animal that has died of its own accord teaches us that we must not benefit from another's misfortune, even when that other is an animal: "All of these things are meant to impress deeply upon us that we must not wrong our fellows, for we were all fashioned by a single Creator; and the time of concession to evil will be followed by one of actively doing good, and man will no longer be capable of raising his sword against a living creature" (*Hapeles*, ibid.).

As we have noted, Rabbi Kook stresses the fact that the hidden enlightenment in these verses "pertains primarily to the future", and that their fundamental goal in the current stage of history is "to help man attain intellectual perfection". But why does the Torah not make the moral ideal the binding norm? Rabbi Kook explains that had the Torah applied "Thou shalt not murder" equally to all living creatures, it would have undermined the fundamental distinction between man and animal, creating the impression of equivalence between human and animal life. Such a view might have had a negative moral impact, possibly leading to cannibalism: "When the animal lust for meat became overpowering, if the flesh of all living beings had been forbidden, then the moral destructiveness, which will always appear at such times, would not have differentiated between man and animal, beast and fowl and every creeping thing on the earth" ("Fragments of Light," p. 318). Had the same law forbidden both animal and human flesh, it would have made little difference to one overcome with lust for meat, whether he murdered a man or a beast: "The knife, the axe, the guillotine, the electric current, would have felled them all alike in order to satisfy the vulgar craving of so-called cultured humanity" (*ibid.* pp. 318–319).

The Torah's failure to explicitly prohibit the slaughter of animals thus serves an educational purpose. It conveys the supreme value of human life, and the obligation to make human beings one's first concern, above all other living creatures:

> In this day and age, when man subjugates man to do him harm, when hatred between nations and strife between families is rife; in an age when morality is debased, and the dignity of man created in God's image is trampled underfoot; in an age such as this, could one possibly demand that man affect kindness toward animals, as if all his accounts with human beings had been settled? (*Hapeles*, p. 658).

The message that Rabbi Kook sought to convey was that the educational scope of the Torah is far greater than that of man. The former embraces eternity, while the latter pertains only to the ephemeral. The principle of "their burnt offerings and their sacrifices shall be acceptable upon mine altar" is still applicable in the current age, inasmuch as only animal sacrifice can prepare the way for the vision of "my house shall be called a house of prayer for all peoples" (*ibid.* 720; and see at length "*Te'amei Hamitzvot Bemishnat Harav*", *Matityah: Sefer He'asor Liyeshivat Bene Akiva Binetanyah*, p. 211 *et seq.*).

It is thus eminently clear that the *maskilim*, in casting off the yoke of religious observance, impede the realization of their own vision. This is also true of their weakening ties to the to the Jewish People: "The Community of Israel is the essence of all existence; an essence that, in this world, flows into the physical Israelite nation ... And there is no movement among the peoples of the world that does not have its equivalent in Israel" (*Orot*, 1, p. 138).

In the Kabbalah, the empirical status of the Jewish People in the physical world is said to correspond to that of the "Community of Israel" (*Knesset Yisra'el*), i.e. the *Sefirah* of *Malkhut* (Kingdom), in the metaphysical world.

The function of the *Sefirah* of *Malkhut*, the final *Sefirah*, is to receive the radical expressions of each of the other *Sefirot*, balance them and create harmony between them: "The Community of Israel is the essence of all that is good and fine in the world" (*Orot*, 3, p. 349).

The Jewish People is thus "the essence of all existence" (*Orot*, 2, p. 152), and is "imbued with the full weight of all spiritual tendencies in all their manifestations" (*Orot Hakodesh*, 2, 423). All expressions of the human spirit are flawed in some way or other, and it is the role of the Jewish People to gather them all, balance them and fashion them into a viable system of normative behavior (*Orot*, 2, 165). This role places Israel at the heart of human culture—needful of the other nations, but all the more needed by them.

> The Holy One, praised be He, bestowed mercy on his world, by not confining his endowments to one place, one person, one people, one land, one generation or one world, but His endowments are diffused, and the quest for perfection, which is the most idealistic striving of our nature, directs us to seek the higher unity, that must finally come in the world. In that day—God will be one and His name one (*Orot*, 2, p. 152, in Bokser, *op. cit.*, p. 24).

In this way Rabbi Kook sought to bring the *maskilim*, who had turned their backs on the Jewish religion, to reconsider their ways. He firmly believed that secularism was a transitory phenomenon, pending only the realization—by the *maskilim* as well—that no great moral idea can ever play a constructive role in human society without first passing through the crucible of the People of Israel in the Land of Israel.

Jacob J. Schacter

Tazri'a

Rabbi Joseph B. Soloveitchik on Marriage, Mitzvot and a Jew's Relationship to God

---

The Lord spoke to Moses saying, Speak to the Children of Israel saying, "When a woman conceives and gives birth to a male..." (Leviticus 12:1–2).

Prior to Revelation, a man would meet a woman in the marketplace. If they would both want him to marry her, he would bring her into his home, have intercourse with her privately, and she would be unto him as a wife. Once the Torah was given, the Jews were commanded that if a man wants to marry a woman, he must first acquire her in the presence of witnesses and then she can be unto him as a wife (Maimonides, *Mishneh Torah, Hil. Ishut* 1:1).

A familiar theme in the teachings of Rabbi Joseph B. Soloveitchik (the Rav) is defining the nature of the religious act, or what he calls the "religious gesture." The Rav points out that this act has two components, each necessary and indispensable. One is the act or physical performance of the *mitzvah* or commandment (in Hebrew, the *ma'aseh ha-mitzvah*), like holding the four species or sitting in a *sukkah* on the holiday of Tabernacles, eating *matzah* on Passover, or the daily recitation of the words that make up the Shema prayer. The second is the fulfillment of the *mitzvah*, the religious or spiritual goal that is attained by the act or the performance (in Hebrew, the *kiyyum ha-mitzvah*).

In most cases, these two components of the *mitzvah* are identical. The *ma'aseh ha-mitzvah* of eating *matzah*, for example, is to eat the *matzah* (the requisite amount in the requisite amount of time with, perhaps, the requisite posture). That represents the *kiyyum ha-mitzvah* as well, achieved via the act itself. One achieves the fulfillment of the *mitzvah* by doing the act of the *mitzvah*. The same applies to taking the four species or counting the *omer* or to most religious commandments. The act also represents the fulfillment; its fulfillment is achieved by performing the act.

There are, however, selected *mitzvot* where the act and the fulfillment are separate from one another, the classic example being prayer. Here the act (*ma'aseh*) is the recital of words found in fixed texts; it is external, public and demonstrable. The fulfillment (*kiyyum*), by contrast, is "in the heart." Prayer is, after all, "service of the heart" (*Ta'anit* 2a); it is internal, private and personal. If one merely recites words, one has not fulfilled the *mitzvah*. This is also the case with regard to the recital of the Shema where the *ma'aseh* or act consists in the verbal declaration of a fixed text, like prayer, while the *kiyyum* or fulfillment is "accepting upon oneself the yoke of the kingdom of heaven," a deeply inner personal experience. Similar, as well, are the *mitzvot* of blowing the *shofar* on Rosh Hashanah and repentance where the act and the fulfillment are separate from one another.

The classic examples of this phenomenon, most often cited in the secondary literature on the subject, are the *mitzvot* of personal mourning and rejoicing on a festival. The Talmud assumes that they are mutually exclusive, a fact reflected in the ruling (*Mo'ed Katan* 14b) that the advent of a festival with its attendant obligation to rejoice cancels personal mourning. But the rationale for this ruling is not self-evident. After all, asked the Rav, the acts or behaviors mandated by both these obligations are not mutually exclusive: a mourner can eat the meat and drink the wine required for one who rejoices on a festival while one who is engaged in this rejoicing may refrain from bathing, greeting people and the like, activities mandated for the personal mourner. The physical acts required by both of these commandments do not stand in opposition to one another. Clearly, concluded Rabbi Soloveitchik,

> the mutual contradiction between mourning and rejoicing does not involve the behavioral details of mourning and rejoicing. These outward acts do not contradict one another and could easily be accommodated together. The contradiction involves the *kiyyum* of the commandments of rejoicing and mourning in their

very essence and in the way they take effect. The essence of
rejoicing is an inner act, the heart's joy; likewise, the nature of
mourning is the inner attitude, the heart's grief. . . These acts,
however, are only the means through which man achieves the *ki-yyum* of the commandments of inner rejoicing or mourning (*And
From There You Shall Seek* [Jersey City, 2008], pp. 195–96, n.
19).

And since a person cannot simultaneously *feel* or *experience* joy
and grief, these two *mitzvot* cannot possibly coexist simultaneously.
It is thus quite obvious that the performance of these *mitzvot* is not
fully discharged via action; an inner personal experiential dimension is required—and, indeed, is indispensable—as well.

This point is well taken. Merely doing the act is not enough. *Mitzvah*
observance, on occasion, involves an inner experience in addition to
an external performance. Both outward behavior and internal religious
experience are necessary for the proper fulfillment of certain *mitzvot*.
(For more on this idea in the teachings of Rabbi Soloveitchik, see David
Shapiro, *Rabbi Joseph B. Soloveitchik on Pesach, Sefirat ha-Omer, and
Shavu'ot* [Jerusalem and New York, 2005], pp. 53–67, and the primary
sources and secondary literature cited there.)

But the issue goes deeper than this. Close to fifty years ago, the
Rav's younger son-in-law, Rabbi Aharon Lichtenstein, underscored his
father-in-law's emphasis on the indispensability of religious experience
in the context of *mitzvah* observance in general, not limited only to those
few examples mentioned above. For the Rav, wrote Rabbi Lichtenstein,
every mitzvah observance must include an element of the internal and
experiential in addition to the external and behavioral, even in those
cases like *matzah*, the four species and *omer* where the act and the fulfillment are coterminous. *Every mitzvah* must combine act and emotion,
behavior and feeling. ("R. Joseph Soloveitchik," in Simon Noveck, ed.,
Great Jewish Thinkers of the Twentieth Century [Clinton, 1963], pp.
295–96.)

In fact, this notion was central to the world view and academic
scholarship of my late teacher and the Rav's older son-in-law, Dr. Isa-
dore Twersky. In an article published in 1974, Dr. Twersky character-

ized Halakhah or "Jewish religious consciousness" as consisting of both "religion in manifestation" and "religion in essence," borrowing from the title of a book by the well-known Dutch Gentile scholar, Gerardus van der Leeuw first published in 1963. Dr. Twersky understood "religion in manifestation" to be the outward act of the *mitzvah* performance. One *manifests* one's commitment to God and Torah by *acting* in a certain way. The act is public, visible, obvious and identifiable. Holding the four species, eating *matzah*, sitting in a *sukkah*, reciting the *Kiddush* on Friday night, building a railing on one's roof (*ma'akeh*) and lighting Shabbat candles are all examples of this category; anyone who looks at the one performing the act knows exactly what she or he is doing.

By contrast, "religion in essence" was understood as the inner, personal, subjective, hidden component of *mitzvah* observance, a focus on what Dr. Twersky called "interior, fluid spiritual forces and motives . . . internal sensibility and spirituality." This element focuses on what the adherent of Halakhah is *feeling* or *experiencing* while performing the *mitzvah* act. After all, the fundamental assumption is that God does not want the halakhic practitioner to be merely a robot or a monkey; God wants the practitioner to be affected, inspired, elevated and even, hopefully, transformed by the *mitzvah* act she or he performs.

And, continued Dr. Twersky, both of these elements are absolutely necessary. "The true essence of halakah and its ultimate consummation," he wrote, consists of both "prophecy and law, charisma and institution, mood and medium, image and reality, normative action and individual perception, objective determinacy and subjective ecstasy." ("Religion and Law," in S. D. Goitein, ed., *Religion in a Religious Age* [Cambridge, 1974], pp. 69–70, and p. 78, n. 2.)

In an earlier article, he formulated this point in the following way: "Halachah itself is a tense, vibrant, dialectical system which regularly insists upon normativeness in action and inwardness in feeling and thought. . . Halachah itself, therefore, in its own behalf, demands the coordination of inner meaning and external observance." ("The Shulhan 'Aruk: Enduring Code of Jewish Law," *Judaism* 16:2 [1967], p. 157.)

And, indeed, this dual nature of the halakhic obligation in general was stressed repeatedly by Rabbi Soloveitchik; in fact, I would characterize it as one of the central components of his life's teachings. The

following represents a small sample of passages in the Rav's writings
where this theme is highlighted.

- I learned from her [my mother] very much. Most of all I
  learned that Judaism expresses itself not only in formal
  compliance with the law but also in a living experience. She
  taught me that there is a flavor, a scent and warmth to *mitzvot*. . . The laws of Shabbat, for instance, were passed on
  to me by my father. . . The Shabbat as a living entity, as a
  queen, was revealed to me by my mother. . . The fathers
  knew much about the Shabbat; the mothers *lived* the Shabbat, experienced her presence, and perceived her beauty and
  splendor. ("A Tribute to the Rebbitzen of Talne," *Tradition*
  17:2 [1978]. p. 77.)
- [There is] a serious educational-philosophical problem
  which has long troubled me. Orthodox youth have discovered the Torah through scholastic forms of thought, intellectual contact and cold logic. However, they have not merited to discover her [the Torah] through a live "experiential"
  feeling which excites and invigorates the heart. They know
  the Torah as an idea, but do not directly encounter her as an
  unmediated "reality," perceptible to "taste, sight and touch."
  Because many of them lack this "Torah-perception," their
  world view of Judaism becomes distorted. . . . In one word,
  they are confounded on the pathways of Judaism, and this
  perplexity is the result of unsophisticated perspectives and
  experiences. Halakhah is two-sided . . . the first is intellectual, but ultimately it is experiential. ("*Al Ahavat ha-Torah
  ve-Geulat Nefesh ha-Dor*," reprinted in Pinhas Peli, ed., *Be-
  Sod ha-Yahid ve-ha-Yahad* [Jerusalem, 1976], 407–08.)
- It is up to the Yeshiva and the teacher to open up the emotional world of Judaism to the students. . . . I can teach my
  students the laws and the philosophy of these Holy Days. I
  am not a bad teacher. However, I cannot transmit my rec-
  ollections to them. If I want to transmit my experiences, I
  have to transmit myself, my own heart. . . . It is exactly what
  is lacking on the American scene. . . There is no true *avo-*

dah she-be-lev, worship of the heart when it is only a mechanical recitation. The American Jew does not experience Rosh Hashanah and Yom Kippur as the Jew of old did. He observes these days, but he does not truly experience their sanctity, and particularly the nearness to God.

This is exactly our greatest need in the United States—to feel and experience God's presence. It is not enough to eat *matzah*; we must feel the experience of the *mitzvah*. One should not only study Torah, but should actually experience it as a great drama and redeeming act which purges the personality. (Aaron Rakeffet-Rothkoff, *The Rav: The World of Rabbi Joseph B. Soloveitchik*, vol. 2 [1999], pp. 169–70.)

• The modern Jew is in dire need of religious experience, of a great ecstasy in living as a Jew and "being involved" in Jewishness. No matter how committed the contemporary Jew is, he is completely unaware of the emotional dimension of the religious act. The lack of warmth and joy in observing the law and practicing Judaism is appalling. He is mostly either over-intellectualized and too sophisticated or superficial and utilitarian in his relationship to the Almighty. (Nathaniel Helfgot, ed., *Community, Covenant and Commitment: Selected Letters and Communications by Rabbi Joseph B. Soloveitchik* [Jersey City, 2005], 337–38.)

These four texts reflect the Rav's repeated insistence that "Judaism" or "Jewishness" involves not just act and behavior but emotion and feeling. The first one describes the profound influence his mother had on his life in sensitizing him to the flavor, scent and warmth of *mitzvot*, complimenting the more technical, legal, intellectual perspective that he learned from his father. In the second, he bemoaned the fact that while young American students of the type that found their way to his classroom at Yeshiva University were able to master the knowledge and logic of classical Jewish texts, they did not succeeded in experiencing the "taste, sight, and touch" of Torah. They know Torah but they do not feel the excitement of Torah and, in his judgment, this will lead to potentially negative consequences. In a most remarkable self-reflective passage, the third text, the Rav took personal responsibility for this state of affairs. In a somewhat self-deprecating formulation which no one took seriously, he took credit for being a good transmitter of the *knowledge of Torah* but faulted himself in failing to convey to his students the *experience of the presence of God*. He felt that he succeeded in conveying to them the technicalities of the laws relating to eating *matzah* on Passover but failed in conveying to them the experience of eating the *matzah* on Passover. And here, like in the last text cited, the frustration of the Rav's is extended to "the American Jew" or "the modern Jew" in general. Commitment and even observance is one thing; feelings, emotions, and "ecstasy" is something else entirely. The former without the latter is insufficient in expressing the fullness of religious engagement. In these passages—and there are others as well—the Rav noted that the "religious gesture" requires not only "formal compliance" but "a flavor, a scent and warmth;" requires not only thought, intellect and logic but "taste, sight and touch." Halakhah, for the Rav, was an experience, and he repeatedly insisted that it include not only external gestures but inner "warmth and joy."

Finally, in a remarkable passage, the Rav associated the indispensable coexistence of act ("religion in manifestation") and emotion ("religion in essence") in the service of God with a similar combination central to the marriage relationship between husband and wife, a relationship outlined in the passage from Maimonides cited at the beginning of this essay and one that, therefore, provides the necessary precondition to the conception of a child described at the beginning of *Parshat Tazri'a*. Rabbi Soloveitchik noted that marriage is "an objective institution and a subjective experience;" the connection between husband and wife entails actions as well as feelings. Similarly, "There are two aspects to the religious gesture in Judaism: strict objective discipline and exalted subjective romance. Both are indispensable." He noted that, "Feelings not manifesting themselves in deeds are volatile and transient; deeds not linked with inner experience are soulless and ritualistic. Both the subjective as well as the objective component are indispensable for the self-realization of the religious personality. . . Judaism is first a discipline and second a romance." ("Marriage," *Family Redeemed* [2000], pp. 39–41.)

The emotional connection suggested in the word "romance" expresses an experience relevant not only to that which exists—or should exist—between wife and husband; it represents also the kind of experience a Jew should strive to have with God. Our connection to our Father in Heaven is predicated on our worship of him through action, of course, but it is also necessary to see it as a relationship—personal, private and intimate—indeed, even romantic.

Naftali Rothenberg

Metzora – "The Law of the Leper"

Guard thy Tongue:
*Halakhah and Ethics in the Writings of the **Hafetz Hayim***

And the leper in whom the plague is, his clothes shall be rent, and the hair of his head shall go loose, and he shall cover his upper lip, and shall cry: 'Unclean, unclean.' All the days wherein the plague is in him he shall be unclean; he is unclean; he shall dwell alone; without the camp shall his dwelling be (Leviticus 13:45–46)

Both *Tazri'a and Metzora* discuss *nega'im*—blemishes that appear on one's body, clothing or the walls of one's home. It is clear from the biblical text that the Torah did not view such "plagues" as ordinary physical illnesses. The afflicted person or owner of the affected clothing or structure must seek out a priest, who will then decide whether the blemishes are due to natural causes, or whether they are *nega'im* requiring his further attention. A leper must be removed from the camp—as in the famous case of Miriam: "And Miriam was shut up without the camp seven days; and the people journeyed not till Miriam was brought in again" (*Num.* 12:15). Only after Miriam was released from her isolation did the Israelites proceed in their journey. A "leprous" garment must be burned outside the camp, and an afflicted house must undergo a process of rehabilitation, consisting primarily of the removal and replacement of the affected stones.

Although it is clear from the text that the plagues addressed in both of these Torah portions are not ordinary illnesses or infections, neither of the portions explains their significance or their causes. They merely describe the blemishes themselves and the laws of ritual purity and impurity associated with them. The Torah does not link the leper or the owner of the leprous garment or house to speaking ill or to any other sin. The Mishnah devotes an entire tractate to the subject, in the order of *Taharot*: the tractate *Nega'im*. In all of its fourteen chapters however, there is not a single mention of the causes or significance of these af-flictions. It is only elsewhere in the tannaitic-halakhic literature that the connection between *nega'im* and the sins of evil speech is established. The *Sifra*, halakhic midrash on the book of Leviticus, reads as follows:

He that owneth the house [shall come and tell the priest]—That he may not send another in his stead. Even if he is old? Even if he is ill? Read rather "*it* shall come and tell the priest"—the priest shall tell how *the plague* came to the house. "Saying"—The priest shall say kind words to him: My son, such plagues are the consequence of evil speech, as it is written "Take heed in the plague of leprosy, that thou observe diligently. Remember what the Lord thy God did unto Miriam, by the way as ye came forth out of Egypt". What does the one have to do with the other? To teach you that Miriam was punished for evil speech. And if thus Miriam, who spoke [ill of] Moses not in his presence, *a fortiori* one who speaks ill of another in his presence (*Sifra*, *Metzora*, 5).

This is the first time that *nega'im* are portrayed as resulting from sins of speech or causing public embarrassment. The priest is charged not only with determining whether the blemish is indeed a *nega*, but also with delivering an admonition. This idea appears again in the *Tosefta*:

How is a blemish examined? [To see] whether it is the size of two (Cilician) beans, and whether it is the prescribed shade of green or red. One [who was afflicted] would come to the priest, and the priest would say to him: Examine your deeds and repent, for such plagues are the result of evil speech and leprosy afflicts only the prideful, and God's punishments are compassionate. If his house is afflicted and he repents, [only] the affected stones are removed; if he does not [repent], the [entire house] must be demolished. If his clothing is afflicted and he repents, [only the affected area] is torn out; if he does not [repent], [the entire gar-ment] must be burned. If his body is afflicted and he repents, he may return [to the camp]; if he does not [repent], he shall dwell alone; without the camp shall his dwelling be (*Tosefta Nega'im*, 6,6).

According to the *Tosefta*, the priest must admonish one comes before him with a *nega*, that he might repent of his sin of evil speech. If he repents, the affliction will disappear and the priest will not be required to quarantine him. Leprosy, according to this source, is a process contingent upon one's descent into sin or penitence from it.

The fact that we have chosen, in this chapter, to focus on the two sources that link *nega'im* to evil speech, may create a false impression regarding the relative importance of this association. We must therefore take note of the fact that these sources are far from central, and did not make a significant impression on Torah scholars throughout the ages. A number of references to the sins of evil speech can be found in the *She'iltot* of Rav Ahai Gaon, but in the matter of their association with *nega'im*, Ahai Gaon follows in the footsteps of the Babylonian Talmud (*Arakhin* 16a), presenting evil speech as *one* of the causes of such afflictions: "*Nega'im* are precipitated by evil speech, murder, false oaths, sexual misconduct, pride, theft and envy" (*She'iltot Derav Ahai, Metzora, she'ilta* 28). In the company of murder, sexual misconduct and theft, evil speech is somewhat eclipsed, as the primary cause of *nega'im*.

Rav Ahai Gaon, as well as other *ge'onim* and *rishonim*, ignores the most important talmudic source on the subject:

Rabbi Yose ben Zimra said: He who speaks ill will be afflicted with *nega'im*, as it is written (*Ps.* 101:5), "Whoso slandereth his neighbor in secret, him will I destroy". Resh Lakish said: What is the meaning of "This shall be the law of the leper (*metzora*)"? This shall be the law of the slanderer (*motzi shem ra*) ... Why must a leper "dwell alone"? He brought discord between man and his wife, between man and his fellow, therefore the Torah said: "alone shall his dwelling be" (*Arakhin* 15b).

Maimonides on the other hand, very clearly associates *negai'm* with the sin of evil speech:

Leprosy is a term shared by a number of matters that bear little resemblance to one another. For the whitening of human skin is called leprosy, and minor hair loss from the scalp or beard is called leprosy, and the altered appearance of clothing and houses is called leprosy. And the altered appearance of clothing and houses that the Torah called leprosy, using the same term, is not a natural occurrence, but a wondrous sign among the Israelites, in order to caution them against evil speech. For when one speaks ill, the walls of his house will change. If he repents, the house will be purified, but if he persists in his wickedness until his home is demolished, the leather couches upon which he sits and lies will change. If he repents, they will be purified, but if he persists in his wickedness until they are burned, the clothes he wears will change. If he repents, they will be purified, but if he persists in his wickedness until they are burned, his skin will change and become leprous. And he will be isolated and left alone, until he no longer engages in the speech of the wicked, which is foolishness and speaking ill. And the Torah cautions us in this regard, saying: "Take heed in the plague of leprosy. Remember what the Lord thy God did unto Miriam, by the way". That is to say: Look at what happened to the prophet Miriam who spoke of her brother who was younger than she, and whom she raised on her knee and whom she saved from the sea [*sic*] at her own peril; and she did not speak ill of him, but was merely mistaken in comparing him to all the other prophets; and he was not angered by her words, as it is written "Now the man Moses was very meek". Nevertheless, she was punished with leprosy. *A fortiori*—wicked foolish people who habitually engage in extravagant talk (*Hilkhot Tum'at Tzara'at*, 16,10).

Maimonides' opinion on the matter seems unequivocal. Even this however, failed to convince readers, as it appears at the very end of the last (sixteenth!) chapter of *Hilkhot Tum'at Tzara'at* ("Laws of Leprous Impurity"). Maimonides generally concludes his work on a given halakhic topic with a brief philosophical note. Readers have thus treated it as little more than an aggadic remark, skirting the main halakhic subject.

The talmudic and midrashic literature contain numerous references to leprosy and *nega'im*. Few of these sources however, associate leprosy with sinful speech. To the sources cited above, we would add: *Sifrei, Deut.* 24:8, which links the leprosy with which Miriam was afflicted to evil speech; *Avot de-Rabbi Nathan* A, 9,3; and a number of other midrashim. This state of affairs is inconsistent with the prevailing outlook among Torah scholars in recent generations, who have viewed the leprosy described in the Torah as inexorably linked to the sins of evil speech. The architect of this outlook is Rabbi Israel Meir Hakohen of Radun—the *"Hafetz Hayim"* (henceforth HH)—author of the books *Hafetz Hayim* and *Shemirat Halashon*. In this sense, it is a modern approach. The way in which Torah scholars and Jewish thinkers throughout the ages—from the geonic period to the late 19th century—read the portions of *Tazri'a* and *Metzora* and studied the tractate *Nega'im* differed substantially from the manner in which these subjects have been approached since the publication of *Hafetz Hayim*. It is difficult for us to discern, some one hundred and twenty years later, because we naturally approach earlier sources through the prism of the HH's writings, and our Weltanschauung has been shaped by the discourse he elicited.

The change in consciousness brought about by the HH was not simply a matter of interpretation. The difference between the isolated references in the *Sifra* or the *Tosefta* to the connection between leprosy and evil speech, and the approach taken by the HH, is primarily one of classification. To the tannaitic authors—and those who studied their teachings over the course of 1,700 years—the association between leprosy and speech was a matter of philosophy rather than Halakhah, even when cited by a halakhic source. To the HH on the other hand, the significance of the association was thoroughly halakhic: Leprosy is the punishment suffered by those who violate the laws of evil speech—the positive and negative precepts and their attendant biblical "curses". The HH established the halakhic significance of the association by means of an innovative halakhic project: a book dedicated entirely to the laws of speech. He thus argued that the association between leprosy and evil speech transcends the merely philosophical or theological. It is, in talmudic terms, halakhic rather than aggadic. Accordingly, he viewed the above *tosefta*—"Examine your deeds and repent, for such plagues are the result of evil speech and leprosy afflicts only the prideful"—and midrash—"The priest shall say kind words to him: My son, such plagues are the consequence of evil speech, as it is written 'Take heed in the plague of leprosy, that thou observe diligently'"—not as aggadic texts included in halakhic sources, as scholars had previously understood, but as Halakhah proper. And this is how he related to the closing passage in Maimonides' "Laws of Leprous Impurity" as well.

In addition to *Hafetz Hayim* and *Shemirat Halashon*, Rabbi Israel Meir wrote another five books and essays on the subject. His other works were primarily intended to exhort the public to guard their speech and eschew slander and gossip. He himself put greater stock in the halakhic framework he had established, and it is that which he sought to emphasize. To this end, he wrote a preface in which he explained the biblical injunctions against evil speech and gossip. It was particularly important to him that Torah scholars and students not treat this area as secondary to the main body of the precepts. He cites three negative biblical precepts pertaining directly to evil speech and gossip:

"Thou shalt not go up and down as a talebearer among thy people"—This prohibition concerns the conveying of non-negative personal information regarding another or the affairs of others. This is the basic definition of "tale-bearing".

Similarly, this precept prohibits one from conveying negative information about one's fellow—even if it is true. This is the definition of "evil speech".

"Thou shalt not utter a false report"—This prohibition applies equally to one who speaks or listens to evil speech.

"Take heed in the plague of leprosy, that thou observe diligently"—In this precept, the Torah commands us not to forget that we must guard against evil speech.

The HH lists fourteen further negative precepts that may be violated—all or in part—by one who engages in evil speech, with each and every word she or he utters.

Beyond these seventeen negative precepts, the failure to guard one's tongue also entails the violation of numerous positive precepts. The HH counts at least fourteen positive precepts that one may violate—all or in part—when one engages in evil speech. And if this were not enough, one who engages in evil speech also incurs three of the biblical "curses":

1. "Cursed be he that smiteth his neighbor in secret", explained by the Midrash and commentators as referring to evil speech.
2. "Cursed be he that maketh the blind to go astray in the way", which includes sins of evil speech.
3. "Cursed be he that confirmeth not the words of this law to do them". If one abandons himself completely to evil speech and gossip, he is considered an "apostate in one matter".

It is on the basis of this broad biblical foundation—comprising seventeen negative precepts, fourteen positive precepts and three curses—that the HH sought to create an elaborate halakhic system of guarded speech. In this, he followed the example of Maimonides, who enumerated all of the 613 biblical precepts in his *Sefer Hamitzvot* ("Book of the Commandments"), as well as listing the relevant biblical precepts at the beginning of each section of the *Mishneh Torah*. In so doing, he sought to demonstrate the explicit and specific biblical origins of Halakhah. Unlike Maimonides however, the HH cited all of his sources—biblical, talmudic and post-talmudic.

The HH was well aware of the difficulty of guarding one's speech, due to human nature—both in terms of interpersonal relations and group behavior. He was far less concerned however, with the psychological aspects of the problem than with the marginalization of the laws and precepts of speech in the Torah literature. He knew that much of the body of law and exegesis on the subject of evil speech and gossip—particularly that which associated evil speech with leprosy—had been relegated to the conceptual and moral realm, and was not generally considered Halakhah per se. His primary goal was thus to change this approach; that Jews in general—and Torah scholars and students in particular—might view the obligation to guard one's speech as an integral part of Torah observance and adherence to the requirements of Halakhah. The distinction between Halakhah and *musar*, or moral rectitude, is unclear when it comes to matters of speech. The HH sought to highlight the fact that his frame of reference was halakhic rather than ethical, although he draws extensively upon Rabbi Jonah Gerondi's quintessentially ethical *Sha'arei Teshuvah* (*Gates of Repentance*):

Let the reader not wonder why, in a number of places—although this entire book is founded upon the principles of Halakhah—I have cited Rabbi Jonah's *Sha'arei Teshuvah*, which is numbered among the books of ethics. For if one examines certain passages of his holy work carefully, one will find that he took great pains never to depart from the realm of the law, and particularly with regard to the laws of evil speech, each and every thing he wrote is rooted in the Talmud ... Nevertheless, for the most part, I have not relied exclusively upon his assertions, except when these imply some halakhic leniency (*Hafetz Hayim*, New York, 5712–1952, p. 5, n.).

Critics of the HH's approach sought to undermine the halakhic basis he strove so hard to establish. They challenged the premise that such matters were in fact the province of Halakhah, an integral part of the 613 precepts and normative halakhic practice. They agreed that pure speech is paramount, but only as a matter of personal piety, properly regarding the need to refine one's moral conduct and philosophical outlook. The critics also questioned the value of a halakhic project of the kind undertaken by the HH, arguing that evil speech is so much a part of accepted behavior and probably of human nature as well, that "it is better that their sins be inadvertent than willful". Informing people of laws they will violate in any case, only serves to aggravate their culpability. The HH rejected this argument, on halakhic grounds:

The prohibitions against evil speech and gossip are explicitly stated in the Torah, and the principle "it is better that their sins be inadvertent than willful" does not apply to explicitly stated precepts. On the contrary, one is obligated to instruct people in the precepts of the Torah and ensure their observance through education. Would anyone consider not teaching the laws of the Sabbath, or the prohibition against eating leaven on Passover, or against theft, or any other precepts that are difficult to observe and widely disregarded, so that those who violate them might not become willful sinners?

The Torah does not accept negative social norms as an immutable force. The HH himself does not recognize the great weakness of the precept of guarding one's tongue, stemming from the fact that gossip and evil speech entail no action, but are "just" talk. This type of injunction incurs a lighter punishment than other negative precepts, as stated in the Talmud: "a negative precept that entails no action is not punishable with lashes" (*Makkot* 2b and parallel texts). Hence the great importance of the association between the laws of *nega'im*—based on the biblical precepts presented in *Tazri'a* and *Metzora*—and the sins of evil speech. The *nega'im* visited upon one who engages in evil speech were meant to show that speech, the words one forms with one's breath, is in fact a tangible and consequential thing, inasmuch as it acts upon reality and may change it for the worse. *Nega'im* are a visual, physical, practical manifestation of something ostensibly intangible—literally "thin air". *Words are an active force*, claims the HH—an assertion clearly supported by the laws of marriage for example, according to which marital status can be changed by words alone. In the case of oaths and vows, the Torah exhorts man to treat his own words with the utmost gravity and to consider a promise an irrevocable act, establishing that "he shall not break his word" (*Num.* 30:3). "A man can create and destroy entire worlds with his words" (preface to *Hovat Hashmirah*, par. 8). The *negai'm* of leprosy demonstrate to one who fails to guard her or his speech, the real power and presence of speech.

In addition to the tangible aspect of *nega'im* that deforms and disfigures, leprosy also constitutes one of the types of ritual uncleanness: "All the days wherein the plague is in him he shall be unclean; he is unclean; he shall dwell alone; without the camp shall his dwelling be" (*Lev.* 13:46). In his commentary on this verse, the HH stresses the relative severity of leprosy as compared to other forms of impurity. The Torah mentions three sources of impurity: dead bodies, issue from the sexual organs and leprosy. Impurity of the dead is considered the most severe, in terms of length and complexity of the purification process. With regard to removal from society however, it is in fact the impurity of the leper that is most severe. One defiled by a corpse was barred only from the camp of the *Shekhinah*, in which the Tabernacle was located, but could reside in the camp of the Levites (where the priests and Levites and their families dwelled, adjacent to the Tabernacle) and the camp of the Israelites. Those who had experienced an "issue" were barred from the camp of the Levites as well (even if they themselves were priests or Levites), but were allowed to reside in the camp of the Israelites. The leper however, whose impurity was the most severe of all and the only type of uncleanness to result from sin, was barred from all three camps. "He shall dwell alone", because his severe impurity precludes all human interaction.

With regard to the leper's purification, the Bible stipulates: "And he shall take the cedar-wood, and the hyssop, and the crimson of the worm". Rashi explains: If he was as proud as the cedar, he must humble himself as the worm and the hyssop, and his sin will be atoned for. In the same vein, the HH explains the verse "his clothes shall be rent, and the hair of his head shall go loose": The leper, in the days of his impurity, must wear torn clothing and leave his hair unkempt "to make him unsightly and humble him before all, that his heart might not be haughty to speak (ill) of another". Beyond the verse's plain meaning, in the spirit of Rashi, the HH also finds evidence of the view of the *Zohar*, that sins of speech spoil one's every good deed or holy act. According to the *Zohar*, the precepts are the finery that clothes the soul when it ascends to the higher worlds. The impurity of evil speech is so destructive, that a person's good deeds are defiled by it, and the words he has uttered in prayer or Torah study or the fulfillment of the commandments are soiled and ruined, so that they are no longer fit to clothe the soul. When the verse states that "his clothes shall be rent", it is intimating that the raiments of his soul will be torn and unfit to wear as he ascends to the heavens. This is echoed in the *Sefer Hayetzirah* (2:4), which asserts, through an inversion of letters, that "There is nothing better than the pleasure (ענג) [of the hereafter], and nothing worse than leprosy (נגע)".

The conditions of the leper's isolation directly correspond to his sin. "He shall cry: 'Unclean, unclean'"—i.e. he must inform those who approach him that he is impure, that they might keep their distance. He who publicly revealed the shame of another must now reveal his own shame in public.

Why are those who engage in evil speech no longer punished with leprosy? According to the HH, *nega'im* are only visited upon those who

live by higher socio-ethical standards than those commonly found today. The Torah addressed a society in which guarding one's speech was
the norm and one who spoke ill of another was a dangerous aberration.
The manifestation of *nega'im* was part of the sanctuary and priesthood
utopia, and was intended to safeguard it. In the current state of destruction and exile however, when *nega'im* no longer appear, the damage
caused by evil speech is far greater:

> Do not wonder at the fact that we see people who engage in evil
> speech yet are not afflicted with *nega'im*... I found the explana-
> tion for this, in part, in the book *Nahal Kedumim*. It is known
> that every punishment that God visits upon man is for his own
> good, that he might be cleansed of his sins or repent of them.
> When the Temple stood, and we had a purifying priest, if one
> stumbled in the sin of evil speech, God would bring upon him
> the punishment of *nega'im* ... That he might be strive thereby
> to change his ways. ... Today however, when we have neither
> Temple nor sacrifices nor purifying priest, were God to afflict
> someone with *negai'm*, he would remain impure forever, unable
> to be cleansed. Therefore, the impurity of the *nega* precipitated
> by this sin adheres only to his soul and cannot be seen on his
> body from without. And this is the meaning of the midrash [on
> the verse] 'Whoso keepeth his mouth and his tongue keepeth
> his soul from troubles' (*tzarot*)—[keepeth] his soul from lep-
> rosy (*tzara'at*)—for the *nega* and the leprosy adhere to the soul
> (*Shemirat Halashon, Sha'ar Hazekhirah*, chap. 6).

In ancient times, when there was a Temple and priests, those who
committed sins of speech could rectify matters. The appearance of
nega'im would give them hope of purification and repentance. Today
however, in the absence of the Temple, *nega'im* do not afflict the house,
clothing or body of one who engages in evil speech, and there is no way
in which one's soul can be purged of this sin. The danger posed by evil
speech is thus greater, and the damage to the soul of one who speaks ill
becomes as "That which is crooked cannot be made straight".

According the HH, all of the tragedies that have befallen the world
in general and the Jewish People in particular have been the result of
evil speech.

The serpent who brought about Adam's downfall, seduced Eve by speaking ill of God, thereby causing them both to violate His command, with devastating consequences. Since it was the sin of the Tree of Knowledge that brought death to the world, death is in fact the result of evil speech. Joseph, who brought evil report of his brothers to their father, was the cause of the Israelites' enslavement in Egypt. The sin of the spies was of course the sin of evil speech: they spread an evil report of the land, bringing future exile and "weeping for generations" upon the people. The deaths of the sages in the days of King Yannai (Alexander Jannaeus) and Shimon ben Shetah were the result of evil speech; as was the torture and execution of the Ten Martyrs. The Second Temple was destroyed because of senseless hatred, the public embarrassment of another and evil speech.

The HH's understanding of the negative ramifications of evil speech lies at he heart of his approach to historical processes and forms the basis of his theology. Sins of speech and carelessness in the guarding of speech are the root causes of all evil in the world, of the destruction of the Temple and the scattering of the Jewish People among the nations. Deliverance from the current state of exile is thus contingent upon our refraining from the sins of evil speech and gossip. Guarding one's tongue will pave the way for future redemption. Criticizing the HH for making unrealistic demands of people is thus tantamount to forswearing redemption and renouncing the messianic ideal. According to the HH, Jewish society must prepare itself for redemption, first and foremost by establishing higher standards of behavior, and by scrupulously observing the laws pertaining to speech. His is not a utopian vision of a golden messianic age in which all will refrain from evil speech, but a practical plan for revolution. In this sense, he was a modern revolutionary, striving to make utopia a reality, in the belief that observance of the laws of speech—first by Torah scholars and then by the public at large—will bring about redemption, hasten the coming of the messiah and the rebuilding of the Temple, and restore the priests to their stations and to the role they are assigned in the portion of *Tazri'a-Metzora*: "to teach when it is unclean, and when it is clean; this is the law of leprosy" (*Lev.* 14:57).

Avigdor Shinan

Aharei Mot – After the Death of the Two Sons of Aaron

An Anonymous Fifth Century Thinker

And the Lord spoke unto Moses, after the death of the two sons of Aaron, when they drew near before the Lord, and died (Leviticus 16:1).

The editor of the *Pesikta de-Rav Kahana* (to whom we shall refer simply as "the editor" or by the name of the work itself) had a wonderful idea: to compile an anthology of homilies, tales and teachings of the Sages, following the cycle of the ancient synagogue calendar.

"Following the cycle of the ancient synagogue calendar"? How so? As we know, the Scriptures are read in the synagogue according to a set pattern: the weekly reading from the Pentateuch, the *haftarot* (reading from the Prophets) and the *megillot* (the five "scrolls")—read publicly over the course of the year, according to fixed rules that leave no room for surprises. Each week has its corresponding Torah portion, each portion its *haftarah* (or *haftarot*, in keeping with the respective customs of the various communities), each holiday its readings, *haftarot* or *megillot*. It is thus possible to know in advance, which readings will be read in the synagogue throughout the year—on the Sabbath, holidays, *Rosh Hodesh* and other special days (such as the Tenth of Tevet or Purim)— or which *haftarot* will be read on various occasions (ordinary Sabbaths, a Sabbath that is also *Rosh Hodesh* or *Rosh Hodesh* eve, a Sabbath that is also a holiday, the Sabbath preceding Passover, following the Ninth of Av, etc.). The same is true of the respective *megillot* (*Song of Songs* on Passover, *Ruth* on Shavuot, etc.).

This was not the case however in *Eretz Yisrael* of the first six centuries of the Common Era—the period over the course of which the *Pesikta de-Rav Kahana* was compiled. With the exception of some of the *megillot* (at least *Esther* on Purim and *Lamentations* on the Ninth

344

of Av), which were read regularly at their appointed times, synagogue readings (from the Pentateuch and Prophets) tended to be quite flexible. Each community followed its own custom, and the entire Pentateuch was read over a period of roughly three years. The latter custom, inaccurately termed the "triennial cycle", allowed each group of worshipers to read the Torah at its own pace, and as far as we know, various communities devoted between 137 and 175 Sabbaths to its completion. Consequently, the division of the Pentateuch into "portions" also varied from place to place, and the Tiberian custom for example, would not have been the same as, shall we say, the Sepphorian custom; and just as the readings from the Pentateuch varied from community to community in Palestine, so too did the *haftarot*. The *haftarah* was sometimes selected on the basis of a connection to the Torah reading, and sometimes for another reason, such as the presence of a bridegroom in the synagogue. In any event, the concept of accepted practice, as we know it today, did not exist in ancient Palestine.

Despite this apparent lack of order and standardization, the talmudic-midrashic period witnessed the development of a somewhat fixed custom with regard to calendar-related readings from Scripture. Although the reading cycles practiced by the various Palestinian communities differed from one another, all (or most) adhered to a single custom at specific times during the course of the year. I refer to holiday and other special Torah readings, such as *Deuteronomy* 25:17–19 ("Remember what Amalek did unto thee ...") on the Sabbath preceding Purim, and *haftarot* such as *Isaiah* 40 ("Comfort ye, comfort ye my people ...") on the Sabbath following the Ninth of Av. Alongside the flexibility and lack of uniformity that characterized the Torah and *haftarah* readings on "ordinary" Sabbaths, the communities of *Eretz Yisrael* would appear to have followed a relatively uniform custom with regard to annual recurrences.

The author of the *Pesikta de-Rav Kahana* drew up a list of such recurrences and dedicated a section of his work to each of them. We thus find sections dedicated to Rosh Hashanah, Yom Kippur, the "Four Portions" (preceding Passover), Passover, the "Seven Sabbaths of Comfort", and so forth. The section corresponding to Yom Kippur (section 26) refers to the Torah reading for that day, which begins with the words

"And the Lord spoke unto Moses, after the death of the two sons of Aaron" (*Lev.* 16:1).

The custom of reading this portion on Yom Kippur obviously stems from the fact that it concerns the service of the high priest in the Sanctuary and the Holy of Holies on this day. The editor of the *Pesikta* however, chose to focus on the opening words of the reading, which refer to the deaths of Nadab and Abihu. He thus constructed an elaborate section on the subject of the brothers' deaths, as a means by which to express his own views.

This section, like all of the sections in the *Pesikta*, adheres to a fixed structure. First come a series of introductions called *petihtot* (six, in this case), apparently taken from sermons delivered on occasions on which *Aharei Mot* was read—i.e. Yom Kippur and the various Sabbaths of the year on which the portion was read as part of the Pentateuch cycle . The editor then develops his central argument, based on various rabbinic teachings, and closes with words of comfort and salvation that leave the reader in a satisfied and hopeful frame of mind. This method of interweaving public sermons and rabbinic teachings resulted in a highly instructive work, in which the editor presents readers with a broad range of ideas. Below, we shall explore the editor's treatment of the story of the deaths of Nadab and Abihu, and the lessons he sought to learn and teach from it. We will discover a thinker who expressed his own unequivocal opinions through the variegated mosaics he fashioned from the words of his predecessors.

Before we begin our analysis, it is worth noting that the very same midrash also appears, word for word, in *Leviticus Rabbah* (ch. 20). Which is the original source? Could they be the work of a single editor who chose to present the same literary unit in two different contexts? For the purposes of this article, it makes little difference. Let it suffice to say that the arguments of those who consider the *Pesikta* the primary source would appear to be the more convincing, and it is this position we have thus chosen to adopt.

The story of the deaths of Aaron's two sons—simultaneously, on a day of rejoicing, before the entire people and before their parents for an act that appears at first sight not to have warranted such a punishment—has fascinated biblical commentators and readers alike. Philo, Josephus, the Sages of the Talmud and Midrash, the medieval commentators and their successors—have all tried to understand exactly what happened on that fateful day, the day of the dedication of the Tabernacle, after fire had come down from before the Lord, causing the people to rejoice at this revelation of divine grace: "And Nadab and Abihu, the sons of Aaron, took each of them his censer, and put fire therein, and laid incense thereon, and offered strange fire before the Lord, which He had not commanded them. And there came forth fire from before the Lord, and devoured them, and they died before the Lord" (*Lev.* 10:1–2). The brothers sinned by ("strange") fire, after fire had descended from heaven, and were punished by fire. Their deaths are mentioned three more times in the Pentateuch: in *Aharei Mot* (16:1)—also the synagogue reading for Yom Kippur, and the subject of this discussion; and twice in the book of *Numbers* (3:4; 26:61). This fourfold repetition further increases the incident's homiletic possibilities. The challenge was eagerly met by a great many preachers, and a good deal of their efforts was incorporated by the *Pesikta*.

The editor, who wrote at a time when there were no longer altar or sacrifice, scapegoat or Holy of Holies, decided to relate to Yom Kippur through the story of the deaths of Aaron's sons, touching upon weighty matters, such as sin and retribution, ways to atonement, and so forth—matters that would undoubtedly have been in the air in the synagogue at this solemn time of year.

The six *petihtot* at the beginning of the section all point to a single question: Why? Why did the two brothers suffer what they suffered? From *petihta* to *petihta*, the editor focuses increasingly on the event itself, further heightening this glaring question. We can reasonably assume that the six *petihtot* were delivered by six different speakers, on six different occasions, and were only assembled, organized and possibly emended by our editor, to suit his stylistic and ideological purposes. The editor was undoubtedly responsible for the choice of *petihtot* cited in his work, and the order in which they appear. He may have gone somewhat further however, leaving his mark on the materials he collected, that they might better express the message he wished them to convey.

The first *petihta* presents six cases from the Bible that substantiate Ecclesiastes' assertion that the righteous and the wicked share a common fate ("event"), i.e. death: "there is one event to the righteous and to the wicked; to the good and to the clean and to the unclean; to him that sacrificeth and to him that sacrificeth not; as is the good, so is the sinner, and he that sweareth, as he that feareth an oath" (*Eccl.* 9:2). Since death itself is the end of all human beings, the author of the *petihta* chose to illustrate his point with pairs of biblical figures who came to the same, unusual end, after having conducted entirely different lives. So for example, he cites Josiah as "him that sacrificeth", and Ahab as "him that sacrificeth not"—yet "the one died by the arrow ... and the other died by the arrow". It would thus appear, indeed, that "there is one event to him that sacrificeth and to him that sacrificeth not". King Zedekiah is "he that sweareth", i.e. one who is quick to take an oath and thus sins in his words, and Samson is "he that feareth an oath"—yet "the one died by the putting out of eyes and the other died by the putting out of eyes". As his final example, the author brings the supporters of Korah, who came to offer incense in their dispute with Moses over his leadership, and were consumed by fire (see *Num.* 16:35); and conversely, Nadab and Abihu, who "came to offer [incense] not in strife, and were consumed by fire". This *petihta* challenges the idea that man's fate is influenced by his deeds. Nadab and Abihu are cited as one of a number of examples of the difficulty in which one who honestly believes in divine retribution, reward and punishment, finds in trying to understand or even justify its application in the world.

The second *petihta* cites a number of examples of another difficult problem: the intermingling of joy and sadness, to the point of calling the meaning of joy itself into question. This passage too begins with a verse from *Ecclesiastes*: "I said of laughter: It is mingled; and of rejoicing: What doth it accomplish?" (2:2)—as if to say, 'what point is there in joy, if it is mixed with sadness?' As an example of such joy intermingled with sadness, the author cites, *inter alia*, the story of a boy who died on the night of his wedding:

> The story is told of a dignitary of Kabul who celebrated his son's wedding on the fourth day of the week, and made a feast for the groom's companions. He said to his son: "Go upstairs and bring us a jug of wine". He went upstairs, was bitten by a snake and died. When he failed to return, the father said: "I will go and see

what has become of my son". He went and found that he had been bitten by a snake and lay dead among the wine-jugs. What did he do? He waited until he guests had eaten and drunk. Once they had eaten and drunk, he said to them: "Did you not come to offer [my son] his bridegroom's blessing? Say the mourner's blessing for him. Did you not come to lead him under his wedding canopy? Come and lead him to his grave". Rabbi Zakai of Kabul spoke the following eulogy of him: "I said of laughter: It is mingled".

The father breaks the terrible news to his guests only after they have finished their meal, when it is time for the bridegroom's blessing. Rather than lead him under the wedding canopy, the father call's upon his son's friends to accompany him to his grave. This heartrending story teaches us that rejoicing and sadness can exist side by side: the feasting guests on the one hand, and the devastated father on the other. This story also clearly brings to mind that of Nadab and Abihu: just as the bridegroom set foot in a place where perhaps he should not have been, and so met his death—so too Aaron's sons; and just as the boy's father responded with silence and resignation, so too it is written of Aaron "And Aaron held his peace".

As his final example of joy mixed with sadness, the author of the second *petihta*, cites the case of Elisheba, daughter of Amminadab, wife of Aaron and mother of Nadab and Abihu, who "rejoiced four times in a single day: she saw her husband as high priest, her brother-in-law (Moses) as king, her brother (Nahshon) as prince [of the Tribe of Judah], and her two sons deputy high priests". Her great joy was transformed into mourning the moment her sons were struck by God's fire, and consumed before her eyes. What sense was there her joy at the high offices attained by her husband, brother-in-law and brother, when her sons came to such a bitter end?

The third *petihta* further develops the ideas raised in the previous *petihtot*. The first *petihta* claimed that the righteous and the wicked share the same fate, while the second asserted that joy and sadness intermingle in our world. The third *petihta* argues that neither the righteous nor the wicked experience real joy in this world. Over the course of the *petihta*, which cites various examples from Scripture, God repeatedly addresses the wicked, saying: "the righteous experience no joy in my world, and you wish to experience joy?!" In support of this assertion, the author cites Adam—who fell from his wondrous state, until he was told: "for dust thou art, and unto dust shalt thou return"; Abraham—who was granted a son after long years of waiting only to be told to sacrifice him, and no sooner did was this tragedy averted than he returned home to discover that his wife had died; and Elisheba daughter of Amminadab, mentioned in the second *petihta*, who rejoiced four times but whose joy was transformed into mourning.

The first three *petihtot* cite numerous examples from the Bible, illustrating man's inability to comprehend the cosmic order: sadness and joy follow or mix with one another, and man's inevitable end offers no apparent indication of divine reward for the righteous or punishment for the wicked. Nadab and Abihu, Aaron and Elisheba, number among the examples, but are not the focus of attention. The fourth, fifth and sixth *petihtot* on the other hand, discuss the brothers and their father directly, focusing on their tragedy. The fourth *petihta* speaks of the greatness of Aaron and concludes with the observation that "after all this glory" he was compelled to see his "young ones" wallowing in their blood, and accept it in silence. The fifth *petihta* extends the scope of the story of Nadab and Abihu, comparing their entry into the sacred precinct to the sacrilege committed by the Roman Emperor Titus, destroyer of the Temple: "Evil Titus entered the Holy of Holies and stabbed the two curtains and left unharmed", while "the sons of Aaron entered [the Tabernacle] to bring an offering and were devoured by fire". How can this be? How can we abide such injustice?! The sixth and final *petihta* serves as a kind of bridge to the body of the section. In this *petihta*, God explicitly states that the killing of Nadab and Abihu was "not good", for "to punish the righteous is not good" (*Prov.* 17:26), although it was justified and they died for their sins; they were "uprightly" (*ibid.*)—that is justly—struck by heaven.

The six *petihtot* thus pose the following weighty questions: Why did Nadab and Abihu die in such a fashion, and what was the nature of the terrible sin for which they paid with their lives? The sixth *petihta* hints at the answer—there are good and "upright" reasons—but fails to elaborate. Details and explanations are wonderfully and cogently provided in the next part of our section, which lists no fewer than a dozen grave sins committed by the brothers—each a capital offense in its own right! With the passage from the *petihtot* to the body of the section, the picture changes completely. Empathy for the brothers is replaced by a damning indictment of their appalling behavior, while the question of theodicy is pithily dismissed in the spirit of "The Rock, His work is perfect; for all His ways are justice" (*Deut.* 32:4).

The twelve sins ascribed by the editor to Nadab and Abihu were gleaned from the entire range of written and oral literature with which he was familiar (a subject I have dealt with at greater length in *Tarbiz* 48 [5739–1979], pp. 201–214). His use of the number twelve would appear to be typological—signifying completion—as if to say that the brothers' sin was consummate. The twelve sins fall—almost certainly intentionally—into two symmetrical groups: six sins "between man and man" and six "between man and God". The first group of sins applies equally to all people in all places at all times. The second group however, pertains only to priests in the performance of their sacred offices. The editor provides evidence of each sin from Scripture, although the verses offered in support of the sins between man and man are dealt with in a creative midrashic, rather than literal, sense. The verses pertaining to the sins between priest and God are much more straightforward, and would appear to be the type of sin to which the Torah itself refers.

These are the sins ascribed by the editor to Nadab and Abihu with regard to their priestly duties: They brought an offering they had not been commanded to bring, they drew too near to the holy place, they brought "strange fire" (a "kitchen fire" rather than sacred fire from the altar), they had drunk wine, they failed to wash their hands and feet before entering the Tabernacle, and they were not wearing all of the required vestments. These six sins of a clearly ritual nature are treated very briefly in the *Pesikta*, and can be seen as a kind of elaboration on the concept of "strange fire"—the ritual sin mentioned explicitly in the biblical text.

Far greater attention is paid to the six socio-ethical sins. They are discussed at greater length, and the editor and his sources go to such lengths to prove them from Scripture, that their efforts appear to have been precipitated by the desire to ascribe these particular sins to Nadab and Abihu. A discussion of how the editor arrived at each and every one of these sins however, is beyond the scope of this article.

The second group of sins concerns all of the figures with whom a man may come into contact over the course of his life: teachers, parents, friends, his wife, children and God. The first of these sins is described as follows: "Nadab and Abihu only died because they gave a halakhic ruling in the presence of their teacher Moses". In Rabbinical times, this was indeed a terrible sin. A student may not determine a Halakhah in his teacher's presence—even if he knows the law, and even if he rules correctly. This is an essential part of the respect and gratitude a student must show toward his teacher. Nevertheless, Nadab and Abihu deemed their offering permissible, without the sanction of their teacher, Moses. The words "which he had not commanded them", which probably mean an offering not required by God, are thus assigned to Moses. The fact that this particular sin is treated first and at considerable length shows the extreme gravity with which it was viewed by the editor of the *Pesikta*—who extended the discussion of these biblical events to the world of the Rabbis:

> The story is told of a student who once gave a halakhic ruling in the presence of Rabbi Eliezer, and he [Rabbi Eliezer] said to Imma Shalom, his wife: "This [student] will not live out the week", and [indeed] he died before the week was out. His students said to him: "Rabbi, are you a prophet?" He said to them: "I am no prophet, neither am I a prophet's son, but so I have been taught, that whoever gives a halakhic ruling before his teacher, incurs death."

Rabbi Eliezer was powerless to help his disciple, who had committed an unpardonable sin. A rabbi cannot, in such cases, waive the respect that is his due. Certain of the student's fate, it is with great sorrow that he tells his wife, Imma Shalom, what has happened. The message is clear. This sin is followed by five other sins of a personal, ethical nature. Nadab and Abihu "did not consult with one another", i.e. each acted of his own accord, convinced that they need not consult with others; "they had no children"; and what is more, "they had no wives", for "they were arrogant. Many women, sat unhappily waiting for them, but they would say: 'Our father's brother is a king, our mother's brother a prince, our father the high priest, and we are deputy high priests. What woman is worthy of us?!'." The word "arrogant" would appear to apply not only to the brothers' refusal to marry, but to all of their ethical sins, for what else but arrogance could bring a man to issue an halakhic rule in front of his teacher or to act without first consulting with others? It is worth noting that the lineage of Nadab and Abihu is mentioned here for the second time in the Midrash. The first time however (in the *petihtot*), it is cited as a source of justified pride and true joy, whereas here it is the basis of wrongful pride.

But that is not all. The Midrash goes on to accuse Nadab and Abihu of another terrible sin: awaiting the deaths of their father Aaron and their uncle Moses, saying "soon these two old men will die and we will assume authority over the people". The author of this tradition viewed this as the sin for which the sons had died in their parents' lifetime, for God said to them: "Boast not thyself of to-morrow; for thou knowest not what a day may bring forth (*Prov.* 27:1)—many foals have died and their skins made into saddlecloths on their mothers' backs". And finally, after listing their sins toward their teacher, friends, wives, offspring and parents, the editor cites the brothers' great arrogance toward God; a sin they committed at the time of the giving of the Torah. This was not the sin of a priest in the performance of his sacred offices, but the sin of a man who is impudent in his behavior toward God, who fixes God with an arrogant stare: "This teaches us that they regaled their eyes upon the *Shekhinah*, like one who looks at his friend while eating and drinking ... For they coarsened their hearts and stood on their feet and regaled their eyes upon God". Nadab and Abihu's manner of looking at the *Shekhinah* (see *Ex.* 24:11) was disrespectful, like one who speaks coarsely to a friend, or when his mouth is full.

With these twelve sins, the editor of the *Pesikta* provides an ample response to the great question posed by the six *petihtot*. What appears at first to be patently unjust, the product of an arbitrary universe, turns out to have been nothing of the sort. There is no reason to pity Nadab and Abihu, who were justly punished for their sins. We must feel sorry for Elisheba and Aaron, and admire the way in which Aaron accepted the terrible blow, but we need not question God or the way in which His world is run.

We now come to the end of the section, which the editor closes on a comforting and optimistic note, in keeping with his practice throughout the *Pesikta*. In order to do so however, after having argued that Aaron's sons were utterly guilty, the editor must resort to a relatively long discussion, in which he revisits—albeit in a different spirit—a number of the elements presented earlier in the section; slowly leading the reader to a very surprising ending.

First, he asserts that God took no pleasure in the deaths of Nadab and Abihu, for "to punish the righteous is not good". On the contrary, although the brothers' last sin took place at the time of the giving of the Torah, they were punished only later, at the time of the dedication of the Tabernacle. The editor explains the delay with a parable:

Like a king who was celebrating the marriage of his daughter and discovered that the groomsmen were guilty of treason. He said: "If I kill them now—I shall disturb my daughter's celebration. Tomorrow will be my celebration, and it would be better [to kill them] at my celebration than at that of my daughter." So God said: 'If I kill Nadab and Abihu now (at the time of the giving of the Torah), I will disturb the celebration of the Torah. Tomorrow will be my celebration (the dedication of the Tabernacle). It would be better [to kill them] at my celebration than at that of the Torah'.

God deferred the brothers' punishment, so as not to spoil the celebration of the Torah on the day of its giving. We thus reencounter motifs seen above: groomsmen on a wedding day, a father celebrating the marriage of a beloved child, joy mixed with (or disrupted by) pain. Unlike the boy who died on his wedding day however, and unlike the joy that was indeed commingled with sadness that evening, the wedding in the parable ends without death—its joy undiminished. The difficult images encountered earlier in the section, in the *petihtot*, are thus mitigated, providing a bridge to the section's closing phrases.

We find further motifs repeated in the section's final passages, when the editor discusses the order of succession to the office of high priest.

Since Nadab and Abihu died—to their discredit—without issue, the high priesthood passed to their younger brothers, Eleazar and Ithamar. This fact serves the editor as a point of departure for a discussion of various aspects of the priesthood, in the context of which he recounts the beautiful tale of a woman named Kimhit:

> The story is told of Shimon ben Kimhit who went to speak with the king on the eve of Yom Kippur, and a stream of [the king's] spittle fell on his clothes and defiled him. His brother Yehudah replaced him as high priest. On that day, their mother saw her two sons [serve as] high priest. The sages said: "Kimhit had seven sons, and they all served in the high priesthood". The sages came before her and said to her: "What good deeds have you performed [that you have been so rewarded]?" She said to them: 'The beams of my house will attest to the fact that they have never seen the hairs of my head'. It is said: "All flours (*kimhaya*) are ordinary flour, but the flour of Kimhit is the finest."

The story takes place on the eve of Yom Kippur, just after the beginning of the holiday. The high priest, as national leader, goes to discuss some matter with a foreign king. During the course of their conversation some of the king's saliva falls on the priest's clothing, rendering him impure and thus unable to fulfill his duties on the holy day. He is replaced by his brother Yehudah, affording their mother the privilege of seeing two of her sons serve as high priest on the same Day of Atonement—one at the beginning of the day and the other in the performance of its holy offices. Furthermore, we learn that during the course of her life, Kimhit saw all seven of her sons serve in this capacity—probably filling in for one another in cases such as the one described in the story. When the Sages sought an explanation for her good fortune, she cited her great modesty (she did not show her hair even in her own home) as the reason she had merited this great honor.

This story seems to overturn everything we have seen so far. Instead of two arrogant sons who failed in their role as priests, we encounter seven sons of a modest and righteous woman who were successful priests. Instead of Elisheba daughter of Amminadab, who witnessed her sons' greatness and saw her joy turn to sorrow, we encounter Kimhit, who saw all of her sons hold high office, without any adversity or suffering. The entire atmosphere of the section is mitigated, the reader prepared for its final message—a surprising one:

> Rabbi Abba bar Zevina said: Why is the account of Miriam's death adjacent to that of the ashes of the [red] heifer? To teach us that just as the ashes of the heifer atone, so the death of Miriam atones. Rabbi Yudan said: Why is [the account of] Aaron's death adjacent to the breaking of the tablets? To teach us that [Aaron's death] was as grievous before the Holy One, blessed be, as the breaking of the tablets. Rabbi Hiya bar Abba said: The sons of Aaron died on the first of *Nissan*. Why [then] are they mentioned on Yom Kippur? To teach us that just as Yom Kippur atones, so the deaths of the righteous atone. How do we know that Yom Kippur atones? Because it is written "For on this day shall atonement be made for you" (*Lev.* 16:30). And how do we know that the deaths of the righteous atone? Because it is written ...

A number of verses are then cited in support of the assertion that the deaths of the righteous atone. For all intents and purposes however, the section ends here, in a decidedly surprising fashion. The proximity of the biblical account of Miriam's death (*Num.* 20) to the injunctions regarding the red heifer (*ibid.* 19) is said to indicate that the death of this righteous woman had the power to atone, both for herself and for her entire generation. Similarly, the proximity of the account of Aaron's death to the story of Moses' breaking of the tablets (see *Deut.* 9:10 and especially 10:6) is said to show that the death of a righteous man is, in the eyes of God, as dire an event as the sin of the Golden Calf and the breaking of the tablets.

Finally, we are told that Aaron's sons died on the first of the month of *Nissan*, the day of the dedication of the Tabernacle—yet the story of their deaths also appears at the beginning of *Aharei Mot*, which deals with the subject of the Day of Atonement. This juxtaposition, according to the *Pesikta*, teaches us that "just as Yom Kippur atones, so the deaths of the righteous atone". Just as Yom Kippur affords atonement to sinners, so the death of a righteous man atones for his own sins and possibly for those of others as well. Nadab and Abihu thus emerge from the section with the designation "righteous" (It is worth noting that they are described in precisely the same way at the very outset of the section, in the first *petihta*, which interprets the verse "there is one event to the righteous and to the wicked" as referring to a case such as theirs. In this sense, the section has an interesting circular structure). Despite all he has written of their twelve sins—each and every one reprehensible and punishable by death—the editor of the *Pesikta* argues that their punishment, their terrible and premature deaths, sufficed to atone for their sins and to warrant their description as righteous. Punishment itself is atonement, allowing those who have received it to begin afresh, like a newborn babe.

In this section, linked to the Torah reading for Yom Kippur, the editor appears to illustrate the principle stated by Rabbi Yishmael (*Mekhilta de-Rabbi Yishma'el, Yitro*, 7):

One who violates a positive precept and repents—is forgiven immediately ... One who violates a negative precept and repents—repentance is not sufficient to atone [for his sin], rather repentance suspends [judgment] and Yom Kippur atones ... And one who incurs death at the hands of Heaven or at the hands of the court and repents—repentance is not sufficient to suspend [judgment] and Yom Kippur is not sufficient to atone, rather repentance and Yom Kippur atone for half and suffering cleanses and atones for half ... One who desecrates the name of Heaven and repents—repentance is not sufficient to suspend [judgment] and Yom Kippur is not sufficient to atone and suffering alone is not sufficient to cleanse, but repentance and Yom Kippur suspend [judgment], and suffering and the day of death cleanse.

Rabbi Yehudah the Patriarch concludes the discussion with the assertion "we thus learn that the day of death atones". The idea is that for each and every sin, there is a prescribed way to atonement: sometimes immediate repentance is sufficient, sometimes both repentance and the atoning power of Yom Kippur are required, sometimes repentance and Yom Kippur must be supplemented with suffering, and sometimes—in the case of one who "desecrates the name of Heaven"—none of these things is enough, and only "the day of death atones". This was precisely the fate Nadab and Abihu, who publicly desecrated the name of Heaven in a number of ways, and whose deaths were their atonement.

One who reads this section of the *Pesikta*, particularly at Yom Kippur, will find a wide variety of topical themes: sin and punishment, sins between man and man as distinct from sins between man and God, theodicy, the possibility of atonement, the role of suffering and even death. These are all topics actively discussed in the synagogue from the beginning of the month of *Elul*, and with greater intensity during the days between Rosh Hashanah and Yom Kippur, leading up to Yom Kippur itself.

In this intricate, varied and instructive section, the editor of the *Pesikta*—a great thinker of Late Antiquity—addresses a number of vital issues in a clear and coherent fashion, transforming the unique event described in the story of Nadab and Abihu into a compelling and timeless lesson in ethical behavior.

Reuven Gerber

Kedoshim – Ye Shall Be Holy

Holiness in the Thought of *Abraham Isaac Kook*

Speak unto all the congregation of the children of Israel, and say unto them: Ye shall be holy; for I the Lord your God am holy (Leviticus 19:2).

Israel Independence Day falls in close proximity to the Sabbath on which we read the portion of *Kedoshim*, the climax of the book of Leviticus, often called "the Book of Holiness". I will try to establish a connection between the two, focusing on the meaning that should be ascribed to holiness in Israel today. I refer of course, to an ideal. Ideals are like stars—we cannot touch them but we are guided by their light. Aspirations are the light of ideals, guiding us to a better future.

For clarity's sake, I shall begin by stating my central thesis.

The meaning of the statement "Ye shall be holy" is the following: Strive toward perfection—seek unity in an ostensibly chaotic world. Man's constant self-perfection is an expression of the profound human need for personal development—in order to achieve a greater sense of peace with oneself, one's family and friends and society as a whole. This is, according to Rabbi Abraham Isaac Hakohen Kook, the ultimate spiritual goal of existence—achieved through participation in the process of "repairing the world" and carrying it to spiritual perfection. The process whereby existence (the macrocosm) and man (the microcosm) develop begins with the lowly, the physical, the simple, and aspires to the complex, the coherent, the unified, the spiritual. The path to perfection rises and falls, coalesces and comes apart, borne slowly higher on the back of experience and the lessons it provides. The creation of such a process—whether of self-perfection or of repairing the world—constitutes sanctification; contrary to those approaches that embrace the credo

"I am, and there is none else beside me", adopting the right of might and exploiting or showing indifference to the other. The spiritual path of one who experiences the mysterious unity of existence and contributes to its perfection is that of sanctification.

In light of the philosophy of spiritual Zionism, including that of Rabbi Kook, I will argue that a unifying, holistic approach to holiness—rather than the separation-oriented approach that prevailed in pre-Zionist times—is best suited to Israeli reality.

In the following passage, for example, Rabbi Kook addresses the prevailing, limited approach to the concept of holiness, and turns it upside down:

The highest form of holiness is the holiness of silence, the holiness of an existence in which man grasps his own insignificance and lives a life of all; wherein he experiences the life of the inanimate, the vegetative and the animal, of the collective entirety of those capable of speech, of each and every person, of every thinking, knowing, grasping and feeling being. And all existence rises up with him to its source, and the source appears always before him and before existence in all its glory, holiness, truth and serenity. And he is suffused with consummate joy, goodness and honesty, strength and beauty, might and power. He is the light of the world, its foundation and its life-force, by his merit the entire world is sustained, yet he is as nothing in his own eyes. *He does not sanctify himself, set himself apart or withdraw. He lives, and his entire life is holy of holies, life of life. His heartbeat, the flow of his blood, the intake of his breath, his look and gaze are true life—life into and through which flows divine power.* If the holy man of silence reduces himself to a limited form of worship, to prayer, to Torah [study], to circumscribed morality and personal exactitude, he will suffer and feel oppressed; a soul filled with the entire universe crushed in a vise, confined to an oppressively narrow space, restricted to a given path, when all paths are open before him, all filled with light, all brimming with life. *The impudence of the messianic era* [ushered in by Zionism] *stems from an internal desire for the supernal holiness of*

silence, which it will in the end attain (Arpelei Tohar, pp. 16–17;
emphasis mine).

In this chapter, I will explain the path that leads to this observation.
The attributes we use to describe God's actions in this world—good,
justice, truth, beauty and the like—are also applied to human endeavors, not necessarily related to the divine. Only the concept of holiness
derives from a uniquely numinous source (see Rudolf Otto, *The Idea of
the Holy*). When we apply this concept to things other than God (e.g.
the Torah, the precepts, the priests, specific actions or places) it is as a
quality emanating from the divine. Holiness in the world flows from the
holiness of God.

The concept of holiness is generally understood as designating separation. This stands in sharp contrast to the perception of holiness as
unity. God himself is apart and it is he who distinguishes between "the
sacred and the profane, between light and darkness, between Israel and
the nations", or in the words of the *Sifra*: "Ye shall be holy—You shall
set yourselves apart". Rashi links this expression to the previous chapter, and explains: "Ye shall be holy—Set yourselves apart from illicit
sexual relations and sin, for wheresoever you find a fence against illicit
sexual relations, there you will find holiness". Nahmanides understands
the exhortation "Ye shall be holy" as a general injunction, including
even those things that are not explicitly forbidden, in the sense of "sanctify yourself even in that which is permitted". Otto too, in *The Idea of
the Holy*, describes God as "wholly other".

The unifying approach on the other hand, attains prominence mainly in the literature of the Kabbalah. Although God is also referred to
as "Nothing" (*Ein*) in the Kabbalah—denoting his complete otherness
from all existence—these mystical works also exhibit a profound understanding of the mystery of the relationship between the holy and our
world. It is from the Nothing that Being flows and emanates. The Nothing is concealed within the world, and that is the meaning of the verse
"the whole earth is full of His glory"; or according to Rabbi Kook: The
holy of holies comprises both the sacred and the profane.

The Jewish concept of marriage or *kiddushin* (literally "sanctification" –tr.) offers further insight into the idea of holiness. According to

Rashi, the essence of *kiddushin* is separation: a woman is sanctified, that is to say, she is forbidden to all but her husband. This is the attitude of Ahasuerus in the book of *Esther*: a wife's beauty is merely a means by which to arouse the jealousy of others. Such is marriage for the sake of social status, but is this really the essence of marriage itself? Most of us marry for the same basic reason—that the *Song of Songs* might be sung between us. Love aspires to unity. When two people marry for love, they are in any case, emotionally detached from all others. The essence of marriage may thus be said to lie in mutual affinity, support, intimacy, and the convergence that precipitates the outpouring of divine abundance, i.e. progeny. Marriage is dedication. This is its paradigmatic, essential meaning.

Hekdesh is something that has been sanctified, or dedicated wholly to God, as we find in *Jeremiah* (1:5): "and before thou camest forth out of the womb I sanctified thee". The aspect of holiness that separates or sets one thing apart from all others is consequential—a practical, external distinction; crucial nonetheless in setting boundaries, framing laws, preserving norms and maintaining order.

How then are we to understand incidents of sanctification described in the Bible—for example, when Joshua is commanded to "sanctify the people" (Jos. 7:13)? To understand this sanctification only in terms of external purification and sexual abstinence is to miss the point. External purity is easily defined and easily commanded. Its purpose however, is to underpin internal change; emotional preparedness is the ultimate goal. Sanctification thus comprises two distinct processes: the internal—preparation of the heart, internal purification and refinement of feeling in anticipation of the encounter with, and dedication to, the divine; and the external—performing the required physical tasks, as a conduit for internal change. In other words, holiness comprises two complementary concepts, one internal and the other external. The external entails fear, boundaries, distance and separation; while the internal fosters closeness and love and devotion.

The term *yihudim* (unifications) also denotes encounter, convergence and integration, and serves to explain the highest of the kabbalistic *kavanot* (meditations): "for the unification of the Holy One, blessed be He, and the *Shekhinah*". Rabbi Kook employs this term in his attempt to define holiness. The perpetual striving toward perfection, according to Rabbi Kook, is the principle of the *yihudim*. The *yihudim* are a practical-spiritual, future-oriented method of attaining perfection that is greater than its component parts. Whenever a veil of separation is removed and unity achieved, integrating distinct and even contradictory elements into a single, harmonious system, life's hidden ideal is brought to light. The principle of sanctification is the secret key to the path of growth and perfection that man should choose to pursue: "the *sitra ahrah*—the 'other side'—dwells in unity and ends in separation, while the 'holy side' dwells in separation and ends in unity, and that unity is called peace" (*Orot Hakodesh* [Lights of Holiness] 2, 441). To return to the example of marriage, it is love that unites the two sexes, and the absence of peace in the relationship is expressed in divorce.

The best illustration of the principle of *yihudim* however, can be found in the movement created by Rabbi Kook himself: religious Zionism (or more accurately, "Zionist religiosity"). This movement unites two antithetical and hostile ideologies—ultra-Orthodoxy and secular Zionism—striving to unite the best of both approaches, despite the fundamental contradiction between them. A meeting of heaven and earth.

It is not the etymology of holiness that is of essence however, but its existential and spiritual significance. As noted above, all holiness derives from the divine. Its internal, joining or converging conception is the product of immanent theology. The love of the *Shekhinah* for the world is like the love of a mother for her children.

The external, separating conception of holiness stems from a transcendent view of God—a God who is distinct from the world, who distinguishes between Israel and the nations, and who revealed himself at Sinai, in a unique breach of the barrier that sets him apart from creation. This world on the one hand, and the world to come on the other. Traditional theology espouses a transcendent approach: "This world is but a passageway to the next. Prepare yourself in the passageway that you might enter the banquet hall". Accordingly, religious life is limited to Torah study and observance.

This was the prevailing approach in the segregated reality of premodern times. In the Age of Enlightenment however, western culture saw the rise of natural religion and Deism, also known as the religion of universal consent. This universal theology asserted the existence of a creator whose will is known through the human mind, and who requires man—as the essence of religion—to behave morally. It viewed revealed religions as myth, indicative only of the journey to the truth that lay beyond them. In such a universal context, Judaism offers no advantage over other religious traditions. On the contrary, its distinctive beliefs—like the founding myths of all revealed religions—are to its disadvantage in relation to natural, rational-universal religion. Belief in the Revelation at Mount Sinai for example, impedes the mind's ability to grasp the notion of perpetual revelation associated with the God of reason. Specific religious requirements too, lead believers to stray from the path of moral rectitude, as dictated by the light of reason. Religious discrimination against women, to cite a relevant example, is seen by many as an expression of moral obscurantism.

This ideological process eventually led to secularism, which argued that inasmuch as nature operates within the principles of natural law, there is no reason to presume the existence of a divine creator. One of the main features of secular thought—alongside denial of God's existence—is the rejection of the hereafter, focusing exclusively on this world. Secularists stressed love of nature, the importance of art, the centrality of education, and the right to freedom and enjoyment; while consigning religion to obscurity.

Nineteenth-century rabbinical leadership sought a response to the sweeping influence of enlightenment, science, human ethics, the arts and the powerful allure of modern culture.

Most traditionalists chose the ultra-Orthodox path pioneered by Rabbi Moshe Sofer ("*Hatam Sofer*"), which simply turned its back on the new world. A minority of rabbis, such as Samson Raphael Hirsch and Rabbi Kook, who followed in his footsteps, chose to internalize the modern revolution. Religious Zionism, as developed by Rabbi Kook, is essentially a process of unification, integrating religious tradition and modern values and the idea of nationalism.

We thus understand the meaning of the phrase coined by Rabbi Kook: "The old will be renewed and the new will be sanctified". As I have claimed in my research, this marked a spiritual revolution, entailing the passage from transcendent to immanent philosophy.

Accordingly, the Jewish People is perceived not as "a people that shall dwell alone", but as a branch of the tree of humanity. All existence aspires to perfection—making painstaking progress, despite terrible setbacks. The essence of civilization is the improvement of the human condition, in myriad ways. It is in this constant striving "upward" that the divine in creation lies. All that is good and does good in man, all that is forthright and just, true and sure, virtuous and seemly, gladdening and uplifting in humankind—stems from the divine within creation:

It is necessary to show how one may enter the palace: by the way of the gate. The gate is the divine dimension disclosed in the world, in all its phenomena of beauty and grandeur, as manifested in every living thing, in every insect, in every blooming plant and flower, in every nation and state, in the sea with its turbulent waves, in the panorama of the skies, in the talents of all creatures, in the thoughts of writers, the imagination of poets and the ideas of thinkers, in the feelings of every sensitive spirit and the heroic deeds of every person of valor ("A Thirst for the Living God", in *Abraham Isaac Kook: The Lights of Penitence, The Moral Principles, Lights of Holiness, Essays, Letters, and Poems*, Ben Zion Bokser ed., Paulist Press, Mahwah, New Jersey, 1978, p. 251)

In other words, the divine is revealed in the everyday spirituality of the world; in physical beauty, in social discourse, in creative imagination, in philosophical truth, in sublime emotion, in all the uplifting forces in a chaotic universe. However, when such upward breakthroughs are the result of efforts to raise up the world as a whole, they arouse debate and conflict, for they necessarily involve change. One must sometimes destroy in order to repair (secular Zionism for example, entails the destruction of the Diaspora). Thus, paradoxically, attempts to better the world actually generate tension and provoke violence. "There is a holiness that builds and there is a holiness that destroys ... From the holiness that destroys there emerge the great warriors who bring blessing to the world. They exemplify the virtue of Moses, the man of the mighty arm, who broke the tablets" (*"Lights of Holiness"*, *ibid.* p. 217). Rabbi Kook's approach embraces both kinds of holiness.

In terms of higher consciousness, the world is illuminated from within, by the divine light it conceals. Providence, previously understood as pertaining primarily to the Jewish People, is henceforth viewed as a universal phenomenon. Zionism provides Diaspora Judaism with the means to break out of the narrow confines of Halakhah, while religious Zionism is marked by a dialectic between traditional and modern values—without, of course, betraying its religious faith. This process comprises two opposing tendencies: the religious—from love of Creator to love of creation; and the secular—love and cultivation of this world. Man's capacity for holiness is directly proportionate to her or his efforts to repair the world.

In opening up to general culture, Judaism strives—in its own, unique way—to raise the ethical and spiritual level of its national existence, as a universal educational paradigm for the family of nations. Judaism too evolves, propelled by the process of historical progress.

> Religion is ... the higher perfection that is infinite and beyond assessment ... and for this reason the Jewish religion may truly be considered as the ideal of religion, the religion of the future, the "I shall be what I shall be" (Exod. 3:14), that is immeasurably higher than the content of religion in the present ("A Thirst for the Living God", *ibid.* p. 267).

How does this relate to holiness? Immanent theology experiences holiness as the core of existence, rather than a separate quality. To sanctify oneself means to love all existence and dedicate oneself to its perfection and exaltation. This is, ostensibly, an innovative approach, influenced—as suggested above—by the secular spirit of love for the physical world. It roots however, can be traced back to Scripture, to the portion of *Kedoshim.*

What is the meaning of the verse "And ye shall be unto me a kingdom of priests, and a holy nation" (*Ex.* 19:6)? Does it mean that Israel is to be a nation apart from all others? Not at all. God is sublime, supernal, ideal existence. Israel is thus commanded to aspire to the holy—as a sublime, supernal social ideal. "Lord, who shall sojourn in Thy tabernacle? Who shall dwell upon Thy holy mountain? He that walketh uprightly, and worketh righteousness ..." (*Ps.* 15:1–2). It is through moral perfection and the harmony of justice and good deeds in a strife-ridden world that one attains holiness, and it is in this fashion that God is sanctified among the Children of Israel, as it is written: "But the Lord of hosts is exalted through justice, and God the Holy One is sanctified through righteousness" (*Is.* 5:16; see also *Lev.* 22:32).

The spirit of our sources, the Torah and the precepts, that requires us to repair a flawed world, does so in order to diminish human suffering. A spiritual view of human suffering engenders a certain ethic: "for ye know the heart of a stranger, seeing ye were strangers in the land of Egypt" (*Ex.* 23:9). Consideration, respect and concern for the other are the very fabric of society. That is why the Bible, according to Nahmanides, includes the categorical imperative "And thou shalt do that which is right and good"—which extends the obligation to act ethically to all areas of life. The sinner on the other hand, is called a *ben beliya'al* or *ben beli-ya'al*—one who lacks the capacity for moral improvement. The violation of basic moral principles results in personal and social ills. Contempt, deceit and violence are the path to human hell.

There are two aspects to immoral behavior. The first is the external, the manifest, the specific wrong—theft affects one's property, violence one's person, false witness one's reputation, and so forth. On another plane however, one's soul is harmed, one's faith in humanity shaken—beginning with the one who has inflicted the harm, but extending to society as a whole. Immorality unravels the fabric of interpersonal relations, the hidden threads of trust and solidarity, eventually resulting in social disintegration. The social fabric is embodied in moral action, which not only meets specific needs, but creates ties between individuals and between the individual and her or his environment. The moral imperative thus comprises two aspects: outwardly it strives to prevent injustice; inwardly, it sustains social cohesion.

At first glance, *Kedoshim* appears to be little more than a random collection of moral teachings. Viewed through Rabbi Kook's unifying, holistic glasses however, each and every verse reflects the idea of universal love and dedication. "Ye shall be holy", as you strive toward harmony on all planes of existence. This aspiration derives from man's desire to imitate his creator. What then is the portion about, and where does it seek harmony?

- In family relationships: Respect between parents and children—domestic harmony (19:3).
- In the prohibition against incestuous relations: (Surprisingly, from a modern perspective, there is no explicit prohibition against sex between a father and daughter, or a man and his wife's sister) (18:6–7).
- In inherent human dignity: "Love thy fellow as thyself" (19:18), love the stranger and do him no wrong (*ibid.* 33–34), "Thou shalt rise up before the grey headed" (*ibid.* 32), "Thou shalt not curse the deaf, nor put a stumbling-block before the blind" (*ibid.* 14).
- In honest human interaction: "Thou shalt not hate thy brother in thy heart" (*ibid.* 17), "thou shalt not bear a grudge" (*ibid.* 18), "thou shalt not stand idly by the blood of thy fellow" (*ibid.* 16), "ye shall not deal falsely, nor lie one to another" (*ibid.* 11).
- In fair labor and commercial practices: Just weights and measures, "Thou shalt not oppress thy neighbor, nor rob him; the wages of a hired servant shall not abide with thee all night" (*ibid.* 13).
- In giving to the poor: Charity—meaning a more just and harmonious distribution of resources. "Thou shalt not wholly reap the corner of thy field, neither shalt thou gather the gleaning of thy harvest … thou shalt leave them for the poor and for the stranger" (*ibid.* 9–10).
- In a balanced approach to the earth and all living organisms: On the one hand, the obligation to plant; on the other, prohibitions against working the land in the seventh year, crossbreeding and eating the fruit of the first three years (*ibid.* 19, 23).
- In dispensing justice: "Ye shall do no unrighteousness in judgment; thou shalt not respect the person of the poor, nor favor the person of the mighty; but in righteousness shalt thou judge thy fellow" (*ibid.* 15).
- In the prohibition against idolatry: Veneration of the multiplicity of forces in nature and the struggle between them (*ibid.* 4).
- In the Sabbath: "And on the seventh day God finished His work which He had made"—i.e. completed, perfected—anticipating

the future state of redemption and harmony. The spirit of the Sabbath itself is often understood in this vein. The Sabbath liberates man from the arbitrariness of worldly existence, replacing it—for an entire day—with the freedom to live in harmony with his surroundings. According to the Rabbis, the Sabbath is one sixtieth part of the world to come; a symbol of future redemption and a foretaste of the experience of harmony in a disunited world.

The meaning of "Ye shall be holy" is therefore not that we set ourselves apart, but on the contrary, that we connect, integrate and unite with creation. Creation is sound, and we are cautioned not to spoil it. It is spoiled when we fear connection and its cost in terms of violence and criminality, and it is repaired through moral behavior. The doctrine of separateness and isolation breeds enmity, while that of unity and its organic morality leads to understanding, convergence, *yihudim* and love.

Thus far, we have described a new-old Jewish cosmology, as developed in the thought of Rabbi Abraham Isaac Kook. Before addressing its far-reaching ramifications, I would briefly like to discuss two commandments. The first of these is the timeless imperative "love thy fellow as thyself: I am the Lord" (*ibid.* 18). How can this commandment possibly be observed? What does "as thyself" mean? As you love yourself? Isn't man "partial to himself", or in the words of the book of Job (2:4): "Skin for skin, yea, all that a man hath will he give for his life". This is a widely-accepted norm.

Many commentators have attempted to explain this commandment. Nehama Leibowitz, in her usual fashion, presents a fascinating debate between them, from which I have chosen to cite the modern approach of Naphtali Herz Wessely: "Every man was created in the image of God. Love him therefore because he is as thyself" (in Nehama Leibowitz, *Studies in Vayikra*, p. 196). The commandment applies to all human beings, for all were created in God's image. And it is this that Rabbi Akiva characterized as 'a great principle in the Torah. It is thus not the individual in our fellow man that we are commanded to love, but her or his inherent humanity, for "in the likeness of God made He him" (Gen. 5:1).

It is important however, to relate to the end of the verse as well. What does it mean that one must love one's fellow man because "I am the Lord"? I will offer a Hassidic-mystical interpretation. The question of self-identification is a profound one. In Hassidic thought, the self resides not in one's clothing or body, thoughts, feelings, desires, or even personality. Your true self is the wellspring of life within you. "I am the Lord", for it is I who created you, who breathed the breath of life into you, into all your fellow beings. God is the original self, and the only self within each and every individual. The entire verse can thus be understood as follows: The commandment to love one's fellow stems from the understanding that all life stems from a single phenomenon, a single primordial force. It is profound consciousness of this primordial identity that arouses empathy and love for the life of another. (As an aside, the expression *ahi* [my brother] that has become so much a part of Israeli speech in recent years would appear to be an indication of the younger generation's receptiveness to this understanding. Similarly, the words of a popular song—"without you I am half a person, with you I am the entire universe"—lend themselves to a mystical interpretation:

"without you"—if I am simply an ego, unattuned to my inner soul—I am only half a person; "with you"—with a soul joined to all other souls, "I am the entire universe."

In Hassidic thought, existential confusion arises from the inability to distinguish between difference and separateness. The differences between men are like those between fingers on the same hand. We differ from one another yet draw our vitality from the same hidden source. Separation—between individuals, genders, societies, nations, and so forth—is entirely external. The experience of internal existence, on the other hand, evokes a sense of closeness. It is this experience that led Hillel to formulate the complementary imperative "That which is hateful to thee, do not unto thy fellow—This is the entire Torah. The rest is commentary. Go and learn" (*Shabbat* 31a). Learn to perfect yourself in the ways of the inner Torah, the Torah of hidden unity, the Torah of love.

One should therefore show respect—and even love—toward the stranger, the ethnic minority residing in your land. "The stranger that sojourneth with you shall be unto you as the home-born among you, and thou shalt love him as thyself; for ye were strangers in the land of Egypt" (19:34). You who were a minority group in Egypt and have first-hand knowledge of the minority experience, do not unto another minority, that which is hateful to you.

The Rabbis limited the application of this simple and logical precept to converts to Judaism ("righteous strangers"), contrary to the plain meaning of the biblical text (just as they limited love of one's fellow to love of "one who is your fellow in the Torah and its precepts"). The biblical commandment exhibits a level of moral development that surpasses even the morality of democracy. The latter is based upon the principle of equality before the law, whereas the Bible demands far more: "Thou shalt love him as thyself"—just as you love the majority group to which you belong. The halakhic interpretation on the other hand, falls short of democratic morality. The challenge is supreme, but it follows naturally from the belief that "the whole earth is full of His glory". Love of creation, as creation, is the heart and soul of faith. The challenge is great, but the path to being a chosen people was never meant to be easy.

Rabbi Kook wrote as follows: "I love everybody. It is impossible for me not to love all people, all nations. With all the depth of my being, I desire to see them grow toward beauty, toward perfection. My love for the Jewish people is with more ardor, more depth. But my inner desire reaches out with a mighty love toward all. There is veritably no need for me to force this feeling of love. It flows directly from the holy depth of wisdom, from the divine soul" (*Arpelei Tohar* p. 22—in Bokser ed., *ibid.* pp. 29–30).

The ramifications of this immanent-spiritual revolution are many:

1. The depth of holiness in man is proportionate to the extent of his real love for the world, and conversely, the more isolation, hatred and violence in the world, the less holiness there is. The need of previous generations to distinguish themselves from Christianity, obscured the Jewish message of love for all beings created in God's image. A Jew should be a loving person.

2. There is a great deal of holiness in the pursuit of peace— among those who seek it in their immediate surroundings and actively pursue it elsewhere. Those who confine them-

selves to the realm of ritual or beliefs that run counter to simple human morality, tend to ascribe inordinate holiness to their actions (see *Orot Hakodesh* [Lights of Holiness] 3, p. 30).

3. Judaism is a process of "repairing the world", i.e. perfecting man and society. The traditional sources are not significant in and of themselves, but only inasmuch as they are imbued with the Jewish spirit and its demand for moral improvement. "Look at the lights, in their inwardness. Let not the names, the words, the idiom and the letters confine your soul. They are under your control, you are not under theirs" (*"Lights of Holiness"*, *ibid.* p. 208).

4. It is not study that is of essence, but worthy action; not ritual, but the act of repairing the world. All who are truly concerned for society—social workers, educators, honest leaders, intellectuals, compassionate rabbis and the like—contribute to the proliferation of holiness.

5. Values—i.e. widely accepted principles that, if adhered to, will diminish suffering—contribute to the betterment of our society. Honoring one's parents, striving for women's equality and children's rights—all diminish suffering. Contemporary Judaism must therefore adhere to modern values, in keeping with the verse "And thou shalt do that which is right and good" (particularly in light of Nahmanides' interpretation, noted above).

6. The holistic approach believes in the constant revelation of all that is good in the world. Religious action is not limited to the "four cubits" of Halakhah. It therefore follows that there is no inherent difference between the religious and the secular (see A.I. Kook, *Massa Hamahanot*). Man is judged purely on the basis of his actions, in accordance with the maxim "your deeds will bring you closer, your deeds will push you away". The dialogue of values between the two groups is an essential part of Israeli Judaism.

7. This approach naturally extends to Israel's Arab citizens as well, to whom the biblical injunctions regarding the stranger

must be applied: "And if a stranger sojourn with thee in your land, ye shall not do him wrong. The stranger that sojourneth with you shall be unto you as the home-born among you, and thou shalt love him as thyself; for ye were strangers in the land of Egypt: I am the Lord your God" (19:33–34). These moral principles should also govern the way in which we relate to the Palestinians. Practical Zionism sought political freedom. We despised living under the yoke of other peoples, and that which is hateful to us let us not do unto our fellows. The path of equivalence—i.e. "I will treat him as he treats me, for he may treat me as I treat him"—is unworthy. Morality requires one to do what is right—"the ideal" rather than "the real". Reality cannot, of course, be ignored, but one must always aspire to righteousness.

8. Tradition gives us the principle of unity and its past expressions, moral values, the cycle of the year and its festivals, and more. Modern culture has provided new values, broad education and the means—such as psychology, sociology and democracy—with which to repair the world. To these, we must add the eastern religions, which have shown the way to exercise and strengthen spirituality. In this great age, one may choose the spiritual path she or he finds most appealing and most suited to her or his own temperament; as Buber said: "repairing the world begins with repairing oneself"—followed by integration into society and striving for its improvement.

9. Pluralism and dialectic contradictions play an essential role in the complex construction of reality—a varied and multifaceted edifice. True morality is intricate and situation-dependent and entails not knowing to what extent a given approach is the right one, as "both [sides] are the words of living man". Rabbi Kook explains:

> Some mistakenly believe that world peace will only be achieved when all views and characters are of one stripe … On the contrary, true peace requires multiplicity … A building is constructed of various materials, employing

various techniques, approaches, methods of training and supervision; for all are the words of the living God and each has its place and its value ... One must search for the inner logic that affords coherence and resolves all apparent contradictions ... The blessing of peace is the unification of all opposites (*Olat Re'iyah* 1, p. 30).

10. Spirituality recognizes a single God or a single creative spirit, within a single world and a single human race that lives a single life. The answer thus lies in the recognition of the hidden unity that enables a variegated world to dwell in peace. This is the significance of man's constant striving for redemption, as reflected in the title of Rabbi Kook's work "*Hazon Hatzimhonut Vehashalom*" (A Vision of Vegetarianism and Peace). Morality thus consists of the countless steps toward repairing the social fabric, drawing upon holiness in order to raise all existence to a higher plane.

Nahum Rakover

Emor – Speak unto the Priests

"I will be sanctified among the Children of Israel"
Rabbi A. I. Kook *on* Kiddush Hashem—
The Sanctification of God's Name

And you shall keep my commandments, and do them: I am the
Lord. And you shall not profane my holy name; but I will be
sanctified among the children of Israel: I am the Lord who sanctifies you (Leviticus 22:31–32).

What do the expressions "You shall not profane my holy name"
and "I shall be sanctified" mean? According to the plain meaning of the biblical text, they refer to the commandments appearing in the preceding verses: "You shall not kill it and its young both
in one day" (22:28), and "When you sacrifice a sacrifice of thanksgiving
unto the Lord … on the same day it shall be eaten" (22:29–30).

Rabbi Abraham Ibn Ezra explained the verse "ye shall not profane
my holy name", as follows: "It is addressed to the *descendants of Aaron*
[the priests], for the passage is contiguous [with the passage concerning
the sacrifice of thanksgiving], and it is they [the descendants of Aar-
on] who are charged not to slaughter" (Ibn Ezra, commentary on *Lev.*
22:31). But perhaps, as Ibn Ezra suggests, it also refers to the preceding
injunction—"you shall not kill it and its young both in one day"—and
thus includes all of Israel: "Or [the commandment is] to *Israel*, mother
and young both in one day" (*ibid.*). The concepts of *kiddush hashem*
(sanctification of God's name) and *hillul hashem* (profanation of God's
name) however, have assumed much greater significance in Jewish tradition—eventually becoming, in the words of J. Blidstein, "a corner-
stone of Jewish halakhic and pedagogic thought" (*Akdamot* 11, p. 123).

I would like to address one aspect of this broad topic—a scenario in
which one is ordered to kill or be killed. In such an eventuality, one may
not kill, even at the cost of one's own life. And if indeed, one lays down

his life rather than killing another—he has thereby sanctified God's name; and conversely, if he kills, he has profaned God's name.

The Talmud (*Sanhedrin* 74a) tells of a man who came before Rava, having been commanded to kill another or be killed himself. The sage ruled that he must lay down his own life rather than kill another, offering the following explanation: "Who is to say your blood is redder [than his]? Perhaps his blood is redder [than yours]!".

Maimonides thus wrote (*Hilkhot Yesodei Hatorah* 5, 4): "One who is required to 'be killed rather than transgress' and allows himself to be killed rather than transgressing—has sanctified God's name ... [and if] he transgresses rather than allowing himself to be killed—he has profaned God's name".

The principle whereby one is obligated to lay down one's own life rather than take the life of another is not based on any authoritative source, such as Scripture, but upon human reasoning. Is Rava's explanation equally valid, however, when a single life is pitted against many? What would Rava say were it not one, but two or three people ordered to kill another or be killed themselves?

Another case is where one is not commanded to actively take the life of another, but is merely thrown against his will at an infant, thereby crushing and killing the child. In such a case, the individual who is thrown does absolutely nothing, not even indirectly, but is rather used by the killer as a weapon. According to the *Tosafot*, one is not required to give up one's own life in such a case, because the principle of "who is to say" applies in the reverse: Who is to say the infant's blood is redder than mine?

What is the law, however, if the killer seeks to throw someone not at one infant, but at a number of infants? Could one still say "who is to say that the infants' blood is redder than mine", or does the blood of many take precedence over the blood of one? These questions are addressed in a number of responsa written by Rabbi Kook to Rabbi Shlomo Zalman Pines (*Mishpat Kohen*, 142–144, 148).

In the first case—when many are ordered to kill one, on the pain of death—it is clear to Rabbi Kook that the doctrine of Rava, "who is to say ...", applies, and the many should not take precedence over the individual. But why should this be so?

According to Rabbi Kook, the lives of many do not take precedence over the life of a single individual because the relative "value" we ascribe to an individual or individuals fails to represent their true or absolute value. A particular individual may be "worth" as much as, or more than, any number of others. The premise that the many outweigh the one is thus untenable, except in matters pertaining to religious precepts, in which such deductive reasoning may, and indeed must, be applied. Such methods are not employed, however, in matters of life and death, such as the question brought before Rava.

So in Maimonides' *Mishneh Torah* (*Hilkhot Sanhedrin* 20,1):
A court may not pass sentence by deduction but only by explicit eyewitness testimony—even if the witnesses saw a man pursuing another, cautioned him and then looked elsewhere; or saw him follow another into a deserted place, and then discovered the latter mortally wounded and the killer holding a sword dripping with blood. Since [the witnesses] did not see him inflict the injury, the court may not condemn him to death on the basis of such testimony. It is of this and similar cases that it is written: "do not slay the innocent and righteous" (*Ex.* 23:7).

Maimonides further elaborates in *Sefer Hamitzvot* (*Lo Ta'aseh*, 290):
The Exalted One therefore commanded that no punishment be exacted unless there are witnesses who can clearly testify to the action in question—evidence that leaves no room for doubt and allows for no other possible explanation. If we refrain from exacting punishment on the basis of very strong probability, the worst that can happen is that we will exonerate a sinner. If, on the other hand, we exact punishment on the basis of deductive reasoning and conjecture, we may one day kill an innocent man, and it is better and more desirable to exonerate a thousand sinners than to kill one innocent man.

Nevertheless, Rabbi Kook identifies circumstances in which the many should be given precedence over the individual:

A. When One is Thrown at a Number of Infants

We raised the question above, regarding one who is to be thrown at a number of infants, in such a manner as to cause their deaths. We have seen that in the case of a single infant, the opinion of the *Tosafot* is that one is not required to forfeit his life, since the principle of "who is to say..." also applies in reverse. When the lives of a number of infants are involved, however, Rabbi Kook suggests that one may in fact be required to sacrifice his own life, adding, however, that "the matter requires further study".

This is so because the case at hand is not a capital one, inasmuch as we neither order nor condone the killing. We merely ask whether one is required to lay down one's own life. Therefore, the matter should be treated as any other halakhic question, and we may employ deductive reasoning and conclude that the lives of many should be given precedence over the life of a single individual. The principle that matters of life and death cannot be determined by deductive reasoning applies only to cases in which we are called upon to decide whether to kill a person, or to charge others to do so. The question regarding one who is to be thrown at a number of infants (on the pain of death), on the other hand, pertains to the realm of precepts (albeit very serious precepts, for which one must "be killed rather than transgress"), where deductive reasoning may be used.

B. Volunteering to Save Many

Another question is whether one may voluntarily lay down his life in order to save the lives many others. Even Maimonides, who ruled that one may not sacrifice his life except when specifically required to do so, would permit such an act were it committed in order to save the lives of many.

C. Precedence in Saving Many

The idea of "weighing" one life against another appears in the Mishnah (*Horayot* 3, 7–8), which establishes an order of precedence for rescue, when only one person can be saved. This would appear to conflict with the principle laid down in the *Tosefta* (*Terumot* 7, 20), whereby one may not deliver an individual to his death in order to save many others: "If a group of people are told by gentiles, 'Surrender one of your number that we might kill him, and if you fail to do so, we will kill you all'—let all be killed and let them not deliver up a single Jewish soul". In this case, the many are threatened that they will all be killed if they fail to surrender one person. Nevertheless, the *Tosefta* rules that one may not surrender even a single individual in order to save the many. If we may give precedence to one person over another when only one can be saved, why can we not surrender one to save many—in effect giving the lives of the many precedence over the life of a single individual?

Rabbi Kook distinguishes between giving precedence in rescue and actually delivering a man to his death. As above, Rabbi Kook explains that one may not send one man to his death in order to save a number of others, because such a preference is based upon deductive reasoning, and matters of life and death may not be decided on the basis of deductive reasoning. We may employ such reasoning, however, when "we do not actively send a man to his death, but merely refrain from acting [on his behalf]; giving precedence to that which we deem more important, whether on the basis of the rules established by the Rabbis when both are equal, or on the basis of our own reasoning and judgment when they are not, carefully weighing their respective levels of wisdom, family status and the like" (*Mishpat Kohen*, 143). With regard to surrendering one man in order to save another, however, Rabbi Kook states: "all of these [rules established by the sages] regarding the estimated value of a life are merely the product of deductive reasoning, and cannot serve as the basis for action in matters of life and death, [in which] the principle of 'who is to say…' remains in force" (*ibid.*).

Thus, according to Rabbi Kook, when one is faced with the choice of saving one or saving many, the many must be given preference over the individual, because that is what deductive reasoning dictates, and since it is not a capital decision, such reasoning may be employed.

What is the law, however, when a person voluntarily lays down his life in order to save another? Is such an act permitted? The answer is a matter of debate between medieval rabbinical authorities.

There are two basic approaches to this question. Maimonides asserts that "One who is required to 'transgress rather than be killed', and allows himself to be killed rather than transgressing—has committed a capital offense" (*Hilkhot Yesodei Hatorah* 5, 4). Rabbi Joseph Karo, on the other hand, reports that "A great many are of the opinion that if he allows himself to be killed rather than transgressing—it is considered a righteous act" (*Kesef Mishneh, ad loc.*).

Maimonides would thus appear to prohibit the saving of another life at the cost of one's own, since he is of the opinion that sacrificing one's life when not required to do so is a capital offense. Rabbi Kook argues, nevertheless, that sacrificing one's own life in such circumstances might be permitted even according to Maimonides, if a distinction is made between the prevention of bloodshed and all other transgressions, as we shall explain below.

Rabbi Kook therefore disagrees with Rabbi Zalman Pines, who opined that one may not sacrifice one's life in order to save the life of another: "And what appears plain to you, that he may not lay down his own life even to save the life of another ... is doubtful to me" (*Mishpat Kohen, ibid.*).

How does Rabbi Kook arrive at this distinction between self-sacrifice for the sake of saving a life and other self-sacrifice? He demonstrates, from the wording of Rashi in his commentary on the tractate of *Sanhedrin*, that the injunction "and live by them" (the principle that one does not have to sacrifice his life in order to refrain from transgressing, in most cases) "pertains not to the individual who acts, counteracts or seeks a ruling, but to all Jewish life, and a case of a life for a life cannot be resolved on the basis of [the principle of] 'who is to say'" (*ibid.*).

If Maimonides, like Rashi, interprets the commandment "and live by them" as a general precept rather than one addressed to the individual, he might also agree that one life may be sacrificed to preserve another, even when there is no obligation to do so. Although he considered "and live by them" to be a binding injunction, precluding voluntary self-sacrifice—in a case involving another life, the law is upheld in the life that is saved:

> There would thus appear to be no reason to prohibit someone from sacrificing his life in order to save the life of another. One would clearly not incur guilt for failing to act [in such a case], for he might invoke [the principle] of "who is to say...". There is however, no reason to prohibit [his doing so], since the pro-

hibition against laying down one's life when not required to do so—even according to Maimonides, who considered it a capital offense—stems from the understanding that the commandment 'and live by them' was not intended to exempt one from the obligation to lay down one's life [when required to do so], but rather to charge him to live by them. Were Maimonides, however, to concede to Rashi that "and live by them" is a general precept, then it is all the same in the eyes of the law whether the life of one Jew is preserved or that of another. And even Maimonides would thus agree, in cases of bloodshed, that one might sacrifice his life for another, if he so desires (*ibid.*).

Elsewhere, however, Rabbi Kook explains Maimonides' approach in a different fashion, implying that one may not sacrifice one's own life to save the life of another. Although Rabbi Kook appears to have been of the opinion that Maimonides too considered "and live by them" optional rather than obligatory—ostensibly permitting one to lay down one's life for the sake of any precept—his position in this matter derived from another source. The Talmud cites the verse "And the Children of Israel shall keep the Sabbath" (*Ex.* 31:16) as one of the sources of the principle that "the duty of saving life supersedes the Sabbath": "Desecrate one Sabbath on his behalf, that he might observe many others" (*Yoma* 85b). According to Rabbi Kook, the latter source is generally accepted in the Talmud and is thus the reason that Maimonides prohibits sacrificing one's own life when not required to do so, "that he might not prevent himself from observing many Sabbaths, as well as many other precepts" (*Mishpat Kohen* 148). Although the same reasoning would appear to apply to cases involving the life of another, the potential to observe many Sabbaths and other precepts may also be ascribed to the one whose life is saved.

The principle whereby one may not deliver one person to his death in order to save many others, raises a further question: Why, in times of war, are individuals called upon to lay down their lives for the sake of others? Moreover, in the case of war, such sacrifice is not voluntary, but compulsory. Why is this the case? Can we infer from the laws of war that the lives of the many do indeed take precedence over the life of a single individual? According to Rabbi Zalman Pines, the obligation to take part in a religiously mandated war teaches us that we are required to endanger our lives for the sake of the Jewish People, although not for the sake of non-Jews.

Rabbi Kook, on the other hand, maintains that we cannot extrapolate from the laws of war, since these do not derive from Torah law, but are in fact exceptions to normative law. For example, he cites the fact that a ruler may engage in "optional", expansionist wars even at the cost of human life.

If the laws of war do not derive from ordinary law, what then is their legal basis? Rabbi Kook suggests that they are subsumed under the Torah's laws of monarchy, the interpretation of which was left to the wisdom of the respective kings.

The laws of war can thus be said to rest on two grounds: 1) the principle of "extraordinary ad hoc legislation", whereby a court may, in the interest of the national collective, institute temporary corrective or preventive measures that deviate from normative Torah law; 2) the laws of monarchy, which grant similar authority to the king.

Rabbi Kook adds the important qualification that such authority need not necessarily be exercised by a king. When there is no king, the legal powers of the monarchy revert to the nation as a whole:

> Moreover, it would appear to be the case, that when there is no king, the legal rights of the monarch revert to the nation, since the laws pertaining to the monarchy also pertain to the nation as a whole. In particular, each and every judge would appear to wield some of the authority of a king—especially in matters of public leadership … A position that is, in any event, supported by reason, for judges and other leaders certainly stand *in loco regis* in public affairs.

Rabbi Kook stressed the *sui generis* nature of the Jewish people, which transcends the sum total of its individual members. While the collective existence of other peoples offers no more than its component parts, the Jewish whole is a thing apart, a value in its own right.

He addresses this issue in his responsum to Rabbi Meir Dan Plotzki (*Mishpat Kohen*, 124), in which he asserts that it was a point of contention between the Rabbis and the Sadducees. The Sadducees ascribed no special significance to the collective, and that is why they interpreted the expression "on the morrow after the Sabbath" (*Lev.* 23:11) to mean the day following the weekly Sabbath, rather than the day following the first day of Passover. The Sadducees failed to grasp the ability of the Jewish people to elevate the festival to the status of "Sabbath" by their monthly determination of the calendar. Similarly, since they made no distinction between individual and collective existence, they also ruled that the daily burnt offering may be brought by any individual.

As evidence of the fact that the Rabbis made a clear distinction between the individual and the collective, Rabbi Kook cites the Mishnah in *Temurah* (1,6), which enumerates "partners" and "the community" separately. The Mishnah would thus appear to consider the community a "legal entity", distinct from the individuals it comprises:

And the Sadducees ruled that an individual may volunteer to bring the daily offering, because they failed to recognize the special sanctity manifested in the collectivity of the Congregation of Israel, as in no other people. The ultimate purpose of every national collective is the welfare of its individual members, but the collective itself lacks independent existence. The body politic among the nations is thus no more than a partnership, or the sum total of the partners' individual shares. Among the Jews, however, community and partnership are two different concepts, as implied by the *Mishnah* in *Temurah* [1,6] 13a: "The community and partners cannot create a *Temurah* [consecrate an animal by intending to substitute it for another consecrated animal]"— for the Jewish community is endowed with sanctity and independent existence that cannot be measured by the share of each individual, but transcends the sum total of its parts. Communal offerings must therefore be made specifically by the community, for that is the significance of the sanctity of the collective.

With regard to the duty of an individual to sacrifice his own life, Rabbi Kook ruled that while one is not obligated to sacrifice his own life to save *many*—as implied by the *Tosefta* regarding a group ordered to surrender one of its number—one *is* obligated to lay down his life for the sake of *the Jewish people*, for there could be no greater justification for extraordinary ad hoc legislation requiring the violation of normative Torah law than the salvation of the Jewish people.

Before addressing Rabbi Kook's approach to the subject, let us note that the obligation to sacrifice one's life for the sake of the Jewish people was a matter of dispute among Torah sages of the previous generation. Rabbi Meir Simhah of Dvinsk maintained that one is not required to sacrifice his life for the sake of others, even for the sake of the Jewish people as a whole. He cites the law that an accidental killer may not leave the city of refuge to which he has fled, even if the entire Jewish people's salvation depends on him. In his treatment of this law, Maimonides adds (*Hilkhot Rotze'ah Ushmirat Nefesh* 7, 8) that if the killer does in fact leave the city of refuge, he may be killed by "the blood avenger". Rabbi Meir Simhah interprets Maimonides' addition as a reason for the prohibition against leaving the city of refuge: for if he leaves, he may be killed, and one is not obligated to endanger his life for the salvation of the Jewish People (*Or Sameah* on Maimonides, *ibid.*).

Rabbi Meir Dan Plotzki, in his book *Keli Hemdah* (*Pinhas*), disagrees with Rabbi Meir Simhah. In his opinion, even those who rule that there is no obligation to place oneself in a potentially dangerous situation in order to save the life of another, would agree that one is required to do so for the sake of the Jewish people. He rejects Rabbi Meir Simhah's interpretation of Maimonides, claiming that were the killer indeed needed to save the Jewish people, the blood avenger would be forbidden to kill him, and he would thus be in no danger. Rather, he explains Maimonides' words as follows: the killer may not leave the city of refuge—and if he does so, the blood avenger is permitted to kill him. And he emphasizes: "God forbid that we should say that one may not place himself in a potentially dangerous situation in order to save the Jewish people". Furthermore, he cites the precedent of Esther: "This is proof that one is obligated to place himself in potential danger as well, since Esther placed herself in danger by entering the palace garden unbidden, which would have resulted in her death, had a miracle not occurred".

Rabbi Plotzki only refers to cases of potential danger, however, and might agree that one is not obligated to place himself in certain danger, i.e. to lay down his life, in order to save the Jewish people—contrary to the opinions of Rabbi Kook and Rabbi Shlomo Zalman Pines.

What is the basis for the obligation to risk one's own life for the sake of the community as a whole? According to Rabbi Kook, it lies in the authority of the Rabbis to suspend positive or negative precepts by "extraordinary ad hoc legislation", in order to check lawlessness and restore general religious observance. In the words of Maimonides (*Hilkhot Mamrim* 2, 4):

> For even biblical precepts may be suspended by any court as an extraordinary ad hoc measure. How so? A court that wishes to introduce additional prohibitions in order to reinforce religious observance may inflict corporal and other punishment unlawfully, but it may not do so in perpetuity and claim that it is Torah law. And so [a court] may temporarily suspend a positive or negative precept in order to restore general religious observance or prevent the Jewish masses from committing other transgressions—in keeping with the exigencies of the day. Just as a physician may amputate an arm or a leg in order to ensure the survival of the whole, so a court may permit the violation of some of the precepts for a time, so that [all] might survive; or in the words of the ancient sages: "Desecrate one Sabbath on his behalf, that he might observe many others".

Rabbi Pines (in his letter dated *Rosh Hodesh Tevet*, 5676) expresses a number of objections to Rabbi Kook's contention that the obligation to sacrifice one's life in order to save the Jewish people derives from the principle of extraordinary ad hoc legislation. His arguments can be summarized as follows:

1. "Only to check breaches in religious observance"—In the examples cited in the Talmud, such ad hoc measures are intended to counter breaches in religious observance or to sanctify the name of heaven; not to save lives.
2. "All is in the hands of God except the fear of God"—It is justified that deviations from normative law should be limited to checking breaches in religious observance. The role

of the court is to save the people from sin, since all but the fear of God—both individual and collective—is in the hands of God. It is not the court's duty to save lives, because that is "in the hands of God".

3. "He that keeps Israel does neither slumber nor sleep" (*Ps.* 121:4).—An approach that permits the violation of the commandments in order to save the Jewish people has the potential to undermine our belief in the divine promise that the keeper of Israel neither sleeps nor slumbers. If we take extraordinary action for the salvation of the Jewish people, it is as if we are saying that God will not save us.

4. Salvation cannot be achieved through sin—Ideologically speaking, "It is inconceivable that the salvation of Israel should come about by means of bloodshed or illicit relations, which the Torah equates with murder". Rabbi Pines supports this assertion with a passage from the Midrash: "How can one who is afflicted be healed by bloodshed?" If the life of a single individual cannot be saved through sin, how much more so the life of the nation, which is the prerogative of Providence.

Rabbi Kook responded as follows:

A. Israel Preceded the Torah

With regard to the claim that the salvation of the Jewish people cannot be considered sufficient cause for extraordinary legislation, Rabbi Kook writes:

I cannot but express my astonishment at that which you have written in objection to my position, stating that the salvation of the Jewish people is not considered sufficient cause for extraordinary legislation ... And I would point out the passage in *Tana Devei Eliyahu Rabbah* 14: "There are two things in the world that I love with all my heart, and these are the Torah and the People of Israel, but I do not know which preceded which." I replied: My son, it is the way of people to say that the Torah came first, as it is written "The Lord made me [Wisdom/Torah] as the beginning of His way" (*Prov.* 8:22). I say however, that Israel came first, as it is written "Israel is the Lords's hallowed portion, His first fruits" (*Jer.* 2:3).

Furthermore, Rabbi Kook explains, that even were Rabbi Pines to espouse the position characterized in the *Tana Devei Eliyahu* as "the way of people", it is still astonishing that anyone would conclude from this that the salvation of Israel is not sufficient cause for extraordinary legislation.

B. The Concept "All is in the Hands of God Except Fear of God" does not Apply to the Jewish People as a Whole

Contrary to Rabbi Pines, who presumes the principle "all is in the hands of God except fear of God" to apply to the collective as well as the individual, Rabbi Kook distinguishes between the two. He maintains, based on the view of Rabbi Isaac Arama in *Akedat Yitzhak* (*Nitzavim*, 99), that the covenant between God and the Jewish People eliminated the community's freedom of choice:

Regarding that which you have written, that "all is in the hands of God except fear of God" refers equally to the individual and the collective, and we are therefore compelled to act in matters pertaining to the fear of God and the upholding of religious observance—even that of the Jewish People as a whole; but are exempt in matters pertaining to the *existence* of the Jewish People: The *Akedah*, on the portion of *Nitzavim*, expounds at length on the nature of the covenant that God forged with Israel in the Plains of Moab, asserting that it was founded upon the elimination of [freedom of] choice from the community as a whole. He [thus] maintains that "all is in the hands of God except the fear of God" refers only to individuals, for just as the Jewish People's existence is ensured in a covenant, so its obligation to uphold its collective commitment to God is ensured in a covenant. And I have found none among the great sages of Israel who disputes this point.

According to the *Akedat Yitzhak*, for the Jewish People as a whole, even "fear of God" is "in the hands of God". Thus, just as our sages are duty-bound to resort to extraordinary legislation in order to check breaches in religious observance—despite the fact that the Jewish People's commitment to uphold its religious obligations is ensured in a covenant—so they must enact extraordinary legislation in order to save the Jewish people, although Jewish existence too is ensured in a covenant. Rabbi Kook therefore concludes: "It is obvious that just as defending the faith as a whole is sufficient cause for extraordinary legislation, so too is the salvation of the nation, which is the foundation of the very Torah and all that is sacred" (*Mishpat Kohen*, 144).

Regarding God's covenant with Israel, whereby no impurity will ever cut the Congregation of Israel off from the divine source, Rabbi Kook elaborates in *Orot Hatehiyah*:

A covenant was forged with the entire Congregation of Israel that it would never be entirely corrupted by the forces of impurity. Impurity may act upon it and mar it, but will never succeed in severing it completely from the divine source of life … The spirit of Israel is bound to the spirit of God to such an extent that even one who says he has no need of the divine spirit, but seeks only the spirit of Israel, the spirit of God lies at the core of his aspirations, even against his will. The individual can detach himself from the source of life, but not so the nation, the entire Congregation of Israel. The nation's heritage—its land, language, history and customs—which it holds dear by virtue of its national spirit, is thus infused with the spirit of God. And if some day such an awakening of spirit should be ascribed to the national spirit alone, attempting to deny the divine spirit that permeates both heritage and its apparent source, i.e. the spirit of the nation, what should the righteous of the generation then do? One cannot rebel against the spirit of the nation and despise its heritage, even if only in speech, for the spirit of God and the spirit of Israel are one. Rather, they must labor arduously to reveal the light and holiness that lies within the spirit of the nation, the divine light in all of these things—that all who hold those thoughts might discover that in [embracing] the collective spirit and its heritage they are in fact immersed, rooted and living in the divine [source of] life, shining with holiness and heavenly valor (*Orot* 63).

C. "He that Keeps Israel Does neither Slumber nor Sleep"

Rabbi Kook demonstrates from the fact that Mordecai suspended the obligation to eat *matzah* on Passover in order to save the Jewish people (*Megilah* 15a), that one may not rely exclusively on the promise: "He that Keeps Israel Does neither Slumber nor Sleep". In other words, from the fact that Mordecai abrogated the commandment of *matzah*, we learn that the reason for the abrogation—the salvation of the Jewish People—is sufficient cause for extraordinary legislation.

This leads Rabbi Kook to a discussion of faith in Providence versus action. Now that we have seen that positive precepts may and indeed must be suspended for the sake of Jewish survival, we also discover that:

Faith in Providence does not release us from the duty to act by any possible means to save the community, and it is up to God to reconcile the seemingly irreconcilable: absolute faith in the Jewish people's continued existence, on the one hand, and the obligation to actively sustain that existence in every way and, *a fortiori*, to remove any danger that might, Heaven forbid, bring about destruction and annihilation. May God preserve us. And these divine mysteries, what concern are they of ours? We must do everything in our power ... And since we do so for the salvation of the Jewish People—which is the very foundation of the Torah and its ultimate purpose—we have all sufficient cause in the world for extraordinary legislation.

Does the promise that the Jewish people as a whole will never disappear from the face of the earth not render self-sacrifice for the sake of national survival redundant? Rabbi Kook responds that indeed, were we permitted to rely solely on God's promise, the abrogation of a positive precept for the sake of national salvation would have been forbidden.

From the fact that we are very plainly obligated to make every effort to save the collective—constrained at times even to violate Torah law to this end—we learn that Providence itself in fact demands that we conduct ourselves in accordance with the Torah, and it is God's will that, whenever the need arises, we act to the best of our ability, and "Salvation belongs to the Lord". Thus, since Israel comes before all, and the Torah too was created for Israel, it is clear that everything that must be done to uphold the Torah must be done to sustain and save the nation as a whole, and this is the basis of [the principle of] extraordinary ad hoc legislation (*Mishpat Kohen*, 148).

D. Positive Outcome by Negative Means
Rabbi Kook goes on to discuss how something positive might be achieved through sinful action. Rabbi Zalman Pines posed this question, based on the midrash that forbids healing by means of one of the three cardinal sins (murder, idol-worship and illicit sexual relations), because sin cannot heal.

Rabbi Kook first addresses the source cited by Rabbi Pines, arguing that this midrash cannot be applied to cases meriting extraordinary legislation (i.e. that involving the continued religious or physical existence of the nation). Regarding the prohibition against bloodshed, Rabbi Kook notes that preferring the life of the Jewish people over that of a single individual is a far simpler matter than choosing between two individual lives; for the principle of "who is to say" ("Who is to say that your blood is redder? Perhaps his blood is redder"), which is the basis for the prohibition in such cases, is not relevant when the very existence of the Jewish people is at stake.

Regarding the ideological argument that the salvation of Israel cannot be achieved by the shedding of innocent blood, Rabbi Kook replied: "By virtue of upholding the words of the Rabbis, it is no longer innocent blood but an offering to God—one who has the privilege of being killed for the salvation of the Jewish People".

Rabbi Pines rebutted that if one who is killed for the sake of the nation is "an offering on the altar of the nation, and his death a privilege", then "we may also justify human sacrifice, and the end does not justify all means".

To this intimation that sacrificing an individual for the sake of the People is in fact human sacrifice, Rabbi Kook replied that as an extraordinary measure, even human sacrifice would be permitted: "In truth, it also is within the authority of a prophet to order human sacrifice. Witness the binding [of Isaac]. For had the prophecy 'Lay not your hand upon the lad' not followed, it would have been done ... And if we find sometimes that we must sacrifice the life of an individual on the altar of the community—we do so as an extraordinary measure, and in extraordinary times one need not adhere to the [norms of the] generations" (*ibid.*).

Note, however, that the question does not apply to laying down one's own life for the sake of the People, but only to sacrificing the life of another for that purpose—hence the example of the binding of Isaac, which proves such a thing to be possible, for "in extraordinary times one need not adhere to the [norms of the] generations". In other words, although the norms of the generations certainly forbid human sacrifice, it is acceptable as an extraordinary measure in extraordinary times.

A fascinating approach to the ideological legitimacy of human sacrifice in Jewish thought can be found in the work of Rabbi J.D. Soloveitchik, who argues that the Torah forbade human sacrifice in practice, but not the *idea* that man must sacrifice himself. Rabbi Soloveitchik, however, places particular emphasis on the concept of self-sacrifice (as opposed to the sacrifice of another):

> The Torah forbade all human sacrifice. The example it uses to describe the abomination of idol-worship is "for even their sons and their daughters they consume with fire on behalf of their Gods" (Deuteronomy 12:31). Yet although the Torah forbade human offerings, it did not invalidate the idea behind it, that man sacrifice his own self—"that it is proper that [man] spill his blood and burn his flesh" (cf. Nahmanides, Leviticus 1:9)— rather than just bring a bull or two pigeons or turtle-doves. God does not seek offerings from man, he seeks man himself. This is the foundation of sacrificial practice and it is on this idea that the story of the binding of Isaac is based. On unconditional self-sacrifice, of body and of soul, the Jewish faith is founded. Juda-

ism does not reject the idea behind human sacrifice. If man is the property of the Holy One, blessed be He, when he hears the voice of God calling to him, "Take now thy son, thine only son ... and offer him ... for a burnt offering upon one of the mountains which I will tell thee of", he has no other choice than did Abraham (Pinchas Peli, *On Repentance: In the Thought and Discourses of Rabbi J.B. Soloveitchik*, Oroth Publishing House, Jerusalem, 1980, p. 266).

Although he considered human sacrifice a theoretical possibility, Rabbi Kook firmly believed God would never render it necessary: "Rather, as long as such an event has not occurred, we may be certain that God will safeguard his people and those who fear him, that such a state of affairs might never come about and that we might never have need of such measures. Such, however, is the law" (*Mishpat Kohen, ibid.*). Murder and illicit relations are no exception to the principle that prohibitions may be violated upon the instructions of a prophet or court in order to counter religious or physical danger to the nation. The only exception is idolatry. And although the need for human sacrifice will never arise, the fact remains that it is permitted according to Halakhah.

Here Rabbi Kook introduces a further element to the discussion: Although it is the principle of extraordinary legislation that provides the legal basis for the violation of commandments for the sake of Jewish people, actual "legislation" (i.e. a court ruling) is not required. It in fact follows, *a fortiori*, from the obligation to save lives—for the sake of which the Talmud (*Yoma 86a*) rules that one must desecrate the Sabbath, and that "One who acts swiftly is to be commended, and one need not seek permission from the court" (*Mishpat Kohen*, 143). If this is the law concerning a single life, says Rabbi Kook, it is eminently clear that permission would be granted were the existence of the Jewish people at stake, and there is therefore no need to seek explicit permission from court. Since a court order is not required in order to save the Jewish people as a whole, Jael was allowed to lie with Sisera, even without having obtained permission to do so from the court.

When such action is required not for the sake of the Jewish people, however, but in order to save many lives, an explicit court order is required.

Summary

We have examined a number of questions pertaining to the obligation to sanctify the name of heaven even at the cost of one's own life. We have focused primarily on the approach espoused by Rabbi A.I. Kook. As we have seen, Rabbi Kook held that the lives of many should not be given preference over a single life, because to do so would be the product of deductive reasoning and cases of life and death cannot be decided on such a basis. Nevertheless, he points out circumstances in which the lives of the many should be preferred over that of a single individual, e.g. in cases of voluntary (as opposed to compulsory) self-sacrifice.

The laws of war, which require the individual to lay down his life for the sake of the many, are an exception to the rule. This obligation does not derive from normative Torah law, however, but from the laws of monarchy and the principle of extraordinary ad hoc legislation.

Another exception is the salvation of the Jewish People as a whole. In this Rabbi Kook gives halakhic expression to his philosophical understanding of the Jewish people as more than just an aggregate of individuals. Contrary to all other nations, which are merely the sum total of their component parts, the Jewish people—according to Rabbi Kook—is a thing apart, a value in its own right. Rabbi Kook thus maintains that one is obligated to lay down his life for the sake of the Jewish People, for there could be no greater justification for extraordinary ad hoc legislation permitting the violation of Torah law than the salvation of the Jewish People.

Benjamin Brown

Behar – And the Lord Spoke Unto Moses in Mount Sinai

The Hazon Ish—Rabbi A.Y. Karelitz:
Faith, Trust in Providence and Obedience to the Word of God

Six years thou shalt sow thy field, and six years thou shalt prune thy vineyard, and gather in the produce thereof. But in the seventh year shall be a Sabbath of solemn rest for the land, a Sabbath unto the Lord; thou shalt neither sow thy field, nor prune thy vineyard. That which groweth of itself of thy harvest thou shalt not reap, and the grapes of thy undressed vine thou shalt not gather; it shall be a year of solemn rest for the land. And the Sabbath-produce of the land shall be for food for you: for thee, and for thy servant and for thy maid, and for thy hired servant and for the settler by thy side that sojourn with thee; and for thy cattle, and for the beasts that are in thy land, shall all the increase thereof be for food. And ye shall keep my commandments, and do them: I am the Lord. And ye shall not profane my holy name; but I will be sanctified among the children of Israel: I am the Lord who sanctifies you (Leviticus 25:3–7).

Behar begins with the Sabbath of the land. The final verses in this passage often lead readers to the conclusion that the Sabbatical year is essentially a social precept, intended to help the weak and poor. Although the practice of land-release lends itself to this interpretation, the passage's opening verses suggest otherwise. Allowing the land to lie fallow reduces agricultural yields, so that the poor and the weak suffer greater deprivation than in other years. For this and other reasons, a number of commentators have attributed religious rather than socio-economic purposes to the Sabbath of the land. Every seventh year, people would renounce the fruits of their labor and com-mend their livelihood to God's grace, thereby expressing their trust in His providence.

In the *musar* literature, we find tension between the concept of *trust* in Providence (*bittahon*), which stems from faith in God and his concern for the welfare of those who fear him; and that of *endeavor*, i.e. man's natural, worldly exertions—particularly in the context of earning a livelihood. The Sabbatical year was thus intended to provide man with the opportunity to abandon the path of endeavor for a period, in order to cultivate the virtue of trust in Providence. This approach is supported by a number of verses later in the chapter:

And if ye shall say: "What shall we eat the seventh year? behold, we may not sow, nor gather in our increase"; then I will command my blessing upon you in the sixth year, and it shall bring forth produce for the three years. And ye shall sow the eighth year, and eat of the produce, the old store; until the ninth year, until her produce come in, ye shall eat the old store (*ibid.* 20–22).

The Torah is aware of the farmer's anxiety at the prospect of the seventh year, but reassures him with a promise: in the sixth year, God will provide harvests sufficient for the seventh and eighth years as well—until the harvests of the ninth year (sown in the eighth year) can be reaped. The farmer must thus dismiss his fears, and place his trust in God and his promise.

One of the most appropriate figures to associate with a discussion of this subject is Rabbi Avraham Yesha'ayahu Karelitz (1878–1953), known as the *Hazon Ish* (the title of his first work, an acronym of the name Avraham Yesha'ayahu). Most secular Israelis are familiar with the *Hazon Ish* by virtue of his historic meeting with Ben-Gurion, in which he used the metaphor of the "full cart", the religious, and the "empty cart", the secular (a metaphor apparently misquoted or misunderstood, but that is another matter). In religious circles however, he is known primarily as one of the greatest halakhic authorities of the 20th century, who made an important contribution to the revival of halakhic interest in precepts pertaining to the Land of Israel—first and foremost, the Sabbatical year. These agricultural precepts, pertaining only to the Land of

Israel, generally attracted little halakhic interest over the ages, due to the lack of Jewish agricultural activity in the Holy Land. With the advent of Zionist settlement, however, they became burning issues for religious farmers.

The Sabbatical year posed the greatest difficulty of all. For recently established farms, not yet on their feet, the suspension of all agricultural activity for an entire year could have meant total financial ruin. In anticipation of the Sabbatical year 5649 (1889), the settlers of the First *Aliyah* asked the rabbis of Lithuania to find a solution—which they did, in the form of a legal fiction of a kind well-established in halakhic tradition. Jewish lands would be sold on the eve of the Sabbatical year to non-Jews, and since the precepts of land-release did not apply to non-Jewish land, the settlers would be permitted to perform all of the tasks forbidden by rabbinic injunction, but not the four actions explicitly prohibited in the Bible—sowing, pruning, reaping and grape-gathering. This "permit of sale" (*heter mekhirah*) was sharply criticized by the rabbis of the Old *Yishuv*, but was renewed in the successive three Sabbatical years, with only minor changes, designed to overcome various halakhic difficulties. Prior to the Sabbatical year 5670 (1910), Rabbi A.I. Kook (1865–1935) wrote his *Shabbat Ha'aretz* (*Sabbath of the Land*), in which he provided an extensive halakhic basis for the permit of sale, as well as a list of permitted and forbidden actions on land that has been sold. Alongside his halakhic arguments however, Rabbi Kook also presented an extra-halakhic consideration: The Zionist settlement enterprise is the beginning of a process of national rebirth, which will culminate in a renaissance of the Jewish spirit and the sincere desire to return to Torah observance—including the precepts of the Sabbatical year. If, God forbid, the Zionist enterprise were to fail, Rabbi Kook maintained, there would be no one to keep the Sabbatical year in any case. If, on the other hand, we suspend the obligation to observe the sabbatical year for a time, in order to support Jewish settlement, the end result will be complete adherence to the Sabbatical laws.

Rabbi Kook was the rabbi of Jaffa and the Jewish colonies, in which capacity he organized the sale of Jewish lands. Later, when the Chief Rabbinate Council for Palestine was established (1921) and Rabbi Kook elected chief rabbi, the Rabbinate regularly arranged the sale of the land, every seven years. The sale permit was henceforth associated with the name of Rabbi Kook, although he was not its author. There is a certain amount of historical justice in this, since it was he who institutionalized the sale and transformed it from an extraordinary *ad hoc* measure into a normative halakhic practice, renewed virtually automatically. Moreover, the religious authority he enjoyed helped gain widespread acceptance. At the time of the *Hazon Ish*'s arrival from Lithuania, in 1933, only a handful of Jews observed the Sabbatical year in its original form, without having recourse to the sale permit. Those who did so belonged, for the most part, to anti-Zionist *haredi* circles.

The *Hazon Ish* was relatively unknown in Palestine. Within a short time of his arrival however, he was discovered by members of the small *haredi* kibbutzim of the *Po'alei Agudat Yisrael* movement, who did not accept the authority of the Zionist chief rabbinate and approached him with their halakhic problems. With regard to the Sabbatical year, the *Hazon Ish* stated unequivocally that the sale permit was a groundless fiction and as such incapable of revoking the sanctity of the land and its produce. Furthermore, he maintained, the sale of land in *Eretz Yisrael* to a non-Jew is prohibited. His book *Hazon Ish al Shevi'it* (*The* Hazon Ish *on the Sabbatical Year*), which appeared in 1937, includes discussions of the unacceptability of the sale permit, definitions of the actions prohibited in the Sabbatical year, and a number of interesting lenient rulings.

One of these discussions concerns the law that one may perform tasks such as watering fruit trees—forbidden only by rabbinic injunction—in order to avert financial loss (*Hazon Ish al Shevi'it*, 18). Based on a careful analysis of talmudic and midrashic sources, Maimonides and the *Tosafot*, the *Hazon Ish* concluded that one must distinguish between ordinary financial loss and "unbearable" loss. If it is a matter of ordinary loss, no work is permitted, even if forbidden only by rabbinic injunction. If, on the other hand, the loss is great and "unbearable", "nearly life-threatening", tasks prohibited only by rabbinic injunction may be performed. Even in such cases however, the license granted is not absolute and applies only to "the public interest, but not in cases of individual loss". It is quite clear that the criteria cited by the *Hazon Ish*—ordinary versus unbearable loss—are imprecise and ill-defined, and might be applied in any number of ways. The *Hazon Ish* however, was not averse to such flexible concepts. On the contrary, he believed that many halakhic concepts cannot be defined in precise terms and can only be understood by meta-literal intuition, acquired through intensive study of the law.

At this point one may ask: Rabbi Kook's permit of sale was also granted only in light of great and "unbearable" loss—that of the community as a whole (i.e. "in the public interest"), and was also limited to tasks forbidden only by rabbinic injunction. Why then did the *Hazon Ish* oppose it so much, while he himself permitted such tasks, even without the sale of the land? There are a number of answers to this question. One of them is that the *Hazon Ish* advocated a case by case approach and rejected the idea of a wholesale permit. Furthermore, in one of his letters from the 1930s, he intimated that the original permit granted to the first settlements might have been halakhically justifiable, since these communities certainly faced a "do or die" situation. Once the community was on its feet however, he viewed the automatic renewal of the permit as a grave departure from the strictures of Halakhah. In a number of his letters, he presents the problem of the Sabbatical year as pertaining primarily to the faith and resolve of the observant farmer. He acknowledges the fact that it poses a serious and difficult challenge, but that is true of all divine service; "and all of the talk of life-threatening circumstances and perils stems from a coldness of heart and insufficient reverence for the Torah and the precepts" (*Kovetz Igrot Hazon Ish*, III, 85).

Here another question arises: How can we even entertain the possibility that farmers who observe the Sabbatical year might reach a state of unbearable, nearly life-threatening loss? God himself promised, as we have seen, that such an eventuality would never come about: "And if ye shall say: 'What shall we eat the seventh year? ...; then I will command my blessing upon you in the sixth year, and it shall bring forth produce for the three years". And if the main purpose of the Sabbatical year is to strengthen the virtue of trust in God and his providence, how can we make halakhic provision for the event that the promise is not kept? Aware of this tension, the *Hazon Ish* embarks on a brief theological digression, in an attempt to resolve this issue.

God's promise "I will command my blessing", explains the *Hazon Ish*, indeed conveys the message "contrary to your worldly understanding that by refraining from work you will incur loss and suffer deprivation, I will command my blessing upon you". This promise is not a categorical guarantee however, and may be withheld "due to sin". The *Hazon Ish* uses the expression "due to sin", which appears a number of times in the Talmud and Midrash (see especially *Berakhot 4a*) precisely in this context: God may withhold a reward promised to those who observe a particular precept, "due to sin". Moreover, says the *Hazon Ish*, the blessing was conferred upon the Jewish People as a whole, and the whole—including its righteous members—may suffer the consequences of the sins of individuals. The biblical promise is far from assured, so that severe, nearly life-threatening loss is a distinct possibility. "Like all the precepts of the Torah, the Sabbatical year is superseded by the obligation to preserve life, in times of siege and war, when there is nothing to eat" (*Hazon Ish*, 18,4). In this fashion, the *Hazon Ish* also explains the assertion that when the Land of Israel was reconsecrated in the days of Ezra, a number of places were left in which the sanctity of the Land would not apply, "that the poor might rely on them in the Sabbatical year" (e.g. *Hagigah* 3b, and elsewhere). Why was this necessary, if God's blessing is assured and "the poor are certainly included in this blessing"? The answer is, as above, that "they did not rely on the blessing in the sixth year ... but saw that poverty was great and the Torah did not say that we must rely on the blessing and make no worldly endeavor" (*ibid.*). On the contrary, despite the promise of God's blessing, "the court may not refrain from doing that which is warranted for the public and for the poor, because of the promise of blessing" (*ibid.*).

The *Hazon Ish* thus claims that the promise has no bearing on our halakhic obligations. Although the Torah promises God's blessing, the very same Torah commands us to care for the poor and the weak—in the form of practical assistance, or "worldly endeavor", not by relying on God's grace or even biblical promises. The promise in no way affects the validity or scope of the halakhic obligation. So, when lives are at stake, the Torah commands us to do whatever is necessary, even when that entails violating the Torah's own precepts; and so in the Sabbatical year, in cases of unbearable, nearly life-threatening financial loss, we are permitted to violate the rabbinic injunctions.

Dr. Zvi Yehuda—who was in his youth, in the 1940s, a student of the *Hazon Ish*—recalls a number of statements in this vein. In a personal interview, in 1998, he told me that the *Hazon Ish* had stressed to him on more than one occasion that one must make a clear distinction between two types of divine utterances: commandments and promises. The commandments are incumbent upon us, and we must therefore study them well and carefully observe them, whereas the promises are incumbent upon God, and we must therefore leave them up to Him and not concern ourselves with them. Why then were the promises given to us alongside the commandments? The reason must be that they, too, entail an obligation for us—the obligation to believe in them. We do not know how they will be fulfilled or in what circumstances, but we must trust in God, that He will keep his word. Although we have no direct written source corroborating Dr. Yehuda's account, the idea itself is implicit in a number of places (including the above text on the Sabbatical year).

This leads us to a deeper understanding of the dispute between the *Hazon Ish* and Rabbi Kook. Rabbi Kook saw the settlement project as an integral part of the redemption process, culminating in the People's return to God. Supporting the settlements was therefore a religious duty, for the sake of which he was prepared to suspend observance of the Sabbatical year. The *Hazon Ish* on the other hand, believed God's promise of redemption to be incumbent upon God himself, who has no need of our "help". Our duty is to observe the commandments, including the precept of the Sabbatical year, and it is they—not the promises—that must govern our actions. This approach demands greater stringency with regard to the sale permit, but allows for greater leniency where there is a danger of severe loss.

What about the virtue of trust in Providence, which the Sabbatical year is supposed to cultivate? When the *Hazon Ish* allows a farmer not to rely on God's blessing, but to take practical steps, to make "worldly efforts", does he not justify the man's lack of faith in the promise and insufficient trust in God? The answer is somewhat complicated, and leads us to another controversy in which the *Hazon Ish* took part, also concerning the virtue of trust in Providence. I refer to the *Hazon Ish*'s dispute with the *Musar* Movement—a religious educational movement that developed in Lithuania in the mid-19th century and went on to gain considerable influence in the world of the *yeshivot*. The central religious ideal of its adherents was ethical improvement, attained by subduing man's baser instincts and instilling higher virtues, such as fear of God, humility, contentment with little, respect for others—and trust in God. Following the death of its founder, Rabbi Israel Salanter (1810–1883), a number of different trends emerged in the movement. The most extreme of these, the "Novardok" (*Novogrudok*) trend, believed that man's natural instincts are deeply rooted, and as such can only be subdued, or "broken", by drastic means. Adherents flouted social conventions and intentionally engaged in unusual behavior, in order to free themselves of external influence. They renounced their possessions, in order to acquire the virtue of contentment with little. They lived lives of deprivation, dressed in rags, and scorned order and cleanliness, in order to internalize their contempt for this world and its vanities. They took a similar approach to trust in Providence. Constantly reiterating their conviction that all is in the hands of Heaven and that man's sustenance for the entire year is decreed at the New Year (*Bava Batra* 10a), they contended that one who truly and sincerely trusts in God's grace, will be preserved from hunger even if he makes no effort whatsoever to obtain his bread. All "worldly endeavor" is pointless, the Novardokers claimed, resorting to extreme *peules*—or exercises—in order to internalize this recognition.

The *Hazon Ish* opposed the *Musar* Movement, and three of the six chapters of his unfinished work, *Hazon Ish al Emunah u-Bittahon* (Hazon Ish *on Faith and Trust*) contain explicit or implicit references to this dispute. The *Hazon Ish*'s central message is simple: meticulous observance of Halakhah, and particularly intensive Torah study, are the best means to ethical improvement. The educational exercises of the *Musar* Movement fail to achieve their goal, and in its younger members lead not to ethical improvement, but mainly to neglect of Torah study and looseness in observing the precepts, under the guise of deep religiosity. It is in this spirit that the *Hazon Ish* develops his own approach to trust in Providence, while sharply criticizing adherents of the *Musar* Movement (*Emunah u-Bittahon*, 2).

There are people, writes the *Hazon Ish*, who believe that trust in Providence is the belief that things will go well for them in the future. This is not however, the true meaning of the term. Trust in Providence is the belief that all things are God's will, and all that comes to pass—the bad as well as the good—is therefore, the way it should be. Here we find a veiled reference to the Novardokers, who saw their trust in Providence as a guarantee that God would provide for them, without any "endeavor" on their part. Nevertheless, adds the *Hazon Ish*, one who trusts in God believes that all bad things may turn out for the best, since they are in God's hands, even if there is no guarantee that this will happen. Therefore, in circumstances when an ordinary person would look to the "rich and powerful" to help him, one who trusts in God looks to "repentance, prayer and charity to repeal the evil decree" (*ibid.* 2,1). Trust in Providence is the application of faith: "faith is the theory and trust in God the practice" (*ibid.* 2). May one therefore rely solely on God, engage exclusively in prayer and refraining from all worldly endeavor? According to the *Hazon Ish*, the answer is no. Halakhah sometimes forbids practical endeavor, sometimes allows it, and sometimes requires it. Thus, for example, "One who sees a man drowning in the river and can save him, but fails to do so, praying [instead] for his delivery—is a murderer" (*Kovetz Igrot Hazon Ish*, III, 62). Later in the same chapter however, the *Hazon Ish* writes that each case must be judged separately, to determine whether practical action is permitted or not. True to his method, he offers no theoretical standard, but refers readers to the halakhic sources to determine whether practical efforts are permitted in a given case, and to what extent. Even the Halakhah itself does not always provide absolute and clearly-defined criteria, according to the *Hazon Ish*. Sometimes it provides only relative, subjective guidelines: one's spiritual stature and the extent of one's trust in God for example, might influence the amount of effort one may exert (see e.g. *Teshuvot u-Khtavim*, OH, 48). This case-by-case approach is a hallmark of the *Hazon Ish*'s halakhic method.

This also explains his position regarding the performance of tasks forbidden by rabbinic injunction during the Sabbatical year, in cases of severe loss. If in a given instance the *Halakhah* permits one to work, it is also permissible from the aspect of the trust in Providence. It does not even contradict the promise that economic support will come from God's blessing, since "the blessing is promised only to those who have made an endeavor or to those exempted from endeavor" (*Hazon Ish al Shevi'it, ibid.*). According to the *Hazon Ish*, this principle applies to livelihood in general, not just in the Sabbatical year. When a man toils and is successful, he must know that his success is not the fruit of his labor, but the result of God's blessing. And if he were to ask why he should toil rather than merely praying for the grace of Heaven—the *Hazon Ish* would reply that he must toil not because it is the source of his livelihood, but because the Torah commanded him to do so (compare *Kovetz Igrot Hazon Ish*, III, 62). When one acts in accordance with Halakhah, even if such action is of a pragmatic nature, it is not for lack of trust in Providence but, on the contrary, an expression of pure faith.

The *Hazon Ish* was a halakhist, not a philosopher. He rarely addresses metaphysical or theological questions, focusing rather on the "dos and don'ts" of Halakhah. This focus on practical observance however, in itself expresses a particular theological approach. All of the minute details that sometimes appear overly technical and petty to the outside observer are, in the opinion of the *Hazon Ish*, the ultimate expression of man's faith in God. He believed that one who obeys God's word gives far greater expression to his faith than one who resorts to permits designed to "help" God fulfill His promises, or one who seeks to strengthen his trust in Providence by prohibiting worldly endeavor when it is permitted by Halakhah.

Tsvia Walden

Behukotai – If Ye Walk in My Statutes

Behukotai? Behukoteinu? Behukateinu? Our Statutes?
My Statues? Our Constitution?
*On the Sabbath and **Abraham Joshua Heschel***

If ye walk in my statutes, and keep my commandments, and do them; then I will give your rains in their season, and the land shall yield her produce, and the trees of the field shall yield their fruit. And your threshing shall reach unto the vintage, and the vintage shall reach unto the sowing time; and ye shall eat your bread until ye have enough, and dwell in your land safely. And I will give peace in the land, and ye shall lie down, and none shall make you afraid; and I will cause evil beasts to cease out of the land, neither shall the sword go through your land. (Leviticus 26:3–6).

At first glance, *Behukotai* makes me rather uncomfortable. It includes a list of conditions—the nonfulfillment of which, it stipulates, will result in a variety of calamities. I, a firm believer in the exclusive use of positive incentives in education, find myself rushing to the biblical commentators for comfort. Nehama Leibowitz (*New Studies in Vayikra*, Jerusalem) is very reassuring. My initial reaction to the portion's menacing tone would seem to be a common one, to the extent that *Behukotai* is often referred to as *parshat hatokhehah*— "the admonition portion." Leibowitz' words, in which I find comfort, are supported by longstanding exegetical tradition, cautioning against a superficial reading of the 30 verses of admonition and the 13 verses of blessing. My heart and eyes however, have already been captivated by two of the admonishing verses (*Lev.* 26:34–35):

Then shall the land be paid her Sabbaths (*shabtotehah*), as long as it lieth desolate, and ye are in your enemies' land; even then shall the land rest (*tishbot*), and repay her Sabbaths (*shabtotehah*). As long as it lieth desolate it shall have rest (*tishbot*); even the rest which it had not (*lo shavta*) in your Sabbaths (*shabtotekhem*), when ye dwelt (*beshivtekhem*) upon it.

The letter sequence *shin-bet-tav* appears seven times in these two verses. The first six correspond to the root *shin-bet-tav* (to rest, cease activity), and the final one—somewhat fraudulently—to the root *yod-shin-bet* (to sit, dwell).

In the minds of Hebrew-speakers today, these letters have three possible meanings: *lishbot* (not to work), *Shabbat* (day of rest), and even *lashevet* (to sit), although the root of the latter, as noted above, derives from another root (*yod-shin-bet*). Here, in these verses of admonition, the root *shin-bet-tav* is used merely in the sense of not working or shutting down, as opposed to a festive and spiritual approach to the day of rest, the Sabbath Queen, or a "palace in time", as Heschel characterizes it in *The Sabbath* (Farrar, Straus and Giroux, New York, 2005).

As if that were not enough, I find that of the four verbs appearing in these two verses, two derive from the root *shin-bet-tav*, while the other two come from the root *resh-tzadi-heh*. Hebrew-speakers will recognize this usage of *resh-tzadi-heh* in the modern idiom *leratzot onesh* (to serve a sentence or punishment), which is virtually the opposite of *lirtzot hofesh* (to seek freedom). I am reminded of the fact that many of my students associate the verb *lirtzot* (*resh-tzadi-heh*)—to want—with the verb *larutz* (*resh-vav-tzadi*), or as one teenager said to me: if you really want (*rotzim*) something, you really run (*ratzim*).

The juxtaposition of *larutz* and *shabbat* takes me thirty years back, to an event ingrained in my memory—the first of its kind in Israel, an ambitious and prestigious undertaking—that in the end never got "to run" but was instead "shut down". It became associated in my mind with the shaping of time in Judaism, and resurfaced when I read these two verses of admonition in *Behukotai*, searching for comfort in them. Like many of my generation, I am a product of the country of my birth, and the passage of time we mark, whether in hours or in years, is that of the land—rife with miracles, celebrations and even a scandal or two.

In 1970, Israel stood on the verge of joining the community of nations in which cars are used not merely to get from place to place, but as a means of going faster than other drivers, in order to win a prize—or

"Grand Prix", as it is called. A group of entrepreneurs decided to hold just such a race in the town of Ashkelon. Some years later, I happened to be in Monte Carlo at the time of the annual race. From my hotel room, it was impossible not to hear the wheezing and screeching of the tiny fancy cars whose drivers hoped to win everlasting fame by defying the laws of gravity. The cars shrill cries cut through the air from time to time, and I was reminded of Samson: "Tell it not in Gath, publish it not in the streets of Ashkelon". The race in question was supposed to serve as a springboard for the development of Ashkelon, a city blessed with many ancient ruins. Like Tel-Aviv, Ashdod and Gaza, Ashkelon is by the sea, but unlike Tel-Aviv it is not bustling, unlike Ashdod it has no port, and unlike Gaza it is not fought over. I would not have known much about the race, had it not aroused heated public debate. I became acquainted with its more interesting facets, those that took place behind closed doors, or more precisely, in the modest living room of my parents, Sonya and Shimon Peres.

Amit Lauzon describes the events as they unfolded:

First to express opposition was MK Shlomo Gross (*Agudat Yisrael*), who said, during the course of a parliamentary debate on the subject of road accidents: "Should we hold car races in order to encourage speeding and in order to encourage young people to see crazy driving? Is this what we really need? ...

In another debate, on the subject of tourism as a matter of fact, MK Menahem Porush called upon the minister of tourism not to grant his auspices to the event, since "The matter is not in our spirit. The tourist attractions of our country are the Western Wall, the tombs of our fathers, the Cave of Makhpelah and the Tomb of Rachel. Not auto races" (*Ynet* 16/4/02).

This story is connected to the portion of *Behukotai*, not because of the roots and verbs that appear in the passage cited above, but because of the way in which it developed and the way in which it ended. The day chosen for the inauguration of the racetrack was, not surprisingly, Saturday; a day on which many people would be free to come and watch the race. My father, who was minister of transportation at the time, was asked not to issue a permit for the race to be held on the Sabbath. It was, it would seem, another manifestation of the well-known Israeli dilemma stemming from the tension between the country's commitment to democracy and its desire to preserve its Jewish character—including safeguarding the Sabbath from being publicly trampled underfoot; albeit, in this case, by means of sophisticated machines.

The religious claim that the event would constitute public desecration of the Sabbath, was met by the organizers with the argument that cancelling the race at the last minute, and especially preventing it from being held on Saturday, would cause them great financial loss. The next question was soon to follow: "How much money are we talking about? Tell us the price of the Sabbath, and we will pay you its ransom".

Lauzon (*ibid.*) describes the public side of the drama—to which I was a witness, as noted above, behind the scenes, and about which I am still ambivalent:

The battle raged to the very last, and it was only on Friday, 22/11/70, that the thousands who had flocked to Ashkelon, were informed that the race would not take place on Saturday. It was agreed that the race would be postponed to Sunday, and that the religious parties would provide the organizers with financial guarantees to cover any eventual losses. In any case, in order to ensure the race's cancellation on Saturday, some 100 religious party leaders chose to spend the Sabbath in Ashkelon, staying at the Ganei Shimshon Hotel. Money, ladies and gentlemen, is never an object.

"By what right can a group of people force its principles on others?" I argued with the passion typical of me in my twenties. To which my father, with the equanimity typical of him at all ages, replied: "That is why the blessing 'who sanctifies Israel and the times' is recited; you cannot ignore the fact that those who want to prevent this race from being held on the Sabbath are prepared to defend their principles even at the cost of bloodshed; and besides, Heschel says ..."

Years later, when I came across the first Hebrew edition of Heschel's small but powerful book, I saw Ilya Schor's wonderful wood engravings (created especially for the book's English edition). Their intricate lines continuously took on new shapes in mind. One minute I heard the small cars accelerating and taking to the air on an unknown course, and the next they seemed to be the ascending virtues of the Sabbath, coming and going, converging and scattering.

The thinker I therefore associate with *Behukotai* is Abraham Joshua Heschel (1907–1972). The interpretation I would like to propose for the word *behukotai* is almost synonymous with "my day" or "my Sabbath", but I would like to adopt it in the plural, i.e. *behukoteinu*. Before explaining my choice however, I would like to keep the reader abreast of two subsequent developments. First, the race was held only once, for reasons unrelated to the Sabbath. A 12-kilometer-long fence was constructed, at a cost of IL150,000—an astronomical sum at the time—but it was unable to contain the crowd. Hooliganism during the first lap led police to ban such events in the future, nipping the newly-born tradition in the bud. Secondly, in January 2004, MK Eliezer 'Cheetah' Cohen, together with members of various parliamentary factions, submitted a bill to allow automobile and motorcycle racing in Israel. How wonderful...

Behukoteinu—I have always been aware of the distinct advantage in growing up Jewish in a land in which language, Book and place are intertwined at the most prosaic level. This advantage means, among other things, that the week begins on *Yom Rishon* (Sunday—lit. 'First Day'), first of the seven days of creation, as recounted in the book of Genesis. And following the days of the week—First, Second, Third, Fourth, Fifth and Sixth, comes *Shabbat*—the Sabbath. It is not merely 'Seventh Day', but the day on which man tells the world: I am stopping. Sabbath of rest. "And on the seventh day God finished His work which He had made; and He rested on the seventh day from all His work which He had made" (Gen. 2:2). In the language of a native-born Israeli, *Shabbat* is not just another day, but a different day—for many, *the* day—although this difference may be marked in many and varied ways. Living according to the Jewish calendar, distinguishing the Sabbath from the other days, you automatically find yourself reenacting creation. "Six days thou shalt do thy work, but on the seventh day thou shalt rest". Heschel defines it as follows:

> The seventh day is the armistice in man's cruel struggle for existence, all truce in all conflicts, personal and social, peace between man and man, man and nature, peace with man; a day on

which handling money is considered a desecration, on which man avows his independence of that which is the world's chief idol. The seventh day is the exodus from tension, the liberation of man from his own muddiness, the installation of man as a sovereign in the world of time (*The Sabbath*, p. 29).

As a native-born Israeli however, your life oscillates between two calendars. On the one hand, the birth-date that determines when every Israeli child must start school follows the Gregorian calendar, as does the end of the school year. School holidays however, are determined entirely by the Jewish calendar. Our fiscal year is Gregorian, but all our fuss, excitement and presents are Jewish. For many of us in fact, there is a kind of tacit agreement regarding the question of what *hukoteinu*—our statues, customs, allotted times—should be. In the meantime, we live in a kind of duality; some would say we are torn by it, or even schizophrenic. On the other hand, our constitution has not even reached the dialogue stage.

Behukotai, in the singular, sounds to me like a condition, almost a threat. "But if ye will not hearken unto me ... and if ye shall reject My statutes (*hukotai*) ... And if ye walk contrary unto me, and will not hearken unto me". I find that difficult to accept. The jealous God is not my God. *Behukoteinu*, in the plural, tempts me, invites me to take part, to share in the responsibility. Yet these two expressions differ from the third—*behukateinu*—a constitution, accepted by all; something that Israel still lacks. What sort of statute-making do I have in mind? What is engraved on the tablet of my heart? How can words be engraved, when the letters that form them are so fleeting?

Behukoteinu appeals to me in the resounding expression *hukat olam*—"its celebration shall be an everlasting statute" (*Ex.* 12:14).

Behukoteinu finds its way to my heart when I hear the verse "Who giveth the sun for a light by day, and the fixed order of the moon (*hukat yare'ah*) and of the stars for a light by night" (*Jer.* 31:34).

Behukoteinu allows me to live in peace with scripture, as I recall the injunction "there shall be one statute (*hukah ahat*) both for you, and for the stranger that sojourneth with you" (*Num.* 15:15).

My choice of the first person plural—"our statutes"—goes hand in hand with my choice of Abraham Joshua Heschel, from whom I learned about the Sabbath's inherent reciprocity:

> With all its grandeur, the Sabbath is not sufficient unto itself. Its spiritual reality calls for companionship of man. There is a great longing in the world. The six days stand in need of space; the seventh day stands in need of man. It is not good that the spirit should be alone, so Israel was destined to be a helpmeet for the Sabbath (Heschel, *The Sabbath*, p. 52).

He has also afforded me a very meaningful insight into what it means to be human:

> This is the task of men: to conquer space and sanctify time ... All week long we are called upon to sanctify life through employing things of space. On the Sabbath it is given to us to share in the holiness that is in the heart of time (p. 101).

With the help of Heschel's interpretation, I discovered another possible reading of the two verses from *Behukotai*, and their effect on me suddenly became clearer; language it seems, merely reveals what is in one's own heart. For me—as one who is aware that her time on this earth is limited and borrowed—portraying the Sabbath Queen as the bride of man who lives in the vastness of space, and not necessarily as the bride of God, offers a path to turning His statues into our statues:

> Then shall the land be paid her Sabbaths, as long as it lieth desolate, and ye are in your enemies' land; even then shall the land rest, and repay her Sabbaths. As long as it lieth desolate it shall have rest; even the rest which it had not in your Sabbaths, when ye dwelt upon it.

I suggest that we find consolation rather than admonition in these verses; incentive rather than threat. At first reading, it appears that the land will rest in an attempt to regain its lost Sabbaths—the sabbatical years that were not observed, that were neglected by its inhabitants. The threat is obvious. If however, the Sabbath is understood not as inactivity, but as punctuating time; not as a locus in space, but as a part of infinity—a part that we may affect and shape—then the land will want to reassert its Sabbaths, and its weekdays will become festive as well; thereby striving to redress desolation and neglect, to make amends to its inhabitants for their exile, and even to tempt them to return.

A subversive reading? Certainly. But also the reading of a loving and pained heart, one that cannot accept the quotidianization of everything, one that abhors the idea that a "soul shall be cut off", one that truly desires the most desirable of days, one in which the Sabbath can come to rest. May it be so.

Bamidbar – Numbers

Gili Zivan

Bamidbar – In the Wilderness of Sinai

*On the Meaning of the Birth of the Jewish People
in the Wilderness: A Look at the Thought of
Rosenzweig, Fromm and Leibowitz*

And the Lord spoke unto Moses in the wilderness of Sinai, in the tent of meeting, on the first day of the second month, in the second year after they were come out of the land of Egypt, saying: "Take ye the sum of all the congregation of the Children of Israel, by their families, by their fathers' houses, according to the number of names, every male, by their polls; from twenty years old and upward, all that are able to go forth to war in Israel: ye shall number them by their hosts, even thou and Aaron." (*Numbers* 1:1–3).

Bamidbar, the first portion in the book of *Numbers*, begins with the divine commandment to Moses to count the Children of Israel. The description of the counting, which takes place "in the second year" after the exodus from Egypt, is followed by a description of the order in which the tribes encamped and travelled in the wilderness, "after their families, by their fathers' houses".

Through the census data and the order of encampment and setting forth, we get a glimpse of the experience of prolonged wandering in the desert: the lack of stability, the sandstorms, the exhausting dryness, the search for life-giving oases, and the ultimate question—"when do we move on?" or "when can we finally stop, pitch our tents and rest?"

Forty years of wandering in the desert before entering settled land—what do they mean? And in the spirit of the question asked by the Midrash: Why was the Torah given in the desert rather than upon entering the Promised Land? Desert is the antithesis of settled land; the opposite of civilization; a place in which man is at the mercy of God no less than at the mercy of man. Is it a place of freedom or a place of fear? Shulamith Hareven beautifully describes the desert experience, afford-

415

ing some sense of the emotions the Hebrews must have felt having fled
their Egyptian masters into the vast desert:

An immense freedom, vast beyond human measure, hung over
everything. The days had no rules and the laws of nature themselves seemed suspended ... There were no masters and no
slaves. There was only the desert, which held no threat, and the
gullies among the rocks ... The silence was palpable. There was
no end of sky ... There were no sounds. A few bleats or whinnies
from the flocks, a few human voices from the gully or the spring,
now and then the sharp screech of some bird. All the sounds of
settled land had been washed from their ears. The shouts of their
taskmasters too (Shulamith Hareven, *Thirst: The Desert Trilogy*;
The Miracle Hater, Mercury House, San Francisco, 1996).

What is the role of the desert? Liberation from the sounds of Egypt?
From the sounds of master and slave? From the sounds of the Nile and
its magicians? The negation of all previous existence in order to create a
new existence? A radical change in scenery, intended to effect profound
change in the identity of those who had come out of Egypt? And what is
the significance of the fact that the people's formative moments did not
occur on its own soil? The exodus, the wanderings, receiving the Torah
in the desert, are the formative memories of Jewish national identity.
What do they mean? What weight have various thinkers given to this
fact? What significance have they ascribed to the story of the birth of the
Jewish People in the desert?

I will attempt to address this question, as it was perceived by three
modern thinkers: Erich Fromm, Franz Rosenzweig and Yeshayahu Leibowitz. First and foremost however, I would like to begin this hermeneutical journey with the Midrash.

The *Tanhuma* explains the protracted wanderings in the desert as
having served an educational purpose. The people, in need of a radical
metamorphosis, a change of habits and perceptions, required forty years
in the desert in order to rid itself of its previous conceptions. The Children of Israel needed to experience life free from the concerns of livelihood and existence, in order to devote their time, resources and energy
to reeducation, learning to internalize the revolution in their faith, or

in the words of the Midrash: "God led them around the desert for forty years. He said: 'If I lead them immediately by a direct route, each will occupy himself with his field and vineyard and they will neglect the Torah. I will lead them rather through the desert, they will eat manna and drink well water, and the Torah will settle in their bodies" (*Tanhuma, Beshalah* 1).

Another midrash explains the desert as a state of mind, a departure from self and self-importance; a state of full attention to the voice of the other—both the transcendent other and the other who stands bedside us. Only one who "makes himself as a wilderness" is able to receive the Torah, able to make room for new and revolutionary ideas, and to fully heed the voice of God revealed at Mount Sinai and his commandments:

> "And the Lord spake unto Moses in the wilderness of Sinai"—
> One who does not make himself as a wilderness free to all cannot acquire wisdom and the Torah, and so it is said "in the wilderness of Sinai" (*Bamidbar Rabbah* 1). That is, only one who can make himself as a wilderness can—like Moses—hear the voice of God speaking to him in the wilderness of Sinai: "And the Lord spake unto Moses in the wilderness of Sinai" (*Num* 1,1).

This idea was further developed by the psychologist and philosopher Erich Fromm, who saw in the wanderings of the Israelites at the dawn of Jewish history, testimony to Judaism's struggle against the god of possessiveness. Forty years of wandering in the desert are forty years of "being", of human experience that does not seek to define itself by means of "having". It is a period in which the ancient Hebrews were taught to recognize a different kind of relationship structure: human relations not based on ownership and possession.

According to Fromm, Biblical Judaism emphasizes the fact that human beings are not property, refusing to define individuals by their possessions or by their ownership of one another:

> The desert is the key symbol in this liberation. The desert is no home: it has no cities; it has no riches; it is the place of nomads who own what they need, and what they need are the necessities of life, not possessions ... life in the desert as preparation for life

of freedom (Erich Fromm, *To Have or to Be*, Harper & Row, New York, 1976, pp. 48–49).

Some of the main symbols of the Jewish festivals, claims Fromm, derive from the desert experience, such as the *sukkah* ("tabernacle")—the temporary dwelling of the nomad; or the *matzah*—the unleavened, hurried bread of the wanderer. Moreover, even when God accedes to the request of the Israelites who longed for the fleshpots of Egypt, he adds an important condition: "they gathered every man according to his eating" (*Ex.* 16:18), thereby prohibiting the Children of Israel from hoarding food. In Fromm's opinion, this commandment is linked to the struggle against possessiveness: "For the first time, a principle is formulated here that became famous through Marx: to each according to their needs. The right to be fed was established without qualification. ... The second injunction is one against hoarding, greed and possessiveness. The people of Israel were enjoined not to save anything till the next morning" (Fromm, pp. 49–50)

The struggle against possessiveness is reflected in another injunction that comes with the granting of the manna: the prohibition against gathering on the Sabbath and the commandment to gather a double portion on Friday both for the Sabbath eve and for the Sabbath itself. According to Fromm, the Sabbath has been central to Jewish life throughout history, due to the struggle it represents, for liberation from the slavery of possessiveness. The Sabbath is not merely a day of rest. It is an expression of life without possessiveness, without transfering any object "from one privately owned piece of land to another" (*ibid.* p. 51), without buying or selling or transfering ownership. "On the Shabbat one lives as if one *has* nothing, pursuing no aim except *being*, that is, expressing one's essential powers: praying, studying, eating, drinking, singing, making love" (*ibid.*). This principle of the Sabbath was greatly emphasized by the philosopher and theologian Abraham Joshua Heschel. In his book, *The Sabbath*, he stresses the place of the Jewish Sabbath as an expression of Judaism's perpetual struggle against the human aspiration to conquer space:

Technical civilization is man's conquest of space. It is a triumph frequently achieved by sacrificing an essential ingredient of existence, namely, time. In technical civilization, we expend time to gain space. To enhance our power in the world of space is our main objective. Yet to have more does not mean to be more. The power we attain in the world of space terminates abruptly at the borderline of time. (*The Sabbath*, Farrar, Straus and Giroux, New York, 2005, p. 3).

The Sabbath is a kind of freeze in the race of material life; a "palace in time", as Heschel calls it: "The meaning of the Sabbath is to celebrate time rather than space. Six days a week we live under the tyranny of things of space; on the Sabbath we try to become attuned to *holiness in time*. It is a day on which we are called upon to share in what is eternal in time, to turn from the results of creation to the mystery of creation; from the world of creation to the creation of the world" (*ibid.* p. 10).

Let us return to the Israelites wandering in the desert and to Fromm's interpretation. Wandering in the desert, like the Sabbath, affords an unusual life, without possessions or property, the object of which is to internalize the idea that man is not defined only by what he owns, or in the words of Fromm—man is what he *is* not what he *has*.

Did the people of slaves in fact succeed in liberating itself from possessiveness and ownership in the wilderness? The hoarding of the manna (*Ex.* 16:20–21) would appear to have been merely the first outbreak of greed. Over the course of the Israelites' wanderings in the desert, it becomes clear that "The Hebrews cannot bear to live without *having*" (*ibid.* p. 52). Indeed Fromm laments the failure of the revolution of the desert generation; one that is also the failure of people everywhere. The failure of our struggle against greed, possessiveness, the accumulation of wealth, and "golden calves" of every kind:

Although they can live without fixed abode, and without food except that sent by God every day, they cannot live without a visible, present "leader."

Thus when Moses disappears on the mountain, the desperate Hebrews get Aaron to make them a visible manifestation of something they can worship: the Golden Calf. Here, one may say, they pay for God's error in having permitted them to take gold and jewelry out of Egypt. With the gold, they carried within themselves the craving for wealth; and when the hour of despair came, the possessive structure of their existence reasserted itself. Aaron makes them a calf from their gold, and the people say: "These are your Gods, O Israel, who brought you up out of the land of Egypt" (Exodus 32:4) (Fromm, *ibid.*).

Fromm addresses the failure of the revolution, also in the context of the conduct of the tribes upon entering the Land, and the development of the Israelite monarchy. He sees the prophets and the sages of the Talmud—particularly Yohanan ben Zakai—however, as carrying on the struggle against the sanctification of space and possessions, It is this struggle that saved the Jewish People from extinction even when it lost its political independence and its Temple was destroyed.

In short, the story of the birth of the Jewish People in the desert bears, according to Fromm, a message regarding the realization of a life of being, as an alternative to self-definition by a life of having. The desert thus represents a lifestyle of self-fulfillment, based on love and the joy of sharing and productive activity, contrary to a lifestyle of possessiveness, power and aggression based on ownership. The story of the Israelites' wanderings in the desert, and their incessant desire for additional sources of food, hoarding, the Egyptian fleshpots or the golden calf—are in fact the essence of human history. The ability to share and give, not only to accumulate, is—in Fromm's opinion—the greatest task that lies before man in consumer and affluent societies: "The realization of the new society ... is possible only if the old motivations of profit, power, and intellect are replaced by new ones: being, sharing, understanding; if the marketing character is replaced by the productive, loving character" (Fromm, p. 201).

The Jewish philosopher Franz Rosenzweig, author of *The Star of Redemption*, offers another explanation of the significance of the birth of the Jewish People in the Sinai Desert. Rosenzweig developed a unique historiosophy in an attempt to understand the unique character of the Jewish People, as compared to other peoples. The Jewish People differs from all other peoples, according to Rosenzweig, inasmuch as its "blood relationship" suffices—without land or soil—to express its eternal message. In his criticism of nationalism and its consequences, Rosenzweig drew upon his personal experiences as a German soldier in the First World War. He argued that the religious singularity of the Jewish People demands that it rise above attachment to land; "for while the earth nourishes, it also binds" (Rosenzweig, *The Star of Redemption*; in Nahum N. Glatzer (ed.), *Franz Rosenzweig: His Life and Thought*, Hacket Publishing Company, 1998, p. 294). The Jewish People that lives in "eternity" rather than "history" needs, in Rosenzweig's view, to overcome the fetters of nationalism, and devote itself to the eternal life of monotheism. The nations of the world, contrary to the Jewish People, strike roots in the earth lest they be swept away:

The peoples of the world are not content with the bonds of blood. They sink their roots into the night of earth, lifeless in itself but the spender of life, and from the lastingness of earth they conclude that they themselves will last. Their will to eternity clings to the soil and to the reign over the soil, to the land. The earth of their homeland is watered by blood of their sons, for they do not trust in the life of a community of blood, in a community that can dispense with anchorage in solid earth (*ibid.*).

Rosenzweig goes on to say that the danger is greatest "whenever a people loves the soil of its native land more than its own life", and "though nine times out of ten this love will save the native soil from the foe and, along with it, the life of the people, in the end the soil will persist as that which was loved more strongly, and the people will leave their lifeblood upon it. ... The soil endures, but the peoples who live on it pass" (*ibid.* 294–295). Land will fail in its role—when a people show greater devotion to the land than to its own singularity and destiny. Such devotion, claims Rosenzweig, can lead a people to extinction.

Two stories seem to lie behind Rosenzweig's harsh vision of the land as enthralling its defenders even to the death, to the point of their annihilation as a people: the story of German nationalism and its victims, as observed by the young German Jewish philosopher Franz Rosenzweig, stationed in the Balkans during the First World War; and on the other hand, the biblical narrative, regarding the birth of the Jewish People, a story with an entirely different message.

The legend of the origins of the Jewish People does not begin with "autochthony", with a homeland, stresses Rosenzweig. The story of the Jewish People begins with the father of the nation, Abraham, who comes from afar, complying with a divine command to leave his country and kindred, and go to a land that God will show him. Later in the biblical narrative, we come upon the Israelites who depart Egypt to go out into the vast wilderness. In other words, the fact that the father of the nation was a "stranger" and that the Israelites became a people while in exile, wandering the desert, landless—expresses the Jewish People's lack of dependence upon the land; its a-historical message and a-nationalistic character.

> This people are a people in exile, in the Egyptian exile and subsequently in that of Babylonia. To the eternal people, home is never home in the sense of land, as it is to the peoples of the world who plough the land and live and thrive on it, until they have all but forgotten that being a people means something besides being rooted in a land. The eternal people has not been permitted to while away time in any home. It never loses the untrammeled freedom of a wanderer who is more faithful a knight to his country when he roams abroad, craving adventure, and yearning for the land he has left behind, than when he lives in that land. In the most profound sense possible, this people has a land of its own only in that it has a land it yearns for—a holy land.

> And so even when it has a home, this people, in recurrent contrast to all other peoples on earth, is not allowed full possession of that home. It is only "a stranger and a sojourner". God tells it: "The land is mine". The holiness of the land removed it from the people's spontaneous reach while it could still reach out for it (Franz Rosenzweig, *ibid.* 295–296).

The holiness of the land, according to Rosenzweig, is thus reflected specifically in the fact that the Jewish People cannot possess its land like other peoples, and that even in the lands in which it resides in the Diaspora, it is never at home. The Jewish People's loyalty to its land

and to the memory of the land it has lost, preclude its assimilation to other lands. That is how the Jewish People becomes a people, in "a thing which, for other peoples, is only one among others yet which to it is essential and vital: the community of blood. In doing this, the will to be a people dares not cling to any mechanical means; the will can realize its end only through the people itself" (*ibid.*).

Rosenzweig thus sees the birth of the Jewish People in the desert a sign of its a-historical singularity: a people that preserves its identity only through its blood relationship and its exceptional nature.

In order to better understand Rosenzweig's position presented above, it is worth noting his approach to modern Jewish nationalism, i.e. Zionism and the subject of *Eretz Yisrael*, in light of his general view of the role and standing of the Jewish People. In *The Star of Redemption*, Rosenzweig compares Judaism to Christianity, claiming that Judaism has already attained eternity, contrary to Christianity, which is charged with the task of disseminating the truth.

He compares Judaism to "fire that feeds on itself", and Christianity to "the rays which shine out into the world and illumine it" (*ibid*. p. 341). Christianity is the rays that go forth throughout the world, striving to bring illumination to idolaters. It therefore fights wars, conquers countries, or in other words—lives within history. Christianity has a messianic mission, while Judaism—as already having attained eternal life—realizes itself in its very existence. The two faiths, Judaism and Christianity, draw upon the same source, like two sisters who need each other; the one expressing the eternal way (Christianity) and the other eternal life (Judaism).

The Jewish People, a kind of "a-historical element cast into history" (Ehud Luz, "*Franz Rosenzweig Vehatziyonut*", *Shdemot* 5733, p. 28), should not take part in history and has no political role to play in the country in which it resides. It must withdraw from the laws of survival of historical peoples. Rosenzweig saw Zionism as a dangerous aspiration toward normalcy (through land). He believed that the Jewish People should build Jewish spiritual organizations, not a Jewish state. Zionism thus correctly identified the Jewish problem—the weakening of Jewish identity—but offered an inappropriate solution.

We thus return to the subject with which we began. Israel's Declaration of Independence states: "The Land of Israel was the birthplace of the Jewish people. Here their spiritual, religious and political identity was shaped". For Rosenzweig however, the opposite is true: the Land of Israel is not the basis of the eternal people's existence. The Jewish People's attempts to cling, like other peoples, to its land, were never consummated, and it therefore returns again and again to its natural state—exile, wandering in the wilderness. Rosenzweig puts it as follows: "from its inception, the history of the Jews passes from one exile to another ... the spirit of exile, the essential foreignness to the land ... is rooted in the history from its beginning" (Rosenzweig, cited in Ranen Omer-Sherman, *Israel in Exile: Jewish Writing And the Desert*, University of Illinois Press, 2006, p. 148).

The final figure whose views I would like to discuss, regarding the birth of the Jewish People in the desert, is Yeshayahu Leibowitz. Leibowitz also addresses the fact that "the Torah was not given in the promised land" (Leibowitz, *Sheva Shanim shel Sihot al Parashat Hashavua*, Jerusalem, 2000, p. 291). The Torah's existence does not depend upon a specific land. The Torah, as the Midrash states, was given "in common land (*demosin*) of the world", a place over which there is no private ownership, a place that belongs to everyone, but to no one in particular. The Midrash emphasizes the fact that the Torah was given in the desert, that "any who wish to partake of it may come and do so"; or in another version—"just as a desert is open to all, so the Torah is open to all". The purpose of the Midrash, according to Leibowitz is:

> To convince those who believe that divine worship is contingent upon *Eretz Yisrael* ... The Torah was given *to man as man*, and not as not as a denizen of *Eretz Yisrael* or any other place. *Eretz Yisrael* is a framework established for the existence of the Jewish People ... under no circumstances however do the precepts or the Torah itself depend upon the Land ... This must be expressed in no uncertain terms for the sake of many good Jews, who strive in their naiveté to turn the people of God into a boorish people of the land (*ibid.* pp. 291–292).

In his poignant style, Leibowitz the Zionist, who lived in sovereign Israel, addressed the danger of sanctifying the land. It would seem that even without adopting Rosenzweig's mystico-existentialist approach to the Jewish People, Leibowitz' thoughts echo Rosenzweig's fear of turning the land from a means to an end.

Indeed, despite the historical remoteness of Rosenzweig's words (who knows whether Rosenzweig would have changed his approach had he lived to see the Holocaust) and their extreme naiveté, the warning they entail is still valid; a warning to a people that had long forgotten its desert experience—not to sanctify soil so dead that it poses a threat to life upon it, not to cling to the land more than to our uniqueness as a people (expressed in Jewish action and values). Leibowitz seeks to emphasize that the Torah is the heritage of all who received it, and is not intended exclusively for those who reside in the Land of Israel. The values and precepts of the Torah are not contingent upon territory, but on the will of the individual who accepts the yoke of Torah.

> Just as Abraham's recognition of God, that is the beginning of Jewish history, occurred outside the Land of Israel, so the Torah was given outside the Land, and there is no doubt that this is meant to convey a great deal; to teach us that accepting the yoke of God's kingdom, His Torah and commandments is a matter that transcends territory. This is another facet of the fact that the Torah was given in the desert (*ibid.*).

Leibowitz, who struggled throughout his life against the sanctification of all things that are not God, e.g. the state, the army and land of Israel—saw the Jewish People's birth in the desert as resonant with Judaism's struggle against all forms of idolatry. Turning the land from a means to an end, sanctifying the state (even a Jewish state), and extreme patriotism can be enslaving, changing an elixir of life into a deadly poison: "Not only was the Torah given outside the Land of Israel, but in the desert that is wholly *hol*, that is both a place of windblown sands, and a place of *hulin*, of the profane and the unsacred" (*ibid.* p. 291).

Fromm's warning also takes on new meaning in light of our having struck roots in the land, becoming a society of property and ownership. Every affluent society faces the danger of falling into the jaws of the golden calf. The definition of the self or the other by means of property and possession is a natural tendency in human-consumerist society. In the story of the desert however, as in the concept of the Sabbath, lies a challenge to adopt a different path to self-definition and a different basis for inter-personal relations.

Shalom Ratzaby

Naso – Take the Sum of the Sons of Gershon also

The Idea of Peace in the Priestly Blessing and in the Thought of A. D. Gordon

And the Lord spoke unto Moses, saying: "Speak unto Aaron and unto his sons, saying: On this wise ye shall bless the Children of Israel; ye shall say unto them: The Lord bless thee, and keep thee; The Lord make His face to shine upon thee, and be gracious unto thee; The Lord lift up His countenance upon thee, and give thee peace. So shall they put My name upon the Children of Israel, and I will bless them" (*Numbers* 6:22–27).

Naso includes a variety of interesting topics. One of its literary, religious and philosophical high points is undoubtedly the Priestly Blessing, also know as the "threefold blessing", so-called for the three concise verses it comprises: "The Lord bless thee, and keep thee; The Lord make His face to shine upon thee, and be gracious unto thee; The Lord lift up His countenance upon thee, and give thee peace". Let us first examine the portion as a whole, in order to better understand the context of the Priestly Blessing.

The first part of *Naso* is a continuation of the section begun in the previous portion, regarding the census of the Levites, the division of labor in carrying, unloading and setting up the Tabernacle, and the replacement of the first-born with the Levites. The first three passages in *Naso* discuss the various parts of the Tabernacle, its furnishings and vessels, entrusted to each of the three Levitic houses: Gershon, Kehath and Merari. The passage concerning the sons of Kehath also includes a description of the duties of the priests in preparing the Tabernacle for travel. Moses and Aaron are cautioned lest they cause the deaths of the sons of Kehath by carelessness with the sacred objects. The section concludes with the census results for each of the houses, as well as the total number of Levites between the ages of thirty and fifty.

427

The following three chapters discuss a variety of laws. The first of these passages (5:2–4), concerns the isolation of those who are unclean: "Command the Children of Israel that they put out of the camp every leper, and every one that hath an issue, and whosoever is unclean by the dead". As noted by the Rabbis, the text refers to three types of isolation: the lepers are put out of all three camps—the camps of the Priests, Levites and Israelites, respectively; those who have had a bodily issue, only from the precinct of the Tabernacle and the Levite camp; and the unclean by the dead—only from the precinct of the Tabernacle.

Next come the laws concerning one who has dealt falsely with another and offerings to the Priests; the law regarding a woman who has committed a trespass against her husband and the ordeal of the bitter waters; the vow of the Nazirite, and finally the commandment to the Priests to bless the people—including the text of the threefold blessing cited above, with the additional charge: "So shall they put My name upon the Children of Israel, and I will bless them" (6,27). This is followed by an account of the gifts offered by the princes on the day of the dedication of the altar, after the Tabernacle had been set up and anointed—gifts that included wagons and teams of oxen for the houses of Gershon and Merari, who were charged with bearing the parts of the Tabernacle; while the sons of Kehath were required to carry the holy vessels on their shoulders. The portion concludes with a description of the manner in which God spoke with Moses: "And when Moses went into the tent of meeting that He might speak with him, then he heard the Voice speaking unto him from above the ark-cover that was upon the ark of the testimony, from between the two cherubim" (7:89).

The arrangement of the sections in *Naso* is puzzling. There appears to be no connection between the *events* described—the parts of the Tabernacle, the roles of the Levites, the dedication of the Tabernacle and the offerings of the princes—and the detailed *laws* that disrupt the narrative description: the isolation of the unclean, the laws of false dealing, restitution and atonement, the case of a woman suspected of unfaithfulness by a jealous husband, the Nazirite vow and the Priestly Blessing. Some of the Rabbis have suggested that these laws were given here, following the census of the Levites and prior to the dedication of the Sanctuary, because they all pertain to the Sanctuary and the Priests.

Especially curious is the section describing the offerings of the princes on the day of the dedication of the Tabernacle. The princes all brought the very same offerings, yet the Bible lists them twelve times, in twelve separate passages—identical but for the names of the respective princes and their tribes. Toward the end of the section, we find an account of all of the gifts and sacrifices brought that day.

Much has been written about the princes, who are described here as "the princes of Israel, the heads of their fathers' houses—these were the princes of the tribes, these are they that were over them that were numbered" (7:2). The Rabbis interpreted the unnecessary repetition of the word *hem* ("these") in the verse, as follows:

These were the princes of the tribes—They were the same as had been appointed over them in Egypt: "And the officers of the Children of Israel, whom Pharaoh's taskmasters had set over them, were beaten, saying: "Wherefore have ye not fulfilled your appointed task in making brick both yesterday and today as heretofore" (*Ex.* 5:14) (*Numbers Rabbah*, 12,16).

The princes, who were the first to bring offerings to the Tabernacle, were thus the officers who had been beaten in Egypt. The moral of this midrash would appear to be that, sooner or later, all good deeds are rewarded.

The topics addressed in *Naso* pertain only to the "end of days" or to the glorious past—'precepts not practiced in our time', in halakhic terms. The Tabernacle, its dedication, the service (*avodah*) of the Levites, the laws of false dealing, offerings to the Priests, the "wife who has gone aside" and the Nazirite—are all of interest only as practices to be resumed in the messianic era or as historical descriptions. The only exception to this is the "Priestly Blessing", which remains a part of religious worship to this day, despite the fact that the priestly lineage is no longer certain. Although none of the other elements in the portion is practiced today, two general concepts have retained their central importance: the concept of divine service (*avodah*) and the concept of peace, with which the Priestly Blessing concludes.

The Rabbis of the Talmud and Midrash, medieval commentators and contemporary biblical scholars have all devoted a great deal of attention to the order and logic of this portion. Ibn Ezra for example, discusses a number of the portion's topics and seeks a connection between them. Regarding the proximity between the description of the census of the Levites and the commandment to send the unclean out of the camp, he writes: "Every one to his service, and to his burden—… And the passage 'that they put out of the camp' immediately follows, because the *Shekhinah* was present in the camps when they set forward and when they encamped" (Ibn Ezra on *Num.* 4:49). Regarding the proximity between the laws of restitution and atonement that must be made when "a man or woman" has committed "a trespass" and the isolation of the unclean, he writes: "And the Children of Israel did so—… And the passage 'a man or woman' immediately follows, because leprosy and bodily issue result when one commits a trespass" (*ibid.* 5:4). In other words, the relationship is ontological: leprosy and bodily issue are the consequence of committing a trespass. He offers the following explanation for the proximity between the ordeal of the bitter waters and restitution for dealing falsely: "If any man's wife goes aside—because she has committed a trespass (*ma'al*) against him" (*ibid.* 12). The connection here is purely associative, as the word *ma'al* ("trespass") appears in both passages. Similarly, Ibn Ezra explains the proximity between the vow of the Nazirite and the ordeal of the bitter waters: "And the man shall be clear from iniquity—… There are those explain the proximity between the passage regarding the Nazirite and that of the wife who has gone aside in that she will have a son who will be a Nazirite, if she was not defiled. But I believe the reason to be that a woman who takes the vow of the Nazirite is the opposite of one who commits a trespass, for most sins are brought about by wine, and a woman who does not dress her hair will not seek to lie with a man" (*ibid.* 31). Here too the relationship is ontological: abstaining from wine keeps one from sin. Regarding the proximity between the vow of the Nazirite and the Priestly Blessing, he explains: "Beside that for which his means suffice—… And the passage of the Priestly Blessing immediately follows that of the Nazirite. Having completed the law of the Nazirite who is holy, [the text] proceeds to the law of the Priests who are holy" (*ibid.* 6:21). The connection here is once again purely associative. Ibn Ezra thus resorts to a number of methods, including word association, passing resemblance and so forth.

Unlike Ibn Ezra, Gersonides (Ralbag) sought a more systematic explanation of the order of the topics in *Naso*. He believed the various passages should be viewed as a progression, from the broad to the specific, from the external to the internal. According to Gersonides, sending the unclean out of the camp was the final stage of a comprehensive process of religious preparation. Regarding its immediate proximity to laws of restitution and atonement for dealing falsely, he writes: "It is as if [the Torah] remembered at this point ... to rid the camp of evil that would lead to conflict and strife, that is one should not hold the money of another unlawfully, taking advantage of one who has no kinsman" (5:5–8). Gersonides here adopts the rabbinic interpretation of the passage as referring specifically to theft from a proselyte, who has no heirs who might claim restitution in his stead.

Gersonides explains the proximity between this passage and the next in the same vein: "And this passage ['If any man's wife go aside'] immediately follows the previous passage, the purpose of which was to eliminate conflict and strife among the Israelites in general, because the purpose of this passage is to eliminate strife from the home. And although domestic peace comes before national peace, as established in political philosophy, the Torah began with the greater but later peace, and concluded with the earlier" (*ibid.*).

Regarding the proximity between the matter of a wife who has gone aside and that of the Nazirite, he remarks:

And this passage immediately follows that of the wife who has gone aside, which regards the elimination of strife and harm in the home, because the purpose of this passage is to subdue the struggle between man and himself and the harm caused thereby, due to the physical passions that lead him to sin. And subduing this struggle comes before domestic peace and political peace, and that is why the Torah placed it last. This passage offers one who is overcome by his [evil] inclination a remedy: that he deprive himself of wine, because wine greatly increases the evil inclination, leading to harm and disgrace in deed and in thought (6:1–21).

And so, with regard to the Priestly Blessing, he concludes: "And after presenting that which will resolve man's battle with his soul and eliminate struggle and conflict from the home and the nation as a whole, [the Torah] presents the Priestly Blessing, which offers wonderful insight into the concept of perfection and true peace" (*Ibid.* 22–27).

In other words, the portion unfolds from the outside in: from national peace to domestic peace, to inner peace ("to subdue the struggle between man and himself and the harm caused thereby"). He thus views the Priestly Blessing as the culmination of all of these passages, offering "wonderful insight into the concept of perfection and true peace", concluding with the words "The Lord lift up His countenance upon thee, and give thee peace".

Although there are other explanations, Gersonides' approach clearly reflects a predominant voice within Judaism, which sees the Torah as a constitution, intended to organize social life in the most perfect way possible. This approach is consistent with the spirit of Judaism, which strives to perfect the world under the reign of the Almighty. This was also the view of Maimonides. Contrary to Rabbi Judah Halevi, he did not consider the unique status of the Land of Israel to be *sui generis*, and although (like Halevi) he viewed prophecy as the epitome of religious fulfillment, he did not believe it required any special ability. It was clearly not the exclusive province of Jews, just as it had clearly not been restricted to the Land of Israel. Such a state of religious perfection however, is contingent upon certain political and social conditions—provided, according to Maimonides, by the Mosaic constitution. The uniqueness of the Jewish People therefore derives from its Torah—produced by the prophet Moses; the perfect legislator. Maimonides thus explained the idea of the messianic era as a time of true, eternal peace, in which all will be able to grasp the divine, "each according to his ability". In other words, the theme of *Naso* is peace: beginning with the service of the Levites and the purification of the camp, followed by domestic and internal peace, and concluding with peace.

As noted, the Priestly Blessing is, according to Gersonides, the climax of the entire portion. Let us now examine the content of this blessing. The passage containing the Blessing begins with a command: "Speak unto Aaron and unto his sons, saying: On this wise ye shall bless the Children of Israel; ye shall say unto them: The Lord bless thee, and keep thee; The Lord make His face to shine upon thee, and be gracious unto thee; So shall they put My name upon the Children of Israel, and I will bless them.'" (6:23–27).

The first blessing—"The Lord bless thee, and keep thee"—appears somewhat repetitive, although, as the commentators have pointed out, the two expressions are not the same. The first to address the subject were the ancient Sages, who offered the following explanation: "With the blessing, a safeguarding—A human king had a slave in Syria and he resided at Rome. The king sent for him, and he came. He gave him a hundredweight of gold, which he loaded, and then departed. Thieves fell upon him and took all he had been given and all that he had. Could he have guarded himself against the thieves? Therefore, 'The Lord bless thee' with wealth, and 'keep thee'—from thieves" (*Numbers Rabbah* 11,5).

Rashi and Ibn Ezra explain this verse in a similar fashion. "The Lord bless thee"—bestowing the good, and "keep thee"—preventing the bad. Most of the commentators understand this blessing as referring primarily to physical needs. Don Isaac Abravanel, for example, writes as follows: "The first blessing concerns physical matters, that he will bless them and pour out much goodness upon them... And it says 'keep thee' after 'bless thee', because 'bless thee' refers to wealth and other material goods, and because wealth often brings harm to its owner, they will also require safeguarding" (*ibid.*).

Most of the commentators interpret the second blessing, "The Lord make His face to shine upon thee, and be gracious unto thee", as referring to spiritual matters. This is primarily due to the appearance of the word *ya'er* ("shine"), because light symbolizes Torah, wisdom, and so forth. There is more to the blessing however than "The Lord make His face to shine upon thee", as the Sages of the Midrash note: "*Viy'huneka*—He will give you the understanding to be gracious and merciful toward one another, as it is written 'and He will show thee mercy, and have compassion upon thee' (*Deut.* 13:18)" (*Numbers Rabbah* 11, 6).

Rashi explained differently: "The Lord make His face to shine upon thee—He will show you a laughing, radiant countenance". In other words, the fact that God will shine his face upon you, is in itself the blessing. Rashi also interprets "and be gracious unto thee" as pertaining to the spiritual and emotional, rather than material realm: "*Viy'huneka*— Will grant you *hen* (grace)". Rabbi S.D. Luzzatto explains the difference between *hen* and *hesed*: "*Hesed* is the quality of the one who shows love and *hen* is the quality of the one to whom it is shown".

The final blessing is "The Lord lift up His countenance upon thee, and give thee peace". The first part of this blessing would seem to mean that God will not become angry with you, will show forbearance toward you, and then he will "give you peace". That is to say that a "lifting up of countenance", clemency and conciliation, is a precondition for peace.

The Talmud in the tractate of *Rosh Hashanah* (17b) tells the story of a woman convert who came before Rabban Gamliel and asked why one verse states that God "regardeth **not** persons (*lo yissa panim*), nor taketh reward" (*Deut.* 10:17), and another "The Lord lift up His countenance (*yissa panav*) upon thee". Rabbi Jose Hakohen replied:

> I will explain by means of a parable. It is like a man who borrowed a [100 denar] from another and fixed a time [of payment] before the king and took an oath on the king's life. The appointed time came and he failed to pay. He came to placate the king. The king said to him: You are forgiven for the slight to me, go and placate your fellow. Here too, one concerns sins between man and God, the other sins between man and man.

In other words, God will forgive those things that concern him, but not slights to others—in keeping with the well-known principle that God cannot forgive sins between man and man. Accordingly, the Rabbis ruled that *Yom Kippur* atones only for sins between man and God, but cannot atone for sins between man and man until the one who has been wronged has been placated (*Yoma* 8,9). "The Lord lift up His countenance upon thee" thus refers to forbearance and forgiveness from God, as a prerequisite for the granting of "peace". The Midrash proposes a similar interpretation (*Numbers Rabbah* 11:7): "Just as they lift up their countenances to me, so I will lift up my countenance to them. What does this mean? I have written in my Torah (*Deut.* 8:10) 'And thou shalt eat and be satisfied, and bless the Lord thy God'—When a Jew sits down with his household and they do not have enough to satisfy their hunger, [yet] they meticulously lift up their faces to me in blessing, even for a portion the size of an olive or the size of an egg—Therefore: 'The Lord lift up His countenance upon thee'."

Here too "lift up His countenance upon thee" is explained as a reference to divine mercy and forbearance, although the interpretation offered by the Midrash differs slightly from that of the Talmud in *Rosh Hashanah*. The Midrash asserts that God will show favor to those who show favor to him, i.e. those who worship him beyond what is required according to the strict letter of the law. The Talmud, on the other hand, explains merely that God will show tolerance in his relationship with man.

It is worth noting, in this context, the interpretation suggested by Rabbi Isaac Arama (Spain; c. 1420–1494), and author of the well-known commentary *Akedat Yitzhak*. Arama viewed the threefold blessing as a progression: the first blessing pertains to the satisfaction of material needs; the second to emotional needs and the ability to relate to others in a nonverbal, empathic manner; and the third blessing to our relationship with God. On the closing of the Blessing, he remarks: "And peace is the essence of the blessings and that is how they end".

The premise that "The Lord lift up His countenance upon thee, and give thee peace" is the culmination of the Priestly Blessing is also supported by the fact that verses gradually increase in length. Furthermore, the emphasis in the third verse is double: "upon thee" and give "thee".

Closer study however, shows that the Priestly Blessing is hardly straightforward. It begins "On this wise ye shall bless the Children of Israel"; yet ends "So shall they put My name upon the Children of Israel, and I will bless them"—that is to say, it is not the Priests who will bless them, but God. Moreover, what exactly does the blessing consist of? At best we might say that the Priests will ask God to bless the Children of Israel, lift his countenance upon them, etc. Is there not a contradiction between the commandment "On this wise ye shall bless" and the statement "I will bless them"? And indeed, what is the Priestly Blessing? These difficulties would appear to be the source of the following Midrash in the *Tanhuma*, as well as similar Midrashim in the *Sifre*:

The Congregation of Israel said before the Holy One, blessed be He: Master of the Universe, why have you told the Priests to bless us? We need only your blessing, and to be blessed from your mouth alone, as it is written "Look forth from Thy holy habitation, from heaven, and bless Thy people Israel" (*Deut.* 26:15). The Holy One, blessed be He replied: Although I have told the Priests to bless you, I too will bless you (*Tanhuma, Num.* 6:22).

Samson Raphael Hirsch thus explained that members of the Jewish priestly caste lack charismatic powers of their own, to bless or to curse. The Priests, he maintained, are merely an instrument by means of which the blessing is pronounced. In this way he also explains the deaths of Nadab and Abihu, who performed their divine service not by God's command, but of their own initiative.

The question posed in the *Tanhuma* however, still remains: "Master of the Universe, why have you told the Priests to bless us? We need only your blessing!" I believe the concept of blessing here should be understood in the manner suggested by Don Isaac Abravanel. In his commentary on the word *barekhu* (bless), he explains that the concept of *berakhah* (blessing) has a number of possible meanings. It may refer to an outpouring of good, as in "and the Lord had blessed Abraham in all things" (Gen. 24:1); or it may designate praise, as in "Wherefore David blessed the Lord" (1 *Chron.* 29:10). Both of these meanings are obvious. To this however, he adds a further meaning: prayer and supplication on behalf of another. One who blesses another does not simply bestow a blessing upon him, but intercedes with God that he might pour out his blessing upon him. That is how we should understand the commandment to the Priests: "On this wise ye shall bless the Children of Israel". The Priest does not bless, but pray.

The question remains however. Why do the Israelites need the priests to pray for them? Why should they not pray for themselves? It is this problem that commentators such as Rabbi Moses Alshekh and Rabbi Isaac Arama—kabbalists as well as exegetes—addressed. Alshekh, who lived in Safed in the 16th century, believed that in the act of blessing, the Priests would prepare the Israelites to receive the blessing. As in the explanation of Samson Raphael Hirsch cited above, the Priests as a caste do not possess any special power to confer blessings. They fulfill a function, and that is to arouse the Israelites to a state of awareness and preparedness to receive the blessing as an outpouring of divine abundance (*shefa*).

This view is shared by Isaac Arama, author of *Akedat Yitzhak*, and his commentator Rabbi Haim Yosef Pollack. They cite the Talmud in the tractate of *Shabbat* (81a), which teaches: "When Moses ascended to heaven, he came upon God as he was tying crowns to the letters. He said to him: Moses, do they not greet (lit. give peace to) one another in your city? He replied: Master of the universe, does a slave greet his master? He said to him: You should have helped me".

In other words, although everything depends upon God's will, it is man's duty to purify and sanctify himself and society as a whole, through his behavior. Divine abundance will only descend upon an individual or society prepared to receive it. Indeed, both Arama and Pollack compare moral behavior to the cultivation of soil: as long as the land is not tilled and sown, the rain and dew fall in vain.

The closing verse of the Priestly Blessing is much clearer, according to this interpretation. Peace does not simply descend from heaven, by God's grace. Man must prepare the ground and create the conditions in which it can reign. The Sages of the Talmud and the Midrash thus perceived peace not as a state of affairs, but as a moral imperative; charging man to "seek peace and pursue it".

We find in the *Mekhilta de-Rabbi Yishma'el*, for example: "One who establishes peace between man and wife, between cities, between nations, between governments, between families … will be spared misfortune" (*Bahodesh*, *Yitro*, 11). Also worth noting are the Rabbinic injunctions introduced "for the sake of peace". The Rabbis stated unequivocally: "Without peace there is nothing … for peace is the equal of all things" (*Sifra*, *Behukotai*, 1). Similarly, we find that peace is the ultimate purpose of prophecy: "The prophets placed naught but peace in the mouths of the people" (*Sifre*, *Numbers*, 42).

The peace with which the Priests bless the Children of Israel is meant to prepare them and to afford them the basis upon which to build peace. Peace is thus a task, achieved not by miracle but by natural means. As in all battles against evil, peace can only be achieved by the proliferation of knowledge. Scripture does not recognize ontic evil; war—which is the opposite of peace and the good—is merely the fruit of ignorance, and can clearly be averted by cultivating knowledge. Maimonides would thus envisage the messianic age as the proliferation of knowledge of God, which would, at the same time, entail the elimination of evil—i.e. war and the absence of peace.

We may thus interpret the blessing of peace with which the Priestly Blessing ends, as follows: the shining of God's face, which is contingent upon man's preparedness, is a precondition for peace. Without knowledge of God, there can be no place for God, and only the shining of God's face, i.e. man's recognition of the divine, can create a space in which there may be knowledge of God. Thus, as long as reality and its demands remain the standard for human behavior, war is inevitable. Only by transcending the boundaries of reality and by knowing God can we achieve peace and eradicate evil. This is how Maimonides perceived the messianic age. Nature will not change, nor will human nature. Jewish sovereignty and adherence to the Torah will create the conditions necessary for the attainment of human perfection that will, in turn, prevent war and animosity. The Mosaic constitution was intended to prepare the individual for knowledge of God, or to create the social and political conditions in which such knowledge might be pursued.

Abraham Bar Hiyya also viewed lack of knowledge of the divine as the cause of war. Unlike Maimonides however, he advocated the cultivation of emotions such as solidarity and empathy, rather than knowledge. Only such emotions, he believed, had the power to relieve "jealousy, hatred and covetousness". He thus offers the following remarks on the precept "love thy fellow as thyself":

And this commandment will be practiced and upheld throughout the world in the days of greatness. And if all denizens of the earth love one another as they love themselves, jealousy and hatred and covetousness will disappear. And these are the causes of war and killing in this world. It is thus written regarding the days of the Messiah: "and they shall beat their swords into plowshares, and their spears into pruning-hooks; nation shall not lift up sword against nation" (Bar Hiyya, *Hegyon Hanefesh Ha'atzuvah* [*Meditation of the Sad Soul*], 4).

Arama takes a different approach; resembling neither that of the great rationalist Maimonides, nor that of the emotional and semi-mystical Bar Hiyya. According to Arama, the root cause of war is man's departure from natural law:

Inasmuch as the laws of the Torah are divine, there can be no doubt as to the natural benefits they confer, for the natural benefits conferred by the restrictions imposed by law and religion are in direct proportion to their proximity to the true nature of things. Laws should thus be changed in accordance with their proximity to the true nature of things or distance from it, for if a particular law is wrong and distant from natural truth, although it may be adhered to somewhat, it will inevitably result in conflict and strife as long as people are dissatisfied with it and do not accept it willingly, leading to great wars and the detriment of society. When the governing laws are close to natural truth however, the benefit of the restrictions imposed on human character is perfect, and society as a whole is perfected, for as the laws that correct them are closer to the truth, the more readily they accept them and dwell together in peace (*Akedat Yitzhak*, 46).

Arama explains here that war is not an end in itself, but a means to other ends. A wise leader will therefore prevent war by creating a social order that takes these ends into account—thereby eliminating the need to resort to violence to achieve them. Arama however, believes it is not enough merely to perfect government and society as a means of achieving peace. We must strive to perfect all of creation:

As it is written in the first chapter of *Sanhedrin* (7a): "One who leaves the court without a cloak (i.e. the court has ruled against him) should sing a song and go on his way". And this was the intention of the prophet (*Is.* 2:4): "And He shall judge between the nations, and shall decide for many peoples; and they shall beat their swords into plowshares, and their spears into pruning-hooks; nation shall not lift up sword against nation, neither shall they learn war any more"—the meaning of which is clearly that conflict and war among the nations until that time are due to the failings of laws that are not in accordance with natural truth. Those who are judged by them are therefore dissatisfied and unwilling to accept them. When justice is perfected by the Messiah, however, and in concord with natural truth, they will dwell in tranquility, and wars and strife will be seen no more (*ibid.*).

A sense of justice is thus inherent to human nature, but will only become fully apparent when world peace is achieved. This conception of peace offers a basis for understanding the reason why the blessing of peace is the culmination of the Priestly Blessing. Arama explains further: "Peace is a necessary common good between people, who need to embrace and cleave to one another. It is like a silver, golden or other thread, by means of which they can be strung together [as a necklace] … to base the rule of law on the substance of the shared necklace and on the perfection of its form … and God is therefore called Peace for peace is His. It is He who binds all of the worlds and creates them in form and state, pleasure and stature". Peace is thus "a necessary good between people, who need to embrace and cleave to one another". When humanity is divided, people—who by their nature need "to embrace and cleave to one another"—are denied the only good.

The idea of peace as a mission and ultimate goal can be found not only in the Talmud, Midrash and traditional literature throughout the ages, but also among the teachers and thinkers of the Second Aliyah—who associated it with the concept of physical labor. *Naso* thus begins with the labor of carrying the Tabernacle, entrusted to the three Levitic houses: Gershon, Kehath and Merari. The task of the sons of Gershon and Merari was to carry the curtains and appurtenances of the Tabernacle. To this end they received from the princes, twelve oxen—an ox from every prince; and six wagons—one from every two princes. The task of the sons of Kehath was different. They were charged with carrying the Tabernacle's sacred objects: the ark, the table of showbread, the golden candlestick and its vessels, the golden altar and the bronze altar.

Due to the holiness of these objects, they were not given tools or means of transport, but rather "bore them upon their shoulders".

The difference between the labors of the sons of Kehath who "bore them upon their shoulders" and those of the other houses, explains Yeshayahu Leibowitz, lay in the difference between labor that concerns appurtenances and labor that concerns ultimate purpose. When the objects of one's labors are tools and instruments that help to achieve the ultimate goal, one may employ various means. When however, the object of one's labors is in itself the ultimate goal, the work cannot be accomplished with the help of aids and devices, but must be performed directly by man. The worker cannot be relieved of his duty by a machine. He must do the work on his own.

Social organization—one of the most active and significant components of cultural life—offers a good example of this principle. The state is a means, designed to achieve peace, security, and other values. These goals cannot be realized by the state itself however. It is man who must achieve them on his own. The state merely provides the framework for their realization. The state offers a number of tools: ministries, laws, enforcement agencies, etc. When it comes to the realization of the values themselves however, that can only be accomplished by man. Similarly, the aids and devices—the wagons and the oxen—pertain only to the curtains, screens, hangings, pins, sockets, bars and pillars that are not employed in the holy service itself, but merely provide a framework within which it can be performed. The objects actually employed in the holy service—the ark, altars, and so forth—must be "born upon their shoulders".

In one form or another, this approach has prevailed within Judaism throughout the ages. The ultimate purpose however, has always lain beyond the present—always spiritual and theurgic. This is manifest in the *Avodah* ("Divine Service") prayer recited on the Day of Atonement, or in the famous words of Simon the Just, one of the last survivors of the Great Assembly: "He used to say: The world stands upon three things, on Torah, on worship (*avodah*), and on acts of kindness". There is also the well-known Hassidic doctrine of *avodah begashmiyut* (divine service by material means), which sanctifies worldly endeavors and spiritualizes them. The principle behind this belief is that when one serves God by physical means one gathers up the "divine sparks" dispersed throughout the material world at the time of creation. What is more, in so doing, one upholds the devotional ideal of "I have set the Lord always before me".

The Second Aliyah, and particularly figures such as Berl Kaznelson and A. D. Gordon, brought about a fundamental change. The ultimate purpose of labor (*avodah*) in their thought and deeds was national and personal salvation. All of the pioneers of the Second and Third Aliyah shared this view of the value of labor. Based on their analysis of Diaspora life, the philosophers of modern nationalism, and the *Maskilim* who preceded them, reached the conclusion that the Jewish People can only be regenerated through "productivization", i.e. a return to the land, or more specifically to a life of labor as a people in its land. *Eretz Yisrael* will not be Jewish—even if the Zionist Organization were to purchase all of the land and obtain the longed-for charter—unless the Jews work the land with their own hands. Only then will it be theirs in the sense that a land is the homeland of a people. Moreover, the Jews will only be a people, in the normal sense of the word, if it resumes a full existence, i.e. engages directly in agriculture and industry. This is not only true of the national collective, but of each and every individual Jew. Only a life of labor and productivity can repair the damage caused by Diaspora life. When these pioneers spoke of labor and the detrimental effects of the Diaspora, they were referring primarily to detachment from the land and from working the land. Productive labor is therefore the only means of restoring the bond between the individual, the People and the land.

A. D. Gordon shared these convictions of the pioneers of the Second Aliyah. Whereas they believed that labor was not an end in itself however, but a means to redemption, Gordon took a very different approach. Labor, according to Gordon, is a prerequisite for "true life". In order to understand this, we must recall the distinction he made between "recognition" and "experience". "Recognition" is the reasoned and detached perception of reality, for the sake of conducting oneself in the world and attaining rational goals. "Experience" on the other hand, is when one knows the world from within, instinctively—inasmuch as man is also a creature of nature and therefore capable of knowing it from within her/

himself. It is worth noting in this context that the nation—the larger unit to which each of us belongs—is a natural and comprehensible unit. Humanity however, is an abstraction that cannot be grasped without the medium of the nation. The path of humanity and being thus passes through the nation, which—by virtue of its language and culture—transforms the individual from biological specimen to civilized man.

According to Gordon, man (and not only Jewish man) has become estranged from nature, since the nation as a whole has also become estranged from nature. The nation is no longer an organic society through which man touches cosmic being, but a utilitarian society, in which the individual fulfills her or his role in the exploitation of nature and its resources; hence man's alienation from nature and all it represents. In order to rectify this, the individual must live with nature, not alongside it or at its expense. Life with nature entails creation, to which man—who is also a creature of nature—must add her or his forces, uplifting, perfecting and assisting nature in its creative efforts.

As Eliezer Schweid explains in a number of places (e.g. *Avot* 1, 1), the individual, according to Gordon, cannot connect with nature when he detaches himself from it on a collective or personal level. This connection can only be made when his life is thrown open to the whole and truly bound to it. In this context we see the value of physical labor. Physical labor requires the application of intellectual as well as physical abilities, i.e. the whole man. It thus repairs the damage inflicted by culture in detaching spirit from matter, body from soul. If possible, such labor should be agricultural, because agriculture combines cognitive human force with the lower forces of nature. In other words, only when man exists within nature, concerned and attentive from within, can he establish a true and authentic bond with nature. Labor, and especially agricultural labor, is thus not merely a means to national or even international renewal, but a remedy for divided modern man—"fissured man", in Gordon's words—alienated from the power of inner recognition as an integral part of nature. On this basis, true society may be founded—by "experience" that allows man to grasp being from within, rather than "recognition" that entails a subject-object relationship. The connection between inner self, nature, and the creative wellspring of the nation must be restored. This can only be achieved however, explains

Gordon, if we transcend the conventions of recognition, and embrace "experience", which marks the juncture between self and the nation, and through the nation, to cosmic being:

> Divergent opinions, like branches and trunks that appear separate, share a hidden but common root for mutual understanding … One who espouses a particular view induces the exponent of an opposing view—to the extent that it is opposing—to creation; not by benevolence but by mutual exchange … Is there anything more uplifting, more conducive to concord and affection, than creation? Is there any richer source of reciprocal love than mutual exchange and shared creation? (Gordon, *"Hilkhot De'ot Umilhemet De'ot"*, *Ha'adam Vehateva*, p. 302).

Clearly, this cannot be accomplished until all barriers between self and cosmic being have been removed, by means of self-knowledge and regeneration from the core. Gordon further explains:

> The most important component of our creation is that each of us must first recreate himself. Each and every one of us must look deeply into his "self" … He will discover that the national rift begins in the soul of each and every individual. Thus, each of us must heal the rifts within his spirit and establish peace within his soul … Then we will discover, by various means, our pure national "self" (Gordon, *Ha'umah Veha'avodah*, p. 543).

The healing of this rift implies peace between the individual and the nation, and the restoration of the bond between the nation, as a unit of nature, and humanity as a whole. Once again, we find a vision of world peace based on labor and creation in conjunction with humanity and the entirety of being. We may thus say, in the spirit of the Priestly Blessing, that Gordon too viewed peace as the ultimate purpose of all personal and national endeavors; peace that begins with the individual, proceeds with the nation and culminates with world peace and perfected humanity.

Hanoch Ben Pazi

Beha'alotkha – When thou Lightest the Lamps

Necessity, Freedom of Choice and the Lesson of the Menorah
Rabbi Yitzchak Hutner

And the Lord spoke unto Moses, saying: "Speak unto Aaron, and say unto him: When thou lightest the lamps, the seven lamps shall give light in front of the *menorah*. And Aaron did so: he lighted the lamps thereof so as to give light in front of the *menorah*, as the Lord commanded Moses. And this was the work of the *menorah*, beaten work of gold; unto the base thereof, and unto the flowers thereof, it was beaten work; according unto the pattern which the Lord had shown Moses, so he made the *menorah*" (*Numbers* 8:1–4).

The *menorah*—the seven-branched candelabrum—is a fundamental symbol in the thought of Rabbi Hutner, used to shed light on many diverse subjects. The importance of the *menorah,* and the symbolism of the precepts associated with it, is addressed primarily in his book on the holiday of Hanukah, the lights of which he associated with the lighting of the *menorah* in the Sanctuary.

Rabbi Hutner typically attempts to identify basic philosophical and existentialist elements in religious exegesis, Midrash and Halakhah. His approach to the "work of the *menorah*" in *Beha'alotekha* is based on a number of dichotomies: necessity and choice, miracle and nature, light and darkness. As we will see below, these dichotomies afford not only religious insight, but also provide a basis for contemporary religious-spiritual experience.

All human activity can be characterized as either necessary—consciously or unconsciously so—or voluntary. Natural or necessary action is bound by the laws of nature and entails a sense of compulsion, difficulty and limitation. Voluntary action on the other hand, gives expression to man's *imago dei*, wherein lies his beauty, his "majesty and glory". Although performed by the body, the radiance of such actions is manifest, for "A man's wisdom maketh his face to shine". "Man is free to choose. He is his own master. The dominion he exercises over his own world rises even up to the heavens, for God Himself is praised thereby" (*Igrot Ukhtavim*, 109).

Rabbi Hutner's treatment of the *menorah* and its moral implications ranges from the personal to the general and the philosophical. It begins with the matter of Aaron's discontent. Rabbi Hutner often highlights a given approach by referring readers to a particular commentary—in this case Nahmanides on the Pentateuch: "See Nahmanides' remarks on the portion of *Beha'alotekha*". The reference is a broad one, covering a wide range of exegetical, homiletic and philosophical issues, which we will cite here only inasmuch as they pertain directly to the subject of this chapter.

His point of departure is midrashic-aggadic, and portrays Aaron as has having been upset by the fact that the princes of all the tribes but his own had taken part in the dedication of the Tabernacle. Every detail is explained as encouragement to Aaron or as illustrating the greatness and importance of the *menorah*: "For when Aaron saw the dedication of the princes, he was saddened that he had not taken part in the dedication, neither he nor his tribe. God said to him: By your life! Your [lot] is greater than theirs—for you light and dress the lamps" (Rashi, *Num.* 8:2).

Why did Aaron take offense, and what was the nature of his feelings? The commentators and the Midrashim upon which they are based offer various explanations, including the following parable: "It is like a king who made a feast and invited all his craftsmen [craft by craft]. There was one whom he loved exceedingly, yet he did not invite with the others. He was distressed and said 'perhaps the king has some complaint against me, that he has not invited me to any of these feasts?!' When the days of feasting were over, the king called the man he loved and said to him: 'I made a feast for all the inhabitants of the land, and I will make a feast entirely for you. Why? Because you are dear to me" (*Numbers Rabbah* 15,3).

The dedication of the altar is compared to a feast to which members of all the crafts have been invited, except the most beloved craftsman— the craftsman of the *menorah*. The altar was dedicated by the princes in an impressive and stately manner, with great pomp and public ceremony, whereas the service of the *menorah* was performed privately, inside the Sanctuary, without fanfare. It is precisely this element of intimacy however, that made the *menorah* the more beloved of the two. Aaron, whose face darkened when he saw the magnificence of the dedication of the altar, was comforted with the intimate "light of the face of the *menorah*". What lights up the face of man more than personal, intimate attention, directed exclusively at him, setting him apart from all others? This is God's gift to man in creating him in his own image.

Moreover, the sacrificial act, according to Rabbi Hutner, belongs to the natural world, governed by law and necessity, with nothing of the miraculous about it: "Simple consumption is elevated by the act of sacrifice" (*Reshimah*, 150). An action that coincides with nature and necessity does not give expression to man's uniqueness, to his freedom of choice. Like all natural actions, the act of sacrifice is limited in time and place: "as long as the Temple stands—they are performed". The *menorah* on the other hand, represents miraculous, voluntary actions, and is not limited in time—it is eternal. The flame of the *menorah* is eternal whereas the flame of the altar is transitory: "God said to Moses: Go say to Aaron fear not, you are destined for something greater. That is why it says 'Speak unto Aaron, and say unto him: When thou lightest the lamps'. The sacrifices are performed only as long as the Temple stands, but the lamps shall forever give light in front of the *menorah*" (*Numbers Rabbah* 15,6).

The lights of the *menorah* thus represent eternity. Rabbi Hutner interprets this on a spiritual-philosophical level, but also on a historical level. The *menorah* was rededicated in the time of the Hasmoneans, and its endurance is manifested in the lighting of candles on this holiday, for posterity: "For the Hasmonean dedication of the *menorah* is greater than the princes' dedication of the Tabernacle, as the Sages said, 'your [lot] is greater than theirs', since nothing remains of the princes' dedication, whereas the Hasmonean dedication has endured throughout the generations in the form of the Hanukah lights" (*Pahad Yitzhak, Hanukah* 6,1, p. 46).

Upon careful reading of Rabbi Hutner's words, we find that the lighting of the *menorah* in the Sanctuary is not sufficient to mollify Aaron. In order to do so, an extraordinary gift is required; one that will leave a lasting impression, for many generations to come. Rabbi Hutner returns to this idea, spinning a thread between the Midrashim (*Midrash Yelamdenu* and *Midrash Rabbah*) and the commentary of Nahmanides: "To evoke the dedication (*Hanukah*) of the lights in the Second Temple … the Hasmonean high priest and his sons" (Nahmanides, *Num.* 8:2). Nahmanides also cites Rabbi Nissim's *Megilat Setarim* to this effect. The force of the dedication of the *menorah* was greater than that of the dedication of the altar, because it included a dimension of "miracles and salvation": "God said to Moses, Speak unto Aaron, and say unto him, there is another dedication involving the lighting of the lamps, at which time I will grant miracles and salvation to Israel at the hands of your descendants, and it shall be called after them, that is the dedication (*Hanukah*) of the Hasmoneans" (Rabbi Nissim ben Jacob, *Megilat Setarim*).

All aspects of the lighting of the *menorah* in the Sanctuary—intimate miraculous and eternal—can be found, according to Rabbi Hutner, in the private lighting of the Hanukah lights in the home: "For the commandment to kindle the Hanukah lights is the continuation of the commandment to light the *menorah*" (*Igrot Ukhtavim*, 17). On Hanukah, the lamps that "shall give light in front of the *menorah*", illuminate each and every home. The dedication of the altar was a unique occasion, and the altar itself was only used for as long as the Sanctuary stood, whereas the dedication of the *menorah* is never-ending, performed anew each year.

Aaron's face, which darkened when he saw that he and his tribe had been excluded from the dedication of the altar, was made to shine anew in the light of the *menorah*: "Majesty and glory are the essence of Hanukah" (*Hanukah* 7, p. 55). The light and illumination of the *menorah* are reflected in man's face: "Majesty and glory … the place in which the light of the soul is manifest in the vessel of the body is its majesty … The light of intelligence is not apparent in the body as a whole. The face is the only place in the human body in which the radiance of the mind shines through. 'A man's wisdom maketh his face to shine'" (*ibid.* p. 57). In Rabbi Hutner's writing, textual analysis leads to symbolic interpretation and philosophical contemplation. He progresses from the passage in *Beha'alotekha*—which he interprets as addressing Aaron, saying "your lot is greater than theirs", shedding the light of majesty and eternity upon him; to the passage's symbolic significance, representing the tension between the "nature" of the altar and the "freedom" of the *menorah*; and finally, to a discussion of the *imago dei* that shines in man's face and ethical conduct.

Man's actions are governed by the dynamics of "necessity" and "choice". "Natural" behavior is "necessary" behavior, while "human" behavior is an expression "choice". To Rabbi Hutner, the act of illumination—unlike other actions—is entirely a matter of choice. This is evidenced not by the kindling of the Hanukah lights, but by the ethical significance of man's shining his face upon the world, illuminating it from the light within himself. This cannot be accomplished simply by lighting the Hanukah candles once or once a year. It requires a day-to-day commitment—in the boundless act of education and in the way in which one treats one's fellow man.

Necessity and choice are reflected in man's actions and represent two different modes of divine agency that, as we will explain below, also entail an internal dialectic. Rabbi Hutner describes it as two systems of divine action in the world, two paradigms of revelation, the one embodied in the "act of genesis" and the other in the Sinaitic revelation: "And the will of God is revealed to us in two configurations: one is the configuration of genesis, of the world created in ten utterances; and the other is the configuration of Sinai, of the Torah given in ten commandments. Both are expressions of God's will" (*Hanukah*, 4, p. 39)

The paradigm reflected in nature and its laws is the paradigm of necessity, while the paradigm reflected in the concept of Torah is the paradigm of choice. They assume similar forms, both as modes of knowledge and as modes of speech. Only choice, however, the most profound expression of freedom, can be said to represent man's innermost essence. Rabbi Hutner identified the human manifestations of these paradigms with two distinct types of wisdom and knowledge: the wisdom of necessity and the wisdom of choice. Natural science is the wisdom of necessity; Torah—which pertains to man's inner being—is the wisdom of choice.

The will of God manifested in Creation is realized in necessity, whereas the will of God manifested in the Torah is realized in choice. "Let there be light" is an utterance realized by means of natural law—i.e. necessity. "Thou shalt not bow down" is a commandment realized by means of free will—i.e. choice. The wisdom of nature is the wisdom of divine will revealed as necessity, and is external compared to the wisdom of the Torah, which is the wisdom of divine will revealed as freedom. That is why the Sages referred to all wisdom apart from the wisdom of the Torah as external. For the Ten Commandments are the inner essence of the ten utterances [with which the world was created]. "Were it not for my covenant day and night, I would not have appointed the ordinances of heaven and earth", that is to say that God only gave us His revelation of necessity that there might be a space in which he might give us His revelation of freedom (*ibid.*).

Rabbi Hutner's approach is not a purely dichotomous one. The relationship between freedom and necessity includes a dialectic element as well. Acts of nature occur within an established order, while man's actions are expressions of freedom. The purpose of creation, effected as necessity, is to provide a medium and an expanse in which "the possible" can exist—to afford a space for revelation, a place in which man can exercise her or his free will. Rabbi Hutner's choice of examples is significant. Both types of wisdom are represented by speech: the wisdom of nature by the ostensibly spiritual utterance "Let there be light", and the wisdom of the Torah by the concrete precept "thou shalt not bow down". The latter specifically prohibits idolatry, but can be understood in a broader sense, banning all forms of enslavement inasmuch as they compromise freedom, and hence choice.

Freedom is thus the cornerstone of creation. Without it there would be no possibility of choice within a world that is entirely necessity and determinism. Freedom and creative freedom are the hidden platform upon which the physical world is built. Creation itself was a product of the will of absolute divine freedom, described as "the primordial light with which the world was created" a light described in the midrash as "visible to the very ends of the earth." The created world could not endure such light however, could not exist in a state of absolute freedom. God therefore hid it away, and it is known as the "hidden light". The initial action of choice and creation in absolute freedom was followed by the action of nature and necessity, founded entirely upon limitations and thus, in effect, the action of law. "The laws of nature are merely limitations; limitations that, in their very essence, stand in contradiction to the primordial light that was the beginning of creation" (*Reshimah*, p. 146).

Natural science, i.e. "external wisdom", addresses laws and limitations that follow the paradigm of necessity. The description of creation as a dialectic of freedom and necessity provides a space in which choice may exist: "The word 'hidden' implies that the type of choice that existed prior to the act of hiding was thereby changed. Choice before the hiding was manifest and explicit; after the hiding, concealed and implicit. And so it is with the hiding of the primordial light" (*ibid.*). The hidden light does not disappear but it is not manifest. It may therefore receive expression in a world of free-willed action, as freedom within nature, in turn founded upon freedom. Rabbi Hutner associates the hidden light with the act of natural illumination reflected in man's face.

Rabbi Hutner thus explains the dual nature of the "hidden light". It may be hidden, leaving action to necessity and the law called "nature", or it may come to light, thereby constituting a "miracle". A miracle is a free act, entirely devoid of necessity –an expression of freedom and choice. This freedom that transcends law and necessity—that emerges from its place of concealment or storehouse—is, according to Hutner, the primary significance of the Torah.

The main function of the Torah and the precepts is to serve as a key to this storehouse. We thus arrive at the wonderful ("milk and honey") principle whereby the laws of the Torah must themselves serve as a key to open the storehouse, and a key must be inserted in a locked door, for it is pointless to use a key on an open door. The laws of the Torah therefore have no place among the miracles, for the laws of the Torah were intended to open the storehouse and thus rightly belong the storehouse. And they will never be contingent upon miracles, for miracles represent the opening of the storehouse and if it is already open, the laws of the Torah serve no purpose there (*ibid.* p. 147).

The "action of freedom" described by Rabbi Hutner is the emergence from the storehouse, or as he calls it the "revelation of divine inspiration". This revelation is the eruption of free will from the confines of law and necessity: "For the revelation of this inspiration is in effect a breach in the storehouse. And every detail of the laws of the Torah that strives to achieve this revelation inherently concerns the place in which the storehouse was breached" (*ibid.*).

The lighting of the *menorah* by Aaron and his descendants is one of the manifestations of this hidden light of will and freedom. Light is not another physical object, one of the things that exists in the natural world, but a "reality distinct from all other realities", an expression of something beyond necessity, beyond natural reality. The Talmud thus asks: "Did He truly require its light? For forty years, the Israelites walked in the desert by His light alone. Rather … it serves to attest before the entire world that the *Shekhinah* dwells among Israel" (*ibid.* p. 148).

The reason the Talmud asks about the light of the *menorah* and not about the sacrifices, of which God has no need either, is because light is not something that man brings to God, but the discovery of something that belonged to God in the first place. Light represents freedom of action inasmuch as it reveals the freedom that lies hidden beneath a world it shows to be deterministic. Light is kindled by removing limitations, by revealing its pre-existence in the fiber of reality, and "human freedom" is revealed by removing the "necessity" and "nature" that inhibit man.

The blessing "Who formest light" in the morning prayer refers not only to the primordial light with which God created the universe, but also to the light that man reveals through his own actions:

And so we learn a great lesson from the words of the *Tur* (Jacob ben Asher). That our light, which is the light of the sun, directly relates, in some fashion, to the primordial light that is currently hidden from us. For if our light were not connected in some way to that primordial light, we would not be able to bless the primordial light and our light with the same word. If these two lights were of entirely different types, we could not bless both of them at the same time, with the words "who formest light". For it is obvious that our blessing "who formest light" is recited specifically at the time of the appearance of our light. And if so, certainly the time of the appearance of our light also pertains to the hidden primordial light. The great lesson hidden in these words is that our light is, in its very essence, a reality apart from all other types of reality in the world. For no other reality can be said to be of the same essence as the primordial light (*ibid.* 148–149).

Rabbi Hutner thus binds together primordial light, the light of the *menorah* and daylight in a single blessing of light. "For they are closely intertwined, and all the more so the service of light in the Temple, i.e. the lighting of the *menorah*, must relate to both kinds of light" (*ibid.* p. 148).

The kindling of the lights constitutes a manifestation of the *Shekhinah*, in the sense that it precipitates the revelation of light and absolute freedom. It is a kind of key for the release of light from its storehouse, for the emergence of will and freedom from the confines of law: "And since the Hanukah light commemorates the light of the *menorah*, if the *menorah* was a testimony before all the world that the *Shekhinah* dwells among Israel, the Hanukah lights too commemorate the presence of the *Shekhinah*, and the aspect of testimony that characterizes the *menorah* extends to the Hanukah lights as well" (*ibid.* 151). The act of kindling the lights is a human one, founded upon the "hidden light"—infinite light confined within the boundaries of necessity. The entire purpose of the precepts is to open this storehouse, the purpose of their observance to create the possibility of freedom. This is the profound sense of the Sinaitic revelation, as Hutner saw it; the possibility of escape from the necessary dominion of the natural and the normal, to the possible and free-willed action.

The most interesting part of Rabbi Hutner's remarks on this subject is his identification of the types of actions that preclude human freedom. He singles out the great philosophies, the universally accepted modern theories, even the world of advertising and the "brainwashing" of the mass media, but also the educational methods that habituate people—or "domesticate" them, in his words—to perform good or bad deeds, or even to observe the religious precepts. Both occlude human light, both occlude free will.

"The guiding principle" or "source of all impurity" in our time, according to Rabbi Hutner, is "contempt for man's humanity". This contempt is directed at that which truly sets man apart—freedom of choice. In dialectic terms, claims Rabbi Hutner, the process of empowerment afforded by free choice will inevitably culminate in the loss of choice— not in the sense of the loss of "man's humanity", but in that the choice will be without inhibitions or difficulties, and will bring man to choose right. Absolute freedom leads to the consummation of man's humanity—manifested in the shining of her or his face.

The modern condition is one of denial, not in the sense of denying God, but in the sense of denying man. The contemporary experience is an attempt to deny man her or his freedom of choice: "The denial of the end of days is denial of the value of man's choice … the source of all the contempt for man's humanity in our time. And we therefore welcome any force that joins the effort to exalt man's humanity and the value of human life" (*Igrot Umikhtavim*, letter 42 [15 *Tamuz* 5724], p. 70–71).

The *menorah* highlights the possibility of choice, because it is neither a unique act nor a perpetual one, but rather expresses the idea of *Beha'alotekha*, "When thou lightest the lamps": denoting periodic inspiration that does not suffer stagnation. The *menorah* does not pertain only to the Temple or to Aaron. On the contrary, it pertains to each and every home, to each and every individual. Hutner explains the verse in *Proverbs* "Educate (*hanokh*) a child in the way he should go, and even when he is old, he will not depart from it" (*Prov.* 22:6) accordingly.

This statement can be interpreted in two ways: "The first approach understands the dictum to mean that a child educated in the way he should go will not depart from that way. The second, deeper approach explains that a child educated in the way he should go will never depart from education. Education itself becomes a way of life, and one who has been educated will never depart from the way of education. According to the first approach, the way that is imparted is perpetual and the process of education fleeting. According to the second approach however, education too is perpetual" (*Hanukah*, 6, p. 46). One approach to education is to make virtue inevitable. Education is thus a formative event, and all who have experienced it will pursue the path of virtue. Rabbi Hutner believed however, that virtue cannot give expression to man's unique quality, if it is not freely chosen. The second mode of education offers no unique formative event, but a "way"—in which man continues to be educated and develop throughout his life. This way includes the possibility of a uniquely human existence, because it incorporates freedom and freedom of choice. Such existence allows man to transcend "nature" and aspire to "humanity": "The princes' dedication of the Tabernacle was in keeping with the first approach. The holiness that was the object of their dedication remains, but the act of dedication was for that time only. The dedication of the Hasmoneans, on the other hand, followed the second approach. The dedication itself became a perpetual tendency, a legacy for generations to come" (*ibid.*).

The "work of the *menorah*", as described in *Beha'alotekha*, stands in contrast to the dedication of the Tabernacle in the portion of *Naso*. The dedication of the altar was a unique event that left no impression beyond its own time. The Hasmonean dedication on the other hand, which is the fuller historical expression of the idea of the *menorah*, is a "legacy for generations to come", since it expresses a perennial desire for renewal and spiritual growth. The crucial test of education in the style of the *menorah* as opposed to education in the style of the altar, is the question of pleasure:

If one wishes to educate a man to take pleasure in divine service, he must teach him to learn, so that the ability to learn might in itself become a permanent part of his life. For if divine service is performed only out of force of habit, the potential for pleasure is denied, for habit kills pleasure. As a wise man once said, constant pleasure is no pleasure at all. Which brings us back to the beginning of our discussion. The dedication of the *menorah* by the Hasmonean Priests—an act of loving devotion which came to redeem the sweet light of Torah—must certainly be an educational act of the kind that imparts the ability to learn, so that the process itself might also be a legacy for generations to come.

For that is the way of all who are taught how to learn; the way of pleasure. Your lot is greater than theirs (*Hanukah* 6, 2).

In conclusion, I would like stress the conceptual leap we have seen here—from the subject of virtue to the importance of pleasure. Pleasure, according to Rabbi Hutner, is synonymous with freedom. An action performed out of necessity cannot give pleasure or express freedom. Pleasure thus derives from the ability to choose and the desire for spiritual improvement.

In his book, *Rav Yitzchak Hutner Zt"l*, Binyomin Ben Chaim provides an interesting illustration of this approach. When Rabbi Hutner first arrived in Israel, Ben Chaim recounts, he was asked about his intention to build up Torah in Israel. He replied "I do not intend to build, I intend to plant" (p. 6). "Building Torah" implies inertness. A building cannot stand of its own accord, but is entirely dependent upon the forces and materials with which it was built. A plant, on the other hand, can strike roots, grow and blossom independently. Similarly, a student must be "able to draw words of profound wisdom from within himself" (*Hanukah* 4, p. 42). Modern education is of the "building" kind—the kind that domesticates and denies free choice. Rabbi Hutner envisioned another sort of education, one that promotes freedom by recognizing the unique character of each and every student.

The lighting of the *menorah* is thus a profound expression of man's freedom of choice, hidden within circumstances and necessity. Spiritual improvement and growth are thus the essence of the kindling of the lights, which express the perennial desire for renewal, manifest in the shining of man's unique face:

> Generally speaking, in no other religious obligation is this element of spiritual improvement an integral part of the observance itself. The exception to this is the obligation to kindle the Hanukah lights. Part of observance of Hanukah is the practice of progressively adding lights, rooted in the principle that one must always increase holiness (*Hanukah* 7, p. 55).

Yoske Achituv

Shelah Lekha – Send thou Men

The Desert as a Formative Memory in the Thought of
Rabbi Hayim of Volozhin

And your children shall be wanderers in the wilderness forty
years ... After the number of the days in which ye spied out the
land, even forty days, for every day a year, shall ye bear your
iniquities, even forty years, and ye shall know my displeasure. I
the Lord have spoken, surely this will I do unto all this evil congregation, that are gathered together against me; in this wilderness they shall be consumed, and there they shall die (*Numbers*
14:33–35).

Not every memory is a formative one. Many experiences and
events sink into oblivion, and even if we do recall them, they
cannot be said to have left an impression on us, in any sense of
the word. Nevertheless—and I assume each of us can confirm this from
personal experience—there are events and experiences that do leave an
impression on one's life. They may occur at any point in time, from the
distant past of childhood to the present—influencing and shaping one's
inner world, affecting lifestyle, behavior, choices and preferences in all
areas of life. They may be spiritual, religious, aesthetic, or traumatic.
Their impact may be conscious or unconscious. In this one might say
that every person carries around the baggage of her or his memories.
Such memories are formative.

Alongside such personal memory, we may also speak of collective
memory. Collective memory too may be formative, in the sense that it
shapes—in different ways and to different extents—the behavior, lifestyle and sense of identity of all who share it. The collective might be
a family, a community or a people. A collective memory too may be
the memory of an uplifting, moving or spiritual event or experience,
or it may be the memory of a disaster or a traumatic event experienced
by all members of the collective. Formative memory is sometimes so

powerful, that the boundaries of the collective are determined by the boundaries of memory.

There is however, a considerable difference between personal and collective memory, in terms of the ways in which they are preserved and the mechanisms by which they are recalled. Collective memory is preserved, transmitted and imparted by means of education and culture—including language, literature, song, ceremony, religious ritual, holidays and other events shared by members of the group. These are associated with the calendar or life-cycle, and serve as "agents of memory' in the collective consciousness. Not all are explicit. Many methods of preserving, transmitting and imparting memory operate in an indirect fashion. Memory—whether personal or collective—is not static. Language and ritual often lose some of their wealth of meaning, consequently weakening memory. At other times, they are refreshed and renewed, reclaiming latent memories and restoring their ability to function as bearers of formative memory.

A classic example of formative collective memory is the story of the exodus from Egypt, transmitted in countless ways: through Scripture, precepts, traditions, holidays, songs and literature. The Passover *Seder* however, stands out above all else; an evening entirely devoted to remembering the exodus, in narrative and ritual intended to be renewed and refreshed every year. The diversity of practices and discussions from generation to generation and even from year to year and table to table, clearly attests to the vitality and dynamism of this unique memory. New emphases and focuses develop, while others that may once have played a prominent role are mitigated or even discarded.

The ways in which the group is actually affected by collective memory is a more complex issue. In the case of the exodus for example, we can list a series of values and modes of behavior that have been shaped by this memory: the idea of freedom, the relationship between God and the Jewish People, responsibility toward strangers, orphans and widows, and so forth. These values and perceptions influence our way of life and our decisions, and serve as a source of inspiration for a wide range of attitudes. There is a system of mutual influence and inspiration between the objects and the agents of memory in religious and national tradition and culture.

The dynamic vitality of memory and the system of mutual inspiration between its agents and objects, together create the subjective dimension of memory, which helps to shape the narrative that is then implanted in the various modes of transmission to future generations.

We must distinguish between collective memory and historiography. Historiography is subject to standards of acceptability, and is supposed to correct itself as new facts emerge. Like all scientific study, historiography is built on facts and findings, and is open to refutation if evidence to the contrary is discovered. Collective memory, on the other hand, which permeates the culture and lifestyle of the collective at every level, need not be supported by facts and findings. These may be vague, and perhaps it is precisely this vagueness that leaves greater room for collective memory to fill in the "gaps".

The literature on the subject is extensive. Let it suffice to mention French-Jewish sociologist Maurice Halbwachs (1877–1945; perished in the Holocaust) who, some seventy years ago, laid the foundations for today's accepted distinctions between collective and historical memory. He viewed collective memory as an organic part of social life, constantly evolving and recast in keeping with the changing needs of society (see M. Halbwachs, *The Collective Memory*). Historian Yosef Hayim Yerushalmi, in his book Zakhor: *Jewish History and Jewish Memory*, points out the central place that Jewish tradition accords the culture of memory, in contrast to the marginal status afforded to historiography, and traces the flow of Jewish collective memory.

Shelah Lekha and the adjacent Torah portions illustrate the variety of ways in which reality may be perceived in the collective memory. Hermeneutical and philosophical traditions have preserved at least two diverse conceptions of the desert period; resulting, *inter alia*, in diverse visions of utopian, Torah-governed society. Below, we will discuss the memory of the desert experience as an idyllic time, and the ethos of the Torah world based on that time, in the thought of Rabbi Hayim of Volozhin. This will be followed by a brief discussion of another approach to memory of the desert period; one that has given rise to an entirely different set of *ethoi*. Anyone seeking legitimization for pluralistic approaches to reality will find them here.

A.

The memory of the period in which we wandered the desert for forty years, which we will address first, pervades the Prophets, the midrashic and exegetical literature, and a wide variety of mystical and ethical works—and continues to do so to this day. This memory is generally marked by a warm and innocent sense of nostalgia, which views the desert period as the golden age of relations between the Jewish People and God, and between the Jewish People and its leader Moses. The following two expressions, ingrained in literature and tradition, are emblematic of this type of desert memory. The first is the expression "youthful affection", based on the verse "I remember for thee the affection of thy youth, the love of thine espousals; how thou wentest after me in the wilderness, in a land that was not sown" (*Jer.* 2:2); and the second is the expression "those who eat manna", based on the dictum "The Torah was not given but to those who eat manna" (see e.g. *Mekhilta de-Rabbi Yishmael, Beshalah*).

"Youthful affection" expresses unbounded loyalty and complete trust in God, like the innocent and all-absorbing love of youth that causes the lovers to become so immersed in the present that they ignore all hardship and misfortune and have no concern whatsoever for the future. This motif appears frequently, as for example in the *Mekhila de-Rabbi Yishma'el*:

> The Israelites did a great thing. The belief they showed in me merited my splitting the sea for them. For they did not say to Moses, how shall we go out into the desert with no provisions for the journey, but believed and followed Moses. Of them the prophet said: "Go, and cry in the ears of Jerusalem, saying [...] I remember for thee the affection of thy youth, the love of thine espousals; how thou wentest after me in the wilderness, in a land that was not sown" (*Vayehi Beshalah*, 3).

Rashi (1040–1105) cites this midrash in his commentary on the verse "neither had they prepared for themselves any victual" (*Ex.* 12:39): "Neither had they prepared for themselves any victual—for the journey. This shows the Israelites' praiseworthiness, for they did not say, how shall we go out into the desert without provisions? They simply believed and went. And that is the meaning of the verse in the Prophets 'I remember for thee the affection of thy youth, the love of thine espousals; how thou wentest after me in the wilderness, in a land that was not sown' (*Jer.* 2:2)".

The Israelites are given credit for this idyllic time, entitling them to "dividends" later on, even in times of rebellion and sin; as we see for example, in the following parable:

> It is like a king who took a wife. He would say: There is no one as beautiful as she, no one as fine, no one as mild-tempered. [One day] her bridesman entered and found her unkempt, the house in disarray, the beds unmade. He said to her: If you could only have heard the way in which your husband praises you in the streets. That praise does not fit these deeds. The bridesman said [to himself]: If he praises her so when she is unkempt, how much more he would praise her were she composed. So the generation of Jeremiah was sinful, and God said to them "I remember for thee the affection of thy youth …". Jeremiah said: If you could only hear what He says of you, "Go, and cry in the ears of Jerusalem … Israel is the Lord's hallowed portion". He said: If he loves them so when they sin, how much more so when they do His will (*Numbers Rabbah* 2:15).

Life in the desert, characterized as an idyllic existence free from worldly responsibility, is cited in rabbinic literature as an example of the ideal conditions for Torah study. We thus find in the *Mekhilta de-Rabbi Shimon ben Yohai* (ch.16): "Rabbi Eliezer says, the Torah was not given for study but to those who ate the manna. How so? A man would sit and study, not knowing whence he would eat and drink and whence he would clothe himself! Hence, the Torah was not given for study but to those who eat manna".

This midrash implicitly justifies or expresses understanding for those who fail to devote themselves to Torah study under ordinary circumstances in which man is not free of worldly concerns and the need to earn a livelihood. The following midrash further strengthens the position that one must enjoy ideal, worry-free conditions if one is to devote oneself to Torah study. The midrash ascribes such reasoning to God himself, and offers an alternative explanation to the one provided in the Bible for the Israelites' protracted wandering in the desert ("for God said: 'Lest peradventure the people repent when they see war, and they return to Egypt.'"):

> The Holy One, blessed be He did not take them by the direct route to the Land of Israel, but through the wilderness. The Blessed One said, if I bring the Israelites to the Land now, each will immediately take up his field and his vineyard, and they will not engage in Torah study! Rather, I will lead them about in the wilderness for forty years, that they might eat the manna and drink water from the well, and the Torah might be absorbed in their bodies. Rabbi Shimon ben Yohai therefore said that the Torah was not given for study but to those who eat manna (*Mekhilta de-Rabbi Yishmael, Beshalah, Petihta*).

A constant motif throughout the generations, the desert period eventually came to represent the ideal of complete devotion to Torah study. Rabbi Jonathan Eybeschuetz offered the following colorful description (1690–1764), based on the above midrash:

> It was not so with the righteous generation of the desert, who ate manna and neither hungered nor worried, for delicate bread was proffered to them day by day, and a child could lead them to collect an omer a head, every man according to his eating, without difficulty, effort or care. And the food was in perfect harmony with the constitutions of those who ate it. It would undergo no constitutional change but would be absorbed directly into the organs, for it would separate into blood and other corporeal elements according to their respective accidents (dispositions) and properties (qualities). There was no need even to excrete waste, and time remained wholly consecrated to God, without impediment or disturbance. And so it was said: "The Torah was not given but to those who eat manna (*Ya'arot Devash*, 2, 16).

The memory of these ideal conditions, enjoyed by the Israelites in the desert, was eventually translated into a normative ideal. It is right and proper that a student—for the sake of Torah study and love of God—

ignore worldly concerns and even responsibility toward his children and household. In this sense, Torah students were expected to be "stout-hearted". We thus find in the commentary of Rabbi Elijah of Vilna (the Gaon; 1720–1797) on *Proverbs* 23:30:

A man of valor is stout of heart in his perfect faith, observing the commandments always and studying the Torah day and night, though he has no bread or clothing in his home, and his children and members of his household cry out to him: provide for us, sustain and support us; and he pays no attention to them whatsoever and does not tremble at their voices ... for all that he loves is as naught before his love for God and his Torah.

The next step in the development of the ethos of Torah study based on the relationship between study and material conditions, was a revolutionary one, taken by the great disciple of the Gaon of Vilna, Rabbi Hayim of Volozhin (1749–1821). Rabbi Hayim of Volozhin should be credited with the creation, in the 19th century, of the "Torah world": the constellation of the Lithuanian yeshivot, representing the *mitnaged* (anti-Hassidic) ethos of Torah study, that persists to this day. The revolution was in essence, an ideological-theological one, based on mystical thought (with older roots, beyond the scope of the present discussion). Henceforth, it is not ideal conditions without material concerns, represented by the desert generation, that ensures Torah study, but Torah study that ensures idyllic existence without material-financial worries. What is more, Torah study guarantees existence itself. Rabbi Hayim of Volozhin developed this approach in his classic treatise, *Nefesh Ha-hayim*, which was to become the canonical work of the Lithuanian yeshivot. This work, like the revolutionary and remarkable undertaking of establishing the Yeshivah of Volozhin, was supposed to provide an appropriate response to the threat posed to the world of Torah and Jewish tradition. The threat, in the eyes of Rabbi Hayim of Volozhin, was that of the Hassidic Movement, which had changed the face of accepted Jewish values and jeopardized the Torah world. Hassidism, dominated by the ideal of *devekut* ("communion with God"), espoused a religious and social ethos that undermined intellectual-elitist Torah scholarship. The Hassidim argued that *devekut* and spiritual ascent were difficult to achieve through dialectic study of the Talmud. Although the obligation to study Torah is an important one, constant and prolonged study can also distance one from the *devekut* experience. Rabbi Menahem Mendel of Peremyshlany thus recommended that Torah students "rest a little from their studies", that they might be free to engage in the spiritual exertions required to achieve *devekut*. It is obviously easier to attain a state of *devekut* reading *Psalms* or ethical and devotional works than by profound study of the Talmud and its commentaries. Indeed Rabbi Hayim of Volozhin complains in his *Nefesh Hahayim* that such circles "set the main part of study each day in books of devotion and ethics … because these works impassion the heart … and the crown of Torah lies abandoned in a corner … and what shall become of the Torah?". (For a more complete picture, see Immanuel Etkes, *Tenu'at Hahasidut Bereshitah* and the second chapter in Rabbi *Israel Salanter and the Musar Movement*). To Hayim of Volozhin, the desert generation indeed represented the ideal reality he sought to recreate:

> And the generation of the desert were privileged daily to eat heavenly bread at an exalted table, and their clothing showed no signs of wear, and they had no need to earn their livelihood in any way. All agree that they were not called doers of God's will unless they looked up with complete honesty and subjugated their hearts only to Torah and to divine service and fear of God, that day and night these things literally did not depart from their mouths, without turning aside at all, even for a brief moment to engage in earning a livelihood. And as the Rabbis of blessed memory said, the Torah was not given but to those who eat manna (*Nefesh Hahayim* 1:9).

Later however, Rabbi Hayim presents an audacious metaphysical cosmology, whereby Torah study itself ensures God's presence in the universe and thus, in turn, guarantees the world's continued existence. The vitality of the world, indeed of the universe, is contingent upon Torah study. Rabbi Hayim develops the kabbalistic idea of an isomorphic relationship between the human body and the soul, and the "body" of the cosmos and God—who is, as it were, the "soul" of the universe. Just as the soul may quit the body when the latter is denied nourishment, so God may, in the absence of "nourishment", quit the world—which would then, heaven forbid, cease to exist. This "nourishment" is none other than Torah study:

> Just as man's soul is bound to and preserved in his body by eating and drinking, without which it would separate and depart from the body, so the Godhead is bound to the worlds ... In order to sustain and preserve them, that his soul might not abhor them, *His will decreed that [this bond] would depend upon the Torah study, precept-observance and prayer of his chosen people*, and that without these things, He would remove His Godhead from them, and they would instantly return to nothingness ... And so, in this vein, it is written in *Midrash Tehilim* (on *Ps.* 103) that just as the soul neither eats nor drinks, so too God neither eats nor drinks. The midrash specifically mentions eating and drinking above other pleasures, teaching us that although the soul itself does not eat or drink, the essence of the bond that makes soul and body as one ... nevertheless depends upon the eating and drinking of the body. So it is [with God], although certainly the Godhead of the one and infinite Lord, blessed be He ... does not eat or drink ... Indeed the essence of God's bond with the worlds, *is as one, like man in every particular and all the organs dedicated to eating; and His will decreed that it should depend upon the good deeds of His holy people. And that is the significance of eating and drinking in the worlds, to nourish and sustain them* and increase the power of their holiness and light through their bond with God, in keeping with His sublime will. All is contingent upon the deed of the chosen people ... that [the worlds] might be worthy of receiving the outpouring of divine light and increased holiness, *like the food that adds strength to the body and refines it* ... And this is the meaning of the saying of the Sages of blessed memory (*Midrash Zuta Shir Hashirim* [Buber], 1,15) "Israel gives sustenance to its Father in heaven" (*Nefesh Hahayim*, 2,6; the emphases are mine).

In this cosmology, Rabbi Hayim of Volozhin lays a heavy responsibility upon the shoulders of every Torah student for the physical existence of the world. Henceforth, one who studies does not do so for himself and his own soul, but the essence of his studies is in fact devotion to others, out of altruistic concern for the welfare of the world. It thus comes as no surprise that the philosopher Emmanuel Levinas (1906–1995), whose ethical approach is rooted in man's infinite duty and responsibility toward the other and toward the world as a whole, found his own thoughts reflected in these passages of *Nefesh Hahayim*, and praised them (in the final chapter of *Nine Talmudic Readings*).

On the other hand, it is easy to see how such a theological-metaphysical approach can serve as a tool of the educational and social ideology of the yeshivah world, justifying their demand for financial support from the state. The giver-receiver relationship is reversed here. It is they who afford security and ensure the material well-being of their environment, and their contribution is infinitely greater than that which society gives them in return.

This approach has inspired many halakhic rulings and responsa regarding the relationship between means of material support and those who study Torah. One expression of this Weltanschauung can be observed in the following responsum by Rabbi Ovadiah Yosef, who was asked to decide the following case: "A student who desires to study Torah and wishes to transfer from an ordinary school to a yeshivah where Torah is studied exclusively throughout the day, and his parents adamantly insist that he transfer to a yeshivah high school, must he obey his parents, due to the commandment 'honor thy father and mother'? (*Yehaveh Da'at* 5:56).

Rabbi Yosef dismisses the student's obligation to obey his parents, citing the ethos of "those who eat manna", and promises that his material well-being will be assured, if his intentions are truly for the sake of heaven, for:

> The righteous shall live by his faith and those who trust in God will suffer no want. And of this they said in *Midrash Tanhuma*, the Torah was not given but to those who eat manna—these are the Torah scholars whose Torah study is their trade, whose only true desire is the Torah, from which their eyes do not depart day and night … and it is they who are granted the crown of Torah. And so the Rabbis said in the tractate of *Beitzah* (15b): God

said, my son, adhere to me and believe in me and I will repay you—for God's support is commensurate with the faith one has in Him. Rabbi Nehorai therefore said, I am abandoning all crafts in the world and will teach my son nothing but Torah. But one whose trust is not strong, and his heart worries and wavers, cannot place his trust in the miraculous.

[And thus in conclusion]:
A student who desires to study Torah, may go to study in a yeshivah where Torah is studied all hours of the day, even if this goes against the wishes of his parents who want him to study in a yeshivah high school. And the obligation to honor one's father and mother does not apply here, for the obligation to study Torah is greater than honoring one's parents (*ibid.*).

B.

The image that arises from the biblical text itself however—in *Shelah Lekha* and the adjacent portions—regarding the relationship between the Israelites and God, and between the Israelites and their leader Moses, is in fact far from flattering. The picture that emerges is one of lack of faith and lack of trust. We find a blatant example of this in the Israelites' hysterical response to the report presented by the spies:
And all the congregation lifted up their voice, and cried; and the people wept that night. And all the children of Israel murmured against Moses and against Aaron; and the whole congregation said unto them: "Would that we had died in the land of Egypt! or would we had died in this wilderness! And wherefore doth the Lord bring us unto this land, to fall by the sword? Our wives and our little ones will be a prey; were it not better for us to return into Egypt?" And they said one to another: "Let us make a captain, and let us return into Egypt" (14:1–4).

Nahmanides, in his commentary on the Pentateuch, sees the Israelites' forty years of wandering in the desert as a forerunner of the period of exile that would follow later in history. The night on which the people cried (*ibid.* 1), was the night of the ninth of Ab, the eve of the destruction of the Temple. That is to say that the seeds of our future exile had already been sown in the desert. The desert period is thus the formative memory of the exile narrative: "The duration [of their exile] was forty years, as a result of the sin of the spies; for all of those forty years were an affliction to them, as it is written 'And thou shalt remember all the way which the Lord thy God hath led thee these forty years in the wilderness, that He might afflict thee' (*Deut.* 8:2), and so 'And He afflicted thee, and suffered thee to hunger' (*ibid.* 3). And it was to them a complete exile in a foreign land, wherein were only serpents, fiery serpents, and scorpions" (Nahmanides, *Ex.* 12:42).

In many midrashim, the Rabbis lay the blame for the tragic unfolding of events during the desert period, not only with the spies themselves, but mainly with the "mixed multitude". Although the "mixed multitude" (*erev rav*) is mentioned only once in the Pentateuch, in the portion of *Beshalah* (*Ex.* 12:38), the concept has "enjoyed" a prominent place in our collective memory—to this very day—as the cause of our prolonged exile and the slowness of redemption to come. So we find in the Midrash: "'And the rabble that was among them fell a lusting'— What is the rabble? Rabbi Shimon bar Abba and Rabbi Shimon ben Menasya offered explanations. One said: these are the strangers who came up with them from Egypt and gathered to them, as it is written 'And a mixed multitude went up also with them' (*Ex.* 12:38)" (*Numbers Rabbah* 15).

The Sages of the Talmud and the Midrash inflate their presence to incredible proportions (at least twice as many as the Israelites themselves), as in the following midrash: "And a mixed multitude went up also with them—One hundred and twenty myriads, according to Rabbi Yishmael; Rabbi Akiva said two hundred and forty myriads; Rabbi Yonatan said three hundred and sixty myriads" (*Yalkut Shimoni, Bo*). The "mixed multitude" has been a constant presence among the Jews, throughout the generations. It is identified, for example, in the wicked or the rich whose hearts are indifferent to the suffering of the poor—as in the following talmudic tale:

> Rabbi Natan bar Abba said: The wealthy of Babylon merit Gehenna. As in the case of Shabbetai bar Marinos, who arrived in Babylon and asked for work, and they would give him none;

food, and they would give him none. He said, these are of the mixed multitude, as it is written, "and show thee mercy, and have compassion upon thee" (*Deut.* 13:18). If one shows compassion to others—know that he is of the seed of our father Abraham. If one does not show compassion—know that he is not of the seed of our father Abraham (*Beitzah* 32b).

The "mixed multitude" continued to play a role in various works of the Kabbalah and the popular *musar* literature, as responsible for the great length of the exile and the fact that the Messiah has not yet come. As in the Talmudic account above, various individuals or social groups against whom it has been expedient to direct the arrows of blame and responsibility throughout history, have been identified with the "mixed multitude". The collective memory thus preserved the "mixed multitude" and did not allow it to sink into the oblivion of a distant past. Its constantly changing presence played an important role in improving Jewish society's self-image, serving practically as a scapegoat. Finally, it is worth noting that the presence of the "mixed multitude" has enjoyed a renaissance in our generation, recognized by some in contemporary secular Jews. This recognition converged with the discussion in certain circles of how one should relate to such Jews. On the basis of the identification of the secular public with the "mixed multitude", some adopted an extremist and uncompromising position, while others adopted a more empathic and conciliatory approach. Both of these positions draw upon metaphysical-kabbalistic sources.

We are thus witness once again to the many faces and dynamic vitality of collective memory, and stand in awe of the fascinating ways in which it affects our religious and national culture.

Avinoam Rosenak

Korah

Are All the Congregation Holy?
A Study of the Philosophies of *A. I. Kook* and *Yeshayahu Leibowitz*

And they assembled themselves together against Moses and against Aaron, and said unto them: "Ye take too much upon you, seeing all the congregation are holy, every one of them, and the Lord is among them; wherefore then lift ye up yourselves above the assembly of the Lord?" (*Numbers* 16:3).

A footnote in one of Yeshayahu Leibowitz' books, describes a meeting that took place in the 1930s, between Leibowitz— then a young student—and an elderly Rabbi A.I. Kook, at the Rabbi's home in Jerusalem. The two discussed the relationship between *Torat emet* ("true Torah") as the Kabbalah is known—to which Leibowitz was completely opposed—and the thought of the greatest of the medieval Jewish philosophers, Maimonides. The antithetical views expressed by the two men in that room at that time, represented positions that have divided Jewish thought for centuries.

Who were these two figures and how can we enter their spiritual and philosophical worlds? I believe the story of Korah and his company affords a key to understanding their respective philosophies. The portion of *Korah* tells of the outbreak of the first rebellion in the Israelite camp. The Bible describes the source of the dispute:

Now Korah, the son of Izhar, the son of Kohath, the son of Levi, with Dathan and Abiram, the sons of Eliab, and On, the son of Peleth, sons of Reuben, took men; and they rose up in face of Moses, with certain of the children of Israel, two hundred and fifty men; they were princes of the congregation, the elect men of the assembly, men of renown; and they assembled themselves together against Moses and against Aaron, and said unto them: "Ye take too much upon you, seeing *all the congregation are holy, every one of them, and the Lord is among them*; wherefore then lift ye up yourselves above the assembly of the Lord?" And when Moses heard it, he fell upon his face (16:1–4).

What is the nature of Korah's argument, that "all the congregation are holy, every one of them, and the Lord is among them"? Does it mean that all heard the voice of God at Sinai (as Rashi explains)? That all first-born are worthy of serving in the Sanctuary, and not only the Levites (as Rabbi Bahye, Hizkuni and Sforno explain)? Or did they wish to abolish the intermediary role of the Priests, who stood between the people and its God (*Gur Aryeh*)? I would like to address a deeper interpretation of the dispute however; one that incorporates all of the above explanations.

The incident of Korah and his company can be seen as part of a conflict that extended well beyond the event itself. The entire rebellion can be viewed as a dispute regarding the meaning of the concept of "holiness"; a dispute that persists to this day, with clear ramifications for our public and religious-cultural lives. The opposing camps in this dispute are led by the two figures mentioned above: Rabbi A.I. Kook and Yeshayahu Leibowitz.

What then is holiness? How can it be defined? Let us look at two well-known approaches to this concept:

A. Sociological-transcendent holiness: According to the socio-logical approach, "holiness" is always a product of normative legal or ritual action that distinguishes between a particular object and all other objects. For example, if one wishes to sanctify a particular room, ac-cording to this model one would have to prohibit or restrict access to the room, by certain people at certain times. The sanctification of time requires that it be differentiated from other times, setting it aside for the performance of certain definitive actions. How does one sanctify a book? By obligating oneself and one's community to stand every time the book is brought into the room, by kissing it every time it passes, by not placing other books on top of it, by fasting when it falls. That is how its holiness (like that of a Torah scroll) is established. A "holy person" would be one who is inaccessible, strange and apart, different in dress or hairstyle, in behavior; a recluse or one who resides far from others, a desert-dweller with an unusual occupation, approachable only with great difficulty. All of these things provide fertile ground for the development of a myth of a "holy man". Sanctification is thus always contingent upon a certain set norms applied to the thing or time we wish to sanctify.

According to this approach, we may speak of holiness on two distinct planes. The first of these is the cultural plane, in which the concept of God plays no role. On this plane, we do not speak of "holiness per se"; all is the fruit of normative action that society or the individual apply to the object they wish to sanctify. At the same time, no culture can do without areas of holiness. For the sake of their own existence, culture and community require loci of holiness that express their fundamental principles.

One could argue however, that this model functions on a religious plane as well. We might say in this context that the "holy", in the full sense of the word is merely the "other" or the divine, the transcendent, the holiness of which stems from its infinite remoteness from everything in the world. God is "apart", and as such, is the paradigm or prototype of the "holy". Henceforth, nothing may be sanctified but in *imitation* of the "holy", and nothing may be *holy* in its own right, but merely *sanctified*. Sanctification is only achieved by emulating the "holy", which will always remain unparalleled. This approach is generally found in philosophical and religious-philosophical works of the Middle Ages, and to a certain extent in the Modern Era as well.

B. Immanent-ontological holiness: The immanent approach is completely different. Holiness, according to this model, pertains to the inherent uniqueness of space and time. An advocate of this approach would argue that a "holy person" is not the product of a normative process within a given socio-cultural context. A holy person is indeed visited by the divine spirit and the divine presence dwells within her/him. There is a profound qualitative difference between a "place" charged with divinity and a place from which the divine is absent. A "holy tree" is distinguished by the miracles effected by its force. So too, the energy within the "holy book", emanates from the forces within its letters and "crownlets". The "holy land" is no less than the "gate of heaven", and the spirit and wisdom of the "holy man" reflect the infinite presence of the divine. Holiness results from the descent of the divine into the physical world, which transforms the quality of the "matter" that it permeates, so that it differs completely from "matter" that lacks divine presence.

One who stands before the "holy" thus feels compelled to *respond* with norms capable of *expressing* the uniqueness of the situation. Normative action does not create the holiness, but arises from an understanding of the nature of the event and the uniqueness of the object. If one were to choose not to respond in a normative fashion, the object would not lose its holiness, but the man would be shamed, having failed to grasp the significance of the presence before him. In other words, one who stands before the holy does not create it, but merely recognizes its presence.

Combined with the monotheistic belief in God's infinity this approach inevitably leads to the realization that "there is no place free of it" (i.e. the divine presence). The question thus arises, how should one conduct her/himself in the knowledge that she or he is perpetually in the presence of God? This approach and the questions it raises lie at the heart of kabbalistic and Hassidic thought.

Leibowitz: Korah, Immanence and Idolatry

Yeshayahu Leibowitz viewed these models as the key to understanding the dispute with Korah and his company. Leibowitz suggests that this dispute represented a radical departure from the concept of holiness imparted by Moses, and elucidated by Maimonides. Leibowitz' preferred the sociological-transcendent conception of holiness, as found in the chapter concerning the commandment that the Children of Israel make "fringes in the corners of their garments": "and do all my commandments, and be holy unto your God" (15:40). You wish to be holy? Do my commandments! Holiness is a function of commitment, action, loyalty and a decision to accept the yoke of heaven. That is not how Korah and his company understood the concept however. They were the first in the Israelite camp to express the immanent-ontological approach to holiness. They held the reins of the rebellion ("Now Korah … with Dathan and Abiram … took men"), and claimed that "all the congregation are holy, every one of them". In the words of Leibowitz:

> The difference between these two types of holiness is the difference between faith and idolatry. The holiness mentioned in the chapter of the fringes is not a fact, but a *challenge*. It does

not say "you are holy", but presents a demand ... "*be* holy". In the religious consciousness of Korah and his company however, "all the congregation are holy, every one of them"—holiness is something we are *given*, something *bestowed* upon us (Leibowitz, *He'arot Leparshiyot Hashavua*, p. 96).

Leibowitz' unequivocal assertion and dichotomous approach pertain not only to the portion of *Korah*, but address a fundamental trend in Jewish thought.

According to Leibowitz, Judaism does not promise—nor should it promise—anything to believers. A believer "is required to take a great task upon himself" (*ibid.* 97) and to expect nothing in return. Abraham—the father who was prepared to sacrifice his son—is thus the quintessential representative of Jewish culture, throughout Leibowitz' works. The binding of Isaac in fact calls into question the very concept of the divine promise. It would have left Abraham without issue; contrary to functional logic. Abraham is therefore, in Leibowitz' opinion, a paragon of faith. His act gives extreme and prominent expression to the nature of Jewish belief, as a decision to submit to God's will, regardless of the consequences for man himself. It is a demanding view, based on a system of normative precepts, without any promise of heteronymous (i.e. external) reward. It is this framework and system of normative loyalty that truly defines "Judaism". Christianity on the other hand, perceives God as a sacrifice made for the sake of man and his needs. Judaism, according to Leibowitz, is not a religion of "values and beliefs" or a "giving religion", in the Christian sense. The latter is "an aid to the satisfaction of man's spiritual needs and emotional doubts; its goal is man. One who accepts this religion is one who is saved" (Leibowitz, *Am Yehudi Umedinat Yisrael*, p. 23). Judaism is a "religion of precepts", "a demanding religion that imposes duties and responsibilities and makes man an instrument of a goal that transcends him ... One who accepts this religion is one who serves God simply because He should be served" (*ibid.*). The distinction is between a culture focused on the sacrifice of the believer for the sake of God, and a culture focused on the crucifixion of God for the sake of man.

Leibowitz' argument against immanent holiness, nonnormative Christian belief and the incident of Korah and his company, is one and the same: all of these religious approaches release man from responsibility for his actions. They impose no task, obligation or effort. With regard to Korah, Leibowitz' asserts: "He is absolutely certain that he has already attained holiness. We have learned, throughout history, that even a scoundrel may take pride in the fact that he is a member of a holy people" (Leibowitz, *He'arot Leparshiyot Hashavua*, p. 97).

It is thus easy to see how, according to Leibowitz, the dispute with Korah and his company is not just a matter of historical interest, but in fact continues to this day—an idea we may illustrate with words of the Midrash, "the sons of Korah did not die" (*Bamidbar Rabbah* 18:20). The sons of Korah are alive and well, and they place their faith in the holiness imparted to Israel. They believe that they have already attained the level toward which man is commanded to strive in the passages of the *Shema* (Leibowitz, *ibid.*).

Leibowitz' remarks are aimed, as he explains, at philosophers and leaders such as Rabbi Judah Halevi, Rabbi Judah Loew (Maharal) of Prague, Rabbi A.I. Kook and David Ben-Gurion. All of these men adopted "the Judaism of Korah, which is very comfortable: every Jew may glory in his membership in the 'Chosen People', which is inherently holy—without incurring any sort of responsibility". This approach, claims Leibowitz, empties "Judaism of its religious content", replacing it with "racist chauvinism" (Leibowitz, *Emunah, Historiya Ve'arakhim*, pp. 116–117). This is not the case, he believes, with Maimonides or Rabbi Joseph Karo (author of the *Shulhan Arukh*). The latter begins his code of Jewish law with the following: "One must summon his strength like a lion to rise in the morning for the service of his creator" (*OH* 1:1)—recognizing that the precepts do not represent a comfortable reality, but a demand we may never be able to fulfill. We are nevertheless charged with the duty to endeavor, each and every morning, to do so.

Clearly, argues Leibowitz, "What is said of the holiness of the people applies equally to the 'holiness of the land'. Raising the land itself to a level of holiness—is blatant idolatry", for:

There is no holiness in the world but sanctification through the precepts ("who hast sanctified us with thy precepts"). And there-

in lies the difference between idolatrous religiosity and true religiosity. Idolatrous religiosity considers the land itself holy; and
I know that this idolatry is greedily eating away at us today …
There is true religiosity however, the meaning of which is: we
are commanded to fulfill a number of obligations with regard to
this land … Holy is only the One who is thrice-called holy. Apart
from Him, nothing else is holy—neither in history nor in nature
nor in man. Things may be sanctified however, through divine
service (Leibowitz, *ibid.* pp. 117–118).

Rabbi Kook: The Blindness of Sociological Ideology
It is no coincidence that Leibowitz and Rabbi Kook clashed specifically in this matter. Rabbi kook was undoubtedly the 20th century's
most charismatic representative of the immanent view. His approach
gave rise to the social cultural and political movement (*Gush Emunim*—
"Bloc of the Faithful"), rooted in the immanent-ontological principle;
much to Leibowitz' chagrin.

Let us take a closer look at Rabbi Kook's philosophy. Here too, I
will use the episode of Korah and his company as a pathway to his Weltanschauung. Indeed, it is impossible to understand Rabbi Kook's work
without the immanent-ontological rationale, on which he also bases
his interpretation of the Korah affair. This time, Korah's sin is not his
immanent-ontological approach to holiness (as Leibowitz maintains),
but his sociological approach and his rejection of the immanent model.
We find two references to Korah in the works of Rabbi Kook. In both
of these place he relates to Korah typologically (i.e. as the prototype of
a philosophical position)—as does Leibowitz—rather than offering a
direct interpretation of the event described in the biblical text. Korah's
sin, according to Kook, lay in his attempt to eliminate the boundaries
of immanent holiness and to decentralize it; on the basis of his rational,
"sociological" argument, he sought to extend holiness to broader circles
than those dictated by the ontological approach.

The immanent-ontological model, according to Rabbi Kook, is what
affords the Priests their separate status. Only they are able to perform
the sacrifices and other Temple rites, and it is only through them that the
Temple service can arouse "divine thought in such a fashion as to render

its life the life of all things" (Rabbi A.I. Kook, *Shemonah Kevatzim*, vol.3, 91:33). Confusing the role of the Priests and that of the other Israelites will spoil the divine service: "A common man who draws near [to perform the holy rites] will open the conduit of this thought-life in a spoiled, twisted and harmful manner that will ultimately result in abstinence from divine life. And this abstinence is a general abstinence, affecting the entire universe" (*ibid.*). In other words, divine service performed by one who seeks to step into the shoes of those chosen to perform such service, will fail, and its spiritual and cultural consequences will be perverse. It is not service in the Temple that makes a Priest a Priest, but his basic-ontological fitness for the role. Those who seek to replace the Priests merely disrupt the conduit of divine service and spoil the entire universe, which depends upon the level and quality of this service. The compatibility between the divine service and the original priestly caste is thus immanent. The priesthood is not based on any sociological distinction, but on a state of ontological compatibility, and is limited to a well-defined and closed circle. It is this that Korah and his company refused to understand. They believed everyone could be compatible, and thus "Korah, who sought to uproot the foundation of priesthood, damaged the foundation of the world, the 'middle bar' of the cosmos, and the earth rose up against him, so that this tendency itself would come to bear witness to the life of divine thought" (*ibid.*).

The same fault is ascribed to Korah in Rabbi Kook's second reference. Here however, the frame of reference is broader. Korah's position is associated not only with the difference between the priesthood and remainder of the Israelites, but with the difference between the Jewish People and the nations as well. Here too the distinction is immanent and ontological, and Rabbi Kook's words reflect the fact that they were written at the height of the First World War. He identifies among the nations a tendency toward "the foundation of wickedness, which divaricates into idolatry and sectarianism" (*Orot* 32–34; *Shemonah Kevatzim* 143:45). It is important to remember that these words (published, as mentioned, during the war) create a certain tension with the general tenor of his work.

What is the nature of this tension, and what role does the figure of Korah play in it? According to Rabbi Kook's description, there is wickedness that cannot be given a place within holiness. This distance and regimentation—that must be maintained—disheartens wickedness, which seeks every possible way to attach itself to holiness. It does so not for the sake of deep personal change, but in pursuit of its own negative ends (*ibid.*). Rabbi Kook thus explains the rejection of Cain's offering. Although Cain truly wished to draw near to the divine, his efforts were repulsed, because God recognized the murderous intent that lay behind them—which indeed he acted upon as soon as he discovered that his offering had been rejected. In other words, *the murder of Abel was not the result of the rejection of Cain's offering but its cause*. According to Rabbi Kook, these tendencies are inherent to the "sectarian" movement (i.e. Christianity), which seeks—like Korah—to undermine the unique character of Israel and the special status of the Sages, based on the sociological approach to holiness, which denies Israel any ontological distinction:

The sole purpose [of Christian sectarianism] is not to sanctify will, life, the material world and its inner essence, by means of the order established by God for that end, *founded upon Israel, the holy nation, that many peoples might draw upon its offshoots—each nation according to its qualities, morality and natural preparation*, historical and racial background, education, geography and economic situation, with all of the accompanying social and individual qualities (*Orot, ibid.*; *Shemonah Kevatzim, ibid.*).

Alongside its condemnation of wickedness, this passage also includes an assertion regarding the role of Israel vis-à-vis the other nations. This assertion however—which also appears in Rabbi Kook's prewar writings—appears to contradict the spirit of his condemnation of sectarianism. These words seem to imply that all facets of existence—"in the absence of a rift between actions and opinions, between mind and imagination; and even the discernible rifts"—unite under "supernal illumination" (*Orot Hakodesh* 2, 411; *Shemonah Kevatizim* 1, par.459:90).

All [thoughts] that arise in the world from the beginning of time to the end of days, *all* are but fractions of aspirations, fractions of recognitions, that eventually combine to form a single whole.

Until perfecting form comes and *gathers all* into its complete perfection, they comprise both good and *evil*, truth and *falsehood, impurity* and purity, the holy and the *profane*. When the light of total unification appears however … then *all* will be recognized for good, for truth, purity and holiness. A world that is wholly Sabbath, wholly good (*ibid*. par.286:104).

In the divine world *all* aspires to the complete good, the wholly perfect, and *all* our intentions are not partial, but universal (*ibid*. par.324:115).

The Jewish People is unique, according to Rabbi Kook, in its spiritual ability to sanctify the *totality* of life and to reveal the inner essence of creation that lies within divine service. Only they can perform this service, and it is an immanent quality that cannot be acquired. Rabbi Kook points this out, not to advocate insularity and withdrawal into the particular. On the contrary, he claims that only by maintaining its separate identity can Israel develop the culture that will, in the future, serve as a source for the universal, in all its variety. We will explain with the help of the following metaphor: The Jewish People is not one of the colors of the cultural spectrum; its role is to create the ray of white light from which the hues of cultural diversity will disperse. Only the Jewish People can create this ray of white light, and any stranger who attempts to do so in their place will spoil it. The process itself is one of separation, on the basis of immanent and ontological premises. Its tendency however is *universal*. Some, like Korah, have failed to grasp the crucial importance of this separation:

Envy among men has done the work of Korah against Israel. *The cry that all the congregation are holy, every one of them, and the Lord is among them showed contempt for the very essence of holiness, for the spiritual ascent and inner preparation necessary* until the holy is truly established in life … You are all holy, all sons of God, there is no difference between peoples, no holy or chosen people, all men are equally holy. This is mankind's 'Korahism', the new jealousy with which it is afflicted, from which the earth reeleth to and fro like a drunken man … and the transgression thereof is heavy upon it, and it shall fall, and not rise again (*ibid.*).

Racism, "A Light unto the Nations" and the Limits of Accepting the "Other"

When Leibowitz described the difference between the divergent positions, he claimed that the uniqueness of the people, according to the immanent approach to holiness, is not acquired through deeds and is independent of any decision or *a priori* commitment—and is therefore particularist and racist. Contrary to Leibowitz' assertion however, the position represented by Rabbi Kook does not develop along chauvinistic and racist lines. Its intention is not that Israel shut itself in its particularist shell and forsake the rest of creation. It does not even purport to conquer and bring about the disappearance of the "other". On the contrary, the ray of white light seeks not to conceal the variegation of the colors of the rainbow, but to *sustain* the entire spectrum and serve as a *medium* for their pluralistic development. These universalistic ideas are however, accompanied by an immanent ontological worldview, without which—Rabbi Kook would argue—they could never be realized. Again, this is a racist premise; claiming that a specific group inherently possesses unique, otherwise unattainable qualities. It is not racist however, in the sense that it does not negate the "other", but rather seeks to serve as a medium or source of energy for the variegated development of all peoples and their cultures.

Nevertheless, Rabbi Kook's words exhibit, as noted above, a deep inner tension; the result of a certain ambivalence with regard to the "other". On the one hand, they recognize the need for the other—*any other*—as a culture that draws its strength from the Jewish People, and of which it is a positive outgrowth. On the other hand, as we have seen, Rabbi Kook points to tendencies of "wickedness, which divaricates into idolatry and sectarianism", seeking only "to defile and pollute" the holy. He sharply condemns such wickedness, and finds no room for it in his world.

The positive facets of the other are to be found, as noted" in Rabbi Kook's prewar writings, in which we also find the *duty* incumbent upon those who possess immanent ontological uniqueness; a *duty* that requires *action* and not just a sense of chosenness—contrary to Leibow-itz' characterization of this approach.

Can this tension within the writings of Rabbi Kook be resolved? Even "sectarianism" is, after all, part of the universe that will one day find its place in the whole that aspires to the complete good. His words can perhaps be reconciled by taking a closer look at the concept of "holiness". According to Rabbi Kook, holiness expresses the ascendancy of the divine in the human spirit. Although this ascendancy is achieved at the expense of man's physical nature, it is not meant to eliminate that nature, but to elevate it to its "intellectual purpose". This harmonious approach *makes it incumbent* upon man to behave with charity, love and forbearance. Conversely, "hatred, stringency and pedantry result when God is forgotten and the holy light wanes" (*Orot Hakodesh* 3,317; *Shemonah Kevatzim* 1, par. 346:120). We are thus far from free to do as we please. This approach clearly distinguishes between observance and transgression, normative action and "destruction of the plants" (apostasy).

Holiness is thus all-embracing, and the "other" [of non-Jewish culture] is a desirable outgrowth of the Jewish world. At the same time however, the activities of the other express the positive when—in their own fashion—they express charity, love and forbearance. When they express hatred and destruction however, they do not draw upon that holiness, and are repulsed.

According to Leibowitz, the positive and the normative can be found only in the obligations of the *Shulhan Arukh* and Maimonides' *Mishneh Torah*—i.e. in the world of Halakhah. According to Rabbi Kook, on the other hand, our obligation is to develop a harmonious and broad-spirited worldview. Man must gain the ability to broaden his heart to include "all chambers and crevices of reality"; and sin is "all moral destruction, in deed and in action, in character and in disposition". These norms, Rabbi Kook argues, "are a great internal torment to all aspects of the soul". Such sins require *repentance*, the essence of which is the healing of "all rifts" (*Orot Hateshuvah* 8, 7; *Olat Re'iyah* 2,364; *Shmonah Kevatzim* 370:126).

What are the Limits of Community

The complexity of Rabbi Kook's approach to the "other" of the nations of the world is echoed in his approach to increasing diversity within the Jewish People. To better understand this matter, let us return to the comparison between Leibowitz and Rabbi Kook. Leibowitz, who vehemently condemned Korah and his immanent approach, claimed that holiness is exclusively the fruit of normative commitment. Judaism is therefore "an institutional religion … in the sense that these institutions—*the precepts*—are themselves the religion, and *it [the religion] does not exist at all beyond these institutions*" (*Yahadut, Am Yehudi Umedinat Yisrael*, p. 14). Again: the precepts and the precepts alone, are the only possible basis for realizing and expressing the uniqueness of the Jewish People within a distinctive religious framework. The difference between Judaism and other cultural groups lies, according to Leibowitz, exclusively in the Torah and the precepts. "We find that it is not the beliefs and opinions that determined the identity of Judaism, but the *religious act* that has sustained its continuity" Thus, any religious approach within Judaism that did not maintain the normative continuity, was swiftly ejected. This is the distinction, in Leibowitz' opinion, between Hassidism—"that did not set out to create a new Halakhah, nor did it do so" and therefore remained a part of Judaism—and Sabbateanism that "marred the precepts" and therefore "separated from the body [of Judaism]" (*ibid.* p. 15).

Rabbi Kook's approach (the Korahism of which Leibowitz accused a number of figures, including Kook) is completely different. Although, as we have seen, immanent-ontological chosenness also entails obligation, this obligation sometimes overrides that of the practical precepts— for the sake of *a higher form of action*:

> Extraordinary individuals, inclined toward knowledge of God, must immerse themselves in it more than in any other branches of Torah and wisdom. And they may not turn away from their high calling for any reason in the world—even if it seems to them that by immersing themselves in knowledge of God they may neglect some aspects of the practical precepts and knowledge of the Torah, or that they may not fulfill their worldly obligations. For all perfection in practice and in Torah (study) is

but a guide [or: a means] to bring man to that supreme quality of pursuing knowledge of God, and once man has attained this sublime quality, he must not forsake profound holiness in order to engage in superficial holiness (*Shemonah Kevatizim* 1, par.80,25–26)

The precepts are thus merely a means by which one may attain higher "knowledge of God", i.e. a harmonious worldview. And if, at a given moment in time, the desire to know the cosmos as a variegated divine whole fails to coincide with the observance of one precept or another, one must not be deterred!

This position receives frequent and even radical expression in the writings of Rabbi Kook, which his students withheld from the general public for many years. We must stress however, that this spiritual current was never intended to undermine the halakhic system. Rabbi Kook envisaged a return to the normative; this time however, in a spirit of total acceptance. We may return to the precepts, but we must first abandon the sense of duty, subservience and conflict with nature. It is interesting to note that these are the very same feelings that Leibowitz ascribes to his "paragon of faith". According to Leibowitz, one who accepts the precepts completely, experiencing only harmony and sublime joy in their observance—without distinguishing between his own desires and his commitment to God—is a self-worshiper, an idolater. Rabbi Kook on the other hand, believed that one may return to divine service through the precepts only after his soul has been enlightened and he has attained a sense of total communion with the supernal:

Surely by the supernal enlightenment of his soul, a soul truly immersed in divine light, all his pathways of knowledge will be expanded, and his heart will fill with the light of justice and the improvement of society; *so that he will find the great blessing and broadness of heart necessary to engage, with true holiness, in the practical aspects of the Torah and worldly affairs as well,* with great success—much greater than the success enjoyed by those immersed solely in practical affairs, who have not achieved the same level of true thirst for knowledge of God (*ibid.*)

What then was the nature of Korah's sin? I do not know. We have seen however, that Scripture is broad enough to sustain opposing views, as long as the exponents of such views remain devoted to its study and feel compelled to use it as a medium for the expression of their ideas.

Benjamin Lau

Hukat – This is the Statute of the Law

The Song of Moses, the Song of Miriam and the Song of the People –
Leadership in a Generation of Transition
*In the Thought of **Rabbi Yitzhak Meir Alter***

Then sang Israel this song: Spring up, O well—sing ye unto it. The well, which the princes digged, which the nobles of the people delved, with the sceptre, and with their staves. And from the wilderness to Mattanah; and from Mattanah to Nahaliel; and from Nahaliel to Bamoth; and from Bamoth to the valley that is in the field of Moab, by the top of Pisgah, which looketh down upon the desert (*Numbers* 21:17–20).

In the portion of *Hukat* we read about the transition of leadership from one generation to the next: nearly the entire old guard that had accompanied Israel from Egypt to the end of its desert wanderings, steps aside in favor of the younger generation. The natural deaths of Aaron and Miriam set the stage. The third and foremost leader, Moses, is punished, and prevented from entering the Promised Land. The three leaders' careers thus come to a close, but the end of Moses' tenure leaves a bad taste.

In the mid-19th century, a drama unfolded in the Hassidic court of Kotsk. There are a number of different accounts of the events of that Sabbath eve in the house of study of Rabbi Menahem Mendel of Kotsk, but they all agree on the fact that an outburst by the Rabbi against his disciples precipitated a period of zealous reclusion, during which time the Rabbi withdrew to the attic of his house, where he remained until his death (some twenty years later). Many of the disciples joined other Hassidic courts. Few remained loyal to their Rabbi. One of Rabbi Menahem Mendel's closest disciples was Rabbi Yitzhak Meir Alter Rothenberg. He was considered a great leader in his own right, and during the period of crisis strove to lead the community along a softer path that became known—following the death of the Rabbi of Kotsk—as the court of Ger.

Rabbi Yitzhak Meir's grandson, whom he raised as a son (following the death of his father, Rabbi Yitzhak Meir's son), succeeded his grandfather as head of the community of Ger, also publishing his grandfather's teachings in his book *Sefat Emet*.

I would like to examine the commentary of Rabbi Yitzhak Meir, founder of the Hassidic dynasty of Ger, on the Torah portion of *Hukat*, in an attempt to find some insight into his experiences regarding the leadership of his master, the Rabbi of Kotsk. His homily on *Hukat* is based on the juxtaposition of certain narrative elements (from the beginning of chapter 20 to the end of the portion): the death of Miriam, the lack of water and Moses' sin, and the Song of Israel at the well.

> And the children of Israel, even the whole congregation, came into the wilderness of Zin in the first month; and the people abode in Kadesh; and Miriam died there, and was buried there. And there was no water for the congregation; and they assembled themselves together against Moses and against Aaron. ... "Take the rod, and assemble the congregation, thou, and Aaron thy brother, and speak ye unto the rock before their eyes, that it give forth its water; and thou shalt bring forth to them water out of the rock; so thou shalt give the congregation and their cattle drink." ... And Moses lifted up his hand, and smote the rock with his rod twice; and water came forth abundantly, and the congregation drank, and their cattle. And the Lord said unto Moses and Aaron: "Because ye believed not in me, to sanctify me in the eyes of the children of Israel, therefore ye shall not bring this assembly into the land which I have given them" (*Num.* 20:1–12).

Many have questioned the lack of proportion between Moses' sin and the terrible punishment he received—never to enter the Land. In search of justification for Moses' punishment, commentators have let their imaginations run wild with regard to his sins: "Moses committed only one sin and the commentators heaped thirteen or more sins upon him, for each of them invented new sins of their own accord" (S.D. Luzzatto in his commentary on *Hukat*. An exhaustive summary of both earlier and later commentators can be found in N. Leibowitz, *Studies in*

Bamidbar). What all the commentaries have in common is the idea that to be punished, Moses had to have committed a sin.

Rabbi Yitzhak Meir, in *Sefat Emet*, takes a different approach. In essence, he claims that the issue here is not one of sin and punishment, but of a test and its results. He bases this conclusion on his understanding of the Song of Israel that follows the striking of the rock. The song appears in the context of a recapitulation of the events of Israel's wanderings in the desert. It is written, regarding one of the places in which the Israelites stopped: "And from thence to Beer; that is the well whereof the Lord said unto Moses: 'Gather the people together, and I will give them water.' Then sang Israel this song: Spring up, O well—sing ye unto it" (*ibid.* 21:16–17).

The verses refer to a place called "Beer", so named for the events surrounding God's commandment to Moses that he gather the people together and give them water. At that place however, Israel also burst into song: "Spring up, O well—sing ye unto it". Rabbi Yitzhak Meir notes the fact that the opening words of this song are reminiscent of the Song of the Sea (*Ex.* 15), with one, very significant difference: while the Song of the Sea begins "Then sang Moses and the children of Israel", the song here begins "Then sang Israel". Moses' absence is glaring. The *Sefat Emet* cites the following explanation offered by his grandfather, Rabbi Yitzhak Meir (the *Hidushei HaRim*):

> That is why Moses is not mentioned in this song, for it is at this point that a new generation truly arose; one that was not drawn to Moses' level of greatness, and that is why it is written "Because ye believed not in me, to sanctify me [in the eyes of the children of Israel], therefore ye shall not bring [this assembly into the land which I have given them]". God forbid that we say that this was simply a punishment meted out to Moses. Rather, it served to prove that these were not the leaders of the generation that would enter the Land of Israel. And Moses, as a result of his very greatness, did not see that the hearts of the Children of Israel would be so moved as to utter song here (*Sefat Emet, Bamidbar, Hukat*, 5638 [1878]).

He repeated the same idea in the year 5650 (1890), with a certain addition:

> And indeed Moses was on a higher level. But the Children of
> Israel were not drawn to his leadership, for the generation of
> those who were to enter the Land had begun. Had Moses been
> able to efface himself in leadership, seeking their counsel, he
> could have entered the Land of Israel. This was in fact proof that
> he was not prepared to assume that kind of leadership ... And
> the Song of the Sea stands out in the holy Torah, inasmuch as
> it is written differently [in the Torah scroll]. And this song does
> not stand out in the Torah, for it is a degree below, on a par with
> the Oral Law. And so in the words of the song—"Spring up,
> O well—sing ye unto it"—its force and inspiration come from
> below; while the essence of Moses' leadership was wholly from
> heaven.

I would like to take a closer look at the words of the *Hidushei HaRim* and try to explain them. The *Tosefta* gives vivid expression to the different styles of leadership affected by the three siblings of the House of Levi: "When Israel departed Egypt they were given three good officers, and these were Moses, Aaron and Miriam. By virtue of these [three] they were given three gifts: a well, a pillar of cloud and the manna. The well by virtue of Miriam, the pillar of cloud by virtue of Aaron and the manna by virtue of Moses" (*Tosefta Sotah* 11,8).

Moses' leadership came from above and was founded upon miracles. His main difficulty—one he bore with him throughout his life, from the Burning Bush to his final appearance before the people—lay in his limited power of speech: "I am not a man of words". The trust that he enjoyed stemmed from the people's clear knowledge that their leader possessed a direct connection with a heavenly force; with the Almighty. One might say that Moses was God's representative on Earth. The gift of the manna—that miraculous food—is emblematic of what Moses gave to Israel. In no way however, did his leadership draw upon the capacities of the people.

One of the most striking examples of Moses' attitude to the spiritual ability of the people can be found in the Song of the Sea. The Sages addressed the precise circumstances of the event (*ibid.* 6,2). It is written "Then sang Moses and the children of Israel", yet the song itself begins in the singular: "I will sing unto the Lord". Rabbi Akiva offers the following explanation:

> When the Israelites came up from the sea they wished to utter song; the holy spirit descended upon them and they sang. How did they sing? Like a child reading the *Hallel* [prayer] before its teacher, repeating each and every phrase after him. Moses said "I will sing unto the Lord" and Israel said "I will sing unto the Lord"; Moses said "The Lord is my strength and song" and Israel said "The Lord is my strength and song'."

This is the song of a charismatic leader who enraptures his followers. They echo his every word. Moses sees them as schoolchildren, lacking independent resources and hence in need of a nursemaid to carry them at all times. How understandable is Moses' cry at the Israelites' complaints in the desert, when he feels he cannot go on: "Have I conceived all this people? have I brought them forth, that Thou shouldest say unto me: Carry them in thy bosom, as a nursing-father carrieth the sucking child?" (*Num.* 11:12). This outburst wells up from the depths of Moses' consciousness; Moses the leader who feels solely responsible for the child he bears in his arms.

Miriam's leadership—symbolized by the gift of the well, whose life-giving waters gush from below (as opposed to rain that comes from above)—stands in sharp contrast to that of her brother Moses. Miriam constantly acts behind the scenes, facilitating the work of existent life forces—without openly appearing on the stage of history.

One of the most beautiful examples of this, highlighting the role of Miriam in the great drama of the exodus from Egypt, appears in relation to the verse "And his sister stood afar off, to know what would be done to him"(*Ex.* 2:4). There is more to this verse than meets the eye. What is clear is that Miriam appoints herself guardian of her younger brother, out of concern for his welfare. The "lead" here is obviously played by Moses, and Miriam's role lies somewhere between that of a supporting actress and an extra. The Sages however, added a further dimension to the story:

Rabbi Amram said in the name of Rav: We are taught that when she was [only] the sister of Aaron she foretold that her mother would give birth to a son who would be a savior to Israel. And when Moses was born, the house was filled with light. Her father arose and kissed her on the head and said to her "daughter, thy prophecy has been fulfilled". And when he was cast into the Nile, her father struck her on the head and said "daughter, where is they prophecy now?" And that is the meaning of "And his sister stood afar off, to know what would be done to him"—to know the outcome of her prophecy (*Sotah* 12b).

It is no ordinary task that Miriam performs, watching over him lest he be harmed by the Egyptians (as explained by Sforno: "for she thought an Egyptian would take him"), but concern for the future of the child floating on the Nile, destined to be the leader and savior of the Children of Israel. Her role is not merely to safeguard the child, but to safeguard the vision of redemption of the Jewish People. Miriam is the elder sister, not only of Aaron and Moses but, in a certain sense, of the entire nation. The midrash that identifies the midwife Puah with Miriam (see e.g. Rashi on *Ex.* 1:15) affords further insight into her character.

The role of the midwife is to help another woman bring life into the world. The midwife herself does not give birth, but encourages, spurs on, reassures and sustains. She stands watch. That is Miriam, who speaks to the mother and encourages her at difficult moments, when the labor pains are at their worst. She is the midwife who soothes and heartens the exhausted mother who has lost faith in her ability to bring her child into the world.

Let us now compare the song that Miriam sings at the sea to that of Moses, as described above. Moses' song begins "Then sang Moses and the children of Israel", and as the Sages explain, he sang and they repeated after him. Miriam went out with all the women and said to them "Sing ye to the Lord, for He is highly exalted". Miriam's song is generally seen as duplicating that of Moses, but upon closer examination we find that it is in fact its exact opposite. In Moses' song, he is both instigator and actor, with the people merely responding. Miriam on the other hand, believes it is the people who must take the lead, and her role as leader is merely to sustain and encourage them: "And Miriam responded (*vata'an*) to them"—it is she who responds to the song of the people!

I now return to *Hukat*. Miriam's leadership, which strove to inspire the people to bring forth their own song, was ahead of its time. The people needed Moses' leadership by virtue of the miraculous; leadership from above. Only after forty years in the desert, there came a new generation that sought to stand on its own feet. The death of Miriam—whose symbol was the well, for her ability to inspire the people to sing its own song—left a void. Who would take Miriam's place?

God gives Moses a chance to change his style of leadership; to take the staff, but speak to the rock rather than striking it. This would have constituted a radical change in his leadership, but Moses cannot escape his own personality and spiritual level. His power as "man of God" will not allow him to "go down" to the people and speak with them. He strikes the rock, as if saying: this is my power.

God's response is completely appropriate—you will not enter the Land because you are not an earthly leader. Joshua, who knows how to approach people, may not be at your level, but he will bring the people into the Land. At this point the people understand that Moses will not replace Miriam. Now, forty years after Miriam's appeal "Sing ye to the Lord, for He is highly exalted", they are doing exactly as she wished them to do. This is also the meaning of the song of Israel; so different from the song of Moses. They break free from Moses' song and burst into their own. The difference between these two songs, as they appear in the Torah scroll, is immediately apparent. The Song of the Sea is written in the form of "half bricks set over whole bricks", and is entirely sacred. The Song of the Well is written in ordinary script, as if devoid of any holy spirit—but it is their song and no one else's, and that is where its importance lies. And so *Midrash Yelamdenu* (in *Yalkut Shimoni, Hukat*, 764):

"Then sang Israel" ... When Israel was about to sing the Song of the Sea, Moses did not allow them to do so of their own accord, but as a boy learns a lesson with his teacher, so Moses recited it with them, as it is written: "Then sang Moses and the children of Israel", like a boy repeating after his teacher. Forty years later, having attained their majority, they began to sing the Song of the Well of their own accord, as it is written: "Then sang Israel". They said: Master of the Universe, it is your task to perform miracles for us and it is our task to sing [before you], as it is written: "The Lord is to save me, and my songs shall we sing" (*Isaiah* 38:20).

This is the essence of Rabbi Yitzhak Meir's homily, as it appears in *Sefat Emet*. The events of his life, the alternative he offered to the leadership of his friend and teacher Menahem Mendel of Kotsk, would seem to shed further light on his teachings. In a certain sense, the leadership of the Rabbi of Kotsk resembled that of Moses: leadership from above. He brought his disciples to the true path, which he himself had found at the court of Yaakov Yitzhak ("the holy Jew") of Przysucha (Peshiskha). Disciples flocked to him to receive the light that shone from him, but in the end, this leader withdrew from his community. He remained exalted and alone.

Rabbi Yitzhak Meir saw himself as far less worthy than his teacher, but his path was a different one. He led his disciples from below, inspiring them to draw upon their own abilities. In his teachings he intimates that every generation requires a different kind of leadership. Charismatic leadership that controls and guides the spirit of the people—"as a nursing-father carrieth the sucking child"—is fitting in its day, but a time comes when the people must carry itself and sing the song of its life; no longer able to live by the miracle and the striking staff; in need of the power of speech, from which a new song may burst forth.

Yossi Turner

Balak

"A People that Shall Dwell Alone"
in the Writings of *Nachman Krochmal*

For from the top of the rocks I see him, and from the hills I behold him: lo, it is a people that shall dwell alone, and shall not be reckoned among the nations (*Numbers* 23:9).

This portion tells of the attempt by Balak, king of Moab, to curse the Israelites, a short time after the exodus. To this end he approached Balaam son of Beor, a sorcerer from the land of Pethor in the east, requesting that he curse the Israelites on his behalf. The curse here is not merely an expression of negative sentiments but a thing of magical power, intended to neutralize Israel's ability to defeat Moab in war:

> And Balak the son of Zippor saw all that Israel had done ... And he sent messengers unto Balaam the son of Beor, to Pethor, which is by the River, to the land of the children of his people, to call him, saying: "Behold, there is a people come out from Egypt; behold, they cover the face of the earth, and they abide over against me. Come now therefore, I pray thee, curse me this people; for they are too mighty for me; peradventure I shall prevail, that we may smite them, and that I may drive them out of the land" (22:2–6).

When we read the story in its present form—the product of later biblical redaction—the verse that describes the Israelites as "a people that shall dwell alone" serves to explain the fact the Balaam is unable to curse them and instead acts as a prophet of God, blessing them in his name. And so it is first written: "And the Lord put a word in Balaam's mouth ... And he took up his parable, and said: From Aram Balak bringeth me, the king of Moab from the mountains of the East: 'Come, curse me Jacob, and come, execrate Israel'" (23:5–7); and then, having explained the circumstances of his arrival in Moab, he replies to Balak's request: "How shall I curse, whom God hath not cursed? And how shall I execrate, whom the Lord hath not execrated? For from the top of the rocks I see him, and from the hills I behold him: *lo, it is a people that shall dwell alone, and shall not be reckoned among the nations*" (*ibid.* 8–9).

The simple meaning of the words "*a people that shall dwell alone*" is that Israel's nature is unlike that of the other nations, in that it is not subject to magic but only to God's will, and that is why Balaam is unable to curse them if God does not will it. By virtue of Israel's special bond with its god, Balaam's magic is ineffectual in their regard: "For there is no enchantment with Jacob, neither is there any divination with Israel". But what is the source of the ability—whether of God himself or of his relationship with the people—to resist the magical force of the curse? Is God portrayed here merely as possessing greater power than the sorcerers of the East? Is the difference between the power of the Israelite god and that of other gods of the ancient Near East purely quantitative—i.e. that he is simply more powerful than they? Or does this ability stem from an entirely different conception of the very nature of the divine and the way in which the God of Israel, as Creator, intervenes in historical reality?

As we will see below, Nachman Krochmal's interpretation of the expression "a people that shall dwell alone" presumes a special relationship with the god of creation at the core of Jewish existence. This approach is not surprising, and is typical of traditional Jewish exegesis. In addition, however, Krochmal appears to have ascribed some truth to the gods and religious beliefs of the nations as well, thereby opening the way for a new and original approach to Jewish Scripture. This would also appear to form the basis of Krochmal's central thesis; that the Jewish People is indeed different from other peoples by virtue of its unique religious faith, but that this uniqueness cannot be realized except through dialogue and exchange with other cultures. We will therefore try to discover the precise meaning of the expression "a people that shall dwell alone" in the Bible, and how this expression relates to the uniqueness of the religious faith of the Jewish People as compared to that of other peoples.

Krochmal lived in Galicia, in the first half of the 19ᵗʰ century. He was influenced by *Haskalah* ideology and the methods of modern historical and philosophical research that characterized the "Science of Judaism" (*Wissenschaft des Judentums*) in the West. Our interest in Krochmal's interpretation of the expression "a people that shall dwell alone" stems from the conflict that has surrounded this expression in the Modern Era, regarding the status of the Jewish People among the nations, and the tension between the uniqueness of Jewish existence and the desire to join with other nations as a full partner in modern culture since the time of emancipation. The Orthodox response to emancipation was marked by a stringent interpretation of the expression "a people that shall dwell alone"; an expression which denies the possibility of Israel and the nations having anything at all in common. As we shall see below, Krochmal's understanding of the phrase bears a certain resemblance to the Orthodox interpretation, inasmuch as he too seeks to emphasize the Jewish People's unique spiritual character—which he ascribes to the religious relationship it has maintained with God over the centuries. As we shall see however, Krochmal's interpretation also presumes, in the manner of Liberal Judaism, dialogue and exchange with the nations of the world in matters of religion and faith.

The portion of *Balak* provides scant information regarding the uniqueness of Jewish faith and offers no explicit comparison between Judaism and other faiths. Nevertheless, such a comparison would seem to lie at the heart of the biblical narrative, and can even be reconstructed on the basis of the ancient literary sources from which the Torah portion of *Balak* developed.

Balak comprises a number of different documents, distinguished by the language and divine names they employ, and the ways in which they portray Balaam, God and the manner of God's revelation. A thorough study of the composite sources of the biblical text of *Balak* is beyond the scope of this chapter. Approached with this idea in mind however, the expression "a people that shall dwell alone" gives the impression of a unique religious response to the pagan orientation of some of the earlier source materials. Read in this fashion the main focus of the story would appear to be the transformation of Balaam from pagan sorcerer to prophet of God. At a certain point in the story, Balaam is portrayed as identifying deeply with Israel, due to its religious singularity—which he discovered when God spoke to him as He is wont to speak with other prophets in the Bible. By virtue of the unique religious character of the People, revealed to him through prophecy, Balaam proclaims the Israelites "a people that shall dwell alone and shall not be reckoned among the nations", adding the supplication "Let me die the death of the righteous, and let mine end be like his" (*ibid.* 10).

What is the nature of the Israelites' religious singularity; what is the nature of their relationship with their god; and what is the nature of this god's power—that evoked such a strong emotional response in Balaam? At different points in the story we find different answers to these questions. In the passage that describes the encounter between Balaam, the ass, and the angel of the Lord (22:21–35), God's power is still perceived as magical—essentially the same as the powers that Balaam himself, as a sorcerer, invokes when he seeks—in Balak's name—to curse the Israelites. In this ancient stratum of the portion of *Balak*, patterns of divine revelation through prophecy that are characteristic of later biblical works had not yet been established. Divine power manifests itself, on the one hand, in the form of an "angel of the Lord" disguised as a warrior: "And the ass saw the angel of the Lord standing in the way, with his sword drawn in his hand" (*ibid.* 23); while on the other hand it is manifest in the wondrous speech of the ass: "And the Lord opened the mouth of the ass, and she said unto Balaam: 'What have I done unto thee, that thou hast smitten me these three times'?". It is interesting that in this stratum of the story, Balaam sees nothing unusual in the fact that the ass has spoken, reacting only to her unruly behavior. In any event, the essence of this part of the story is God's anger at Balaam's having agreed to go with Balak's messengers to curse Israel. In this too the religious approach reflected in this document differs from that of the later redactors. We cannot say that God revealed his will to Balaam, or that Balaam heard the commanding voice of God. Even God's will is not really His "will"—expressed as a commandment to his creatures—but rather His anger which in its most primitive form is exhibited as the "desire to kill". Only the threat posed by the angel standing before him, disguised as a warrior, threatening his life with a drawn sword, brings Balaam to conclude that he has aroused God's anger: "Then the Lord opened the eyes of Balaam, and he saw the angel of the Lord standing in the way, with his sword drawn in his hand; and he bowed his head, and fell on his face ... And Balaam said unto the angel of the Lord: 'I have sinned; for I knew not that thou stoodest in the way against me; now therefore, if it displease thee, I will get me back'." (*ibid.* 31; 34)

In the passages associated with later biblical redaction, on the other hand, God appears directly—as for example in chapter 22, verses 8–12. This stratum of the story is also based on Balak's request that Balaam accompany his messengers to go and curse the Israelites in his name. Here however, God himself—through prophecy—instructs Balaam as to how he should reply: "And he said unto them: 'Lodge here this night, and I will bring you back word, as the Lord may speak unto me' ... And God came unto Balaam ... And God said ... 'Thou shalt not go with them; thou shalt not curse the people; for they are blessed'."

The difference between God's appearance to Balaam in this passage and his wondrous manifestation in the older text, is striking. Here, God appears directly to Balaam. He speaks to him and communicates His will to him in the clearest possible terms. As we shall see, in this stratum of the story, God's revelation through prophecy is not a unique event, but is repeated a number of times. The direct revelation of God's word to Balaam is thus a characteristic element of the story's later redaction. And so we find in chapter 22, 15–20:

> And Balak sent yet again princes, more, and more honorable than they ... And Balaam answered and said ... "I cannot go beyond the word of the Lord my God, to do any thing ... Now therefore, I pray you, tarry ye also here this night, that I may know what the Lord will speak unto me more". And God came unto Balaam at night, and said unto him: "If the men are come to call thee, rise up, go with them; but only the word which I speak unto thee, that shalt thou do.

As noted above, this is the context in which the expression "a people that shall dwell alone" should be understood, and this is, it would seem, the main theological innovation of the story, as shaped by the biblical redactors. "And God met Balaam ... *And the Lord put a word in Balaam's mouth* ... And he took up his parable, and said ... For from the top of the rocks I see him, and from the hills I behold him: lo, it is a people that shall dwell alone, and shall not be reckoned among the nations." The refashioning of Balaam, so that he appears in the story's later version as a prophet of God rather than a sorcerer, is at the heart of the story, and serves as the basis upon which Israel's unique character is displayed in contrast to the peoples of Balak and Balaam: "For there is no enchantment with Jacob, neither is there any divination with Israel". Israel's uniqueness stems from the fact that its destiny is not determined by pagan sorcery, but by the word and will of the god of creation, revealed through prophecy.

In light of the above, let us now take a look at Nachman Krochmal's interpretation of "a people that shall dwell alone". At first glance, Krochmal's treatment of the expression appears incidentally in the historiographical portion of his book; that is, as an explanation of the destruction of the First Temple and the expulsion of the Jews from the Kingdom of Judah. Indeed the context in which it is mentioned is part of a much broader philosophical and historiographical discussion. Nevertheless, Krochmal's treatment of the expression within a historiographical context is an important component of his overall conception of the relationship between Israel and the nations, which is one of the book's central themes. He writes as follows:

Although the worship of foreign gods did not prevail in Judah as it did among the ten tribes, they did adopt certain practices and revert to the "high places" there as well. Some wicked kings such as Ahaz, Manasseh and Jehoiakim, believed that they could improve their fortunes by worshiping many gods, like the nations. They failed to understand that Israel can have no delivery or salvation but through adherence to the Lord their God, free of all traces of idolatry [and] preserving their special niche as it was given to them. This niche is inexorably linked to the People's continued existence, its happiness and prosperity, and is what keeps us from following the mores of the nations. … These foolish kings failed to understand what the prophet of the nations understood regarding the spirituality of this people, when he said: *lo, it is a people that shall dwell alone, and shall not be reckoned among the nations.* And this explains how the entire structure was destroyed, step by step (*Moreh nevukhei hazman* [Guide for the Perplexed of Our Time], 49).

Krochmal thus attributes the destruction of the First Temple to the fact that Israel's leaders failed to understand what Balaam understood in the portion of *Balak*: that the fate of the people depends upon God's will, expressed in His precepts and revealed through prophecy; and that following foreign ways, against God's will, will necessarily lead to its downfall. Krochmal however, also espouses the opposite view. Elsewhere, in a discussion regarding the circumstances of the creation of the Jewish People, he claims that the tribes of Israel had to descend to Egypt before becoming a people so that, *inter alia*, they might come into contact with cultural and civilizational paradigms previously unknown to the family of Abraham; that is, in order to be come a people, the tribes of Israel needed to descend into Egypt in order to learn aspects of their civilization:

> And Providence decreed that the holy family should descend to Egypt and sojourn there ... And it was the desire of Providence that our nation should dwell among them, that we might become, as promised, a great nation. The [tribes] would not fully have become a nation, with all the attendant resources and abilities, had they remained in the lands of Canaan where, at the time of their arrival, there were no worthy structures, even to the pagan gods (*ibid.* 42–43).

The question arises, how can Krochmal claim both that destruction results when Israel forgets that she is "a people that shall dwell alone", and at the same time maintain that interaction with other cultures is a precondition for her existence as a people? The answer is that Krochmal indeed perceived the Jewish People as different from other peoples, in that its relationship with its god—as reflected in its national heritage—is the essence of its existence. For the sake of its continued existence however, it must also interact with its non-Jewish cultural environment, since the God of Israel is the God of all creation. That is to say, even the founding and sustaining principles of the nations are recognized by Israel as part of God's works. Indeed, discussion of the cultural assets of all peoples and their cosmic significance is ordinarily considered a topic of discussion in the realm of general philosophy and not a matter emphasized in Jewish religious discourse. And yet, according to Krochmal, these should also be considered from a particularly Jewish and Torah oriented perspective precisely because the Torah's ultimate purpose is to bring about the recognition of God in all creation (compare *ibid.* 272).

According to Krochmal, Jewish existence, as it has developed throughout history, is in effect a crystallization of "divine self-realization". The Jewish People thus has a cosmic purpose: it effects a process through which all things will ultimately be recognized in light of the biblical belief in the God of creation. Accordingly, the Jewish People— which must continue to exist until this purpose is achieved—was meant, from its very inception, to develop and express its faith in all areas of religion and culture, while maintaining a constant dialogue with other world-cultures. For if, God forbid, Israel were to cease to exist before having successfully applied the principles of its belief in creation to the cultures of all peoples, then God's own process of self-realization would never reach completion.

Let us consider this principle in the context of Krochmal's overall philosophy, as expressed in his *Guide for the Perplexed of Our Time.* According to Krochmal, "it has been a matter of paramount importance to our nation throughout the ages, that through [our] striving we might achieve distinct impressions as to [the nature of] our inner-self and essence; that is of the collective Jewish soul ... in accordance with the circumstances and the vagaries of time" (*ibid.* 34). Krochmal sought to clarify the nature of Israel's existence so that we might know how to shape its culture in the present, with the advent of modernity. As a historian, he chose to examine the history of the Jewish People using modern culture's critical methodology. He presumed however, that such historical analysis would not suffice to unearth the secret of Jewish existence over the ages, without examining its findings in light of its traditional, Torah-oriented conceptions concerning of God—including those which pertain to the development of its age-old self-perception as the people of God.

Krochmal believed that the reality of every people is founded upon an "idea", which determines its distinctive forms of social, cultural and political existence. He termed the founding "idea" of a people, its "spiritual principle" and maintained that "all concepts", "legal moral and linguistic, as well as books of wisdom and images of the divine … are diffused within each nation, more or less completely" and that "these are the spiritual heritage and principles that come to be possessed by the group as a whole … disseminated, over time, to the multitudes" (*ibid.* 35). This is the dimension of Jewish existence that justifies the description of the Jewish People as "a people like all other peoples": all aspects of Jewish cultural existence, including its unique religious culture, are determined by an "idea", borne in the national consciousness. According to Krochmal, however, that "idea" or "spiritual principle" upon which Jewish existence is founded—is both human and divine, since it is a part of God's infinite becoming. The way in which the "spiritual principle" that governs Jewish consciousness acts upon it thus differs from the way in which the spiritual principles determine the history of other peoples. Regarding other peoples, Krochmal writes:

And its god or genius will also be especially renowned for this spiritual quality. For example, the genius of a nation that rules by the sword will be the spirit of valor, to which it will direct its worship; and so the spirit of craftsmanship and industry, the spirit of beauty, justice, cunning, knowledge … each of these principles is … symbolized by some striking element of creation, and by the celestial bodies closest to the earth … For example: the Sun—to symbolize the realization or "bringing to light" of all potential; Saturn—education; Jupiter—the spirit of justice; Mars—the spirit of valor; Venus—the spirit of beauty. The nation may thus draw and sculpt every spirit in images and other symbols: the image of a thinking man; the image of a conquering hero—Baal; the image of a supple and nursing [woman]—Ashtoreth; the image of a figure bearing the scales of justice, and so forth (*ibid.*).

Regarding the People of Israel, on the other hand, he asserts:

And the prophet declares "not like these is the portion of Jacob; for He is the creator of all things, and Israel is the tribe of His inheritance; the Lord of hosts is His name". That is to say that

He is Absolute Spirit and He alone is the source of all spiritual beings and encompasses them all. For each of these, in its own specific existence is finite and ephemeral, and has no Absolute Reality or Being except in the Lord, blessed be He, i.e. in its adherence to the hosts of heaven and earth (*ibid.* 37).

The idea upon which the existence of any people, Israel included, is founded—is embodied in the image of the divinity it worships. The gods of the nations however, are not the God of creation. They are not infinite and absolute divinity, the reality of which necessarily encompasses all others, but the unjustified raising up of specific details of creation sanctified by each individual people to the status of the divine, or to the level of absolute reality.

This is the key to understanding Krochmal's approach to the verse in the portion of Balak describing Israel as "a people that shall dwell alone". The basic nature of the Jewish People differs completely from that of all other peoples because of its collective role as bearer of the cosmic process through which God Himself is to achieve self-realization. In regard to the historical dynamic whereby national expression is given to the "spiritual principle" that lies as the basis of its existence, on the other hand, Israel is no different than the other peoples of the world. For Israel, as for the other peoples, the spiritual principle upon which it is founded may serve as the basis for a secular historiographical examination of its inner character.

This is further elucidated in Krochmal's discussion of the question: why the ancient peoples that appeared on the stage of history, at about the same time as the Jewish People, have become extinct, while the Jewish People, on the contrary, lives on in its unique way to this very day?

For even when we said that no nation is completely lost and destroyed until the spirit that sustains it departs ... our intention was that the spirit ceases to exist in relation to a specific time and place ... and in this sense the spirit itself is also finite and will certainly be lost ... In truth however, it is not lost entirely, but rather, when a nation is great and accomplished, many impressions of its spirit remain to the end of time; its artistry and poetry, books and laws, are bequeathed to the entire human race and imbue its general spirit, wherein it is given manifest expression throughout history ... And since Divine Providence decided to choose the source from which we derive, that is the holy patriarchs, and to select from their descendants, generation after generation, a single family—the 12 tribes of Jacob—and to increase their number until they became an entire nation unto themselves ... Divine wisdom saw fit to guide this nation and perfect it, that it might be a kingdom of priests. That is, to teach the great and absolute faith of the Torah to the human race, until all spiritual elements and principles are revealed in it ... since all spiritual principles depend upon God, and rely upon Him for their truth. Thus, in all our deeds as a nation and in every sublime and good spirit that is revealed among us, we shall know in our hearts and profess with our mouths that God lives among us and it is from Him that these things derive; that all spirituality springs from Him and emanates from His spirit. And this is the true meaning ... of the verse "that I may dwell among them", because I am with you and my spirit dwells among you, and the true meaning of the name *Shekhinah* (Divine Presence) and of the dictum that the *Shekhinah* abides with Israel. And so you may grasp the meaning of the phrase 'when they were exiled to Babylon .. when they were exiled to Elam, the *Shekhinah* [went] with them (*ibid*. 36–38).

God, according to Krochmal is a spiritual being that becomes the founding principle of all existence when His thoughts are concretized in the context of world-cultures. Some of God's primeval infinity can be discerned in the passage of knowledge, belief, and values from people to people, as well as in the manner in which these continue to shape mankind even after the peoples who originally bore them disappear from the world stage. At a certain point in the discussion, Krochmal asserts that all peoples undergo three stages or epochs in their collective existence: "growth and development", "vigor and enterprise" and "decline and annihilation". The first period corresponds to the period of Israel's inception, as described by Krochmal, prior to the exodus. This is a period in the life of a nation, in which the "idea" upon which its existence is founded first appears in a specific group consciousness, determining the cultural patterns that will characterize it over the course of its historical development. The second period marks the peak of the life cycle of every people. In this phase, its cultural, social and political achievements fully realize the "idea" that defines its identity. The third period is characterized by a process of national dissolution which continues until the people are no more. This is a period in which individual consciousness gradually diverges from the spiritual orientation that once stood at the heart of the collective existence, until nothing is left save a distant memory preserved in the books of ancient history. However, since the spiritual ethos that sustained the people in the past is part of God's self-realization, it will necessarily continue to influence and shape human culture by influencing additional national cultures even after the people which originally bore that idea has disappeared The Jewish People however, according to Krochmal, is eternal because the "idea" that shapes its culture is the idea of the infinite God Himself.

What is the crux of the claim Krochmal advances in this discussion, and what bearing does it have on his interpretation of the biblical verse which refers to Israel as "a people that shall dwell alone"? Indeed, Krochmal perceived the Jewish People as unique, by virtue of its singular religious heritage. But it is precisely this singularity that obligates Israel to interact with other cultures. Krochmal thus combines a traditional, particularist approach with a universalistic one, typical of modern humanism. Indeed, Krochmal asserts that Judaism has always possessed a unique divine truth which is properly associated with prophecy, and he views all developments in Jewish religious thought over the centuries as a continuing revelation of the very same divine truth that was initially revealed through prophecy in the biblical period. This truth however, presupposes the existence of partial truths contained in the spirits of other peoples, so that even Judaism's religious truth cannot be realized without interaction between Israel's spirit and that of the nations. Moreover, the realization of the potential for profound, divine truth implanted in Israel from the beginning, is contingent upon the gradual absorption of the spiritual achievements of other peoples, and their reinterpretation in light of the infinite parameters of the Jewish belief in the God of creation; and although Israel was the first people to recognize the single all-encompassing divine truth, this truth is also the ultimate purpose of all of mankind. On the one hand, Judaism needs dialogue and exchange with the rest of humanity, so that the idea upon which its existence is founded may finally become the essence of all human existence. On the other hand, mankind—if it is to attain its ultimate goal—needs Judaism as a guide, by virtue of its ability to renew itself within time, even as other peoples fade and disappear.

The Jewish People is thus indeed a "people like all other peoples". Like all peoples, it develops on the basis of its own "spiritual principle", and it does so while interacting with other peoples. It is also however, "a people that shall dwell alone", because it alone—from its historical beginnings—possesses God's infinite "truth", and it alone continues to exist after all other peoples of the world have come and gone.

Yedidyah Yitzhaki

Pinhas

*Zealotry and Tolerance in Religion and the Jewish Religion
In the Thought of Spinoza, Locke and A.I. Kook*

Pinhas, the son of Eleazar, the son of Aaron the priest, hath turned my wrath away from the children of Israel, in that he was very jealous for my sake among them, so that I consumed not the children of Israel in my jealousy. Wherefore say: Behold, I give unto him my covenant of peace (*Numbers* 25:11–12).

The portion begins with the story of Pinhas, the son of Eleazar, the son of Aaron the priest, who was jealous for the sake of God, and killed Zimri the son of Salu, "a prince of a fathers' house among the Simeonites". Zimri had committed harlotry with a Midianite woman, Cozbi, the daughter of Zur ("head of the people of a fathers' house in Midian"), in honor of the Baal of Peor. The story of Zimri and Pinhas is divided between two Torah portions, spanning the 18 verses of chapter 25—nine at the end of the portion of *Balak*, regarding the circumstances of Pinhas' act and its consequences, and nine at the beginning of *Pinhas*, regarding the reward he is promised.

Balak tells another story—the wonderful tale of Balaam, who was a contemporary of Moses and, although not an Israelite, heard the voice of God. *Pinhas* covers many different topics: the counting of the Children of Israel after the plague provoked by their misdeeds with the daughters of Moab, instructions for the division of the Land among the Israelite tribes, the story of the daughters of Zelophehad, an intimation of Moses' death and Joshua's acceptance of the leadership, as well as laws pertaining to the festival sacrifices.

It is thus no wonder that the story of Pinhas and his jealousy is often neglected in sermons and discussions of the portion that bears his name. The choice of *haftarah* (weekly reading from the *Prophets*) however, appears to reflect the opinion that Pinhas' jealousy is in fact the essence of the Torah portion. The *haftarah* of *Pinhas* recounts the story of Elijah

506

at Mount Horeb, following his massacre of 450 prophets of Baal and 400 prophets of Asherah (1 *Kings* 19). The clear connection between the two episodes lies in the words of Elijah, when God asks him: "What doest thou here, Elijah?" The prophet's reply—"I have been very jealous for the Lord, the God of hosts"—echoes God's characterization of Pinhas' action: "in that he was very jealous for my sake among them". I believe the story of Pinhas deserves particular attention today, considering the topicality of the subject of religious zealotry and the related issue of tolerance.

The connection between Pinhas' jealousy and the story of Elijah is treated extensively in the talmudic and midrashic literature. The Midrash even goes as far as claiming that the two figures were in fact one and the same: "God changed the name of Pinhas to that of Elijah" (*Pirke de-Rabbi Elazar*); and more explicitly, "Pinhas is Elijah" (Rashi on *Bava Metzia* 114b). This could mean that a centuries-old Pinhas reappeared in the person of Elijah. The midrash however, states that "Pinhas is Elijah", rather than "Elijah is Pinhas", implying that it was in fact Elijah who appeared in the form of Pinhas, six centuries before his own birth—just as he assumes many different forms in the Midrash and popular legend, centuries after his ascent by a whirlwind into heaven.

The story of Pinhas' jealousy is mentioned again, hundreds of years later, in the First Book of the Maccabees. According to the account there, King Antiochus ordered the Jews

> to follow customs strange to the land, to profane Sabbaths and festivals, to defile the sanctuary and the priests, to build altars and sacred precincts and shrines for idols, to sacrifice swine and other unclean animals, and to leave their sons uncircumcised. They were to make themselves abominable by everything unclean and profane, so that they would forget the law and change all the ordinances (1 *Macc.* 1:45–49, NRSV).

Mattathias the Hasmonean, a priest from Modi'in, rejects the suggestion of the king's officers that he set an example for his people, in obeying the king's commands:

> "Even if all the nations that live under the rule of the king obey him, and have chosen to obey his commandments, everyone of

them abandoning the religion of their ancestors, I and my sons and my brothers will continue to live by the covenant of our ancestors. Far be it from us to desert the law and the ordinances. We will not obey the king's words by turning aside from our religion to the right hand or to the left". When he had finished speaking these words, a Jew came forward in the sight of all to offer sacrifice on the altar in Modein, according to the king's command. When Mattathias saw it, he burned with zeal and his heart was stirred. He gave vent to righteous anger; he ran and killed him on the altar. At the same time he killed the king's officer who was forcing them to sacrifice, and he tore down the altar. Thus he burned with zeal for the law, just as Phinehas did against Zimri son of Salu (*ibid.* 2:19–26).

The connection to *Pinhas* is explicit: Mattathias' jealousy for God and the Torah is compared to the jealousy of Pinhas and his action against Zimri son of Salu.

What these three stories—of Pinhas, Elijah and Mattathias—have in common is jealousy for God's unity. According to the biblical text, Moses commanded the judges to slay all who had "joined themselves unto the Baal of Peor" and not specifically those who had committed harlotry with the daughters of Moab (25:5); Elijah slew the prophets of Baal and Asherah; and Mattathias killed the Jew who sought to offer sacrifice to "foreign gods", by order of King Antiochus. In all three cases, jealousy is accompanied by bloodshed. The Midrash (*Numbers Rabbah* 20:26) mentions the possibility that Pinhas may have killed Zimri for his act of harlotry with the Midianite woman: "He [Pinhas] saw the act and recalled the law: One who lies with an Aramean (var. Cuthaean) woman, zealots strike him down" (see also *Sanhedrin* 81b). In parentheses, let us say that this is more warning than law, or perhaps it affords zealots license to strike down anyone who fails to preserve the "purity of the race", without trial, without discussion. It is puzzling nonetheless, because Rebecca, the daughter of Bethuel, was an Aramean, as were the matriarchs Rachel and Leah, and even our ancient forebear Jacob is called a "wandering Aramean" (*Deut.* 26:5). The Rabbis discuss the apparent contradiction between the law against contact with the Midianites and the fact that Moses's wife was a Midianite, and his father-in-law Jethro (a priest of Midian) even advised him in his leadership. What is more, many great and important men were guilty of having lain with or committed harlotry with foreign women, yet they escaped severe punishment. These difficulties are somewhat mitigated if we accept the interpretation that the great sin for which the Israelites were afflicted with the terrible plague was not harlotry but idolatry. Furthermore, such harlotry was, in itself, idolatry—part of the fertility cult of Ashtoreth. Solomon too was punished because his foreign wives had "turned away his heart" after their gods, and not for the very fact of having married them.

Just as three points determine a plane, so these three events on the plane of Jewish history—in the mythological time before the conquest of the Land, in the time of the Kingdom of Israel and the First Temple, and at the height of the Second Temple period—establish a clear and unequivocal fact, to which we will relate at this point without passing moral judgment: Judaism sees itself as a zealous, intolerant religion. In all three cases jealousy is cited as the protagonists' primary motivating factor, and all three actions draw lavish praise and reward. Pinhas' jealousy is rewarded with "everlasting priesthood" for him and all his descendants. Elijah, although compelled to transfer his spirit of prophecy to Elisha, ascends to heaven in a whirlwind and goes on to become a central figure in redemption mythology and popular legend. Mattathias becomes the founding father of a royal dynasty, and later plays a prominent role in Zionist mythology. Boris Schatz' well-known sculpture "Mattathias"—which is captioned "Whoso is on the Lord's side, let him come unto me" and depicts the Hasmonean priest wielding a sword, having just slain the Jew who wished to sacrifice to the Greek gods—is one of the earliest and most important artistic works of Zionist culture.

Judaism's zealotry or jealousy, as reflected in the above examples, has disturbed many thinkers, particularly since such jealousy entails bloodshed. Professor Yeshayahu Leibowitz addresses this subject at length both with regard to Pinhas and with regard to Elijah (see Leibowitz, *Sheva Shanim Shel Sihot al Parashat Hashavua* pp. 724–730). He cites many sources, including the statement by Naphtali Zevi Yehudah Berlin (Netziv) that "One may be jealous for the sake of God only if he is free of all human jealousy". In other words, only pure jealousy for God's sake, unmarred by personal interest, can be justified. Leibowitz cites a midrash regarding the dialogue between God and Elijah at Horeb, from which he concludes that "one should not be more jealous for the sake of the Lord of hosts than the Holy One is jealous for His own sake". The verses themselves may attempt to justify the bloody actions of the jealous, but they express no reservations with regard to jealousy *per se*. Pinhas' action, according to the biblical account, was a reaction to an open and explicit provocation by "one of the children of Israel", Zimri son of Salu: "And, behold, one of the children of Israel came and brought unto his brethren a Midianitish woman in the sight of Moses, and in the sight of all the congregation of the children of Israel" (25:6). Elijah's action against the prophets of Baal and Asherah can be seen as self-defense and a reaction to the desecration of God's sancta and the murder of His prophets: "I have been very jealous for the Lord, the God of hosts; for the children of Israel have forsaken Thy covenant, thrown down Thine altars, and slain Thy prophets with the sword; and I, even I only, am left; and they seek my life, to take it away" (1 *Kings* 19:10). Mattathias too reacted to Antiochus' "evil decrees", following an explicit provocation: "a Jew came forward in the sight of all to offer sacrifice on the altar in Modein, according to the king's command" (1 *Maccabees* 2:23). The provocation occurred "in the sight of all"—just as the act that provoked Pinhas was perpetrated "in the sight of Moses and in the sight of all the congregation of the children of Israel". In all three cases, the "zealot" does not initiate the conflict, but merely responds to the actions of his adversary. As noted above, although some "justification" is offered for the blood that is spilled, no reservations are expressed regarding religious zealotry in and of itself.

Although traditional Judaism—in all its many streams and forms—considers Judaism a zealous faith, and its truth absolute, unquestionable and immutable, recent generations—over the past two hundred years or so—have witnessed a tendency to view Judaism as a tolerant faith, wholly devoid of zealotry. Historically speaking, this tendency reflects Jewish efforts to embrace the democratic and liberal spirit of the modern age, in the wake of 17th and 18th century European Enlightenment and its philosophical interest in the subject of religious tolerance.

The monotheistic religions, Judaism foremost, have never been particularly tolerant. On the contrary, religious zealotry is inherent to these faiths, by virtue of their very monotheism. Polytheism on the other hand, has an inbuilt capacity for tolerance: where there are many gods, there is room for more. Coercion is also inherent to the monotheistic religions, as exemplified—at least as far as Judaism is concerned—in the words of Rabbi Avdimi bar Hama: "This teaches us that the Holy One, blessed be He held the mountain over their heads like an inverted tub, and said to them: If you accept the Torah—good; if not—there you will be buried" (*Shabbat* 88a).

Christianity and Islam followed Judaism's lead in this matter, increasing the element of coercion in their respective faiths even further. On the other hand, champions of Jewish tolerance highlight the lack of a missionary ethos in Judaism, the fact that it is a "culture of debate", citing the words of the Rabbis regarding the disputes between the schools of Hillel and Shamai: "Both are the words of the living God" (*Eruvin* 13b). Regarding the element of religious coercion, they often cite the verse (referring to wisdom, in the original source) "Her ways are ways of pleasantness, and all her paths are peace." (*Prov.* 3:17). Such champions of Jewish tolerance admit however, that it does not extend beyond the boundaries of Judaism itself. Even the verses and dicta that intimate universal tolerance, such as Rabbi Akiva's famous maxim "Beloved is man for he was created in the image of God" (*Avot* 4,14), are reduced by the halakhists to tolerance toward Jews. Some, for example, interpret the "fellow" in the universal imperative "love thy fellow as thyself" (*Lev.* 19:18) to mean "thy fellow in religious observance". Some "broad-minded" individuals extend the commandment to include all Jews (See D. Dishon, *Tarbut Hamahloket Bimkorot Hayahadut, Sovlanut Le'or Mekorot Yisrael*, p. 16). Others, of course, have remained faithful to the universality of this commandment or of Hillel's encapsulation of the essence of Judaism in the phrase "that which is hateful to you, do not unto your fellow" (*Shabbat* 31a)—taking "fellow" to mean "your fellow man".

As noted, a philosophical interest in religious and political tolerance lay at the heart of the European Enlightenment of the 17th and 18th centuries. The term "tolerance" originated in the "religious wars" waged between Catholics and Protestants in the 16th and 17th centuries. As a result of these wars, rulers of different faiths agreed to tolerate one another and to recognize the possibility of peaceful coexistence between the two religions. Over time, the concept was extended to include all religions and freedom of thought in general. The demand for tolerance reflected opposition to the unity of church and state, whereby the state was perceived as the temporal arm of religion. The principle of temporal subordination to religious authority was widespread in the Middle ages and is still espoused in a number of states today. In the 17th century however, philosophers began to question its validity, and in the name of religious tolerance, demanded the separation of church and state. This movement included such prominent figures as Thomas More, Spinoza, Bayle, Locke, Voltaire, Schelling, Mendelssohn, Kant and Hegel.

Baruch Spinoza (1632–1677) was one of the first to raise the subject of religious and political tolerance, particularly in his Theologico-Political Treatise, published in 1670. Spinoza addresses the issue of tolerance in the context of a broader discussion of the relationship between religion and state. Based on a thorough analysis of the essence and workings of the state—including a study of the "Hebrew state", as described in the Bible—Spinoza concludes that: "it is impossible to deprive men of the liberty of saying what they think"; "such liberty can be conceded to every man without injury to the rights and authority of the sovereign power"; "every man may enjoy this liberty without detriment to the public peace"; "no inconveniences arise therefrom which cannot easily be checked"; "every man may enjoy it without injury to his allegiance"; "laws dealing with speculative problems are entirely useless"; and finally, "not only *may* such liberty be granted without prejudice to the public peace, to loyalty, and to the rights of rulers, but that it is even *necessary*, for their preservation" (Spinoza, Theologico-Political Treatise XX,71–76 –tr. R. H. M. Elwes).

"Wherefore, as we have shown", Spinoza writes, "the safest way for a state is to lay down the rule that religion is comprised solely in the exercise of charity and justice, and that the rights of rulers in sacred, no less than in secular matters, should merely have to do with actions, but that every man should think what he likes and say what he thinks" (ibid. 81). We may also conclude from this that every man should be able to act in accordance with his views and beliefs, on condition that he does not "injure the authority of his rulers"—assuming they are guided by the spirit of reason. Spinoza sees the limits of tolerance in tolerance itself. Tolerance must not be shown toward those who fail to show tolerance toward others.

Spinoza's approach is not pluralistic. He believes in the existence of a single absolute truth, founded upon reason, but which lies beyond the grasp of "the common people", who generally prefer imagination to reason, and are rife with superstition, prejudice, phantoms, illusions and foolishness of all kinds, as a result of the adversity and fear to which they are subject in their lives. Nevertheless, Spinoza opposed any attempt to make "absolute truth" a cause for repression and coercion. Every person has the right to hold opinions and to live by them, even if they are entirely untrue, as long as he obeys the laws of the state and upholds them in all his actions. Spinoza explains that tolerance must be shown to everyone, specifically because the masses hold wrong views, for if everyone could grasp the "absolute truth", there would be no need for tolerance. On the other hand, the state must act in the spirit of reason, and encourage the masses to behave rationally, if not out of conviction, then out fear, force of habit or imitation of others.

John Locke (1632–1704), a contemporary of Spinoza, also addressed the subject of tolerance from the point of view of political philosophy. In *A Letter Concerning Toleration*, published in 1689, Locke asserts the need for the complete separation of church from state, of religious ritual and ecclesiastical law from state law. He argues that "The care of souls cannot belong to the civil magistrate, because his power consists only in outward force: but true and saving religion consists in the inward persuasion of the mind, without which nothing can be acceptable to God" (*The Works of John Locke in Nine Volumes*, Rivington, London, 1824, vol.5, p. 11). Nor does the church have the right to compel others to adhere to its doctrines, since it is, according to Locke, "a voluntary society of men, joining themselves together of their own accord in order to the public worshipping of God, in such a manner as they judge acceptable to him, and effectual to the salvation of their souls" (ibid. p. 13). The laws of a religious society must therefore necessarily be limited to matters pertaining solely to the proper functioning of the church. Nor may government give any one church authority over another, since there is no way to determine which church possesses the truth to which all lay exclusive claim. Even if it could be decided which church professes the true faith, "there would not accrue thereby unto the orthodox any right of destroying the other. For churches have [no] jurisdiction in worldly matters" (*ibid.* p. 19). The same would apply to "idolatry", according to Locke, for if we presume that civil government has the right to kill idolaters, idolaters would, by the same principle, have the right to kill Christians: "If it be once permitted to introduce any thing into religion by the means of laws and penalties, there can be no bounds put to it; but it will in the same manner be lawful to alter every thing, according to that rule of truth which the magistrate has framed unto himself" (ibid. p. 35). Locke then turns to another matter, directly related to our discussion. Regarding the claim that according to "law of Moses", idolaters must be annihilated, he replies that the law of Moses was given only to the Jews and does not obligate Christians. Moreover, even in the "Jewish commonwealth"—where religious law was the law of the land, enforced by the civil authorities—the law forbidding idolatry applied only to Jews. It did not apply to members of other peoples, even those who resided in the Land of Canaan, because idolatry was an offense against God's sovereignty, which applied only to the Jews in Canaan. The limits of tolerance, according to Locke are more problematic. Political government, he maintains, is not bound to tolerate opinions that undermine the welfare of society and its foundations, nor is it bound to tolerate religion that presumes to interfere in matters of government or demands loyalty to a foreign sovereign. And lastly, "Those are not at all to be tolerated who deny the being of God" (ibid. p. 47), since removing God from "promises, covenants and oaths" dissolves them, and since one cannot claim tolerance in the name of religion while at the same time destroying all religion. In other words, tolerance disappears when it comes to opinions that stand in contradiction to the religion of the civil power; and this applies to opinions, as well as actions.

Spinoza presumed all religious belief to be rooted in error, since it is inspired by the forces of imagination and emotion rather than those of reason, but that every man has the right to his own error, in which he may believe and to which he may give expression. Moses Mendelssohn (1729–1786) on the other hand, claimed (particularly in *Jerusalem*) that all religions contain some truth and are therefore equal to one another. Mendelssohn accepts the assertions of his predecessors regarding church and state, i.e. that coercion is the exclusive province of the state, while religion has only the power of persuasion. Tolerance between religions, according to Mendelssohn, rests upon that which they have in common by definition; more specifically, the rational and moral principles common to all religions. Differences between religions are not intrinsic, but stem from the subjective historical differences between peoples. Each of the monotheistic religions therefore, reflects a part of the religion of universal truth—the "religion of reason", and as such must be shown tolerance and respect. In this sense, claims Mendelssohn, Judaism is preferable to the other monotheistic religions, because it recognizes the element of truth in each, and does not strive to convert their members. Christianity and Islam on the other hand, do not recognize each other or Judaism, or the truth in each, seeking rather to convert members of the other faiths to their own—an approach that can only be justified with regard to religions that run counter to the "religion of reason".

Mendelssohn follows in the footsteps of Locke when he responds to the claim regarding the clear element of coercion in Jewish religion, reflected both in religious law and in Jewish community practice. He repeats the assertion that the Jewish religion and the Jewish state were one and the same—religious law was also state law, and could therefore be imposed by force. Regarding the coercion practiced by Jewish communities, Mendelssohn maintained that it was an aberration, brought about by the circumstances of Diaspora life; one that should be eliminated, by cancelling the authority afforded to religious communities by the state.

Mendelssohn's approach, like that of Spinoza, presumes the existence of a single "true religion": "the religion of reason". Neither however, sees any possibility of establishing this truth in everyday life. According to Spinoza, the masses are incapable of grasping the truth in reason, because they are governed by their emotions; while Mendelssohn attributes this inability to the historical circumstances particular to each and every human society, which lead them to perceive truth in a unilateral manner. Both thinkers may thus be said to view religion itself, historically speaking, as inherently pluralistic and as such a force for tolerance and mutual respect between the various faiths.

A completely different approach to religious tolerance can be found in the thought of Rabbi Abraham Isaac Kook (1865–1935). Rabbi Kook's ideas are not set forth in a systematic fashion, as "words fitly spoken", but appear in bits and pieces scattered throughout his written works, in numerous essays, aphorisms, letters, poems, parables, etc. It is thus easy to find support in his writings for contradictory positions. In one place he will describe non-Jews as inferior beings, closer to beasts than men, while advocating love of humanity and "all peoples" in another (see *Musar Avikha Umidot HaReiyah, "Ahavah", 56). Rabbi Kook is renowned for his tolerant attitude to secular Zionism, and some speak of his pluralistic approach to Judaism in general—a position for which there is ample support in his writings. Nevertheless, many of his polemical works are far from liberal or pluralistic. Thus, for example, Rabbi Kook does not approve of "freedom of opinion" (*ibid. Hofesh*):
The aspiration to freedom of opinion has a good side and a bad side, a pure side and an impure side. The good side manifests itself when this aspiration transcends the limitations of imagination and physical desire. Opinion then freely follows its path and brings joy to man and society. The bad side manifests itself when freedom of opinion is guided by man's natural inclinations—determined by temperament and imagination, physical desire and all that is base and brutish in man. Then freedom of opinion leads to the terrible disfigurement of man's humanity, destroying all that is precious in life and uprooting Majesty and Eternity from man's soul, both individually and collectively; "whoso pleaseth God shall escape from her" (*Ecc.* 7:26).

In other words, as long as "freedom of opinion" leads one to ideas that coincide with those espoused by Rabbi Kook himself, all is well and good. If however, one should happen to arrive at different conclusions by virtue of "freedom of opinion", according to one's own nature and inclination, that is the "bad side" of such "freedom". Elsewhere, Rabbi Kook presents "freedom of opinion", along with other "achievements" of modernity, as running counter to the one and only truth of Judaism: "Let it be known to the enlightened world—with all its knowledge, with all its modernity, with all its doubts, with all its material decadence, with all its scientific experimentation, with all its freedom of opinion—that in fact, there is only one everlasting truth" (*Orot HaReiyah*, "*Sham'u Amim Yirgazun*"). It is interesting to compare Rabbi Kook's approach to that of Spinoza, regarding the tendency of "the masses" to follow their hearts rather than the dictates of reason. According to Spinoza, it is precisely the "error" that results from this tendency that mandates tolerance and freedom of opinion, since the need for these only arises with regard to opinions with which we disagree, opinions rooted in "error". There is no need for freedom of opinion and no need to show tolerance toward opinions with which we concur.

Rabbi Kook divided mankind into two categories—Jews and non-Jews: "The difference between the Jewish soul ... and the souls of all non-Jews of all [spiritual] levels, is greater and more profound than the difference between a human soul and that of a beast" (*Orot*, 156). The Jews are "the center of the universe and the center of mankind", and they alone bear the one, eternal, absolute truth. This truth is, of course, "supernal truth", embodied by the Jewish People, which is "the people of God" (*ibid.* 62). Thus, if Rabbi Kook can be said to advocate tolerance and pluralism of any kind, it is only within the boundaries of Jewish society.

Rabbi Kook's famed tolerance toward Zionist secularism is generally explained in one of two ways. On the one hand, it is portrayed as a tactical approach, intended to bring secular Jews closer to religious faith, while affording them a preordained role in the process of national redemption—an approach referred to in secular circles as the "Messiah's donkey" approach. Secular views are indeed characterized by Rabbi Kook as "unlawful opinions" that should be given no license whatsoever (see *Igrot HaReiyah* 1, 172). That is to say, tolerance should be shown to those who espouse secular ideas, but not to the ideas themselves. On the other hand, Rabbi Kook's writings also reveal a multifaceted approach to truth. It is not quite pluralism, since the core of his philosophy remains the single absolute truth, manifested in the Jewish people. Man, whose vision is necessarily limited, may only grasp part of this infinite and indefinite truth. Such partial conceptions however, are elements of the whole and absolute truth, and steps along the road to its discovery (see *Orot Hakodesh* 1, 17–18). In this way, even "pioneer" Zionism may be tolerated, since it acts in the cause of Jewish unity, which is the ultimate goal of Jewish existence and part of the absolute truth—but only for a time. In the end, this brand of secularism and all its values will converge with faith and be subsumed by it. Rabbi Kook summarizes this viewpoint as follows, in his chapter on tolerance:

Tolerance of opinions when it stems from a pure heart, free of all wickedness, will not dampen the ardor of holy sentiment—including that of simple faith, the source of all joy—but will rather broaden and increase ardor for the sake of Heaven. Tolerance is endowed with very great faith—to the point of recognizing that the soul cannot possibly be devoid of all holy light, for the life of the living God imbues all life. Therefore, even where action appears destructive and opinions heretical, the heart and depths of the soul conceal holy life-light, revealed in the good that we find even in many aspects of our own spoiled ranks, afflicted with heresy and consumed with doubt. And from this knowledge and great faith and holiness comes the tolerance to enfold all in a thread of grace. "I will surely assemble, O Jacob, all of thee" (*Micah* 2) (*Musar Avikha Umidot HaReiyah*, 84).

Rabbi Kook thus dos not view pioneer Zionism as authentically Jewish, since it is in his opinion, one of the "spoiled ranks, afflicted with heresy and consumed with doubt", nor does he show tolerance toward it. He accepts the secular "pioneers"—for "the good that we find" in them—but utterly rejects their views, which he considered dangerous. On the one hand, this is certainly not tolerance in the liberal or pluralistic sense, open to different and even aberrant opinions. On the other hand, Rabbi Kook's approach is not the jealousy of Pinhas, Elijah and Mattathias either. Nevertheless, those who call themselves disciples of Rabbi Kook have adopted from his work precisely those elements that lead to religious and nationalist zealotry, and possibly bloodshed. Although Rabbi Kook's thought may contain the seeds of extreme zealotry, it can be said of such zealots that they have distorted his message to serve their own ends. In any event, the jealousy of Pinhas is still alive and well, flying the banner of intolerance and anti-pluralism.

Reuven Gerber

Matot – And Moses spoke unto the Heads of the Tribes

The Pioneer Spirit and Self-Fulfillment
in the Thought of A. D. Gordon

And every armed man of you will pass over the Jordan before the Lord, until He hath driven out His enemies from before Him (*Numbers* 32:21).

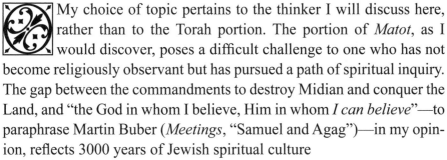My choice of topic pertains to the thinker I will discuss here, rather than to the Torah portion. The portion of *Matot*, as I would discover, poses a difficult challenge to one who has not become religiously observant but has pursued a path of spiritual inquiry. The gap between the commandments to destroy Midian and conquer the Land, and "the God in whom I believe, Him in whom *I can believe*"—to paraphrase Martin Buber (*Meetings*, "Samuel and Agag")—in my opinion, reflects 3000 years of Jewish spiritual culture

In light of today's religious fanaticism, which I believe distorts "Jewish morality", I would like to discuss the thought of A. D. Gordon. Since Gordon did not engage in biblical exegesis, we will explore his views on the issues raised in the portion of *Matot*, as they appear in his writings. Gordon belonged to the school of "spiritual Zionism", which perceives Judaism as an essence that evolves through dialogue with the progressive values of every era. (Rabbi A.I. Kook aptly described this process in the phrase "The old will be renewed and the new will be sanctified"—*Igrot HaReiyah* 1, 214).

The topics addressed in *Matot* (*Num*. 30–32) are three: 1) The laws of vows; 2) the fulfillment of God's commandment to kill the Midianites, men and women, and divide the spoils—as revenge for their having led the Israelites to worship the Baal of Pe'or; and 3) the settlement of the sons of Gad, Reuben and half of Manasseh, on the eastern bank of the Jordan, in exchange for their promise to serve as a vanguard in the conquest of the Land.

The portion begins with the laws of vows: "And Moses spoke unto the heads of the tribes of the children of Israel, saying: This is the thing which the Lord hath commanded. When a man voweth a vow unto the Lord, or sweareth an oath to bind his soul with a bond, he shall not break his word; he shall do according to all that proceedeth out of his mouth" (30:2–3). This is followed by the laws concerning vows made by women, which could be annulled by fathers or husbands who, in keeping with the practice of the day, exercised control over their lives.

We are immediately reminded of the story of Jephthah's daughter. In light of human weakness and the fear that such terrible events might be repeated, the Rabbis instituted the practice of "release from vows". One may be released from a vow for one of two reasons—"remorse" and "opening"—explained as follows, by Rabbi J. B. Soloveitchik:

> The release of "remorse" is based on emotional factors—no error or change has occurred in the vow, but, in me, myself. If, for instance, yesterday it seemed important to me to live in a beautiful home, to transfer to a rich neighborhood, it now seems to me to be pointless and absurd. In contrast, the release by "opening" is based on reason. In this case a person comes to a sage seeking release because his reason has deepened, it is more mature than it was before, and he now understands more than he did previously (*On Repentance*, p. 210).

The *Kol Nidrei* prayer, recited on the eve of Yom Kippur, effects just such a process. What is important for the purposes of this discussion however, is that the practice runs counter to the plain meaning of the Torah, and was not employed in biblical times—witness Jephthah's daughter. The Sages of the Mishnah candidly admit that, "The release from vows floats in the air and is without basis; the laws of the Sabbath, the festival sacrifices and the misuse of consecrated property are like mountains hanging on a thread, for they comprise many laws based on little Scripture" (*Hagigah* 10a). The Sages thus saw fit to limit the application of the biblical precept. They rejected the notion that this commandment—as an expression of God's will—should take precedence over human life, as in the case of Jephthah's daughter. This is an example of the creative and bold approach adopted by the Rabbis, in response to the cultural reality of their day.

This innovative and dynamic approach to religious law was supplanted however, over the course of a long and arduous exile—particularly among Eastern European Jews—by fanatical ultra-Orthodoxy. Yosef Aharonovitch tells of Gordon's first encounter with fanatical Hassidism, as a young man, in the town of Obodovka. Although an observant Jew himself, Gordon was treated like an apostate by these Hassidim (Introduction to *Kitvei A. D. Gordon, Mivhar Ketavim* p. 32).

What is the source of religious fanaticism? Jealousy is a natural human emotion. It evokes loyalty, ownership, a sense of superiority over others, and is particularly strong in cases of romantic love. Considered from this perspective, fanaticism—or religious jealousy—is also a natural emotion. People who are loyal to their gods jealously defend their honor—all the more so in the case of a single god, Creator of a single world, who revealed himself to a single people, from whom He demands complete obedience.

Fanaticism as appropriate religious behavior can be found, for example, in the story of the golden calf: "Then Moses stood in the gate of the camp, and said: 'Whoso is on the Lord's side, let him come unto me.' And all the sons of Levi gathered themselves together unto him. And he said unto them: 'Thus saith the Lord, the God of Israel: Put ye every man his sword upon his thigh, and go to and fro from gate to gate throughout the camp, and slay every man his brother, and every man his companion, and every man his neighbor'. And the sons of Levi did according to the word of Moses; and there fell of the people that day about three thousand men ... And the Lord smote the people, because they made the calf, which Aaron made" (*Ex.* 32:26–35). Is it not however, reasonable to claim that the root of religious fanaticism lies in God's own jealousy, as described in the Bible? Thus, for example, in the previous portion: "And the Lord spoke unto Moses, saying: 'Phinehas, the son of Eleazar, the son of Aaron the priest, hath turned my wrath away from the children of Israel, in that he was very jealous for my sake among them, so that I consumed not the Children of Israel in my jealousy. Wherefore say: Behold, I give unto him my covenant of peace;

and it shall be unto him, and to his seed after him, the covenant of an everlasting priesthood; because he was jealous for his God, and made atonement for the children of Israel'" (25:10–14).

The word jealousy is used to refer both in reference to God and as justification for the act that won Phinehas everlasting priesthood. This kind of fanaticism stands out in the second topic addressed in *Matot*—the massacre of the Midianites in God's name. The critical modern reader is not shocked by the fact that the Bible presents the terrible things that are said and done as God's will. The Israelites were not the only people of that time to portray their horrifying deeds as the will of their god. Nor are we shocked by the fact that today, after centuries of biblical criticism, there are still Orthodox Jews who believe that every word in the Torah was said to Moses at Mount Sinai. There are men and women of simple faith—in all senses of the word—in all religions. The profound shock that we experience stems from the relevance of this and similar biblical texts to current reality—a reality in which, as so often in Jewish history, a small group of extremists strives to impose its views on the large moderate majority, in the name of God's jealousy.

The third topic that of the conquest of the Land, has some bearing on the circumstances of Gordon's life. The labor-oriented Second Aliyah, of which Gordon was a leading light, based its claim to the Land of Israel, *inter alia*, on the historical settlement of the Land by the Israelite tribes. This only serves to highlight however, the vast difference between the conquest as described in the bible and the "conquest of labor" in Gordon's time.

In the Bible, the Israelites are commanded by God to annihilate the seven peoples of Canaan: "And when the Lord thy God shall deliver them up before thee, and thou shalt smite them; then thou shalt utterly destroy them; thou shalt make no covenant with them, nor show mercy unto them" (*Deut.* 7:2); "and ye shall possess it, and dwell therein" (*ibid.* 11:31); "thou dispossessest them, and dwellest in their land" (*ibid.* 12:29). The Rabbis try to mitigate the commandment somewhat: "The commandment is to kill them if they do battle against us, but if they wish to make peace then we shall make peace. We may not however, leave the land in their hands or in the hands of any other people. Similarly, these peoples [were not killed] if they turned and fled, as it is said of the Girgashite, that they turned and went away" (*Yerushalmi, Shevi'it* 6:1)

The secular aliyot on the other hand, pursued a policy of land purchase. In this too, as we know, there was an element of dispossession—the dispossession of the *fellahin*, the tenant farmers. Gordon however—who immigrated to Palestine late in life and viewed agricultural labor as a spiritual opportunity—called upon the pioneers to eschew undue force:

> It is now commonly said that the right to a land can only be acquired through blood. This is one of the sophisms that have been naturalized among all peoples, whom the common idea of justice has allowed to behave like bloodthirsty animals—one of the accepted lies. With blood and fire the freedom of a people is taken from them and they are, along with the land, temporarily enslaved, for as long as the enslaver's strength does not wane; but the land will always remain in the hands of those who live on it and cultivate it ... Land is acquired by living, working and creating in it. And so we too may acquire or regain the right to our land. We have a historical right to the land, and that right remains only as long as another creative, living force has not taken full possession of it (*"Avodateinu Me'atah"*– an essay written following the publication of the Balfour Declaration).

The Bible Concealed within our Soul

A critical examination of the portion of *Matot* may help explain the middle road suggested by Gordon with regard to Scripture. At one end of the ideological spectrum, stood figures such as M. J. Berdyczewski, who sought a "change of values", or Y. H. Brenner, who claimed to have "freed himself from the hypnosis of the Bible." At the other end, were the ultra-Orthodox. The former sought modern Jews alienated from their Judaism, the latter Judaism alienated from modernity. But what should a modern, critical-minded person with a religious spirit do? Gordon offers the following solution:

> Note, my friend, that I am not referring here to the Bible's historical value, but to the value of the opinions and poetry it contains. Indeed, the great value of the Bible to us lies not so much

in what it said, but in what it did not say; in what we or future generations will draw from it and from it alone—from the Bible concealed within our soul (A. D. Gordon, *Hayahadut Vehanatzrut*).

This fascinating statement, to which Gordon himself gives special prominence in his essay, encapsulates his attitude to the Bible. Reading this statement, it feels as if our entire understanding of the concept "Bible" has left the high road, rolled over twice and set out again on a new road, toward an unknown destination. Unlike his contemporaries, who approached the Bible in search of historical justification for their return to the land of the Bible, Gordon stressed its spiritual dimension—"the opinions and poetry it contains". Just when we expect him to elaborate however, to point out the opinions he considers particularly central, he changes direction, switching from the past to the future: "the great value of the Bible to us lies not so much in what it said, but in what it did not say; in what we or future generations will draw from it". OK, you say to yourself, automatically translating Gordon's words into a modern secular slogan: "the Bible need not be seen as revelation, but rather as a source of human inspiration". Then comes the second change in direction: "and from it alone—from the Bible concealed within our soul". In other words, not merely a source of inspiration, but actual revelation. The revelation however, is not the words of a transcendent god, but the Torah concealed like light within the human soul. You now realize that Gordon has travelled a great distance from a straightforward reading of the Bible and you look inward, in an attempt to understand where he wishes to take you. Like the kabbalists, Gordon interprets the essence of the Bible in a new-old way. Unlike them however, he believes in the Bible "concealed within our soul" without believing in a "lawgiving" God. Where has he taken us? Can we describe the Bible, in Gordon's view, as a "spiritual runway"?

A look at Gordon's life, confirms this feeling. Gordon was a Torah scholar who "pursued a path of continuous inquiry" (a better term than "apostatized" or "lost his faith", when describing a spiritual man like Gordon). He was firmly rooted in Judaism, but opposed Hassidic fanaticism during the religious period of his life, in the Diaspora, and gradually shed the yoke of Halakhah following his arrival in Palestine.

Many of the pioneers of the Second Aliyah were former yeshivah students. It was the modern zeitgeist, sweepingly secular, influenced by science, positivist philosophy, biblical criticism, and especially God's Nietzschean demise. Gordon however, contrary to most members of the Second Aliyah, did not pit the profane against the sacred, but sought a new way.

Gordon's singularity, as a member of the Second Aliyah, lay not in his physical efforts, but in the pioneering nature of his spiritual philosophy. Anyone who examines his work closely will come to the conclusion that he was both material pioneer—like the other members of his group—and spiritual pioneer. His long hours of toil in the fields were marked by moments of fulfillment and joy. He could not help but try to convey the fruit of his spirit to those around him and those who shared his views. In the small hours of the night, after a long and arduous day's work, he would sit by lamplight and stitch his words into ponderous essays. His devotion to agricultural labor, like that of his fellow pioneers, stemmed from his total submission to an inner life that recognized the value of physical labor in nature. Gordon was a unique figure; a pioneer who incorporated a connection to nature, the construction of a homeland, manual labor, suffering and spiritual joy. As a result of this unique combination, A. D. Gordon became a symbol of self-fulfillment for his generation.

Like the label "religion of labor" this reflects a partial and superficial understanding of his ideas. At this level, self-fulfillment means the way in which one applies oneself to the path one has chosen in life. The members of Gordon's generation saw in him what they saw in themselves—a pioneer who chose to serve in the vanguard, in order to prepare with her or his physical labor, the Jewish People's return to its land.

Gordon's thought however, affords two further, deeper insights into the essence of self-fulfillment. The first, stresses the word "fulfillment", while the second—the deeper of the two—places greater emphasis on the word "self". The first demands profound self-knowledge, the second "living intuition". Gordon considered self-knowledge the means by which the "timbre" of personality—i.e. the distinctive tone of voice that accompanies a common language—is expressed. Similarly, Gordon believed that human beings differ from one another (Nietzsche from Tolstoy, for example) not in their rational thought—which we all share, but in their unique, prerational personalities. Collective rationality is thus merely the means by which we express our individuality. In this sense, one's specific life and its reflection in one's thought is in fact self-fulfillment. In other words, one must seek self-fulfillment not in the pioneering collective, but in the development of one's own spiritual individuality. On a deeper level however, one must strive to experience the essence of the "spiritual ground" in which our spiritual seeds germinate and grow. The fulfillment of one's unique self provides the means by which to describe the part of spiritual totality that is closest to one's soul. True self-fulfillment is the experiential encounter of consciousness with the "self" from which it derives.

At this point, we must offer a brief explanation of Gordon's role as a spiritual pioneer, i.e. the core of his philosophy. To this end, we will discuss the Hebrew concept of *havayah* or "living intuition", coined by Gordon, his attitude to the eastern religions, and finally his attitude to Jewish tradition.

As noted, it was Gordon who first suggested the concept of *havayah*. Over the years, its original meaning has been forgotten, and it has assumed the familiar sense of an event that leaves an impression on one's soul. Gordon created his neologism by combining the words *havayah* (existence) and *hayim* (life). He sought a term for the faculty of "preconscious consciousness", the ever-present flow of preverbal consciousness. In a state of living intuition (*matzav havayati*), consciousness (pure rather than subjective) experiences its source, its unity with the totality of the cosmos. *Havayah* is to man, explains Gordon, like the spinning of the earth to those on the planet's surface. The influence is constant, but precisely for that reason, because it is so essential, like oxygen, we are not aware of its existence. *Havayah* might also be called "pure consciousness"—i.e. consciousness free of cognitive and linguistic content, form and structure. Gordon compares it to the sea, before having put forth waves, vegetation and fish. At the same time however, the rational element in consciousness, which operates according to logical principles, shows that pure consciousness is "meta-rational"—the "source of reason" and the creative forces at work in the world. *Ḥavayah* is thus true self-fulfillment, inasmuch as it unites pure self and all manifestations of the essential in reality.

Gordon's intuition-belief in universal, meta-rational consciousness—which he calls "hidden intellect", greatly resembles the belief of eastern religions in a non-personal creative and sustaining force. Gordon himself, who was aware of this resemblance, denied any connection between his *ḥavayah* and Buddhism, and rejected the Buddhist concept of nirvana, as running counter to nature and the cosmos. (In my opinion however, due to cultural conditions at the time, little was known of these philosophies. Meditation, with which many today are familiar, seeks to develop the ability transcend ordinary consciousness, in order to achieve a state of pure consciousness.) Gordon himself experienced the *ḥavayah* of unity simply by being and working in nature. He therefore concluded that labor is the surest path to the *ḥavayah* of unity with the nature of reality. Labor is like the circulatory system in the body of society. It is through labor that man is able to contribute to the constant growth in nature. The following passage regarding the *ḥavayah* of redemption hidden within nature, further explains this important concept in Gordon's philosophy:

> And when, O Man, you will return to Nature, you will open your eyes, and you will gaze straight into the eyes of Nature, you will see therein your own image, and you will know that you have returned to yourself, that when you have hidden from nature you have hidden from yourself … On that account your life was cut in two—a very small fraction of existence and a very large part of no-existence—of work, of labor, of restlessness. "Sabbath" and the "Eve of Sabbath". You did not think, and it did not occur to you that there is no Life in a life ready-made, if there is not Life in its preparation, for nature also lives within the preparation of Life, within the creation of Life ("Man and Nature", *Selected Essays*, pp. 247–249).

The true religious *ḥavayah*, according to Gordon, is that of unity with the stream of cosmic life. The dimension of redemption however, raises the question of Gordon's attitude to the traditional Jewish sources. He maintained that the Torah spoke in terms of "the word of God", in an effort to convey this *ḥavayah*. The problem arises in religion, when myth is taken for fact. So for example, the intention of the biblical story of "the tree of life and the tree of knowledge" was to give expression to the rift that had arisen between the capacity to experience unity and detailed consciousness. Those who sanctify the content of the Torah as truth, err in their religious consciousness.

Research has shown that, despite his disdain for the literal interpretation of Scripture, Gordon was greatly influenced by Hassidic thought (for a remarkable analysis of the Hassidic sources in Gordon's work, see Avraham Shapira, *Or Hahayim Be "Yom Ketanot"*). For example, Gordon use of the term "hidden intellect" to refer to the divine—derives from Hassidic mysticism. Gordon's approach to tradition would thus appear to be ambivalent. He draws heavily upon rabbinic hermeneutical literature—particularly Hassidic works; yet rejects the accepted religious worldview. This apparent contradiction is easily resolved. The language and literature of the nation are the idiom employed by the souls of its members who, by means of the religious literature, sought to suggest the idea of the spiritual *ḥavayah*—Gordon's very intention. Like Gordon however, the religious literature is unable to verbalize the unitary preconscious *ḥavayah*, but can only refer to it indirectly, in the esoteric language of *remez* and *sod*. The religious literature at its height not only evokes love for its esoteric message and desire for the *ḥavayah*, but it also affords a bridge of words by which one may approach its intimacy; like the knowledge with which "Adam knew Eve".

Gordon felt a deep affinity for Scripture and key concepts in the religious literature that reflect a living approach to the *ḥavayah* of unity and its moral laws. He did not follow the path of strained interpretation, which attempts to wrap its inventions in a mantle of quotations taken out of their original context. He did not resort to biblical exegesis in order to persuade readers that his philosophy was in fact merely a link in a continuous chain. We can only guess what his views on the topics addressed in *Matot* might have been. He would probably have seen the cruel treatment of the Midianites as an expression of the base feelings that man experiences when greatly removed from the *havayah* of unity with the cosmos, and the religious sanctity that the biblical author ascribes to the war, as a complete distortion of spirituality (furthermore, as a socialist, he would certainly have been outraged by the generous gifts afforded from the general spoils to the ruling religious class). The commandment to destroy the seven peoples of Canaan is certainly in the category of things best looked back on from a distance, as we take to the spiritual heights. The halakhic development allowing the dissolution of vows on the other hand, could serve as an example of dialogue between the Bible and the soul of the Rabbinic reader, who added something to Scripture that it had not yet said. The comparison clearly demonstrates a process of moral refinement over the course of spiritual history, at the juncture between that which has been written and that which has been said in response to it (see also Ahad Ha'am, *"Hamussar Hale'umi"*, *Al Parashat Derakhim*, vol.2, p. 49). As we rise up and delve into our inner selves, our feelings are refined, and our hearts are touched by sublime emotions of compassion and brotherhood.

Gordon's *havayah* of cosmic unity cannot be transmitted. Knowledge can be conveyed to others, but "living intuition" can only be implied. Words are the road signs of the spiritual world, and that is the ultimate goal of Gordon's wonderful works. It is up to each and every one of us to decide where we stand with regard to the essence of holiness; to choose between the biblical God revealed to his prophets and the *havayah* of unity.

Personally, I believe that Jewish education must recognize this process of moral perfection—from the Bible to Halakhah to spiritual-Zionist philosophy to the present day. The road that leads from the Bible to modern thought is our runway, as we strive to ascend to spiritual heights.

Gordon, like his friend A.I. Kook, was a modern Jewish mystic. By virtue of his Jewish education on the one hand and his spiritual growth on the other—he was able to experience and create the kind of holistic approach we associate with the "New Age" movement today. His position—at the crossroads between tradition and western progress, presaging holistic Jewish spirituality and espousing modern values—is certainly a fitting educational approach for our time.

Alas, at a time when Scripture and its various commentaries are enjoying a renaissance even at nonreligious institutions, Gordon's teachings are completely disregarded. Young people, both religious and secular, travel all the way to the Himalayas in search of similar spiritual philosophies and their exponents. The eastern philosophies however, appear to lack the dimension of spirituality through work, creative and productive activity within the context of real life. When emphasis is placed exclusively on immersing oneself in the spiritual, it entails a tendency to existential passivity, which is inappropriate to the western society in which we live. The philosophy of Gordon and the mature philosophy of Rabbi Kook, which sought to bring about a spiritual revolution and was also consigned to oblivion, were developed in light of the encounter between Jewish mystical spirituality and western culture. These and similar philosophies developed by the school of spiritual Zionism should be taught, as a spiritual foundation for Israeli society.

Michael Zvi Nehorai

Mas'ei—These are the Journeys of the Children of Israel

Eretz Yisrael in the Thought of *Rabbi Isaac Jacob Reines*

And the Lord spoke unto Moses in the plains of Moab by the Jordan at Jericho, saying: "Speak unto the children of Israel, and say unto them: When ye pass over the Jordan into the land of Canaan, then ye shall drive out all the inhabitants of the land from before you, and destroy all their figured stones, and destroy all their molten images, and demolish all their high places. And ye shall drive out the inhabitants of the land, and dwell therein; for unto you have I given the land to possess it" (*Numbers* 33:50–53).

 The verse "And ye shall drive out the inhabitants of the land, and dwell therein" has been a source of halakhic and political debate, particularly from the time of Maimonides (1138–1204) to the present. The question arises: Should this verse be treated as a divine promise to be fulfilled in the end of days, or as one of the 613 precepts that Jews are required to observe throughout the ages? Maimonides does not number dwelling in the Land among the precepts, leading many commentators to conclude that he espoused the former position. Nahmanides (1194–1270) on the other hand, concludes from this verse, that dwelling in the land is a positive precept, numbered among the 613.

Some six centuries later, in the early days of the Zionist movement, the debate reawakened in a different form: Is it permitted or prohibited to initiate action that would bring about an exodus from the Diaspora and a return to the Land of Israel? The parties to the debate were the religious Zionists—led by Rabbi Isaac Jacob Reines (1839–1915), founder of the Mizrachi movement—and the *haredim*, led by the Torah sages of the day. The latter group vehemently opposed the very existence of the Zionist movement headed by Dr. Theodor Herzl.

The debate in fact persists to this day in the State of Israel—after more than a century of Zionism. It is therefore worth examining the formation and development of these positions, and the extent to which historical reality has substantiated their initial claims. In order to better understand the respective positions, we will cite a passage from Reines' own work, in which he summarizes the arguments regarding the religious legitimacy of the Zionist movement, using the following, seemingly innocent parable:

A young man of good family ... suffered great pain ... and fits of trembling ... until all who saw him believed he would not live ... [His parents] stopped at nothing to deliver him from his illness, summoning all the physicians in the land ... But alas, even the wisdom of the greatest doctors failed them and the ablest among them were helpless, and the force of the illness to crush this lovely young man under its heel was in no way diminished ... So all who loved him came together to discuss the matter, and decided to bring from a great distance a singularly remarkable physician, unparalleled in all the world ... also renowned as a holy man of God, who had seen visions from the Almighty and had told things that were to come thereafter, and all he said came to pass ... When this great doctor came and had examined the unfortunate patient carefully, he opened his mouth and said: Know this, honored gentlemen! As a physician ... I must tell you the truth, that my efforts to heal him would be in vain, for the air in this land greatly aggravates his incurable disease and he will never recover here. The air that can bring him succor and a cure for his illness can be found in such and such a distant land, which lies beyond deserts and great seas, and all who travel there are exposed to great danger ... for the roads are plagued by highwaymen.

Furthermore, I can tell you that despite the great danger his illness appears to pose ... you may be certain that you will not lead him to the grave, and even when he is seized with trembling and his limbs are racked with convulsions ... be not discouraged for him, for they will pass and the patient will return to his constant illness, which will not take him to the grave, even if it continues for many years. When he had finished saying these things, he said to them: Now I must caution you on two matters with regard to the patient: … I have considered the matter carefully and have concluded that there is no stratagem or contrivance against this illness , and even if you see that charlatans … succeed in their actions and the illness eases its grip on the patient from day to day, beware lest you delude your hearts with false hopes, for it will not endure … it is but a false remedy … and before long the convulsions will return with greater violence than ever before … Remember, he will live with his illness …until the time is ripe to go to that distant land I have mentioned, to find relief and be restored to health. This is my first caution.

The second matter of which I feel I must warn you … A bitter thought might occur to you, to try to take him to that land, that he might find relief and be restored to health. I therefore charge you, upon your oaths, that you will not attempt to do so, for not only will you not help him, you will endanger your own lives and the patient's life, and you will bring disaster upon yourselves and upon him.

In order to ease your suffering and grief somewhat, I will tell you that I am able to see the future, and I see by my prophetic spirit that one day some men will take pity on the patient and carry him on their shoulders to that land where he will regain his strength and his health. You, sirs, however! Do not try to hasten the process, but rather wait calmly and quietly and fortify the patient with [faith in] God, thereby instilling in him the courage to endure his suffering … so that even if [his salvation] is late in coming, he will yet await it. And with these words, he took his leave (Reines, *Or Hadash al Tziyon*, 113–114).

Rabbi Reines leaves no room for speculation regarding the moral of this tale. The sick lad is the Jewish People, persecuted and oppressed in exile. The holy man, the doctor and prophet who cautions and promises, represents Scripture and the rabbinic literature, which state as follows:

1. The Jewish People will suffer terribly in exile—"And among these nations shalt thou have no repose, and there shall be no rest for the sole of thy foot" (*Deut.* 28:65).
2. The torments of exile will never pose a threat to the existence of the Jewish People—"And yet for all that, when they are in the land of their enemies, I will not reject them, neither will I abhor them, to destroy them utterly" (*Lev.* 26:44).
3. The exile will come to an end one day, when God will gather the dispersed of Israel from among the nations and lead them to the Land of Israel—"And then the Lord thy God will turn thy captivity, and have compassion upon thee, and will return and gather thee from all the peoples, whither the Lord thy God hath scattered thee. (*Deut.* 30:3).

All agree that the above three points are entirely in the hands of God. This is not the case however, with regard to the two cautions that accompany them. The first of these cautions against seeking "natural stratagems and political artifices to remove the burden of exile from their shoulders", i.e. do not be fooled by the illusion that the torments of exile can be resolved by rebelling against the nations or trying to assimilate in their midst. Illusions of this kind are likely to make things "worse than before" (*Or Hadash al Tziyon*, 115). The Talmud in the tractate of *Ketubot* (111a) infers from Scripture, three oaths to which God adjured Israel: not to "ascend the wall" (i.e. forcibly, and in an organized fashion –tr.), not to rebel against the nations of the world, and not to hasten the end. Rabbi Reines extends these oaths to include the stipulation that Jews in the Diaspora not attempt to ease their suffering by attempting to attenuate their Jewish identity. Reines here follows in the footsteps of Rabbi Judah Halevi, who wrote: "If the majority of us ... would learn humility towards God and His Law from our low station, Providence would not have forced us to bear it for such a long period" (*Kuzari* 1,115 –tr. H. Hirschfeld). The second caution, according to Rabbi Reines, is that no attempt be made to ascend to Zion by force—"They must await the wondrous end, when God will cause his voice to be heard from Mount Zion in a great blast of the *shofar*, and the redeemed will pass over and come with singing unto Zion"; or in the words of Halevi: "If we bear our exile and degradation for God's sake, as is meet, we shall be the pride of the generation which will come with the Messiah, and accelerate the day of the deliverance we hope for" (*ibid.*); and "Were we prepared to meet the God of our forefathers with a pure mind, we should find the same salvation as our fathers did in Egypt" (*ibid.* 2,24).

The essence of the debate concerns the practical halakhic application of these two cautions. The following is Rabbi Reines' view on the matter, from which we may also deduce the views of his opponents:

In this too there is something that remains unclear, and that is whether we are permitted to seek sure means of transport even before the awakening from above, for the miraculous passage promised to us by the prophets (the cautions we have mentioned refer only to a situation of danger and should not be applied to situations in which there is no danger). There is no doubt however that we are not only permitted [to do so], but are duty-bound to try to improve our situation ... by sure and lawful means according to Jewish law. And since, moreover, the transfer the Zionist movement seeks to effect is by no means universal, and at best we can only hope to transfer a large number of our people to Zion, why should we not engage in this matter? The hope of redemption does not preclude seeking and taking action, and those who think that where there is hope there can be no room for action show that they do not understand the meaning of the word hope.

Rabbi Reines refers here to the passage in *Ketubot*, cited above, regarding the oaths to which God adjured Israel—not to "ascend the wall" or rebel against the nations. In order to dispel any suspicion that he might have questioned the validity of this talmudic teaching, Rabbi Reines opines that the talmudic "cautions", or oaths, only apply to situations in which taking such action might be dangerous. When no danger is entailed however, no one could possibly deny the fact that we are obligated to do everything in our power to improve our circumstances. In his book *Or Hadash al Tziyon*, Rabbi Reines devotes a great deal of attention to these oaths, maintaining that they are indeed of practical, halakhic significance. In a lengthy halakhic discourse, he argues that both Maimonides and Nahmanides would agree that the commandment to dwell in the land of Israel is not applicable, unless it can be fulfilled by means of actions that entail no danger, such as the purchase of lands from their owners. The only point on which they disagree is whether the injunction to engage in such action is biblical (Nahmanides) or rabbinic (Maimonides). Rabbi Reines therefore dismisses outright any possibility of conquest by force, and maintains that such an option had never occurred to Nahmanides:

> Nahmanides attempts to prove there that this precept [to conquer and settle the Land] also applies today ... It is clear that he did not mean that we are commanded to conquer by war, for the Children of Israel have been adjured for the duration of the exile to distance themselves from all plots of rebellion and treachery, Heaven forbid. It is therefore manifestly clear that his intention was to consensual acquisition ... [which] is also a religious obligation. For according to his approach, as we have explained, all that is conquest is considered a religious obligation ... inasmuch as it is a means to obtaining and settling the land ... Acquisition with the consent of the owners is thus a religious obligation because it is a means of settling the Land (*ibid.* 18–19).

Rabbi Reines concluded that the intentions of the Zionist movement were "by no means universal, and at best we can only hope to transfer a large number of our people to Zion". He believed that Nahmanides' ruling (unlike that of Maimonides)—that the commandment to conquer the Land applies to all generations—refers to conquest by purchase, not war.

He was thus fully aware of the teachings in *Ketubot* and their validity, yet concluded that there is no halakhic impediment to Zionist activity. Such activity does not constitute rebellion against the nations, since it does not purport to supplant the Messiah and gather the exiles, but only those persecuted individuals in need of asylum. The Torah therefore does not allow, but rather requires each and every Jew to act "by sure and lawful means according to Jewish law" to alleviate the suffering of the Children of Israel.

Another argument with which Rabbi Reines had to contend concerned the halakhic prohibition against associating with "the wicked", i.e. the secular leadership of the Zionist movement. Rabbi Reines replied that one must distinguish between those who join the movement and the movement itself. Ideally, the *haredim* should have been the first to the bear the standard of the Zionist movement. The fact that it was the secular who flocked to it only affirms its great value:

The pogroms and attacks were like a public proclamation that there could no longer be any hope of improving the condition of Israel among the nations, and it is this that gave rise to the Zionist movement. Of course, only the irreligious and the innovators were surprised by the pogroms and attacks, and all their hopes to be as all the nations were proven false; but this came as no news to those who fear God and tremble (*haredim*) before Him, for they were never deceived by the chimera of assimilation among the nations, and longed only for the end of days ... It was therefore only natural that the irreligious should be the first to be deeply shaken by these pogroms and attacks, seeing in them the end to all their hopes. And they were therefore imbued with a new spirit, a spirit of national pride, and became the first to act for the sake of the Holy Land. Clearly, in light of all this, we no longer saw travail and vanity in the Zionist movement. On the contrary, following the awakening of the irreligious to this great and holy matter, it is the sacred duty of the *haredim* to join forces with them and become as one for the 'work of service and the work of bearing' upon the mountains of Zion.

This is then Rabbi Reines' reply to the objection that one may not associate with the "wicked": The secular abandoned the yoke of Torah and the precepts in the expectation that non-Jewish society would welcome them with open arms. In so doing, they violated one of the above cautions. To their great disappointment however, they were rejected by non-Jewish society, which continued to treat them as undesirable Jews. The assimilationists' intuitive response was to lend their support to Zionism, that they might quit the lands of the nations. Those who "tremble before the Lord" on the other hand, had long ago lost their sense of national pride. They took for granted the fact that they, as Jews, were destined to suffer humiliation. It is therefore to the credit of the nonreligious, says Rabbi Reines, that they joined a movement that is a source of strength and resolve for all who seek to regain their national pride and return to their Jewish roots.

Judging by the way in which Jewish history has unfolded since that time, the approach taken by Rabbi Reines would appear to have been the more prescient of the two. The fact is that the Zionist movement laid the foundations for the state of the Jews, which provided asylum to tens of thousands of survivors of the flames of the European Holocaust. The *haredim* however, also foresaw many of the upheavals that have occurred since then in the Jewish national ethos, first and foremost—disillusionment and a reevaluation of the talmudic homily of the three oaths.

Devarim – Deuteronomy

Hagai Dagan

Devarim – These are the Words

The Human God and the Divine God
Hans Jonas

These are the words which Moses spoke unto all Israel beyond the Jordan; in the wilderness, in the Arabah, over against Suph, between Paran and Tophel, and Laban, and Hazeroth, and Di-za-hab. It is eleven days journey from Horeb unto Kadesh-Barnea by the way of mount Seir (*Deuteronomy* 1:1–2).

Devarim can read as a lesson and a prophecy, intermingled with Moses' admonitions to Israel. Its stated rationale is: "beyond the Jordan, in the land of Moab, took Moses upon him to expound this law" (1:5). It is a kind of recapitulation, a review of events up to that point, explaining the logic behind them and offering insights for the future, for the period that will follow the crossing of the Jordan and entry into the Land.

Moses mentions, among other things, the affair of the spies and that which is portrayed in this context as the sin that kindled God's wrath against the Israelites—their fear of the future, of the sons of the Ana-kim and the fortified Canaanite cities. Such faintness of heart however, appears completely human and natural. It is the fear and hurt of no-madic tribes in the presence of those who dwell in safety; the fear of the precarious, when confronted with the complacent and the stable. This fear, which also includes a sense of inferiority and of one's own wretchedness, is beautifully described in Shulamith Hareven's *Thirst* trilogy, which depicts the settlement of the Land, not as a campaign of conquest—as in the book of *Joshua*—but as a hesitant and gradual flow of hapless nomads to the margins of Canaanite society, a process ac-companied by doubts concerning God and the entire founding narrative. The other side of this coin of fear is the terror of townsmen and villag-ers at the specter of marauding desert tribes. The Bible however, tells the nomads' story and the story of the god who rebukes them, exhorts

541

and admonishes them—a god who comes from Paran and from Horeb, a desert god, a nomad's god, a god who will not abide human weakness and fear. His hallmark is detachment and uprooting—from Aram-Naharaim and from Egypt—and journeys with vague, distant and hidden destinations, beyond seemingly endless deserts; places that inevitably belong to other peoples, other tribes, who must be annihilated—men, women and children (3:6–7). He is impervious to longings for flesh-pots, cucumbers and melons, to the need for something tangible and joyous (the calf), and he is impervious to fear of the unknown.

The faith and loyalty he demands are absolute and entail a commitment to storm the fortified walls of Canaan's cities with narrowed eyes and clenched teeth. The fear that these walls evoke in the hearts of the people, weary of wandering, deserts and promises, angers him so much that, even after they have repented and shown willingness to rush into battle, he is still not satisfied. Moses describes it as follows: "Then ye answered and said unto me: 'We have sinned against the Lord, we will go up and fight, according to all that the Lord our God commanded us'. And ye girded on every man his weapons of war, and deemed it a light thing to go up into the hill-country. And the Lord said unto me: 'Say unto them: Go not up, neither fight; for I am not among you'" (1:41–42). They go into battle anyway, perhaps to exonerate themselves and prove that they are indeed loyal, and are thoroughly defeated. "And ye returned and wept before the Lord; but the Lord hearkened not to your voice, nor gave ear unto you" (1:45).

This story embodies the people's future relationship with God. *Deuteronomy* is not only a relatively late work, but it is also a didactic work, which strives to establish a determined pattern of relations with the divine, and a specific approach to the meta-historical covenant forged at Horeb. God is bound to ensure the welfare and normal progression (perhaps regression?) of the People along the path of history, while the People itself is required to worship God and observe His precepts, with complete faith in his message and absolute obedience to the words of his messengers. Incidentally, while this is generally portrayed as an exclusive covenant between the one God and his one chosen people, chapter two would seem to imply that He fought the wars of other peoples as well: the Edomites (descendants of Esau), Moabites and Amonites

(2:1–23). In other words, God has other chosen peoples, and the Israelites are merely one component in God's broad historical plan.

This in no way detracts from the importance of the covenant or the direness of its violation. The consequences of violating the covenant, of not upholding God's commandments or even doubting His promises can be terrible indeed. In this portion, God simply allows the Israelites to go to war and suffer defeat at the hands of their enemies. Here, the characteristics that God will later assume—as a harsh, vindictive deity, in whose eyes no price is too great for having disobeyed Him or questioned His authority—begin to take shape. He is authoritarian, overbearing and patriarchal. To use a somewhat clichéd image, He does not treat his people as a mother would a child—protecting and defending it no matter what, even when it disobeys her—but like those inflexible fathers who are prepared to abandon their children and inflict terrible punishments upon them when they violate the tribal codes of honor, the sacred hierarchy or the absolute loyalty they are expected to show the fathers of the tribe or the nation. Although omnipotent, He does not intervene on behalf of his people, allowing them to be defeated and slaughtered—beyond all the afflictions that await them if they continue to disobey him, described in excruciating detail in *Deuteronomy* 28.

According to this rationale, the course of Jewish history is one of complete submission to God—even when His commands appear absurd or entail great suffering—or of even greater suffering, when His will or precepts are disobeyed. It is sometimes hard to tell which of the two types of suffering is responsible for the people's tribulations: the one that is an integral part of the difficult and inexplicable path of chosenness, or the one that is caused by deviating from that path. Only one thing remains absolutely clear, and that is that suffering is suffering. The longer it has persisted—in fact, coloring the entire history of the people in its collective memory and in the mythological-historical consciousness reflected in its writings—the more it has given rise to hermeneutic, homiletic, and linguistic attempts to justify it and the God identified with it, so that we are no longer able to tell which way is the right way and whether a way of less suffering is even possible.

It is no accident that Judaism gave rise to Christianity, which is founded entirely upon the glorification and deification of suffering.

The Christian god, who descended to earth and became flesh to atone through suffering for the sins of men, is identified almost completely with suffering. He does not remain outside and cause suffering (without suffering himself). He does not maintain his earlier separateness—the transcendence by virtue of which he created the world from without—but descends to the world and identifies with its suffering. The Jewish god on the other hand, continues to inflict suffering upon his chosen people, but does not suffer with them. In light of this rather cruel and cynical pattern, a good deal of midrashic acrobatics are required to claim that this god—despite his apparent wickedness and virtual indistinguishability from Satan—still seeks the good of his people; a good that is relegated to some indefinite age of redemption.

As the catastrophes that befell the People intensified, this pattern of divine behavior became increasingly difficult to justify. The logic of *Devarim* however, offers a convenient solution: tragedy befalls Israel when it defies God, who then abandons his children and ceases to dwell among them, hides his "face" from them, and so forth. This is as true for the casualties sustained in the disastrous war against "the Amorites that dwell in that hill-country" (1:44) as it is for the millions who perished in the years 1939–1945. One can always find "sins" or "iniquities" if one looks hard enough, just as the Rabbis did for example, in the case of the Ten Martyrs (who were tortured and executed by the Romans).

The logic of theodicy—in effect the justification of suffering—is transparent, clear, consistent, solid, embarrassingly simple, cynical and hand-wringingly callous. And indeed, many continued to adhere to this logic, even after the Holocaust. There is no amount of suffering, no matter how great, that can shake their conviction. A few others, like Rabbi Kalonymos Shapira (the Hassidic rabbi of Piaseczno), departed very slightly from this position. He speaks of God weeping in the hidden "inner chambers" of heaven, unable to come to Israel's aid. Here we begin to see a crack in the conceptual wall of an omnipotent divinity who simply abandons his people to its fate, undefended by providence. This idea was taken much further by Jewish theologian Hans Jonas.

Jonas addressed the subject in his essay "The Concept of God after Auschwitz" (*Der Gottesbegriff nach Auschwitz*), based on a lecture he gave on that subject at Tübingen University in 1984. Jonas' point of departure was the realization that the evil of the Holocaust was so great that we can no longer speak of God in the old theological terms. The wholesale destruction of the Jewish People, as well as the Roma and many millions of Russians, and what is worse, the boundless suffering inflicted upon individuals—so many, yet individuals nonetheless—completely shatters the concept of God as both Lord of history and a caring God. Such evil in the present can no longer be justified with a vague promise of future good. A God who, as Lord of history, causes such suffering in the present and justifies it as a sacrifice on the altar of future redemption—from which those who are suffering now will not benefit in any case—cannot be anything but evil. If we are to relate to God as good, the concept must be profoundly shaken up. In other words, we must retell God's story from the very beginning if we are to exonerate him or relate to him in any way after the Holocaust.

Jonas therefore suggests that we abandon concepts of divine transcendence and majesty, in favor of a "suffering God", who experiences creation and shares in its suffering. This God is passive and limited, having renounced his omnipotence in the very act of creation, which—contrary to the medieval Jewish conception—was not *ex nihilo*, but the product of God's self-limitation and self-imposed immanence. In identifying with creation, the Godhead reconstituted itself as a becoming God—becoming rather than being; and creation itself is a kind of adventure, upon which God embarked not as an observer or a "hidden hand", but as an unreserved participant, risking his entire being in the process. Jonas thus rejects the medieval concepts of divine oneness, unity, immutability and transtemporality. He also suggests that the unquestioned superiority of being over becoming is rooted in Platonic-Aristotelian tradition, as incorporated into Judeo-Christian (as well as medieval Arab) thought, which ascribed being to God and becoming to our world. A return to the concept of becoming divinity is, in Jonas' opinion, a return to the authentic language and imagery of the Bible, freeing these from the artificially imposed constraints of Hellenic ontology.

A self-effacing God, who identifies with the world and with man's suffering to such an extent, would appear to be a rather Christian God. Jonas concedes this fact, but notes that a similar approach can be found in the Lurianic concept of *tzimtzum* (contraction), which maintains that God must withdraw "from Himself into Himself" in order to make "room within Himself" for the creation of the worlds.

The idea of a hidden (or hiding) God is unacceptable to Jonas as an explanation or justification of the Holocaust, inasmuch as it stands in direct contradiction to the concept of a revealed, commandment and law-giving God. It also contradicts the idea of God as good (i.e. moral), for something cannot be said to be "good" if its goodness is not apparent. Jonas incisively observes that the three aspects generally attributed to the monotheistic God—omnipotence, morality (absolute goodness), and intelligibility (a quality that stems from his relation with man and the world and his being a revealed divinity)—cannot co-exist. For if God is good and all-powerful, how can he allow evil to happen? Put another way: if he is both good and omnipotent, yet allows evil to happen, he necessarily ceases to be intelligible. Jonas therefore suggests that we eliminate divine omnipotence, in order to preserve divine goodness. A suffering God is a good God, despite the existence of evil, because he also suffers at its hand, yet is powerless to prevent it.

According to Jonas' theodicy, the Holocaust is a series of events that is—as part of world and human history—*also an integral part of God himself.* This idea, which combines pantheism, Christianity and Lurianic Kabbalah, is a radical and heroic attempt to preserve some sort of theology after Auschwitz. What Jonas does not explain is why we need theology at all after Auschwitz.

Speculating on the divine would appear to be a human need—a need so strong (at least in people like Jonas) that even the Holocaust has failed to eradicate it; demonstrating that nothing ever will. God will continue to live in their midst, even after the concept itself has undergone a revolutionary transformation. Or should I say perhaps, that God will continue to hover between life and death in their midst; for what kind of God emerges from Jonas' new theology? A helpless God, known not for his strength but for his weakness, and for his inability to do anything on our behalf. His role ended with creation, and we are now, for all intents and purposes, alone. Or perhaps we are not alone, but only in the sense that we are aware of a presence in our midst that suffers with us and feels our pain—unlike the God of *Devarim*, who deserted his people and ceased to dwell among them.

Why do we need such a presence? So that we are never entirely alone, some might say. But there is more to it than that. Jonas' God may indeed be seen as a good and well-intentioned God who is powerless against evil and whose only function since creation (or perhaps since eternity) has been his own quiet (but evident) existence, alongside the victims of evil. Such a God may alleviate a sense of existential loneliness among his believers and highlight by his very existence the fact that man bears exclusive responsibility for his own life and ability to choose good. A consistent approach to the concept of free choice almost certainly leads to a divinity of this kind. Any other type of God would necessarily limit choice in some way.

Jonas' God can also be seen in a far more radical light. God, in forfeiting his ability to intervene from without, identified completely with the world and with human reality—good and evil alike. Auschwitz itself is thus an integral part of God: not only the tortured, the imprisoned, the enslaved and the murdered, but the SS and Ukrainian guards as well. God is Auschwitz. God is the idea that gave birth to Auschwitz. God is creation and everything in it.

The question remains however: do we really need such a divinity? In what sense, and for what purpose? Does it hold out the possibility of rehabilitating discredited theologies, or does it merely highlight their inevitable failure?

In any event, the path that leads from a God who abandons his people at the foot of the Amorite hills to a God who abandons his people at the railroad platform at Auschwitz, is one that renders the entire concept of God redundant, or produces a theological indictment so grave that no defense—revolutionary as it may be—can possibly lay to rest.

Marla L. Frankel

Va'ethanan – And I Pleaded with the Lord

"You are to inculcate them in your children
and are to speak of them"
The Educational Commitment of **Rabbi Samson Raphael Hirsch**

You are to inculcate them in your children and are to speak of them in your sitting in your house and in your walking in the way, in your lying-down and in your rising-up.

You are to tie them as a sign upon your hand, And they are to be as for bands between your eyes. You are to write them upon your doorposts of your house and on your gates (*Deuteronomy* 6:7–9).

In *Va'ethanan* we find a lengthy entreaty by a leader who is about to depart from his people and is concerned for its future. Moses' discourse expresses his deep desire to bequeath to the people, a constitution based on the covenant forged with God at Sinai in order that it shape their character as they are about to take possession of the land. Many expressions repeated throughout the portion of *Va'ethanan* emphasize the constitution rooted in the covenant, including: "And now, O Israel, hearken to the laws and the regulations, that I am teaching you to observe" (Deut.4:1); "And you are to keep His laws and His commandments that I command you today" (*ibid.* 40); "These are the precepts, and the laws, and the regulations, which Moses declared to the children of Israel, when they went out of Egypt" (*ibid.* 45; as well as 5:1; 6:1; 7:1).

Va'ethanan also abounds with passages that stand at the core of the religious heritage of the Jewish people: "Know today, and lay it up in your heart, that the Lord, He is God in heaven above and upon the earth beneath; there is none else" (4:39); "And this is the law which Moses set before the children of Israel" (*ibid.* 44); "Hear, O Israel: the Lord our God, the Lord is one" (6:4); the *ve'ahavta* passage (*ibid.* 5–9); "When

548

your child asks you on the morrow, saying: What are the precepts, the laws and the regulations that the Lord our God has commanded you?" (*ibid.* 20); "For you are a people holy to the Lord your God, it is you that the Lord has chosen to be for Him a specially-treasured people from all the peoples that are on the face of the soil." "For you are a people holy to the Lord your God, and it is you that the Lord has chosen to be for him a specially treasured people from all the peoples that are on the face of the earth" (14:2); and of course, the Ten Commandments (5:6–17). These passages provide us with an opportunity to examine Rabbi Samson Raphael Hirsch's approach to fundamental concepts of Jewish tradition:

> Samson Raphael Hirsch never shaped his thoughts into a systematic philosophy, nor did he ever confront the liberal philosophy of religion systematically. Essentially, he was not a philosopher and most likely did not want to be one. Although he began a religio-philosophical work entitled *Moriah*, which contained his teachings about duties (and was to preceed *Horeb*) he never completed it and eventually abandoned it altogether. In several hundred articles in his periodical *Jeschurun*, as well as in his *Commentary on the Pentateuch*, Hirsch expressed his views on many religious and social issues. But he never managed a methodical summation. As an educator devoted to the individual and to the community, he was much more concerned with creating an educational system than with articulating a rigorous system of thought. He sought to work on behalf of tradition, getting lost souls engaged in Judaism, strengthening their will to observe the divine word; he wanted to create people who "with ardor and love clung to the name 'Jew'." Hirsch's pedagogic ethos guided his pen and so deprived him of the detached contemplation of the philosopher (M. Breuer, *Modernity within Tradition: The Social History of Orthodox Jewry in Imperial Germany*, Columbia University Press, New York, 1992, p. 56).

Even if Hirsch, as Breuer claims, never formulated a systematic philosophy, we will attempt to draw a portrait of Hirsch and his worldview, based on his *Commentary on the Pentateuch*. We will try to understand whether it was indeed his "pedagogic ethos", as Breuer writes,

that "guided his pen" in the *Commentary on the Pentateuch* as well—
and if so, how. We will focus primarily on Hirsch's commentary on
Va'ethanan, but will consult other works as well, in order to bring our
conclusions into greater relief.

Hirsch's first work, *Neunzehn Briefe über Judentum* (*Igrot Tsafon.
The Nineteen Letters on Judaism*), was written in the form of an exchange of letters between two young men: Benjamin—spokesman for
the "perplexed"; and Naphtali—representing the views of traditional Judaism. In the following excerpt from the Second Letter, Hirsch
(through Naphtali) presents his "credo" regarding the study of Bible:

> But, before we open it, let us consider how we shall read it. Let
> us not read it for the purpose of conducting philological and an-
> tiquarian investigations, or to find support and corroboration for
> the antediluvian or geological hypotheses, or in the expectation
> of unveiling super mundane mysteries. It is as *Jews* that we must
> study the Torah, looking upon it as a Book given us by God that
> we may learn from it to know what we are and what we should
> be in this our earthly existence. It must be to us *Torah*; that is, a
> source of instruction and guidance in God's world, a generator
> of spiritual life within us (S.R. Hirsch, *Igrot tsafon. The Nine-
> teen Letters on Judaism*, P. Feldheim, New York, 1960, p. 28).

Thus, according to Hirsch, it is not for the sake of philological, historical or scientific inquiry that a Jew approaches the study of Bible, but
in order to know himself and the path he must follow. A Jew must view
the Torah as a God-given gift, and so will posit the Book's uniqueness
(and unity). Obviously, Hirsch was not opposed to study of the sciences
or the arts. On the contrary, he favored such study and founded institutions in which he strove to foster general education alongside Jewish
education. "The curriculum he envisaged when he founded his school
in 1852 was based upon the equivalence of Jewish and general *Bildung*,
and it more or less kept the two areas in balance", because he believed
that Judaism and general knowledge were not antithetical, but "in a
most profoundly true sense: one" (Breuer, p. 110).

With regard to Bible however, and particularly the Pentateuch, Hirsch demanded "Torah study", rejecting higher criticism and its scientific

tools. He also opposed the historical-developmental approach to Judaism that formed the basis of the "Science of Judaism" (*Wissenschaft des Judentums*). His attitude to the various fields of Jewish studies was determined by a single criterion: their contribution to the preservation and strengthening of "Jewish life". Hirsch asked: "How many scholars of the *selihot, yotzrot* and *piyutim*—still arise early to recite them?" (E. Schweid, "*Hayahadut Kemahut Al-Historit: Mishnato Shel Shimshon Refael Hirsch*" in *Toldot Hehagut Hayehudit Ba'et Hahadshah*, Keter and Hakibutz Hameuhad, Jerusalem and Tel-Aviv, 1977, p. 293). As one who rejected the historical approach adopted by the Reform, he also denied attempts to explain the Biblical text on the basis of its development (chronologically or geographically).

Va'ethanan begins with Moses' plea that he be allowed to enter and see the land beyond the Jordan, and God's absolute refusal to accede to his request (3:23–29). God's refusal is of course based on the events recounted in *Numbers* 20:12. In his *Commentary on the Pentateuch*, Hirsch explains Moses' sin and the punishment he received:

If Moses' excitement sprang from the bitter feeling that the whole of his devoted work for the people had been in vain, that the attitude of the people towards him was still that of המרים (rebels): no confidence, no response to efforts to alter their minds to being more fully convinced; if such as excitement could be regarded as a stressing of his own personality not quite in keeping with the frame of mind of a Moses, and which should in all cases recede into the background in consideration of his mission coming from God, and—surely the hardest of all trials—should never have lost patience as long as God remained patient; if one cannot take away from it a momentary doubt existing in Moses' mind of the ultimate success of God's mission of the people being finally won over to accomplish their mission and purpose on earth; should not all this together be able to be taken as a momentary sinking of the אמונה [?] ... And should not then the opposite demand: the demand never for a moment to lose consciousness of God being the decisive One whom nothing can hinder in absolutely achieving His purpose ... be able to be regarded as the highest form of קידוש השם (sanctification of God's name)? And

from that point of view does not לא האמנתם בי להקדישני (you had
no faith in Me to sanctify Me) hit the very essence of the lapse,
the impatient passion of Moses, in its real innermost nature? ...
But the impressive fact remains ... on account of such a small,
easily understood, momentary weakness in their אמונה, the leaders had to suffer the same fate that was meted to the generation
of the wilderness for their continuous lack of אמונה (faith). The
grave of the great leader at the very border of the Promised Land
to which he had at last brought his people, next to the graves of
those who died in the wilderness, now bears everlasting witness
to the impartial justice of the Divine rule, in the scales of which
the slightest errors of the great saintly men, so close to God in
their service, weigh equally to the worst sins of ordinary mortals
(S.R. Hirsch, *The Pentateuch*, Judaica Press, Gateshead, 1982,
p.).

According to Hirsch, Moses' strong independent personality is
closely linked to the weakening of his faith. The bending of individual
will (including that of a prophet) before God's will is, in Hirsch's opinion, a fundamental concept, and it is in this light that he understands the
sequence of *Va'ethanan*. For immediately following God's rejection of
Moses' plea, we read "And now, O Israel, hearken to the laws and the
regulations, that I am teaching you to observe; in order that you may
live, and enter and possess the land which the Lord, the God of your
fathers, is giving to you" (4:1), Essentially the same exhortation is repeated later in the chapter: "And you are to keep His laws, and His commandments, that I command you today, that it may go well with you,
and your children after you, in order that you prolong days upon the soil,
which the Lord thy God is giving you, all the days to come" (*ibid.* 40).

Rather than providing a detailed description of all of the "laws and
regulations" however, the Bible focuses extensively on the subject of
idolatry (3:16; 19; 25; 28)—beginning with the injunction "You are not
to add to the word that I am commanding you, and you are not to sub-
tract from it, in keeping the commandments of the Lord your God that I
am commanding you" (4:2). According to Hirsch, there is a significant
connection between idolatry and the prohibition against adding to the

Torah or diminishing it. Idolatry, Hirsch believes, is but "that arrogance which thinks it can better God's commands by carrying out one's own ideas of what should be done" (he cites the example of Saul who diso-beyed God's commandment to utterly destroy Amalek). Hirsch explains the prohibition "you shall not add" as an admonition to the entire nation against instituting new precepts, in addition to those commanded by God in the Written and the Oral Law. Toward the end of the *parasha*, on the words "when we care to observe all this commandment" (6:25), Hirsch remarks that "we can only discharge the mission of our life if we keep the Torah as מצוה (commandment), all, ... carefully, unstinted and unaltered ... We have no right either to abrogate anything nor to reform anything". For according to Hirsch, such is the way of idolatry: "which does not place everything, one's whole fate and one's whole life under the One Only God, but places at His side some glorification of oneself ... and allows that to sway one's fate, and oracles to decide one's deeds" (*Commentary*, *Deut.* 4:3).

Does Hirsch's exegesis echo his polemic with the Reform—a con-temporary movement raising the banner of change, seeking to legitimize adding to and subtracting from Mosaic Law? Indeed it does. Although he does not mention his adversaries by name, throughout his commentary on *Va'ethanan*—a portion concerned with "laws and regulations"—we find Hirsch's numerous arguments against the beliefs embodied in the Reform. Similarly, we read in the fifth of *The Nineteen Letters*:

Not that should be deemed good or evil which is agreeable or disagreeable to man, or pleasant or unpleasant to his sensual na-ture.

For the task of man lies not in the gratification of his own im-pulses and lusts, nor in ambitions, self-aggrandizement and ca-price. Instead, he is to elevate all his power, his desires and the demands of his body to be the means of carrying out the will of God (p. 42).

Schweid sums up Hirsch's view as follows:

Man's personal happiness is an idolatrous element of modern humanism. To make the pursuit of personal happiness life's ul-

timate goal is to deny one's moral obligation ... The concept of
obligation is inherently rooted in recognition of a commanding
authority above man ... Man's ability to make moral distinctions
and judgments is limited. The little we know of the world and
of ourselves does not allow us to determine what course of action would be beneficial to us and to all creation. Without divine
revelation we cannot know the correct path. Therefore, only recognition of divine sovereignty and the revelation of divine will
can enable man to fulfill his destiny. 'Torah from Heaven' is thus
essential to man's humanity (Schweid, *ibid.* pp. 291–310).

The beginning of *Va'ethanan* thus embodies an important principle
in the thought of Samson Raphael Hirsch: the submission of individual
desire to the sovereign will of God. Any attempt by the individual to
subvert divine command, to add to it or detract from it, is seen by Hirsch
as man worshiping man—and is therefore a form of idolatry.

For Hirsch, the significance of the divine revelation at Sinai lies not
only in the actual covenant forged between the people and its God, but
in the validation it affords Jewish belief as such: "You yourself *have
been made to see*, to know that the Lord, He is God; there is none else
beside Him" (4:35). In his *Commentary*, Hirsch explains:

> Your consciousness of God is no belief but a knowledge, and
> your knowledge rests on no report, nor on any conclusions
> which your minds come to, *your knowledge of God rests on the
> certainty of the actual experience of all of you together simulta-
> neously having had the direct actual evidence of your own sens-
> es.* אתה הראת לדעת : your own eyes were given enough to see
> for you to *know* that God, Who was revealed to you under that
> Name ... is the one real God Whom the rest of mankind seek and
> believe in under such manifold delusive images. אין עוד מלבדו,
> and that apart from Him alone, there is nothing that has exist-
> ence on itself alone.

And elsewhere:

> But everything rests on the fundamental fact of God's revela-
> tion of the Law which the whole nation itself witnessed, and

the direct guarantee of the Divinity of the Torah and the supernatural Personality of God. It is therefore, in the very first place,
this historical thoroughly fundamental fact, the revelation of the
Lawgiving on Sinai, proven by the evidence of our own senses,
which must always be kept vivid in our minds and in our hearts,
and be handed down to our children, generation by generation
to be taken to heart with equal certainty. Based in actual experience, an experience made simultaneously by a whole nation, is
the unparalleled unique foundation for the historical fact of the
revelation on Sinai (*Commentary, Deut.* 4:9).

According to Breuer, it is evident from the above that Hirsch followed in the footsteps of Rabbi Judah Halevi, who "rejected philosophical speculation as a means for reaching knowledge of God" (Breuer,
ibid. p. 59). However, Hirsch did not follow the medieval philosopher
entirely. Breuer explains: "The spell of the Enlightenment made him
balk at Halevi's quasibiological interpretation of Jewish peoplehood"
(*ibid.*).

Hirsch saw the Jewish people as the chosen people, which he explains in terms of exclusive ownership. On the verse "So now if you will
hearken, yes hearken to my voice and keep my covenant, you shall be
to me a special treasure from among all peoples. Indeed all the earth is
mine" (*Ex.* 19:5), Hirsch writes: "We must become exclusively His possession in every phase of our being, that our whole existence and all our
desires be dependent on Him, that we give no place to aught but Him to
have any influence on the direction of our lives and actions." According to Hirsch, the chosenness of the Jewish people was "more a concept
of ought than of fact". Breuer claims that Hirsch believed that "with
respect to the potential realization of normative obligation, all people
were fundamentally equal", and therefore, "Wherever Halevi took wing
into irrationalism, Hirsch stayed wrapped up in rationalism".

Hirsch understood however, that the acceptance of normative obligation at Sinai cannot be taken for granted, but requires study and
understanding, and offers the following explanation:

שמע את, "listen to", not "obey" ... את החקים ואת המשפטים אשר
אנכי דבר באוזניכם היום, the laws governing your moral and social

behavior which I present to you this day according to their contents for you to apprehend and understand them. למוד : שמירה
and עשיה, that is the sum of all that the Torah demands from us.
למוד to appropriate that which we are told, by studying to really
understand it; שמירה, conscientiously to keep it present in our
mind, and only to act under the dictates of such conscientious-
ness; and עשיה, carrying it out, which is of course, the purpose,
indeed the basis of the whole of it. Mere theoretical knowledge
without practical fulfillment has no value, it does not even attain
the right knowledge, if it is only striven for as an intellectual
game and not with the serious intention of carrying it out (*Commentary, Deut.* 5:1).

In his commentary on the Ten Commandments, Hirsch remains
faithful to two very different goals, which he hopes to instill in his readers: (1) "to appropriate that which we are told, by studying to really understand it"; and (2) "to conscientiously carry it out". It is worth noting
here that Hirsch emphasizes that:

The Ten Commandments have in no wise any greater holiness
or greater importance than any other commandment in the Torah
... God clearly and expressly proclaimed them as being merely
a preparatory introduction to the whole following, real giving of
the Law ... this revelation on Sinai is expressly stated to have for
its object solely the preparation of the people for the whole of
the rest of the lawgiving which was to be transmitted to them by
Moses (*Commentary, Ex.* 20:14).

For example we can cite the fourth commandment: "Keep the day
of the Sabbath, by hallowing it, as the Lord your God commanded you"
(Deut. 5:12). In his lengthy commentary on the Ten Commandments (on
Exodus), Hirsch discusses the philosophical significance of the commandment in both its sources (*Ex.* 20:7; *Deut.* 5:12), and only then does
he relate to its normative aspects, i.e. actual observance of the Sabbath
precepts. The following is an excerpt from his commentary on *Exodus*
20:7:

The first institution of the Sabbath for mankind, only established it as a spiritual commemoration for remembrance, to keep it in mind. But as such it became entirely lost to mankind. To bring the Sabbath back and to preserve it, Israel was given the command of שמירה, the concrete, physically noticeable keeping of the Sabbath as a symbol of its spiritual content. It is just this שמירה, rather than the זכירה which latter should already have been the common possession of all mankind, which is the specific Jewish Law of Sabbath. Accordingly, he who takes away the שמירה (observance) from our Sabbath and imagines he can satisfy himself with the זכירה (remembrance) is denying the whole Jewish Sabbath, and is destroying the whole institution which God has established in Israel for the purpose of ensuring Sabbath for the whole of mankind.

Thus, study, contemplation and remembrance are precursors to the commandment, the observance of which is the ultimate goal. Following the rabbinical teaching "'Remember' (*Ex.* 20:7) and 'Observe' (*Deut.* 5:12) were said in a single utterance" (*Shevuot* 20b), Hirsch stresses the "identification of זכירה (*zekhirah*—"remembrance") and שמירה (*shemirah*—"observance") ... considered ... as one inseparable unity" (*ibid.*). Hirsch lists a number of Sabbath laws that derive from his understanding of the word *zakhor*, meaning perpetual remembrance. Hirsch suggests that the word *zakhor* as it appears in *Exodus* 20:7, is not an imperative, but is to be understood in the aoristic tense:

It is not limited just to the duration of the day itself but extends beyond it, yea, even to all times. Hence, first of all the order זכרהו על היין בכניסתו (Pesachim 106a) "declare the great, the sanctifying meaning of the day at its entry by קידוש"... further in the Mechilta: מכאן שמוסיפין מחול על הקדש, that we are to let the sanctity of the Sabbath at its beginning reach over into the weekday, to cease work before the entry of the Sabbath ... finally in the Mechilta: לא תהא מונה כדרך שאחרים מונין אלא מונה לשם שבת; not to call the days of the week as others do ... but to count everyday from the standpoint of Sabbath (*ibid.*).

In citing these laws directly from their Talmudic and midrashic sources, Hirsch reiterates his belief in the unity of the Written and the Oral Torah. As noted above, he has no need for any further hermeneutical tools—beyond those provided by rabbinical literature, that are "a source of instruction and guidance in God's world, a generator of spiritual life within us" (*The Nineteen Letters*, p. 28).

In his brief commentary on the Ten Commandments in *Va'ethanan*, Hirsch addresses the differences between the two versions of the commandments, in light of varying historical circumstances:

For, in the change to having to live for oneself in the impending decentralization, and the consequent activities of wresting one's independence from nature and human competition, the Sabbath was to be impressed above all in its שמירה aspect, in its twenty-four hour sacrifice of ceasing work in acknowledging homage to God. So that those who henceforth would feel relegated to their own יד and their own זרוע, their own "strength and power", should not forget the truth that every ounce of strength and every grain of power, and all that they might come to think was their own production, comes from God and belongs to God ... That is also why the whole sphere of the power and strength of a man's personality is still more completely described by ושורך וחמורך וכל בהמתך [a description lacking in *Exodus*—M. F.] ... and on the other hand, all the members of this sphere of man's power are joined to him by the copulative ו in complete equality with his own personality to place themselves with him at the feet of God on Sabbath—ועבדך, not עבדך, and that is why here למען ינוח עבדך ואמתך כמוך is stressed as a special visible consequence of the God-acknowledging festival of Sabbath when Man calls a halt to the exercise of his "strength and powers.

It is interesting to compare these remarks to Hirsch's discussion of the Friday evening ceremonial *Kiddush*, in his commentary on the Prayer Book. He explains the custom of reciting the *Kiddush* in the synagogue as a vestige of the ancient practice of inviting guests to partake of the Sabbath meal in the synagogue, but emphasizes the importance of reciting the *Kiddush* specifically in the home as a declaration of man's absolute submission to his maker:

"Remember the Sabbath day, to keep it holy" (*Ex.* 20:7). The sole purpose of this commandment is to charge Israel not to 'forget' the Sabbath day, as the remainder of the human race has forgotten it. It is incumbent upon us, every Sabbath, to evoke its purpose of bringing holiness among us—to us and to all that is ours. Although we have already mentioned its holy purpose and its ancient constitution (*Vayekhulu Hashamayim*—"Thus the heavens") in the synagogue, the holiness of the Sabbath should be recognized and praised primarily in our home lives.... Renouncing our independence and pride in domination will then not cast a shadow on our happiness. Bending our own volition, property and being to God's will, surrendering our insignificant and transient aspirations and achievements to the great will of God, will raise our heads, help us to transcend all hardship and will truly bring us joy in our existence; the joy that lies in living our lives before God (S. R. Hirsch, Commentary on the *Siddur* [Heb.], p. 253).

In Hirsch's opinion there is thus no significant difference between studying the Prayer Book used in divine worship and studying the Torah in the classroom or study hall. The purpose of study in both cases is to lead the student to religious observance. In addition, Hirsch makes no distinction between Bible as the subject of academic study and the Torah read in the synagogue (and at home). His subsequent comments on the Sabbath reveal a characteristic hermeneutical approach; one we have already observed above:

תעבוד; Not as self-glorification, but as "service" shalt thou consider thy powers of construction and the master over the materials of this world. As service performed in the Kingdom of God, as service to thy God, and as performed at His bidding, for His world. It was לעבדה ולשמרה to serve it and to keep it that he placed you in it; to raise it, by appropriating its materials, changing and transforming them out of the sphere of blind physical existence into the realm of human purposes, to serve and further God's aim for the world. In this spirit ועשית כל מלאכתך art thou to accomplish all thy work. We have already defined the idea of מלאכה (*Gen.* 2:2). Just as מלאך is a personal creature who carries out the will and message of someone else, so is מלאכה any material or thing that is made of service to carry out the will or order of anybody's mind. עשית מלאכה is the transformation of thing or of some material into being our מלאך i.e., to impress on something or material such a permanent state or condition, that henceforth it is qualified to serve the purpose that we desire it to have—we make it serve *our* will and our purpose. Every עשית מלאכה is exercising our mastery over the matter of this world. And this mastery of ours we are to exercise only as "service" תעבוד (*Commentary, Ex.* 20:9).

"You are not to do any work" (Deut. 5:14)—the Sabbath is not desecrated by one who fails to go to synagogue, participate in public worship or hear the rabbi's sermon, but by one who does work on that day:

One that profaneth it shall surely be put to death; for whosoever doeth any work therein, that soul shall be cut off from among his people (*Ex.* 31:2). ... The whole idea of Sabbath has been distorted and the whole laws of Sabbath undermined by the translation "thou shalt not do any work". When Jews began to be disloyal to the oath they took at Sinai, which swore "to bring life into line with the Torah" and altered it to "bring the Torah into line with Life" ... [T]he essential idea of the word מלאכה seems to be—as indeed its etymological derivation from מלאך has told us—not the greater or lesser amount of bodily fatigue but the intelligent carrying out of an intention. ... לא תעשה כל מלאכה means "thou shalt not perform any constructive work". Thou shalt not carry out thy intention on any thing, make no thing the bearer of thy purpose, thy ideas; in general, thou shalt not produce, not construct! (*ibid.*)

In his interpretation of "Six days you shall serve, and are to make all your work" (*Ex.* 20:9), Hirsch goes beyond the verse's plain meaning. He interprets the word "serve" (*taavod*) to mean actual, physical labor—but that too must be performed for the sake of Heaven; "not as self-glorification, but as service to God". This idea also arises from Hirsch's assertion (cited above) that all man's thoughts must be dedicated to God. Hirsch's commentary would thus appear to be circular—the same ideas are repeated over and over again albeit in various textual contexts. This hermeneutical approach is rooted in Hirsch's belief in the unity of the biblical text and its ideas on the one hand, and his desire to educate his generation, on the other hand.

In his commentary on "and make all your work" (*ibid.*), Hirsch's tendency toward midrashic interpretation is even more blatant. He explains the word *melakhah*—work—as deriving from the word *malakh*—angel or messenger and therefore concludes that work is essentially "a mission". *Melakhah* is thus not "labor and toil" but rather "any material or thing that is made of service to carry out the will or order of anybody's mind". This method, which Schweid terms "philological Midrash" "bases broad philosophical constructs on the etymological proximity between words with very different meanings". The interpretations may seem arbitrary, Schweid notes, "but their intention is to offer a comprehensive symbolic understanding of all biblical precepts ... In any event, he manages to infuse seemingly mundane and meaningless verses with a surprising wealth of meaning, of a kind that appeals to the reason and best intentions of the enlightened humanist" (Schweid, p. 301).

Towards the end of his commentary on the Sabbath commandment we hear echoes of Hirsch's debate with the Reform, which sought to adapt the Torah to reality, rather than adapting reality to Torah. The former insists on transforming Judaism, while the latter strives to transform the people. Naphtali expresses a similar view in the Seventeenth Letter:

> Let us truly "reform." Yes, let us strive with all our power, with all the good and noble qualities of our character to reach this height of ideal perfection. Reform! ... It must be education and progress of time to the high plane of the torah, not the lowering of the torah to the level of the age, cutting down the towering summit to the sunken grade of our own lives. ... Merely to seek greater ease and comfort in life through the destruction of the

eternal code set up for all time by the God of Eternity, is not, and never can be, the "reform" which we need. Judaism seeks to lift us up to its own high plane. We must never attempt to drag it down to our own level (*The Nineteen Letters* pp. 112–113).

Hirsch's focus on the philosophical aspect of the Sabbath and only then on its practical observance is consistent with his commentary on all of the commandments. His goal is to bring the reader to understand the significance of the biblical text in the context of his or her own life. Moreover, he strives to impart the internal logic of the commandments and the connection between them—an idea that appears no fewer than four times in his commentary on the commandments in *Exodus*. Note the following:

> [Among] the first five commandments, אנכי and לא יהיה לך proclaim the knowledge and acknowledgement of God as the One Who is responsible for our fate and the guide of all our acts, in their positive and negative signification respectively; in לא תשא this knowledge and acknowledgement is set as the whole basis of our individual and social life; in זכר homage to this idea is ensured by the ever-recurring act of cessation of work; and in כבד את אביך ואת אמך its continuous transmission through the ages is ensured by the influence of the home. Now the following five commandments proclaim the result of this knowledge and acknowledgement in our social life. If God is the One Who is solely responsible for your fate in life and is to be the Guide of all your actions, then every one of your fellow-men must be considered as standing equally under His care, and every one of your actions towards him comes under His observation. Every man at your side is placed where he is by God's Direction and, equally with yourself, has all human rights granted by Him, so that all his possessions, his life, his wife, his freedom, his happiness, his honor, and his property must all be considered as sacred to him. Thou shalt not take his life, nor break up his marriage, nor rob him of his freedom, nor smirch his honor and his happiness by false evidence, more, thou shalt not even allow thyself to covet anything which makes

the home of thy fellow-man, and that includes everything which he can call his own!

The fifth section of *Va'ethanan*, which deals with education, opens with verses that serve as an introduction to the *Shema*, emphasizing the role of the father in transmitting Torah to his children (6:2—"in order that you may hold the Lord your God in awe, by keeping all his laws and his commandments that I command you, you and your child, and your child's child, all the days of your life and in order that your days may be prolonged."). For Hirsch, transmission is effected through the word *veshamata*—"Hear therefore" (*ibid*. 3 and 4, in the form *shema*). At Sinai, knowledge of God was based upon sight. Since that time however, such knowledge has been founded upon hearing.

> But this revelation of Himself, making Himself perceptible (*sic*) on earth, God only did once, when laying the foundation for the creation of His People, so that it could be a means of conviction from generation to generation, from community to community, and remain by direct tradition the indisputable basis on which, for all eternity, every son of Israel has to build up all his thinking and doing (*Commentary, Deut*. 6:4).

And in his introduction to the *Shema*:

> the sentence which expresses the Jewish consciousness of the "oneness of God" ... And as a result of this consciousness, sentences are added which, wherever the Jew may live, educate his child, live his private and public life, when he lies down and gets up, prepares his hand for deeds, his mind for thoughts, build his house, fixes his doors, they bring to his mind the mission of his life, the purpose of his education, the purpose of his homely and public efforts, the principles behind his deeds, the axioms for his thoughts and the dedication of the whole of his private and public life, and which sentences he accordingly has to repeat daily, early and late.

Hirsch thus harnesses the philosophical-theological declaration to that which is required of man in practical terms. As Schweid observes:

"The affirmation of tenets or philosophical truths is worthless. The Torah teaches man to accept the yoke of heaven".

Hirsch's commentary on the word "one" in verse 4 is one of his most
poetic:

"What is laid down here as the very first fundamental truth of
our knowledge for us ever to take to heart, the אחדות of our
God is nothing but the positive denial of all ancient and modern polytheistic ideas and false opinions. In the midst of all the
greatest contradictory appearance of the manifold presentations
of nature, history and our own inner selves, a contradictory variety which, more than anything else begat—and begets—the
polytheistic erroneous conception, this אחד expresses the fact,
the truth:—of the whole of this apparent antagonism—heaven
to earth, personal to universal, what one pursues to what one
avoids, endures and conquers, constructive forces and materials
to destructive ones, all the changes of day and night, of becoming and reverting, of blooming and withering, of living and dy-
ing, of having and losing, of eating and starving, of rising and
falling, loving and hating, of joy and sorrow, the contrasts of
freedom and subjection, of spiritual and material, of heavenly
and earthly, out of which human beings feel themselves wo-
ven—it is One single One, God alone Who created and holds all
these contrasts, arranges them and guides them, Who formed all
these contrasts, arranges them and guides them, Who formed all
these contrasts about us and in us, from Whom all our joy and all
our sorrow comes, our spirit and our body, He created our bodies and invested them with spirit from His spirit, and personality
from His own, and freedom of will from His Free-will ... This
was the view of the dual nature of the world taken by the old
Parseeism ... to which Isaiah in Ch, XLV,6 had to bring the Word
of God that "from the rising of the sun to the setting thereof they
may know that there is nothing that occurs without Me, I am
God, and there is none else. It is I that form the light and create
darkness; I make peace and create badness, I God do all this".

As Hirsch notes, the contrasts that mark our existence, emanating from God, can also be found within man's own soul. He further elaborates upon this idea in his commentary on the words "with all your heart"—that is, with both the good and the evil inclination, for both—the base and the sensual, the noble and the moral, stem from God. Were it not for the allurement of evil, we would not be worthy of the name "man":

> With the absence of the יצר הרע our whole moral worth would be buried ... Yea, in truth, none of our inclinations are in themselves good or bad. All of them, the most sensuous of the sensuous ones, the most spiritual of the spiritual ones become good or bad according to whether or not they are used within the limits and for the purpose which God has allotted to each one of them, or misused, going beyond the limits, neglecting the purposes, or changing them for other purposes than those which God has set for them. So that to love God with the whole of our heart means :—to keep our whole mind—with all inclinations and in every direction—dedicated exclusively to accomplishing the Will of God, and to use every one of our efforts in His service that such mastery and use of them brings us nearer and nearer to Him (*ibid.*).

Hirsch writes that "consciousness of the "Oneness" of God ... unites the whole of our being ... to one single unity of what we are and what we desire"—to love God and ultimately to "give ourselves up entirely" to Him. It is this notion, Breuer asserts, that distinguishes Hirsch from Kant in his "tenacious adherence to the heteronomy of divine law, revealed *to* a person, not *in* him" (Breuer, p. 62).

"And these words" (6:6) Hirsch explains as referring to "the whole teachings of the Torah": "Clearly the text of the verses וכתבתם and וקשרתם can only be the object of שמע ואהבת. On the other hand ושיננתם and ודברת בם ... allow one to refer to the whole teachings of the Torah as being the subject for teaching of the young and for expressing of the thoughts of the adults". The key however, according to Hirsch, lies in the verse: "You are to inculcate them into your children, and are to speak of them in your sitting in your house, and in your walking in the way, and in your lying down and in your rising up" (6:7); the first part of which—"you are to inculcate them into your children, and are to speak of them"—he explains as follows: "Then the instruction is given regarding the teaching of the Torah, first to imprint it in short, sharp, concise sentences and then impress it by conversing and debating on it: **כ"שבת** (Written Law) and **פ"שבת** (Oral Law) and similarly **משנה** (Mishnah) and **גמרא** (Gemara)".

In his explanation of the first word, *"veshinantam"*—"you are to inculcate them into your children", Hirsch once again takes up the debate against advocates of Reform (whom he believes are confused):

> From that we can also draw the admonition for us, when we transmit the knowledge of the Torah, to our children ... to implant in them their obligation to [the Mitzvot] of the Torah with the whole sharpness of their definite orders, and not let them be weakened by compromising for so-called necessary considerations of the times we live in and subjective expediences".

On the second word, *vedibarta*—"and are to speak of them"—he addresses the form that study of Torah should take:

> They, the teachings of the Torah are to form the real subjects of our mental occupation, we are not to cultivate them as a side-issue, nor from the standpoint or for the standpoint of other scientific study, and equally indeed take care not to introduce into the sphere of our Torah-studies foreign matter and ideas which have grown on the soil of other scientific hypotheses. We are altogether always to bear in mind the specific higher level of our knowledge which differs from all other scientific knowledge through its Divine origin and not place it on the same level as the other sciences, as if it, too, rested on the basis of human knowledge.... these sentences of the Sifri quite clearly do not demand completely ignoring all scientific knowledge gained in other spheres, on the contrary, they rather presuppose having knowledge of them, but they give us the only correct standpoint from which our occupying ourselves with them, can be benefi-

cial to us, and they warn us of the danger the neglecting such a standpoint would bring to our mental life of study for true knowledge (*Commentary, Deut.* 6:7).

That is to say, that although it is desirable for a Jew to study general subjects, these should not be allowed to shape his worldview. A Jew must "firmly stand on the rock of his Judaism", from which standpoint he may acquire universal knowledge, "no matter what its spiritual source" (Breuer, p. 73).

Hirsch then goes on to discuss the laws pertaining to the *Shema*, as presented in the Talmud. We find Hirsch's two goals, as cited above ("to appropriate that which we are told, by studying to really understand it"; and "to conscientiously carry it out") in this section as well; with regard to the *Shema* and the laws of *tefillin* and *mezuzah*. Following a lengthy philosophical discourse on the symbolic meaning of these precepts, he presents a detailed overview of the laws of *tefillin* and *mezuzah*; laws concerning the form of the *tefillin*, and how each of its two "boxes" is made; where and how they are worn on the head and arm; the materials from which they are made—leather and parchment from a ritually clean animal; aspects of the scribe's craft and the notion of "perfect writing"—who is worthy of writing *tefillin* and *mezuzot*, the writing of the Torah scroll, its holiness, and so forth.

Hirsch's approach to the precepts of *tefillin* and *mezuzah* as they appear in this *parasha*, can be summarized as follows:

The acknowledgement of the "oneness" of God, the giving up of the whole of our lives and wishes to this One God with all our heart and all our soul and all our fortune which we are daily to bring to mind as being the whole of our life's task and the theme of our own education and of our educating our children, this we are to bind on our hands as a symbol of "binding duty", and bind on our forehead as a symbol of "directing our eyes and thoughts" (*ibid., Deut.* 6:8).

However, this is only possible, so long as the Jew preserves his or her Jewish identity. In this manner, Hirsch manages to link all that has

been said thus far, to the sixth and final section of *Va'ethanan*. He reiterates his belief that Jewish education is contingent upon the Jewish
identity of both parents:

> But this heritage of the Torah, attracting and bringing up our
> children for our eternal life's task is frustrated beforehand if they
> are born under non-Jewish influence, if they are conceived in
> non-Jewish wombs, rocked on the knees of a non-Jewish father,
> if a non-Jewish father's or mother's teachings and example form
> their minds and characters if our married life and family life
> is penetrated with non-Jewish elements. This endangering our
> mission at the root of our whole future is what the following
> verses come to counter (*ibid., Deut.* 7:1).

According to Hirsch, the holiness of the Jewish people and its status
as a "chosen" people must not be regarded as a mandate for disengage-
ment from other nations, but as an imperative to mend the world in the
manner of His kingdom (*bemalchut shadai*):

> כי עם קדוש אתה, for you are a "holy" people. The zenith of the
> mission of other nations is themselves, keeping their national
> existence is the highest purpose of the united nation. But the
> mission of your national union lies exterior to itself, it does not
> belong to itself, it belongs to God, it has to place itself, with all
> its relationships, with every phase of its individual, family and
> public life "prepared and ready" for certain purposes and tasks
> which are indicated by God its Lord and Master. Hence it has
> to keep out of all its connections everything which would work
> against these purposes. "A holy nation art thou, belonging to
> One God, thy God" (*ibid., Deut.* 7:6).

In this passage, as in many others throughout Hirsch's works, we are
witness to the complex nature of his approach to Israel and the nations.
On the one hand, Hirsch advocated for Jewish involvement in economic, social and cultural life, but on the other hand, he envisioned a Jew as
"living beyond his time, in order to influence his time" (Schweid, 303).

In the introduction to his commentary on the book of Genesis, Hirsch cites three main goals: (a) to strive to understand the Bible without

recourse to other disciplines; (b) to prove that the sources of the Written and Oral and Law are one and the same; and (c) to construct the foundations of Judaism based upon the Bible, as a guide and measure of all things pertaining to man, nature and history.

Hirsch's attempt to understand the Bible without recourse to other disciplines led to "midrashic philology" and to the interpretation of the biblical text in light of other sacred texts; his desire to prove that both sources of the Written and Oral Law are one led him to engage in elaborate discussions of the rational underlying precepts and the details of normative commandments; and his goal "to construct the foundations of Judaism based upon the Bible, as a guide and measure of all things pertaining to man, nature and history", nurtured a constant debate with the Reform.

Our study of Hirsch's commentary on *Va'ethanan* reveals a number of the foundations of Judaism which he sought to establish as a guide for the Jew of his generation: subjugation of individual will to divine demands; God's revelation as unequivocal testimony determining the Jew's relationship with his maker and the world; acceptance of the "yoke" of the commandments willingly and thoughtfully; the role of the father in transmitting the Jewish ideological and halakhic heritage to his children; "mending the world" as the task of the Jewish people among the nations.

In effect, Hirsch's "pedagogic ethos" led to his putting *nishma*—"let us hear" before *na'aseh*—"let us do"—in providing the ideological explanation behind every precept. Schweid's characterization of Hirsch's approach in *The Nineteen Letters* would seem to apply to Hirsh's *Commentary on the Pentateuch* as well:

> His attitude to those who seek to study is a positive one, like that of an educator who believes that if a student learns, if he understands, he will be convinced. The role of the educator is to reveal the hidden light within Halakhah. One must have faith in the traditional sources. A student need only grasp the sublime moral meaning of the precepts of the Torah, and he will recognize their validity only inasmuch as they are revelations of the divine will—he will then be convinced and committed (Schweid, 294).

Hirsch interpreted biblical text as a rabbi deeply committed to the welfare of his community; a community bewildered by the charms of enlightenment and the spirit of emancipation. However, Hirsch's commentary on *Va'ethanan* fails to convey the full complexity of his philosophy of *Torah im derekh eretz* ("Torah accompanied with worldly involvement"), or his significant contribution in forging a path for Orthodox Judaism from his time to the present day. *Va'ethanan*, with its focus on shaping the character of the Jewish people, impelled Hirsch to relate to the "Torah" part of his equation alone, in the hope of captivating his readers with its practical but eternal message.

Alvin I. Schiff

Ekev—Because Ye Hearken to these Ordinances

Retribution and Love of Man in the Commentaries of **Rabbi Ovadiah Sforno**

And it shall come to pass, because ye hearken to these ordinances, and keep, and do them, that the Lord thy God shall keep with thee the covenant and the mercy which He swore unto thy fathers (*Deuteronomy* 7:12)

Ovadiah ben Jacob Sforno stands out among the biblical commentators, as a multifaceted and multipurpose exegete. In his exegetical method, he stresses the plain meaning of the biblical text, coupled with philosophical and scientific ideas. Sforno was also fond of allegory and parables, taking a broad view of the text in order to grasp its entire meaning, rather than limiting himself to comments on individual verses.

Sforno was an independent thinker and rejected Aristotelian philosophy. He considered Maimonides' admiration for the renowned Greek philosopher, misplaced. He treated all men with respect and tried to inculcate his community with love of mankind. He based his approach to converts to Judaism on the verse "Yea, He loveth the peoples, all His holy ones—they are in Thy hand" (*Dt.* 33:3). His exegetical method was rooted in his belief in the inner logic and connectedness of the Torah—without linguistic superfluity. He believed that the Torah had been given to the Children of Israel in order to make them a holy nation, and he sought to bring to the attention of his fellow Jews—and through them to the entire world—the value of divine love and mercy. The portion of *Ekev*—in all its 111 verses—addresses many different topics. It begins with the proclamation to the Israelites "And it shall come to pass, because ye hearken to these ordinances … that the Lord thy God shall keep with thee the covenant and the mercy which He swore unto thy fathers".

Sforno, in keeping with his preference for literal exegesis, does not see this as promise of recompense for observance of the precepts *per se*—certainly not in the manner of a father who admonishes his children: "If you are good children and do all that I ask, I will give you ample reward". The Israelites are asked to fulfill the commandments out of love, without hope of recompense. Only then will "the Lord thy God keep with thee the covenant".

According to Sforno, God will keep His covenant throughout the generations, as promised in Genesis: "And I will establish My covenant between Me and thee and thy seed after thee throughout their generations for an everlasting covenant, to be a God unto thee and to thy seed after thee" (*Gen* 17:7). The bond between God and the Jewish People is eternal and immediate: "For indeed inasmuch as He is to us a God whose influence is immediate, eternal reality that flows from him is [also] immediate, as it is written: 'whatsoever God doeth, it shall be for ever' (*Ecc.* 3:14)". And conversely, "transient reality" does not come directly from God, but "through an intermediary". The difference between those who are immediately bound to God and those whose bond to Him requires an intermediary is that the former are rewarded in the World to Come, while the latter receive their reward in this world only.

In this vein, Sforno explains why God promises to keep "the mercy that He swore unto thy fathers", as well as His covenant with them. Is the covenant itself not sufficient? Sforno argues that a covenant obligates both sides, so that God's response to the actions of the Israelites would not be an act of mercy, but the fulfillment of an obligation. What then is the difference between covenant and mercy? Sforno explains that God's mercy regards the good that He bestows upon is in this world, whereas true, ultimate recompense will be given in the World to Come.

Sforno implies that the beginning of *Ekev* is in fact a continuation of the final verses of the portion of *Ve'ethanan*, in which Moses informs the Israelites: "Know therefore that the Lord thy God, He is God; the faithful God, who keepeth covenant and mercy with them that love Him and keep His commandments to a thousand generations" (7:9). This is followed by "Thou shalt therefore keep the commandment, and the statutes, and the ordinances", which establishes God's commitment to uphold the covenant originally forged with Abraham, with the Children of Israel—His descendants "to a thousand generations". The Torah then goes on to discuss the matter further in the portion of *Ekev*. The reward that is promised is: "and He will love thee, and bless thee, and multiply thee". Like Rashi in Genesis (*Lekh Lekha* 12:3), Sforno explains the word *uverakhekha* to mean "wealth", adding the qualification "wealth for transitory life"—the result of God's mercy in this world, in the Land of the Fathers.

Sforno believes that Jews who engage in the ephemeral, in the amassing of wealth in this world, have a special purpose. When Moses instructs Aaron regarding the kindling of the *menorah* in the Tabernacle, he says to him: "When thou lightest the lamps, the seven lamps shall give light in front of the candlestick" (*Numbers* 8:2). Sforno explains that only "when the flame of each of the six lamps turns to the middle branch, then the seven lamps shall give light". Furthermore, the three lamps to the right represent the "right-goers"—"those who engage in eternal life"; while the three lamps on the left represent the "left-goers"—"those who engage in worldly matters and assist the right-goers". Only when the right-goers and the left-goers join together do they "cast supernal light upon Israel" and only then do they "perform the will of God, blessed be He", as we find in the case of the Israelites at Mount Sinai: "And all the people answered together, and said: 'All that the Lord hath spoken we will do'." Sforno highlights the unity of action expressed in the words "the people answered together". The left-goers, who engage in worldly affairs, are like the wealthy tribe of Zebulun, which supported the tribe of Issachar in its Torah study (see Nahmanides on *Num.* 2:1–9).

Divisions within the Jewish community of Bologna in Sforno's time distressed him greatly, and in his commentary on the words "the seven lamps shall give light in front of the candlestick" he tried to emphasize the importance of cooperation and fellowship. Indeed in his positive approach to the Jewish People as a whole—i.e. to all Jews—he set a shining example for all generations.

Sforno demonstrates his talent for concise explanation in his commentary on the Torah's use of the word *mishpatim* (ordinances) at the beginning of the portion: "because ye hearken to these ordinances". His succinct remark is: "For by justice (*mishpat*) the land is established", based on the verse "The king by justice (*mishpat*) establisheth the land" (*Prov.* 29:4). Without justice the king cannot reign and the affairs of the kingdom cannot be conducted in an equitable manner. For this reason, the King of kings—the Holy One, blessed be He—sought, from the very beginning, to establish Israel's existence in its land on solid ground—on the principles of justice.

The first verse in chapter 8 thus reads: "All the commandment which I command thee this day shall ye observe to do, that ye may live, and multiply, and go in and possess the land which the Lord swore unto your fathers". Sforno explains that God uses the word "commandment" here in order to persuade the Israelites not to follow the laws of the nations and not to worship foreign gods: "For the masses wish to attain transitory success, which falls into three categories: longevity, progeny and wealth. By observing the commandments you will achieve all of these things and that is why ye shall observe to do them" (Sforno, *ad loc.*). The Israelites thus knew that the reward for observing the precepts includes all of the things for which idolaters (the "masses") strive. Rest assured, he tells his readers, you will obtain all that the masses wish to obtain, if only you observe God's commandments.

The connection between keeping the commandments and inheriting the land is reiterated a number of times throughout the portion, along with the importance of faith in God's justice. The Torah cautions the Israelites against the consequences of failing to observe the precepts: "And it shall be, if thou shalt forget the Lord thy God … ye shall surely perish". Sforno explains the forgetfulness that leads to nonobservance, as follows: "And this will happen when you attribute your success to your own efforts and fail to bless God for it" (*ibid*). Furthermore, he explains, God's promise to uphold His covenant (7:12) assures Israel that it will reap the benefits in this world as well as the next. Conversely, if the commandments are not observed, the loss will be twofold.

The Torah closes this subject with the words "because ye would not hearken"—paralleling the language of the portion's opening verse: "because ye hearken" (7:12). Later in the portion, Moses retells the story of the golden calf and the role he played in that crisis, when he entreated God to forgive the people. Consequently, he recounts: "At that time, the

Lord said unto me: 'Hew thee two tables of stone like unto the first'" (10:1). Sforno explains Moses' intention as follows: "Despite all of my prayers, the restoration was incomplete, for in place of the tablets fashioned by God, He said to me 'hew thee'—you Moses will fashion the second tablets and not I".

Maimonides also understands this verse (10:1) as the continuation of the proclamation to Israel in the previous chapter, regarding the "the two tablets of stone written with the finger of God". Sforno also interprets the words "hew thee" in this vein, stressing that the first tablets were fashioned by God (*Ex.* 32:16), while the second were the work of man. This demonstrates that the original sanctity of the tablets was not maintained.

At the end of the portion in his second conversation with the Israelites in the book of *Deuteronomy*, Moses reiterates the importance of loving God and keeping his commandments and the consequences of doing so. Here Moses adds that observance of the precepts is a precondition for dwelling in the land, as it is written: "and that ye may prolong your days upon the land, which the Lord swore unto your fathers to give unto them and to their seed, a land flowing with milk and honey" (11:9). Sforno explains: "For if your sons do not keep the commandments, they will swiftly be exiled from it, before 'ye shall have been long in the land', as evidenced by the verse 'and ye perish quickly from off the good land which the Lord giveth you'" (*ibid.* 17).

The use that Sforno makes of the word *venoshantem* ("and ye shall have been long on the land"), is based on the talmudic teaching in *Sanhedrin* (38a). The Sages show that the numeric value of the word *venoshantem* is 852, noting that Israel would be exiled from their land for 852 years after the conquest in the days of Joshua. Here they are warned that if they do not observe the precepts, exile would come sooner. This is the meaning of the verse in *Ekev* "and the anger of the Lord be kindled against you, and He shut up the heaven … and ye perish quickly from off the good land which the Lord giveth you" (*ibid.*), which would appear to be a message for future generations as well.

In the portion's final passage, the Torah concludes the subject of precept observance with a blessing: "For if ye shall diligently keep all this commandment which I command you, to do it … then will the Lord drive out all these nations from before you, and ye shall dispossess nations greater and mightier than yourselves." (*ibid.* 22–23).

Sforno explains the concept "will drive out" to mean that God will "allow you to earn a livelihood without grief so that you will be able to do His will" (*ibid.* 23) In other words, you will not have to bother overmuch to support your families, and so you will be able to serve God in tranquility. This idea is indeed a fitting ending to the portion of *Ekev*.

Einat Ramon

Re'eh – Behold, I Set before You This Day

*Women in Ritual and Feminine Divinity: The Distinction between Paganism and Idolatry in the Thought of **Judith Plaskow***

Ye shall surely destroy all the places, wherein the nations that ye are to dispossess served their gods, upon the high mountains, and upon the hills, and under every leafy tree. And ye shall break down their altars, and dash in pieces their pillars, and burn their Asherim with fire; and ye shall hew down the graven images of their gods; and ye shall destroy their name out of that place (*Deuteronomy* 12:2–3).

Feminist theology, within the broader context of Jewish thought, received its first systematic expression in 1990 with the publication of Judith Plaskow's *Standing Again at Sinai*. One of the most widespread criticisms of the book was the claim that the attempt to restore feminine images of God to Jewish prayer constitutes a radical departure from Jewish tradition. The inclusion of feminine divine imagery in prayer, it was argued, violates the prohibition against idolatry—in the sense that it is a throwback to pagan religion, which included the worship of female deities. This opposition prevented serious discussion of the important issue that Plaskow raised in her book—the moral implications of divine imagery. Some two years later, and probably as a result of the reactions to the book, Plaskow again addressed the issue of the Torah's condemnation of paganism, and the theological and moral significance of this stance.

Plaskow's article "Jewish Anti-Paganism" (*Tikkun* 6(2), p. 66) begins with a quotation from *Exodus* (34:12–14), but draws on many other sources as well—including the portion of *Re'eh*—which condemn the religion and gods of the Canaanite peoples and stress the deep moral contrast between paganism and the service of God. The exhortation not to go "after other gods, which ye have not known" (11:28) is reiterated three times in *Re'eh*. Prominence is given to the obligation to break down "their altars" and destroy the names of the gods of these nations "out of that place" (12:3), stressing that inheriting the land and dwelling in it are contingent upon the total rejection of "every abomination to the Lord, which He hateth, have they done unto their gods; for even their sons and their daughters do they burn in the fire to their gods" (*ibid.* 31).

In her criticism of the Bible's attitude to paganism, Plaskow postulates that the description of the pagan religions with which the ancient Hebrews struggled, like the dichotomy between divine service and idolatry, reflect a polemic approach fraught with historical distortions. "The Jewish caricature of paganism cuts us off from aspects of our own history", she writes, noting the importance of physical images of the divine, such as the cherubim in the Holy of Holies, in Jewish tradition. Like us, the Rabbis reflected on the meaning of the verse in *Re'eh* concerning the pilgrimage festivals: "Three times in a year shall all thy males appear before the Lord thy God in the place which He shall choose; on the feast of unleavened bread, and on the feast of weeks, and on the feast of tabernacles" (16:16). The syntax of the phrase "shall appear before" is unusual and raises the question of whether the purpose of such pilgrimages was to see God or to be seen by Him (or possibly both). The Talmud answers after its usual fashion: "When Israel would make the pilgrimage, the curtain before the Holy of Holies would be drawn aside and they would be shown cherubim which were intertwined, and they would be told: behold God's love for you is as the love between male and female" (*Yoma* 54a). And Rashi explains: "They adhered to one another and embraced one another as a man embraces a woman". Even if the Talmud's representation of the cherubim is not historically accurate, it is worth noting that the expression "shall appear before the Lord" creates a certain tension within *Re'eh* between the struggle against idolatry and evidence of ancient Near-Eastern influence upon the Hebrew Temple cult and concept of the divine.

According to Plaskow, the view that Judaism and paganism are wholly incompatible, denies us the chance to wonder what the Jewish religion lost in its struggle against paganism, and where one may find continuity between paganism and ancient Judaism. Plaskow's approach, characteristic of feminist theologians—Christian and Jewish alike—relates to the loss of feminine imagery of deity present in the pagan religions, and the exclusion of women as priests in monotheistic cult worship. Plaskow notes that biblical anti-pagan polemics obscure the connection between the development of monotheism and the elimination of those elements that were, in her opinion, so vital to the religious lives of women and their sense of belonging to religion.

While Plaskow advocates tolerance toward paganism—particularly modern pagan religions and cults engendered by the ecological "New Age" movement and its emphasis on the sanctity of the earth and nature—she does view some religious phenomena as expressions of idolatry, which she denounces without reservation. A clear example of this kind of idolatry, according to Plaskow, is the glorification of hierarchical male God imagery and the complete addiction to it. *Adhering to a limited range of images of the divine is in itself an expression of idolatry*, inasmuch as it reduces infinite divinity to a being characterized exclusively by male traits. Indeed, many of the midrashim on the revelation at Sinai teach that unlike finite beings, God comprizes an infinity of characteristics, qualities and aspects, since "God's ways are not the ways of men" (*Exodus Rabbah, Yitro*, 28,5), and since at the time of the revelation God's voice was heard on Mount Sinai "each according to his ability" (*ibid.* 29,1). Plaskow thus explains the meaning of monotheism, as a unity that comprises a multiplicity of images of the divine. Hence the importance of expanding the imagery of deity in the language of prayer, to include feminine and nonhierarchical natural imagery of the divine.

Plaskow is correct in asserting that certain aspects of the Torah's portrayal of pagan religion—like New Testament portrayals of the Pharisees—are no more than superficial caricatures, which should be approached critically. Recent studies concerning the role of women in religious ritual in biblical times show, for example, that the interpretation of the word *kedeshah* in the sense of "harlot" (Gen. 38:21) is found only in biblical Hebrew, as part of the biblical campaign against paganism. Bible scholar Mayer Gruber, in his book *The Motherhood of God and Other Studies*, points out that in Assyrian, Ugaritic and Phoenician documents (from which we learn about the religions of the ancient Near East) the term *kedeshah* signifies a holy or consecrated person, without any sexual connotations. The *kedeshot*, according to a wide variety of such texts, were midwives, nursemaids, priestesses who sang and danced in the temples of the Assyrian God Adad, diviners or archivists. Although in Mesopotamian ancient texts *kedeshot* are alluded to as harlots, there is no evidence associating them with ritual prostitution or prostitution of any kind in other ancient Near Eastern texts.

In his article on maternal images of God in Second Isaiah, Gruber supports the criticisms leveled by Plaskow and other religious feminists at the patriarchal imagery employed by the prophets Jeremiah and Ezekiel. These prophets also frequently resort to pornographic images of the People of Israel as a harlot, in order to highlight the participation of women in foreign cults, like that of the "queen of heaven" (*Jer.* 7:18) or of Tammuz (*Ezek.* 8:14). The adherence of Hebrew women to various pagan fertility cults in biblical times is supported by archaeological evidence, discovered at the City of David. In Gruber's opinion, Second Isaiah's frequent use of maternal images of God—such as the comparison of God to a woman in labor, in *Isaiah* 42:14: "now will I cry like a travailing woman, gasping and panting at once"—reflects the prophet's profound understanding of the hearts and minds of people of all kinds, and the sense of alienation evoked in women by the patriarchal rhetoric of Jeremiah and Ezekiel. While the two earlier prophets failed in their war against paganism, Second Isaiah, according to Gruber (*ibid.*), was in fact successful in his efforts to attract "Also the aliens, that join themselves to the Lord, to minister unto Him, and to love the name of the Lord … for my house shall be called a house of prayer for all peoples" (*Is.* 56:6–7).

Nevertheless, Plaskow's portrayal of the earlier pagan religions as less patriarchal and less brutal than biblical monotheistic religion is historically inaccurate and poses a number of theological and philosophical difficulties. In the absence of textual evidence, we have no information regarding the nature of goddess religion and worship in prehistoric cultures. Lotte Motz, in her study of female deities in the mythologies of ancient cultures around the world, points out that the images associated with these goddesses and their relationships with male gods were extremely varied—including hierarchical and martial images alongside stereotypical images of women in patriarchal society. Plaskow also ignores archaeological evidence and extra-biblical documentation of infant and child sacrifice in ancient pagan ritual. A cemetery for infants discovered at the Tunisian site of Carthage for example, attests to the fact that the Phoenician cult of Asherah (or *Tanit,* the equivalent of the Canaanite Asherah), included the sacrifice of children to Moloch. In this sense, biblical portrayals would appear to rest on solid historical ground.

As noted above, Plaskow's arguments are also problematic from a philosophical and theological perspective. Her basic premise—that symbols of the divine that reflect the gender of female worshipers will ensure their sense of belonging to the religious community—is narrowly based on the theories of Feuerbach, Nietzsche and Freud: that symbols of the divine reflect the identity of worshipers and its projection upon their conception of the divine. Recent studies have shown however, that religious symbols are extremely varied and complex, and represent different things in different societies. Patriarchal, male societies often assign great importance to feminine symbols of divinity—both for their erotic and heterosexual significance, as in the kabbalistic system of the *sefirot* for example, and for the identification of the male community with values that are considered "feminine".

Another question is why Plaskow raises no objections to the historical-theological view, widely-held among Christian feminists, that Hebrew monotheism begat—with the decline of pagan religions—the patriarchal social structure and its accompanying values. Plaskow was one of the first theologians to question the second part of the Christian claim: that Jesus, through his gospel of "liberation", restored the egalitarian message that had declined with the rise of Hebrew monotheistic culture. Plaskow maintained that this approach merely reflects the anti-Semitism that permeates Christian theology—even feminist Christian theology—although it is doubtful whether her remarks have had any real impact. She does not however, question the basic premise of Western feminist thought in this regard—i.e. the association between patriarchy and monotheism—and she ignores certain aspects in which Hebrew women would seem to have had an advantage, in terms of ritual authority, over their pagan counterparts. (Many sacrifices were not slaughtered by priests but by members of the general public—men or women; contrary to pagan practice at the time—as emerges from various ancient Near Eastern documents—which restricted the slaughter of animals for sacrifice to male priests). She also ignores the pagan origins of the laws of purity and impurity, or is unaware of them (see Gruber pp. 66–68), and sees these taboos as expressions of a uniquely Jewish approach to female sexuality as unclean and a source of exclusion from the foci of religious power (Plaskow, *ibid.* pp. 174–175). Plaskow's erroneous identification of ancient pagan religion with modern paganism and the peaceful cult of the earth mother espoused by modern women of the "New Age", merely romanticizes the ancient religions and the patriarchal societies in which they developed. In other words, she fails to apply to these religions, the same suspicious, critical method that she applies to Jewish sources.

Nevertheless, Plaskow's theological distinction between pagan symbols of the divine and "idolatry" (denoting moral depravity), follows in a venerable exegetical tradition, established by the Renaissance talmudic scholar Menahem Meiri and pursued by a number of modern thinkers, on the basis of Hegelian philosophical principles. While Hermann Cohen and Leo Baeck, for example, saw paganism as the moral and religious antithesis of Judaism, Aaron David Gordon and Franz Rosenzweig (like Hegel) viewed paganism as a first and necessary step in the religious development of the human spirit.

In his essay "The Human and Nature", A. D. Gordon notes that pagan religion, in which man worships nature, is a first step in the development of human consciousness, whereby: "It is as if the sense of oneness of man's soul with the soul of the world teaches man—children—to think and feel humanness, abstract thought, and the rational but also emotional ability to particularize and to generalize" (A. D. Gordon, "*Ha'adam Vehateva*", *Mivhar Ketavim*, Jerusalem, p. 82). At the same time, he sees the personality cults of religious leaders and any attempt to exploit nature and other human beings as "idolatrous slavery," or an expression of the moral depravity identified in Jewish tradition with the concept of "idolatry" (*avodah zarah*), to which Jews and even members of other faiths can descend.

Like Gordon, Rosenzweig saw in the pagan world, the foundations of God's pure revelation. Unlike Gordon however, the pagan religion to which Rosenzweig related was that of Ancient Greece. Toward the end of the first part of *The Star of Redemption*, Rosenzweig writes: "A shimmering glitter of *perhaps* extends over gods, worlds, and men" (Franz Rosenzweig, *The Star of Redemption*, Translation by Barbara E. Galli, University of Wisconsin Press, Madison, 2005, p. 96). The weighty foundations for revelation were laid in the classical, pagan world, but they lacked light, movement, flow, since, as we find in a later essay (from 1928–1929), entitled "A Note on Anthropomorphism" (F. Rosenzweig, "*Al Ha'antropomorfism*", *Naharayim*, tr. Yehoshua Amir, p. 40): "Paganism is merely the momentary embodiment of true Revelation of the true God in a tangible image of divinity". While the "raw materials" into which revelation breathed the spirit of life had been in existence from the dawn of pagan civilization, the true extent of the bond and the love between God and man only became a part of cosmic existence with the revelation at Sinai (Rosenzweig, pp. 96–98). And God's perpetual desire for revelation has continued to pulse in the world ever since.

What then has Plaskow added to the theological discussion regarding the differences between paganism and idolatry? On one level, she extends the boundaries of tolerance to include, not only Christianity and Islam—a step already taken by Maimonides with regard to Islam and by Menahem Meiri with regard to Christianity—but also nature religions and the beliefs and views held by modern pagan groups. Although they may seem strange or inauthentic to those who adhere to ancient Jewish tradition, it is important to stress the fact that, judging by the writings of the leaders of these new religions, their rituals and teachings do not include wild sexual behavior, and they preach messages of peace and equality. In this sense, Plaskow follows in the pluralistic religious footsteps of the American Jewish philosopher, Rabbi Prof. Mordecai M. Kaplan.

On another, more important level, Plaskow's thought stresses the way in which the participation of women in religious ritual has posed a threat to male religious establishments. Even more threatening is the leading role that women have taken in reshaping Jewish theology and imagery of the divine "in their image and in their likeness". Women who have demanded an equal role to men in all facets of religious life have frequently been labelled "idolaters" by Jewish religious establishments, from biblical times to the present. Plaskow's hope, like that of other Jewish feminists, is that we will finally see this patriarchal hoax and false accusation exposed in our generation—to be replaced by a just society, in which the status of women, as equal partners in the divine image, is faithfully reflected in Jewish ethics, Halakhah and prayer.

Hannah Kasher

Shoftim—Judges and Officers Shalt Thou Make Thee

"For the Tree of the Field Is Man"
Ecology in the Thought of **Rabbi Joseph Ibn Kaspi**

When thou shalt besiege a city a long time, in making war against it to take it, thou shalt not destroy the trees thereof by wielding an axe against them; for thou mayest eat of them, but thou shalt not cut them down; for is the tree of the field man, that it should be besieged of thee? Only the trees of which thou knowest that they are not trees for food, them thou mayest destroy and cut down, that thou mayest build bulwarks against the city that maketh war with thee, until it fall (*Deuteronomy* 20:19–20).

In the following chapter, we will discuss the well-known analogy "for the tree of the field is man", which creates a link between man and one of the components of his natural environment. From an ecological perspective, the "tree of the field" is unique, inasmuch as our interaction with it is not governed by any moral obligation—i.e. it is not seen to suffer when it is harmed, as would a human being or an animal.

The discussion will comprise two parts. In the shorter of the two, we will briefly examine the biblical context of the analogy and some of the ways in which it has been interpreted. In the second, longer part, we will introduce the ecological views of Rabbi Joseph Ibn Kaspi, based on his understanding of these verses.

The biblical text addresses a commandment to soldiers who wish to construct wooden siegeworks. In order to do so, they must, presumably, cut down trees in the environs of the besieged city. They are therefore commanded not to cut down fruit trees—"for thou mayest eat of them". It is unclear whether this explanation pertains to the morality and decency of such behavior, or whether it is simply a matter of expediency. As

a moral obligation, it can be understood as a mark of man's gratitude to
the tree, as it were, for the fruit it provides. The utilitarian interpretation
is of course that a fruit tree might serve as a source of food during the
siege, and it would therefore be short-sighted to cut it down. Only those
trees that are clearly not fruit trees—"the trees of which thou knowest
that they are not trees for food" may be destroyed. The reasoning offered by the text itself has been understood, alternatively, as a question
or a statement: "for [is] the tree of the field man"/ "for the tree of the
field [is] man".

If it is understood as a question—a rhetorical question, implying a
negative response—it suggests no equivalence between tree and man.
The Midrash *Tannaim* (Deuteronomy 20, 19) explains the injunction as
an expression of "ethical combat": [Is a tree like a man? Of course not!]
"For a man sees his killer and flees" [while a tree stands helpless]. Rashi
presents the cutting down of a tree as an act of gratuitous destruction:
"For is a tree [like] a man, to be besieged, to be tormented by hunger and
thirst, like the townspeople? Why should you destroy it?"

Even as a statement, the verse is explained in a number of different
ways. One interpretation, reads: "For [the life of] man [depends upon]
the tree of the field" (see *Sifre, Devarim,* 203, and Ibn Ezra *ad loc.*).
Another (Rashbam), proposes the following reading of the entire verse:
"Thou shalt not destroy the trees thereof [the distant fruit trees] by wielding an axe against them; for thou mayest eat of them, and thou shalt not
cut them down [but rather those trees that are near to the city and serve
as places of concealment]; for [to] the tree of the field man will come [to
hide] from thee under siege." The circumstances described according to
this interpretation are quite different: The intention in cutting down the
trees is not to construct ramparts, but to clear the area around the city of
potential hiding places. In these interpretations, the statement "for the
tree of the field is man" may express a positive sentiment, but certainly
does not create an analogy between man himself and the tree of the field.

The interpretation of the phrase as an analogy between man and
tree necessarily takes the expression out of its original context. Man is
sometimes compared to a tree: "If he is a worthy Torah scholar—'thou
mayest eat of him, and thou shalt not cut him down'; and if not—'him
thou mayest destroy and cut down'" (*Ta'anit* 7a). And trees are some-

times compared to man: "Even trees that bear no fruit will one day be called to account ... 'For the tree of the field is a man'—Just as man is called to account [for his actions], so trees are called to account " (Genesis *Rabbah* 26). Either way, the identification of man with the tree of the field offers a counterweight to the approach that man is unparalleled in all creation.

Anthropocentrism, with all it entails, is the prevailing approach in human society. Presenting man as the center of the universe also leads, inadvertently, to the convenient conclusion that all that surrounds him was created solely for his benefit. If so, there is nothing morally wrong with the exploitation of all other creatures—even to the point of killing them—in order to better satisfy man's needs. Nevertheless, from time to time, we come across a philosopher, among those whose thought is rooted in traditional sources, who holds the diametrically opposed position, known today as "deep ecology". This approach goes beyond utilitarian ecological discourse, which seeks to limit man's exploitation of the environment because such behavior compromises the needs of mankind's own future generations—asserting instead that such exploitation infringes upon the rights of other creatures, which must also be treated as ends in themselves.

We find clear signs of such "deep ecology" in the writings of Rabbi Joseph Ibn Kaspi—including his interpretation of the verse "for the tree of the field is man" as an analogy between man and tree. Ibn Kaspi considered himself a disciple of Maimonides, and indeed in the writings of Maimonides we begin to see a certain deviation from elitist anthropocentrism, toward biocentrism. In his *Commentary on the Mishnah*, a work Maimonides wrote as a young man, he discusses the purpose of the earth, and claims that "All that exists beneath the sphere of the moon was created exclusively for man" (*Maimonides*, introduction to the *Commentary on the Mishnah*, ch.8). Note, only that which exists "beneath the sphere of the moon" was created for man's sake, contrary to the opinion of Rabbi Bahya Ibn Pakuda, who claimed in *Duties of the Heart* (*Gate of Unity*, ch.6) that the celestial bodies themselves were only created to serve man. Maimonides further explains, in the introduction to the *Commentary on the Mishnah*, how plants and animals were meant to serve man's needs:

For all types of animal—some for his food, such as sheep and cattle and others, and some for his benefit other than food, such as donkeys to carry that which he cannot carry himself, and horses—to traverse great distances in a short time … And so the trees … and the grasses … and every grass and every tree and every type of animal, from the elephant to the worm, would not be, were it not of some benefit to man.

According to Maimonides, human society as well, was only created to serve the wise and to satisfy their physical and social needs (*ibid.*). In the *Guide for the Perplexed*, written some twenty years after the *Commentary on the Mishnah*, Maimonides reiterates his belief that "Man is merely the most noble… in this nether world" (*Guide for the Perplexed* III,12 –tr. S. Pines), but does not make man the purpose of all creation. He agrees with Aristotle, that "plants were brought to existence only for the sake of animals" (*ibid.* 13; Aristotle, *On Plants* 1,2), without asserting that plants and animals were created in order to serve man. Moreover, he terms the anthropocentric explanation that "the ape was created in order that man should laugh at it"—"ravings" (*ibid.* 25). The explanation that Maimonides offers is that all things created are ends unto themselves, and God created the world in all its fullness and variety because existence is undoubtedly preferable to nonexistence.

Ibn Kaspi goes much further than the *Guide* in this. He even sought to blur the traditional hierarchical order, stressing instead man's community with and likeness to his environment. This is reflected in his various commentaries on the Torah—both his earlier works (*Sefer ha-Sod*; *Tirat Kesef*), and his later commentary (*Matsref la-Kesef*). His approach is based on Aristotle's doctrine of categories, as expounded in *Kitzur Sefer Hamavo Le-Porfirius* (*A Summary of Porphyry's Isagoge*), which he included in his *Tzeror Hakesef*. There, he suggests a distinction between "genus" and "species":

We will explain these things together, for they correlate with one another, and are like father and son, for the 'genus' is like the father, and the "species" is like the son. Both are common to many, differing only in extent, for the "genus" extends to more things than the "species". For example: Animal and Man. Animal is the "genus", and Man is the "species" ... And so in the case of Substance and Organism (lit. "growing") ... And behold the wise Porphyry created an order of genera and species—called the "Porphyrian Tree" in the *category of the substance*. For he placed many genera above the species of man, in many stages. The uppermost genus is Substance—and from it Material and Non-material—and from it Organism and Non-organism. And after Organism—Animal and Non-animal. And after Animal— Rational (lit. "speaking") and Non-rational. And the Rational is man.

The stages can be represented as follows:

Substance (uppermost genus)				
Material (Body)				Nonmaterial
Organism			Nonorganism	
Animal		Nonanimal		
Rational=Man	Nonrational			

Porphyry uses family relationships to illustrate the hierarchy:
Father = the genus Material, the genus Organism, the genus Animal
Son = the genus Organism, the genus Animal, the species Man

Porphyry himself wrote a book in praise of vegetarianism, in which he presents the following argument, which he attributes to Theophrastus:
Those that are generated from the same sources, I mean from the same father and mother, are said by us to be naturally allied to each other... Hence, I think we should say, that Greek is allied and has an affinity to Greek, and Barbarian to Barbarian, and all men to each other ... Thus also we must admit that all men have an affinity, and are allied to each other. And, moreover, the principles of the bodies of all animals are naturally the same. I do not say this with reference to the first elements of their bodies; for plants also consist of these; but I mean the seed, the flesh,

and the conascent genus of humors which is inherent in animals. But animals are much more allied to each other, through naturally possessing souls, which are not different from each other... For, as Euripides says, they have all of them the same food and the same spirit, the same purple (*sic*) streams; and they likewise demonstrate that the common parents of all of them are Heaven and Earth... Nor because some animals are savage, is their alliance to us to be on this account abscinded. For some men may be found who are no less, and even more malefic than savage animals to their neighbors, and who are impelled to injure any one they may meet with ... Hence, also, we destroy such men; yet we do not cut them off from an alliance to animals of a mild nature. Thus, therefore, if likewise some animals are savage, these, as such, are to be destroyed, in the same manner as men that are savage; but our habitude or alliance to other and wilder animals is not on this account to be abandoned. But neither tame nor savage animals are to be eaten; as neither are unjust men (Porphyry, *On Abstinence from Animal Food*, Book 3, 25–26 –tr. Thomas Taylor).

Porphyry calls man's superiority over the animals into question by creating an analogy between them, based on their behavior: tame animals and decent men on the one hand, savage animals and wicked men on the other. Man's affinity with all animals is not broken, and none should be eaten. Nevertheless, such affinity is only extended to animals, since—in promoting vegetarianism—he allows the consumption of plants. Kaspi cited financial constraints as the reason for his own abstention from meat (*Tirat Kesef* 33), and also considered himself a brother and fellow of "the cabbage and the horseradish":

And I would say that one of the reasons that the Giver of our Torah commanded us to show compassion to other creatures—as [our Rabbis] of blessed memory said: "[The duty of relieving] the suffering of animals is a biblical law" (*Shabbat* 128b)—is to teach us that we humans are very close to them, we and they—are children of a single father, because we share a single genus. This runs counter to the belief of the masses who lack natural science and are therefore ignorant of many truths, and that is the reason for their mistaken pride. And the Giver of the Torah was not satisfied with all of His commandments until he informed us in all of them that we are living organisms, that we might know that we and the vegetables, like the cabbage and the horseradish, are brothers, and we share a single father. Therefore, he charged us not to cut down fruit trees, as it is written in the Torah. And it says, by way of explanation: "for the tree of the field is man" (*Deut.* 20:19), that is to say that man is the tree of the field, which is another species in the genus Organism, as it is written "All flesh is grass" (*Is.* 40:6). And our Rabbis of blessed memory said: "Men are like the grasses of the field (*Sanhedrin* 102a). And this is the reason that He first commanded us with regard to a city, in which there are animate creatures: 'proclaim peace unto it" (*Deut.* 20:10), for it is to our advantage that they live, that they might be slaves to assist us, like horses and mules, and sheep and cattle. The seven [Canaanite] peoples however, are irredeemable, for they are savage animals, like wolves and leopards that hunger for prey—and we cannot but slay them (*Tirat Kesef*).

Kaspi explains the injunctions against animal suffering and cutting down fruit trees as attempts by the Torah to impart to man a correct cognizance of reality. This cognizance—that the human species is like other animal species inasmuch as they are "sons" of the genus Animal, which is, like other organic species, a son of the genus Organism—may help man to avoid the sin of pride. Unlike Porphyry, Kaspi extends brotherhood and fellowship to plants as well, and the criterion he proposes is far less demanding than Porphyry's. Like Porphyry however, he creates a strong analogy—here and in other contexts—between human beings and the various kinds of animals: domesticated beasts and predators. This "deep ecology" is further developed in his later commentary on the Torah (*Matsref la-Kesef*), in which he analyses the system of precepts in terms of the various levels of reality.

For our perfect Torah wished to give us perfect opinions, that is to impart to us knowledge of reality, to the best of our ability.

And in so doing had two intentions: One—to inform us of our own level of reality, and consequently, to free us from haughtiness and pride. And that is: that our overall genus is Substance, and below that—Organism; and below Organism—Animal; and below Animal—Rational, that is Man and human individuals. And this includes the reality of the world of the elements. And the masses remain foolish in of all this, and in our pride we boast of a false endowment and believe that there is no relation between ourselves and the other animate creatures, and even the plants such as the cabbage and other vegetables, and even the fields. Therefore, in order to dispel all of this folly, we were given various precepts, some pertaining to lifeless matter, some to living organisms, some to animate creatures, and some rational beings. And great and careful attention was paid to that which belongs to Rational [genus]—which is the final species (in the Porphyrian hierarchy): Man. And God commanded us to show compassion to all human beings, regardless of the people to which they may belong, with the exception of the seven peoples, who are like savage beasts. And so the commandment concerning a beautiful captive: "thou shalt not deal with her as a slave" (*Deut.* 21:14). *A fortiori* with members of our own faith … and then with other people who are not of our faith, as we have explained. And after having dealt so extensively with all members of the human species, He commanded us with regard to all of the animal species: "because thy soul desireth to eat flesh" (*Deut.* 12:20)—that we should not kill them needlessly, but only for food, since it is in man's nature to desire flesh. For the original intention was that we should not eat meat, but would be satisfied with plants, and therefore in the beginning we were only permitted the grass of the field. And after the flood, the eating of animals proliferated, which is like eating our father, for they are our close genus. The Torah therefore commanded us to show them compassion, as we are reminded: "it and its young" (*Lev.* 22:28), and "Thou shalt not seethe a kid in its mother's milk" (*Ex.* 23:19), and "If a bird's nest chance to be before thee in the way" (*Deut.* 22:6). And could the Torah have restricted us further, it would have done so. But since over-affinity for the Animal genus would have lessened our affinity for the Rational genus, [the Torah] weakened and minimized precepts commanding love and compassion toward [animals]. And so, the precepts concerning animals are followed by those regarding the genus of Organism, such as the precept "thou shalt not destroy the trees thereof" (*Deut.* 20:19). And because they are further removed, their precepts are weaker. And so, the precepts pertaining to living organisms are followed by those that concern the Material in the fields, as we are commanded with regard to the Sabbatical year, to give some rest to the earth, for out of it we were taken. And because it is further removed, its precepts are weaker. And the essence of the matter is that the Giver of our Torah sought, in these things, to impart to us knowledge of a great part of lower reality through knowledge of the uppermost genus (Substance) of the ten higher genera (Substance and its nine "accidents"). And He imparted to us modesty and humility, that we might know and have before us always that we are like the donkey and the mule, and even the cabbage and the pomegranate, and even the lifeless stone. He also imparted to us in this, the quality of mercy, that is to show mercy to every good man, for the entire world was not created but for the sake of this imperative (*Matzref la-Kesef* 293–294).

Kaspi's explanation of the precepts that concern nature follows the Maimonidean view that the divinity of the Law is measured by the accurate knowledge of reality that it affords (*Guide for the Perplexed* II: 40; III: 26). Such knowledge, as we have seen, protects man from the arrogance spawned by the incorrect view that he is distinct from the rest of creation. Despite this fellowship of creation, there is a direct correlation between one's obligations and the generic or specific status of their object. With regard to the earth, which is an inert body, we are commanded to observe the Sabbatical year, in awareness of our affinity with it: "to give some rest to the earth, for out of it we were taken" (based on Gen. 3:19). Our obligation to growing things is reflected in the prohibition against destroying trees, in the portion of *Shoftim*. This interpretation creates a certain problem however, inasmuch as the Bible clearly distinguishes between trees that bear fruit, which may not be cut down; and those that do not bear fruit, which may be used to construct the bulwarks of siege warfare.

A number of the precepts concerning animals pertain specifically to the relationship between animals and their offspring: the prohibition against slaughtering an animal and its young on the same day, seething a kid in its mother's milk, and taking eggs or chicks in the presence of the mother bird. In this context of behavior toward animals, Ibn Kaspi expresses the opinion that the Torah may not have gone far enough, "and could the Torah have restricted us further, it would have done so". The original plan, as reflected in the command to Adam, was that man should eat "the grass of the field" (based on Gen. 3:18), since we would "be satisfied with plants". Permission to eat meat was granted only after the flood, as a concession to human nature, which "desires flesh". Kaspi expresses his reservations regarding this practice, in highly emotive family terms: "which is like eating our father, for they are our close genus". Here Kaspi employs a different family relationship than the one suggested in his earlier commentary, *Tirat Kesef*: "We and they—are children of a single father, because we share a single genus". In other words, man and animals are brothers, inasmuch as they are different species within the same genus: Animal. Here on the other hand, he presents the animal as man's father—based on its identification with the genus Animal ("our close genus"), which is above the species Man in the Aristotelian hierarchy. Kaspi's approach to human beings also depends upon their closeness and status: preference is given to "members of our own faith", while the Canaanite peoples are like savage beasts. As a rule, we must "show compassion to all human beings, regardless of the people to which they belong". Kaspi also relates to the special status of the wise—seen by Maimonides as the purpose of creation—who must be treated with "mercy" (apparently different from "compassion"), and whom he characterizes as "good", adding that "the entire world was not created but for the sake to accompany him".

Indeed, in another context, Ibn Kaspi stresses man's dual responsibility. Man must be humble, yet he must also realize the intellectual potential that sets him apart from the animals, on the other. Kaspi explains the biblical metaphor "thou worm Jacob" (*Is.* 41:14) in this light:

> To inform us that we are of the Animal genus and similar to the lowest of the creeping things. And we are like them in every way, unless we realize our intellectual potential. And all this to instill in us the more deeply and the more essentially, the quality of humility; and to awaken us to acquire intelligence and the intelligibles wherein we differ from the worms. And from this the sum and substance, which are mercy and clemency, or rest and respite from work, for animals, plants and minerals (*Adnei Kesef* 1,151).

Alongside the imperative to realize God's intellectual image in man, Kaspi highlights the importance of humility as one of the underlying reasons for the precepts. As a deep ecologist, he calls for a sense of constant awareness: "that we might know and have before us always that we are like the donkey and the mule, and even the cabbage and the pomegranate, and even the lifeless stone" (*Matsref la-Kesef*).

With this analogy, which compares man to animals, plants and lifeless matter, we may return to the expression with which we began—"for the tree of the field is man"; in its broader sense, transcending the specific context of the biblical verse. The deep affinity between man and the rest of creation becomes brotherhood, and man's primacy entails greater responsibility, rather than greater privilege.

Rachel Elior

Ki Teze—When Thou Goest Forth

"The betrothed damsel cried, and there was none to save her":
The Fate of Rape Victims in the Bible and in the Poetry
of Dalia Rabikovitz

But unto the damsel thou shalt do nothing; there is in the damsel no sin worthy of death; for as when a man riseth against his
neighbor, and slayeth him, even so is this matter. For he found
her in the field; the betrothed damsel cried, and there was none
to save her (*Deuteronomy* 22:26–27).

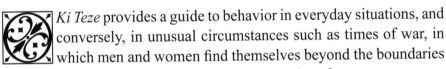 *Ki Teze* provides a guide to behavior in everyday situations, and
conversely, in unusual circumstances such as times of war, in
which men and women find themselves beyond the boundaries
of accepted social norms. *Ki Teze* presents a series of precepts concerning relations between men and women, the rights of men with regard to
women, and the duties of women toward men.

In *Ki Teze*, women are portrayed as belonging to one (or more) of
13 different categories: betrothed women (20:7); spoils of war with a
city that refuses to make peace (*ibid.* 14); captives "of goodly form",
desired as wives (21:10–14); women within polygamous marriage (*ibid.*
15–17); women accused of not having been virgins at the time of their
marriage, and hence of "harlotry" prior to marriage (22:13–21); women
accused of "harlotry" during marriage (*ibid.*); betrothed women raped
in an inhabited area (23:24); betrothed women raped in an uninhabited area (*ibid.* 25–27); raped virgins (*ibid.* 28–9); prostitutes (*ibid.* 18);
women who have married, divorced, remarried and divorced a second
time (24:1–4); widows (*ibid.* 17–20); and objects of levirate marriage
(25:5–10).

This detailed list fails to recognize women as autonomous beings,
but rather discusses the status of women solely in relation to men, as:
virgins, betrothed, married, co-wives, rape victims, divorcees, prostitutes, widows and objects of levirate marriage. *Ki Teze* addresses various

596

relationships of ownership and possession between men and women, as seen from a male perspective, upheld by divine command. The balance of power between the sexes is reflected in the different sexual rights afforded to men and women, in the different levels of modesty required of the respective sexes, and in the language that ascribes different verbs to the rights of men and to the duties of women. The exclusive privileges of men in forming and dissolving conjugal bonds are reflected in expressions such as *take, lay hold, come to, desire, send away, torment, find an unseemly thing, perform levirate duty*. The status of women on the other hand, is marked by such terms as: *go astray* (*Num.* 5:12); *act unfaithfully* (*ibid.*); *defilement* (*Deut.* 24:4 and *Num.* 5:1–31); *harlotry* (*Deut.* 22:21); and *an unseemly thing* (*ibid.* 24:1).

Taking, laying hold, lying with, desiring, tormenting and sending away are all unilateral actions permitted to men only: "If any man take a wife" (*Deut.* 22:13); "If a man find a damsel that is a virgin ... and lay hold on her, and lie with her ... then the man that lay with her shall give unto the damsel's father fifty shekels of silver, and she shall be his wife" (*ibid.* 29). A man's right to fulfill his desires without the consent of his partner is also one-sided: a man may plunder the women of his enemy; a man may lie with a beautiful captive whom he desires, and take her as his wife—an action described in the very same passage as a torment to her; a man may marry a number of women without the consent of his first wife, although the law forbids preferring the sons of a beloved wife to those of a despised wife with regard to inheritance, requiring that the rights of the firstborn be safeguarded. The Bible also addresses the issue of a father entitled to compensation when his daughter is maligned (*ibid.* 19), whereas the daughter herself is not entitled to any compensation from her slanderous husband. The passage further elaborates upon the duty of women to safeguard their virginity and the right of a husband to his wife's virginity (*ibid.* 14–19). A young woman found by her husband not be a virgin is executed by stoning, on the charge of harlotry (*bid.* 20–21); and when a married women sins with another man, both she and the man who lay with her are put to death (*ibid.* 22).

The marriage relationship—rooted in the principles of acquisition and social convention—applies only to the chaste and modest virgin, taken possession of, and subsequently placed under the protection of her husband, for the purpose of perpetuating his seed. The attitude to men, as noted, is completely different. Men are permitted—under various circumstances—additional sexual liaisons, with women belonging to groups or categories over which force and desire have the upper hand. The first of these categories is that of the *helpless*—a raped virgin, a captive taken by force, a female servant, concubine or slave, compelled to acquiesce to her master's will. The second category is that of the woman who *deviates from the social convention of conjugal protection, subjugation, ownership and obedience*, i.e. the prostitute, harlot, wanton, rebellious or deviant woman, who will consent to sex in exchange for money, or chooses to enter a relationship outside the confines of marriage-ownership. Prostitution, polygamy and forced sex outside of marriage, with unprotected women (spoils of war, captives, raped women, female servants), are permitted to men and afforded social and legal sanction, whereas women are forbidden to engage in any sex beyond the confines of marriage-ownership. The punishment for women who engage in forbidden relationships—characterized as deviation, adultery and harlotry—is death; and those suspected of such behavior are subjected to the humiliating ordeal of the "bitter waters".

A woman, who oversteps the boundaries of marriage and her husband's exclusive ownership over her body and her sexuality, becomes an adulteress, a deviant, a harlot and a rebellious wife. Men, who are unsatisfied with marriage on the other hand, may have recourse to polygamy, the harem, divorce, abandonment, sex with female servants and slaves, captive women or prostitutes. As noted above, all of these options are socially sanctioned, as frequently illustrated by biblical narrative.

Thus, according to biblical law, men and women belong to different legal categories, from which derive *different* punishments for the *same* actions. There are no masculine equivalents in the Bible of such terms as: "one who has gone astray" (*sotah*), harlot (*zonah*), maidservant (*amah*), female slave (*shifhah*), concubine (*pilegesh*), "woman of goodly form" (*eshet yefat to'ar*), or one who has been raped (*ne'eneset*). In other words, these concepts are emblematic of the balance of power between men and women, and determine the status of women in an aggressive male world, in which men and women have different rights with regard to their bodies and the satisfaction of their desires both within and beyond the family structure. The punishments prescribed for breaking the law concerning sovereignty over one's body and violations of that sovereignty thus differ as well.

The legal code pays particular attention to rape victims, determining their fate in accordance with the nature of the place in which the act took place, the victim's proprietary status of (a virgin who is not betrothed, one who is betrothed, a married woman), and the identity of the rapist—perceived alternately as tormentor, murderer or bridegroom. A woman who is raped in a city, and was not heard to cry out, is stoned to death, along with the rapist who tormented her (*Deut.* 22:21–24). In other words, both the attacker—who has committed the sin of rape—and the attacked—the innocent victim of the rape, suspected of collusion because she failed to cry out—are punished in the same fashion, despite the fundamental difference between them: he acted with malice, in order to satisfy his desires by force, while she was coerced to participate in violent sex, in which she had no part other than that of helpless victim. On the other hand, a woman who is raped in the field, in an uninhabited place, is spared punishment and suspicion: "But unto the damsel thou shalt do nothing; there is in the damsel no sin worthy of death; for as when a man riseth against his neighbor, and slayeth him, even so is this matter. For he found her in the field; the betrothed damsel cried, and there was none to save her" (*ibid.* 26–27); and the rapist is put to death: "the man only that lay with her shall die" (*ibid.* 25).

Rape in the field, embodying violence against the helpless, perpetrated beyond the reach of civilization and social convention, beyond speech, voice or hearing, in the realm of speechless violence and the silence of primal desires, brings to mind the story of Cain and Abel: "And Cain spoke unto Abel his brother. And it came to pass, when they were in the field, that Cain rose up against Abel his brother, and slew him" (Gen. 4:8). Her shout or cry, unheard by anyone except the dull-eared rapist, is reminiscent of "the voice of thy brother's blood crieth unto me from the ground" (*ibid.* 10). It is the cry of injustice, the desperate plea for help, unheard by man, but heard in heaven, beyond time and space.

The *Temple Scroll*, written in the last centuries BCE and discovered among the Dead Sea Scrolls at Qumran, offers another version of the biblical rape scenarios (the interpolation in brackets follows *Deut.* 22):

[If there be a damsel that is a virgin betrothed unto a man, and a man find her in the city, and lie with her] then they shall both be brought out unto the gate of that city and unto the *s*[] and they shall be stoned with stones that they die: the damsel, because she cried not, being in the city; and the man, because he hath tormented his neighbor's wife; so thou shalt put away the evil from the midst of thee.

But if the man find her in the field, in a place distant and concealed from the city, and the man take hold of her, and lie with her; then the man only that lay with her shall die. But unto the damsel thou shalt do nothing; there is in the damsel no sin worthy of death; for as when a man riseth against his neighbor, and slayeth him, even so is this matter. For he found her in the field; the betrothed damsel cried, and there was none to save her (Elisha Qimron (ed.), *Megilat Hamikdash*, Jerusalem, 1966, 91).

As we see in the biblical text pertaining to the rape of a virgin, the penalty incurred by the rapist is determined by the extent of the damage to property and ownership rights rather than to the girl herself. The wording in the Bible—"If a man find a damsel that is a virgin, that is not betrothed"—differs from that of the *Temple Scroll*, which reads: "And if a man entice a virgin that is not betrothed and is [permitted] to him according to the law, and lie with her, and be found, then the man that lay with her shall give unto the damsel's father fifty shekels of silver, and she shall be his wife, because he hath tormented her; he may not put her away all his days" (*ibid.*).

According to the *Temple Scroll* version of the text, the sin here is one of deliberate seduction: "And if a man entice a virgin that is not betrothed"; contrary to the biblical version that employs neutral language: "If a man find a damsel that is a virgin, that is not betrothed"—and involves force: "and lay hold on her, and lie with her". In both cases, the rape results in the payment of compensation to the girl's father, as the owner of the damaged and hence devalued property. The opinion of the girl forced to spend the rest of her life with the man who raped her, her wishes, her preferences, her voice and her feelings, are not taken into

account. The rapist, who has forced himself on a girl who was not betrothed—and thus still subject to her father's authority—is not punished
with death, but rather constrained to negotiate a financial settlement,
leading to a socially accepted and legally sanctioned marriage with the
victim.

The sexual prohibitions applied to men pertain, for the most part,
to illicit relations with near of kin, sexual contact with whom is characterized as uncleanness, abomination and lewdness—associated with
the laws of ritual purity, and intended to preserve the purity of descent
and safeguard proprietary rights. The *Temple Scroll* includes a further
passage (not included in *Ki Teze*), listing the various sexual relations
prohibited due to nearness of kin—similar to Leviticus 18–20.

A man shall not take his father's wife, and shall not uncover
his father's skirt. A man shall not take his brother's wife, and
shall not uncover the skirt of his brother, son of his father or
son of his mother, for it is uncleanness. A man shall not take his
sister, daughter of his father or daughter of his mother; it is an
abomination. A man shall not take his father's sister or his mother's sister, for it is lewdness. A man shall not take his brother's
daughter or his sister's daughter, for it is an abomination (*ibid.*).

These taboos however, which form the basis of the social order, remain within the limits of patriarchal interests. Alongside the restrictions
it imposes, the text sanctions coerced relations with women lacking pa-
ternal or conjugal-proprietary protection; women who may be taken by
force of desire and lust (spoils of war, beautiful captives), money (concubines, servants, slaves, co-wives, prostitutes) or rape (raped in the city
or in the field).

We thus find that the boundaries of family ownership, the nearness
of kin governed by incest taboos, must not be violated. Women who are
not forbidden kin, or otherwise protected by recognized proprietary relationships however, may be taken by force of rape or money. It is interesting to note that later traditions permit relations with forbidden kin as
well. A medieval kabbalistic treatise entitled *Reasons of the Commandments* written by Joseph of Hamdan in the 13th century claims for example that *Forbidden Relations are the Sceptre of the King*, asserting that

the high-ranking are, under certain conditions, exempt from the sexual prohibitions. This was in fact the practice among royal families in antiquity (e.g. the Cleopatras—daughters of the Ptolemaic dynasty who married their brothers and bore them children—and the Incas; while the Roman emperor Caligula and his sister Drusilla were rumored to have been lovers). Another well-known example is that of anarchistic mystical cults (such as the Donmeh and the Frankists), whose leaders declared themselves royalty or "sons of God" to whom forbidden relations are permitted; based on the verse "that the sons of God saw the daughters of men that they were fair; and they took them wives, *whomsoever they chose*" (Gen. 6:2). These historical cases illustrate the significance of the sexual taboos and the justifications found for their violation.

The laws prohibiting sexual relations due to consanguinity are intended to distinguish between near kin with whom sex is forbidden, and those who are not closely related, with whom sex is permitted. These injunctions place the taboo that creates a sexual barrier between those who are *naturally* close, at the foundation of *culture*, religion and law.

It is this tension between culture and nature—at the heart of holiness, matrimony and conjugal-proprietary rights—that determines the bounds of convention. Women who lack consanguinity and the protection afforded by family and ownership—remain vulnerable.

The *Temple Scroll* offers an interesting version of the laws concerning a captive "woman of goodly form"—attesting to the cultural restraints imposed upon the force of desire, upon female defenselessness and male violence; the normative limits placed upon the desire for possession. According to the *Temple Scroll*, the captor is required to shave the captive woman's head, cut her nails, and allow her to mourn, before claiming his right—as a soldier and a captor—to lie with her; a right that does not include the captive woman's participation in the ritual life of her husband-captor:

> When thou goest forth to battle against thine enemies, and I will deliver them into thy hands, and thou wilt carry them away captive, and see among the captives a woman of goodly form, and have a desire unto her, and would take her to thee to wife, then thou shalt bring her home to thy house; and thou shalt shave her head, and pare her nails; and put the raiment of her captivity

from off her, and she shall remain in thy house, and bewail her father and her mother a full month; after that thou mayest go in unto her, and be her husband, and she shall be thy wife. Thy sacred food she shall not touch up to seven years, and of thy peace-offerings she shall not eat until seven years have passed; then she shall eat thereof (*The Temple* Scroll, 88).

The law recognizes the chaotic reality of war, in which women are abducted by men, and establishes a procedure whereby captive women are removed from their natural state of defenselessness, and brought into the sphere of culture. The law addresses itself exclusively to men, affording them far-reaching rights over women's bodies; while the women in question are denied status, the right of consent or refusal—in effect, sovereignty over their own bodies. These laws are all marked by fundamental inequality, and the granting of unreserved privilege to one side. Such is the case with the laws of *sotah* ("If any man's wife go aside ... she being defiled—*Num.* 5:11–31). A "spirit of jealousy" is sufficient grounds for a husband to cast a shadow of guilt upon his wife, without the usual burden of evidence, whereby guilt is established by testimony and all are presumed innocent until proven otherwise. And so with the laws of adultery, such as the law pertaining to the daughter of a priest who has "played the harlot", who is burnt with fire—a punishment the author of the *Book of Jubilees* applied to all women charged with adultery. The laws of divorce too, recognize only male initiative and power of decision, without any recourse to common sense, clarification or negotiation. The marriage relationship is thus characterized by unilateralism and a complete disregard for the female perspective on sex and marriage-ownership—reflected in exclusive recognition of male attitudes to conjugal and proprietary rights, suspicion, unfaithfulness-defilement, jealousy, punishment and justice, finding "an unseemly thing" and sending away the accused party.

These laws, in their various forms, are founded upon four priestly postulates, which stipulate: 1) the sanctity of the text and the law, which are divine; 2) the sanctity of the author of the text, and the eternal and incontestable validity of his words, as enshrined in the text; 3) uncritical obedience on the part of those to whom the law is addressed and who are charged with its observance; and 4) the innate sanctity of the priests, "keepers of the charge of the sanctuary", and their right to act as judges and arbiters. All four components of this approach to the establishment of authority and social norms in the first and second millennia BCE, underwent far-reaching change in Late Antiquity, and throughout the subsequent period—associated with Rabbinical tradition in the first millennium CE, and with philosophy and Kabbalah in the second millennium.

The sacred *text* underwent a process of canonization that circumscribed its content and sealed off the sources of its inspiration. This process gave rise to diverse retellings of the Law, alternately expanding or reducing its application through exegesis, Midrash, halakhah and aggadah, Oral Law, traditions of the fathers, mystical and philosophical traditions, as well as historical change. With the closing of the canon in the second century CE, the sanctified *author* ceased to be the sole source of the Law—directly revealed in the word of God. Interpretation of the divine word from a human perspective, on various planes of meaning (in a developing Oral Law and constantly expanding body of law), superseded the divine authority (the Written Law) that had been closed and sealed in the canon. The *subjects* of the Law ceased to be obedient recipients of the word of God, compelled to observe a divinely revealed law with which they could not argue, becoming rather, active readers, participants, even critics and creative commentators, banishing the supernatural God from discussions concerning everyday life. (On man's changing status and sovereignty of decision vis-à-vis divine authority, see the story of Akhnai's oven, *Bava Metzia* 59a). The *subjects* of the Law also rejected priestly hegemony, in the name of divine law; claiming instead, their own right to understand, weigh, choose, expand, reduce and reformulate details of the law pertaining to human reality.

This complex process began with a democratic revolution by the Rabbis against the hegemony of a priesthood that demanded recognition of the aforementioned postulates. Until the destruction of the Temple, the priesthood also claimed heavenly authority and privileges with regard to sacred time, place and cult, by virtue of an innate right stemming from their divine selection (the sons of Levi, the seed of Aaron, most holy, "And of Levi he said ... They shall teach Jacob thine ordinances, and Israel thy law"; "For the priest's lips should keep knowledge, and they should seek the law at his mouth; for he is the messenger of the Lord of hosts").

This revolution entailed wrenching hegemony over the sacred from the privileged few, to make it the province of the many. Cultural history is thus the extension of the boundaries of the sacred to the human: that is, extending the partnership between God and man, stretching the boundaries of man's autonomy and freedom of choice with regard to the limits of her or his existence.

The Rabbis broke down the boundaries of exclusive authority over knowledge, replacing hereditary priestly hegemony based on divine chosenness, with a democratic system that ascribed no importance to lineage, status, or divine appointment. People from all walks of life—by virtue of their freedom, wisdom, experience and knowledge (as opposed to lineage and birth)—were thus able to take part in the creation of the Oral Law, a product of the human mind, rather than divine revelation ("the crown of Torah is open to all"; "henceforth, incline thine ear, and hear the words of the Sages"; "incline after a majority"; "it is a custom of our fathers in our hands"; "there are seventy facets to the Torah"). The Rabbis limited the scope of their revolution however, extending it to men only.

This decisive step, that broadened the sources of authority and demanded wider participation in scholarship, leadership, and the right to interpret and pass judgment, occurred among men known in Antiquity as Fathers, Pharisees, Sages and Rabbis. These groups, replaced divinely ordained, exclusive, priestly hegemony based on the Written Law—with inclusive human law rooted in oral tradition and the Oral Law, added to the written law. The Sages however, like their predecessors the priests, did not allow women to take part in the revolutionary changes they had wrought.

The men extended the bounds of culture and freedom, access to the public voice, public leadership, knowledge, study, law and ritual, to include all male members of the community. Women on the other hand, continued to represent nature that must be tamed, separated, enclosed within the precincts of home and family; within the limits of guarded nakedness, modesty and the sacredness of marriage; within the boundaries of fertility, ownership, sexual objectification, child-rearing and marital servitude. Unlike men, for whom the limitations upon participation and freedom of interpretation had been expanded, women remained bound by the plain meaning of the law, maintaining their inferior position as obedient listeners denied the right to argue or interpret, subject to patriarchal hegemony. This hegemony determined that "a woman's voice is nakedness", forbidding them to use their voices in public, and claimed that "women are light-minded", i.e. their judgment is not worthy of consideration in the sphere of public leadership, knowledge, law, justice and authority—which remained the exclusive province of men. The Sages continued to assert that "a woman is a vessel", that "a woman's only purpose is to beget sons", and "a man may do whatever he pleases with his wife" (*Nedarim* 20a). Male hegemony perpetuated this physical subjugation by means of marriage at a very young age, frequent births, strict laws of modesty, and exclusion from study and the acquisition of knowledge—in the spirit of the maxim "If one teaches his daughter Torah, it is as if he has taught her foolishness" (*Mishnah, Sotah* 3,4).

Women's lives continue to be governed by the old order: a sacred text upon which their perspective has no bearing; a sacred author whose words are addressed to men only; a duty to listen and to obey; a judicial authority to which they must submit without the freedom of interpretation or change. They are excluded from spiritual life because they are denied autonomy over their own bodies, as well as the possibility of acquiring knowledge or sharing in the sovereignty enjoyed by members of the Jewish community. They are deprived of the joy of study and the freedom of interpretation; barred from public discourse, written memory, law-making and the administration of justice. All of these things were afforded to men only. Moreover, the Sages would appear to have denied women opportunities they had previously enjoyed. In their world, there were no women prophets, poets, judges or leaders— something that is taken for granted in the Bible. On the contrary, women like Deborah, Miriam, Huldah and Abigail who had enjoyed respect and admiration in biblical times, are denigrated in the Talmud (see e.g. *Megilah* 14b). The Sages constantly disparaged women, condemned them to lives governed wholly by biology, and daily recited the blessing "Blessed art thou who hast not made me a woman".

In the 20th century, women in various parts of the world began to reject patriarchal hegemony—including the duty to silently obey a law that required their confinement to the realm of home and family, ownership and fertility, and excluded them from the public sphere and loci of authority and knowledge. They were no longer prepared to allow men to control their sexuality; to treat it as a commodity bought and sold by men ("bride-price of virgins"; "A woman is acquired in three ways"; *tashmish*—sexual "use"). They began to protest against the exclusion of women from circles of study, teaching and authority, public life and leadership. They rejected the authority of legal texts, written, transmitted and interpreted without the participation of women. (Note the connection between the word "authority" and the word "author", and in Hebrew, between words deriving from the concept *samkhut*—authority:—as well as *mismakh*—document: and *bar-samkha*—authorized-applied only to men from talmudic times until quite recently, reflecting their exclusive control over authority and knowledge. To this day, Orthodox discourse possesses no feminine forms of the terms: *rav*—rabbi, *dayan*—rabbinical judge, *talmid hakham*—Torah sage, *posek*—halakhic authority, *sofer*—scribe, *ilui*—Torah prodigy, *parnas*—community leader, or *sheliah tzibur*—prayer leader). They also rebelled against their status as "still life"—i.e. without voice; demanding a place in the cultural arena, in which to make themselves heard and express their point of view, to reexamine the laws that govern their lives, to play an active role in the institutions that provide leadership and administer justice, and to recount their historical narrative. From the moment they understood the relationship between control of their sexuality and control of their destiny; between subjugation of the body and subjugation of the spirit; women began to change the boundaries of the socially acceptable taken for granted in patriarchal society. This new approach, which seeks to add "her-story" to "his-story", until recently the only vantage point on the history of human culture, has found diverse expression, both spoken and written—manifest in the growing body of women's literature on the Bible, cultural criticism, history of the law, participation in social life and reinterpretation of tradition. The social, cultural, historical and legal status of women is thus no longer seen from an exclusively male perspective, but in a more complex fashion, drawing upon the perspectives of both sexes with regard to the range of human issues evoked by control over body and soul. This change, that denies any one group a monopoly over truth, demands a new hermeneutical sensitivity, mindful of the perspectives of those whose voice had not been heard until recently.

In this context, I have chosen to highlight a poetic interpretation of one of the laws in *Ki Teze*, that immortalizes the silence of the raped, in the voice of the absent "hoverer". The poem draws attention to the various perspectives: that of the silent attacker, of the victim who cries out but whose cry goes unheard, and of society that keeps silent, preferring neither to see nor hear.

Dalia Rabikovitz gives poetic expression to the verses that relate to the fate of a woman raped in the field and, as in all great poetry, examines the subject from an unexpected angle: from the perspective of society that is a silent witness to rape, seeing but not seeing, hovering but never touching. She attests, through the speaker in the poem, to the inherent horror in the relationship between helpless innocence and malicious evil; between trusting, childish weakness—embodied in the little shepherd girl in the mountains—and plotting, violent, silent, adult power—embodied in the man who comes up the mountain. The poem's originality lies in the fresh perspective it offers on society's inability to contend with a hard hand used against a helpless girl. The silence of the rapist and society stand in sharp contrast to the silent cry of the girl whom no one hears.

Hovering At a Low Altitude

I am not here
I am in the clefts of eastern mountains
Dotted with ice
In a place where grass does not grow and shadows lie scattered on the hillside
A small shepherd girl with a flock of goats
black
She suddenly appeared
From an invisible tent

She will not live to see the end of the day, that girl
And she arose so early that little one
To pasture...
Her neck is not stretched forth
Her eyes are not enlarged with paint, nor are they wanton
She does not ask, from whence shall my help come

I am not here
I have been in the mountains for many days
The light will not scorch me, the cold will not bite
I should not be shocked
I have seen worse in my life.

I gather up my dress and hover
Very close to the ground.
What was she thinking that girl?
Wild-looking, unwashed
Bending for a moment on her knees
Her cheek as soft as silk
Frostbite on the back of her hand,
Seemingly distracted
But in fact quite alert
And she has only a few hours left.

I was not thinking about such things.
My thoughts swaddled me in down.
I have found a very simple method.
Neither tread nor flight
Hovering
At a low altitude.
But as the afternoon waned
Many hours
After sunrise
That man came up the mountain
As if climbing his own business.
And the girl was very close to him

And there was no one there but them.
And if she tried to hide or cry out
There is nowhere to hide in the mountains.

I am not here
I am atop the wild and terrible mountains
On the outskirts of the east.

A trivial matter. No need to elaborate
It is possible, if you leap and hover
To circle at wind speed.
I can take flight and say to myself:
I haven't seen a thing.
And the little one's eyes just bulged in their sockets
Her mouth dry as baked clay,
When a hard hand grabbed her hair and held her
Without a shred of pity.

(Dalia Rabikovitz, *Kol Hashirim Ad Koh*, p. 219–221)

"I have seen nothing", says the voice in the poem, representing the blind eye society turns to the outrages perpetrated by enslaving men against enslaved women, by sacrificing men against sacrificed women, by powerful men against helpless women, by rapists against the women they rape, by murderers against the women they kill. The constant succession of power, physical strength, force, injustice, harm, pain, rape and death that society silently ignores, is directly related to the cry that goes from the one end of the earth even unto the other end of the earth. "The voice of thy brother's blood crieth unto me from the ground", in the poem becomes the voice of thy sister's blood—raped in the field with no one to hear her cry.

The description of rape and murder in the field, implicit and reserved, is heightened by the fact that it is a mirror image of the descriptions of love in the *Song of Songs*. There too we find a shepherd girl, a flock of goats, and flowing hair tied with love imagery, mountains in which the sun shines, mountains of myrrh and frankincense. The lovers in the *Song of Songs* however, are unconcerned with the law and unhindered by its bonds. They seek out and desire one another, as their love flows from the wellsprings of their hearts. They utter words of love and devotion, poetry and passion for a lover's ear, on equal footing, without controller and controlled, compeller and compelled, rapist and raped. In contrast to the curse in Genesis: "and thy desire shall be to thy husband, and he shall rule over thee"—at the heart of the patriarchal order; *Song of Songs* presents a different order, one of love, choice and freedom, of "I am my beloved's, and his desire is toward me" (7:11). In Dalia Rabikovitz' poem on the other hand, the protagonists do not speak, but merely voice the silent cry of those who have no common language or culture; only the alienation of extreme violence, of "and he shall rule over thee"—over your spirit, your body, your childhood and your youth, your life and your death.

The dramatic resonance of Rabikovitz' description is further heightened by its inverse relationship to the language of the prophets. In contrast to the sinful daughters of Zion, described in Isaiah as walking "with stretched-forth necks and wanton eyes" (*Is.* 3:16), Rabikovitz writes of the little girl in the field who is wholly innocent: "her eyes are not enlarged with paint, nor are they wanton". She also echoes—in reverse—Jeremiah's description of the forsaken daughter of Zion: "that thou enlargest thine eyes with paint? In vain dost thou make thyself fair; thy lovers despise thee, they seek thy life" (*Jer.* 4:30). The gulf between the shepherd girl's unconscious innocence and the danger she faces in the mountains, the danger to her unprotected body and soul, is expressed in the phrase: "that little one ... she does not ask, from whence shall my help come". This stands in contrast to the psalm that promises divine providence and heavenly protection for the helpless: "I will lift up mine eyes unto the mountains: from whence shall my help come? My help cometh from the Lord ... The Lord shall keep thee from all evil; He shall keep thy soul" (*Ps.* 121:1–2;7).

The ancient traditions that tacitly accept the rape of unprotected women by violent men, offering legal and social sanction for the rape of captive women and unbetrothed girls, servants and concubines, "women of goodly form" and slaves, did not remain within the confines of the biblical world.

The Patriarchal order—that affords men various avenues for the satisfaction of their sexual desires by means of power, violence and money—has remained in force even where it would appear to have been superseded. It is applied to weak groups in society, whose consent is not required for such acts of oppression, and whose silencing is considered acceptable. Evidence of a system that implicitly and explicitly recognizes male control over the female body, can be found in many contemporary expressions, such as "sex slave", "gang rape", "domestic violence", "call girl", "brothel" and "bride-price"—still paid to fathers in return for their daughters' virginity, in parts of modern society. Even in the Modern Era, soldiers in various armies have been given license to rape enemy women in the early days of occupation, and rape—with and without license—has been perpetrated on a wide scale in the wars of the last decade, in Europe (Chechnya, Albania, Kosovo, Yugoslavia), Africa (Rwanda), and Asia. Beyond the terrible harm inflicted upon the women themselves, rape also gives rise to the chilling phenomenon of unwanted children.

In 2003, some 7,000 complaints of rape and other sexual offenses were filed in Israel (source: Israel Police), and in 2004, the hotlines of Israel's rape crisis centers received more than 21,000 calls (5,578 of which were from women reporting rape or sexual assault for the first time). These statistics demand a reevaluation of the significance of cultural continuity that enables such violence to persist in today's world, and raise questions regarding the effect of the past on the present.

Ancient laws that allowed men to possess women by force, also allowed them to silence women and exclude them, treating their bodies as the prerogative of male aggression, with no regard for the wishes of the women themselves. The roles that these laws have played in shaping legal and social constructs have been addressed at length in the field of social history. All of the above would appear to warrant the critical examination of society's formative sacred texts, from various perspectives, both female and male; as well as the analysis of their place in contemporary law and the reality that derives therefrom, in terms of the boundaries of the reasonable and the possible. Such critical examination could serve to clarify the extent to which the past exerts an influence on the present—leading to a better understanding of the basic patterns of consciousness and culture that demand reevaluation.

Christoph Schmidt

Ki Tavo—When Thou Art Come in unto the Land

*The Theopolitical Discourse of **Hermann Cohen***
In the Book, Religion of Reason: Out of the Sources of Judaism

---

A wandering Aramean was my father, and he went down into Egypt, and sojourned there, few in number; and he became there a nation, great, mighty, and populous (*Deuteronomy* 26:5).

Hermann Cohen is not a biblical commentator in the classical sense, and his approach to the Torah and Scripture is a product of the philosophical-ethical question of the status of the individual opposite the law. In his great work, *Religion of Reason: Out of the Sources of Judaism* (1919), Cohen seeks, on the one hand, to afford universal philosophical validity to the Torah and Halakhah, and on the other, to demonstrate that philosophy needs the Torah if it is to resolve the problem of the individual. When Cohen reads the Torah, he tries not only to illustrate this duality between theology and philosophy, but also proposes a critical political theology; a theology based on the problems of the Jewish individual in modern society, but one that also offers a response to the cultural perplexities of his day. For the most part, Cohen's answers are equally applicable today, in our post-modern age, which also turns to ethics and theology in search of a solution to the problem of the individual as Other. In this chapter, I will try to outline the basic elements of this unique political theology, through Cohen's commentary on the portion of *Ki Tavo*. Cohen does not relate to specific Torah portions, and *Ki Tavo* is no exception. His references appear within the broader context of his ethical-philosophical discussion, in relation to the problem of the individual versus the law. Let us therefore reconstruct his field of reference, that is the web of sources that he cites in relation to the verses of this portion, in order to place them within the framework of his theopolitical discourse. In the *Religion of Reason: Out of the Sources of Judaism*, Cohen focuses on three verses from *Ki Tavo*:

Cursed be he that perverteth the justice due to the stranger, fatherless, and widow (27:19).

When thou hast made an end of tithing all the tithe of thine increase in the third year, which is the year of tithing, and hast given it unto the Levite, to the stranger, to the fatherless, and to the widow, that they may eat within thy gates, and be satisfied, then thou shalt say before the Lord thy God: "I have put away the holyed things out of my house, and also have given them unto the Levite, and unto the stranger, to the fatherless, and to the widow, according to all Thy commandment which Thou hast commanded me; I have not transgressed any of Thy commandments, neither have I forgotten them" (26:12–13).

A wandering Aramean was my father, and he went down into Egypt, and sojourned there, few in number; and he became there a nation, great, mighty, and populous. And the Egyptians dealt ill with us, and afflicted us, and laid upon us hard bondage. And we cried unto the Lord, the God of our fathers, and the Lord heard our voice, and saw our affliction, and our toil, and our oppression. And the Lord brought us forth out of Egypt with a mighty hand, and with an outstretched arm, and with great terribleness, and with signs, and with wonders. And He hath brought us into this place, and hath given us this land, a land flowing with milk and honey (*ibid.* 5–9).

Cohen's remarks on these three verses seem rather straightforward. Their selection however, reflects the central ethical aspect of Cohen's reading: the relation of the judicial system, i.e. the law, to the individual; and the structure of memory, which is essential to bridging the gap between the poles of individual and law. Cohen uses these verses as examples of the way in which the Torah approaches this problem: the first verse in a discussion of the Torah's relation to the individual as Other, that is the nonnative, the noncitizen; and the second in a discussion of the Torah's relation to the individual, oppressed on a socio-economic plane. In other words, Cohen uses the first two verses as a basis for a discussion of the law's relation to individuals who do not "naturally" benefit from it. The third verse serves as (a further) example of the structure of memory, in its primary function as a bridge between extremes.

But why is the law's relation to the individual and the individual's relation to the law so important, and how does this problem lead the Kantian philosopher Hermann Cohen to the Torah? How can the Torah help to resolve this ethical-philosophical problem?

Cohen, as the founder of the Neo-Kantian school (late 19th—early 20th century), consummated his philosophical work in the book *Religion of Reason: Out of the Sources of Judaism*. Kant too brought his critical philosophy to a close with a philosophical interpretation of religion (Christianity)—*Religion Within the Limits of Reason Alone* (1793)—in which he bases religion upon the ethics of autonomous subject, i.e. the law of self-determination (the categorical imperative). It was to be expected that Cohen would seek to reduce the Jewish religion to autonomous ethics, or what Kant termed "practical reason". Indeed Cohen followed in Kant's footsteps when he identified Judaism with autonomous ethics—something every Jewish theologian from Saul Ascher (*Leviathan*, 1790) to Moritz Lazarus (*The Ethic of Judaism*, 1898–1911) has done. Cohen however, discovered a fundamental problem with this law of autonomy and freedom; one that engaged many philosophers of his time (such as Georg Simmel, Max Scheler, György Lukács, Martin Heidegger): "The case that comes under a law is not the individual", writes Cohen, raising the question: Does the law of autonomy—which is the underlying law of culture—truly serve the needs of the individual whose freedom it establishes? Cohen interprets this relation as an act of self liquidation, since all that is specifically individual is submitted to the law. But against the existential case of individuality versus the law he stresses first of all the basic socio-political tension that stems from the attempt to apply universal law within a concrete and particular nation state. The law of freedom is universally valid—"everywhere and at all times", as Kant asserted, but in real political and social conditions however, the individual and entire groups may find themselves beyond the jurisdiction of the law, as people who are not perceived as citizens of the state or as citizens whose socio-economic circumstances exclude them, *de facto*, from the community of citizens. In pointing out these two problems, Cohen does not question the validity of ethical law, but seeks to expose the dialectic that accompanies it in the socio-political context. Here Cohen reiterates Karl Marx' criticism of bourgeois society, which raises the banner of universal freedom, in order to safeguard its own specific economic interests. He does so however, not from Marx' materialistic perspective, but from an idealistic-Kantian perspective, which he seeks to expand—through Jewish theology.

This gap between the individual and the law is typical not only of the dialectic of enlightened culture, i.e. the tension between utopia and reality, but is also a distinctive feature of the Jewish political experience within this same bourgeois modern-secular culture. Jews achieved equal rights through the Jewish emancipation movement—they became full subjects of the law. The price they paid for this juridical emancipation however, was emancipation from their own Judaism. The Jewish experience can serve thus as an example of the socio-political tension that inevitably accompanies attempts to apply the law, but also of the fundamental, "philosophical" problem—of the law as representing the individual (the human and Jewish experience of alienation of the individual from the law finds its most impressive literary expression in Kafka's parable *Before the Law*).

As already mentioned the structural-philosophical dimension of the individual's relation to the law also has a clearly existential aspect, when the individual consistently feels that the general law does not reflect the full range of possibilities presented in his own life and experience. The "infinite" meaning of individuality cannot be subsumed to the "totality" of the law. Man needs the law of freedom to ensure his existence in the social sphere. But exercising this freedom heightens the question of the very "meaning of existence" and the meaning of "all this"—a question traditionally answered by religion. In the Modern Era however, religion itself has become a system based entirely on the same autonomous law, and as such, can no longer provide an answer.

These problems, which pertain in fact to the legitimacy of modern secular culture, led Cohen to attempt to reestablish the Jewish religion, as a bridge between the problem of individuality on the existential level and the status of individuality on the socio-political level. When Cohen explores the realm of ethics through the *Sources of Judaism*, he insists on maintaining a modern, philosophical (Kantian) cultural framework, unlike many thinkers of his day—on the right and the left—who concluded, from the tension between the law and the individual, that the social structure of bourgeois society must be dismantled. Moreover, he always places the socio-political problem before the existential problem, contrary to the existentialists themselves, who, for the most part, ignore the socio-political problem. According to Cohen, there is a big difference between an individual who already enjoys the benefits of law and freedom and raises the question of "the meaning of life" or "the meaning of being" (as Heidegger called it), and an individual who, as a noncitizen, foreigner and other, is outside the sphere of influence of the law. Although Cohen can be considered one of the first existential philosophers, he insists on the priority of the socio-political question, which is indeed the main focus of his concern. Cohen rejected the fashionable discourse of his time, which saw the alienation of the self from the law as a "tragedy of culture", and even a sign of the "decline of culture", which must be overcome by anti-cultural strategies designed to promote a return to more authoritarian political structures (the remainder of the chapter will deal exclusively with the socio-political aspect of the problem).

Cohen's recourse to Jewish theology stemmed primarily from his understanding of the socio-political significance of the problem of individuality. His reading of Jewish sources is thus geared toward the establishment of a critical-political theology—not only to resolve the "dialectic of enlightenment" and culture, but also the unique status of the Jew in modern culture, as the embodiment of a society that lies beyond political and national sovereignty. It is here that the Torah plays its decisive role in the framework of Cohen's thought because the Torah addresses the socio-political problem schematically, in the figures of the stranger, the widow and the orphan. Cohen's political theology focuses on these representatives of "Otherness", in an attempt to develop theology as a necessary complement to autonomous ethics.

The stranger, the orphan and the widow, which always appear in the Torah together, not only represent the problem of individuality, which the law tends to ignore, but draw a distinction between two different types of individuality. The stranger represents the man who does not "belong", who is not native-born and as such is beyond the law. The orphan and the widow represent the problem of poverty, the socio-economic state that prevents one from enjoying the benefits of the law. Cohen's principal objective is to emphasize the importance of Torah, in general, and prophetic instruction, in particular, as a platform for the resolution of a substantive problem that besets human society, at large, and modern society, especially: the relationship of the law to the individual.

We now turn to the first type: the stranger, discussed by Cohen in reference to the verse "Cursed be he that perverteth the justice due to the stranger, fatherless, and widow" (27:19). In theory, the Torah establishes the contrast between Jew and non-Jew (stranger) in such a fashion that the Jew is first a human being and only then a descendant of Abraham, thereby assuring the discussion's universal context. The Torah however, does not leave the discussion at this general level, but rather directs all attention to a historical-political situation in which universalism is no longer assured. Indeed, in the context of the Jewish state, the contrast between those who "belong" and those who "do not belong" returns with a vengeance. The stranger is considered an idolater in the Torah and as such, a real enemy, so that the political contrast that gives rise to the tension between Jew and non-Jew reawakens as the ultimate tension: between friend and foe Israel's relation to the stranger is thus, in Cohen's opinion, one of a "state of emergency", created as a result of the monotheistic mission to all humanism. The problem of the Other's individuality thus appears, in its sharpest form here. The Torah does not make do with general universalism or a theoretical view of the problem of politics, but departs from the extreme case in which the stranger is an "enemy of God". This extreme situation, writes Cohen, questions the brotherhood of man, as formulated in the commandment "love thy fellow". Cohen evokes Rabbi Akiva's "great principle" in defense of Judaism against Christian claims that the principle of "love thy fellow" is limited in the Torah to love of one's national fellow, and that only Christianity extended this principle beyond the boundaries of national community.

When Cohen cites the verse "Thou shalt not abhor an Edomite, for he is thy brother; thou shalt not abhor an Egyptian, because thou wast a stranger in his land" (23:8), he not only seeks to demonstrate the special relation to the stranger and the foreigner, and even to the enemy but, as noted above, challenges Christian polemics against Judaism as a national religion. The gap between citizen and noncitizen is bridgeable—Cohen returns time and again to this biblical strategy—through memory. Memory is not meant specifically to recall the Jewish People's own suffering as strangers in Egypt, but to prepare the ground for practical and legal conclusions regarding the status of strangers and the real treatment they receive. The granting of equal rights is a function of the historical comparison between the status of the Jew now and then, and the knowledge that history can turn the tables, that those who belong and those who do not may once exchange places.

The Torah therefore establishes "One law shall be to him that is home-born, and unto the stranger that sojourneth among you" (*Ex.* 12:49), and constantly reminds us of the danger that the weak, the minority, will be marginalized by the laws of the community ("And a stranger shalt thou not wrong, neither shalt thou oppress him; for ye were strangers in the land of Egypt"—*ibid.* 22:20). Only Jewish theology offers a solution to the problem of the individual, inasmuch as it is God who ensures the just existence of the whole, i.e. of the entire community. This is the significance of the special status of the stranger in the Torah, which is a function of the fact that the "God of gods, and Lord of lords, the great God, the mighty, and the awful ... loveth the stranger, in giving him food and raiment" (*Deut.* 10:17–18).

Clearly, the challenge of monotheism—the other as an idolater and an enemy—is not resolved in a satisfactory manner, when the Other is only granted legal status if he accepts the Noahide Laws—that is, if he is willing to renounce his "idolatry" and his "Otherness". Cohen manages however, in this discussion, not only to highlight the Torah's dialectic awareness in terms of relations between the universal and the particular, but also to repulse the traditional Christian argument regarding the principle of "love thy fellow" in the Torah as restricted to the national fellow. Furthermore, Cohen is not satisfied merely to demonstrate the stranger's legal status as an equal citizen, because he is extremely aware of the fact that legal status and socioeconomic reality are not symmetrical where "minorities" are concerned. He insists that this juridical equality must also apply to the equitable distribution of land, between the native-born and the stranger (citing *Ezekiel* 47:21–22).

Above all, Cohen seeks to establish the connection between the biblical and universal principle of "love thy fellow" and European natural law, which, from the days of John Selden and Johann David Michaelis, has been firmly rooted in the biblical approach. The idea of Jewish theocracy is thus defended against claims (following Spinoza) that it is a particular political legal framework that runs counter to universal European legal culture. Moreover, with its unique awareness of the universal point of departure and the dialectic of the law and the individual, this theology becomes a paradigm for modern culture, which—although it espouses universality—in fact tends to ignore the problem of the individual, the stranger and Other, within the framework of enlightened order. Modern culture, which rests upon the law of autonomy, can only fulfill itself—maintains Cohen—when its "truth" is not based "on the identity and union of religion and state", but on the union of "state and law". In choosing the term "theocracy", Cohen connects to the modern German tradition, which sees in the kingdom of liberty and freedom, the realization of the Kingdom of Heaven, within the framework of human history and politics. This is the tradition of German enlightenment—from Lessing, Hölderlin and Hegel to Heine, Moses Hess and Ernst Bloch—that aspired to political utopia, based on Christian, messianic (Christological) theology. Here especially Cohen and Lessing have a number of things in common: both adopt this theopolitical program, both are very aware of the potential contradictions in attempting to translate and transfer the "theological" to the "political", and both are extremely conscious of the importance of the socio-politically extraneous, to the establishment of this ideal messianic order within the framework of European culture. Contrary to Lessing however, Cohen derives his theocratic principles from the *Sources of Judaism*.

It is only in light of the Torah's legislation regarding the foreigner and the stranger, to which Cohen ascribes so much importance in his conception of theocracy, that we can understand why he also included the curse from the portion of *Ki Tavo* (27:18). In incorporating this passage in his complex array of citations from "the sources", Cohen in effect stresses the fact that the legitimacy of the entire legal system is measured by its relation to the marginalized. Where the Other is not afforded equal and dignified treatment, the entire system fails, and with it, certainly, its claim to "theocracy". Here, the curse from *Ki Tavo* becomes the curse of modern enlightened culture, in perpetual danger of distorting its universal utopia in favor of the constraints of power and control, and of turning it into an ideology of the powerful. The curse is thus a warning against the "dialectic of enlightenment" that Cohen seeks to remedy by means of the "Jewish sources", i.e. in the context of Jewish political theology based on the Torah and its prophetic interpretation.

The stranger represents the problem of the non-Jew and the noncitizen, while the orphan and the widow, as noted, represent the socioeconomically marginalized within the legal system. Cohen views poverty as the greatest threat to the existence of human society. Poverty, writes Cohen, is "culture's ultimate crisis", since it radically undermines all morality. Contrary to the aesthetic approach to suffering—which seeks solutions to the "tragedy of culture", only "with sublime feelings of compassion that are in fact illusions", this crisis requires a kind of compassion that translates into practical action. Cohen's juxtaposition of the aesthetic approach and the practical, theology-based approach is by no means a coincidence. This juxtaposition is meant to remind the reader that modernity, in aspiring to emancipation from all heteronomous authority (God, king and nature), gradually reduced the principle of religious love. From love of one's fellow *per se*, society passed to love of one's fellow as a means to self-love, incorporating the Other only to the extent that she or he suits the needs and interests of the self, on a sensual, erotic, economic and social level. Nietzsche saw the spectator's aesthetic thrill in the face of tragedy merely as a moment of self-overcoming.

Cohen cautions against an aesthetic approach to suffering in general and to the "tragedy of culture"—which creates the suffering of the poor and the alienated—in particular. He insists upon a practical compassionate approach to the suffering, the paradigm for which he finds in the unique social laws of the Torah. Cohen cites the verse "When thou comest into thy neighbor's vineyard, then thou mayest eat grapes until thou have enough at thine own pleasure; but thou shalt not put any in thy vessel" (23:25), as an example of a more equitable system of social distribution. The tithing confession also falls into this category: "When thou hast made an end of tithing all the tithe of thine increase in the third year, which is the year of tithing, and hast given it unto the Levite, to the stranger, to the fatherless, and to the widow, that they may eat within thy gates, and be satisfied, then thou shalt say before the Lord thy God: 'I have put away the holy things (*hakodesh*) out of my house, and also have given them unto the Levite, and unto the stranger, to the fatherless, and to the widow, according to all Thy commandment which Thou hast commanded me; I have not transgressed any of Thy commandments, neither have I forgotten them'" (26:12–13). Here Cohen stresses the significance of the word "holy" ("I have put away the holy things"), which he identifies with social assistance. He also identifies the sacred in Kantian tradition with autonomous morality, from which we conclude that the freedom of one who recognizes the freedom of all of society's subjects, compels her/him to extend assistance to those who, for economic reasons, are unable to fully realize their own. Holiness, according to Cohen, signifies that man, as an autonomous subject, needs the help and support of many in order to attain freedom, and that the giving of such assistance is both an admission that the giver too relies upon the help of others, and a expression of gratitude for it. Holiness, in Cohen's philosophy, denotes not only the utmost state of autonomous morality with regard to the individual, but also the precondition for the very possibility of autonomy. It indicates that establishing subjectivity—autonomy—is secondary to subjectivity's dependence upon the treatment of others. The declaration before one's creator of having "put away the holy things", is an act of recognition of the precedence of the Other—God, one's fellow—to one's own independence and autonomy. Cohen therefore links this "holiness" (*kedushah*) to the verse "Ye shall be holy (*kedoshim*); for I the Lord your God am holy". Just as God establishes the relation to the Other, so man must realize the unique relation of holiness within the community.

"Holiness is morality, and is distinct not only from knowledge of nature but from all natural force and power", adds Cohen. Holiness thus has clearly political significance, as the moral realm beyond necessary concern for economic and political independence, i.e. natural survival, which is also the mark of politics, power and sovereignty. In this sense, holiness also characterizes the unique status of the Jewish People in the Diaspora.

Our brief review of the principles of Cohen's commentary on the Torah would be incomplete without considering his approach to this singular problem. When the Torah addresses the problem of ethics from the perspective of the law's relation to the individual, it represents, in effect, the political constitution of the Jewish People, with its unique approach to the stranger, the poor and so forth. Exile inverts the relation of the law to the individual and the relation of the state to the outsider, because the Jewish polity loses its status as a sovereign nation. Cohen perceives this loss as a kind of "Copernican turn", from an ethical-theological perspective: "Peoples thus have their gods and their states. Israel's isolation must necessarily lead to the loss of statehood. With this loss, begins its social distress, which is the social equivalent of poverty" (Cohen, 143). The loss of political sovereignty makes the Jewish nation itself a paradigm for poverty, claims Cohen—that is, the model of the nonbelonging, the outcast in search of shelter. As such, the Jew becomes a symbol of the demand for implementation of the universal program, at the level of each and every individual. While the Egyptian and Babylonian exiles were a matter of historical-political fate, the exile that followed the destruction of the Second Temple bears special religious-ethical significance. The Jewish People must assume the task of representing monotheistic theology, in its true theopolitical sense, among the nations—that is, to serve as a symbol of exile, as a "not-yet-completed" political-cultural state. The exile of the Jewish People draws attention to the exile of culture, as a "not-yet completed project". By virtue of its status, the Jewish People tends toward a critical view of any situation in which the aspiration to universalism yields to the dictates of power and control. As a people without sovereignty, the Jewish People is particularly sensitive to all the flaws and faults of society—because these flaws affect its own fragile status within society, but also because of its universalist rejection of all idolatry, which is in essence the reduction of the universal to the particular. The role of the Jewish People is to shatter the myths and mythologies that beget social injustice. Neither the nations nor modern culture welcome this mission. On the contrary, it further alienates the Jew, heightening his Otherness. Cohen's eschatology, in effect, entails the martyrization of the Jew and the Jewish People. According to Cohen, the Jewish People is the "servant of God, who bears all the sins of the world, for the sake of its redemption". In this, Cohen clearly sought to present a modern Jewish interpretation of the prophecy of Isaiah, cited by Christian exegetes as one of the sources of their Christology.

The shift in theopolitical perspective that Cohen affects here is a product of his ethical approach, which relegates the Jewish People to existence without political sovereignty; the existence of the stranger, the poor and the orphan in modern society. Although it might seem very harsh after the Holocaust and the establishment of the sovereign Jewish state, Cohen truly believed this to be the theopolitical role of the Jewish People in exile, thereby offering an original interpretation of the importance of memory in the Torah.

Memory is supposed to remind Jews of the time when they were strangers in Egypt, dependent upon the good will of a host country—in order to elicit in them, a positive attitude to the stranger in their midst. This is the traditional function of memory in the Torah; not, as Cohen constantly stresses, to recall our own suffering, unless this furthers the practical goal of providing help and support to the stranger. The memory of the period in which Israel was enslaved reflects—in the very passage from slavery to citizenship—the structure of history, as the stage on which kingdoms and states rise and fall, on which there is never true equality between people and mankind is always divided into rulers and slaves. Cohen believed that modern culture—based on the law of freedom and universal equality in the spirit of Kant and the French Revolution—indeed stands in the way of the great utopian vision of unity and cooperation, as suggested by the foundation of the League of Nations in the aftermath of the First World War. He believed that cyclical history—the history of the constant rise and fall of power—was about to end, and that a messianic prospect had opened up, in which freedom would truly be established on a universal basis. In this historical situation, the Jews were meant to consciously choose the role of stranger in the midst of their respective nations, that is, to insist on their status as a people without sovereignty, in order to hasten the messianic age—the era of ideal European society that would follow the renunciation of power and control. Although Cohen merely hinted at this, he saw in the political circumstances of his time, a truly messianic opportunity to realize theocracy in the form of a free socialist society. Historical memory, which preserves the fact of Jewish slavery in Egypt—translated in the Torah into a legal system that respects the stranger, the orphan and the widow as full juridical subjects—imposes a duty upon Jews at this crucial moment in time. It compels them to remain outside of the system of power and control, and to refuse the temptations of the assimilationist bourgeoisie and the national political idea of Zionism, in order to fulfill the purpose of history as theocracy.

Not only were Cohen's messianic hopes proven false, but Europe itself became the arena of unprecedented violence and murder. Nevertheless, Cohen's focus on the problem of the stranger and the weak has not lost its importance. In the age of globalization, which has a messianic dimension of its own, culture faces the very same problems that Cohen viewed as the point of departure for all political theology. And even within the national-Zionist context, these problems have become fundamental issues that, if not resolved, will also preclude the resolution of the question of legitimacy.

Chaniel Farber

Nitzavim—Ye Are Standing this Day

*Redemption and the Ingathering of the Exiles
in the Writings of the **Hafetz Hayim***

> And shalt return unto the Lord thy God, and hearken to His voice
> according to all that I command thee this day, thou and thy chil-
> dren, with all thy heart, and with all thy soul; that then the Lord
> thy God will turn thy captivity, and have compassion upon thee,
> and will return and gather thee from all the peoples, whither the
> Lord thy God hath scattered thee (*Deuteronomy* 30:2–3).

Nitzavim—only 40 verses long—is one of the shortest portions
in the Torah. It has no positive or negative precepts. It consists entirely of the words of exhortation and encouragement
that Moses spoke to the Children of Israel on the day of his death, lest
they stray from the path of God's Law and commandments. *Nitzavim*
is usually read on the Sabbath preceding Rosh Hashanah and, in most
cases, together with the portion of *Vayelekh*. Only when the first day of
Rosh Hashanah falls on a Monday or a Tuesday, are the two portions
read separately—*Nitzavim* before the holiday and *Vayelekh* on the Sabbath between Rosh Hashanah and Yom Kippur. Rabbi Jacob ben Asher,
author of the *Arba'ah Turim*, offers the following mnemonic (*Orah
Hayim* 429): *Ba-G Hamelekh Pat Vayelekh*—that is to say, when Rosh
Hashanah (*Hamelekh*—[day of] the king) falls on Monday or Tuesday
(*Ba"g -bet/gimmel*—Monday or Tuesday) "בג המלך" "פת וילך", the portions are broken like bread (*pat*), and *Vayelekh* is not attached to *Nitzavim*.

Nitzavim comprises three main parts: (1) Moses' leave-taking: final
words of caution, as his role comes to an end, just before his death. He
cautions the Israelites against violating the covenant with God and failing to observe his Law, and the terrible consequences such behavior
would entail (29:9–8); (2) Moses' final words of comfort: if the Israelites repent, God will have mercy on them, and the dispersed of Israel

626

will return to their place (30:1–14); (3) The possibility of choice: Moses explains to the People, the significance of the choice between life and good and death and evil, concluding "therefore choose life, that thou mayest live, thou and thy seed" (*ibid.* 15–20).

The portion begins with the assembly that Moses convoked before God, prior to his death, in order to bring them into God's covenant:

> Ye are standing this day all of you before the Lord your God: your heads, your tribes, your elders, and your officers, even all the men of Israel, your little ones, your wives, and thy stranger that is in the midst of thy camp, from the hewer of thy wood unto the drawer of thy water; that thou shouldest enter into the covenant of the Lord thy God--and into His oath--which the Lord thy God maketh with thee this day; that He may establish thee this day unto Himself for a people, and that He may be unto thee a God, as He spoke unto thee, and as He swore unto thy fathers, to Abraham, to Isaac, and to Jacob (29:9–12).

Who stood there? All types of people, from all walks of life, as a single unit before God, without discrimination and without internal division; complete, compact unity. The expression "standing" reflects stability and strength, as in the expression "my sheaf arose, and also stood upright" (Gen. 37:7), used by Joseph when recounting his dream to his brothers, presaging his future leadership. Three generations stand here together: the elders—adults at the time of the Exodus; their children—now adults—who left Egypt as children; and the "little ones"—the new generation, born in the desert.

The younger generation can transmit the message to future generations. Not only transmit, but even compel the people to uphold the covenant with God. To the elders he says: "for ye know how we dwelt in the land of Egypt" (29:15); to their children: "and how we came through the midst of the nations through which ye passed" (*ibid.*). In the land of Sihon, Moab and Midian, the Children of Israel saw and went after their idols and "detestable things". That is why they are called upon to renew the covenant and abjure these sins.

The reproaches of Israel's Sages and spiritual leaders over the generations have been severe, directed both at that part of the People that is filled with knowledge and understanding and at that part that strays from the true path, casting off wisdom and the precepts. This is the role of spiritual leaders, to reprove, preach and explain, to all Jews, the value of the precepts and their ancient heritage. Such was the approach of Rabbi Israel Meir Hakohen of Radun, better known as the "*Hafetz Hayim*", in ethical matters: to direct every Jew to the path of complete Judaism, including all parts of the Torah, and to help each person achieve all-encompassing personal spiritual growth (Rabbi Dov Katz, *Tenuat Hamusar*, Introduction).

The *Midrash Tanhuma* (ed. Buber; *Nitzavim* 2,48) offers the following explanation of why the portion of *Nitzavim* immediately follows the passage of the curses in the portion of *Ki Tavo*: "For the Israelites had heard one hundred curses minus (one or) two, spoken in this portion, in addition to the forty-nine in the book of Leviticus. They grew pale and said, who can withstand all of these things? Moses immediately convoked them and reassured them ... but when they suffer afflictions, the Jews succumb and pray, as it is written 'I will lift up the cup of salvation, [and call upon the name of the Lord]'."

The leader's reproaches were meant to reassure the People that even if they should experience a spiritual decline and fail to heed the voice of God and be punished for it—their afflictions will not last forever, for in the end they will repent: "and then the Lord thy God will *return* thy captivity, and have compassion upon thee, and will *return* and gather thee from all the peoples, whither the Lord thy God hath scattered thee" (30:3).

This verse of comfort, and particularly its repetition of the word "return" (*veshav*), attracted the attention of the biblical commentators. So Rashi (1040–1105), the great expositor of the Bible and the Babylonian Talmud, who lived in Europe at the time of the First Crusade, writes as follows:

> And then the Lord thy God will return thy captivity—It should have said *veheshiv* (the transitive form—as opposed to the intransitive *veshav*). Our Rabbis learned from this (*Megilah* 29a) that the *Shekhinah* dwells, as it were, with Israel in the adversity of exile. And when they are redeemed, *He dictated His own redemption*, that He will return with them. *Furthermore, the day*

of the ingathering of the exiles is a great and difficult task, as if He himself must take each and every one of them by the hand. As it is written, "and ye shall be gathered one by one, O ye children of Israel" (*Is.* 27:12). *And so we find regarding the exiles of other nations as well*: "Yet will I return (*veshavti*) the captivity of Moab" (*Jer.* 48:47).

Rashi's commentary, as noted, is based on the Talmud in the tractate of *Megilah* (29a):

We have learned, Rabbi Shimon bar Yohai said: Come and see how dear Israel are to God—wherever they have gone into exile—the *Shekhinah* [has gone] with them, as it is written "And then the Lord thy God will return thy captivity". It does not say *veheshiv* (tr.) but *veshav* (intr.), to show that God returns with them from their places of exile.

To take Rashi's interpretation a little further, the words *et shevutkha* ("thy captivity") can mean *im shevutkha* ("with thy captivity"); "He dictated his own redemption"—that God told Moses to write in the Torah, "the Lord will return (*veshav*)", that is to say that He would be "redeemed" with them; and that it is not only the ingathering of Israel's exiles that is difficult, but the gathering of any scattered people.

"Furthermore, the day of the ingathering of the exiles is a great and difficult task". Rashi here offers a second explanation of the word *veshav*, which appears twice in the verse, and of the entire phrase "and will return and gather thee" (had they been gathered before?!).

Rashi refers to the difficulty of the process of the ingathering of the exiles, which will occur bit by bit—as stated in the Jerusalem Talmud (Ms. Leiden, *Berakhot* 4a): "The redemption of Israel is thus, little by little at first". Redemption will be effected on an individual basis, person by person, exile by exile, directly by God (as in the exodus from Egypt—not through a messenger or intermediary).

"And so we find regarding the exiles of other nations as well". According to Rashi's second explanation, *veshav* does not mean that God himself will return with the Jewish People, but is a transitive form of *shav*, denoting repetition. In other words, the return will occur in stages—as implied later in the verse by the phrase "and will return and gather thee" (30:3). This interpretation is further supported by the fact that this form of *shav* is used with regard to other nations as well, of whom one could not say that God "returns" with them.

The 14th century Spanish philosopher and halakhist Rabbi Nissim ben Reuben Gerondi (RaN), also remarks on the repetition of the word *veshav* (return) in the verse "And then the Lord thy God will return thy captivity ... and will return and gather thee" (*Derashot HaRaN* p. 177). The RaN explains that God will first make his people "find favor in the eyes of the peoples among whom they are captive, that they might ease the yoke of exile", and only then will complete redemption come about.

Nahmanides on the other hand, relates to the essence of the first "return", which—although precipitated by punishment and suffering, is the product of true *repentance (return) and contemplation*. Only such *complete* (to use Nahmanides' own term) return has the power to rise even to the Heavenly Throne itself. We thus learn the force of repentance, for it can hasten redemption. In support of this assertion, he cites the words of Isaiah (59:20): "And a redeemer will come to Zion, and unto them that return from transgression in Jacob, saith the Lord". In other words, when the Jewish People returns to God and purifies its actions, the redeemer will come. Nor does redemption occur only in the Land of Israel, for the *Shekhinah* resides with the Jewish People in exile.

The ingathering of the exiles is so difficult, that God Himself must hold the hand of each and every person. This is in keeping with the vision of the prophet Zephaniah (3:20): "At that time will I bring you in, and at that time will I gather you; for I will make you to be a name and a praise among all the peoples of the earth, when I turn your captivity before your eyes, saith the Lord". God Himself will return with the People, and that is the meaning of "before your eyes". It is a promise to the people that they will witness with their own eyes, the coming and returning of the *Shekhinah* with them.

This will be to Israel's great credit in the eyes of the nations, and so the prophet says: "for I will make you to be a name and a praise among all the peoples of the earth". Noteworthy in this context is Don Isaac Abravanel's interpretation of *Deuteronomy* 30:3. Abravanel, who lived through the expulsion from Spain in 1492, also wondered at the verse's repetition of the word "return": "To say 'and then the Lord thy God will return thy captivity, and have compassion upon thee, and will return and gather thee' is redundant, for it would have been enough merely to say 'and then the Lord thy God will return thy captivity'." He explains this duplication as referring to two distinct groups of Jews in exile, on the basis of his experience in 15th-century Portugal and Spain. Some Jews withstood all of the trials and tribulations of the Inquisition. Many others however, publicly renounced their faith, while remaining loyal to the Torah and its precepts in secret. It is with these crypto-Jews in mind, that he wrote: "'And thou shalt think in thy heart' (30:1)—*In your heart* and not *in your mouth*, since they cannot make their return and their faith public 'among all the nations, whither the Lord thy God hath driven thee', because they are intermingled with them and considered like them; *but in their hearts* they will return to God. It is to the other part of our people however, the Jews who observe their faith publicly, that the verse relates when it says, 'and shalt return unto the Lord thy God, and hearken to His voice'. They may return publicly, just as they never renounced their faith. Then God will accept their repentance. That is the meaning of the verse 'and then the Lord thy God will return thy captivity, and have compassion upon thee, and will return and gather thee from all the peoples'. Of the *anusim* (the 'crypto-Jews') the verse says 'and will return and gather thee'. The word 'compassion' however, does not refer to their return, for they have not suffered like the others".

Rabbi Bahye ben Asher of Saragossa explains the ingathering of the Jewish People from among the nations in a different fashion. Rabbi Bahye ben Asher Ibn Haliwa was a 13th-century Spanish exegete and kabbalist, and close disciple of Rabbi Solomon ben Adret (Rashba). In his commentary on the Torah, he employs four distinct methods of interpretation: *peshat* (plain or literal meaning), midrash (homiletic interpretation), *sekhel* (a philosophical-allegorical approach), and *kabbalah* (esoteric meaning). In his commentary on *Nitzavim*, Rabbi Bahye explains the "dispersed" (*nidahim*) as a reference to the ten tribes of Israel, exiled by the king of Assyria (722 BCE)—who constitute a majority within the Jewish People. Following the ingathering of the dispersed, there will be another ingathering, of the tribes of Judah and Benjamin (the "Babylonian" exile of 586 BCE). That is why the word "return"

appears twice in the verse (30:3), denoting the ingathering of two exiles. Similarly, we find in the book of Isaiah: "Yet I will gather others to
him, beside those of him that are gathered"(56:8). According to Amos
Hakham, in his commentary on *Isaiah*, in the *Da'at Mikra* series, the
reference is to the proselytes, whose numbers will be added to those of
the exiles of Israel.

The *Hafetz Hayim* (1838–1933), who lived in the second half of the
19th century, until a short time before the outbreak of the Second World
War, was well-acquainted with European anti-Semitism, and foresaw
the future. He concerned himself not only with current affairs, but believed with all his heart that he was living in the time of the "footsteps
of the Messiah" (the days preceding the coming of the Messiah), and
that we must prepare ourselves for imminent redemption. This is clearly
apparent in his remarks on the verse "And then the Lord thy God will
turn thy captivity, and have compassion upon thee …" (*Hafetz Hayim
al Hatorah*):

> This is the promise of redemption that will come in the near
> future, and we must expect it every day. And this is one of the
> questions that man is asked on Judgment Day: "Did you await
> salvation?" And if he (the Messiah) shall tarry—await him, for
> he will surely come. And one of the greatest impediments to
> this belief is the state of our people among the nations in recent
> years, for we are to them, an object of scorn and derision. And
> we are now the lowest and most despised in their eyes, and many
> ask how such a lowly nation can possibly rise up as a symbol
> and glory before all?

In the years 5650–5651 (1890–1890), at the time of the Second Aliyah, when land was purchased in Palestine, vineyards planted and the
first *moshavot* (colonies)—Petah Tikva, Zikhron Ya'akov, Rehovot and
others—established, the *Hafetz Hayim* wrote to his son that he believed
that these events marked the beginning of the ingathering of the exiles,
which precedes the coming of the Messiah, and that one should purchase
land in the Holy Land and settle there. Since he himself was unable to
do so, he wrote, he considered himself duty-bound to do something else
in order to prepare for the redemption.

He maintained that with the People's return to its land, the Temple would be rebuilt and the Priests would be called upon to perform the sacrificial cult. As a *kohen*, he believed it was his duty to study the laws of sacrifices and ritual purity (rarely studied in the *yeshivot*, due to their lack of practical applicability). He therefore began to study the talmudic order of *Kodshim* (in which the Temple and the sacrifices are discussed), with the intention of putting its laws to practical use (*Kol Kitvei Hafetz Hayim Hashalem* vol.1 (*Mikhtavim*): "*Ma'amar Rodef Tzedakah Vahesed*", 1; "*Ma'amar Zikhru Torat Moshe*", 30).

He devoted two years to the study of the tractate *Zevahim* (Sacrifices), with all its commentaries, publishing his own halakhic glosses. Having obtained the consent of the great sages of his time, he spent thirty five years writing a commentary on the entire order of *Kodshim*, which he entitled *Likutei Halakhot*. As part of this project, he established at his *yeshivah* in Radun, a *kollel Kodshim*—an institute devoted entirely to the study of the laws of the Temple and the sacrifices—that there might be a cadre of knowledgeable priests ready to perform the divine offices as soon as the Temple is built.

The *Hafetz Hayim* was self-taught, a man whose intellectual and spiritual development came from within, from his unique personal world. He was one of the greatest exponents of *musar* of his time, in theory as well as practice. This is evident in his books *Hafetz Hayim* and *Shemirat Halashon*, which call for greater observance of the prohibitions against evil speech, as well as ethical behavior in general, charity and kindness, fear of God, and emphasising the positive in one's fellow man—principles by which the *Hafetz Hayim* lived his entire life. Some attribute his commitment to the subject of ethical speech to his exposure, as a young man, to the sermons of Rabbi Israel "Salanter" (Lipkin), founder of the *Musar* Movement, to whom he owed a great deal, and whose methods he applied in his books. His concept of "love of Torah" was unique, and is described by his son, Rabbi Aryeh Leib, as follows:

The Torah is our soul, and how can one live without a soul? There is nothing, no matter how difficult, that one will not do for the sake of his own life. He should therefore study God's Torah all his days, that he might merit eternal life. For man doth not live by bread only, and in the World to Come he will need

bread from heaven, which is the Torah he has learned in this
world"(*Meir Einei Yisrael* 1,32).

Accordingly, the *Hafetz Hayim* was untiring in his efforts—in his
comments on the Torah, his reproofs and moral exhortations on the
one hand, and love for the Jewish People and the Torah on the other.
In a number of places in his writings, he reviews the entire history of
the Jewish People, from its earliest beginnings to his own time. His
commentary on *Deuteronomy* 30:3 for example, includes the following
scholarly account of Jewish history:

> In truth, if we look closely, we will see that all of God's inter-
> action with our People has been in this fashion, in the manner
> of "and lifteth up the needy out of the dunghill" (*Ps.* 113:7), to
> give greater prominence to the miracle of our existence, for "is
> anything too hard for Him"?

Abraham begat Isaac when he was 100 years old, an age at
which such a thing would not have been possible naturally. And
so Sarah said: "shall Sarah, that is ninety years old, bear?" (Gen.
17:17). And that is the meaning of the words of the prophet Isaiah "Look unto Abraham your father, and unto Sarah that bore
you" (51:2)—in other words, witness the miracles that I performed for them. Our father Jacob produced twelve tribes, and
struggled with an angel and prevailed, after Eliphaz had robed
him of everything so that he crossed the Jordan with nothing
but his staff in his hand, and after he had worked in the house of
Laban, day and night for fourteen years.

Joseph rose to the monarchy after having suffered in prison for
twelve years. Moses was subject, from the day of his birth, to
trials and tribulations—cast him into the river—and in the end,
he became God's messenger to redeem the People of Israel and
give them the Torah.

Israel was lowly and despised in Egypt, as it is written, "And
they were adread because of the Children of Israel" (*Ex.* 1:12),

and each of them was forced to make 400 brick per day, as it is said in the name of the *Rokeah* (Rabbi Eleazar ben Judah of Worms, 12th century), and terrible decrees were issued against them, so that any who saw them in their enslavement could not believe that these slaves would go out with a high hand before the eyes of all the world, and moreover, that Pharaoh himself would arise in the middle of the night to plead with them, saying "Rise up, get you forth from among my people" (*Ex.* 12:31).

And for fifty days to Mount Sinai to receive the Torah and they made very great achievements. More than all the prophets that later arose among the Jews, as the Rabbis said: "a handmaiden at the [Red] Sea saw wonders that [even] Ezekiel did not see" (*Mekhilta, Beshalah* 15:2).

And so, any who saw Israel in the days of Haman, after it had already been "written and sealed with the king's ring... to destroy, to slay, and to cause to perish, all Jews, both young and old, little children and women, in one day, even upon the thirteenth day of the twelfth month" (*Esth.* 3:13). Who would have believed then, who would have said that on that very day, the Jews would rule over them as they pleased, and instead of the fear and terror that they felt at the first—fear of them would fall on all the peoples? And that many from among the peoples of the land would become Jews, and that Haman, next unto King Ahasuerus, who had meant to hang Mordecai upon a tree, would himself be hung on the very same tree, and Mordecai would be next unto the king, in his place (*Hafetz Hayim al Hatorah* p. 277).

Following his recapitulation of Jewish history, the *Hafetz Hayim*—as a man of *musar* and reproof, but also of comfort and encouragement—opens a window to our own time, with an eye to the future. How relevant his words are even today:

And so it is in our time as well, when we see the Jewish People given for spoil in almost every country, let our hearts not fail. For on the contrary, it is a sign that God will swiftly redeem us and raise us up from the dunghill and we will be renowned in praise and glory throughout the world, rather than constantly despised in the eyes of all. And the following verses will be fulfilled in us: "I will give thanks unto Thee, for Thou hast answered me", and "the stone which the builders rejected is become the chief corner-stone" (*Ps.* 118:21–22); and in *Isaiah* "Whereas thou hast been forsaken and hated ... I will make thee an eternal excellency, a joy of many generations" (60:15). And one who has the heart to understand will see in a shining glass, how great is God's providence, for in His compassion, He does not allow the destroyer to destroy us. We must therefore, learn the future from the past. For the trials that come upon us increase, we must strengthen ourselves in perfect faith, that in the end, our triumph will go forth as brightness, and all peoples will recognize and know that there is none like our people, Israel, a nation one in the earth, and the Lord, blessed be He, will comfort Zion and our People, and will swiftly send us his Messiah (*ibid.* p. 168).

The *Hafetz Hayim* concludes on an optimistic note, with words of reassurance, worthy of a great leader and of his generation, who lived in perfect faith and complete adherence to the Thirteen Principles, as stated by Maimonides:

And any one who does not believe in [the Messiah] or does not await his coming, not only does he deny all of the other prophets, but the very Law of Moses, for the Torah bore witness to him, as it is written (*Deut.* 30:3–5) "And then the Lord thy God will turn thy captivity, and have compassion upon thee, and will return and gather thee from all the peoples... If any of thine that are dispersed be in the uttermost parts of heaven ... And the Lord thy God will bring thee into the land (*Hilkhot Melakhim* 11,1).

The explicit in the Torah (the Pentateuch) include all of the words of all of the prophets, and it is fitting of the activities of the *Hafetz Hayim* through his behavior and his books, to bring the Jewish People from true return to God to upcoming redemption. We will conclude this chapter with the words of Rabbi Abraham Isaac Hakohen Kook:

The renewal of the desire in the people as a whole to return to its land, to its essence, to its spirit and way of life—in truth, there is a light of penitence in all this. Truly this comes to expression in the Torah: "And you shall return to the Lord your God" (Deut. 30:2)... The penitence spoken is always an inner penitence, but it is covered over by many screens. No impediments or lack of completion can keep the higher light from reaching us... And all this will culminate in a penitence that will bring healing and redemption to the world (Lights *of Penitence* 17, in B.Z. Bokser ed., *Abraham Isaac Kook: The Lights of Penitence, The Moral Principles, Lights of Holiness, Essays, Letters, and Poems*, pp. 126–127).

According to the traditional exegesis and Orthodox theology, re-pentance—or "return"—is an essential and existential part of the proc-ess of redemption of each and every individual and of the Jewish People as a whole.

Lea Mazor

Vayelekh – And Moses Went

Moses' Departure in Light of Scripture and in Light of
Shulamith Hareven's "The Miracle Hater"—*Modern Scripture and Midrash*

And Moses went and spoke these words unto all Israel. And he said unto them: 'I am a hundred and twenty years old this day; I can no more go out and come in; and the Lord hath said unto me: Thou shalt not go over this Jordan (*Deuteronomy* 31:1–2).

Four of the five books of the Pentateuch are marked by the gigantic figure of Moses. The story of his birth is interwoven, in tradition, with the birth of the People of Israel in the land of Egypt; and the story of his life is thereafter interwoven with that of the People. Moses was the Israelites' leader: he took them out of slavery in Egypt, led them in the desert for forty years, gave them the Torah, mediated between them and God, and led the conquest of the eastern bank of the Jordan. The story of his life comes to a close with the end of the period of wandering in the desert, when the Children of Israel stand in the plains of Moab, on the threshold of the Promised Land.

Moses was a hundred and twenty years old when he died (34:7). The portion of *Vayelekh* describes the final year of his life and the preparations that he made in anticipation of his death. The shadow of death approaches and is cast over the entire portion. It is mentioned five times in the portion, with increasing urgency. First, Moses tells the Israelites that he is old and weak, and can no longer serve as their leader: "I am a hundred and twenty years old this day; I can no more go out and come in" (31:2); then, God tells him, explicitly, that his days are nearing their end: "Behold, thy days approach that thou must die" (*ibid.* 14). The next reference to the matter no longer speaks of approaching "days", but of death itself: "And the Lord said unto Moses: 'Behold, thou art about to sleep with thy fathers" (*ibid.* 16); and finally, Moses addresses events following his death: "behold, while I am yet alive with you this day, ye have been rebellious against the Lord; and how much more after my death? … For I know that after my death ye will in any wise deal corruptly" (*ibid.* 27–29). Knowing that the Children of Israel will rebel against him, God commands Moses to write a song that will serve as a witness against them. The introduction to the song appears in *Vayelekh*, and the song itself in the portion of *Ha'azinu*. The story of Moses' death is recounted in *Ha'azinu* and *Vezot Haberakhah*. God commands Moses to go up to the mountain upon which he will die (32:49–50), Moses blesses the Children of Israel before his death (33:1), goes up to Mount Nebo and dies there (34:1–7).

The story of Moses' final days (chapters 31–34) forms a distinct unit within the book of *Deuteronomy*; a unit comprising narrative interlaced with oratory, poetry and prophecy, while the rest of *Deuteronomy* consists mostly of Moses' orations to the people. This unit concludes the book of *Deuteronomy*, and with it the story of the entire Pentateuch.

The Pentateuch recounts the early history of the People of Israel, beginning with the three forefathers to whom, and to whose seed, God promised the land of Canaan. The children of Israel went down to Egypt, where they became a people. Moses delivered them from their Egyptian bondage, led them in the desert for forty years, and after an arduous and event-filled journey, brought them to the threshold of the Promised Land. But the land was not empty. It was inhabited by "a people great and tall", who resided in well-fortified cities (1:28) and had to be fought and annihilated in order to win the land. The Israelites became dispirited, and it was at this juncture that it was decreed that Moses—the only leader they had ever known—would not be allowed to cross the Jordan (3:27; 4:21–22; 31:2) which, in the story, is more of a symbolic than a physical boundary. The Jordan, in the story, is a divider of space, time and imagery. On the one side, the desert, and on the other—the land flowing with milk and honey; on the one side, wanderings, and on the other—settlement on the land; on the one side a great vision, struggling against stubborn resistance, and on the other—the unknown.

Moses knew that he was about to leave behind a people that did not yet have a land of its own, and whose religious identity had not yet been internalized. How would this young faith in a single god survive in an established pagan environment? How would the people uphold God's

Law after the demise of the leader who gave it to them? *Vayelekh* deals with Moses' feverish preparations for the time that would come after his departure, focusing on three main topics: leadership, conquest and the Law.

The Bible is in the habit of placing parting words in the mouths of leaders, prior to their deaths. Joshua and Samuel made parting speeches (Jos. 23; 1 Sam. 12), David, on his deathbed, gave Solomon a legacy to uphold (1 *Kings* 2:1–9), and Jacob took leave of his sons with poetic words of prophecy regarding the "end of days" (Gen. 49). *Vayelekh* includes all of these elements: parting speeches (*Deut.* 31:1–6; 9–14;24–26), a legacy to Moses' successor, Joshua (*ibid.* 7–8), and an introduction to the prophetic poetry of the "end of days" (38–29). The inclusion of all of these parting forms in the description of a single leader is a literary device to convey the thoroughness and extensiveness of the preparations preceding the leader's death. This is also reflected in the portion's narrative thread: Moses appoints Joshua as his successor, writes down the words of the Law in a book—which he entrusts to the Levites, with instructions for its safekeeping, gives the Priest instructions for the cycle of its public reading, exhorts the People to observe its precepts, teaches the Children of Israel the prophetic song that they must transmit orally from generation to generation, convokes a great assembly, at which conveys the words of the song.

The three main topics addressed by Moses—leadership, conquest and the Law—appear throughout the portion, with varying degrees of emphasis. At the beginning of the portion, emphasis is placed on the two most pressing issues at that moment: leadership and conquest. Moses informs the People of his imminent departure, appoints Joshua in his place, and offers words of encouragement in anticipation of the upcoming conquest. Moses tells the People that the change in leadership is by divine command: "and the Lord hath *said unto me*: Thou shalt not go over this Jordan" (31:2), and "Joshua, he shall go over before thee, *as the Lord hath spoken* (*ibid.* 3). The command to which Moses is referring, appears at the beginning of *Deuteronomy* (ch. 3)—as witnessed by the great similarity in language:

3:27 And the Lord said unto me ...
Get thee up into the top of Pisgah ...
and behold with thine eyes; for thou shalt not go over this Jordan

31:2 And the Lord hath said unto me Thou shalt not go over this Jordan

3:28 But charge courage him	Joshua and strengthen him and encourage him
31:7 And Moses called courage	unto Joshua Be strong and of good courage
	and said unto him
3:28 for	he shall go over before this people
31:3	he shall go over before thee

It is recounted, at the end of *Deuteronomy*, that Moses went up "unto mount Nebo, to the top of Pisgah" (34:1) and died there, and the book of *Joshua* begins with the words: "Now it came to pass after the death of Moses the servant of the Lord, that the Lord spoke unto Joshua the son of Nun, Moses' servant, saying: 'Moses My servant is dead; now therefore arise, go over this Jordan, thou, and all this people, unto the land which I do give to them, even to the children of Israel'" (Jos. 1:1–2).

From the context of *Deuteronomy* 3, we learn the reason for "Thou shalt not go over this Jordan" (31:2). God denied Moses the possibility of entering the Promised Land as a punishment for the sin of the spies. "But the Lord was wroth with me for your sakes" (3:26, and in greater detail in 1:22–38). Moses' punishment, according to this explanation, is part of a collective punishment imposed by God upon the entire desert generation. The Torah offers another explanation however. Moses (and his brother Aaron) were barred from entering the Promised Land as a personal punishment for the "waters of Meribah" affair (*Num.* 20:8–13; 27:12–14; *Deut.* 32:49–52). *Vayelekh* suggests a third explanation: Moses cannot enter the Promised Land, due to his advanced age (31:2).

This explanation differs from the other two in that it does not attribute Moses' inability to enter the Land to sin of any kind. The reason for the change in leadership prior to the conquest is purely biological.

Central issues in biblical thought have often produced varying traditions, and just as there are a number of traditions regarding the reason for Moses' inability to enter the Promised Land, so there are a number of traditions regarding the appointment of Joshua. Joshua's appointment, according to *Deuteronomy* 31:2–8, was a public one, conferred before all of Israel. Moses defined his role—to bring the People to the Land and to cause them to inherit it—strengthened his spirit and promised him that God was with him, adding various terms of encouragement.

In *Vayelekh*, we find another tradition of Joshua's appointment, whereby Joshua was appointed directly by God, in Moses' presence alone. "And the Lord said unto Moses: 'Behold, thy days approach that thou must die; call Joshua, and present yourselves in the tent of meeting, that I may give him a charge [appoint him].' And Moses and Joshua went, and presented themselves in the tent of meeting. And the Lord appeared in the Tent in a pillar of cloud; and the pillar of cloud stood over the door of the Tent." (31:14–15). The story continues in verse 23: "And he gave Joshua the son of Nun a charge, and said: 'Be strong and of good courage; for thou shalt bring the children of Israel into the land which I swore unto them; and I will be with thee'." (On the theory that the contiguity of the passage was interrupted by a "textual accident", and on the literary history of the entire portion, see Alexander Rofé, "*Hiburah shel Parshat Vayelekh*" [The Composition of the Portion of *Vayelekh*], *Mavo Lesefer Devarim*, pp. 198–215).

The events described in verses 14–15 and 23 read like a legend, in which a servant takes his master's place. From *Exodus* 33 we learn that Joshua was Moses' servant (*mesharet*), and that his role was to guard the Tent of Meeting, which stood outside the camp (*ibid.* 11). In this tent, God would appear to Moses from time to time and speak to him "face to face, as a man speaketh unto his friend" (*ibid.*). And here, when Moses is about to die, Joshua is called to the Tent of Meeting, where God appears to him and appoints him to succeed his master. Joshua's divine revelation and direct appointment by God, raises him to the level of a leader-prophet.

Joshua's private, almost clandestine appointment in the Tent of Meeting, stands in direct contradiction to the tradition in 31:7–8, and to the rest of the portion, characterized by public and dramatic events: Moses addresses the entire People (1–6; 30), the Priests the sons of Levi and all the elders of Israel (9–13), teaches the song to the Children of Israel (22), commands the Levites (25–27) and summons all the elders of the tribes and the officers (28).

Another tradition regarding the appointment of Joshua can be found in the book of *Numbers*. According to this tradition, it was *Moses* who asked God to appoint a leader in his stead, and God suggested Joshua. Joshua's appointment is conferred in a ritual ceremony, in which Moses lays his hands on him before Eleazar the Priest and the entire community, and "puts of his honor upon him" (*Num.* 27:12–23).

The two traditions of Joshua's appointment in *Vayelekh* are clearly of a military nature. In the Tent of Meeting, God says to Joshua: "Be strong and of good courage; for thou shalt bring the children of Israel into the land which I swore unto them; and I will be with thee" (31:23)—which is a slightly shorter version of the words that **Moses** said to Joshua, according to the previously recounted tradition: "Be strong and of good courage; for thou shalt go with this people into the land which the Lord hath sworn unto their fathers to give them; and thou shalt cause them to inherit it. And the Lord, He it is that doth go before thee; He will be with thee, He will not fail thee, neither forsake thee; fear not, neither be dismayed" (*ibid.* 7–8). Following Moses' death, we are told, God repeated these words of promise and encouragement to Joshua: "There shall not any man be able to stand before thee all the days of thy life; as I was with Moses, so I will be with thee; I will not fail thee, nor forsake thee. Be strong and of good courage; for thou shalt cause this people to inherit the land which I swore unto their fathers to give them" (Jos. 1:5–6).

Moses' words to the People (31:2–6) are also of a military nature, as befits the circumstances. The Israelites are about to embark upon a war of conquest and must be imbued with courage, passion and belief in their ability to defeat their enemies (compare 20:1–4). Moses' speech is filled with slogans of encouragement and promises of divine assistance. As an illustration and sign of things to come, he mentions their recent victory over Sihon and Og, kings of lands to the east of the Jordan. The fate of the peoples of Canaan must be like that of Sihon and Og. Israel must destroy the peoples of Canaan and do to them "according unto all the commandment which I have commanded you" (31:5; 7:2–4).

Moses addresses two distinct stages that will come about following his demise. The first and more immediate stage is that of the conquest. Later however, once they have settled in the Land, their main difficulty will be maintaining their religious identity. They will have to fear God and observe his precepts, but Moses knows that they will not succeed, and will therefore suffer great evils. Once he has addressed the People and appointed Joshua, Moses turns to the issue of preserving God's Law for future generations, who will not have witnessed God's wonders with their own eyes (31:13; see also 11:2–9). He writes down the Law and the prophetic song (19; 22; 24), and establishes methods of instilling them in future hearts and minds. The Priests the sons of Levi are charged with the task of assembling the People once every seven years in order to read the Law before them (the commandment of *hakhel*). Men, women, children and the stranger within thy gates, will come together in the place that will be designated for divine worship ("in the place which he shall choose"), will hear the words of the Law and learn to fear God. Moses had no illusions regarding the future. He knew that the People was stiff-necked and rebellious, and would therefore violate the covenant it had forged with God and go after other gods. The result would be that God would hide his countenance from them and great evils would be visited upon them. Moses writes the song, teaches it to the People and instructs them to transmit it to future generations ("for it shall not be forgotten out of the mouths of their seed", 21), that it might serve as a "witness" (19; 20).

Moses' discourses reflect the approach that history is guided by the principle of retribution: faithfulness to God will ensure the continued existence of the People on its land; the worship of other gods will entail severe punishment. The song and the Law are intended to teach the People that great adversity is not the result of God's powerlessness, but of their own sins. *Vayelekh*, which begins with great enthusiasm, with words of encouragement and promises of military victory—ends on a grave note. The possibility of repentance is not mentioned. There is no forgiveness, no comfort.

Shulamith Hareven's novella *The Miracle Hater* is a modern midrash on the exodus and subsequent wandering in the desert, drawing both upon Scripture and upon the midrashic literature. It was published in 1983 and again in 1996 as part of *Thirst: The Desert Trilogy* (first published in English in 1988, translated by Hillel Halkin). In the following pages, we will take a look at Hareven's approach, in *The Miracle Hater*, to the main elements of the portion of *Vayelekh*, as described above.

The Miracle Hater comprises two intertwined plots: a historical one, centered on the figure of Moses; and a biographical one, centered on the figure of Eshkhar—one of the many who had left Egypt. The inner, biographical story is the essence of the novella, and it unfolds on the basis of the historical plot.

Scriptural tradition describes the exodus, Israel's becoming a people and the message of monotheism, from the point of view of "the management"—God and Moses. Seen from this perspective, Israel was a stiff-necked, cranky and rebellious people. Hareven tried to look at events from the point of view of the people, who bore the brunt of the great revolution. The resulting image is one of a group of people who spent years wandering through the desert—tired, hungry, parched and ill, without ever understanding the processes of which they were a part. They were concerned only with survival in the present, while Moses spoke to them of eternity and bushes: "Although they did not understand him, they nodded politely, without arguing. If the man wanted to talk about burning bushes, let it be burning bushes (*Thirst* p. 12). Opposite Moses, the hero of the biblical saga, Hareven portrays Eshkhar—the outcast, living on the margins of society "watching detachedly" (*ibid*. p. 37). His name, which means "buckthorn", attests to his character: a common shrub. If a "hero" is someone who exerts a great deal of influence on society and history, and an "anti-hero" is someone on a more human scale, whose interests mostly lie inward, then Moses is a hero and Eshkhar is a classic anti-hero. This anti-hero is the protagonist of Hareven's novella.

At the heart of *The Miracle Hater* lies the oedipal love story between Eshkhar and Baita, who was like mother, sister and desired woman to him. Baita raised Eshkhar from the time of his birth, when she herself was only five years old, and they grew up as one. They left Egypt together and wandered the desert together, until Baita reached the age of marriage and the men of the tribe gave her in marriage to a young Ephraimite named Zavdi. Frustrated and furious, Eshkhar fled to the distant flocks, and a year or two later, Baita set out to find him. The painful attempt to consummate their love ended in disaster. Baita was deadly afraid of her parents, of Zavdi and of Moses, who "had ways of finding out everything in the world" (p. 41). In the end, she falls ill and dies. The lovers' final meeting takes place in a dream. Baita bids Eshkhar farewell, but not before giving her blessing to his budding relationship with Dina. Eshkhar and Dina gradually build a stable family, and give birth to a son, Yotam. With him, and their other children, they cross the Jordan and enter the Land.

The story of Eshkhar and his relationships with the two women in his life can be understood on a number of different levels, and symbolizes the complexity of the relationship between those who left Egypt and their two homelands: their biographical homeland on the one hand (Egypt), and their historical homeland on the other (the Land of the Fathers). Baita represents the land of their land of origin and Dina represents the land of their destination. It is no coincidence that Dina bears the name of a figure from the time of the Fathers, and "Baita" (or "Baithah") is a play on the name "Bithiah"—the daughter of Pharaoh (1 *Chron.* 4:18) who, according to the Midrash, pulled Moses from the Nile (see e.g. *Megilah* 13a; *Sanhedrin* 31b).

The traditions of the Israelites' wandering in the desert are all deeply rooted in the notion that Egypt was a cruel house of slavery, and that the People's longings for Egypt were nothing more than manifestations of their ungratefulness (e.g. *Ex.* 16:2–3; *Num.* 11). Hareven's novella challenges this sweeping assumption and opens feelings of the people—for whom Egypt was a land flowing with light and honey, of fertile land and fish-filled waters (p. 4; 18). The people loved Egypt, but were unable to truly connect with it and make it theirs, because they were a foreign body in its midst, like a humpback, like Eshkhar whom Baita bore on her back when he was a baby (p. 9). Eshkhar loved Baita with every fiber of his being, but only with Dina could he "come to the rest and to the inheritance", because he and Dina shared an ancient, ancestral bond. Between Eshkhar and Baita-Egypt on the other hand, there was no common blood, because she was not his biological mother. His natural place was thus in the ancient Land of the Fathers that awaited him at "the end of all their journeys" (p. 61).

The novella hints at an overriding principle that directs history and guides man, even if she or he is are not aware of it. This principle creates a hidden connection between beginning and end, between wakening and weakening. The desert journeys were not only "journeys toward", but also journeys "away from". Eshkhar, the People, and Moses, all suffered from Lot's wife syndrome: those who look back will be frozen in their tracks and denied the possibility of attaining their goal-purpose. Eshkhar reached the Land. Moses did not. The Bible, as shown above, offers various explanations of the fact that Moses never entered the Land. Hareven adopts the natural explanation—his venerable age—to which she adds a more intrinsic reason, inspired by the Midrash: Moses did not enter the Land, because he remained bound to Egypt. Moses' tragedy lay in the fact that although he succeeded in taking Israel out of Egypt, he was unable to take Egyptianness out of himself:

> Rabbi Levi said—He said before Him: Master of the universe, the bones of Joseph entered the Land, but I may not? God said to him: He who admitted his land is buried in his land, and he who did not admit his land is not be buried in his land. Where does it say that Joseph admitted his land? His mistress said (Gen. 40:15) "See, he hath brought in a Hebrew unto us …", and he did not deny it, but asserted that (*ibid.* 40:15) "I was stolen away out of the land of the Hebrews". And he was buried in his land, as it is written (Jos. 24:32): "And the bones of Joseph, which the children of Israel brought up out of Egypt, buried they in Shekhem". You [Moses], who did not admit your land are not buried in your land. How so? The daughters of Jethro said (*Ex.* 2:19): "An Egyptian delivered us out of the hand of the shepherds", and he heard and was silent. Therefore, he was not buried in his land (*Deuteronomy Rabbah* 2,8).

Moses appears in *The Miracle Hater* as a superhuman, asexual, afamilial, asocial figure. The people did not understand him. They told fantastic stories about him: "Some said that he had two hearts in his breast, one Hebrew and one Egyptian, and that he had murdered the Egyptian one so as to leave no trace of it. Some even swore they had seen the scar on his chest. Yet although he did not quite seem a Hebrew like the rest of them, there was nothing obviously Egyptian about him either. Egypt was all eloquence and ceremony, whereas he had trouble talking, and spoke the Hebrew language quite clumsily ... Sometimes an Egyptian word slipped into his speech, causing him to blush all over" (pp. 11–12, see also p. 17). Hareven stresses the influence of his Egyptian childhood on his life and his identity: "His Egyptian childhood oppressed him; he was unable to free himself of it. He talked to them about eternity, that of life and that of death. He was forced to resort to Egyptian" (p. 12).

Eshkhar too grappled with the idea of eternity, and went to the elders that they might explain to him: "He knew, of course, that there was nothing to the beliefs of the Egyptians, and that the Hebrews did not think that there was any *ba* or *ka* who came to take your soul when you died. Yet the question bothered him whether or not one was born again after death" (p. 22). Eshkhar managed to free himself of Egyptian belief. Moses did not. And when he got old: "His mind was failing. Sometimes, imagining that *ba* and *ka* had come to take his soul, he harangued them that he was a Hebrew, not an Egyptian, and that they should go somewhere else. Sometimes he shouted that he must, must enter the land and that no force in heaven or on earth could stand in his way. In his more lucid moments he sought to impose more and more laws on them, a never-ending Torah. Yet even his intimates no longer bothered to write them down. They knew that his hour was nigh; one way or another, everything was already up to Joshua" (p. 59).

Hareven condenses a world of meaning into this one paragraph. Moses' desperate cry that he must enter the land is based on *Deuteronomy* 3:23–26. He pleads with God to allow him to cross the Jordan, to see the Land from up close, and God refuses, saying: "Let it suffice thee; speak no more unto me of this matter" (*ibid.* 26). But Moses, according to the novella, must enter the land, and "no force in heaven or on earth could stand in his way" (*p.* 59). The heaven and earth motif is taken from the Midrash:

> When Moses saw that the decree against him had been sealed,
> he began to fast and drew a small circle and stood within it and

said: I will not move from here until You annul that decree! What [else] did Moses do at that time? He donned sackcloth and covered himself in ash and stood in prayer and supplication before the Holy One, blessed be He, until *heaven and earth* and the order of creation shook (*Deuteronomy Rabbah* 11,10). Similarly, When Moses saw that [God] would pay him no heed, *he went to heaven and earth* and instructed them to beg for mercy. They said to him, if we could beg for mercy for you, we would beg for mercy for ourselves (*Midrash Tanhuma, Va'ethanan* 6).

In *Vayelekh*, we learn that Moses appointed Joshua and then finished writing the Torah. "And the Lord said unto Moses: 'Behold, thy days approach that thou must die; call Joshua, and present yourselves in the tent of meeting, that I may give him a charge' (31:14). The appointment is described in verse 23, after which it says "And it came to pass, when Moses had made an end of writing the words of this law in a book, until they were finished, that Moses commanded the Levites" (24–25). Moses appears here, as he does throughout *Vayelekh*, a man at the height of his spiritual faculties—lucid, planning, active, creating and implementing.

The novella paints a very different picture. Joshua has been making all the decisions for some time now, and the people no longer listen to Moses and his Torah, because his mind is failing. Here too, Hareven draws upon the Midrash. The *Tanhuma* (*Va'ethanan* 6) comments as follows on 31:4:

He said to him, so I have decided and so is the way of the world, to each generation its teachers and to each generation its leaders. Until now, it was your role to serve me, and now your role is lost and it is the hour of Joshua your student to teach… And the Israelites came to Moses to learn Torah … A heavenly voice said to them: learn from Joshua, accept him as your teacher and sit before him. Joshua sat at the head, with Moses at his right hand and Aaron at his left. And Joshua would sit and teach before Moses. Rabbi Shmuel bar Nahmani said in the name of Rabbi Yonatan, when Joshua said, "blessed is He who has chosen the righteous", Moses' legacy of wisdom was taken from him and given to Joshua, and Moses no longer knew what Joshua was teaching. When the Israelites arose, they asked Moses to explain [the lesson]. He said to them, I do not know the answer. And Moses stumbled and fell. At that time Moses said, "Master of the universe, until now I have sought life, now my soul is Yours."

How did Joshua get the job? According to Hareven, he was forced on Moses:

One day *Nun* came to Moses. He spoke Egyptian and importuned him greatly, thrusting an obsequious hand into his belt to make him yield. He had brought his son Joshua with him; let Moses take him as his aide and bodyguard to protect him from the crowds that were so lovingly, glad-handedly free with him that soon they would kill him with affection. Moses would rather have declined but ended up by agreeing. From then on anyone wishing to see him had first to get past Joshua, who sat by the flap of his tent (p. 17).

Eshkhar wanted to see Moses, and when he reached the leader's tent, he found Joshua barring the way to Moses and to justice:

Joshua was sitting by the flap of the big tent, his curled sidewhiskers gracing his broad moonface... Spotlessly groomed, dressed all in white, he looked with disdain at the thin, grimy boy whose face was smeared with dirt and tears... Eshkhar let loose a tirade of words ... justice, justice, justice. The thinnest of smiles flitted over Joshua's chill lips without passing from them to the eyes, and he said: We work miracles. Justice is not our concern. Whereupon he rose to his feet, his large white moonface filling the boy's field of vision. For an instant Eshkhar longed to poke his fist into its insolence and did not dare (p. 23).

The scene is based on the contrast between black and white, with color and essence reversed. It is the black Eshkhar who is pure as the driven snow, and the white-faced, white-clothed Joshua whose soul is black. This passage echoes the talmudic comparison between Moses and Joshua, which claims that Joshua was Moses' inferior: "And thou shalt put of thy honor upon him (*Num.* 27:20)—And not all thy honor.

The elders of that generation said: The face of Moses was like the sun, the face of Joshua like the moon. Woe to such shame, woe to such disgrace" (*Bava Batra* 75a).

Vayelekh ends with the distressing image of the Israelites as a rebellious and stiff-necked people, and in *Ha'azinu,* God commands Moses to go up to the mountain where he will die, and says to him "For thou shalt see the land afar off; but thou shalt not go there" (32:52). The end of the desert journey in *The Miracle Hater* is very different; soft and appeased. Eshkhar sees the land far off and goes there: "Eshkhar kept back. The Land stretched out before him along the horizon" (p. 59). All of a sudden, he senses a strange presence behind him, and is afraid to turn around: "someone smiling and forbearing who expected something of him without his knowing what it was… you are close now, Eshkhar, very close; just one more little effort and you will understand. But he could not understand… then, all at once, like a man who has not done so for years, he began to laugh…" (pp. 59–60). The time had arrived for Eshkhar, Dina and the children to enter. "They kept on crossing the river, household after household, family after family, men, women, and many children, those born in the desert and those who had walked all the way from Egypt. They crossed over in good order, helping each other, the good, the bad, the cruel, and the indifferent, the law-makers and the law-abiders" (p. 60).

In Hareven's novella, contrary to *Vayelekh*, there is no military context, no preparations for conquest and annihilation, and no miracles. Hareven is the miracle hater. When they entered the Land, the waters of the Jordan did not stand as a wall, the Children of Israel did not cross over on dry land, and the ark of the Lord and his Priests did not go before them. People just crossed the water and clambered onto the other shore. And when they came into the land, they tried to draw it all into themselves, through its colors, smells and sounds that were so different from those of the desert: "It was all so new, fresh and sparkling. Their senses swooned before the sudden shock of oleander and flame trees, bees and turtledoves, the strong odors and the barking of the dogs… There were butterflies . There were low-flying birds plummeting among the fruit trees. The people looked and looked, dumbstruck, and still they could not look enough. (p. 62).

Hareven believes that "Myths that are taken in their literal sense for too long, tend to lose their meaning or cease to be relevant, and in the end become contemptible" (*Mashiah o Knesset: Massot Uma'amarim*, pp. 108–109). In order to preserve them, they must be interpreted. An intellectual must engage in myth maintenance. "Constant interpretation and the duty of explication are the clear and natural province of the intellectual" (*ibid.* 109).

The approach that "there are seventy facets to the Torah" is well-established in Jewish tradition. In a Torah built layer upon layer, the reader is free to search and interpret. Exegetes throughout the ages, writers and philosophers, have read the Torah in keeping with their own needs and those of their age. Through processes of selection and change, acceptance and debate, they have formulated their values and beliefs and tried to disseminate them. Recognizing the plurality of voices in Scripture and its many debates leads to the understanding that the roots of the midrashic process lie in Scripture itself.

"What we need now is to humanize this myth, to understand it in human terms", wrote Hareven of the Sinaitic myth (*ibid.* 108)—something she accomplished in *The Miracle Hater*. She retold the story of the exodus from Egypt, from the moment of departure to the moment of arrival in the Land, taking a special interest in ordinary people who were, in the eyes of the authors of the Torah, a faceless mass known as "The Children of Israel". If the emphasis in the Torah is on the relationship between the People and God, the emphasis in Hareven's *Miracle Hater* is on relationships between people. From the way in which she treats the figure of Joshua we see the contempt she has for those who abuse power. Her compassion is reserved for the weak whose voices are not heard: the outcasts, the disfigured, the betrayed, the abandoned, the children and the lost.

With wisdom, wonderful, compact, musical language, and an inspired capacity for plot and character development, Hareven tells the story of the exodus from Egypt in her own unique way.

My deepest gratitude to the late Shulamith Hareven who, during her illness, gave generously of her time, listened attentively to my thoughts on her book and discussed them with me.

Moshe Sokolow

Ha'azinu – Give Ear Ye Heavens

"I Kill and I Make Alive": *Exile and Redemption in the Thought of Rabbi Solomon Ephraim Luntschitz*

See now that I, even I, am He, and there is no god with me; I kill, and I make alive; I have wounded, and I heal; and there is none that can deliver out of my hand (*Deuteronomy* 32:39).

And [Moses] prophesized in this song—which is a true and faithful witness against us—all the adversity that befalls us in this exile (Nahmanides, *Sefer Hage'ulah*).

In this chapter, I will present some of the elements that make up the thought of Rabbi Solomon Ephraim Luntschitz (RaShAL), author of the famous commentary *Keli Yakar* on the Pentateuch. RaShAL is considered one of the finest homileticists of the early Modern Era. His keen observations and penetrating homilies addressed social problems within the Jewish community, and he would appear to have paid a heavy price for his uncompromising moral integrity.

Although it would be anachronistic to label him a "Zionist," the subjects of exile and redemption are extremely prominent in his works, as compared to other rabbis of his time. Toward the end of the chapter we will see how RaShAL integrated the centrality of the Land of Israel and the importance of returning to it into his commentary on the portion of *Ha'azinu*.

Let us first take a look at his approach to exile and redemption, as reflected in the song of *Ha'azinu*. We intend to address two questions that are in fact four: (1) What is the cause of exile and its long duration; and (2) what is the nature of redemption and how can it be hastened? Before we attempt to answer these questions, we must first take a glimpse at the thought of RaShAL as it pertains to the matter at hand. The key to understanding RaShAL's homiletic philosophy is the concept of duality and his struggle against it. From "In the beginning..." to "... in the sight of all Israel" (the first and last verses of the Torah –tr.), he relates to the world and to all the forces within it, as to opposites in need of reconciliation and unification. Deeply familiar with the mythological mindset, RaShAL knew that the Torah was completely at odds with pagan dualism, and sought to provide his readers with the means to bridge the ostensible gaps and to put the world back on its unitary footing.

RaShAL was wont to say: "Make God sovereign over all the apparent opposites in the world which have led many to apostasy, to say that two opposites cannot possibly derive from a single source" (*Keli Yakar*, *Lev.* 2:13). The Torah does not deny the existence of chaos. On the contrary, it concedes from the very beginning that formlessness and void (*tohu vavohu*) are the state in which the world was before it took on its current semblance of order. The Torah's goal is to teach us how to resolve the apparent contradictions in creation, and how not to relate to its contrasts as to powers over which we have no control, thereby avoiding the responsibility of dealing with them. In his commentary on Genesis 38:18, RaShAL compares exile to the darkness of the primordial abyss, noting that just as the world passed—via creation—from darkness to light, so Israel are destined to pass from the darkness of oppression to the shining light of redemption.

By nature, man, too, is a "dual" being, comprising an earthly-brutish element ("dust of the ground") and a sublime-celestial element ("breath of life"). He has the ability however, through Torah, to overcome the disparity between them, and even cause them to work together. The divergence of these two elements and the subjugation of the sublime-celestial element to its earthly-brutish counterpart, turn back the process of creation and annul the intentions of the creator, or in the words of RaShAL: "Because the heavenly and the earthly are opposites, they require a medium to bind them together, and that is man, who is composed of both matter and form. And this fusion is effected through the Torah, for without Torah, man is like a beast, with no element of the heavenly" (*ibid. Deut.* 32:1).

To be more precise, RaShAL maintains that man comprises three elements: "Soul from heaven and body from earth, made clay by means of water." Earth (*eretz*), sea (*yam*) and heaven (*shamayim*), also form the acronym "*ish*" (*aleph-yod-shin*)—man. Elsewhere (*Olelot Efraim*

2,231), RaShAL teaches, using these same letters, that if one cancels the earthly in himself (*aleph*), the other two elements still form the word "*yesh*" (*yod-shin*)—is, exists. If however, one cancels the heavenly (shin), all that remains is "*i*" (*aleph-yod*)—null, nought. We thus see that RaShAL saw man as a microcosm.

In this worldview, the heavens and the earth in the song of *Ha'azinu* play a central role. According to the Rabbis of the Talmud and the Midrash, as cited by Rashi on *Deuteronomy* 32:1, heaven and earth are called as witnesses to the song's admonishments—specifically chosen for this task "because they are eternal." RaShAL in his commentary, repeats his previous explanation: "And the reason is that the existence of heaven and earth is contingent upon the Torah ... Therefore, one who engages in Torah-study establishes peace between the upper and lower retinues, that they might not oppose one another, for that which is between unites them (*Keli Yakar*, *Deut.* 32:1).

God made creation conditional upon acceptance of the Torah (*Shabbat* 88a: "Why is there an additional *heh* [in the word *ha-shishi* in Gen. 1:31]? To teach us that the Holy One, blessed be He, made a condition with all of creation, saying: If Israel accepts the Torah, you will continue to exist. And if not, I will return you to formlessness and void"). Therefore, in the very fact of their continued existence, heaven and earth attest to the success of the Jewish People in preserving their union, through Torah.

Four things bring about exile, according to RaShAL (*Olelot Efraim* 2,24 p. 55b): *Envy and discord*—of which he says: "And this evil quality of strife between us, not only did it cause the destruction of two temples by virtue of senseless hatred, but many other destructions and expulsions and devastations and tribulations have befallen the People of God for the lack of peace." Furthermore, RaShAL raises a question, which is especially poignant today: "How can God restore us to the Holy Land? If it [strife] was the cause of our exile, we can certainly not return until it is removed from our midst." *Adulation*—which he defines as an expression of the lack of peace and spiritual perfection. "And if so, [a group] among whose members there is no peace, certainly cannot reside in the Holy Land, as we have explained above." Elsewhere, he writes: "Even great men [i.e. rabbis] flatter the wicked, [thinking] that

they might, through them, achieve honor and positions of authority."
Pride: From the verse "The Lord reigneth; He is clothed in pride" (*Ps.*
93:1), RaShAL teaches that pride befits God alone, "And it is unseemly
that the raiment of the king should be worn by any other"—especially in the Holy Land, which is governed wholly by Providence. Of all
man's animal weaknesses, pride is of particular concern to RaShAL. It
is pride, he writes, that causes the rich to amass wealth and treat their
poor brethren with suspicion. And it is pride that causes parents to give
their children a poor education, unsuited to their developmental needs.
For example, RaShAL criticizes the prevailing curriculum of his day
which pointlessly began talmudic studies with the tractates of *Hulin* and
Eruvin, simply because it afforded parents the opportunity to boast. He
also criticized the *pilpul* method of study (an approach based on elaborate argumentation and subtle differentiation –tr.), which he saw as little
more than intellectual showmanship. Pride causes people to be selfish,
to ignore communal needs and to forget that they reside in exile. *Slander*: The Torah barred the spies from entering the Land of Israel "lest
they persist in their evil speech in the Holy Land."

Each of these four negative qualities however, has a positive counterpart, capable of repairing the damage they cause and hastening redemption. The counterpart of envy is *peace*; of adulation—*honesty*; of
pride—*humility*; of slander—*guarding one's tongue*. Elsewhere (*Olelot
Efraim* 2, 71), RaShAL draws a parallel between these four qualities
and the four things by virtue of which "our fathers were delivered from
Egypt" (according to *Exodus Rabbah*): they did not change their names,
mode of dress or language, and they refrained from evil speech.

In one of the autobiographical references scattered throughout his
works, RaShAL writes: "Here I, the least of my tribe, sit and wonder all
my days, and even at night my heart does not rest, the thoughts emerging urgently and fitfully. I wonder at this people—scattered, broken and
abandoned, over the face of the earth. Each focused on the task of earning a livelihood, and no one notices, no one seeks or asks, how long
these constant and incomprehensible tribulations will go on" (*Olelot
Efraim*, introduction to part 3).

He blames the exile itself and its duration on three groups. *The
wealthy*: RaShAL railed at the rich more than any other group within the

Jewish community. In a sermon on the Israelites' travels in the desert, he maintained that the standard of Dan was the last to break camp because the Danites were wealthy, "And they would travel last, for the acquisition of wealth is the least of all acquisitions, because it is replaceable, and there is nothing of it that man can carry to protect him from the heat of the Day to Come" (*Ir Giborim* 2, *Bamidbar*). Elsewhere, RaShAL explains the commandment to let nothing remain of the paschal lamb— and similarly, the manna—as a censure of materialism: "For such is the end of all money-gathering fools. In the end, they will be ruled over by maggots, and they will burn on the Day to Come ... For one who acquires many ephemeral goods is no better than a poor man in the next world, and one who has few such goods is not a whit the worse for it. On the contrary, he is better off—for the ease of the burden of sin he bears" (*Olelot Efraim* 2, *Noah*). According to RaShAL, wealth causes people to love exile and despair of salvation: "That is the wealthy of the land, whose rings are silver, and who have filled their sacks with as much silver as they can carry. And most of them live tranquilly and intermingle with the nations. And are far from seeking salvation, for they lack nothing and know nothing of man's travail." *The wicked*—of whom RaShAL writes: "They are vain and light fellows who follow their desires, killing sheep and slaying oxen, and [pursuing] other delights. And salvation is far from the wicked as well, for at that time the destruction of sinners and evildoers will become apparent, and why should they seek to hasten the day of their own misfortune?" (*ibid. Noah*). *The leaders*: Even RaShAL's colleagues, the rabbis and communal leaders, did not escape his censure, mainly for their refusal—due to their jealousy of one another—to join together "to repair the breaches of the generation." He thus held them responsible for delaying redemption. Regarding his custom of preaching on market days in the town of Lublin, he writes: "And there it was my wont to speak against kings; 'Who are the kings? The Rabbis' (based on *Gittin* 62a). And afflicted at the edge of the camp by rulers and outcasts alike, I shall not turn away for any, although I am persecuted because of this ... and have made many enemies" (*ibid.* intro.).

According to RaShAL (*ibid.* 234), the song of *Ha'azinu* presents three elements "that lie at the heart of all sin". *Arrogance and conceit*: A kind of insolent pretense that prevents man from regretting his actions and repenting from them, encouraging him to reject all admonitions. This can be seen in the verse "Do ye thus requite the Lord, O foolish people and unwise" (32:6), as he explains: "That sometimes observance can become a transgression and a stumbling-block ... and for this reason our penitence has not been accepted throughout ... the duration of this exile ... For every act of observance is a falsehood, performed not for the sake of heaven, the intention of most being to show themselves off before their peers, that they might be praised for their actions and their Torah" (*Orah Lahayim* 39,2). If this ailment is to be remedied, one must actively seek out reproof, as intimated in the following verse: "ask thy father, and he will declare unto thee, thine elders, and they will tell thee" (*ibid.* 7). *Treating sin lightly and denying its consequences*: This is reflected in the verse "Is corruption His? No; His children's is the blemish; a generation crooked and perverse" (*ibid.* 5). This includes the category of sins "that people commit habitually," such as tale-bearing, evil speech, vain oaths, mockery and levity (RaShAL also discusses this verse in his "Homily for the Days of Awe" [*Orah Lahayim* 77–78], where he explains that "the damage that man causes by his sins is ultimately to himself, not to God"). *Lustfulness*: This element comprises all desires in the world—the "gentile desires" (i.e. material desires) that confuse the mind. These are mentioned in the verse "He made him ride on the high places of the earth, and he did eat the fruitage of the field" (*ibid.* 13), and particularly the desire for wine, addressed in the following verse: "and of the blood of the grape thou drankest foaming wine." RaShAL charges wine "which comes from the grape" with being "the partner of Samael, who is Satan, who is the evil inclination." RaShAL notes that the letters of the Hebrew word for grape, *A-N-B*, immediately follow the letters *S-M-A* (as in Samael), in the alphabet. Elsewhere, he sharply condemns the widespread practice of drinking to inebriation on the holiday of Purim: "They drink and become inebriated until they can no longer tell the difference between cursed Haman and blessed Mordecai, until they empty their bodies of vomit and excrement, as one empties a barrel of refuse ... Is this what a day of celebration dedicated to God should be? From what source do they derive such despicable customs?" (*Olelot Efraim* 2,309).

It is worth noting the parallel between these three elements and the three groups upon whom RaShAL blames the exile: Lustfulness is the fault of the wealthy; treating sin lightly—of the wicked; arrogance—of the leaders.

Redemption, according to RaShAL—in keeping with his general, duality-oriented approach—is twofold: "Redemption of the body from subjugation and adversity, and the redemption of the soul in matters of the spirit" (*Keli Yakar* Gen. 35:10). These two aspects of redemption, the national-material and the spiritual-religious, were both realized in the exodus from Egypt, which serves as a paradigm for the final redemption. When Moses was sent to tell the Israelites of their redemption, God gave him "the four redemptive expressions" (*Ex.* 6:6–8). RaShAL associates each of these expressions with a spiritual or material aspect of slavery—corresponding to the four expressions used in the "Covenant of the Pieces" (Gen. 15:13): 1) "I will bring you out from under the burdens of the Egyptians" addresses their affliction ("and they shall afflict them"); 2) "I will deliver you from their bondage" addresses their servitude ("and shall serve them"); 3) "I will redeem you with an outstretched arm" addresses their state of foreignness ("thy seed shall be a stranger"); 4) "I will take you … and I will be to you a God" addresses their distance from God ("in a land that is not theirs").

To this he adds: "And that is why it was decreed that we should drink four cups on Passover, corresponding to our salvation from these four ills." RaShAL also explains the thirty-year discrepancy between the prophecy ("four hundred years") and its fulfillment ("And it came to pass at the end of four hundred thirty years"), as follows: "And I would say that they were given these additional thirty years because there were many who did not want to leave Egypt … For God said to Abraham, 'thy seed shall be a stranger'—a stranger and not an inhabitant, and in vain they sought to be inhabitants of the land, never to depart" (compare *Keli Yakar* on Gen. 47:28 [157a]).

In his remarks on the relationship between the name "Jacob" and the name "Israel" RaShAL identifies three distinct redemptions—Egypt, Babylon and the redemption that is yet to come—stressing the need to mend our ways, in order to hasten redemption.

For at the time of the redemption from Egypt, their merit was not sufficient to be taken out 'with a high hand', and they needed to go by subterfuge and deceit ["And it was told ... that the people had fled"]... And in Babylon, theirs was not a complete redemption but they were merely taken cognizance of ["flee ye from the Chaldeans"] ... At the time of the final redemption, however, after all sin will have been completely purified by the length of this exile, their merits will suffice to go out with a high hand—on the plain [*mishor*—symbolized by the name 'Israel'] and not by subterfuge [*okba* -'Jacob'] and not in haste (*ibid.* Gen. 35:10).

The return to the Land of Israel is indeed the remedy for exile and it enables Israel to exist both nationally and religiously. In his commentary on the covenant forged in the plains of Moab, he explains: "'If any of thine that are dispersed be in the uttermost parts of heaven'—For when Israel reside among the nations, they are dispersed from the commandments. 'From thence will the Lord thy God gather thee'—This is the ingathering of the exiles. 'And from thence will He fetch thee'— To him, to help you observe the commandments" (*ibid. Deut.* 30:1). RaShAL finds intimations of this twofold redemption in the song of *Ha'azinu* as well: "And I will offer some further explanation of the matter of redemption intimated in these verses, and that is the meaning of 'See now that I, even I, am He, and there is no god with me; I kill, and I make alive; I have wounded, and I heal; and there is none that can deliver out of my hand' (*Deut.* 32:39)". He explains the repetition of the word "I" (*ani*)—which is reminiscent of the repetition "I, even I, am He that comforteth " (*Is.* 51:12), and also "Comfort ye, comfort ye my people" (*ibid.* 40:1)—as a clear reference to the redemption that is to come, which "will be twofold: physical redemption and spiritual redemption. Physical, that is subjugation to the nations; and spiritual that is subjugation to the evil inclination, which will be eliminated at that time." Let us conclude with RaShAL's final words on *Ha'azinu*:

And this is the meaning of the Rabbis' assertion that we learn the principle of resurrection from this verse—that is redemption, for in exile we are like the dead. And at the time of redemption, God will make us live etc. For he has already resurrected us from the exiles of Egypt and Babylon, but these redemptions were not eternal. And on the third day (based on *Hosea* 6:2), which is a reference to the third redemption, he will make us live for all eternity before him.

Naftali Rothenberg

Vezot Haberakhah – And This is the Blessing

*The King, Heads of the People and the Tribes of Israel: Equality before the Law in the "**Meshekh Hokhmah**" – Commentary by Rabbi Meir Simhah Hakohen of Dvinsk*

Moses commanded us the Torah, an inheritance of the congregation of Jacob. And there was a king in Jeshurun, when the heads of the people were gathered, all the tribes of Israel together (*Deuteronomy* 33:4–5).

In *Vezot Haberakhah*, a leader takes leave of his people. Some leaders carefully plan their departure from office in such a fashion as to highlight their achievements on behalf of the people, their contribution to the common good, and their place in history. As a leader who had completed his mission, Moses could have done the same. He liberated his people from slavery in Egypt, brought them before Mount Sinai to receive the Torah, raised a new generation of free people and led them to the threshold of the Land of Israel. And that is where God informed him that he would have to step down (32:52—the final verse of the portion of *Ha'azinu*): "For thou shalt see the land afar off; but thou shalt not go thither into the land which I give the children of Israel". This too is a boon to a visionary leader: the opportunity to see his goal accomplished, though he himself may not be a direct participant.

In a culture that exalts personal fulfillment, and in which the masses are more interested in a leader's "personal story" than in her or his real accomplishments, Moses' fate is seen as a terrible tragedy. Moses however, gives no thought to himself, but turns to his final task: "And this is the blessing wherewith Moses the man of God blessed the children of Israel before his death" (33:1). The leader departs with a blessing—not one, but many blessings: to the Children of Israel as a whole and to each and every individual tribe. The blessing begins with a general message, setting forth that which is common to all of Israel—the Torah given by

God at Sinai—and the blessings of Torah and faith are addressed to the entire people. At this point, I would like to cite Rabbi Meir Simhah of Dvinsk—author of *Meshekh Hokhmah*—on the verse that prefaces this chapter:

> For the Torah makes no distinction between great or small, and even Moses was bound by all of the prohibitions and punishments, just like anyone of Israel; and the lofty merit of a soul—even one that sojourned in the spiritual heavens, like Moses—cannot abrogate a single personal precept. As it is written: "Moses commanded us the Torah, an inheritance", that is a perpetual inheritance, without deviation, God forbid; "the congregation of Jacob", that is for the entire community without distinction. And [the verse] states that Moses' status was that of a king in Jeshurun, and just as a king must observe all of the Torah, turning not from a precept to the right hand or to the left, so was Moses (*Meshekh Hokhmah, Vezot Haberakhah*).

In his interpretation, Rabbi Meir Simhah establishes three principles: the perpetuity of the laws of the Torah; equality before the law; and the equal obligation of a king (Moses) toward the law. The word *morashah* ("inheritance") comes to emphasize the fact that the Torah was given to the Jewish People as a perpetual inheritance for future generations, from which stems the perpetuity of its laws; the expression *kehilat ya'akov* ("congregation of Jacob") comes to teach the principle of equality of all Jews before the law; and the verse "And there was a king in Jeshurun, when the heads of the people were gathered"—in asserting that the king is bound by the law like any other member of the people, comes to intensify the message of equality before the law. Even Moses, who was like a king, was not permitted to deviate from the law, and so—all subsequent kings and rulers.

Those who assert the equality of all human beings before the law, base their position on reason and morality. This is not the point of departure of the *Meshekh Hokhmah*, who accepts the rational and moral argument, but does not consider it a sufficient basis. Others cite convention: such is the practice in the tribe or people, that the law is the same for everyone, or that the accepted norm in a given society is that even its strongest members, and even its rulers—who wield power—are subject to the law. The rational and moral arguments in favor of equality, as well as those based on claims that "such is our custom" and "so it should be", are problematic inasmuch as they rely upon an insufficient and limited source of authority that can be undermined by those in positions of power.

The fundamental question is whether our obligation to observe the precepts of the Law is based upon the claim that our forefathers Abraham, Isaac and Jacob accepted the laws of the Torah in an egalitarian fashion, and that this practice has been observed by the Jewish People since ancient times. According to the Midrash, the Patriarchs voluntarily observed all of the precepts of the Torah, although they had not been commanded to do so. Nonetheless, this is not the reason that we are required to observe the precepts. We do not circumcise our sons because it is an ancient custom first established by our father Abraham, but because the Torah given to Moses at Sinai, and through him to the entire Jewish People, commands us to do so. Equality before the law thus derives from a religious principle that affords the law complete and independent primacy: the giving of the Torah at Mount Sinai by divine revelation to Moses, witnessed by all of Israel. This principle lends special status to the laws of the Torah, to which nothing further may be added, even by the prophets, as asserted by the Midrash (*Sifra, Behukotai* 5,13): "'These are the commandments'—henceforth a prophet may introduce no innovation". Rabbi Meir Simhah adopts the view of Maimonides, as set forth in his *Introduction to the Mishnah* and in his halakhic works:

> It is clearly and explicitly stated in the Torah that it is a commandment that stands for ever and all eternity and cannot be changed or diminished from or added to, as it is written "All this word which I command you, that shall ye observe to do; thou shalt not add thereto, nor diminish from it". And it is written "but the things that are revealed belong unto us and to our children for ever, that we may do all the words of this law"—teaching us that we are commanded to observe all of the words of the Torah for all eternity. And so: "It shall be a perpetual statute throughout your generations", and "It is not in heaven"—teach-

ing us that henceforth a prophet may introduce no innovation. And therefore, if anyone should come—whether of Israel or the nations—and perform a sign or wonder, and say that God has sent him to add a precept or diminish one or interpret one of the precepts in a way that we had not heard from Moses, or say that the precepts given to Israel are not eternal and for all generations, but precepts for a time, he is a false prophet, for he has come to deny the prophecy of Moses, and he must be put to death by strangling, for deliberately speaking in God's name that which he was not commanded. For the Holy One, blessed be He commanded Moses that these precepts belong unto us and to our children for ever, and God is not a man, that He should lie (Maimonides, *Hilkhot Yesodei Hatorah* 9,1).

The perpetuity of the law, of "a commandment that stands for ever and all eternity", makes the absence of change the first measure of true prophecy and a true prophet. No one is above the law, not even a prophet, who may not add to or diminish from it—because he himself is bound by its precepts and their absolute nature. This subjection to the law is a primary expression of—and necessary condition for—the truth of a prophet's words, and any subversion of this obligation automatically invalidates the prophecy. The *Meshekh Hokhmah* expresses this view, based on a verse in *Vezot Haberakhah*:

Prior to the giving of the Torah, if a prophet came offering signs and wonders, it was possible to entertain doubt as to whom one should give greater credence? Since the giving of the Torah however, all of the signs and all of the prophets in the world cannot detract a single element from our sacred religion. And this is the meaning of "Moses commanded us the Torah, an inheritance of the congregation of Jacob": that the commandments were no longer as they were prior to the giving of the Torah, when they could easily be revoked, as they were not yet permanent.

In other words, were the law to derive its force from the practices of the patriarchs, and a prophet were to come later and show signs and wonders and add to or detract from it, there would be no reason to question his authority. For why would he have any less authority than the patriarchs? The latter accepted the law out of a sense of personal recognition and on the strength of their prophecy; and so a later prophet would attempt to change the law, add to or detract from it, on the strength of his prophecy and the depth of his recognition. Since however, subjection to the law does not derive from convention—that is Jewish practice since the time of the patriarchs—but from the giving of the Torah, a prophet may no longer change the law. Thus it is written: "Moses commanded us the Torah, an inheritance of the congregation of Jacob"—immutable, inherited as it was given.

"An inheritance of the congregation of Jacob" has a further meaning, inasmuch as it establishes the absolute nature of the law and its equal application to all. The Torah was given to the People of Israel at Mount Sinai, in a public act, thereby removing it from the realm of the individual, where it had been before Sinai, when it was observed by the Patriarchs and others. The *Meshekh Hokhmah* illustrates this point with the story of Moses' killing of an Egyptian whom he had seen strike a Hebrew. Moses took the law into his own hands when he saw the way in which the Egyptian was treating one of his brethren, and endangered his own life in order to punish him. In the absence of a binding legal framework, Moses decides to risk his life in order to save that of a member of his people. Before the giving of the Torah, Rabbi Meir Simhah stresses, he was permitted to take this responsibility upon himself. Following the giving of the Torah however, there is law and justice, and no one can appoint himself judge and executioner or, above all, endanger his own life by taking such an initiative, outside the framework of a judicial system.

We thus learn that a precondition for equality before the law is the existence of an independent judicial system. The subjection of the king or others who wield power, to the law is meaningless if the judicial system does not act independently. The judges must represent the law, not the king. Thus, if a ruler or ruling class can revoke its own subjection to the law, the principle of equality remains an empty husk. So we find in the Mishnah: "The king may neither judge nor be judged, testify nor be testified against" (Sanhedrin 2, 2).

In the context of this far-reaching pronouncement, the Gemara (*BT* Sanhedrin 19a) distinguishes between two types of kings: those who accept the authority of the law and allow themselves and their transgressions to be judged by it; and those who use their power to escape justice and whom the court is powerless to compel. The former may also judge others, while it is with regard to the latter that the Mishnah rules that "The king may neither judge nor be judged, testify nor be testified against".

A king of the House of David would judge the people and would be judged himself, if he had transgressed. This is also supported by the words of Jeremiah (*Jer.* 21:12): "O house of David, thus saith the Lord: Execute justice in the morning, and deliver the spoiled out of the hand of the oppressor, lest my fury go forth like fire, and burn that none can quench it, because of the evil of your doings". That is because the kings of the House of David accepted the authority of the judicial system to judge them for their transgressions, as it is written (*Zephaniah* 2:1): "*Hitkosheshu vekoshu*—Gather yourselves together, yea, gather together". The *amora* Resh Lakish explained: "*Hitkosheshu vekoshu*—first correct thyself, then correct others" (playing on the similarity between the Hebrew verbs *kashesh* and *kashet* –tr.). In order to be able to judge others, one must first be subject to law and justice, setting a personal example and not placing oneself above the law.

Moses thus chooses to open his series of blessings to the Children of Israel with the principle that all, including the king (i.e. Moses himself) are equal before the law: "Moses commanded us the Torah, an inheritance of the congregation of Jacob. And there was a king in Jeshurun, when the heads of the people were gathered, all the tribes of Israel together" (*Deut.* 33:4–5). Only then does he proceed to the specific blessings to each and every tribe, as if saying that the fulfillment of the individual blessings is contingent upon the realization of the general blessing—that the king will be subject to all of the precepts of the Torah, like any member of the Congregation of Jacob. If not, the harmony of "all the tribes of Israel together" will be upset, and the blessings of the respective tribes will be unfulfillable. The principle of equality before the law henceforth becomes the responsibility of Jewish kings and rulers. If they accept the authority of the law, blessings will be conferred upon Israel: "when the heads of the people were gathered, all the tribes of Israel together". Such a state of affairs however, is by no means assured. There will be kings and rulers who will consider themselves above the law, and such negative behavior on their part will have far-reaching ramifications, undermining appropriate conduct in society as a whole.

The Gemara cited above (*ibid*. 19a–b) ascribes the Mishnah's ruling—that a king may not judge or be judged—to an incident in which a slave of King Yannai (Alexander Jannaeus) killed a man. Since a slave-owner is responsible for the actions of his slave, the Torah established that the *ha'ada'ah* (deposition) in the case of a crime committed by a slave must be conducted in the presence of his owner. The president of the court, Shimon ben Shetah, summoned King Janai together with his slave. Janai complied and sat before the court:

> Shimon ben Shetah said to him: King Yannai, stand on your feet and you will be testified against, and it is not before us that you stand but before He who spoke and the world came into being that you stand, as it is written (*Deut.* 19:17): "Then both the men, between whom the controversy is, shall stand before the Lord". He [King Yannai] said to him [Shimon ben Shetah]: "Not at your behest, but at that of your colleagues" [whom he knew—as Sadducees who owed their appointment to the Sanhedrin to him—would not dare to challenge him]. He [Shimon ben Shetah] looked to his right, and they turned their gaze to the ground; looked to his left, and they turned their gaze to the ground. Shimon ben Shetah said to them: "Are you engrossed in thought? May the master of thought exact retribution from you. Instantly, the angel Gabriel came and struck them to the ground, dead. It was then established that: A King may neither judge nor be judged, testify nor be testified against".

The Mishnah thus tries to contend with improper behavior on the part of a king, by excluding such a king from the judicial system. This approach, which affords rulers special privileges, stems from the desire to preserve the authority of the judicial system—at least as far as those who cannot undermine its authority are concerned, i.e. the general public. The special privileges and immunity granted to those in power, that derive from this approach are not limited to totalitarian or semi-totalitarian regimes, past and present, but can also be found in today's democratic states. Officials at various levels enjoy special privileges: from immunity and its inherent inequality, through complex hearings prior to indictment—enabling those in power to escape prosecution—to the nonapplication of certain laws to a president or other leaders.

Rabbi Meir Simhah of Dvinsk did not believe in the long term ability of a society to exist in strength and health, while maintaining two parallel standards of justice: one for kings and men of power, and another for the rest of the public. Real equality before the law can only be founded upon belief in the divine origin of the Torah: "The Lord came from Sinai". Moses asserts that the authority of the law does not derive from his own "kingship"; although "Moses commanded us the Torah", he received it from "The Lord [who] came from Sinai ... at His right hand was a fiery law unto them". This Torah is therefore "an inheritance of the congregation of Jacob". As the Mishnah in *Avot* (1:1) states: "Moses received the Torah at Sinai and passed it on ..."—he is receiver and conveyor, himself subject to the law and its minutiae, without immunity or special privileges of any kind.

There is a clear discrepancy between the *Meshekh Hokhmah*'s interpretation, and the pragmatic position taken by the Mishnah in Sanhedrin. Moses establishes a moral ideal to which we must aspire, and every monarch, president or leader is judged by the extent to which she or he approaches that ideal. According to the Torah, it is personally incumbent upon every Jewish king to write a Torah scroll:

> And it shall be, when he sitteth upon the throne of his kingdom, that he shall write him a copy of this law in a book, out of that which is before the priests the Levites. And it shall be with him, and he shall read therein all the days of his life; that he may learn to fear the Lord his God, to keep all the words of this law and these statutes, to do them; that his heart be not lifted up above his brethren, and that he turn not aside from the commandment, to the right hand, or to the left; to the end that he may prolong his days in his kingdom, he and his children, in the midst of Israel (*Deut.* 17:18–20).

This precept clearly and explicitly reflects the king's subjection to the law, and its purpose is to provide him with a means by which he may achieve the principle of equality before the law: constant Torah study. The Sages of the Mishnah explained as follows: "And he shall write a Torah scroll in his own name. When he goes out to war—he shall take it with him; when he sits in judgment—it shall be with him; when he takes his meals—it shall be before him" (*Sanhedrin* 2,4)".

If, during the course of his royal duties, a king begins to believe that he is entitled to special privileges, his reading of the Torah scroll will remind him at all times that he—like all of Israel—is fully bound by the laws of the Torah. If he reads the Torah all the days of his life, he will learn fear of Heaven and observance of the law. He will also learn "that his heart be not lifted up above his brethren"; that he is accorded no special privileges with regard to the precepts of the Torah. If he conducts himself in this fashion, he will "prolong his days in his kingdom, he and his children, in the midst of Israel". In other words, the promise that his reign will endure is accompanied by a further message: in the eyes of the law, he is "in the midst of Israel", as one of the people. This is how the *Meshekh Hokhmah* interprets the verse "And there was a king in Jeshurun, when the heads of the people were gathered—all the tribes of Israel together"—all are equal before the law.

Biographies

Isaac Abravanel
(*Vayigash*)
Castile, 1437—Venice, 1508. Leader of Portuguese and Spanish Jewry until the Expulsion, Renaissance political philosopher and biblical exegete, treasurer to the king of Portugal, advisor to the king of Castile and, following the Expulsion, advisor to the rulers of Naples and Venice. He wrote many books, including a commentary on Maimonides' *Guide for the Perplexed*. His commentary on the Torah is written almost entirely in the spirit of neo-Platonic philosophy. In his messianic works, he sought to comfort the Conversos and the Jews expelled from Spain and Portugal.

Shmuel Yosef Agnon
(*Terumah*)
Galicia, 1888—Jerusalem, 1970. One of the new Hebrew literature's greatest story-tellers, winner of the Nobel, Bialik and the Israel prizes. He emigrated to Palestine in 1908, left for Germany in 1913 and returned to Palestine in 1924, settling in Jerusalem. Agnon's roots lay both in the "Science of Judaism" and in German literary circles. In his works, he describes the social milieus of Galicia, Germany, Jaffa and Jerusalem. His unique style was greatly influenced by traditional Jewish sources, particularly the aggadic literature and popular Hassidic tales. He treats a wide variety of subjects and presents a complex and multi-faceted Weltanschauung. His works have been the subject of numerous studies in Israel and abroad, most of which discern a bipolarity, whereby earlier generations and their values are cast in an ironic light, while his own generation is examined in light of traditional Jewish values.

Yitzhak Meir Alter—"*Hidushei HaRim*"
(*Hukat*)
Poland, 1799–1866. Founder of the Hassidic Dynasty of Ger. Born to a rabbinical family descendent from Rabbi Meir (Maharam) of Rothenburg. Known at a young age as the "*ilui* (prodigy) of Warsaw", he was

sought as a student by all the great rabbis of Poland. At a certain point, he joined the Hassidic court of Peshischa (Przysucha), which emphasized values of scholarship and independent thought. He went on to become a "disciple-companion" of Rabbi Menahem Mendel of Kotsk, who had radicalized the traditions of Peshischa, establishing truth, determination and courage of spirit as the basic principles of Hassidism. When the Rabbi of Kotsk shut himself up in his room, Rabbi Yitzhak Meir became the group's undisputed leader, establishing his court in the town of Ger (Góra Kalwaria) and attracting of thousands of new adherents to the way of Kotsk.

Elia Benamozegh
(*Lekh-lekha*)

Leghorn, 1822–1900. Born to parents of Moroccan origin. He served as rabbi and preacher in Leghorn, Italy and taught theology at the city's rabbinical seminary. He wrote extensively in Hebrew, Italian and French. In his work, he sought to demonstrate the similarities between Judaism and other religions. His main assertion was that the Torah spread throughout the ancient world, leaving traces in the religions and mythologies of many different peoples. His commentary on the Torah reflects this approach, as well as a thorough knowledge of archaeology, anthropology, history and philology. His best-known work is *Israël et l'humanité*.

Ber Borochov
(*Ki Tissa*)

Russia, 1881–1918. The first theoretician of Socialist Zionism and one of the founders of the Po'alei Zion Party. He received a general, Russian education, and taught himself European languages, philosophy, sociology and economics. His philosophical efforts were, for the most part, devoted to providing Zionism with a Marxist basis. He ardently supported Po'alei Zion's participation in the World Zionist Organization. Borochov was also leading expert on the Yiddish language, publishing a comprehensive study of its linguistic roots, and advocating the standardization of Yiddish orthography.

Martin Buber

(*Beshalah, Mishpatim*)

Vienna, 1878—Jerusalem, 1965. A leader of German Jewry until 1938, at which time he emigrated to Palestine. Together with Franz Rosenzweig, he translated the Bible into German. He edited various Jewish periodicals, wrote books on Hassidism and his famous *Ich und Du*, in which he laid the foundation for his dialogical approach to relations between man and man, and between man and God. He was a leading member of Brit Shalom and advocated the establishment of a bi-national state in Palestine. In 1958, he was awarded the Israel Prize. His hermeneutic approach to the Bible in the book *Moses: The Revelation and the Covenant* is that one must "listen to God's voice as it emanates from Scripture" and conduct a "dialogue" with that voice.

Hermann Cohen

(*Ki Tavo*)

Germany, 1842–1918. German Jewish philosopher. He attended the rabbinical seminary in Breslau, where his teachers included Zacharias Frankel and Graetz. He studied philosophy at the universities of Breslau and Berlin, and was subsequently appointed professor ordinarius at the University of Marburg. He is known as one of the founders of the Neo-Kantian "Marburg School". During his tenure at the Hochschule für die Wissenschaft des Judentums in Berlin, Cohen devoted most of his efforts to the field of Jewish thought. He developed Kantian theory in a unilateral direction, regarding all consciousness as *a priori*. In his Jewish thought, he attempted to combine ethics, religion and the idea of the Divine. Cohen rejected Zionism, and engaged in a famous dispute with Martin Buber on the subject.

Yitzhak Danziger

(*Noah*)

Berlin, 1916—Tel-Aviv, 1979. Painter and sculptor. He emigrated to Palestine in 1923, where he studied under Ze'ev Ben-Zvi, attended London University's School of Fine Arts, and eventually became a professor of architecture. He taught art in Haifa and Tel-Aviv and was awarded the Dizengoff Prize in 1945/46. Danziger settled in Tel-Aviv in 1929.

His sculpture *Nimrod* became a symbol of the Canaanite Movement in the 1940s. He died in a traffic accident in 1979.

Eliyahu Eliezer Dessler

(*Vayetze*)

Lithuania 1892—Bnei-Brak, 1954. One of the most influential voices in the 20th century Lithuanian *Musar* movement. He served as a rabbi in London, and founded the Orthodox community at Gateshead. In 1948 he accepted the position of *mashgiah ruhani* (spiritual supervisor/mentor) at the Yeshivah of Ponevezh, in Bnei-Brak, and went on to develop a unique ethical-intellectual philosophy. He was greatly influenced by kabbalistic and Hassidic thought—particularly that of Chabad-Lubavitch—as well as modern philosophy. His writings and lectures were published in the *Mikhtav Me'eliyahu* series.

Sigmund Freud

(*Shemot*)

Moravia, 1856—London, 1939. Austrian Jewish psychiatrist, father of psychoanalysis and one of the greatest thinkers of the 20th century. He believed that the root of psychological disorders lay in the repression of desire and sexual experiences, both real and imagined. In his book, *The Interpretation of Dreams*, published in 1899, he analyzed the content of dreams in terms of experiences stemming from unconscious conflict between the three constituents of the mind: the id, the ego, and the superego.

Erich Fromm

(*Bamidbar*)

Germany, 1900—U.S., 1980. Psychoanalyst, social philosopher and writer. Fromm completed his studies in psychology, sociology and philosophy at Heidelberg, Munich and the Psychoanalytic Institute of Berlin. In 1933, he fled to the United States. He taught at many different universities, holding positions at the University of Michigan's Psychiatric Institute, the medical school of the National Autonomous University of Mexico (UNAM), and elsewhere. His many published works on society and psychology include: *The Sane Society, Forgotten Language,*

The Crisis of Psychoanalysis, You Shall Be as Gods, Psychoanalysis and Zen Buddhism, The Art of Loving and *To Have or to Be.*

Gersonides, see Levi ben Gershom

Aaron David Gordon
(*Hayei Sarah, Naso, Matot*)
Podolia, 1856—Deganyah, 1922. Scion of an important, scholarly family. As a young man, Gordon studied extensively on his own. He married at the age of 18, and was an ardent supporter of the Hovevei Zion movement. Sadly, he suffered the loss of five of his seven children. He worked, unenthusiastically, as an estate clerk for 23 years, suffering from the lack of direct contact with nature. To compensate for this emotional frustration, he dedicated himself to the education of youth in his town. Upon the death of his parents, he fulfilled his Zionist aspirations, settling in Palestine in 1904, at the age of 48. In Palestine, he worked as a manual laborer—no easy task for him—with various pioneer groups. He came to be seen as a model figure, a philosopher in the spirit of the Bible and the Rabbinic teachings, a "repairer of the world"—through the perfection the individual soul, out of a sense of admiration for nature, simplicity, agricultural labor, and the belief that man's intrinsic worth outweighs all considerations of social and political standing.

Israel Meir Hakohen of Radun—"*Hafetz Hayim*"
(*Metzora, Nitzavim*)
Russia 1839–1933. One of the greatest rabbis of Eastern Europe in the generation immediately preceding the Holocaust, famed for his piety. He studied at the yeshivot of Vilna and taught for a time in the town of Vasilishok in the Vilna district. In 1869, he founded a yeshivah in the town of Radun, and four years later, published his first book—*Hafetz Hayim*—on the laws of evil speech. In 1876 he published the ethico-philosophical context of these laws, in a work entitled *Shemirat Ha-lashon*. He was greatly concerned with the spiritual state of the Jewish people and devoted most of his life to writing works of guidance and homiletics for the Jewish masses. His most important halakhic work was the *Mishnah Berurah*, on the *Orah Hayim* section of Joseph Karo's

Shulhan Arukh. He was known for his remarkable humility and rigorous observance of the laws of speech. Later in life, he became the spiritual leader of the Eastern European Agudat Yisrael Movement, founded in 1912.

Meir Simha Hakohen of Dvinsk
(*Vezot Haberakhah*)
Lithuania, 1843–1926. Preeminent Lithuanian rabbi of the early 20th century, halakhic authority and biblical exegete. In his youth, he studied at Eishishok and Bialystok, and in 1888 was appointed rabbi of Dvinsk; a position he held for nearly forty years. Evidence of his dedication can be found in his refusal to abandon the community during the First World War. His *Or Sameah* on Maimonides is considered a classic of Torah literature. His highly original thought is clearly reflected in his commentary on the Torah, *Meshekh Hokhmah*.

Shulamith Hareven
(*Vayelekh*)
Warsaw, 1931—Jerusalem, 2003. Author and essayist, one of the most prominent Hebrew writers of the second half of the 20th century. Hareven (Riftin), who was born to a left-wing Zionist family, emigrated to Palestine in 1940 and attended school in Jerusalem. At the age of 17, she joined the Haganah and served as a medic in Israel's War of Independence. She was one of the founders of Israel Army Radio and, during the War of Attrition, warned against the erosion of Israel's moral fiber. She wrote reviews, poems, stories and novellas, and translated many books and plays. Her best-known works include *Thirst: The Desert Trilogy* and *City of Many Days*. Her works have been translated in to 21 languages and have received glowing reviews in the world's leading newspapers. In 2002, she published her literary autobiography: *Yamim Rabim: Otobiografiyah* (Many Days: An Autobiography).

Abraham Joshua Heschel
(*Behukotai*)
Poland, 1907—U.S., 1972. One of the greatest Jewish theologians of the 20th century. A scion of pre-eminent Polish Hassidic families on both

his father's and his mother's side, he received a traditional yeshivah education, and was ordained to the rabbinate. He later moved to Berlin, where he earned a doctoral degree. He also attended the Hochschule für die Wissenschaft des Judentums, where he received liberal rabbinical ordination, and later taught Talmud. His first position in the United States was at the Reform Movement's Hebrew Union College in Cincinnati. He then joined the faculty at Conservative Judaism's Jewish Theological Seminary, where he taught Jewish ethics and Kabbalah.

Samson Raphael Hirsch
(*Va'ethanan*)
Hamburg, 1801—Frankfurt am Main, 1888. Rabbi, author, leader and philosopher of Orthodox Judaism in Germany, founder of the "*Torah im Derekh Eretz*" movement. He studied classical languages, history and philosophy at the University of Bonn. In 1830 he was appointed rabbi of Oldenburg, where he remained for eleven years. It was during this time that he wrote his most influential works: *Nineteen Letters on Judaism* and *Horeb*. In 1841 he was elected rabbi in Hanover, and fought for equality for the Jews of Austria and Moravia. In 1851 he was appointed rabbi of the Adath Jeschurun community in Frankfurt am Main, a position he held for thirty-seven years. In Frankfurt, he founded his elementary, middle and high school for girls and boys, based on his educational approach of *Torah im Derekh Eretz*—Torah with secular studies. He opposed Reform, but also opposed the old haredi approach. His views became the prototype for Neo-Orthodoxy, in Germany—from his time and until the Holocaust, and in its various forms throughout the world today.

Yitzhak Hutner
(*Vayehi, Beha'alotekha*)
Warsaw, 1906—Jerusalem, 1980. Haredi rabbi and intellectual. The variety of places in which he studied and taught attest to his broad horizons and multifaceted personality. He attended the yeshivot of Hevron and Slobodka, but also studied the sciences and was an autodidact in a wide variety of fields. He began his teaching career at Mesivta Yeshiva Rabbi Chaim Berlin in New York, later heading the yeshivah's post-high school Kollel Gur Aryeh. His writings include works of Halakhah

and Jewish thought—which he termed "the laws of opinions as the duties of the heart"—as well as a scholarly edition of Hillel ben Eliakim's commentary on *Midrash Sifra*.

Hans Jonas
(*Devarim*)
Germany, 1903—U.S., 1993. Jonas studied philosophy and comparative religion with Martin Heidegger and Protestant theologian Rudolf Bultmann, specializing in Gnosticism, early Christianity and phenomenology. In the 1930s he went to Palestine, where he attended the Hebrew University of Jerusalem. During the Second World War, he served in the British army, and later in the Israel Defense Forces. In 1951, he emigrated to Canada and then the United States. His work is imbued with a deep sense of respect for freedom and the value of human life, and addresses a variety of topics: from religious thought to the philosophy of biology. He placed particular emphasis on the decline of western culture and the acute need to revive humanism. His magnum opus, *The Imperative of Responsibility*—which focuses on man's ethical needs in a technological age—sold 200,000 copies worldwide, and exerted a considerable influence on Germany's green movements.

Mordecai M. Kaplan
(*Vayakhel*)
Lithuania, 1881—U.S., 1983. Philosopher, founder of the Jewish Reconstructionist Movement. He studied at the Jewish Theological Seminary in New York, where he received ordination and subsequently taught for over fifty years. At the heart of his philosophy lies the concept of "Judaism as a Civilization", which transcends national and territorial boundaries, and which—like all civilizations—adapts itself to time and place. The Jewish religion is the highest expression of the Jewish cultural genius, the essence of which is the perfection of human conduct and moral values. As such however, it does not negate the other, secular components of culture, as part of the overall experience of Jewish spirituality.

Abraham Isaiah Karelitz—"*Hazon Ish*"
(*Behar*)

Kosava, Lithuania, 1878—Bnei-Brak, 1953. One of the 20th century's pre-eminent halakhic authorities and a leading figure in the development of *haredi* Judaism in Israel. The *Hazon Ish* never studied in a yeshivah nor was he an ordained rabbi. Nevertheless, he devoted his life to Torah study and the writing of novellae, attaining mastery over the entire body of the talmudic literature. He arrived in Palestine in 1933, settling in the town of Bnei-Brak, where he published prolifically and gained increasing recognition as a halakhic authority. His stringent rulings regarding the Sabbatical (*shemitah*) year, the application of ancient values to modern circumstances, and the use of electricity on the Sabbath, have become landmarks of halakhic literature. Following the establishment of the State of Israel he was considered the leading representative of rabbinical authority in public life. He encouraged the *haredi* public to devote all of its talents and energies to rebuilding the "Torah world" destroyed in the Holocaust, in Israel.

Joseph Ibn Kaspi
(*Shoftim*)

Provence, 1280–1340. Philosopher, exegete, and grammarian. Ibn Kaspi's literary efforts were devoted, for the most part, to the application of the Maimonidean approach, whereby the true meaning of Scripture corresponds to the conclusions of philosophical inquiry. To this end, he wrote more than 20 books on the subjects of language, logic, ethics, theology and biblical exegesis. His work, well-written and often witty, is marked by a somewhat radical theology. This approach was sharply criticized by the sages of his generation, including the poet Kalonymus ben Kalonymus, who accused him of irreverence. His works include replies to his detractors.

Søren Kierkegaard
(*Vayera*)

Denmark, 1813–1855. Although he led a completely uneventful life, his writings attest to a stormy internal existence. He is considered the father of existentialism, particularly religious existentialism. In one of the most famous episodes of his life, he renounced his engagement to the only woman he ever loved, Regine Olsen. This renunciation is associated with the value of "perpetual renunciation" that is, in Kierkegaard's opinion, a prerequisite for authenticity. His complex relationship with his father and his criticism of the religious establishment and the Danish press also influenced his work. His work is very different in style from the technical and systematic philosophies he criticized, integrating elements of prose, poetry and theatre.

Abraham Isaac Hakohen Kook
(*Shemini, Kedoshim, Emor, Korah, Pinhas*)
Griva, Latvia, 1865—Jerusalem, 1935. One of the greatest Torah scholars, intellectuals, and spiritual leaders of recent times, a halakhic authority, and Palestine's first Ashkenazi chief rabbi. He studied at the Yeshivah of Volozhin, where he began to develop as a highly original thinker. In 1904 he went to Palestine to assume the post of chief rabbi of Jaffa and the surrounding Jewish agricultural settlements. It is at this time that he began to formulate his unique approach to Zionism. His complex philosophy combines a strong mystical current with elements of modern thought. One of the authors of Jewish nationalism in the spirit of the Torah, he is considered the spiritual father of religious Zionism. His vast literary legacy includes works of Halakhah, philosophy, and Kabbalah, as well as commentaries on the Talmud and the Midrash. His best-known works include: *Orot* (*Lights*), *Orot Hakodesh* (*Lights of Holiness*), and collections of his letters.

Nahman Krochmal
(*Balak*)
Galicia, 1758–1840. Philosopher and historian, one of the founders of the "Science of Judaism" (*Wissenschaft des Judentums*) movement. He surrounded himself with leading members of the Haskalah, with whom he conducted "Socratic conversations". His thought was greatly influenced by Maimonides, Ibn Ezra, Kant and Hegel. His work was entirely devoted to investigating the relationship between philosophy and religion, and in placing Judaism in a unique historical light. His well-known work, *Moreh Nevukhei Hazman* (Guide for the Perplexed

of the Time), is a cautious and partial summary of his philosophy, edited posthumously by Leopold (Yom Tov) Zunz and published in Lemberg in 1851.

Avraham Krol
(*Pekudei*)
Lodz, Poland, 1912—Jerusalem, 1983. Ordained by Rabbi Hayim Ozer Grodzinski of Vilna and considered a prodigy. Miraculously, he survived the Second World War in Warsaw, together with his wife and daughter. After the Holocaust, he settled in Paris and later Brussels, where he served as rabbi. In 1967, he went to Israel, where he was appointed rabbi of Jerusalem's *Ohel Aharon* synagogue in Jerusalem. Thousands came from all over Israel and the Diaspora to attend his lectures, and he frequented the greatest Torah sages of his time. His published works are *Befikudekha Asihah* on the weekly Torah portions and *Mimayenei Haberakhot* on the talmudic tractate of *Berakhot*.

Nehama Leibowitz
(*Noah, Vayishlah, Miketz*)
Riga, 1905—Jerusalem, 1997. Biblical scholar, exegete and teacher. In 1919 her family settled in Berlin, where she completed her PhD and studied Judaism and pedagogy. In 1930, she emigrated to Palestine. She was a professor of Bible at Te-Aviv University, and taught for many years at the Mizrachi Teachers Seminary, and at many schools and *Hesder* yeshivot. In 1942, she began distributing study sheets on the weekly Torah portion, which enjoyed wide circulation. Leibowitz also commented on the Torah readings on Israel radio. She was awarded the Israel Prize for Education, in 1956. One of the leading Bible teachers of the 20th century, Leibowitz was seen as a role model for many educators in the field of Bible studies.

Yeshayahu Leibowitz
(*Miketz, Bamidbar, Korah*)
Riga, 1903—Jerusalem, 1994. Scientist, philosopher and one of the great Jewish intellectuals of the 20th century. He studied at the universities of Berlin and Basel and taught in a number of departments at the

Hebrew University of Jerusalem, in both the sciences and the humanities. His areas of interest were extremely varied, but his greatest influence lay in the fields of religious belief, Jewish hermeneutics, ethics and the philosophy of science. Yeshayahu Leibowitz was a "popular philosopher", in the sense that his views were widely known and exerted a marked influence on public discourse. Leibowitz stimulated public debate in matters of ethics and politics, war and peace, religion and the state. He served as a "reprover in the gate", demanding that Israeli society take stock of its goals and ethos.

Emmanuel Levinas
(*Vayikra*)
Lithuania, 1905—France, 1995. French Jewish philosopher. Born in Kovno to a modern traditional family. In 1923, he began to study philosophy at the University of Strasbourg, where he was influenced by the thought of Husserl and Heidegger. In 1930, he became a French citizen and, until the 1960s, served as director of the École Normale Israélite Orientale, in Paris. He intensified the dialogical aspect of existentialist theory, going from reciprocity to obligation and asserting that "absolute responsibility for the other" is the essence of human existence in God's image. Levinas is seen as the philosopher who placed the ethical question above the ontological. His thought stemmed from his sharp criticism of Heidegger, and developed in the context of his radical reformulation of the question of subjectivity, in which he placed the other's otherness above the identity of the self.

Levi ben Gershom—Gersonides or Ralbag
(*Tzav*)
Provence, 1288–1344. Neo-Aristotelian philosopher, biblical exegete, physician, mathematician and astronomer, who made important discoveries in these areas. Born to a family of scholars, famed in Jewish and non-Jewish circles for his scientific and literary achievements. In his commentary on the work of Averroes and in his *Wars of the Lord*, he disputes elements of Maimonidean philosophy. His exegetical works are imbued with the spirit of his philosophy and include practical lessons (*to'aliyot*) drawn from the biblical texts.

John Locke
(*Pinhas*)

England, 1632–1704. English philosopher, who joined the Royal Society in 1688, together with Isaac Newton. Founder of the empiricist school of philosophy, which affirms that all knowledge is based on experience. He wrote numerous treatises in the fields of philosophy, political science, theology, economics and education. His treatises on tolerance and government greatly influenced liberal democratic thought. He argued that government derives its sovereignty from the people, by contract, and that the people therefore have the right to bring down any government that fails to live up to its obligation to safeguard the fundamental rights of the people.

Solomon Ephraim Luntschitz—*Keli Yakar*
(*Ha'azinu*)

Poland, 1550—Prague, 1619. Rabbi and author, one of the greatest homilists of the early Modern Era. In his youth, he studied under Rabbi Solomon Luria (Maharshal) in Lublin, and in 1604 was appointed head of the rabbinical court and yeshivah at Prague—a position he held until his death. Luntschitz also spoke at of meetings of the Council of Four Lands in Lublin, which helped him to publish a number of his works, including *Olelot Efraim, Ir Gibborim, Amudei Shesh* and *Orah le-Hayim*. His most celebrated work is his commentary on the Torah, *Keli Yakar*, which combines plain interpretation of the text, with homilies and reproof against various social injustices and the indifference of the rabbis to them. It is also a commentary on Rashi, and has been included in the popular *Mikra'ot Gedolot* edition of the Pentateuch.

Samuel David Luzzatto
(*Va'era*)

Trieste, 1800—Padua, 1865. Historian, philosopher and biblical exegete, teacher and poet, one of the founders of the "Science of Judaism". In his youth, he completed the entire Talmud, and wrote poetry in Hebrew and Italian. At the age of 21, he translated the *Siddur* (Prayer Book) into Italian. He taught at the rabbinical seminary of Padua and corresponded with Jewish scholars from all over Europe. Throughout his life, he sought the middle road between scientific study and faith. He wrote commentaries on *Isaiah, Jeremiah, Ezekiel, Proverbs, Ecclesiastes* and *Job*, as well as many works of philosophy, grammar and poetry. In his monumental commentary on the Pentateuch, he strove both to explain the plain meaning of the texts and to contend with prevailing theories of biblical criticism.

Maimonides, see Moses B. Maimon

Moses Mendelssohn
(*Beshalah*)
Dessau, 1729—Berlin, 1786. German Jewish philosopher, spiritual leader of the Jewish Enlightenment. He received a traditional education, and his knowledge of Jewish sources was extensive, earning him the respect of the rabbis of his generation. He studied languages, science and particularly philosophy, and subsequently earned his living as a bookkeeper. Greatly influenced by Gottfried Wilhelm Leibniz, Mendelssohn's approach to religion, as to all things, was a rational one. He distinguished between faith and conduct, since social conduct requires a certain amount of coercion, whereas faith cannot be coerced. His best-known works are *Phädon* and *Jerusalem*. In conjunction with a team of scholars, he produced a German translation of the Pentateuch, to which he added his famous *Bi'ur*.

Moses ben Maimon—Maimonides
(*Hayei Sarah, Miketz*)
Spain, 1136—Egypt, 1204. The most famous Jewish figure of the Middle Ages, the greatest halakhic authority of all times, a leading rationalist Aristotelian philosopher, scientist and scholar, leader of Egyptian Jewry. His best-known works are: *Treatise on Logic, Hayad Hahazakah* (*Mishneh Torah*), *Commentary on the Mishnah* and *Guide for the Perplexed*. Beyond Aristotle and Plato, Maimonides drew upon the thought of the Muslim Scholastics of his generation: Al-Farabi, Ibn Bajjah and Avicenna. His views on Halakha and philosophy have been the subject of Jewish scholarship from his time to the present day.

Moses ben Nahman—Nahmanides
(*Bo, Hayei Sarah*)
Girona, 1194—Acre, 1270. One of the greatest of the medieval sages, rabbi and author, philosopher and kabbalist, biblical exegete, poet and physician. His students at the yeshivot of Girona included halakhic masters such as Solomon ben Adret and Aaron Halevi of Barcelona. He enjoyed considerable influence over Jewish public life in Catalonia, and was often consulted by the Crown. In addition to his works on the Talmud and Halakhah, later in life, he wrote a commentary on the Torah, in which he focused on the broader context of the biblical texts and their deeper meaning. The commentary is sometimes philological, but more frequently kabbalistic, and addresses philosophical interpretations of Scripture proposed by Nahmanides' contemporaries, including Maimonides, in his *Guide for the Perplexed.*

Nahman of Breslov
(*Vayeshev*)
Medzhibozh, 1772—Uman, 1810. Grandson of the Ba'al Shem Tov and companion of Rabbi Levi Yitzhak of Berditchev. His Hassidic teachings emphasize uncompromising faith and psychological introspection, focusing on one's personal failings and their correction. His best-known works are: *Likutei Moharan, Sippurei Ma'asiyot,* and *Likutei Tefilot.* Today, nearly two hundred years after his death, his approach and teachings are the subject of many and varied interpretations, as well as the focus of considerable academic interest.

Nahmanides, see Moses b. Nahman

Pesikta de-Rav Kahana
(Anonymous thinker to whom the author ascribes a philosophical system)
(*Aharei Mot*)
Galilee, second half of the fifth century CE. A Torah scholar who took it upon himself to redact the work known to us as the *Pesikta de-Rav Kahana*, from a wealth of source materials. We know absolutely nothing of the redactor himself. Even the time and place in which he lived

are a matter of conjecture. His work however, speaks for itself and for its creator, showing that he was no mere anthologist, but an articulate author with a clear philosophical point of view.

Judith Plaskow
(*Re'eh*)

Professor Judith Plaskow is one of the most prominent feminist religious thinkers in the world today and a pioneer in the field of feminist Jewish theology. The subject of her dissertation, at Yale University, was the relevancy of the religious thought of two leading American Protestant theologians—Reinhold Niebuhr and Paul Tillich—to the lives of women. In her many articles lectures and public appearances and in her classic book, *Standing Again at Sinai* (1989), Plaskow has developed a foundation for feminist Jewish thought, rooted in a religious, rather than halakhic thought. Plaskow was one of the founders of the *Havurah* movement in the United States and of the *B'not Esh* community—home to many noted Jewish feminists. She is co-editor of the *Journal of Feminist Studies in Religion* and teaches modern Jewish thought at Manhattan College.

Dalia Rabikovitz
(*Ki Teze*)

Ramat Gan in 1936—Tel Aviv 2005. Israeli Poet, studied at the Hebrew University of Jerusalem, and was a teacher for a number of years. Dalia Rabikovitz is a winner of the Bialik Prize and the Prime Minister's Prize. In 1999, she was awarded the Israel Prize for Poetry. Her poems are, on the one hand, personal reflections—on orphanhood, impossible love and the desperate struggle for existence—and on the other hand, expressions of universal truths and common experience. This convergence of the personal and the universal, together with a unique combination of rich, "high" language with everyday speech, is characteristic of her work, and has made hers the most important and outstanding voice in contemporary Hebrew poetry.

Isaac Jacob Reines
(*Mas'ei*)

Pinsk, 1839—Lida, 1915. Preeminent Lithuanian rabbi and ardent supporter of the *Hibat Zion* movement. He studied at the yeshivot of Volozhin, Eishishok and Telz, served as rabbi in the towns of Shavkyany (Saukenai) and Sventsyany (Svencionys) in the district of Vilna, and from 1884 until his death, as the rabbi of Lida. Reines was familiar with the scientific works of the Haskalah, and sought to apply a logical approach to Talmud study. He explained his methodology in *Hotem Tokhnit* and other works. In Lida, he founded a yeshivah, the first of its kind, at which both religious and secular studies were taught. This was considered an audacious move, and drew sharp criticism from many of his rabbinical colleagues. In 1902 he founded the Mizrachi Movement and became its first leader.

Franz Rosenzweig
(*Yitro, Bamidbar*)

Germany, 1886–1929. Born in Kassel to an assimilated and wealthy family of merchants. He studied medicine, history and philosophy, and was a student of Hermann Cohen at the Hochschule für die Wissenschaft des Judentums in Berlin. In 1912, he earned a doctoral degree, for his dissertation *Hegel and the State*. According to his own account, at the age of 23, he nearly converted to Christianity. A Yom Kippur experience at a small Eastern European synagogue in Kassel led him to change his mind, and he wrote to a friend: "I will remain a Jew". This dramatic shift was the beginning of his return to Judaism and laid the foundations for his magnum opus *The Star of Redemption*. In this work, Rosenzweig attacks German idealism and elaborates upon the God-world-man relationship, as well as the relationship between Christianity and Judaism and their respective roles in the world. His essays have appeared in Hebrew, in *Naharayim: Mivhar Ketavim* (Yehoshua Amir, ed.), and in English, in *Franz Rosenzweig: His Life and Thought* (Nahum N. Glatzer, ed.).

Ovadiah Sforno

(Ekev)

Italy, 1470–1550. Rabbi, biblical exegete and physician. He was frequently consulted on halakhic matters by the rabbis of his generation, and is cited extensively by Ashkenazi ethicists. He studied philosophy, mathematics, philology and medicine in Rome. He subsequently settled in Bologna, where he founded a yeshivah and strove to maintain peaceful relations within the local Jewish community—particularly between Ashkenazi and Sephardic factions. As a physician, he maintained close ties with Henry II of France. Sforno wrote many works of philosophy and grammar, but is best-known as a biblical exegete. His commentary emphasizes the plain meaning of the text, with additional philosophical and scientific insights. Though a philologist, he avoided philological interpretations. His interpretations are quite innovative in places and relate to sociological conditions in his community of Bologna.

Joseph B. Soloveitchik

(Tazri'a)

Berlin, 1903–Boston, 1993. One of the most outstanding talmudists of the 20th century as well as one of its most important and influential Jewish thinkers. Scion of one of the most prominent rabbinic families in Lithuania and a graduate of the Philosophy Department at the University of Berlin, Rabbi Soloveitchik influenced thousands of students at Yeshiva University's affiliated Rabbi Isaac Elchanan Theological Seminary where he taught for over four decades and through his original writings and spellbinding public presentations played a leading role in the dynamic resurgence of Orthodox Judaism in America.

Baruch Spinoza

(Beshalah, Tetzaveh, Pinhas)

Amsterdam, 1632—Hague, 1677. Jewish philosopher, born into a family of *Conversos*. A pioneer in the field of Jewish theology, he was influenced primarily by medieval stoicism and Cartesian philosophy, and laid the philosophical foundations of modern humanism. He believed that God exists within nature, and that the laws of nature are God's laws (pantheism). He criticized the tenets of religion and called for free-

dom of thought and spirit. He also developed new approaches to Scripture and is considered by some, the father of modern biblical criticism.
At the age of 24, he was excommunicated by the Amsterdam Jewish
community, for his "opinions and deeds". His most famous works are
the *Theologico-Political Treatise* and *Ethics*. In modern times, Nahum
Sokolov and David Ben-Gurion called for a reversal of Spinoza's excommunication and the inclusion of his works in the spiritual heritage
of the Jewish People.

Hayim of Volozhin
(*Shelah Lekha*)
Lithuania, 1749–1821. A student of Rabbi Elijah (the Gaon) of Vilna,
and one of the leading Torah sages of his generation. In 1802, he founded the Yeshivah of Volozhin, which would become a model for all the
Lithuanian yeshivot. At Volozhin, he introduced a rational *peshat* (plain
meaning) oriented method of study, inspired by the Vilna Gaon, and
imparted a deep sense of commitment to learning as well as extensive
knowledge of both the Written and the Oral Law. A preeminent leader of
Lithuanian Jewry, he concerned himself with the spiritual and physical
welfare of his own community, as well that of the burgeoning community in *Eretz Yisrael*. His best-known work is *Nefesh Hahayim*, which
he wrote in the spirit of Rabbi Elijah's kabbalistic teachings, as a counterweight to the mystical thought and practices of the nascent Hassidic
movement.

Avraham B. Yehoshua
(*Bereshit*)
A.B. Yehoshua was born in Jerusalem in 1936, the fifth generation of
a Jerusalemite family. He graduated from the Hebrew University of Jerusalem, and currently teaches Hebrew and comparative literature at
Haifa University. He has published many books, including anthologies
of short stories and plays. Among his best-known novels are: *The Lover,
A Late Divorce, Five Seasons, Mr. Mani, Open Heart, The Liberated
Bride* and a historical novel entitled *Journey to the End of the Millennium*. He has also published three works of nonfiction—essays on ideology, Zionism, and literature: *Between Right and Right, The Wall and*

the Mountain, The Terrible Power of a Minor Guilt. He has received the Bialik Prize and the Israel Prize for Literature (1995) as well as numerous international awards. His works have been translated into some twenty languages.

Rabbi Yohanan and Rabbi Shimon ben Lakish
(*Toledot*)

Two Palestinian *amoraim* of the second generation, who lived in the third century CE. Rabbi Yohanan headed the yeshivah at Tiberias and Resh Lakish, a few years his junior, was his friend and disciple. One of the most celebrated pairs of talmudic teachers, Rabbi Yohanan and Resh Lakish disputed countless matters of Halakhah and Aggadah between them. Equally celebrated however, was their wonderful friendship and its tragic end, as recounted in the Talmud (*Bava Metzia* 84d). Rabbi Shimon ben Lakish was known for his acuity and was surnamed "uprooter of mountains". His integrity and courage were legendary, and he even clashed with the patriarch, Rabbi Judah ha-Nasi, with whom he later studied and whose words he frequently cited.

List of Authors

Yoske Achituv, The Yaacov Herzog Center for Jewish Studies, Ein Tzurim

Dr. Irit Aminof, Oranim Academic College of Education

Rabbi Prof, Yehoyada Amir, Hebrew Union College, Jerusalem

Prof. Hamutal Bar-Yosef, Poet and literary researcher, Ben-Gurion University of the Negev

Dr. Hanoch Ben Pazi, Department of Philosophy, Bar-Ilan University; Seminar Hakibbutzim Teachers College, Tel-Aviv

Dr. Yotam Benziman, department for political sciences, Hebrew University of Jerusalem; research fellow at the Van Leer Jerusalem Institute

Dr. Benjamin Brown, Department of Jewish Philosophy, Hebrew University of Jerusalem; The Van Leer Jerusalem Institute.

Dr. Hagai Dagan, Writer and lecturer in Jewish philosophy, Sapir College and Ben-Gurion University of the Negev

Prof. Rachel Elior, Department of Jewish Philosophy, Hebrew University of Jerusalem; senior fellow at the Van Leer Jerusalem Institute

Rabbi Dr. Chaniel Farber, Road Safety Education, Ariel University Center of Samaria

Dr. Marla L. Frankel, Department of Bible and Jewish Philosophy, David Yellin College of Education; Melton Center for Jewish Education in the Diaspora, Hebrew University of Jerusalem

Dr. Pnina Galpaz-Feller, Department of Ancient Eastern Studies and Bible, Schechter Institute of Jewish Studies, Jerusalem

Dr. Reuven Gerber, Department of Jewish Philosophy, Levinsky College of Education; David Yellin College of Education

Prof. Warren Zev Harvey, Department of Jewish Philosophy, Hebrew University of Jerusalem

Dr. Gitit Holzman, Department of Jewish Philosophy, Oranim Academic College of Education

Prof. Hannah Kasher, Department of Philosophy, Bar-Ilan University

Avi Katzman, Journalist and cultural critic, Mandel Foundation, Jerusalem

Rabbi Dr. Benjamin Lau, Head of the Women's Beit Midrash at Beit Morasha; school Rabbi at Himmelfarb High School; rabbi of the Ramban Synagogue in Jerusalem

Dr. Bryna Levy, Head of the Department of Bible Exegesis at Matan— Women's Institute for Torah Studies, Jerusalem

Dr. Lea Mazor, Department of Bible, Hebrew University of Jerusalem

Prof. Michael Zvi Nehorai, Department of Jewish Philosophy, Bar-Ilan University; Lifshitz Religious College of Education

Prof. David Ohana, Ben-Gurion University of the Negev

Hava Pinhas-Cohen, Poet and lecturer in literature and art

Prof. Nahum Rakover, The Jewish Legal Heritage Society; former Deputy Attorney General, Ministry of Justice

Rabbi Dr. Einat Ramon, Jewish Philosophy and Gender Studies, Schechter Institute of Jewish Studies, Jerusalem

Prof. Shalom Ratzaby, Department of Jewish History, Tel-Aviv University.

Dr. Avinoam Rosenak, Head of the Department of Jewish Philosophy, Hebrew University of Jerusalem; research fellow at the Van Leer Jerusalem Institute.

Prof. Michael Rosenak, Melton Center for Jewish Education in the Diaspora, Hebrew University of Jerusalem; the Mandel Foundation, Jerusalem

Rabbi Shimon Gershon Rosenberg (Shagar) Z"L, Head of Yeshivat Siach Yitzchak, Efrat

Rabbi Prof. Naftali Rothenberg, Senior research fellow at the Van Leer Jerusalem Institute; Rabbi of Har Adar

Prof. Alvin I. Schiff, Azrieli School of Jewish Education, Yeshiva University, New York

Prof. Christoph Schmidt, Head of the Department of German Literature, Hebrew University of Jerusalem; research fellow at the Van Leer Jerusalem Institute

Dr. Jacob J. Schacter, University Professor of Jewish History and Jewish Thought, Yeshiva University

Dr. Ben Z. Schreiber, Department of Information and Statistics, Bank of Israel; Bar-Ilan University

Prof. Eliezer Schweid, Department of Jewish Philosophy, Hebrew University of Jerusalem

Prof. Avigdor Shinan, Department of Hebrew Literature, Hebrew University of Jerusalem, Prof. Yitzhak Becker Professor of Jewish Studies.

Prof. Moshe Sokolow, Azrieli School of Jewish Education, Yeshiva University, New York.

Rabbi Yeshaya Steinberger, Lecturer, Yeshivat Hakotel; rabbi of the Ramat Sharet and Denya neighborhoods, Jerusalem

Dr. Shlomo Tikochinski, Department of Jewish History, Hebrew University of Jerusalem and Van Leer Jerusalem Institute

Prof. Yossi Turner, Department of Jewish Philosophy, Schechter Institute of Jewish Studies, Jerusalem

Yair Tzaban, Former Member of Knesset and Minister of Immigrant Absorption; Chair of Meitar College of Judaism as Culture; founder and Director of the Lamda Association for Modern Jewish Culture

Dr. Tsvia Walden, Psycholinguist, Director of the Institute for Whole Language and Computers, Beit Berl College.

Dr. Shmuel Wygoda, Lecturer at the Yaacov Herzog College, Alon Shevut; research fellow, the Van Leer Jerusalem Institute

Prof. Elhanan Yakira, Head of the Department of Philosophy, Hebrew University of Jerusalem.

Dr. Erella Yedgar, Lecturer in Bible, Efrata College of Education and Lifshitz Religious College of Education.

Dr. Yedidyah Yitzhaki, Department of Jewish Literature, Bar-Ilan University, Seminar Hakibbutzim Teachers College, Tel-Aviv, and Jordan Valley and Safed colleges

Dr. Gili Zivan, Director of the Yaacov Herzog Center for Jewish Studies, Ein Tzurim.